TEN ON TEN

Major Essayists on Recurring Themes

TEN ON TEN

Major Essayists on Recurring Themes

Robert Atwan

BEDFORD BOOKS *of* ST. MARTIN'S PRESS · BOSTON

FOR BEDFORD BOOKS
Publisher: Charles H. Christensen
Associate Publisher: Joan E. Feinberg
Managing Editor: Elizabeth M. Schaaf
Developmental Editor: Jane Betz
Production Editor: Deborah Liehs
Copyeditor: Cynthia Insolio Benn
Text Design: Claire Seng-Niemoeller
Cover Design: Richard Emery Design, Inc.
Cover and Interior Art: Inkwash portraits by Tom Hughes after photographs:
James Baldwin by J. Phil Samuell; Joan Didion by Jerry Bauer;
Annie Dillard by Renée DeKona, Stephen Jay Gould by Friedman/Black Star,
George Orwell from Historical Pictures Service; Cynthia Ozick by
Julius Ozick, © Cynthia Ozick; Lewis Thomas by Helen Marcus;
Alice Walker from Wide World Photos; Virginia Woolf from
The Hogarth Press; and E. B. White by Donald E. Johnson.

Library of Congress Catalog Card Number: 90–61137

6   5   4   3   2

f   e   d   c   b   a

For information, write: St. Martin's Press, Inc.
175 Fifth Avenue, New York, NY 10010

Editorial Offices: Bedford Books *of* St. Martin's Press
29 Winchester Street, Boston, MA 02116

ISBN: 0–312–06236–2

ACKNOWLEDGMENTS

JAMES BALDWIN, "Autobiographical Notes," "Equal in Paris," and "Notes of a Native
Son" from *Notes of a Native Son* by James Baldwin. Copyright © 1955, renewed
1983, by James Baldwin. Reprinted by permission of Beacon Press. "Here Be
Dragons" (originally published as "Freaks and the American Ideal of Manhood"

*Acknowledgments and copyrights are continued at the back of the book on pages 520–522, which
constitute an extension of the copyright page.*

 The text of this book has been printed on recycled paper.

Preface for Instructors

TEN ON TEN is designed for writing instructors who want to concentrate on several major essayists in depth, yet prefer to do so in a practical compositional context. Therefore, while the book features ten outstanding modern essayists, its fifty-five selections are grouped not by author but by theme. I believe that this thematic organization offers teachers a more useful way to shape a writing course, since composition students are more accustomed to — and I think more interested in — responding to general topics than to individual authors.

The collection as a whole, however, encourages responses to both individual authors and general themes. The book can be used conveniently as *both* an in-depth and a thematic reader. The collection is also appropriate for courses on the essay as a literary genre.

As an in-depth reader, *Ten on Ten* introduces composition students to ten distinguished twentieth-century essayists. Although some of these writers have established major reputations in other genres, they are not authors who have tossed off an occasional essay or two between novels; all of the writers collected here view the essay as an important literary form. Each has written numerous essays, each has published several collections of essays, and each has brought a unique literary talent to bear on the genre. To facilitate an appreciation and understanding of the individual essayists, a thorough introduction to each author is included in the book's appendix.

Yet many instructors who want to focus on several major writers and high-quality essays may still prefer to base their writing assignments on a variety of themes and topics rather than on individual authors. I think *Ten on Ten* will appeal to these instructors. The book's ten themes cover a wide range of subjects that should be both familiar and provocative. The themes, moreover, were not arbitrarily chosen and imposed upon the collection. The book proceeded in a bottom-up rather than a top-down fashion. I started with the essayists I wanted to include, and I let their essays find their own arrangement. In systematically going through the works of the ten writers, I discovered that nearly all of them had touched on the same themes. This, of course, was not surprising. Since Montaigne, essayists have been drawn to certain themes and topics: everyday family life, education, travel, intellectual and emotional epiphanies, gender and identity, the lives of impressive or inspiring people, science and progress, the natural world, language and writing. In constructing a course around these various themes, instructors will find that they can introduce their students to a wide assortment of compositional topics and types, and at the same time cover a set of enduring themes that have traditionally characterized the essay as a literary genre. Inviting students themselves to write on these themes will encourage them to become essayists in their own right.

A word about the essayists and essays: I selected the essayists, all prominent writers, not simply because of their individual literary talents but also because they offered the diversity of backgrounds and professions that I regard as essential for a well-balanced and versatile college text. It's important to expose first-year composition students to good writers, but it's also important that they see that good writers can be a diverse lot. The writers in *Ten on Ten* represent a variety of interests, and they approach the essay from several different perspectives — not only from literature and criticism but from journalism, science, medicine, religion, and politics as well as from the cultural perspectives of racial, sexual, and ethnic identity. Though any collection of major essayists will naturally include a high percentage of strongly voiced, personal essays, *Ten on Ten* offers a sufficient amount of expository, critical, and argumentative prose for instructors who want to move from personal experience papers to compositions that grapple more with information and public issues. The table of contents moves roughly in that direction.

To make this collection as useful as possible for a composition course, I built into *Ten on Ten* several types of instructional material:

1. *A general introduction that encourages students to consider what the essay is — both as the kind of writing they will be asked to do and as a serious literary genre with a long tradition.* The introduction raises a number of essential questions about the essay that I hope will recur throughout the course as students grow closer and closer in their reading and writing to a critical appreciation of this elusive form.

2. *A brief introductory note before each essay to orient the student reader to the particular work.* These headnotes often provide important contextual information that I believe is necessary for a fuller appreciation of the essay, especially for older essays whose implicit occasion or historical background is no longer clear to the general reader.

In keeping with this contextual information, the essays were carefully read for references or allusions that seemed out of the range of the ordinary information that would be expected of today's general reader. I provided footnotes for any item that I thought was not immediately understandable from the text alone. Though any given footnote may strike an instructor as so obvious as to be condescending ("Who doesn't know who Benjamin Disraeli is?"), it's important to remember that even a reference which seems obvious to one well-educated person may be opaque to another equally well-educated person ("Who in God's name is Eugene Aram?"). In general, I used my own classroom experience as a guide and glossed details that I thought would be unfamiliar to the average freshman or sophomore. I'm not embarrassed to add that much of what I glossed I didn't know myself, or casually thought I knew until I looked it up.

3. *Several questions focusing on style, language, and rhetorical strategy after each selection to stimulate thought and discussion.* These questions are not just routine discussion questions. Written in the form of commentary, many of them introduce students to important critical terms and concepts, and then ask them to consider these in response to a specific question about the essay. Although some questions ask about content, their main thrust is to get the student as close as possible to the author's style and strategy. Many of the questions send the student back to the essay for a rereading.

4. *Writing assignments after each chapter.* These encourage students to make connections between various essays and to write their own essays in response to the theme.

5. *A comprehensive biographical and critical essay about each writer to facil-itate an appreciation and understanding of the individual essayists.* Researched and written by Jack Roberts, the essays offer both students and instructors a convenient and relatively thorough guide to the ten essayists and their work. Each of Roberts's entries concentrates on the writer as essayist. Per-tinent remarks by the writer on the essay and relevant critical commentary are brought together in a way that will encourage and assist more extended criticism. For further study, a list of the writer's notable publications and an annotated bibliography of selected criticism follow each entry.

I hope instructors will enjoy using *Ten on Ten* as much as I enjoyed assembling and editing it. I hope, too, that this collection will showcase the modern and contemporary essay as a dynamic and versatile literary form, one that will appeal to students — as great essays do — both intellectually and imaginatively. E. B. White once sadly claimed that in the world of letters the essayist "must be content in his self-imposed role of second-class citizen." I sometimes worry that teachers of essays find themselves in the same position within the world of the English Department. I believe that this volume proves that the essay can hold its own in any literary company.

It is always a pleasure for me to acknowledge the splendid staff at Bedford Books. *Ten on Ten* began with Bedford's publisher, Charles H. Christensen, who suggested less than a year ago that I work on a collection of major modern essayists arranged thematically. Chuck and Bedford's As-sociate Publisher, Joan E. Feinberg, then lent the project their usual unerring guidance. Once again I thank my editor, Jane Betz. She possesses every quality a good editor should have — literary judgment, industry savvy, and let's not forget such matters as patience and efficiency. But she also brings

to the job some qualities that editors aren't required to have: a keen sense
of humor and an uncanny ability to keep a book on a tight schedule without
ever exuding a sense of apocalyptic doom. Other people at Bedford also
deserve my gratitude: Deborah Liehs performed another masterly production
job at an incredible pace, and Terri Walton not only lent ample production
assistance but helped secure permissions as well. Beth Castrodale was always
there to help out in a pinch; she also put together the annotated table of
contents. The book's copyeditor, Cynthia Benn, offered many incisive suggestions and did her best to keep my commentary politically correct; any
deviations from that evasive ideal are my own responsibility. A special thanks
to Claire Seng-Niemoeller, who provided the elegant design. I think readers
will be delighted with Tom Hughes's admirable ink drawings of the book's
ten authors.

I especially want to thank my good friend Jack Roberts for his fine
essays on the essayists. As instructors who specialize in the genre realize, the
form has received relatively little critical attention. In many respects, the ten
entries Roberts contributed to this volume are groundbreaking; taken together, they provide a compact introduction to the twentieth-century essay.
We both hope that they will stimulate further critical response to the genre.
Jack Roberts also prepared the Instructor's Manual for this book. Teachers
will find there an abundance of useful classroom suggestions as well as an
extension of the critical discussions of the essay found throughout the volume.

I'm also grateful for the ideas and advice I've received from a friend
and one of my former teachers, Alexander J. Butrym. Chairman of the Seton
Hall University English Department, Professor Butrym has recently edited
one of the few critical books on the essay, *Essays on the Essay: Redefining the
Genre* (The University of Georgia Press, 1989).

Finally, I extend my appreciation to my wife, Hélène, and my children,
Gregory and Emily, for enduring yet another rigorous schedule. Thanks guys!

Robert Atwan
South Orange, N.J.

Contents

3. Heroes and Heroines 105

Joan Didion, John Wayne: A Love Song 107

"When John Wayne rode through my childhood, and perhaps through yours, he determined forever the shape of certain of our dreams."

Annie Dillard, The Stunt Pilot 115

"When Rahm flew, he sat down in the middle of art and strapped himself in. He spun it all around him."

E. B. White, Will Strunk 126

"He was a memorable man, friendly and funny. Under the remembered sting of his kindly lash, I have been trying to omit needless words since 1919."

Stephen Jay Gould, The Streak of Streaks 133

"DiMaggio's hitting streak is the finest of legitimate legends because it embodies the essence of the battle that truly defines our lives. . . . He cheated death, at least for a while."

Virginia Woolf, Ellen Terry 141

"Which, then, of all these women is the real Ellen Terry? How are we to put the scattered sketches together? Is she mother, wife, cook, critic, actress, or should she have been, after all, a painter?"

Alice Walker, Looking for Zora 147

"It was impossible for me to cry when I saw the field full of weeds where Zora is. . . . there is a point at which even grief feels absurd. And at this point, laughter gushes up to retrieve sanity."

4. Teaching and Learning 163

George Orwell, St. Cyprian's 165

"At St. Cyprian's the whole process was frankly a preparation for a sort of confidence trick. Your job was to learn exactly those things that would give an examiner the impression that you knew more than you did know."

Cynthia Ozick, Washington Square, 1946 173

"I first came down to Washington Square on a colorless February morning in 1946. I was seventeen and a half years old and was carrying my lunch in a brown paper bag, just as I had carried it to high school only a month before."

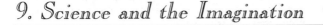

TEN ON TEN

Major Essayists on Recurring Themes

What Is an Essay?

W E USE the word *essay* in many different ways. The term can refer to practically any piece of nonfiction prose, from a five hundred word newspaper column protesting a gasoline tax to a formal academic treatise promoting a new theory of the universe. A magazine review of the latest Arnold Schwarzenegger film and a long article in a financial journal on the origins of the Federal Reserve system may both call themselves essays. A dentist writes an essay defending a new style of braces; a college admission office asks students to submit a personal essay with their applications. Look the word up in the subject heading of your library's catalogue and you'll find entries describing so many different kinds of writing that you might conclude the word had no meaning at all.

Given this widely indiscriminate use of the word, it is easy to forget that the essay is first and foremost a form of literature. The term was introduced by a sixteenth-century French magistrate, Michel de Montaigne, who temporarily retired from official life in the 1570s, and set up a room in his chateau where he began writing and publishing a series of short prose works that he called *essais*. He published three volumes of essays in all, the last in 1588, and with these books assumed his place among the most respected writers of any age. Montaigne's works were quickly translated into English, and by the seventeenth century the essay was well established as a mode of literature.

Montaigne not only devised the essay, but his work still remains central to our understanding of the form. To consider, therefore, what an essay is in its true literary context, it helps to begin with Montaigne's own conception of what he was writing. What did the man who coined the term mean by it?

As it turns out, Montaigne was too much the essayist to define systematically what he meant by "essay." Any rigid, air-tight definition would have been completely out of character and certainly out-of-keeping with his eccentric manner of composition. To understand Montaigne's idea of an essay, we must first of all realize that he gave it no definition. For Montaigne, essays were to be understood in practice and not in theory. To this day, the essay has eluded strict definition and theoretical interpretation. Unlike fiction, poetry, or drama, the essay as a genre has inspired a relatively small body of literary criticism.

That does not mean, of course, that we can't try to extract from his writings some idea of what Montaigne intended his essays to be. Though composed over four hundred years ago, Montaigne's essays nevertheless set the genre on its modern course, and nearly every practitioner of the form has paid tribute to Montaigne's influence. "It is," says Lewis Thomas, "one of the encouraging aspects of our civilization that Montaigne has never gone out of print." For E. B. White, Montaigne was a reliable source of inspiration: ". . . when I am discouraged or downcast I need only fling open the door of my closet and there, hidden behind everything else, hangs the mantle of Michel de Montaigne. . . ."

What keeps Montaigne's writing so fresh and relevant? Let's begin with the word *essay* itself. In Old French *essai* meant an attempt, a test, or a trial. Montaigne often uses the word as a verb — to *essay* something still means to attempt it, to give it a test or a tryout. (Though the word also has this meaning in English, it is more commonly used here to indicate a form of writing. In France you would use the verb "essayer" routinely — to say, for example, that you were test-driving a new car.) Montaigne thus viewed the essay as a trying out of ideas rather than a fully shaped formulation of them. This literal sense of the essay as a tryout or an experiment has remained over the centuries a dominant feature of the form.

"Essay" has other connotations, all of which are important to understanding the genre. After inventing this new type of writing, Montaigne didn't give it an impressive label; instead, he deliberately used an everyday French word that would reinforce his writing's casual manner. Montaigne wanted his readers to know that he wasn't preparing treatises or formal compositions on various topics. A treatise would cover a subject in a thorough, organized, point-by-point fashion, would adhere to a prearranged set of rules concerning diction, style, and format, and would follow a closely reasoned argument. Today, the treatise is best seen in the form of dissertations, scholarly monographs, and even some longer term papers. Montaigne had no patience with this kind of writing; he also distrusted it. He liked to stray from his subject, violate the conventions for orderly transitions, use colloquial language, and flaunt his self-contradictions. The essay, as will be amply seen in this collection, still retains this informal and flexible approach to subjects.

Montaigne also chose the word "essay" to suggest the modesty of his literary task. He warned his readers not to expect a systematic treatment of any subject; the essays were, after all, only his impromptu thoughts and reflections. And along with the modesty of his project went a personal modesty. Montaigne continually downplayed his abilities and achievements. He distrusted his own ideas, claimed he had a deficient memory, and flatly stated that his "ruling quality" was "ignorance." His humor is often at his own expense. In establishing his modesty from the start, Montaigne set an example that has endured among essayists. Writers in this genre characteristically see themselves as people with failings, and they usually are not afraid or ashamed to portray their personalities in an unflattering light. George Orwell and E. B. White often display the same modest traits; they are keenly aware of their limitations, unusually self-critical.

The essayist's modesty, however, is at times ironical. People pretend to be modest (what we call "false modesty") for many different reasons — to make themselves seem more credible, or less boastful, or to appear less important than they think they really are. Since essayists are usually writing about themselves, they must find ways to offset what might look like an irritating egoism and self-absorption. Montaigne was well aware of this inherent problem, and his self-effacing comments might be viewed as an effective tactic: to make himself the center of attention without seeming to do so. George Orwell opens his most famous essay, "Shooting an Elephant," in a way that both establishes his importance and downplays it in the same sentence: "In Moulmein, in Lower Burma, I was hated by large numbers of people — the only time in my life that I have been important enough for this to happen to me." He ends his essay with an unflattering remark that undercuts any heroism the reader might attribute to him. Why did he shoot an elephant? He did it "solely to avoid looking a fool."

The tension between self-effacement and self-importance is only one of the internal conflicts experienced by essayists. Perhaps the most influential thing Montaigne did was to make himself the center of his work. As he says in the preface to his essays: "I want to be seen here in my simple, natural, ordinary fashion, without straining or artifice; for it is myself I portray." Though there had been autobiographical works before his, the nature and extent of Montaigne's self-disclosure was something new in world literature. Yet we know that the "I" on the page can never be identical to the "I" of real life. When we write about ourselves we inevitably wind up revealing one thing and suppressing something else; recounting this experience but distorting that one; remembering one incident while fabricating another. These problems are an inherent aspect of personal writing. The "self" we portray in our writing is not necessarily the self we exhibit to others, nor is it necessarily the self that we think we truly are.

In reading essays — even those primarily concerned with issues and ideas — we are often exposed to the first person singular. In this collection, a number of the essays are not only *in* the first person, they are *about* the first person. Joan Didion, Alice Walker, Virginia Woolf, and James Baldwin are essayists who have meticulously examined their personal identities in writing. For these writers and many other modern essayists, an identity does not precede the writing, but is created in the act of writing. In Alice Walker's "Beauty: When the Other Dancer Is the Self," writing is a means to self-discovery and self-creation. This idea of a personal identity generated by the process of writing also goes back to Montaigne. Montaigne wanted an essay to stand as the enactment of its own composition; in other words, the process of writing was more important to him than the finished product, and he wanted the essays to reflect that aesthetic priority. Throughout his work, Montaigne invites his readers to catch him in the act of writing. He wants us to observe the essay as it unfolds.

As a genre, the essay is oriented to the reader. We might say that it is the most "user-friendly" of literary forms. Montaigne opened his book not with a formal preface but with a casual note "To the Reader," and throughout the essays he often addressed his readers directly as though they were companions in the act of writing. Montaigne was intent upon establishing a friendly relation with his readers; in fact, he said that he began writing essays as a way of filling the conversational gap left by the untimely death of a close friend. This conversational model was again one of Montaigne's legacies. Out of it grew what is still called the "familiar" essay, a type of informal essay marked by the intimate relationship the writer assumes toward the reader.

If the first person singular is important to the essayist, so is the first person plural. In no other genre is the pronoun "we" so significant. Indeed, it's possible to argue that in no other genre do we need to pay such close attention to personal pronouns in general as in the essay. In paragraph after paragraph, we continually come across "I," "you," and "we," and it is crucial how the reader responds to these words. As the reader, are you sure who the writer's "we" refers to? Is it to a specific group? Or is it an editorial "we"? If so, do you feel included in it? Does the writer's "you" indicate a specific individual or does it refer to you as the reader? Or does it refer to the writer? And what about the essay's "I": is it an autobiographical "I" or one invented for the purposes of the essay? Because the essay is so closely related to its reader, you should form the habit of asking yourself such questions as these repeatedly in your reading.

The essay hasn't remained a static form since Montaigne. It has been shaped and reshaped over the centuries as its leading writers have each invested it with their own style and concerns. The history of the English and American essay has been especially affected by changes in publishing technology and by the new audiences that emerged with each transformation. With the steady improvement of the printing press in the seventeenth century, the essay in the hands of polemical writers like Jonathan Swift and Daniel Defoe grew into a popular form of pamphlet literature. In the eighteenth century, such writers as Joseph Addison, Benjamin Franklin, and Samuel Johnson fashioned "the periodical essay" in response to the rise of an urban newspaper press. Their polite, witty, and often instructive essays became the model for much of today's newspaper columns and editorials. In the nineteenth century, the genre was profoundly shaped by the spread of general-interest magazines, which featured the "familiar" style of such important essayists as William Hazlitt, Charles Lamb, and Robert Louis Stevenson, whose work, particularly Hazlitt's, opened up new territory for the modern essay. Hazlitt not only reinvigorated the conversational mode and introduced a lively, mercurial style, he also pioneered many of the types of essays that abound in today's magazines and make up a good percentage of this collection: the short biographical portrait, the journalistic essay, the lyrical or imagistic essay. A reader could pick up a recent issue, say, of *The New Yorker* magazine and trace a fair portion of its contents to the influence of William Hazlitt.

This very brief summary of the essay's history is meant to suggest its rich literary heritage, a heritage that the modern essayists in this volume have consciously or unconsciously acknowledged. In this book, you will find the spirit of Montaigne and his successors fully alive, for essays are still being composed in a conversational and improvisational style and with an open-minded skepticism, a distrust of intellectual systems, an emphasis on experimentation and self-exploration. Essayists still value a humane spirit, shun academic pretense, and often display a noticeable lack of confidence in experts and specialists. And we find essayists still reflecting on, still probing, the same enduring themes that preoccupied earlier generations of essayists: family life, memorable characters, education, travel, nature and the animal kingdom, the relationship of men and women, the relationship of science and culture, and — since the essay has perennially been a self-reflective form — language and the act of writing itself.

But our modern essayists are more than the passive recipients of recurrent themes and literary inheritances. They have themselves broken new ground and expanded the boundaries of the traditional essay. In responding to mass media and mass entertainment, to more culturally diverse populations, to depth psychology, to other types of literary and visual experimentation, and to numerous forms of twentieth-century oppression, the modern essayist lost something of the older essayist's amiability and gentility. With writers like Virginia Woolf, George Orwell, and James Baldwin the personal essay took on serious issues with a sense of cause and urgency. In the essays of E. B. White — though he retained a good degree of the older, more relaxed manner — we frequently encounter moods of depression and morbid anxiety, emotions that often play beneath the surface of what appears to be a congenial personality. Joan Didion has grafted a reflective essayist's manner to the methods of a tough-minded journalist and has produced uneasy essays that expose a disintegrating social order. Lewis Thomas and Stephen Jay Gould have successfully managed to create literary essays out of nearly intractable nonliterary material. Cynthia Ozick brilliantly finds an essayistic way to balance a profound literary knowledge, a tough moral vision, and an eloquent personal voice. Alice Walker uses the essay in advocacy of women and African Americans, but does so in an intricately composed mosaic fashion without sacrificing the creative resources she brings to her fiction. Annie Dillard, for whom the essay is a strict and demanding art form, crafts an intense and illuminating essay that suddenly dissolves the boundary between the self and the natural world. Having lost much of its old-fashioned belletristic manner (though Cynthia Ozick tries to revivify that great tradition), the essay now makes use of more disparate methods and material than it once did. Today's essayists freely incorporate the imagery of lyric poetry, the narrative techniques of short fiction, the strategies of journalism, and the data of informative articles.

In their rethinking and reshaping of the essay, modern and contemporary writers have undoubtedly made it a more challenging literary form to define than it ever was. That challenge, I hope, will be experienced in your reading *and* writing, and will be one of the principal pleasures of this book.

1

Moments of Insight

E. B. WHITE
Once More to the Lake

"Once More to the Lake" is perhaps the most commonly anthologized essay in our literature. Why this is so is an interesting matter for speculation. For many years, White had a reputation as one of America's supreme stylists; he had even co-authored a best-selling book called The Elements of Style *that is still considered authoritative. But White wrote many essays that demonstrate his literary craft and style, and yet none has been so consistently reprinted. The appeal of "Once More to the Lake," then, must have something to do with its subject — the eerie connection that a father feels toward his son as he brings the boy back to the magical summer place where many years earlier* his *father took him when he was a child. White wrote this essay for his monthly column in* Harper's *magazine in 1941.*

ONE SUMMER, along about 1904, my father rented a camp on a lake in Maine and took us all there for the month of August. We all got ringworm from some kittens and had to rub Pond's Extract on our arms and legs night and morning, and my father rolled over in a canoe with all his clothes on; but outside of that the vacation was a success and from then on none of us ever thought there was any place in the world like that lake in Maine. We returned summer after summer — always on August 1st for one month. I have since become a salt-water man, but sometimes in summer there are days when the restlessness of the tides and the fearful cold of the sea water and the incessant wind which blows across the afternoon and into the evening make me wish for the placidity of a lake in the woods. A few weeks ago this feeling got so strong I bought myself a couple of bass hooks and a spinner and returned to the lake where we used to go, for a week's fishing and to revisit old haunts.

I took along my son, who had never had any fresh water up his nose and who had seen lily pads only from train windows. On the journey over to the lake I began to wonder what it would be like. I wondered how time would have marred this unique, this holy spot — the coves and streams, the hills that the sun set behind, the camps and the paths behind the camps. I was sure that the tarred road would have found it out and I wondered in what other ways it would be desolated. It is strange how much you can remember about places like that once you allow your mind to return into the grooves which lead back. You remember one thing, and that suddenly reminds you of another thing. I guess I remembered clearest of all the early mornings, when the lake was cool and motionless, remembered how the bedroom smelled of the lumber it was made of and of the wet woods whose scent entered through the screen. The partitions in the camp were thin and did not extend clear to the top of the rooms, and as I was always the first up I would dress softly so as not to wake the others, and sneak out into the sweet outdoors and start out in the canoe, keeping close along the shore in the long shadows of the pines. I remembered being very careful never to rub my paddle against the gunwale for fear of disturbing the stillness of the cathedral.

The lake had never been what you would call a wild lake. There were cottages sprinkled around the shores, and it was in farming country although the shores of the lake were quite heavily wooded. Some of the cottages were owned by nearby farmers, and you would live at the shore and eat your meals at the farmhouse. That's what our family did. But although it wasn't wild, it was a fairly large and undisturbed lake and there were places in it which, to a child at least, seemed infinitely remote and primeval.

I was right about the tar: it led to within half a mile of the shore. But when I got back there, with my boy, and we settled into a camp near a farmhouse and into the kind of summertime I had known, I could tell that it was going to be pretty much the same as it had been before — I knew it, lying in bed the first morning, smelling the bedroom, and hearing the boy sneak quietly out and go off along the shore in a boat. I began to sustain the illusion that he was I, and therefore, by simple transposition, that I was my father. This sensation persisted, kept cropping up all the time we were there. It was not an entirely new feeling, but in this setting it grew much stronger. I seemed to be living a dual existence. I would be in the middle of some simple act, I would be picking up a bait box or laying down a table fork, or I would be saying something, and suddenly it would be not I but my father who was saying the words or making the gesture. It gave me a creepy sensation.

We went fishing the first morning. I felt the same damp moss covering ⁵ the worms in the bait can, and saw the dragonfly alight on the tip of my rod as it hovered a few inches from the surface of the water. It was the arrival of this fly that convinced me beyond any doubt that everything was as it always had been, that the years were a mirage and there had been no years. The small waves were the same, chucking the rowboat under the chin as we fished at anchor, and the boat was the same boat, the same color green and the ribs broken in the same places, and under the floor-boards the same fresh-water leavings and débris — the dead helgramite, the wisps of moss, the rusty discarded fishhook, the dried blood from yesterday's catch. We stared silently at the tips of our rods, at the dragonflies that came and went. I lowered the tip of mine into the water, tentatively, pensively dislodging the fly, which darted two feet away, poised, darted two feet back, and came to rest again a little farther up the rod. There had been no years between the ducking of this dragonfly and the other one — the one that was part of memory. I looked at the boy, who was silently watching his fly, and it was my hands that held his rod, my eyes watching. I felt dizzy and didn't know which rod I was at the end of.

We caught two bass, hauling them in briskly as though they were mackerel, pulling them over the side of the boat in a businesslike manner without any landing net, and stunning them with a blow on the back of the head. When we got back for a swim before lunch, the lake was exactly where we had left it, the same number of inches from the dock, and there was only the merest suggestion of a breeze. This seemed an utterly enchanted sea, this lake you could leave to its own devices for a few hours and come back to, and find that it had not stirred, this constant and trustworthy body of water. In the shallows, the dark, water-soaked sticks and twigs, smooth and old, were undulating in clusters on the bottom against the clean ribbed sand, and the track of the mussel was plain. A school of minnows swam by, each minnow with its small individual shadow, doubling the attendance, so clear and sharp in the sunlight. Some of the other campers were in swimming, along the shore, one of them with a cake of soap, and the water felt thin and clear and unsubstantial. Over the years there had been this person with the cake of soap, this cultist, and here he was. There had been no years.

Up to the farmhouse to dinner through the teeming, dusty field, the road under our sneakers was only a two-track road. The middle track was missing, the one with the marks of the hooves and the splotches of dried, flaky manure. There had always been three tracks to choose from in choosing which track to walk in; now the choice was narrowed down to two. For a moment I missed terribly the middle alternative. But the way led past the tennis court, and something about the way it lay there in the sun reassured me; the tape had loosened along the backline, the alleys were green with plantains and other weeds, and the net (installed in June and removed in September) sagged in the dry noon, and the whole place steamed with midday heat and hunger and emptiness. There was a choice of pie for dessert, and one was blueberry and one was apple, and the waitresses were the same country girls, there having been no passage of time, only the illusion of it as in a dropped curtain — the waitresses were still fifteen; their hair had been washed, that was the only difference — they had been to the movies and seen the pretty girls with the clean hair.

Summertime, oh summertime, pattern of life indelible, the fadeproof lake, the woods unshatterable, the pasture with the sweetfern and the juniper forever and ever, summer without end; this was the background, and the life along the shore was the design, the cottagers with their innocent and tranquil design, their tiny docks with the flagpole and the American flag floating against the white clouds in the blue sky, the little paths over the roots of the trees leading from camp to camp and the paths leading back to the outhouses and the can of lime for sprinkling, and at the souvenir counters at the store the miniature birch-bark canoes and the post cards that showed things looking a little better than they looked. This was the American family at play, escaping the city heat, wondering whether the newcomers in the camp at the head of the cove were "common" or "nice," wondering whether it was true that the people who drove up for Sunday dinner at the farmhouse were turned away because there wasn't enough chicken.

It seemed to me, as I kept remembering all this, that those times and those summers had been infinitely precious and worth saving. There had been jollity and peace and goodness. The arriving (at the beginning of August) had been so big a business in itself, at the railway station the farm wagon drawn up, the first smell of the pine-laden air, the first glimpse of the smiling farmer, and the great importance of the trunks and your father's enormous authority in such matters, and the feel of the wagon under you for the long ten-mile haul, and at the top of the last long hill catching the first view of the lake after eleven months of not seeing this cherished body of water. The shouts and cries of the other campers when they saw you, and the trunks to be unpacked, to give up their rich burden. (Arriving was less exciting nowadays, when you sneaked up in your car and parked it under a tree near the camp and took out the bags and in five minutes it was all over, no fuss, no loud wonderful fuss about trunks.)

Peace and goodness and jollity. The only thing that was wrong now, really, was the sound of the place, an unfamiliar nervous sound of the outboard motors. This was the note that jarred, the one thing that would sometimes break the illusion and set the years moving. In those other summertimes all motors were inboard; and when they were at a little distance, the noise they made was a sedative, an ingredient of summer sleep. They were one-cylinder and two-cylinder engines, and some were make-and-break and some were jump-spark, but they all made a sleepy sound across the lake. The one-lungers throbbed and fluttered, and the twin-cylinder ones purred and purred, and that was a quiet sound too. But now the campers all had outboards. In the daytime, in the hot mornings, these motors made a petulant, irritable sound; at night, in the still evening when the afterglow lit the water, they whined about one's ears like mosquitoes. My boy loved our rented outboard, and his great desire was to achieve singlehanded mastery over it, and authority, and he soon learned the trick of choking it a little (but not too much), and the adjustment of the needle valve. Watching him I would remember the things you could do with the old one-cylinder engine with the heavy flywheel, how you could have it eating out of your hand if you got really close to it spiritually. Motor boats in those days didn't have clutches, and you would make a landing by shutting off the motor at the proper time and coasting in with a dead rudder. But there was a way of reversing them, if you learned the trick, by cutting the switch and putting it on again exactly on the final dying revolution of the flywheel, so that it would kick back against compression and begin reversing. Approaching a dock in a strong following breeze, it was difficult to slow up sufficiently by the ordinary coasting method, and if a boy felt he had complete mastery over his motor, he was tempted to keep it running beyond its time and then reverse it a few feet from the dock. It took a cool nerve, because if you threw the switch a twentieth of a second too soon you would catch the flywheel when it still had speed enough to go up past center, and the boat would leap ahead, charging bull-fashion at the dock.

We had a good week at the camp. The bass were biting well and the sun shone endlessly, day after day. We would be tired at night and lie down in the accumulated heat of the little bedrooms after the long hot day and the breeze would stir almost imperceptibly outside and the smell of the swamp drift in through the rusty screens. Sleep would come easily and in the morning the red squirrel would be on the roof, tapping out his gay routine. I kept remembering everything, lying in bed in the mornings — the small steamboat that had a long rounded stern like the lip of a Ubangi, and how quietly she ran on the moonlight sails, when the older boys played their mandolins and the girls sang and we ate doughnuts dipped in sugar, and how sweet the music was on the water in the shining night, and what it had felt like to think about girls then. After breakfast we would go up to the store and the things were in the same place — the minnows in a bottle, the plugs and spinners disarranged and pawed over by the youngsters from the boys' camp, the Fig Newtons and the Beeman's gum. Outside, the road was tarred and cars stood in front of the store. Inside, all was just as it had always been, except there was more Coca Cola and not so much Moxie and root beer and birch beer and sarsaparilla. We would walk out with a bottle of pop apiece and sometimes the pop would backfire up our noses and hurt. We explored the streams, quietly, where the turtles slid off the sunny logs and dug their way into the soft bottom; and we lay on the town wharf and fed worms to the tame bass. Everywhere we went I had trouble making out which was I, the one walking at my side, the one walking in my pants.

One afternoon while we were there at that lake a thunderstorm came up. It was like the revival of an old melodrama that I had seen long ago with childish awe. The second-act climax of the drama of the electrical disturbance over a lake in America had not changed in any important respect. This was the big scene, still the big scene. The whole thing was so familiar, the first feeling of oppression and heat and a general air around camp of not wanting to go very far away. In midafternoon (it was all the same) a curious darkening of the sky, and a lull in everything that had made life tick; and then the way the boats suddenly swung the other way at their moorings with the coming of a breeze out of the new quarter, and the premonitory rumble. Then the kettle drum, then the snare, then the bass drum and cymbals, then crackling light against the dark, and the gods grinning and licking their chops in the hills. Afterward the calm, the rain steadily rustling in the calm lake, the return of light and hope and spirits, and the campers running out in joy and relief to go swimming in the rain, their bright cries perpetuating the deathless joke about how they were getting simply drenched, and the children screaming with delight at the new sensation of bathing in the rain, and the joke about getting drenched linking the generations in a strong indestructible chain. And the comedian who waded in carrying an umbrella.

When the others went swimming my son said he was going in too. He pulled his dripping trunks from the line where they had hung all through the shower, and wrung them out. Languidly, and with no thought of going in, I watched him, his hard little body, skinny and bare, saw him wince slightly as he pulled up around his vitals the small, soggy, icy garment. As he buckled the swollen belt suddenly my groin felt the chill of death.

FROM READING TO REREADING

1. At the center of this essay is what White calls "a creepy sensation." We ordinarily use the word "creepy" to describe moments of horror or fear. Though the atmosphere and setting of the essay seem perfectly relaxing, what causes White to feel this sensation? Is there anything frightening or horrible in his experience?

2. "Sensation" is an apt term for much of the experience of the essay. Note White's constant use of sensory details, of hearing, seeing, touching, and so on. How do these sensory images contribute to the overall effect of the essay, and how do they prepare us for the final paragraph?

3. Many essays contain moments of sudden realization or illumination. Critics, borrowing the word from the novelist James Joyce, often refer to such moments as epiphanies. The last paragraph of White's essay is an example of an epiphany. What do you think White suddenly recognizes?

GEORGE ORWELL
An Episode of Bed-wetting

In 1947, a few years before he died, George Orwell wrote a long autobiographical essay about his early education that he ironically called "Such, Such Were the Joys." Between 1911 and 1916, Orwell attended St. Cyprian's, an expensive, private preparatory school for boys on the Sussex coast of England. Many of the students went on from St. Cyprian's to either Harrow or (as Orwell did) to Eton. But Orwell's reminiscences of St. Cyprian's are not those of an enthusiastic alumnus; in fact, he felt he couldn't publish the essay because, aside from its length (it's about forty pages long), he thought it was "too libellous to print." "Such, Such Were the Joys" appeared posthumously in 1952 in an American periodical, Partisan Review, *to which Orwell had been a regular contributor. The essay is divided into six relatively self-contained sections, the first of which is reprinted here (another section appears in Part 4, "Teaching and Learning"). The text is taken from Orwell's original typescript, which differs from the American version mainly in its use of names and nicknames.*

SOON AFTER I ARRIVED at St Cyprian's (not immediately, but after a week or two, just when I seemed to be settling into the routine of school life) I began wetting my bed. I was now aged eight, so that this was a reversion to a habit which I must have grown out of at least four years earlier.

Nowadays, I believe, bed-wetting in such circumstances is taken for granted. It is a normal reaction in children who have been removed from their homes to a strange place. In those days, however, it was looked on as a disgusting crime which the child committed on purpose and for which the proper cure was a beating. For my part I did not need to be told it was a crime. Night after night I prayed, with a fervour never previously attained in my prayers, "Please God, do not let me wet my bed! Oh, please God, do not let me wet my bed!", but it made remarkably little difference. Some nights the thing happened, others not. There was no volition about it, no consciousness. You did not properly speaking *do* the deed: you merely woke up in the morning and found that the sheets were wringing wet.

After the second or third offence I was warned that I should be beaten next time, but I received the warning in a curiously roundabout way. One afternoon, as we were filing out from tea, Mrs W —— , the Headmaster's wife, was sitting at the head of one of the tables, chatting with a lady of whom I knew nothing, except that she was on an afternoon's visit to the school. She was an intimidating, masculine-looking person wearing a riding-habit, or something that I took to be a riding-habit. I was just leaving the room when Mrs W —— called me back, as though to introduce me to the visitor.

Mrs W —— was nicknamed Flip, and I shall call her by that name, for I seldom think of her by any other. (Officially, however, she was addressed as Mum, probably a corruption of the "Ma'am" used by public schoolboys to their housemasters' wives.) She was a stocky square-built woman with hard red cheeks, a flat top to her head, prominent brows and deep-set, suspicious eyes. Although a great deal of the time she was full of false heartiness, jollying one along with mannish slang ("*Buck* up, old chap!" and so forth), and even using one's Christian name, her eyes never lost their anxious, accusing look. It was very difficult to look her in the face without feeling guilty, even at moments when one was not guilty of anything in particular.

"Here is a little boy," said Flip, indicating me to the strange lady,   5
"who wets his bed every night. Do you know what I am going to do if you wet your bed again?" she added, turning to me. "I am going to get the Sixth Form to beat you."

The strange lady put on an air of being inexpressibly shocked, and exclaimed "I-should-*think*-so!" And here there occurred one of those wild, almost lunatic misunderstandings which are part of the daily experience of childhood. The Sixth Form was a group of older boys who were selected as having "character" and were empowered to beat smaller boys. I had not yet learned of their existence, and I mis-heard the phrase "the Sixth Form" as "Mrs Form." I took it as referring to the strange lady — I thought, that is, that her name was Mrs Form. It was an improbable name, but a child has no judgement in such matters. I imagined, therefore, that it was *she* who was to be deputed to beat me. It did not strike me as strange that this job should be turned over to a casual visitor in no way connected with the school. I merely assumed that "Mrs Form" was a stern disciplinarian who enjoyed beating people (somehow her appearance seemed to bear this out) and I had an immediate terrifying vision of her arriving for the occasion in full riding kit and armed with a hunting-whip. To this day I can feel myself almost swooning with shame as I stood, a very small, round-faced boy in short corduroy knickers, before the two women. I could not speak. I felt that I should die if "Mrs Form" were to beat me. But my dominant feeling was not fear or even resentment: it was simply shame because one more person, and that a woman, had been told of my disgusting offence.

A little later, I forget how, I learned that it was not after all "Mrs Form" who would do the beating. I cannot remember whether it was that very night that I wetted my bed again, but at any rate I did wet it again quite soon. Oh, the despair, the feeling of cruel injustice, after all my prayers and resolutions, at once again waking between the clammy sheets! There was no chance of hiding what I had done. The grim statuesque matron,

Margaret by name, arrived in the dormitory specially to inspect my bed. She pulled back the clothes, then drew herself up, and the dreaded words seemed to come rolling out of her like a peal of thunder:

"REPORT YOURSELF to the Headmaster after breakfast!"

I put REPORT YOURSELF in capitals because that was how it appeared in my mind. I do not know how many times I heard that phrase during my early years at St Cyprian's. It was only very rarely that it did not mean a beating. The words always had a portentous sound in my ears, like muffled drums or the words of the death sentence.

When I arrived to report myself, Flip was doing something or other at   10
the long shiny table in the ante-room to the study. Her uneasy eyes searched me as I went past. In the study the Headmaster, nicknamed Sambo, was waiting. Sambo was a round-shouldered, curiously oafish-looking man, not large but shambling in gait, with a chubby face which was like that of an overgrown baby, and which was capable of good humour. He knew, of course, why I had been sent to him, and had already taken a bone-handled riding-crop out of the cupboard, but it was part of the punishment of reporting yourself that you had to proclaim your offence with your own lips. When I had said my say, he read me a short but pompous lecture, then seized me by the scruff of the neck, twisted me over and began beating me with the riding-crop. He had a habit of continuing his lecture while he flogged you, and I remember the words "you dir-ty lit-tle boy" keeping time with the blows. The beating did not hurt (perhaps, as it was the first time, he was not hitting me very hard), and I walked out feeling very much better. The fact that the beating had not hurt was a sort of victory and partially wiped out the shame of the bed-wetting. I was even incautious enough to wear a grin on my face. Some small boys were hanging about in the passage outside the door of the ante-room.

"D'you get the cane?"

"It didn't hurt," I said proudly.

Flip had heard everything. Instantly her voice came screaming after me:

"Come here! Come here this instant! What was that you said?"

"I said it didn't hurt," I faltered out.   15

"How dare you say a thing like that? Do you think that is a proper thing to say? Go in and REPORT YOURSELF AGAIN!"

This time Sambo laid on in real earnest. He continued for a length of time that frightened and astonished me — about five minutes, it seemed — ending up by breaking the riding-crop. The bone handle went flying across the room.

"Look what you've made me do!" he said furiously, holding up the broken crop.

I had fallen into a chair, weakly snivelling. I remember that this was the only time throughout my boyhood when a beating actually reduced me to tears, and curiously enough I was not even now crying because of the pain. The second beating had not hurt very much either. Fright and shame seemed to have anaesthetised me. I was crying partly because I felt that this was expected of me, partly from genuine repentance, but partly also because of a deeper grief which is peculiar to childhood and not easy to convey: a sense of desolate loneliness and helplessness, of being locked up not only in a hostile world but in a world of good and evil where the rules were such that it was actually not possible for me to keep them.

I knew that the bed-wetting was (a) wicked and (b) outside my control. The second fact I was personally aware of, and the first I did not question. It was possible, therefore, to commit a sin without knowing that you committed it, without wanting to commit it, and without being able to avoid it. Sin was not necessarily something that you did: it might be something that happened to you. I do not want to claim that this idea flashed into my mind as a complete novelty at this very moment, under the blows of Sambo's cane: I must have had glimpses of it even before I left home, for my early childhood had not been altogether happy. But at any rate this was the great, abiding lesson of my boyhood: that I was in a world where it was *not possible* for me to be good. And the double beating was a turning-point, for it brought home to me for the first time the harshness of the environment into which I had been flung. Life was more terrible, and I was more wicked, than I had imagined. At any rate, as I sat snivelling on the edge of a chair in Sambo's study, with not even the self-possession to stand up while he stormed at me, I had a conviction of sin and folly and weakness, such as I do not remember to have felt before.

In general, one's memories of any period must necessarily weaken as one moves away from it. One is constantly learning new facts, and old ones have to drop out to make way for them. At twenty I could have written the history of my schooldays with an accuracy which would be quite impossible now. But it can also happen that one's memories grow sharper after a long lapse of time, because one is looking at the past with fresh eyes and can isolate and, as it were, notice facts which previously existed undifferentiated among a mass of others. Here are two things which in a sense I remembered, but which did not strike me as strange or interesting until quite recently. One is that the second beating seemed to me a just and reasonable punishment. To get one beating, and then to get another and far fiercer one on top of it, for being so unwise as to show that the first had not hurt — that was quite natural. The gods are jealous, and when you have good fortune you should conceal it. The other is that I accepted the broken riding-crop as my own crime. I can still recall my feeling as I saw the handle lying on the carpet — the feeling of having done an ill-bred, clumsy thing, and ruined an expensive object. *I* had broken it: so Sambo told me, and so I believed. This acceptance of guilt lay unnoticed in my memory for twenty or thirty years.

20

So much for the episode of the bed-wetting. But there is one more thing to be remarked. This is that I did not wet my bed again — at least, I did wet it once again, and received another beating, after which the trouble stopped. So perhaps this barbarous remedy does work, though at a heavy price, I have no doubt.

FROM READING TO REREADING

1. As an essayist, Orwell strongly emphasized personal honesty and truthfulness. Notice, for example, the opening sentence of his essay. How does the parenthetical detail immediately confront us with Orwell's desire to be as accurate as possible? Can you find other such details in the episode?

2. Corporal punishment is rarely administered in schools today and will strike many as — to use Orwell's term — "barbarous." But consider Orwell's rather complex attitude toward his punishment. Does he feel it was entirely unjustified? Which aspects of his punishment does he feel were undeserved; which deserved?

3. The moment of insight or of sudden illumination represents one of the great themes of the personal essay. But such moments are rare in life and can easily be overdone in literature. Imagine reading a writer who seemed to have one in every essay; we are soon distrustful of someone who concludes every experience with "Suddenly I realized that . . ." or "All at once I understood that. . . ." Orwell is a writer who is clearly uncomfortable in claiming such melodramatic moments. How does he convey his unease with such moments in this episode? And how does his disclaimer contribute to his credibility?

ALICE WALKER

Beauty: When the Other Dancer Is the Self

"I have always been a solitary person," Alice Walker claimed in a 1973 interview, "and since I was eight years old (and victim of a traumatic accident that blinded and scarred one eye), I have daydreamed — not of fairy tales — but of falling on swords, of putting guns to my heart or head, and of slashing my wrists with a razor. For a long time I thought I was very ugly and disfigured. . . ." In "Beauty: When the Other Dancer Is the Self," written ten years after this suicidal confession, she confronts these feelings again through a series of vivid memories that culminate in a healing moment of self-discovery. The essay, as have many others by the author, appeared originally in Ms. *magazine. It was also reprinted as the final essay in her well-known collection,* In Search of Our Mothers' Gardens, *a volume dedicated to her daughter Rebecca, "Who saw in me/what I considered/a scar/And redefined it/as/a world."*

I T IS A BRIGHT SUMMER DAY in 1947. My father, a fat, funny man with beautiful eyes and a subversive wit, is trying to decide which of his eight children he will take with him to the county fair. My mother, of course, will not go. She is knocked out from getting most of us ready: I hold my neck stiff against the pressure of her knuckles as she hastily completes the braiding and beribboning of my hair.

My father is the driver for the rich old white lady up the road. Her name is Miss Mey. She owns all the land for miles around, as well as the house in which we live. All I remember about her is that she once offered to pay my mother thirty-five cents for cleaning her house, raking up piles of her magnolia leaves, and washing her family's clothes, and that my mother — she of no money, eight children, and a chronic earache — refused it. But I do not think of this in 1947. I am two-and-a-half years old. I want to go everywhere my daddy goes. I am excited at the prospect of riding in a car. Someone has told me fairs are fun. That there is room in the car for only three of us doesn't faze me at all. Whirling happily in my starchy frock, showing off my biscuit-polished patent-leather shoes and lavender socks, tossing my head in a way that makes my ribbons bounce, I stand, hands on hips, before my father. "Take me, Daddy," I say with assurance; "I'm the prettiest!"

Later, it does not surprise me to find myself in Miss Mey's shiny black car, sharing the back seat with the other lucky ones. Does not surprise me that I thoroughly enjoy the fair. At home that night I tell the unlucky ones all I can remember about the merry-go-round, the man who eats live chickens, and the teddy bears, until they say: that's enough, baby Alice. Shut up now, and go to sleep.

It is Easter Sunday, 1950. I am dressed in a green, flocked, scalloped-hem dress (handmade by my adoring sister, Ruth) that has its own smooth satin petticoat and tiny hot-pink roses tucked into each scallop. My shoes, new T-strap patent leather, again highly biscuit-polished. I am six years old and have learned one of the longest Easter speeches to be heard that day, totally unlike the speech I said when I was two: "Easter lilies / pure and white / blossom in / the morning light." When I rise to give my speech I do so on a great wave of love and pride and expectation. People in the church stop rustling their new crinolines. They seem to hold their breath. I can tell they admire my dress, but it is my spirit, bordering on sassiness (womanishness), they secretly applaud.

"That girl's a little *mess*," they whisper to each other, pleased.   5

Naturally I say my speech without stammer or pause, unlike those who stutter, stammer, or, worst of all, forget. This is before the word "beautiful" exists in people's vocabulary, but "Oh, isn't she the *cutest* thing!" frequently floats my way. "And got so much sense!" they gratefully add . . . for which thoughtful addition I thank them to this day.

It was great fun being cute. But then, one day, it ended.

I am eight years old and a tomboy. I have a cowboy hat, cowboy boots, checkered shirt and pants, all red. My playmates are my brothers, two and four years older than I. Their colors are black and green, the only difference in the way we are dressed. On Saturday nights we all go to the picture show, even my mother; Westerns are her favorite kind of movie. Back home, "on the ranch," we pretend we are Tom Mix, Hopalong Cassidy, Lash LaRue (we've even named one of our dogs Lash LaRue); we chase each other for hours rustling cattle, being outlaws, delivering damsels from distress. Then my parents decide to buy my brothers guns. These are not "real" guns. They shoot BBs, copper pellets my brothers say will kill birds. Because I am a girl, I do not get a gun. Instantly I am relegated to the position of Indian. Now there appears a great distance between us. They shoot and shoot at everything with their new guns. I try to keep up with my bow and arrows.

One day while I am standing on top of our makeshift "garage" — pieces of tin nailed across some poles — holding my bow and arrow and looking out toward the fields, I feel an incredible blow in my right eye. I look down just in time to see my brother lower his gun.

Both brothers rush to my side. My eye stings, and I cover it with my   10
hand. "If you tell," they say, "we will get a whipping. You don't want that

to happen, do you?" I do not. "Here is a piece of wire," says the older brother, picking it up from the roof; "say you stepped on one end of it and the other flew up and hit you." The pain is beginning to start. "Yes," I say. "Yes, I will say that is what happened." If I do not say this is what happened, I know my brothers will find ways to make me wish I had. But now I will say anything that gets me to my mother.

Confronted by our parents we stick to the lie agreed upon. They place me on a bench on the porch and I close my left eye while they examine the right. There is a tree growing from underneath the porch that climbs past the railing to the roof. It is the last thing my right eye sees. I watch as its trunk, its branches, and then its leaves are blotted out by the rising blood.

I am in shock. First there is intense fever, which my father tries to break using lily leaves bound around my head. Then there are chills: my mother tries to get me to eat soup. Eventually, I do not know how, my parents learn what has happened. A week after the "accident" they take me to see a doctor. "Why did you wait so long to come?" he asks, looking into my eye and shaking his head. "Eyes are sympathetic," he says. "If one is blind, the other will likely become blind too."

This comment of the doctor's terrifies me. But it is really how I look that bothers me most. Where the BB pellet struck there is a glob of whitish scar tissue, a hideous cataract, on my eye. Now when I stare at people — a favorite pastime, up to now — they will stare back. Not at the "cute" little girl, but at her scar. For six years I do not stare at anyone, because I do not raise my head.

Years later, in the throes of a midlife crisis, I ask my mother and sister whether I changed after the "accident." "No," they say, puzzled. "What do you mean?"

What do I mean?   15

I am eight, and, for the first time, doing poorly in school, where I have been something of a whiz since I was four. We have just moved to the place where the "accident" occurred. We do not know any of the people around us because this is a different county. The only time I see the friends I knew is when we go back to our old church. The new school is the former state penitentiary. It is a large stone building, cold and drafty, crammed to overflowing with boisterous, ill-disciplined children. On the third floor there is a huge circular imprint of some partition that has been torn out.

"What used to be here?" I ask a sullen girl next to me on our way past it to lunch.

"The electric chair," says she.

At night I have nightmares about the electric chair, and about all the people reputedly "fried" in it. I am afraid of the school, where all the students seem to be budding criminals.

"What's the matter with your eye?" they ask, critically.   20

When I don't answer (I cannot decide whether it was an "accident" or not), they shove me, insist on a fight.

My brother, the one who created the story about the wire, comes to my rescue. But then brags so much about "protecting" me, I become sick.

After months of torture at the school, my parents decide to send me back to our old community, to my old school. I live with my grandparents and the teacher they board. But there is no room for Phoebe, my cat. By the time my grandparents decide there *is* room, and I ask for my cat, she cannot be found. Miss Yarborough, the boarding teacher, takes me under her wing, and begins to teach me to play the piano. But soon she marries an African — a "prince," she says — and is whisked away to his continent.

At my old school there is at least one teacher who loves me. She is the teacher who "knew me before I was born" and bought my first baby clothes. It is she who makes life bearable. It is her presence that finally helps me turn on the one child at the school who continually calls me "one-eyed bitch." One day I simply grab him by his coat and beat him until I am satisfied. It is my teacher who tells me my mother is ill.

My mother is lying in bed in the middle of the day, something I have never seen. She is in too much pain to speak. She has an abscess in her ear. I stand looking down on her, knowing that if she dies, I cannot live. She is being treated with warm oils and hot bricks held against her cheek. Finally a doctor comes. But I must go back to my grandparents' house. The weeks pass but I am hardly aware of it. All I know is that my mother might die, my father is not so jolly, my brothers still have their guns, and I am the one sent away from home. 25

"You did not change," they say.

Did I imagine the anguish of never looking up?

I am twelve. When relatives come to visit I hide in my room. My cousin Brenda, just my age, whose father works in the post office and whose mother is a nurse, comes to find me. "Hello," she says. And then she asks, looking at my recent school picture, which I did not want taken, and on which the "glob," as I think of it, is clearly visible, "You still can't see out of that eye?"

"No," I say, and flop back on the bed over my book.

That night, as I do almost every night, I abuse my eye. I rant and rave 30 at it, in front of the mirror. I plead with it to clear up before morning. I tell it I hate and despise it. I do not pray for sight. I pray for beauty.

"You did not change," they say.

I am fourteen and baby-sitting for my brother Bill, who lives in Boston. He is my favorite brother and there is a strong bond between us. Understanding my feelings of shame and ugliness he and his wife take me to a local hospital, where the "glob" is removed by a doctor named O. Henry. There is still a small bluish crater where the scar tissue was, but the ugly white stuff is gone. Almost immediately I become a different person from the girl who does not raise her head. Or so I think. Now that I've raised my head I win the boyfriend of my dreams. Now that I've raised my head I have plenty of friends. Now that I've raised my head classwork comes from my lips as faultlessly as Easter speeches did, and I leave high school as valedictorian, most popular student, and *queen,* hardly believing my luck. Ironically, the girl who was voted most beautiful in our class (and was) was later shot twice through the chest by a male companion, using a "real" gun, while she was pregnant. But that's another story in itself. Or is it?

"You did not change," they say.

It is now thirty years since the "accident." A beautiful journalist comes to visit and to interview me. She is going to write a cover story for her magazine that focuses on my latest book. "Decide how you want to look on the cover," she says. "Glamorous, or whatever."

Never mind "glamorous," it is the "whatever" that I hear. Suddenly all I can think of is whether I will get enough sleep the night before the photography session: if I don't, my eye will be tired and wander, as blind eyes will.

At night in bed with my lover I think up reasons why I should not appear on the cover of a magazine. "My meanest critics will say I've sold out," I say. "My family will now realize I write scandalous books."

"But what's the real reason you don't want to do this?" he asks.

"Because in all probability," I say in a rush, "my eye won't be straight."

"It will be straight enough," he says. Then, "Besides, I thought you'd made your peace with that."

And I suddenly remember that I have.

I remember:

I am talking to my brother Jimmy, asking if he remembers anything unusual about the day I was shot. He does not know I consider that day the last time my father, with his sweet home remedy of cool lily leaves, chose me, and that I suffered and raged inside because of this. "Well," he says, "all I remember is standing by the side of the highway with Daddy, trying to flag down a car. A white man stopped, but when Daddy said he needed somebody to take his little girl to the doctor, he drove off."

I remember:

I am in the desert for the first time. I fall totally in love with it. I am so overwhelmed by its beauty, I confront for the first time, consciously, the meaning of the doctor's words years ago: "Eyes are sympathetic. If one is blind, the other will likely become blind too." I realize I have dashed about the world madly, looking at this, looking at that, storing up images against the fading of the light. *But I might have missed seeing the desert!* The shock of that possibility — and gratitude for over twenty-five years of sight — sends me literally to my knees. Poem after poem comes — which is perhaps how poets pray.

ON SIGHT

I am so thankful I have seen
The Desert
And the creatures in the desert
And the desert Itself.

The desert has its own moon
Which I have seen
With my own eye.
There is no flag on it.

Trees of the desert have arms
All of which are always up
That is because the moon is up
The sun is up
Also the sky
The Stars
Clouds
None with flags.

If there were flags, I doubt
the trees would point.
Would you?

But mostly, I remember this: 45

I am twenty-seven, and my baby daughter is almost three. Since her birth I have worried about her discovery that her mother's eyes are different from other people's. Will she be embarrassed? I think. What will she say? Every day she watches a television program called *Big Blue Marble.* It begins with a picture of the earth as it appears from the moon. It is bluish, a little battered-looking, but full of light, with whitish clouds swirling around it. Every time I see it I weep with love, as if it is a picture of Grandma's house. One day when I am putting Rebecca down for her nap, she suddenly focuses on my eye. Something inside me cringes, gets ready to try to protect myself. All children are cruel about physical differences, I know from experience, and that they don't always mean to be is another matter. I assume Rebecca will be the same.

But no-o-o-o. She studies my face intently as we stand, her inside and me outside her crib. She even holds my face maternally between her dimpled little hands. Then, looking every bit as serious and lawyerlike as her father, she says, as if it may just possibly have slipped my attention: "Mommy, there's a *world* in your eye." (As in, "Don't be alarmed, or do anything crazy.") And then, gently, but with great interest: "Mommy, where did you *get* that world in your eye?"

For the most part, the pain left then. (So what, if my brothers grew up to buy even more powerful pellet guns for their sons and to carry real guns themselves. So what, if a young "Morehouse [1] man" once nearly fell off the steps of Trevor Arnett Library because he thought my eyes were blue.) Crying and laughing I ran to the bathroom, while Rebecca mumbled and sang herself to sleep. Yes indeed, I realized, looking into the mirror. There *was* a world in my eye. And I saw that it was possible to love it: that in fact, for all it had taught me of shame and anger and inner vision, I *did* love it. Even to see it drifting out of orbit in boredom, or rolling up out of fatigue, not to mention floating back at attention in excitement (bearing witness, a friend has called it), deeply suitable to my personality, and even characteristic of me.

That night I dream I am dancing to Stevie Wonder's song "Always" (the name of the song is really "As," but I hear it as "Always"). As I dance, whirling and joyous, happier than I've ever been in my life, another bright-faced dancer joins me. We dance and kiss each other and hold each other through the night. The other dancer has obviously come through all right, as I have done. She is beautiful, whole and free. And she is also me.

[1] *Morehouse:* Morehouse College, a black men's college in Atlanta, Georgia.

FROM READING AND REREADING

1. Alice Walker's essay contains a rich texture of imagery that becomes more apparent with rereading. Details that at first seem casual — such as the mention of her father's "beautiful eyes" in the first paragraph — take on fuller significance once we know how the essay proceeds. Can you identify another such imagistic detail and locate a related image elsewhere in the essay?

2. Though Walker is dealing with events in her past, she uses the present tense throughout the essay. What is the effect of this, on both the writer and the reader? How does it affect your sense of time in the essay? Try rewriting the opening paragraph in the past tense: What difference do you think it makes?

3. At several points in the essay, Walker introduces italicized comments. Consider the purpose and meaning of these comments. Why are they italicized? Whose comments are they? How do you think they are intended to be read? Why aren't all of these comments in the present tense? How do they affect the time frame of the essay?

STEPHEN JAY GOULD
The Median Isn't the Message[1]

Suppose you discover that you have a serious illness and are medically informed that victims of your illness have an "eight months median mortality." Would you conclude that you had only eight months to live? If so, you would in all likelihood be making a fatal error. It was an error that Stephen Jay Gould — a biological scientist and one of America's finest essayists — did not make after he learned in 1982 that he had a "rare and serious cancer." Armed with good spirits and trained in statistics, Gould interpreted his dire "eight months" prognosis optimistically — and scientifically. In "The Median Isn't the Message," Gould demonstrates how the knowledge of statistics, a subject that many of us find deadly boring, can lead to insights that can save our lives.

M Y LIFE has recently intersected, in a most personal way, two of Mark Twain's famous quips. One I shall defer to the end of this essay. The other (sometimes attributed to Disraeli),[2] identifies three species of mendacity, each worse than the one before — lies, damned lies, and statistics.

Consider the standard example of stretching truth with numbers — a case quite relevant to my story. Statistics recognizes different measures of an "average," or central tendency. The *mean* is our usual concept of an overall average — add up the items and divide them by the number of sharers (100 candy bars collected for five kids next Halloween will yield 20 for each in a just world). The *median*, a different measure of central tendency, is the halfway point. If I line up five kids by height, the median child is shorter than two and taller than the other two (who might have trouble getting their mean share of the candy). A politician in power might say with pride, "The mean income of our citizens is $15,000 per year." The leader of the opposition might retort, "But half our citizens make less than $10,000 per year." Both are right, but neither cites a statistic with impassive objectivity. The first invokes a mean, the second a median. (Means are higher than medians in such cases because one millionaire may outweigh hundreds of poor people in setting a mean; but he can balance only one mendicant in calculating a median).

---

[1] *The Median* . . . : Gould's title alludes to "the medium is the message," a well-known statement about the impact of electronic media on human perception coined by (Herbert) Marshall McLuhan, author of *Understanding Media* (1964).

[2] *Disraeli*: Benjamin Disraeli (1804–1881), British novelist and prominent conservative political figure who became prime minister in 1868.

The larger issue that creates a common distrust or contempt for statistics is more troubling. Many people make an unfortunate and invalid separation between heart and mind, or feeling and intellect. In some contemporary traditions, abetted by attitudes stereotypically centered upon Southern California, feelings are exalted as more "real" and the only proper basis for action — if it feels good, do it — while intellect gets short shrift as a hang-up of outmoded elitism. Statistics, in this absurd dichotomy, often become the symbol of the enemy. As Hilaire Belloc [3] wrote, "Statistics are the triumph of the quantitative method, and the quantitative method is the victory of sterility and death."

This is a personal story of statistics, properly interpreted, as profoundly nurturant and life-giving. It declares holy war on the downgrading of intellect by telling a small story about the utility of dry, academic knowledge about science. Heart and head are focal points of one body, one personality.

In July 1982, I learned that I was suffering from abdominal mesothe-   5
lioma, a rare and serious cancer usually associated with exposure to asbestos. When I revived after surgery, I asked my first question of my doctor and chemotherapist: "What is the best technical literature about mesothelioma?" She replied, with a touch of diplomacy (the only departure she has ever made from direct frankness), that the medical literature contained nothing really worth reading.

Of course, trying to keep an intellectual away from literature works about as well as recommending chastity to *Homo sapiens*, the sexiest primate of all. As soon as I could walk, I made a beeline for Harvard's Countway medical library and punched mesothelioma into the computer's bibliographic search program. An hour later, surrounded by the latest literature on abdominal mesothelioma, I realized with a gulp why my doctor had offered that humane advice. The literature couldn't have been more brutally clear: mesothelioma is incurable, with a median mortality of only eight months after discovery. I sat stunned for about fifteen minutes, then smiled and said to myself: so that's why they didn't give me anything to read. Then my mind started to work again, thank goodness.

If a little learning could ever be a dangerous thing, I had encountered a classic example. Attitude clearly matters in fighting cancer. We don't know why (from my old-style materialistic perspective, I suspect that mental states feed back upon the immune system). But match people with the same cancer for age, class, health, socioeconomic status, and, in general, those with positive attitudes, with a strong will and purpose for living, with commitment to struggle, with an active response to aiding their own treatment and not just a passive acceptance of anything doctors say, tend to live longer. A few

[3] *Hilaire Belloc* (1870–1953): English poet and essayist, known for his light verse and dedication to Catholicism.

months later I asked Sir Peter Medawar, my personal scientific guru and a Nobelist in immunology, what the best prescription for success against cancer might be. "A sanguine personality," he replied. Fortunately (since one can't reconstruct oneself at short notice and for a definite purpose), I am, if anything, even-tempered and confident in just this manner.

Hence the dilemma for humane doctors: since attitude matters so critically, should such a somber conclusion be advertised, especially since few people have sufficient understanding of statistics to evaluate what the statements really mean? From years of experience with the small-scale evolution of Bahamian land snails treated quantitatively, I have developed this technical knowledge — and I am convinced that it played a major role in saving my life. Knowledge is indeed power, in Bacon's [4] proverb.

The problem may be briefly stated: What does "median mortality of eight months" signify in our vernacular? I suspect that most people, without training in statistics, would read such a statement as "I will probably be dead in eight months" — the very conclusion that must be avoided, since it isn't so, and since attitude matters so much.

I was not, of course, overjoyed, but I didn't read the statement in this vernacular way either. My technical training enjoined a different perspective on "eight months median mortality." The point is a subtle one, but profound — for it embodies the distinctive way of thinking in my own field of evolutionary biology and natural history.

We still carry the historical baggage of a Platonic heritage that seeks sharp essences and definite boundaries. (Thus we hope to find an unambiguous "beginning of life" or "definition of death," although nature often comes to us as irreducible continua.) This Platonic heritage, with its emphasis on clear distinctions and separated immutable entities, leads us to view statistical measures of central tendency wrongly, indeed opposite to the appropriate interpretation in our actual world of variation, shadings, and continua. In short, we view means and medians as the hard "realities," and the variation that permits their calculation as a set of transient and imperfect measurements of this hidden essence. If the median is the reality and variation around the median just a device for its calculation, the "I will probably be dead in eight months" may pass as a reasonable interpretation.

But all evolutionary biologists know that variation itself is nature's only irreducible essence. Variation is the hard reality, not a set of imperfect measures for a central tendency. Means and medians are the abstractions. Therefore, I looked at the mesothelioma statistics quite differently — and not only because I am an optimist who tends to see the doughnut instead of

10

---

[4] *Bacon*: Francis Bacon (1561–1626), British philosopher, scientist, and the first great English essayist.

the hole, but primarily because I know that variation itself is the reality. I had to place myself amidst the variation.

When I learned about the eight-month median, my first intellectual reaction was: fine, half the people will live longer; now what are my chances of being in that half. I read for a furious and nervous hour and concluded, with relief: damned good. I possessed every one of the characteristics conferring a probability of longer life: I was young; my disease had been recognized in a relatively early stage; I would receive the nation's best medical treatment; I had the world to live for; I knew how to read the data properly and not despair.

Another technical point then added even more solace. I immediately recognized that the distribution of variation about the eight-month median would almost surely be what statisticians call "right skewed." (In a symmetrical distribution, the profile of variation to the left of the central tendency is a mirror image of variation to the right. In skewed distributions, variation to one side of the central tendency is more stretched out — left skewed if extended to the left, right skewed if stretched out to the right.) The distribution of variation had to be right skewed, I reasoned. After all, the left of the distribution contains an irrevocable lower boundary of zero (since mesothelioma can only be identified at death or before). Thus there isn't much room for the distribution's lower (or left) half — it must be scrunched up between zero and eight months. But the upper (or right) half can extend out for years and years, even if nobody ultimately survives. The distribution must be right skewed, and I needed to know how long the extended tail ran — for I had already concluded that my favorable profile made me a good candidate for that part of the curve.

The distribution was, indeed, strongly right skewed, with a long tail (however small) that extended for several years above the eight month median. I saw no reason why I shouldn't be in that small tail, and I breathed a very long sigh of relief. My technical knowledge had helped. I had read the graph correctly. I had asked the right question and found the answers. I had obtained, in all probability, that most precious of all possible gifts in the circumstances — substantial time. I didn't have to stop and immediately follow Isaiah's injunction to Hezekiah — set thine house in order: for thou shalt die, and not live. [5] I would have time to think, to plan, and to fight.

One final point about statistical distributions. They apply only to a prescribed set of circumstances — in this case to survival with mesothelioma under conventional modes of treatment. If circumstances change, the distribution may alter. I was placed on an experimental protocol of treatment and, if fortune holds, will be in the first cohort of a new distribution with high median and a right tail extending to death by natural causes at advanced old age.

[5] *set thine house* . . . : Alludes to a verse in the Old Testament, Isaiah 38:1.

It has become, in my view, a bit too trendy to regard the acceptance of death as something tantamount to intrinsic dignity. Of course I agree with the preacher of Ecclesiastes that there is a time to love and a time to die [6] — and when my skein runs out I hope to face the end calmly and in my own way. For most situations, however, I prefer the more martial view that death is the ultimate enemy — and I find nothing reproachable in those who rage mightily against the dying of the light.

The swords of battle are numerous, and none more effective than humor. My death was announced at a meeting of my colleagues in Scotland, and I almost experienced the delicious pleasure of reading my obituary penned by one of my best friends (the so-and-so got suspicious and checked; he too is a statistician, and didn't expect to find me so far out on the left tail). Still, the incident provided my first good laugh after the diagnosis. Just think, I almost got to repeat Mark Twain's most famous line of all: the reports of my death are greatly exaggerated.

[6] *time to love* . . . : Another Old Testament allusion, Ecclesiastes 3:1–8.

FROM READING AND REREADING

1. Writers often use the personal essay as a way to shape a moral lesson. "The Median Isn't the Message" is as much about human attitudes as it is about a personal victory over death. What is Gould's moral? What does it have to do with our intellectual life?

2. It's quite common for essayists to start an essay with an apt quotation. Inexperienced writers use such quotations passively; they simply plug them in and that's that. But experienced writers, like Gould, know how to use quotations actively; their quotations play a key role in the overall composition. How does Gould create a twist to the age-old essayistic convention of an opening quotation? How does his use of an opening quotation give him a structural as well as a thematic opportunity?

3. Note that Gould's first question after surgery pertains to reading. Consider all of the other references to reading in the essay. Why is the act of reading significant to Gould's experience? In what way is it connected to insight?

ANNIE DILLARD
Total Eclipse

Annie Dillard's work has consistently demonstrated that the essay is, like fiction or poetry, a branch of imaginative literature. "Total Eclipse," one of her finest essays, contains ample proof of her literary powers. Here you will find the climactic intensity of a short story, the interwoven imagery of poetry, and the meditative processes of the personal essay. Like many of Dillard's essays, "Total Eclipse" centers on personal insight; but it also resembles much of her work in that the insight — as is the case of so many true insights — is not easily named or articulated. Written in 1981, "Total Eclipse" was collected in Dillard's Teaching a Stone to Talk, *a volume that surely ranks as one of the outstanding essay collections of the past twenty-five years.*

1

IT HAD BEEN LIKE DYING, that sliding down the mountain pass. It had been like the death of someone, irrational, that sliding down the mountain pass and into the region of dread. It was like slipping into fever, or falling down that hole in sleep from which you wake yourself whimpering. We had crossed the mountains that day, and now we were in a strange place — a hotel in central Washington, in a town near Yakima. The eclipse we had traveled here to see would occur early the next morning.

I lay in bed. My husband, Gary, was reading beside me. I lay in bed and looked at the painting on the hotel room wall. It was a print of a detailed and lifelike painting of a smiling clown's head, made out of vegetables. It was a painting of the sort which you do not intend to look at, and which, alas, you never forget. Some tasteless fate presses it upon you; it becomes part of the complex interior junk you carry with you wherever you go. Two years have passed since the total eclipse of which I write. During those years I have forgotten, I assume, a great many things I wanted to remember — but I have not forgotten that clown painting or its lunatic setting in the old hotel.

The clown was bald. Actually, he wore a clown's tight rubber wig, painted white; this stretched over the top of his skull, which was a cabbage. His hair was bunches of baby carrots. Inset in his white clown makeup, and in his cabbage skull, were his small and laughing human eyes. The clown's glance was like the glance of Rembrandt in some of the self-portraits: lively, knowing, deep, and loving. The crinkled shadows around his eyes were

(margin annotation: Repetition is reassuring ↓ like counting you know)

32

string beans. His eyebrows were parsley. Each of his ears was a broad bean. His thin, joyful lips were red chili peppers; between his lips were wet rows of human teeth and a suggestion of a real tongue. The clown print was framed in gilt and glassed.

To put ourselves in the path of the total eclipse, that day we had driven five hours inland from the Washington coast, where we lived. When we tried to cross the Cascades range, an avalanche had blocked the pass.

A slope's worth of snow blocked the road; traffic backed up. Had the 5 avalanche buried any cars that morning? We could not learn. This highway was the only winter road over the mountains. We waited as highway crews bulldozed a passage through the avalanche. With two-by-fours and walls of plyboard, they erected a one-way, roofed tunnel through the avalanche. We drove through the avalanche tunnel, crossed the pass, and descended several thousand feet into central Washington and the broad Yakima valley, about which we knew only that it was orchard country. As we lost altitude, the snows disappeared, our ears popped; the trees changed, and in the trees were strange birds. I watched the landscape innocently, like a fool, like a diver in the rapture of the deep who plays on the bottom while his air runs out.

The hotel lobby was a dark, derelict room, narrow as a corridor, and seemingly without air. We waited on a couch while the manager vanished upstairs to do something unknown to our room. Beside us on an overstuffed chair, absolutely motionless, was a platinum-blond woman in her forties wearing a black silk dress and a strand of pearls. Her long legs were crossed; she supported her head on her fist. At the dim far end of the room, their backs toward us, sat six bald old men in their shirtsleeves, around a loud television. Two of them seemed asleep. They were drunks. "Number six!" cried the man on television, "Number six!"

On the broad lobby desk, lighted and bubbling, was a ten-gallon aquarium containing one large fish; the fish tilted up and down in its water. Against the long opposite wall sang a live canary in its cage. Beneath the cage, among spilled millet seeds on the carpet, were a decorated child's sand bucket and matching sand shovel.

Now the alarm was set for six. I lay awake remembering an article I had read downstairs in the lobby, in an engineering magazine. The article was about gold mining.

In South Africa, in India, and in South Dakota, the gold mines extend so deeply into the earth's crust that they are hot. The rock walls burn the miners' hands. The companies have to air-condition the mines; if the air conditioners break, the miners die. The elevators in the mine shafts run very slowly, down, and up, so the miners' ears will not pop in their skulls. When the miners return to the surface, their faces are deathly pale.

number 6

Early the next morning we checked out. It was February 26, 1979, a   10
Monday morning. We would drive out of town, find a hilltop, watch the
eclipse, and then drive back over the mountains and home to the coast. How
familiar things are here; how adept we are; how smoothly and professionally
we check out! I had forgotten the clown's smiling head and the hotel lobby
as if they had never existed. Gary put the car in gear and off we went, as
off we have gone to a hundred other adventures.

It was before dawn when we found a highway out of town and drove
into the unfamiliar countryside. By the growing light we could see a band of
cirrostratus clouds in the sky. Later the rising sun would clear these clouds
before the eclipse began. We drove at random until we came to a range of
unfenced hills. We pulled off the highway, bundled up, and climbed one of
these hills.

2

The hill was five hundred feet high. Long winter-killed grass covered
it, as high as our knees. We climbed and rested, sweating in the cold; we
passed clumps of bundled people on the hillside who were setting up telescopes and fiddling with cameras. The top of the hill stuck up in the middle
of the sky. We tightened our scarves and looked around.

East of us rose another hill like ours. Between the hills, far below, was
the highway which threaded south into the valley. This was the Yakima
valley; I had never seen it before. It is justly famous for its beauty, like
every planted valley. It extended south into the horizon, a distant dream of
a valley, a Shangri-la. All its hundreds of low, golden slopes bore orchards.
Among the orchards were towns, and roads, and plowed and fallow fields.
Through the valley wandered a thin, shining river; from the river extended
fine, frozen irrigation ditches. Distance blurred and blued the sight, so that
the whole valley looked like a thickness or sediment at the bottom of the
sky. Directly behind us was more sky, and empty lowlands blued by distance,
and Mount Adams. Mount Adams was an enormous, snow-covered volcanic
cone rising flat, like so much scenery.

Now the sun was up. We could not see it; but the sky behind the band
of clouds was yellow, and, far down the valley, some hillside orchards had
lighted up. More people were parking near the highway and climbing the
hills. It was the West. All of us rugged individualists were wearing knit caps
and blue nylon parkas. People were climbing the nearby hills and setting up
shop in clumps among the dead grasses. It looked as though we had all
gathered on hilltops to pray for the world on its last day. It looked as though
we had all crawled out of spaceships and were preparing to assault the valley
below. It looked as though we were scattered on hilltops at dawn to sacrifice

virgins, make rain, set stone stelae in a ring. There was no place out of the wind. The straw grasses banged our legs.

Up in the sky where we stood the air was lusterless yellow. To the   15
west the sky was blue. Now the sun cleared the clouds. We cast rough shadows on the blowing grass; freezing, we waved our arms. Near the sun, the sky was bright and colorless. There was nothing to see.

It began with no ado. It was odd that such a well-advertised public event should have no starting gun, no overture, no introductory speaker. I should have known right then that I was out of my depth. Without pause or preamble, silent as orbits, a piece of the sun went away. We looked at it through welders' goggles. A piece of the sun was missing; in its place we saw empty sky.

I had seen a partial eclipse in 1970. A partial eclipse is very interesting. It bears almost no relation to a total eclipse. Seeing a partial eclipse bears the same relation to seeing a total eclipse as kissing a man does to marrying him, or as flying in an airplane does to falling out of an airplane. Although the one experience precedes the other, it in no way prepares you for it. During a partial eclipse the sky does not darken — not even when 94 percent of the sun is hidden. Nor does the sun, seen colorless through protective devices, seem terribly strange. We have all seen a sliver of light in the sky; we have all seen the crescent moon by day. However, during a partial eclipse the air does indeed get cold, precisely as if someone were standing between you and the fire. And blackbirds do fly back to their roosts. I had seen a partial eclipse before, and here was another.

What you see in an eclipse is entirely different from what you know. It is especially different for those of us whose grasp of astronomy is so frail that, given a flashlight, a grapefruit, two oranges, and fifteen years, we still could not figure out which way to set the clocks for Daylight Saving Time. Usually it is a bit of a trick to keep your knowledge from blinding you. But during an eclipse it is easy. What you see is much more convincing than any wild-eyed theory you may know.

You may read that the moon has something to do with eclipses. I have never seen the moon yet. You do not see the moon. So near the sun, it is as completely invisible as the stars are by day. What you see before your eyes is the sun going through phases. It gets narrower and narrower, as the waning moon does, and, like the ordinary moon, it travels alone in the simple sky. The sky is of course background. It does not appear to eat the sun; it is far behind the sun. The sun simply shaves away; gradually, you see less sun and more sky.

The sky's blue was deepening, but there was no darkness. The sun   20
was a wide crescent, like a segment of tangerine. The wind freshened and blew steadily over the hill. The eastern hill across the highway grew dusky

and sharp. The towns and orchards in the valley to the south were dissolving into the blue light. Only the thin river held a trickle of sun.

Now the sky to the west deepened to indigo, a color never seen. A dark sky usually loses color. This was a saturated, deep indigo, up in the air. Stuck up into that unworldly sky was the cone of Mount Adams, and the alpenglow was upon it. The alpenglow is that red light of sunset which holds out on snowy mountaintops long after the valleys and tablelands are dimmed. "Look at Mount Adams," I said, and that was the last sane moment I remember.

I turned back to the sun. It was going. The sun was going, and the world was wrong. The grasses were wrong; they were platinum. Their every detail of stem, head, and blade shone lightless and artificially distinct as an art photographer's platinum print. This color has never been seen on earth. The hues were metallic; their finish was matte. The hillside was a nineteenth-century tinted photograph from which the tints had faded. All the people you see in the photograph, distinct and detailed as their faces look, are now dead. The sky was navy blue. My hands were silver. All the distant hills' grasses were finespun metal which the wind laid down. I was watching a faded color print of a movie filmed in the Middle Ages; I was standing in it, by some mistake. I was standing in a movie of hillside grasses filmed in the Middle Ages. I missed my own century, the people I knew, and the real light of day.

I looked at Gary. He was in the film. Everything was lost. He was a platinum print, a dead artist's version of life. I saw on his skull the darkness of night mixed with the colors of day. My mind was going out; my eyes were receding the way galaxies recede to the rim of space. Gary was light-years away, gesturing inside a circle of darkness, down the wrong end of a telescope. He smiled as if he saw me; the stringy crinkles around his eyes moved. The sight of him, familiar and wrong, was something I was remembering from centuries hence, from the other side of death: yes, *that* is the way he used to look, when we were living. When it was our generation's turn to be alive. I could not hear him; the wind was too loud. Behind him the sun was going. We had all started down a chute of time. At first it was pleasant; now there was no stopping it. Gary was chuting away across space, moving and talking and catching my eye, chuting down the long corridor of separation. The skin on his face moved like thin bronze plating that would peel.

The grass at our feet was wild barley. It was the wild einkorn wheat which grew on the hilly flanks of the Zagros Mountains, above the Euphrates valley, above the valley of the river we called *River.* We harvested the grass with stone sickles, I remember. We found the grasses on the hillsides; we built our shelter beside them and cut them down. That is how he used to look then, that one, moving and living and catching my eye, with the sky so dark behind him, and the wind blowing. God save our life.

From all the hills came screams. A piece of sky beside the crescent sun was detaching. It was a loosened circle of evening sky, suddenly lighted from the back. It was an abrupt black body out of nowhere; it was a flat disk; it was almost over the sun. That is when there were screams. At once this disk of sky slid over the sun like a lid. The sky snapped over the sun like a lens cover. The hatch in the brain slammed. Abruptly it was dark night, on the land and in the sky. In the night sky was a tiny ring of light. The hole where the sun belongs is very small. A thin ring of light marked its place. There was no sound. The eyes dried, the arteries drained, the lungs hushed. There was no world. We were the world's dead people rotating and orbiting around and around, embedded in the planet's crust, while the earth rolled down. Our minds were light-years distant, forgetful of almost everything. Only an extraordinary act of will could recall to us our former, living selves and our contexts in matter and time. We had, it seems, loved the planet and loved our lives, but could no longer remember the way of them. We got the light wrong. In the sky was something that should not be there. In the black sky was a ring of light. It was a thin ring, an old, thin silver wedding band, an old, worn ring. It was an old wedding band in the sky, or a morsel of bone. There were stars. It was all over.

3

It is now that the temptation is strongest to leave these regions. We have seen enough; let's go. Why burn our hands any more than we have to? But two years have passed; the price of gold has risen. I return to the same buried alluvial beds and pick through the strata again.

I saw, early in the morning, the sun diminish against a backdrop of sky. I saw a circular piece of that sky appear, suddenly detached, blackened, and backlighted; from nowhere it came and overlapped the sun. It did not look like the moon. It was enormous and black. If I had not read that it was the moon, I could have seen the sight a hundred times and never thought of the moon once. (If, however, I had not read that it was the moon — if, like most of the world's people throughout time, I had simply glanced up and seen this thing — then I doubtless would not have speculated much, but would have, like Emperor Louis of Bavaria in 840, simply died of fright on the spot.) It did not look like a dragon, although it looked more like a dragon than the moon. It looked like a lens cover, or the lid of a pot. It materialized out of thin air — black, and flat, and sliding, outlined in flame.

Seeing this black body was like seeing a mushroom cloud. The heart screeched. The meaning of the sight overwhelmed its fascination. It obliterated meaning itself. If you were to glance out one day and see a row of mushroom clouds rising on the horizon, you would know at once that what you were seeing, remarkable as it was, was intrinsically not worth remarking. No use running to tell anyone. Significant as it was, it did not matter a whit. For what is significance? It is significance for people. No people, no significance. This is all I have to tell you.

In the deeps are the violence and terror of which psychology has warned us. But if you ride these monsters deeper down, if you drop with them farther over the world's rim, you find what our sciences cannot locate or name, the substrate, the ocean or matrix or ether which buoys the rest, which gives goodness its power for good, and evil its power for evil, the unified field: our complex and inexplicable caring for each other, and for our life together here. This is given. It is not learned.

The world which lay under darkness and stillness following the closing   30 of the lid was not the world we know. The event was over. Its devastation lay round about us. The clamoring mind and heart stilled, almost indifferent, certainly disembodied, frail, and exhausted. The hills were hushed, obliterated. Up in the sky, like a crater from some distant cataclysm, was a hollow ring.

. You have seen photographs of the sun taken during a total eclipse. The corona fills the print. All of those photographs were taken through telescopes. The lenses of telescopes and cameras can no more cover the breadth and scale of the visual array than language can cover the breadth and simultaneity of internal experience. Lenses enlarge the sight, omit its context, and make of it a pretty and sensible picture, like something on a Christmas card. I assure you, if you send any shepherds a Christmas card on which is printed a three-by-three photograph of the angel of the Lord, the glory of the Lord, and a multitude of the heavenly host, they will not be sore afraid. More fearsome things can come in envelopes. More moving photographs than those of the sun's corona can appear in magazines. But I pray you will never see anything more awful in the sky.

You see the wide world swaddled in darkness; you see a vast breadth of hilly land, and an enormous, distant, blackened valley; you see towns' lights, a river's path, and blurred portions of your hat and scarf; you see your husband's face looking like an early black-and-white film; and you see a sprawl of black sky and blue sky together, with unfamiliar stars in it, some barely visible bands of cloud, and over there, a small white ring. The ring is as small as one goose in a flock of migrating geese — if you happen to notice a flock of migrating geese. It is one 360th part of the visible sky. The sun we see is less than half the diameter of a dime held at arm's length.

The Crab Nebula, in the constellation Taurus, looks, through binoculars, like a smoke ring. It is a star in the process of exploding. Light from its explosion first reached the earth in 1054; it was a supernova then, and so bright it shone in the daytime. Now it is not so bright, but it is still exploding. It expands at the rate of seventy million miles a day. It is interesting to look through binoculars at something expanding seventy million miles a day. It does not budge. Its apparent size does not increase. Photographs of the Crab Nebula taken fifteen years ago seem identical to photographs of it taken yesterday. Some lichens are similar. Botanists have measured some ordinary lichens twice, at fifty-year intervals, without detecting any growth at all. And yet their cells divide; they live.

The small ring of light was like these things — like a ridiculous lichen up in the sky, like a perfectly still explosion 4,200 light-years away: it was interesting, and lovely, and in witless motion, and it had nothing to do with anything.

It had nothing to do with anything. The sun was too small, and too cold, and too far away, to keep the world alive. The white ring was not enough. It was feeble and worthless. It was as useless as a memory; it was as off kilter and hollow and wretched as a memory.

When you try your hardest to recall someone's face, or the look of a place, you see in your mind's eye some vague and terrible sight such as this. It is dark; it is insubstantial; it is all wrong.

The white ring and the saturated darkness made the earth and the sky look as they must look in the memories of the careless dead. What I saw, what I seemed to be standing in, was all the wrecked light that the memories of the dead could shed upon the living world. We had all died in our boots on the hilltops of Yakima, and were alone in eternity. Empty space stoppered our eyes and mouths; we cared for nothing. We remembered our living days wrong. With great effort we had remembered some sort of circular light in the sky — but only the outline. Oh, and then the orchard trees withered, the ground froze, the glaciers slid down the valleys and overlapped the towns. If there had ever been people on earth, nobody knew it. The dead had forgotten those they had loved. The dead were parted one from the other and could no longer remember the faces and lands they had loved in the light. They seemed to stand on darkened hilltops, looking down.

4

We teach our children one thing only, as we were taught: to wake up. We teach our children to look alive there, to join by words and activities the life of human culture on the planet's crust. As adults we are almost all adept at waking up. We have so mastered the transition we have forgotten we ever learned it. Yet it is a transition we make a hundred times a day, as, like so many will-less dolphins, we plunge and surface, lapse and emerge. We live half our waking lives and all of our sleeping lives in some private, useless, and insensible waters we never mention or recall. Useless, I say. Valueless,

I might add — until someone hauls their wealth up to the surface and into the wide-awake city, in a form that people can use.

I do not know how we got to the restaurant. Like Roethke, "I take my waking slow." Gradually I seemed more or less alive, and already forgetful. It was now almost nine in the morning. It was the day of a solar eclipse in central Washington, and a fine adventure for everyone. The sky was clear; there was a fresh breeze out of the north.

The restaurant was a roadside place with tables and booths. The other eclipse-watchers were there. From our booth we could see their cars' California license plates, their University of Washington parking stickers. Inside the restaurant we were all eating eggs or waffles; people were fairly shouting and exchanging enthusiasms, like fans after a World Series game. Did you see . . . ? Did you see . . . ? Then somebody said something which knocked me for a loop.

A college student, a boy in a blue parka who carried a Hasselblad, said to us, "Did you see that little white ring? It looked like a Life Saver. It looked like a Life Saver up in the sky."

And so it did. The boy spoke well. He was a walking alarm clock. I myself had at that time no access to such a word. He could write a sentence, and I could not. I grabbed that Life Saver and rode it to the surface. And I had to laugh. I had been dumbstruck on the Euphrates River, I had been dead and gone and grieving, all over the sight of something which, if you could claw your way up to that level, you would grant looked very much like a Life Saver. It was good to be back among people so clever; it was good to have all the world's words at the mind's disposal, so the mind could begin its task. All those things for which we have no words are lost. The mind — the culture — has two little tools, grammar and lexicon: a decorated sand bucket and a matching shovel. With these we bluster about the continents and do all the world's work. With these we try to save our very lives.

There are a few more things to tell from this level, the level of the restaurant. One is the old joke about breakfast. "It can never be satisfied, the mind, never." Wallace Stevens[1] wrote that, and in the long run he was right. The mind wants to live forever, or to learn a very good reason why not. The mind wants the world to return its love, or its awareness; the mind wants to know all the world, and all eternity, and God. The mind's sidekick, however, will settle for two eggs over easy.

The dear, stupid body is as easily satisfied as a spaniel. And, incredibly, the simple spaniel can lure the brawling mind to its dish. It is everlastingly

[1] *Wallace Stevens* (1879–1955): Prominent American poet whose work often deals with our perception of nature; quoted above is another distinguished American poet, Theodore Roethke (1908–1963).

funny that the proud, metaphysically ambitious, clamoring mind will hush if you give it an egg.

Further: while the mind reels in deep space, while the mind grieves 45 or fears or exults, the workaday senses, in ignorance or idiocy, like so many computer terminals printing out market prices while the world blows up, still transcribe their little data and transmit them to the warehouse in the skull. Later, under the tranquilizing influence of fried eggs, the mind can sort through this data. The restaurant was a halfway house, a decompression chamber. There I remembered a few things more.

The deepest, and most terrifying, was this: I have said that I heard screams. (I have since read that screaming, with hysteria, is a common reaction even to expected total eclipses.) People on all the hillsides, including, I think, myself, screamed when the black body of the moon detached from the sky and rolled over the sun. But something else was happening at that same instant, and it was this, I believe, which made us scream.

The second before the sun went out we saw a wall of dark shadow come speeding at us. We no sooner saw it than it was upon us, like thunder. It roared up the valley. It slammed our hill and knocked us out. It was the monstrous swift shadow cone of the moon. I have since read that this wave of shadow moves 1,800 miles an hour. Language can give no sense of this sort of speed — 1,800 miles an hour. It was 195 miles wide. No end was in sight — you saw only the edge. It rolled at you across the land at 1,800 miles an hour, hauling darkness like plague behind it. Seeing it, and knowing it was coming straight for you, was like feeling a slug of anesthetic shoot up your arm. If you think very fast, you may have time to think, "Soon it will hit my brain." You can feel the deadness race up your arm; you can feel the appalling, inhuman speed of your own blood. We saw the wall of shadow coming, and screamed before it hit.

This was the universe about which we have read so much and never before felt: the universe as a clockwork of loose spheres flung at stupefying, unauthorized speeds. How could anything moving so fast not crash, not veer from its orbit amok like a car out of control on a turn?

Less than two minutes later, when the sun emerged, the trailing edge of the shadow cone sped away. It coursed down our hill and raced eastward over the plain, faster than the eye could believe; it swept over the plain and dropped over the planet's rim in a twinkling. It had clobbered us, and now it roared away. We blinked in the light. It was as though an enormous, loping god in the sky had reached down and slapped the earth's face.

Something else, something more ordinary, came back to me along about 50 the third cup of coffee. During the moments of totality, it was so dark that drivers on the highway below turned on their cars' headlights. We could see the highway's route as a strand of lights. It was bumper-to-bumper down there. It was eight-fifteen in the morning, Monday morning, and people were driving into Yakima to work. That it was as dark as night, and eerie as hell, an hour after dawn, apparently meant that in order to *see* to drive to work, people had to use their headlights. Four or five cars pulled off the road. The rest, in a line at least five miles long, drove to town. The highway ran between hills; the people could not have seen any of the eclipsed sun at all. Yakima will have another total eclipse in 2086. Perhaps, in 2086, businesses will give their employees an hour off.

From the restaurant we drove back to the coast. The highway crossing the Cascades range was open. We drove over the mountain like old pros. We joined our places on the planet's thin crust; it held. For the time being, we were home free.

Early that morning at six, when we had checked out, the six bald men were sitting on folding chairs in the dim hotel lobby. The television was on. Most of them were awake. You might drown in your own spittle, God knows, at any time; you might wake up dead in a small hotel, a cabbage head watching TV while snows pile up in the passes, watching TV while the chili peppers smile and the moon passes over the sun and nothing changes and nothing is learned because you have lost your bucket and shovel and no longer care. What if you regain the surface and open your sack and find, instead of treasure, a beast which jumps at you? Or you may not come back at all. The winches may jam, the scaffolding buckle, the air conditioning collapse. You may glance up one day and see by your headlamp the canary keeled over in its cage. You may reach into a cranny for pearls and touch a moray eel. You yank on your rope; it is too late.

Apparently people share a sense of these hazards, for when the total eclipse ended, an odd thing happened.
When the sun appeared as a blinding bead on the ring's side, the eclipse was over. The black lens cover appeared again, backlighted, and slid away. At once the yellow light made the sky blue again; the black lid dissolved and vanished. The real world began there. I remember now: we all hurried away. We were born and bored at a stroke. We rushed down the hill. We found our car; we saw the other people streaming down the hillsides; we joined the highway traffic and drove away.
We never looked back. It was a general vamoose, and an odd one, for when we left the hill, the sun was still partially eclipsed — a sight rare enough, and one which, in itself, we would probably have driven five hours to see. But enough is enough. One turns at last even from glory itself with a sigh of relief. From the depths of mystery, and even from the heights of splendor, we bounce back and hurry for the latitudes of home.

FROM READING TO REREADING

1. In reconstructing a personal experience, an essayist is faced with an apparently infinite array of narrative options. Most people, however, routinely render their accounts in a step-by-step temporal sequence, as though the clock and calendar were the most essential elements of a story. Note that Dillard's method roughly follows a chronological sequence, but it's not one she religiously adheres to. If you were rewriting her essay in a more conventional fashion, with which of her sentences or paragraphs would you begin? What effect does she gain by not beginning in a conventional manner?

2. When James Joyce used the word *epiphany* to describe sudden moments of insight, he observed that epiphanies can take the form of overhearing a casual or spontaneous remark that has a significance greater than the speaker intended. Where does Dillard introduce such a remark and what importance does it have?

3. What is going on in paragraph 52? Where are Dillard's images coming from? Try to identify each of the images in the paragraph; what, for example, do the winches, scaffolding, and air conditioning refer to? What connection does this paragraph bear to the essay as a whole? What is its connection to the eclipse?

Some point everything will
go, get out fall, ride the wave

VIRGINIA WOOLF

The Moment: Summer's Night

A few essays earlier, Stephen Jay Gould noted that we don't live in a world of "clear distinctions and separated immutable entities," but rather one of "variation, shadings, and continua." His comment is relevant not only to the biological sciences (of which he was speaking) but to the essay as a literary genre. With its capacity for assimilating the diverse techniques of fiction, poetry, philosophy, journalism, scholarship, and so forth, the modern essay has shown little respect for the usual literary or disciplinary boundaries. Gould's point also alerts us to an interesting internal conflict that lies at the heart of many great essays. At the same time that the essayist is attracted to such sharply dramatic themes as "moments of insight," he or she is equally attracted to the "variation, shadings, and continua" that make such moments almost impossible to isolate and define. A classic example of an essay that explores the mind's movement between the distinct and the indistinct is Virginia Woolf's enigmatic "The Moment: Summer's Night." Not published until after her death and rarely anthologized (perhaps because of its puzzling quality), the essay represents an ambitious attempt to capture something which is virtually impossible in art: what a single moment feels like as it flickers through our consciousness.

THE NIGHT WAS FALLING so that the table in the garden among the trees grew whiter and whiter; and the people round it more indistinct. An owl, blunt, obsolete looking, heavy weighted, crossed the fading sky with a black spot between its claws. The trees murmured. An aeroplane hummed like a piece of plucked wire. There was also, on the roads, the distant explosion of a motor cycle, shooting further and further away down the road. Yet what composed the present moment? If you are young, the future lies upon the present, like a piece of glass, making it tremble and quiver. If you are old, the past lies upon the present, like a thick glass, making it waver, distorting it. All the same, everybody believes that the present is something, seeks out the different elements in this situation in order to compose the truth of it, the whole of it.

To begin with: it is largely composed of visual and of sense impressions. The day was very hot. After heat, the surface of the body is opened, as if all the pores were open and everything lay exposed, not sealed and contracted, as in cold weather. The air wafts cold on the skin under one's clothes. The soles of the feet expand in slippers after walking on hard roads. Then the sense of the light sinking back into darkness seems to be gently putting out with a damp sponge the colour in one's own eyes. Then the leaves shiver now and again, as if a ripple of irresistible sensation ran through them, as a horse suddenly ripples its skin.

But this moment is also composed of a sense that the legs of the chair are sinking through the centre of the earth, passing through the rich garden earth; they sink, weighted down. Then the sky loses its colour perceptibly and a star here and there makes a point of light. Then changes, unseen in the day, coming in succession seem to make an order evident. One becomes aware that we are spectators and also passive participants in a pageant. And as nothing can interfere with the order, we have nothing to do but accept, and watch. Now little sparks, which are not steady, but fitful as if somebody were doubtful, come across the field. Is it time to light the lamp, the farmers' wives are saying: can I see a little longer? The lamp sinks down; then it burns up. All doubt is over. Yes the time has come in all cottages, in all farms, to light the lamps. Thus then the moment is laced about with these weavings to and fro, these inevitable downsinkings, flights, lamp lightings.

But that is the wider circumference of the moment. Here in the centre is a knot of consciousness; a nucleus divided up into four heads, eight legs, eight arms, and four separate bodies. They are not subject to the law of the sun and the owl and the lamp. They assist it. For sometimes a hand rests on the table; sometimes a leg is thrown over a leg. Now the moment becomes shot with the extraordinary arrow which people let fly from their mouths — when they speak.

"He'll do well with his hay."   5

The words let fall this seed, but also, coming from that obscure face, and the mouth, and the hand so characteristically holding the cigarette, now hit the mind with a wad, then explode like a scent suffusing the whole dome of the mind with its incense, flavour; let fall, from their ambiguous envelope, the self-confidence of youth, but also its urgent desire, for praise, and assurance; if they were to say: "But you're no worse looking than many — you're no different — people don't mark you out to laugh at you": that he should be at once so cock-a-hoop and so ungainly makes the moment rock with laughter, and with the malice that comes from overlooking other people's motives; and seeing what they keep hid; and so that one takes sides; he will succeed; or no he won't; and then again, this success, will it mean my defeat; or won't it? All this shoots through the moment, makes it quiver with malice and amusement; and the sense of watching and comparing; and the quiver meets the shore, when the owl flies out, and puts a stop to this judging, this overseeing, and with our wings spread, we too fly, take wing, with the owl, over the earth and survey the quietude of what sleeps, folded, slumbering, arm stretching in the vast dark and sucking its thumb too; the amorous and the innocent; and a sigh goes up. Could we not fly too, with broad wings and with softness; and be all one wing; all embracing, all gathering, and these boundaries, these pryings over hedge into hidden compartments of different colours be all swept into one colour by the brush of the wing; and so visit in splendour, augustly, peaks; and there lie exposed, bare, on the spine, high up, to the cold light of the moon rising, and when the moon rises, single, solitary, behold her, one, eminent over us?

Ah, yes, if we could fly, fly, fly. . . . Here the body is gripped; and shaken; and the throat stiffens; and the nostrils tingle; and like a rat shaken by a terrier one sneezes; and the whole universe is shaken; mountains, snows, meadows; moon; higgledy-piggledy, upside down, little splinters flying; and the head is jerked up, down. "Hay fever — what a noise! — there's no cure. Except spending hay time on a boat. Perhaps worse than the disease, though that's what a man did — crossing and recrossing, all the summer."

Issuing from a white arm, a long shape, lying back, in a film of black and white, under the tree, which, down sweeping, seems a part of that curving, that flowing, the voice, with its ridicule and its sense, reveals to the shaken terrier its own insignificance. No longer part of the snow; no part of the mountain; not in the least venerable to other human beings; but ridiculous; a little accident; a thing to be laughed at; discriminated out; seen clearly cut out, sneezing, sneezing, judged and compared. Thus into the moment steals self-assertion; ah, the sneeze again; the desire to sneeze with conviction; masterfully; making oneself heard; felt; if not pitied, then somebody of importance; perhaps to break away and go. But no; the other shape has sent from its arrow another fine binding thread, "Shall I fetch my Vapex?" [1] She, the observant, the discriminating, who keeps in mind always other instances, so that there is nothing singular in any special case — who refuses to be jumped into extravagance; and so sceptical withal; cannot believe in miracles; sees the vanity of effort there; perhaps then it would be well to try here; yet if she isolates cases from the mists of hugeness, sees what is there all the more definitely; refuses to be bamboozled; yet in this definite discrimination shows some amplitude. That is why the moment becomes harder, is intensified, diminished, begins to be stained by some expressed personal juice; with the desire to be loved, to be held close to the other shape; to put off the veil of darkness and see burning eyes.

Then a light is struck; in it appears a sunburnt face, lean, blue-eyed, and the arrow flies as the match goes out:

"He beats her every Saturday; from boredom, I should say; not drink;   10 there's nothing else to do."

The moment runs like quicksilver on a sloping board into the cottage parlour; there are the tea things on the table; the hard windsor chairs; tea caddies on the shelf for ornament; the medal under a glass shade; vegetable steam curling from the pot; two children crawling on the floor; and Liz comes

---

[1] *Vapex*: Presumably a product to relieve hay fever symptoms.

in and John catches her a blow on the side of her head as she slopes past him, dirty, with her hair loose and one hairpin sticking out about to fall. And she moans in a chronic animal way; and the children look up and then make a whistling noise to imitate the engine which they trail across the flags; and John sits himself down with a thump at the table and carves a hunk of bread and munches because there is nothing to be done. A steam rises from his cabbage patch. Let us do something then, something to end this horrible moment, this plausible glistening moment that reflects in its smooth sides this intolerable kitchen, this squalor; this woman moaning; and the rattle of the toy on the flags, and the man munching. Let us smash it by breaking a match. There — snap.

And then comes the low of the cows in the field; and another cow to the left answers; and all the cows seem to be moving tranquilly across the field and the owl flutes off its watery bubble. But the sun is deep below the earth. The trees are growing heavier, blacker; no order is perceptible; there is no sequence in these cries, these movements; they come from no bodies; they are cries to the left and to the right. Nothing can be seen. We can only see ourselves as outlines, cadaverous, sculpturesque. And it is more difficult for the voice to carry through this dark. The dark has stripped the fledge from the arrow — the vibrations that rise red shiver as it passes through us.

Then comes the terror, the exultation; the power to rush out unnoticed, alone; to be consumed; to be swept away to become a rider on the random wind; the tossing wind; the trampling and neighing wind; the horse with the blown-back mane; the tumbling, the foraging; he who gallops forever, no-whither travelling, indifferent; to be part of the eyeless dark, to be rippling and streaming, to feel the glory run molten up the spine, down the limbs, making the eyes glow, burning, bright, and penetrate the buffeting waves of the wind.

"Everything's sopping wet. It's the dew off the grass. Time to go in."

And then one shape heaves and surges and rises, and we pass, trailing ¹⁵ coats, down the path towards the lighted windows, the dim glow behind the branches, and so enter the door, and the square draws its lines round us, and here is a chair, a table, glasses, knives, and thus we are boxed and housed, and will soon require a draught of soda-water and to find something to read in bed.

FROM READING TO REREADING

1. This is not an easy essay to follow, even after several readings. But try to identify the various elements of language that make it difficult to read. In what ways, for example, is the conversation confusing? These confusions are, of course, deliberate on Woolf's part. Consider her artistic intentions in this essay: What aspects of consciousness does she want to convey?

2. Woolf apparently did not compose her essay entirely for aesthetic purposes. How do problems of class and gender arise in the essay? How important do they seem to the "moment"?

3. Though Woolf's essay seems to issue from an intensely subjective consciousness, notice that she never uses the first person singular. Why do you think she opted not to use "I"? What pronouns does she use? How do we obtain a sense of the person whose consciousness is at the center of the essay? In what ways would the essay be different if a more sharply identifiable "I" were present?

From Reading to Writing

1. Both Annie Dillard and Alice Walker show us in their essays how a sudden insight can be connected to a casual or chance remark. The ancient Greeks consulted oracles to interpret the prophetic nature of such remarks, believing that an apparently trivial saying might contain a powerful meaning (people still get a kick out of fortune cookies, and some people still open the Bible at random or consult the *I Ching*). Have you ever experienced a sudden insight from a random or chance comment? If so, write a personal essay describing the experience and the insight it led to.

2. Most of the essays in this chapter deal with a loss of boundaries and confusions of personal identity. Examine the essays by E. B. White and Virginia Woolf in this context. How does each essayist treat conventional distinctions and ordinary boundaries? After considering the many ways that the two essays resemble each other, write a critical essay discussing how each writer uses landscape and atmosphere to reinforce his or her central theme.

√ 3. Both George Orwell's and Stephen Jay Gould's essays contain tough-minded moral lessons. We have all had experiences in which we feel we've learned something significant about human nature. Write an essay in which you describe how something out of your control — an illness, punishment, or some other kind of adversity — led to an important insight into the human condition.

2

The Fabric of the Family

JOAN DIDION
On Going Home

When Thomas Wolfe gave his last novel the title You Can't Go Home Again, *he coined one of the unforgettable phrases of American literature. Wolfe's message — that we can't recapture the memory of time and place, of our youth and our home — is often alluded to in contemporary prose and poetry, and the theme has been adroitly handled by many different writers, especially essayists. In "On Going Home," Joan Didion refers directly to Wolfe's words, reminding us of how difficult it is to revisit the homes we've grown up in after we've left and established families of our own. When she wrote this essay in 1967, Didion, then in her thirties, saw herself as part of an older generation to whom Wolfe's phrase truly meant something; she wonders if those born after World War II (the "baby-boomers") have entered a world too fragmented for them to feel any nostalgic attachment to home and family. Didion's own ambivalence toward family values can be felt throughout the essay, as she moves back and forth between connection and disconnection with those around her. "On Going Home" originally appeared in* The Saturday Evening Post, *a fact many readers at the time found surprising, since that magazine has always been closely associated with traditional family values, so much so that its covers continually featured Norman Rockwell's portraits of American domestic life.*

I AM HOME for my daughter's first birthday. By "home" I do not mean the house in Los Angeles where my husband and I and the baby live, but the place where my family is, in the Central Valley of California. It is a vital although troublesome distinction. My husband likes my family but is uneasy in their house, because once there I fall into their ways, which are difficult, oblique, deliberately inarticulate, not my husband's ways. We live in dusty houses ("D-U-S-T," he once wrote with his finger on surfaces all over the house, but no one noticed it) filled with mementos quite without value to him (what could the Canton dessert plates mean to him? how could he have known about the assay scales, why should he care if he did know?), and we appear to talk exclusively about people we know who have been committed to mental hospitals, about people we know who have been booked on drunk-driving charges, and about property, particularly about property, land, price per acre and C-2 zoning and assessments and freeway access. My brother does not understand my husband's inability to perceive the advantage in the rather common real-estate transaction known as "sale-leaseback," and my husband in turn does not understand why so many of the people he hears about in my father's house have recently been committed to mental hospitals or booked on drunk-driving charges. Nor does he understand that when we talk about sale-leasebacks and right-of-way condemnations we are talking in code about the things we like best, the yellow fields and the cottonwoods and the rivers rising and falling and the mountain roads closing when the heavy snow comes in. We miss each other's points, have another drink and regard the fire. My brother refers to my husband, in his presence, as "Joan's husband." Marriage is the classic betrayal.

Or perhaps it is not any more. Sometimes I think that those of us who are now in our thirties were born into the last generation to carry the burden of "home," to find in family life the source of all tension and drama. I had by all objective accounts a "normal" and a "happy" family situation, and yet I was almost thirty years old before I could talk to my family on the telephone without crying after I had hung up. We did not fight. Nothing was wrong. And yet some nameless anxiety colored the emotional charges between me and the place that I came from. The question of whether or not you could go home again was a very real part of the sentimental and largely literary baggage with which we left home in the fifties; I suspect that it is irrelevant to the children born of the fragmentation after World War II. A few weeks ago in a San Francisco bar I saw a pretty young girl on crystal take off her clothes and dance for the cash prize in an "amateur-topless" contest. There was no particular sense of moment about this, none of the effect of romantic degradation, of "dark journey," for which my generation strived so assiduously. What sense could that girl possibly make of, say, *Long Day's Journey into Night*? [1] Who is beside the point?

That I am trapped in this particular irrelevancy is never more apparent to me than when I am home. Paralyzed by the neurotic lassitude engendered by meeting one's past at every turn, around every corner, inside every cupboard, I go aimlessly from room to room. I decide to meet it head-on and clean out a drawer, and I spread the contents on the bed. A bathing suit I wore the summer I was seventeen. A letter of rejection from *The Nation*, an aerial photograph of the site for a shopping center my father did not build in 1954. Three teacups hand-painted with cabbage roses and signed "E.M.," my grandmother's initials. There is no final solution for letters of rejection from *The Nation* and teacups hand-painted in 1900. Nor is there any answer to snapshots of one's grandfather as a young man on skis, surveying around Donner Pass in the year 1910. I smooth out the snapshot and look into his face, and do and do not see my own. I close the drawer, and have another cup of coffee with my mother. We get along very well, veterans of a guerrilla war we never understood.

---

[1] *Long Day's Journey into Night*: An intense, four-and-a-half-hour-long autobiographical drama of family discord written by Eugene O'Neill and first produced posthumously in New York in 1956.

Days pass. I see no one. I come to dread my husband's evening call, not only because he is full of news of what by now seems to me our remote life in Los Angeles, people he has seen, letters which require attention, but because he asks what I have been doing, suggests uneasily that I get out, drive to San Francisco or Berkeley. Instead I drive across the river to a family graveyard. It has been vandalized since my last visit and the monuments are broken, overturned in the dry grass. Because I once saw a rattlesnake in the grass I stay in the car and listen to a country-and-Western station. Later I drive with my father to a ranch he has in the foothills. The man who runs his cattle on it asks us to the roundup, a week from Sunday, and although I know that I will be in Los Angeles I say, in the oblique way my family talks, that I will come. Once home I mention the broken monuments in the graveyard. My mother shrugs.

I go to visit my great-aunts. A few of them think now that I am my 5
cousin, or their daughter who died young. We recall an anecdote about a relative last seen in 1948, and they ask if I still like living in New York City. I have lived in Los Angeles for three years, but I say that I do. The baby is offered a horehound drop, and I am slipped a dollar bill "to buy a treat." Questions trail off, answers are abandoned, the baby plays with the dust motes in a shaft of afternoon sun.

It is time for the baby's birthday party: a white cake, strawberry-marshmallow ice cream, a bottle of champagne saved from another party. In the evening, after she has gone to sleep, I kneel beside the crib and touch her face, where it is pressed against the slats, with mine. She is an open and trusting child, unprepared for and unaccustomed to the ambushes of family life, and perhaps it is just as well that I can offer her little of that life. I would like to give her more. I would like to promise her that she will grow up with a sense of her cousins and of rivers and of her great-grandmother's teacups, would like to pledge her a picnic on a river with fried chicken and her hair uncombed, would like to give her *home* for her birthday, but we live differently now and I can promise her nothing like that. I give her a xylophone and a sundress from Madeira, and promise to tell her a funny story.

FROM READING TO REREADING

1. Notice that Didion begins her essay with a reference to a typical family ritual — a first birthday party. Note, too, however, that the birthday party, which is the immediate occasion for the essay, receives very little narrative or descriptive attention. Why do you think this is so? What is Didion saying about the place of such rituals in our lives? What other kinds of family rituals are brought into the essay? How are they treated?

2. Note how many instances in the essay pertain to language: Didion's husband writes "D-U-S-T" on surfaces throughout her family's home; her brother refers to her

husband as "Joan's husband" even in his presence. What other aspects of speech and language can you find in the essay? Consider how these references contribute to the overall climate of communication.

3. Didion's power as an essayist is due in no small part to her use of suggestive details — she refers to specific objects or situations that not only give concreteness to her prose but carry with them larger thematic resonance. Consider, for example, the bottle of champagne mentioned in the final paragraph. What is the effect of describing it as having been "saved from another party"? What does this detail suggest about the general mood surrounding her child's birthday? What other similar details can you find in the essay?

JAMES BALDWIN
Notes of a Native Son

It is often forgotten that in 1943, while the United States was hard at war with Germany and Japan, two of the bloodiest race riots of the century erupted in Detroit and Harlem. Although a direct cause of the Harlem riot was the shooting of a black soldier by a New York City police officer, community anger had already been aroused by the prejudiced treatment of blacks in the armed forces. It is against this violent historical backdrop that James Baldwin recalls his troubled relationship with his father and examines his growing awareness of himself as a black American. Like his father, Baldwin was a minister (he began preaching as a teenager), but, unlike his evangelistic father, Baldwin soon grew disenchanted with religion. Writing this essay in Paris years later, Baldwin remembers his father's funeral and describes his efforts to forge a new sense of identity as he discovers resemblances to a father he barely knew. Baldwin's title contains a play on words: "son" refers both to himself and to Richard Wright's seminal 1940 novel of African American experience, Native Son.

1

ON THE 29TH OF JULY, in 1943, my father died. On the same day, a few hours later, his last child was born. Over a month before this, while all our energies were concentrated in waiting for these events, there had been, in Detroit, one of the bloodiest race riots of the century. A few hours after my father's funeral, while he lay in state in the undertaker's chapel, a race riot broke out in Harlem. On the morning of the 3rd of August, we drove my father to the graveyard through a wilderness of smashed plate glass.

The day of my father's funeral had also been my nineteenth birthday. As we drove him to the graveyard, the spoils of injustice, anarchy, discontent, and hatred were all around us. It seemed to me that God himself had devised, to mark my father's end, the most sustained and brutally dissonant of codas. And it seemed to me, too, that the violence which rose all about us as my father left the world had been devised as a corrective for the pride of his eldest son. I had declined to believe in that apocalypse which had been central to my father's vision; very well, life seemed to be saying, here is something that will certainly pass for an apocalypse until the real thing comes along. I had inclined to be contemptuous of my father for the conditions of his life, for the conditions of our lives. When his life had ended I began to wonder about that life and also, in a new way, to be apprehensive about my own.

I had not known my father very well. We had got on badly, partly because we shared, in our different fashions, the vice of stubborn pride. When he was dead I realized that I had hardly ever spoken to him. When he had been dead a long time I began to wish I had. It seems to be typical of life in America, where opportunities, real and fancied, are thicker than anywhere else on the globe, that the second generation has no time to talk to the first. No one, including my father, seems to have known exactly how old he was, but his mother had been born during slavery. He was of the first generation of free men. He, along with thousands of other Negroes, came North after 1919 and I was part of that generation which had never seen the landscape of what Negroes sometimes called the Old Country.

He had been born in New Orleans and had been quite a young man there during the time that Louis Armstrong, a boy, was running errands for the dives and honky-tonks of what was always presented to me as one of the most wicked of cities — to this day, whenever I think of New Orleans, I also helplessly think of Sodom and Gomorrah. My father never mentioned Louis Armstrong, except to forbid us to play his records; but there was a picture of him on our wall for a long time. One of my father's strong-willed female relatives had placed it there and forbade my father to take it down. He never did, but he eventually maneuvered her out of the house and when, some years later, she was in trouble and near death, he refused to do anything to help her.

He was, I think, very handsome. I gather this from photographs and 5 from my own memories of him, dressed in his Sunday best and on his way to preach a sermon somewhere, when I was little. Handsome, proud, and ingrown, "like a toe-nail," somebody said. But he looked to me, as I grew older, like pictures I had seen of African tribal chieftains: he really should have been naked, with war-paint on and barbaric mementos, standing among spears. He could be chilling in the pulpit and indescribably cruel in his personal life and he was certainly the most bitter man I have ever met; yet it must be said that there was something else in him, buried in him, which lent him his tremendous power and, even, a rather crushing charm. It had something to do with his blackness, I think — he was very black — with his blackness and his beauty, and with the fact that he knew that he was black but did not know that he was beautiful. He claimed to be proud of his blackness but it had also been the cause of much humiliation and it had fixed bleak boundaries to his life. He was not a young man when we were growing up and he had already suffered many kinds of ruin; in his outra- geously demanding and protective way he loved his children, who were black like him and menaced, like him; and all these things sometimes showed in his face when he tried, never to my knowledge with any success, to establish contact with any of us. When he took one of his children on his knee to play, the child always became fretful and began to cry; when he tried to help one of us with our homework the absolutely unabating tension which emanated from him caused our minds and our tongues to become paralyzed, so that he, scarcely knowing why, flew into a rage and the child, not knowing why, was punished. If it ever entered his head to bring a surprise home for his children, it was, almost unfailingly, the wrong surprise and even the big watermelons he often brought home on his back in the summertime led to the most appalling scenes. I do not remember, in all those years, that one of his children was ever glad to see him come home. From what I was able to gather of his early life, it seemed that this inability to establish contact with other people had always marked him and had been one of the things which had driven him out of New Orleans. There was something in him, therefore, groping and tentative, which was never expressed and which was buried with him. One saw it most clearly when he was facing new people and hoping to impress them. But he never did, not for long. We went from church to smaller and more improbable church, he found himself in less and less demand as a minister, and by the time he died none of his friends had come to see him for a long time. He had lived and died in an intolerable bitterness of spirit and it frightened me, as we drove him to the graveyard through those unquiet, ruined streets, to see how powerful and overflowing bitterness could be and to realize that this bitterness now was mine.

When he died I had been away from home for a little over a year. In that year I had had time to become aware of the meaning of all my father's bitter warnings, had discovered the secret of his proudly pursed lips and rigid carriage: I had discovered the weight of white people in the world. I saw that this had been for my ancestors and now would be for me an awful thing to live with and that the bitterness which had helped to kill my father could also kill me.

He had been ill a long time — in the mind, as we now realized, reliving instances of his fantastic intransigence in the new light of his affliction and endeavoring to feel a sorrow for him which never, quite, came true. We had not known that he was being eaten up by paranoia, and the discovery that his cruelty, to our bodies and our minds, had been one of the symptoms of his illness was not, then, enough to enable us to forgive him. The younger children felt, quite simply, relief that he would not be coming home anymore. My mother's observation that it was he, after all, who had kept them alive all these years meant nothing because the problems of keeping children alive are not real for children. The older children felt, with my father gone, that they could invite their friends to the house without fear that their friends would be insulted or, as had sometimes happened with me, being told that their friends were in league with the devil and intended to rob our family of everything we owned. (I didn't fail to wonder, and it made me hate him, what on earth we owned that anybody else would want.)

His illness was beyond all hope of healing before anyone realized that he was ill. He had always been so strange and had lived, like a prophet, in such unimaginably close communion with the Lord that his long silences which were punctuated by moans and hallelujahs and snatches of old songs while he sat at the living room window never seemed odd to us. It was not until he refused to eat because, he said, his family was trying to poison him that my mother was forced to accept as a fact what had, until then, been only an unwilling suspicion. When he was committed, it was discovered that he had tuberculosis and, as it turned out, the disease of his mind allowed the disease of his body to destroy him. For the doctors could not force him to eat, either, and, though he was fed intravenously, it was clear from the beginning that there was no hope for him.

In my mind's eye I could see him, sitting at the window, locked up in his terrors; hating and fearing every living soul including his children who had betrayed him, too, by reaching towards the world which had despised him. There were nine of us. I began to wonder what it could have felt like for such a man to have had nine children whom he could barely feed. He used to make little jokes about our poverty, which never, of course, seemed very funny to us; they could not have seemed very funny to him, either, or else our all too feeble response to them would never have caused such rages. He spent great energy and achieved, to our chagrin, no small amount of success in keeping us away from the people who surrounded us, people who had all-night rent parties to which we listened when we should have been sleeping, people who cursed and drank and flashed razor blades on Lenox Avenue. He could not understand why, if they had so much energy to spare, they could not use it to make their lives better. He treated almost everybody on our block with a most uncharitable asperity and neither they, nor, of course, their children were slow to reciprocate.

The only white people who came to our house were welfare workers   10
and bill collectors. It was almost always my mother who dealt with them, for my father's temper, which was at the mercy of his pride, was never to be trusted. It was clear that he felt their very presence in his home to be a violation: this was conveyed by his carriage, almost ludicrously stiff, and by his voice, harsh and vindictively polite. When I was around nine or ten I wrote a play which was directed by a young, white schoolteacher, a woman, who then took an interest in me, and gave me books to read and, in order to corroborate my theatrical bent, decided to take me to see what she somewhat tactlessly referred to as "real" plays. Theater-going was forbidden in our house, but, with the really cruel intuitiveness of a child, I suspected that the color of this woman's skin would carry the day for me. When, at school, she suggested taking me to the theater, I did not, as I might have done if she had been a Negro, find a way of discouraging her, but agreed that she should pick me up at my house one evening. I then, very cleverly, left all the rest to my mother, who suggested to my father, as I knew she would, that it would not be very nice to let such a kind woman make the trip for nothing. Also, since it was a schoolteacher, I imagine that my mother countered the idea of sin with the idea of "education," which word, even with my father, carried a kind of bitter weight.

Before the teacher came my father took me aside to ask *why* she was coming, what *interest* she could possibly have in our house, in a boy like me. I said I didn't know but I, too, suggested that it had something to do with education. And I understood that my father was waiting for me to say something — I didn't quite know what; perhaps that I wanted his protection against this teacher and her "education." I said none of these things and the teacher came and we went out. It was clear, during the brief interview in our living room, that my father was agreeing very much against his will and that he would have refused permission if he had dared. The fact that he did not dare caused me to despise him: I had no way of knowing that he was facing in that living room a wholly unprecedented and frightening situation.

Later, when my father had been laid off from his job, this woman became very important to us. She was really a very sweet and generous woman and went to a great deal of trouble to be of help to us, particularly during one awful winter. My mother called her by the highest name she knew: she said she was a "christian." My father could scarcely disagree but during the four or five years of our relatively close association he never trusted her and was always trying to surprise in her open, Midwestern face the genuine, cunningly hidden, and hideous motivation. In later years, particularly when it began to be clear that this "education" of mine was going to lead me to perdition, he became more explicit and warned me that my white friends in high school were not really my friends and that I would see, when I was older, how white people would do anything to keep a Negro down. Some of them could be nice, he admitted, but none of them were to be trusted and most of them were not even nice. The best thing was to have as little to do with them as possible. I did not feel this way and I was certain, in my innocence, that I never would.

But the year which preceded my father's death had made a great change in my life. I had been living in New Jersey, working in defense plants, working and living among southerners, white and black. I knew about the south, of course, and about how southerners treated Negroes and how they expected them to behave, but it had never entered my mind that anyone would look at me and expect *me* to behave that way. I learned in New Jersey that to be a Negro meant, precisely, that one was never looked at but was simply at the mercy of the reflexes the color of one's skin caused in other people. I acted in New Jersey as I had always acted, that is as though I thought a great deal of myself — I had to *act* that way — with results that were, simply, unbelievable. I had scarcely arrived before I had earned the enmity, which was extraordinarily ingenious, of all my superiors and nearly all my co-workers. In the beginning, to make matters worse, I simply did not know what was happening. I did not know what I had done, and I shortly began to wonder what *anyone* could possibly do, to bring about such unanimous, active, and unbearably vocal hostility. I knew about jim-crow but I had never experienced it. I went to the same self-service restaurant three times and stood with all the Princeton boys before the counter, waiting for a hamburger and coffee; it was always an extraordinarily long time before anything was set before me; but it was not until the fourth visit that I learned that, in fact, nothing had ever been set before me: I had simply picked something up. Negroes were not served there, I was told, and they had been waiting for me to realize that I was always the only Negro present. Once I was told this, I determined to go there all the time. But now they were ready for me and, though some dreadful scenes were subsequently enacted in that restaurant, I never ate there again.

It was the same story all over New Jersey, in bars, bowling alleys, diners, places to live. I was always being forced to leave, silently, or with mutual imprecations. I very shortly became notorious and children giggled behind me when I passed and their elders whispered or shouted — they really believed that I was mad. And it did begin to work on my mind, of course; I began to be afraid to go anywhere and to compensate for this I went places to which I really should not have gone and where, God knows, I had no desire to be. My reputation in town naturally enhanced my reputation at work and my working day became one long series of acrobatics designed to keep me out of trouble. I cannot say that these acrobatics succeeded. It began to seem that the machinery of the organization I worked for was turning over, day and night, with but one aim: to eject me. I was fired once, and contrived, with the aid of a friend from New York, to get back on the payroll; was fired again, and bounced back again. It took a while to fire me for the third time, but the third time took. There were no loopholes anywhere. There was not even any way of getting back inside the gates.

That year in New Jersey lives in my mind as though it were the year   15 during which, having an unsuspected predilection for it, I first contracted some dread, chronic disease, the unfailing symptom of which is a kind of blind fever, a pounding in the skull and fire in the bowels. Once this disease is contracted, one can never be really carefree again, for the fever, without an instant's warning, can recur at any moment. It can wreck more important things than race relations. There is not a Negro alive who does not have this rage in his blood — one has the choice, merely, of living with it consciously or surrendering to it. As for me, this fever has recurred in me, and does, and will until the day I die.

My last night in New Jersey, a white friend from New York took me to the nearest big town, Trenton, to go to the movies and have a few drinks. As it turned out, he also saved me from, at the very least, a violent whipping. Almost every detail of that night stands out very clearly in my memory. I even remember the name of the movie we saw because its title impressed me as being so patly ironical. It was a movie about the German occupation of France, starring Maureen O'Hara and Charles Laughton and called *This Land Is Mine*. I remember the name of the diner we walked into when the movie ended: it was the "American Diner." When we walked in the counterman asked what we wanted and I remember answering with the casual sharpness which had become my habit: "We want a hamburger and a cup of coffee, what do you think we want?" I do not know why, after a year of such rebuffs, I so completely failed to anticipate his answer, which was, of course, "We don't serve Negroes here." This reply failed to discompose me, at least for the moment. I made some sardonic comment about the name of the diner and we walked out into the streets.

This was the time of what was called the "brown-out," when the lights in all American cities were very dim. When we reentered the streets something happened to me which had the force of an optical illusion, or a nightmare. The streets were very crowded and I was facing north. People were moving in every direction but it seemed to me, in that instant, that all of the people I could see, and many more than that, were moving toward me, against me, and that everyone was white. I remember how their faces gleamed. And I felt, like a physical sensation, a *click* at the nape of my neck as though some interior string connecting my head to my body had been cut. I began to walk. I heard my friend call after me, but I ignored him. Heaven only knows what was going on in his mind, but he had the good sense not to touch me — I don't know what would have happened if he had — and to keep me in sight. I don't know what was going on in my mind, either; I certainly had no conscious plan. I wanted to do something to crush these white faces, which were crushing me. I walked for perhaps a block or two until I came to an enormous, glittering, and fashionable restaurant in which I knew not even the intercession of the Virgin would cause me to be served. I pushed through the doors and took the first vacant seat I saw, at a table for two, and waited.

I do not know how long I waited and I rather wonder, until today, what I could possibly have looked like. Whatever I looked like, I frightened the waitress who shortly appeared, and the moment she appeared all my fury flowed towards her. I hated her for her white face, and for her great, astounded, frightened eyes. I felt that if she found a black man so frightening I would make her fright worth-while.

She did not ask me what I wanted, but repeated, as though she had learned it somewhere, "We don't serve Negroes here." She did not say it with the blunt, derisive hostility to which I had grown so accustomed, but, rather, with a note of apology in her voice, and fear. This made me colder and more murderous than ever. I felt I had to do something with my hands. I wanted her to come close enough for me to get her neck between my hands.

So I pretended not to have understood her, hoping to draw her closer. 20 And she did step a very short step closer, with her pencil poised incongruously over her pad, and repeated the formula: ". . . don't serve Negroes here."

Somehow, with the repetition of that phrase, which was already ringing in my head like a thousand bells of a nightmare, I realized that she would never come any closer and that I would have to strike from a distance. There was nothing on the table but an ordinary water-mug half full of water, and I picked this up and hurled it with all my strength at her. She ducked and it missed her and shattered against the mirror behind the bar. And, with that sound, my frozen blood abruptly thawed, I returned from wherever I had been, I *saw*, for the first time, the restaurant, the people with their mouths open, already, as it seemed to me, rising as one man, and I realized what I had done, and where I was, and I was frightened. I rose and began running for the door. A round, pot-bellied man grabbed me by the nape of the neck just as I reached the doors and began to beat me about the face. I kicked him and got loose and ran into the streets. My friend whispered, *"Run!"* and I ran.

My friend stayed outside the restaurant long enough to misdirect my pursuers and the police, who arrived, he told me, at once. I do not know what I said to him when he came to my room that night. I could not have said much. I felt, in the oddest, most awful way, that I had somehow betrayed him. I lived it over and over and over again, the way one relives an automobile accident after it has happened and one finds oneself alone and safe. I could not get over two facts, both equally difficult for the imagination to grasp, and one was that I could have been murdered. But the other was that I had been ready to commit murder. I saw nothing very clearly but I did see this: that my life, my *real* life, was in danger, and not from anything other people might do but from the hatred I carried in my own heart.

2

I had returned home around the second week in June — in great haste because it seemed that my father's death and my mother's confinement were both but a matter of hours. In the case of my mother, it soon became clear that she had simply made a miscalculation. This had always been her tendency and I don't believe that a single one of us arrived in the world, or has since arrived anywhere else, on time. But none of us dawdled so intolerably about the business of being born as did my baby sister. We sometimes amused ourselves, during those endless, stifling weeks, by picturing the baby sitting within in the safe, warm dark, bitterly regretting the necessity of becoming a part of our chaos and stubbornly putting it off as long as possible. I understood her perfectly and congratulated her on showing such good sense so soon. Death, however, sat as purposefully at my father's bedside as life stirred within my mother's womb and it was harder to understand why he so lingered in that long shadow. It seemed that he had bent, and for a long time, too, all of his energies towards dying. Now death was ready for him but my father held back.

All of Harlem, indeed, seemed to be infected by waiting. I had never before known it to be so violently still. Racial tensions throughout this country were exacerbated during the early years of the war, partly because the labor market brought together hundreds of thousands of ill-prepared people and partly because Negro soldiers, regardless of where they were born, received their military training in the south. What happened in defense plants and army camps had repercussions, naturally, in every Negro ghetto. The situation in Harlem had grown bad enough for clergymen, policemen, educators, politicians, and social workers to assert in one breath that there was no "crime wave" and to offer, in the very next breath, suggestions as to how to combat it. These suggestions always seemed to involve playgrounds, too. Playground or not, crime wave or not, the Harlem police force had been augmented in March, and the unrest grew — perhaps, in fact, partly as a result of the ghetto's instinctive hatred of policemen. Perhaps the most revealing news item, out of the steady parade of reports of muggings, stabbings, shootings, assaults, gang wars, and accusations of police brutality, is the item concerning six Negro girls who set upon a white girl in the subway because, as they all too accurately put it, she was stepping on their toes. Indeed she was, all over the nation.

I had never before been so aware of policemen, on foot, on horseback,   25
on corners, everywhere, always two by two. Nor had I ever been so aware of small knots of people. They were on stoops and on corners and in doorways, and what was striking about them, I think, was that they did not seem to be talking. Never, when I passed these groups, did the usual sound of a curse or a laugh ring out and neither did there seem to be any hum of gossip. There was certainly, on the other hand, occurring between them communication extraordinarily intense. Another thing that was striking was the unexpected diversity of the people who made up these groups. Usually, for example, one would see a group of sharpies standing on the street corner, jiving the passing chicks; or a group of older men, usually, for some reason, in the vicinity of a barber shop, discussing baseball scores, or the numbers, or making rather chilling observations about women they had known. Women, in a general way, tended to be seen less often together — unless they were church women, or very young girls, or prostitutes met together for an unprofessional instant. But that summer I saw the strangest combinations: large, respectable, churchly matrons standing on the stoops or the corners with their hair tied up, together with a girl in sleazy satin whose face bore the marks of gin and the razor, or heavy-set, abrupt, no-nonsense older men, in company with the most disreputable and fanatical "race" men, or these same "race" men with the sharpies, or these sharpies with the churchly women. Seventh Day Adventists and Methodists and Spiritualists seemed to be hobnobbing with Holyrollers and they were all, alike, entangled with the most flagrant disbelievers; something heavy in their stance seemed to indicate that they had all, incredibly, seen a common vision, and on each face there seemed to be the same strange, bitter shadow.

The churchly women and the matter-of-fact, no-nonsense men had children in the Army. The sleazy girls they talked to had lovers there, the sharpies and the "race" men had friends and brothers there. It would have demanded an unquestioning patriotism, happily as uncommon in this country as it is undesirable, for these people not to have been disturbed by the bitter letters they received, by the newspaper stories they read, not to have been enraged by the posters, then to be found all over New York, which described the Japanese as "yellow-bellied Japs." It was only the "race" men, to be sure, who spoke ceaselessly of being revenged — how this vengeance was to be exacted was not clear — for the indignities and dangers suffered by Negro boys in uniform; but everybody felt a directionless, hopeless bitterness, as well as that panic which can scarcely be suppressed when one knows that a human being one loves is beyond one's reach, and in danger. This helplessness and this gnawing uneasiness does something, at length, to even the toughest mind. Perhaps the best way to sum all this up is to say that the people I knew felt, mainly, a peculiar kind of relief when they knew that their boys were being shipped out of the south, to do battle overseas. It was, perhaps, like feeling that the most dangerous part of a dangerous journey had been passed and that now, even if death should come, it would come with honor and without the complicity of their countrymen. Such a death would be, in short, a fact with which one could hope to live.

It was on the 28th of July, which I believe was a Wednesday, that I visited my father for the first time during his illness and for the last time in his life. The moment I saw him I knew why I had put off this visit so long. I had told my mother that I did not want to see him because I hated him. But this was not true. It was only that I *had* hated him and I wanted to hold on to this hatred. I did not want to look on him as a ruin: it was not a ruin I had hated. I imagine that one of the reasons people cling to their hates so stubbornly is because they sense, once hate is gone, that they will be forced to deal with pain.

We traveled out to him, his older sister and myself, to what seemed to be the very end of a very Long Island. It was hot and dusty and we wrangled, my aunt and I, all the way out, over the fact that I had recently begun to smoke and, as she said, to give myself airs. But I knew that she wrangled with me because she could not bear to face the fact of her brother's dying. Neither could I endure the reality of her despair, her unstated bafflement as to what had happened to her brother's life, and her own. So we wrangled and I smoked and from time to time she fell into a heavy reverie. Covertly, I watched her face, which was the face of an old woman; it had fallen in, the eyes were sunken and lightless; soon she would be dying, too.

In my childhood — it had not been so long ago — I had thought her beautiful. She had been quick-witted and quick-moving and very generous with all the children and each of her visits had been an event. At one time one of my brothers and myself had thought of running away to live with her. Now she could no longer produce out of her handbag some unexpected and yet familiar delight. She made me feel pity and revulsion and fear. It was awful to realize that she no longer caused me to feel affection. The closer we came to the hospital the more querulous she became and at the same time, naturally, grew more dependent on me. Between pity and guilt and fear I began to feel that there was another me trapped in my skull like a jack-in-the-box who might escape my control at any moment and fill the air with screaming.

She began to cry the moment we entered the room and she saw him lying there, all shriveled and still, like a little black monkey. The great, gleaming apparatus which fed him and would have compelled him to be still even if he had been able to move brought to mind, not beneficence, but torture; the tubes entering his arm made me think of pictures I had seen, when a child, of Gulliver, tied down by the pygmies on that island. My aunt wept and wept, there was a whistling sound in my father's throat; nothing was said; he could not speak. I wanted to take his hand, to say something. But I do not know what I could have said, even if he could have heard me. He was not really in that room with us, he had at last really embarked on his journey; and though my aunt told me that he said he was going to meet Jesus, I did not hear anything except that whistling in his throat. The doctor came back and we left, into that unbearable train again, and home. In the morning came the telegram saying that he was dead. Then the house was suddenly full of relatives, friends, hysteria, and confusion and I quickly left my mother and the children to the care of those impressive women, who, in Negro communities at least, automatically appear at times of bereavement armed with lotions, proverbs, and patience, and an ability to cook. I went downtown. By the time I returned, later the same day, my mother had been carried to the hospital and the baby had been born.

3

For my father's funeral I had nothing black to wear and this posed a nagging problem all day long. It was one of those problems, simple, or impossible of solution, to which the mind insanely clings in order to avoid the mind's real trouble. I spent most of that day at the downtown apartment of a girl I knew, celebrating my birthday with whiskey and wondering what to wear that night. When planning a birthday celebration one naturally does not expect that it will be up against competition from a funeral and this girl had anticipated taking me out that night, for a big dinner and a night club afterwards. Sometime during the course of that long day we decided that we would go out anyway, when my father's funeral service was over. I imagine *I* decided it, since, as the funeral hour approached, it became clearer and clearer to me that I would not know what to do with myself when it was over. The girl, stifling her very lively concern as to the possible effects of the whiskey on one of my father's chief mourners, concentrated on being conciliatory and practically helpful. She found a black shirt for me somewhere and ironed it and, dressed in the darkest pants and jacket I owned, and slightly drunk, I made my way to my father's funeral.

The chapel was full, but not packed, and very quiet. There were, mainly, my father's relatives, and his children, and here and there I saw faces I had not seen since childhood, the faces of my father's one-time friends. They were very dark and solemn now, seeming somehow to suggest that they had known all along that something like this would happen. Chief among the mourners was my aunt, who had quarreled with my father all his life; by which I do not mean to suggest that her mourning was insincere or that she had not loved him. I suppose that she was one of the few people in the world who had, and their incessant quarreling proved precisely the strength of the tie that bound them. The only other person in the world, as far as I knew, whose relationship to my father rivaled my aunt's in depth was my mother, who was not there.

It seemed to me, of course, that it was a very long funeral. But it was, if anything, a rather shorter funeral than most, nor, since there were no overwhelming uncontrollable expressions of grief, could it be called — if I dare to use the word — successful. The minister who preached my father's funeral sermon was one of the few my father had still been seeing as he neared his end. He presented to us in his sermon a man whom none of us had ever seen — a man thoughtful, patient, and forbearing, a Christian inspiration to all who knew him, and a model for his children. And no doubt the children, in their disturbed and guilty state, were almost ready to believe this; he had been remote enough to be anything and, anyway, the shock of the incontrovertible, that it was really our father lying up there in that casket, prepared the mind for anything. His sister moaned and this grief-stricken moaning was taken as corroboration. The other faces held a dark, noncom-mittal thoughtfulness. This was not the man they had known, but they had scarcely expected to be confronted with *him;* this was, in a sense deeper than questions of fact, the man they had not known, and the man they had not known may have been the real one. The real man, whoever he had been, had suffered and now he was dead: this was all that was sure and all that mattered now. Every man in the chapel hoped that when his hour came he, too, would be eulogized, which is to say forgiven, and that all of his lapses, greeds, errors, and strayings from the truth would be invested with coherence and looked upon with charity. This was perhaps the last thing human beings could give each other and it was what they demanded, after all, of the Lord. Only the Lord saw the midnight tears, only He was present when one of His children, moaning and wringing hands, paced up and down the room. When one slapped one's child in anger the recoil in the heart reverberated through heaven and became part of the pain of the universe. And when the children were hungry and sullen and distrustful and one watched them, daily, growing wilder, and further away, and running headlong into danger, it was the Lord who knew what the charged heart endured as the strap was laid to the backside; the Lord alone who knew what one *would* have said if one had had, like the Lord, the gift of the living word. It was the Lord who knew of the impossibility every parent in that room faced: how to prepare the child for the day when the child would be despised and how to *create* in the child — by what means? — a stronger antidote to this poison than one had found for oneself. The avenues, side streets, bars, billiard halls, hospitals, police stations, and even the playgrounds of Harlem — not to mention the houses of correction, the jails, and the morgue — testified to the potency of the poison while remaining silent as to the efficacy of whatever antidote, irresistibly raising the question of whether or not such an antidote existed; raising, which was worse, the question of whether or not an antidote was desirable; perhaps poison should be fought with poison. With these several schisms in the mind and with more terrors in the heart than could be named, it was better not to judge the man who had gone down under an impossible burden. It was better to remember: *Thou knowest this man's fall; but thou knowest not his wrassling.*

While the preacher talked and I watched the children — years of changing their diapers, scrubbing them, slapping them, taking them to school, and scolding them had had the perhaps inevitable result of making me love them, though I am not sure I knew this then — my mind was busily breaking out with a rash of disconnected impressions. Snatches of popular songs, indecent jokes, bits of books I had read, movie sequences, faces, voices, political issues — I thought I was going mad; all these impressions suspended, as it were, in the solution of the faint nausea produced in me by the heat and liquor. For a moment I had the impression that my alcoholic breath, inefficiently disguised with chewing gum, filled the entire chapel. Then someone began singing one of my father's favorite songs and, abruptly, I was with him, sitting on his knee, in the hot, enormous, crowded church which was the first church we attended. It was the Abyssinia Baptist Church on 138th Street. We had not gone there long. With this image, a host of others came. I had forgotten, in the rage of my growing up, how proud my father had been of me when I was little. Apparently, I had had a voice and my father had liked to show me off before the members of the church. I had forgotten what he had looked like when he was pleased but now I remembered that he had always been grinning with pleasure when my solos ended. I even remembered certain expressions on his face when he teased my mother — had he loved her? I would never know. And when had it all begun to change? For now it seemed that he had not always been cruel. I remembered being taken for a haircut and scraping my knee on the footrest of the barber's chair and I remembered my father's face as he soothed my crying and applied the stinging iodine. Then I remembered our fights, fights which had been of the worst possible kind because my technique had been silence.

I remembered the one time in all our life together when we had really 35
spoken to each other.

It was on a Sunday and it must have been shortly before I left home. We were walking, just the two of us, in our usual silence, to or from church. I was in high school and had been doing a lot of writing and I was, at about this time, the editor of the high school magazine. But I had also been a Young Minister and had been preaching from the pulpit. Lately, I had been taking fewer engagements and preached as rarely as possible. It was said in the church, quite truthfully, that I was "cooling off."

My father asked me abruptly, "You'd rather write than preach, wouldn't you?"

I was astonished at his question — because it was a real question. I answered, "Yes."

That was all we said. It was awful to remember that that was all we had *ever* said.

The casket now was opened and the mourners were being led up the aisle to look for the last time on the deceased. The assumption was that the family was too overcome with grief to be allowed to make this journey alone and I watched while my aunt was led to the casket and, muffled in black, and shaking, led back to her seat. I disapproved of forcing the children to look on their dead father, considering that the shock of his death, or, more truthfully, the shock of death as a reality, was already a little more than a child could bear, but my judgment in this matter had been overruled and there they were, bewildered and frightened and very small, being led, one by one, to the casket. But there is also something very gallant about children at such moments. It has something to do with their silence and gravity and with the fact that one cannot help them. Their legs, somehow, seem *exposed*, so that it is at once incredible and terribly clear that their legs are all they have to hold them up.

I had not wanted to go to the casket myself and I certainly had not wished to be led there, but there was no way of avoiding either of these forms. One of the deacons led me up and I looked on my father's face. I cannot say that it looked like him at all. His blackness had been equivocated by powder and there was no suggestion in that casket of what his power had or could have been. He was simply an old man dead, and it was hard to believe that he had ever given anyone either joy or pain. Yet, his life filled that room. Further up the avenue his wife was holding his newborn child. Life and death so close together, and love and hatred, and right and wrong, said something to me which I did not want to hear concerning man, concerning the life of man.

After the funeral, while I was downtown desperately celebrating my birthday, a Negro soldier, in the lobby of the Hotel Braddock, got into a fight with a white policeman over a Negro girl. Negro girls, white policemen, in or out of uniform, and Negro males — in or out of uniform — were part of the furniture of the lobby of the Hotel Braddock and this was certainly not the first time such an incident had occurred. It was destined, however, to receive an unprecedented publicity, for the fight between the policeman and the soldier ended with the shooting of the soldier. Rumor, flowing immediately to the streets outside, stated that the soldier had been shot in the back, an instantaneous and revealing invention, and that the soldier had died protecting a Negro woman. The facts were somewhat different — for example, the soldier had not been shot in the back, and was not dead, and the girl seems to have been as dubious a symbol of womanhood as her white counterpart in Georgia usually is, but no one was interested in the facts. They preferred the invention because this invention expressed and corroborated their hates and fears so perfectly. It is just as well to remember that people are always doing this. Perhaps many of those legends, including Christianity, to which the world clings began their conquest of the world with just some such concerted surrender to distortion. The effect, in Harlem, of this particular legend was like the effect of a lit match in a tin of gasoline. The mob gathered before the doors of the Hotel Braddock simply began to swell and to spread in every direction, and Harlem exploded.

The mob did not cross the ghetto lines. It would have been easy, for example, to have gone over to Morningside Park on the west side or to have crossed the Grand Central railroad tracks at 125th Street on the east side, to wreak havoc in white neighborhoods. The mob seems to have been mainly interested in something more potent and real than the white face, that is, in white power, and the principal damage done during the riot of the summer of 1943 was to white business establishments in Harlem. It might have been a far bloodier story, of course, if, at the hour the riot began, these establishments had still been open. From the Hotel Braddock the mob fanned out, east and west along 125th Street, and for the entire length of Lenox, Seventh, and Eighth avenues. Along each of these avenues, and along each major side street — 116th, 125th, 135th, and so on — bars, stores, pawnshops, restaurants, even little luncheonettes had been smashed open and entered and looted — looted, it might be added, with more haste than efficiency. The shelves really looked as though a bomb had struck them. Cans of beans and soup and dog food, along with toilet paper, corn flakes, sardines, and milk tumbled every which way, and abandoned cash registers and cases of beer leaned crazily out of the splintered windows and were strewn along the avenues. Sheets, blankets, and clothing of every description formed a kind of path, as though people had dropped them while running. I truly had not realized that Harlem *had* so many stores until I saw them all smashed open; the first time the word *wealth* ever entered my mind in relation to Harlem was when I saw it scattered in the streets. But one's first, incongruous impression of plenty was countered immediately by an impression of waste. None of this was doing anybody any good. It would have been better to have left the plate glass as it had been and the goods lying in the stores.

It would have been better, but it would also have been intolerable, for Harlem had needed something to smash. To smash something is the ghetto's chronic need. Most of the time it is the members of the ghetto who smash each other, and themselves. But as long as the ghetto walls are standing there will always come a moment when these outlets do not work. That summer, for example, it was not enough to get into a fight on Lenox Avenue, or curse out one's cronies in the barber shops. If ever, indeed, the violence which fills Harlem's churches, pool halls, and bars erupts outward in a more direct fashion, Harlem and its citizens are likely to vanish in an apocalyptic flood. That this is not likely to happen is due to a great many reasons, most hidden and powerful among them the Negro's real relation to the white American. This relation prohibits, simply, anything as uncomplicated and satisfactory as pure hatred. In order really to hate white people, one has to blot so much out of the mind — and the heart — that this hatred itself becomes an exhausting and self-destructive pose. But this does not mean, on the other hand, that love comes easily: the white world is too powerful, too complacent, too ready with gratuitous humiliation, and, above all, too ignorant and too innocent for that. One is absolutely forced to make perpetual qualifications and one's own reactions are always canceling each other out. It is this, really, which has driven so many people mad, both white and black. One is always in the position of having to decide between amputation and gangrene. Amputation is swift but time may prove that the amputation was not necessary — or one may delay the amputation too long. Gangrene is slow, but it is impossible to be sure that one is reading one's symptoms right. The idea of going through life as a cripple is more than one can bear, and equally unbearable is the risk of swelling up slowly, in agony, with poison. And the trouble, finally, is that the risks are real even if the choices do not exist.

"But as for me and my house," my father had said, "we will serve the 45 Lord." I wondered, as we drove him to his resting place, what this line had meant for him. I had heard him preach it many times. I had preached it once myself, proudly giving it an interpretation different from my father's. Now the whole thing came back to me, as though my father and I were on our way to Sunday school and I were memorizing the golden text: *And if it seem evil unto you to serve the Lord, choose you this day whom you will serve; whether the gods which your fathers served that were on the other side of the flood, or the gods of the Amorites, in whose land ye dwell: but as for me and my house, we will serve the Lord.* I suspected in these familiar lines a meaning which had never been there for me before. All of my father's texts and songs, which I had decided were meaningless, were arranged before me at his death like empty bottles, waiting to hold the meaning which life would give them for me. This was his legacy: nothing is ever escaped. That bleakly memorable morning I hated the unbelievable streets and the Negroes and whites who had, equally, made them that way. But I knew that it was folly, as my father would have said, this bitterness was folly. It was necessary to hold on to the things that mattered. The dead man mattered, the new life mattered; blackness and whiteness did not matter; to believe that they did was to acquiesce in one's own destruction. Hatred, which could destroy so much, never failed to destroy the man who hated and this was an immutable law.

It began to seem that one would have to hold in the mind forever two ideas which seemed to be in opposition. The first idea was acceptance, the acceptance, totally without rancor, of life as it is, and men as they are: in the light of this idea, it goes without saying that injustice is a commonplace. But this did not mean that one could be complacent, for the second idea was of equal power: that one must never, in one's own life, accept these injustices as commonplace but must fight them with all one's strength. This fight begins, however, in the heart and it now had been laid to my charge to keep my own heart free of hatred and despair. This intimation made my heart heavy and, now that my father was irrecoverable, I wished that he had been beside me so that I could have searched his face for the answers which only the future would give me now.

FROM READING TO REREADING

1. Baldwin's essay is filled with images of personal and public conflict. How are these conflicts enhanced by the essay's emphasis on oppositions such as black/white, birth/death, father/son, or love/hate? Can you detect how Baldwin's sensitivity to opposition is reflected in the ways in which he structures his sentences?

2. While attending his father's funeral, Baldwin recalls a brief exchange he once had with his father: "My father asked me abruptly, 'You'd rather write than preach, wouldn't you?' I was astonished at his question — because it was a real question. I answered, 'Yes.' " By relating this incident, Baldwin raises another area of tension and opposition — that between speech and writing. Consider the points in the essay where this relationship is explored. In your opinion, has Baldwin's early experience as a preacher influenced his writing in significant ways?

3. In the final paragraph, Baldwin summarizes the essay's main issues in the form of a *paradox*. A Greek term that literally means "beyond what is thought," the term is commonly used by critics to characterize a statement that appears to be self-contradictory but actually expresses something true. In what ways can paradox be said to shape Baldwin's thinking throughout the essay?

E. B. WHITE
Aunt Poo

Anyone's family, of course, consists of more than its immediate members; it extends into stepparents, grandparents, aunts and uncles, and in-laws. We may not even know some of the people in our family. In "Aunt Poo," for example, E. B. White writes fondly of his wife's aunt, a spirited woman he never met. He knows Aunt Poo from family stories and from her own privately circulated memoir, which she painstakingly composed for her nieces. It's important to remember as you read the essay that White wrote it in 1942, while the United States was at war with Japan.

IN OUR LIVING ROOM, in a great old-fashioned frame, there hangs a painting of a lady and a dog. This picture rather dominates the room, and I have become quite fond of the lady. It is not a great painting, but it is rather a pleasing one. You can look at it again and again and not tire of it. The lady is of Victorian mold. She is young. She sits with one elbow cocked on the table next her chair, gazing down quizzically at her little dog. The artist responsible for this unsung work of art is my wife's aunt, a lady of eighty-five years, whose career as a painter was somewhat broken into in middle life when she laid aside her brushes and married a Japanese.

I have never met this fabulous aunt. She went to Tokyo and, except for a couple of brief visits, never came back. But she seems vivid enough — one of those semi-fictional characters you acquire by marriage and through much hearsay, just as you acquire, by slow degrees, the whole childhood history of the person you marry and at length feel that you know the child. I feel that I know Puss quite well, or Aunt Poo as she is invariably called by her three nieces, who cling with New England grit to the whimsical name by which she was known in the nursery. Although eighty-five, she is still beset by the enormous vigor which has filled her lifetime. At any rate she recently completed, in time to get it to America before all communication with Japan ceased, a volume of her memoirs, including a family history covering the years 1680 to 1908. I have just been reading it. Only three copies exist (one for each niece); for in fact it is not a printed book at all but is a typed book — typed by her single-spaced, on heavy drawing paper, and beautifully bound in an old brocade handed down from her husband's ancestors. Since in her scheme of bookmaking there had to be three copies of this monumental work, Aunt Poo had to run it through her typewriter three times, an appalling task. You see, if she had merely made an original and two carbons she would have been left with an unthinkable problem in discrimination: the problem of deciding which of her three nieces was to get the original, which the first carbon, which the second. Rather than face this distasteful dilemma, and because any book of hers, even a bound typescript, must meet certain standards of craftsmanship, she laboriously executed it three times, punching away night after night in the settlement house over which she presides in the slum district of Tokyo, minding her margins and neatly pasting in photographs by way of illustration.

To have so close a link with the enemy as Aunt Poo is both sobering and salutary. In war one tends to dehumanize the foe and to take pleasure in the thought of the dropped bomb. The presence in Tokyo of a member of the family, while it in no way lessens our determination to win, somewhat tempers our blood lust; we drop our bombs rather gingerly, trusting that our old aunt is dodging with the same skill and courage with which, at the age of four in Minnesota, she was dodging musket fire in the Indian uprising while her father rode two hundred miles on horseback to the rescue of a besieged garrison of whites in Fort Abercrombie. I feel that these new bombs will not prove an impossible burden at the end of so spectacular a career, but they will tear at her heart, since they bring into conflict the two great loves of her life, her ancestral New England and her adopted Nippon.

The story of her marriage to the Japanese and of the founding of the settlement house called Yurin-En is one which I hesitate to tell, since it is just family stuff; yet it is unique and timely and perhaps worth a try.

There was always something about Aunt Poo which was vaguely excit- 5 ing, according to my wife's account. Poo was the member of the family who had thrown off conventions and become an artist. She had been to Paris. She was Bohemia, in Suburbia. Strong-minded, sentimental, domineering, she had a flair for giving life (for little girls anyway) a certain extra quality. She was a great one to make an occasion of a day. Any sort of anniversary inflamed her. It would suddenly occur to her that today was Lincoln's Birthday, or the Ides of March, or Decoration Day, and in no time at all the house would tremble with the violence of redecoration or cookery or charades. She had the gift of celebration. There was no day so drab but, under Poo's fiery tutelage, could be whipped into a carnival.

She had been to Paris. She had had a studio in New York. In those days the very word *studio* was drenched with glamorous meaning. But despite her art and her wanderings, the great preoccupation of the first half of her life was her family, to belong to which seemed a career in itself. Her father, her mother, her sister, and her brother — to these she gave much of her energy and most of her thoughts. Within a relatively short space of time all four died, leaving her alone, and it was then that she bought a house in Woodstock, Connecticut, where the second phase of her life began.

Woodstock itself meant nothing in particular — her people had been rooted in the colder soil of Maine, in the little towns of Fryeburg, Naples, Bridgton, in Saco, and in the metropolises of Portland and Boston. Her infancy had been spent in the frontier town of St. Cloud, Minnesota, her childhood on a farm in Naples. But Woodstock contained a cousin, and to Woodstock she went to settle down for the long agreeable grind of spinster-hood. She applied herself rather briskly to fixing up the place, which she named Apple End, and rather desultorily to painting. She had come into a little money and could afford a cook. She could afford one but she couldn't seem to find one. In desperation she turned to the Springfield Y.M.C.A. Training School, among whose students were a few Orientals learning to be athletic directors in the American manner. It was summertime, and classes were over for the year.

As a result of her inquiry there arrived at Apple End one Hyozo Omori, a young Japanese of distinguished lineage, frail, aesthetic, and anxious to earn a little money. He had a slight beard which, with his delicate features and sensitiveness, gave him a Christlike appearance. He was shown the kitchen and given a rough idea of his duties: he was to cook the meals and serve them and tidy up. He seemed polite but worried.

It became apparent almost immediately that Mr. Omori and a kitchen were strangers of long standing. Aristocracy stuck out all over him. Although his efforts at cooking were preposterous, his conversation was charming. Aunt Poo saw in him a man who had been waited on all his life and who was clearly unsuited for any sudden reversal. So she set to and prepared Mr. Omori's meals for him, and as soon as possible engaged a large colored woman to carry some of the rapidly mounting household burden.

Mr. Omori, it must be said, offered to leave, but she urged him to stay on and assume duties of a more wispy sort — poking about the flower garden and exchanging views on poetry. He consented. For a while the domestic situation at Apple End was confused; the Japanese student was unwilling to sit at table with the colored woman, and the mistress of the house was disinclined to sit at table with the Japanese student. Everybody was eating off trays, in aseptic splendor. 10

> In this way [writes Aunt Poo in her memorial volume] began my acquaintance with Hyozo Omori, a gentleman of ancient lineage and culture who, like most of the Japanese students of that day, regarded all Americans as quite inferior in culture but were quite ready, given a respect for all honest work, to earn money from us in a perfectly impersonal way, making a contact with unpleasant things for a moment for convenience, without feeling oneself degraded.

I take it what slight momentary degradation Mr. Omori had been subjected to during his first few days at Woodstock was forgotten in the ensuing weeks. Aunt Poo and he liked the same books. Together they walked in the garden and talked of Japanese art — which Mr. Omori knew a great deal about — and he told her of his two ambitions in life: to found a settlement house in Tokyo, and to increase the stature of the Japanese race.

In the fall he returned to Springfield, she to Boston. They corresponded. He visited her several times, and finally asked her to marry him. She decided after a while to accept.

The news exploded like a time bomb in the house in a Boston suburb where my wife was then living as a young girl. Since Poo's immediate family were all dead, the conventional and decent thing of course would be to have her married under her brother-in-law's roof. But to a Japanese!

"What will the papers do with this?" groaned Papa, who had troubles enough of an Occidental nature without an involvement with the Rising Sun.

The *Boston American*, already banned from the house on general principles, broke the story with a mild flourish. Family councils were held behind closed doors. The girls, bursting with direct questions, were put off with evasive answers. It was a time of incredible consternation and embarrassment. But my wife's father was no quitter. He announced to the children that the wedding, if indeed their aunt was determined to go through with it, would be "under our roof." This took courage of a high order.

Meantime Mr. Omori was introduced to the household and made some- 15 thing of a hit with his nieces-to-be. He showed them how to make tea in the Japanese fashion, green tea served in cups without handles. Gracefully, politely, they would sip it and nibble on the little rice cakes, which were slightly sweet. Mr. Omori seemed genuinely attached to his New England fiancée and regarded her with amazement and humorous delight. His culti- vated mind and his gentle manner were disarming to a considerable degree, and his appearance was celestial. He lacked only a halo. Aunt Poo, by contrast, appeared more earthly than ever, with her plump and friendly frame.

They were married in the parlor. The girls were delighted to have a wedding in their house and to have the mantelpiece transformed into an altar by the addition of some Mrs. Humphry Ward roses. The couple left imme- diately for Tokyo on their wedding trip. It was the first of October, 1907.

> Since then I have lived thirty years and more in Japan, more than one-third of my life, and have never regretted that daring [writes Aunt Poo in the memoirs]. There is something in the Japanese character that can be understood by one of Puritan stock. They like simplicity, even a sort of severity of life. There is no pretense about them. In manners they are punctilious. At heart they are very kind. I do not say that I have never had homesick moments, but I truly loved my husband's beautiful spirit. When he could no longer do for his country what he so much wished to do, I tried in my small way to supply his place, and perhaps Japan is now my home as New England could not be now; and that other life is now not to me unloved, nor dead, but separated as death does separate, in a way never to be put together again.

That was written in 1939. Mr. Omori died in 1912, five years after the marriage.

One of the things he had "so much wished to do" for his country was, as I have mentioned, to increase the stature of the Japanese race, whose diminutive size he found out of keeping with their large destiny. It seemed like a detail worth correcting. First, however, he and his wife set about realizing his major aim — the Tokyo settlement house, which soon became a reality and has for a quarter of a century been an institution of considerable importance, the Hull House of Tokyo.

The other goal was less easy, but Mr. Omori made a start. What he did was to organize the first Japanese team ever to enter the Olympic Games; he hoped that participation in sports would sooner or later result in bigger bodies for his little countrymen. Proudly he escorted his team to Stockholm, over the trans-Siberian railway, and took Aunt Poo along. The whole junket seems, at this date, curiously roundabout and tinged with musical-comedy intrigue. I haven't any idea whether Uncle Hyozo was dreaming, even then, of Pearl Harbor and the straits before Singapore. My wife doubts that he was. In a way it doesn't make any difference. The Japanese are still little fellows, for all the competition they met at the games.

The team returned by way of Siberia but Aunt Poo and Uncle Hyo   20 continued west, turning up in the Boston suburb bearing some aquamarines from the Urals as gifts for the girls. It was plain, by that time, that Mr. Omori was a sick man. He was, in fact, in an advanced tubercular stage. The doctor ordered him to quit traveling, but Mr. Omori was not a man to be ordered about. He announced that he and his wife were returning immediately to Tokyo, and together they set out. The couple got as far as San Francisco and there he died.

San Francisco must have been a sort of crossroads for Aunt Poo. One way pointed back to New England, to her beloved villages and the elms and the kinsfolk. It was the clearer way. The other pointed to the Orient. Aunt Poo apparently never hesitated. She turned west across the Pacific, escorting her husband's body home, and there she remained to carry on the settlement house which was her husband's dearest desire.

The flyleaf of the memoirs is inscribed: "To my dear niece K —— S —— W —— , a tribute to our common past." The story is one of the most revealing I have ever read. Page by page one learns what it was that nourished her through her busy and useful years in a foreign land. It was her extraordinary sense of the past, her deep sense of family. It was New England in Japan. As time went on she became thoroughly involved in life at 370 Kashiwagi, Yodobashi, Tokyo. She translated *Lady Murasaki* into English. In the earthquake of 1922 she performed heroic service and was decorated by the government. But through it all the sense of the past grew stronger rather than weaker. Her letters flowed in an endless stream, keeping the past alive. Now and again she would request that something be sent her — a root from a common field flower, a recipe for an ancestral pie. Her thoughts returned constantly to the Maine villages of her childhood, to the snowberries and blush roses under the windows of the house in Naples, to the syringa and the spiraea, to the living room with Hannah knitting and sister reading with the kitten in her lap.

I don't know what the war is doing to her. Intellectually it is an impossible situation. She has always stood up for Japan and has felt that everything Japan did was right — even the "China incident" as she called it. For her nieces, who saw nothing "incidental" in the ravaging of China, correspondence with Aunt Poo was becoming increasingly difficult when it was shut off altogether.

At any rate I find it, as I say, salutary to read in the neat typing of this very old lady the findings of her thirty years' ministering to the poor people of an alien race, her insistence on their good qualities. It is a valuable antidote to the campaign of hate which war breeds; for somehow I don't believe that hate is the answer to our troubles. Hate is a mere beginner of wars. To end them, we shall have to marry our indignation with our faith.

Author's note. Since the above was written, word has been received of Aunt   25
Poo's death. Details are lacking, but she is reported to have died of natural causes. Against the backdrop of war and Japanese brutality, the story of Mrs. Omori's life seems unreal, and her long years of work in the slums of Tokyo take on the quality of a bitter jest. They were never this to her; but it is significant, perhaps, that in the last years before the war her thoughts turned away from the new currents around her in Japan and back to New England on the strong tide of emotion which took the form of her memoirs for her nieces.

FROM READING TO REREADING

1. The war with Japan plays a significant part in White's essay. In what ways might the war have inspired him to write about Aunt Poo in the first place? How does the war affect his attitudes toward the Japanese?

2. "I have never met this fabulous aunt," White admits from the start. Note the use of the word "fabulous." How do people normally use the word? How is White using the term? Does he mean "fantastic" or "terrific"?

3. In composing a brief character sketch of someone, we usually look for a few specific details about the person that convincingly establish his or her personality. These could be gestures, expressions, habits, favorite possessions, or any number of other details. We want to offer readers an individual person, not a cluster of abstractions. What specific details does White introduce about Aunt Poo that help us form a vivid picture of her personality?

CYNTHIA OZICK
The Seam of the Snail

One of the standard rhetorical means of constructing an essay is by comparison and contrast: the writer considers something in terms of its resemblances to and/ or differences from something else. This rhetorical method seems also to be an essential part of family discourse, as we tend to identify ourselves both in comparison with and in contrast to other family members. In "The Seam of the Snail," Cynthia Ozick provides us with a classic illustration of how a child perceives and defines herself in relation to her similarities and differences from a parent. Ozick's essay was entitled "Excellence" when it appeared in Ms *magazine in 1985.*

I N MY DEPRESSION CHILDHOOD, whenever I had a new dress, my cousin Sarah would get suspicious. The nicer the dress was, and especially the more expensive it looked, the more suspicious she would get. Finally she would lift the hem and check the seams. This was to see if the dress had been bought or if my mother had sewed it. Sarah could always tell. My mother's sewing had elegant outsides, but there was something catch-as-catch-can about the insides. Sarah's sewing, by contrast, was as impeccably finished inside as out; not one stray thread dangled.

My Uncle Jake built meticulous grandfather clocks out of rosewood; he was a perfectionist, and sent to England for the clockworks. My mother built serviceable radiator covers and a serviceable cabinet, with hinged doors, for the pantry. She built a pair of bookcases for the living room. Once, after I was grown and in a house of my own, she fixed the sewer pipe. She painted ceilings, and also landscapes; she reupholstered chairs. One summer she planted a whole yard of tall corn. She thought herself capable of doing anything, and did everything she imagined. But nothing was perfect. There was always some clear flaw, never visible head-on. You had to look underneath, where the seams were. The corn thrived, though not in rows. The stalks elbowed one another like gossips in a dense little village.

"Miss Brrrroooobaker," my mother used to mock, rolling her Russian *r*'s, whenever I crossed a *t* she had left uncrossed, or corrected a word she had misspelled, or became impatient with a *v* that had tangled itself up with a *w* in her speech. ("*Vvv*entriloquist," I would say. "*Vvv*entriloquist," she would obediently repeat. And the next time it would come out "wiolinist.") Miss Brubaker was my high school English teacher, and my mother invoked her name as an emblem of raging finical obsession. "Miss Brrrroooobaker," my mother's voice hoots at me down the years, as I go on casting and recasting sentences in a tiny handwriting on monomaniacally uniform paper. The loops of my mother's handwriting — it was the Palmer Method [1] — were as big as soup bowls, spilling generous splashy ebullience. She could pull off, at five minutes' notice, a satisfying dinner for ten concocted out of nothing more than originality and panache. But the napkin would be folded a little off center, and the spoon might be on the wrong side of the knife. She was an optimist who ignored trifles; for her, God was not in the details but in the intent. And all these culinary and agricultural efflorescences were extracurricular, accomplished in the crevices and niches of a fourteen-hour business day. When she scribbled out her family memoirs, in heaps of dog-eared notebooks, or on the backs of old bills, or on the margins of last year's calendar, I would resist typing them; in the speed of the chase she often omitted words like "the," "and," "will." The same flashing and bountiful hand fashioned and fired ceramic pots, and painted brilliant autumn views and vases of imaginary flowers and ferns, and decorated ordinary Woolworth platters with lavish enameled gardens. But bits of the painted petals would chip away.

Lavish: my mother was as lavish as nature. She woke early and saturated the hours with work and inventiveness, and read late into the night. She was all profusion, abundance, fabrication. Angry at her children, she would run after us whirling the cord of the electric iron, like a lasso or a whip; but she never caught us. When, in seventh grade, I was afraid of failing the Music Appreciation final exam because I could not tell the difference between "To a Wild Rose" and "Barcarole," she got the idea of sending me to school with a gauze sling rigged up on my writing arm, and an explanatory note that was purest fiction. But the sling kept slipping off. My mother gave advice like mad — she boiled over with so much passion for the predicaments of strangers that they turned into permanent cronies. She told intimate stories about people I had never heard of.

Despite the gargantuan Palmer loops (or possibly because of them), I   5 have always known that my mother's was a life of — intricately abashing word! — excellence: insofar as excellence means ripe generosity. She burgeoned, she proliferated; she was endlessly leafy and flowering. She wore red hats, and called herself a gypsy. In her girlhood she marched with the suffragettes and for Margaret Sanger [2] and called herself a Red. She made me laugh, she was so varied: like a tree on which lemons, pomegranates, and prickly pears absurdly all hang together. She had the comedy of prodigality.

---

[1] *Palmer Method:* A method of teaching handwriting that dominated American elementary schools for decades.

[2] *Margaret Higgins Sanger* (1883–1966): Public health reformer who began a famous crusade for birth control in 1912 and four years later established the first birth control clinic in the United States, which eventually developed into the Planned Parenthood Federation.

My own way is a thousand times more confined. I am a pinched perfectionist, the ultimate fruition of Miss Brubaker; I attend to crabbed minutiae and am self-trammeled through taking pains. I am a kind of human snail, locked in and condemned by my own nature. The ancients believed that the moist track left by the snail as it crept was the snail's own essence, depleting its body little by little; the farther the snail toiled, the smaller it became, until it finally rubbed itself out. That is how perfectionists are. Say to us Excellence, and we will show you how we use up our substance and wear ourselves away, while making scarcely any progress at all. The fact that I am an exacting perfectionist in a narrow strait only, and nowhere else, is hardly to the point, since nothing matters to me so much as a comely and muscular sentence. It is my narrow strait, this snail's road; the track of the sentence I am writing now; and when I have eked out the wet substance, ink or blood, that is its mark, I will begin the next sentence. Only in treading out sentences am I perfectionist; but then there is nothing else I know how to do, or take much interest in. I miter every pair of abutting sentences as scrupulously as Uncle Jake fitted one strip of rosewood against another. My mother's worldly and bountiful hand has escaped me. The sentence I am writing is my cabin and my shell, compact, self-sufficient. It is the burnished horizon — a merciless planet where flawlessness is the single standard, where even the inmost seams, however hidden from a laxer eye, must meet perfection. Here "excellence" is not strewn casually from a tipped cornucopia, here disorder does not account for charm, here trifles rule like tyrants.

I measure my life in sentences pressed out, line by line, like the lustrous ooze on the underside of the snail, the snail's secret open seam, its wound, leaking attar. My mother was too mettlesome to feel the force of a comma. She scorned minutiae. She measured her life according to what poured from the horn of plenty, which was her own seamless, ample, cascading, elastic, susceptible, inexact heart. My narrower heart rides between the tiny twin horns of the snail, dwindling as it goes.

And out of this thinnest thread, this ink-wet line of words, must rise a visionary fog, a mist, a smoke, forging cities, histories, sorrows, quagmires, entanglements, lives of sinners, even the life of my furnace-hearted mother: so much wilderness, waywardness, plenitude on the head of the precise and impeccable snail, between the horns. (Ah, if this could be!)

FROM READING TO REREADING

1. Consider the original title of Ozick's essay: "Excellence." In what way is the essay about excellence? How is Ozick's mother's "excellence" different from her own?

2. Ozick uses the word *seam* in both literal and figurative ways. How many different meanings of the word can you find in the essay? In what senses does the term apply to both her mother and herself? What does the image "seam of the snail" mean literally? What does it mean figuratively?

3. One implicit effect of most comparisons is that one side usually gets preferred over another. Do you think Ozick falls into this trap or avoids it? Do you think she presents her mother's habits as superior to her own, her own as superior to her mother's, or does she see no superiority on either side?

ALICE WALKER
In Search of Our Mothers' Gardens

In one of English literature's most memorable poems, "Elegy Written in a Country Churchyard" (1751), Thomas Gray wrote the famous lines: "Full many a gem of purest ray serene,/The dark unfathomed caves of ocean bear:/Full many a flower is born to blush unseen,/And waste its sweetness on the desert air." As Gray contemplates the many anonymous people buried in an obscure cemetery, he speculates about those who died ("Some mute inglorious Milton here may rest") without realizing their artistic or creative potentials. Alice Walker's "In Search of Our Mothers' Gardens," which originally appeared in Ms magazine in 1973, represents a modern reworking of Gray's theme. In this often-anthologized essay, Walker, like Gray, speculates about all of those whose creative lives were channeled into nonliterary forms of expression. But for Walker, anonymity is more than an occasion for detached contemplation; it is an integral part of her own family heritage and it reaches to the roots of her African American experience.

> I described her own nature and temperament. Told how they needed a larger life for their expression . . . I pointed out that in lieu of proper channels, her emotions had overflowed into paths that dissipated them. I talked, beautifully I thought, about an art that would be born, an art that would open the way for women the likes of her. I asked her to hope, and build up an inner life against the coming of that day. . . . I sang, with a strange quiver in my voice, a promise song.
> — "Avey," Jean Toomer, *Cane*
> *The poet speaking to a prostitute who falls asleep while he's talking.*

W HEN THE POET Jean Toomer [1] walked through the South in the early twenties, he discovered a curious thing: black women whose spirituality was so intense, so deep, so *unconscious*, they were themselves unaware of the richness they held. They stumbled blindly through their lives: creatures so abused and mutilated in body, so dimmed and confused by pain, that they considered themselves unworthy even of hope. In the selfless abstractions their bodies became to the men who used them, they became more than "sexual objects," more even than mere women: They became "Saints." Instead of being perceived as whole persons, their bodies became shrines: What was thought to be their minds became temples suitable for worship. These crazy Saints stared out at the world, wildly, like lunatics —

---

[1] *Jean Toomer* (1894–1967): A black poet, novelist, and a leading figure of the Harlem Renaissance who wrote *Cane* in 1923.

or quietly, like suicides; and the "God" that was in their gaze was as mute as a great stone.

Who were these Saints? These crazy, loony, pitiful women?

Some of them, without a doubt, were our mothers and grandmothers.

In the still heat of the post-Reconstruction South, this is how they seemed to Jean Toomer: exquisite butterflies trapped in an evil honey, toiling away their lives in an era, a century, that did not acknowledge them, except as "the *mule* of the world." They dreamed dreams that no one knew — not even themselves, in any coherent fashion — and saw visions no one could understand. They wandered or sat about the countryside crooning lullabies to ghosts, and drawing the mother of Christ in charcoal on courthouse walls.

They forced their minds to desert their bodies and their striving spirits sought to rise, like frail whirlwinds from the hard red clay. And when those frail whirlwinds fell, in scattered particles, upon the ground, no one mourned. Instead, men lit candles to celebrate the emptiness that remained, as people do who enter a beautiful but vacant space to resurrect a God.

Our mothers and grandmothers, some of them: moving to music not yet written. And they waited.

They waited for a day when the unknown thing that was in them would be made known; but guessed, somehow in their darkness, that on the day of their revelation they would be long dead. Therefore to Toomer they walked, and even ran, in slow motion. For they were going nowhere immediate, and the future was not yet within their grasp. And men took our mothers and grandmothers, "but got no pleasure from it." So complex was their passion and their calm.

To Toomer, they lay vacant and fallow as autumn fields, with harvest time never in sight: and he saw them enter loveless marriages, without joy; and become prostitutes, without resistance; and become mothers of children, without fulfillment.

For these grandmothers and mothers of ours were not Saints, but Artists; driven to a numb and bleeding madness by the springs of creativity in them for which there was no release. They were Creators, who lived lives of spiritual waste, because they were so rich in spirituality — which is the basis of Art — that the strain of enduring their unused and unwanted talent drove them insane. Throwing away this spirituality was their pathetic attempt to lighten the soul to a weight their workworn, sexually abused bodies could bear.

What did it mean for a black woman to be an artist in our grandmothers' time? In our great-grandmothers' day? It is a question with an answer cruel enough to stop the blood.

Did you have a genius of a great-great-grandmother who died under some ignorant and depraved white overseer's lash? Or was she required to bake biscuits for a lazy backwater tramp, when she cried out in her soul to paint watercolors of sunsets, or the rain falling on the green and peaceful pasturelands? Or was her body broken and forced to bear children (who were more often than not sold away from her) — eight, ten, fifteen, twenty children — when her one joy was the thought of modeling heroic figures of rebellion, in stone or clay?

How was the creativity of the black woman kept alive, year after year and century after century, when for most of the years black people have been in America, it was a punishable crime for a black person to read or write? And the freedom to paint, to sculpt, to expand the mind with action did not exist. Consider, if you can bear to imagine it, what might have been the result if singing, too, had been forbidden by law. Listen to the voices of Bessie Smith, Billie Holiday, Nina Simone, Roberta Flack, and Aretha Franklin, among others, and imagine those voices muzzled for life. Then you may begin to comprehend the lives of our "crazy," "Sainted" mothers and grandmothers. The agony of the lives of women who might have been Poets, Novelists, Essayists, and Short-Story Writers (over a period of centuries), who died with their real gifts stifled within them.

And, if this were the end of the story, we would have cause to cry out in my paraphrase of Okot p'Bitek's great poem:

> O, my clanswomen
> Let us all cry together!
> Come,
> Let us mourn the death of our mother,
> The death of a Queen
> The ash that was produced
> By a great fire!
> O, this homestead is utterly dead
> Close the gates
> With *lacari* thorns,
> For our mother
> The creator of the Stool is lost!
> And all the young men
> Have perished in the wilderness!

But this is not the end of the story, for all the young women — our mothers and grandmothers, *ourselves* — have not perished in the wilderness. And if we ask ourselves why, and search for and find the answer, we will know beyond all efforts to erase it from our minds, just exactly who, and of what, we black American women are.

One example, perhaps the most pathetic, most misunderstood one, can   15
provide a backdrop for our mothers' work: Phillis Wheatley, [2] a slave in the 1700s.

---

[2] *Phillis Wheatley* (ca. 1754–1784): A slave in a prosperous Boston family; published her first poetry at the age of thirteen and enjoyed an international reputation, acclaimed by such figures as Voltaire, George Washington, and Benjamin Franklin. She died, however, in poverty and obscurity.

Virginia Woolf, in her book *A Room of One's Own,* wrote that in order for a woman to write fiction she must have two things, certainly: a room of her own (with key and lock) and enough money to support herself.

What then are we to make of Phillis Wheatley, a slave, who owned not even herself? This sickly, frail black girl who required a servant of her own at times — her health was so precarious — and who, had she been white, would have been easily considered the intellectual superior of all the women and most of the men in the society of her day.

Virginia Woolf wrote further, speaking of course not of our Phillis, that "any woman born with a great gift in the sixteenth century [insert "eighteenth century," insert "black woman," insert "born or made a slave"] would certainly have gone crazed, shot herself, or ended her days in some lonely cottage outside the village, half witch, half wizard [insert "Saint"], feared and mocked at. For it needs little skill and psychology to be sure that a highly gifted girl who had tried to use her gift of poetry would have been so thwarted and hindered by contrary instincts [add "chains, guns, the lash, the ownership of one's body by someone else, submission to an alien religion"], that she must have lost her health and sanity to a certainty."

The key words, as they relate to Phillis, are "contrary instincts." For when we read the poetry of Phillis Wheatley — as when we read the novels of Nella Larsen or the oddly false-sounding autobiography of that freest of all black women writers, Zora Hurston — evidence of "contrary instincts" is everywhere. Her loyalties were completely divided, as was, without question, her mind.

But how could this be otherwise? Captured at seven, a slave of wealthy, [20] doting whites who instilled in her the "savagery" of the Africa they "rescued" her from . . . one wonders if she was even able to remember her homeland as she had known it, or as it really was.

Yet, because she did try to use her gift for poetry in a world that made her a slave, she was "so thwarted and hindered by . . . contrary instincts, that she . . . lost her health. . . ." In the last years of her brief life, burdened not only with the need to express her gift but also with a penniless, friendless "freedom" and several small children for whom she was forced to do strenuous work to feed, she lost her health, certainly. Suffering from malnutrition and neglect and who knows what mental agonies, Phillis Wheatley died.

So torn by "contrary instincts" was black, kidnapped, enslaved Phillis that her description of "the Goddess" — as she poetically called the Liberty she did not have — is ironically, cruelly humorous. And, in fact, has held Phillis up to ridicule for more than a century. It is usually read prior to hanging Phillis's memory as that of a fool. She wrote:

> The Goddess comes, she moves divinely fair,
> Olive and laurel binds her *golden* hair.
> Wherever shines this native of the skies,
> Unnumber'd charms and recent graces rise [*My emphasis*]

It is obvious that Phillis, the slave, combed the "Goddess's" hair every morning; prior, perhaps, to bringing in the milk, or fixing her mistress's lunch. She took her imagery from the one thing she saw elevated above all others.

With the benefit of hindsight we ask, "How could she?"

But at last, Phillis, we understand. No more snickering when your stiff, struggling, ambivalent lines are forced on us. We know now that you were not an idiot or a traitor; only a sickly little black girl, snatched from your home and country and made a slave; a woman who still struggled to sing the song that was your gift, although in a land of barbarians who praised you for your bewildered tongue. It is not so much what you sang, as that you kept alive, in so many of our ancestors, *the notion of song.*

Black women are called, in the folklore that so aptly identified one's status in society, "the *mule* of the world," because we have been handed the burdens that everyone else — *everyone* else — refused to carry. We have also been called "Matriarchs," "Superwomen," and "Mean and Evil Bitches." Not to mention "Castraters" and "Sapphire's Mama." When we have pleaded for understanding, our character has been distorted; when we have asked for simple caring, we have been handed empty inspirational appellations, then stuck in the farthest corner. When we have asked for love, we have been given children. In short, even our plainer gifts, our labors of fidelity and love, have been knocked down our throats. To be an artist and a black woman, even today, lowers our status in many respects, rather than raises it: and yet, artists we will be.

Therefore we must fearlessly pull out of ourselves and look at and identify with our lives the living creativity some of our great-grandmothers were not allowed to know. I stress *some* of them because it is well known that the majority of our great-grandmothers knew, even without "knowing" it, the reality of their spirituality, even if they didn't recognize it beyond what happened in the singing at church — and they never had any intention of giving it up.

How they did it — those millions of black women who were not Phillis Wheatley, or Lucy Terry or Frances Harper or Zora Hurston or Nella Larsen or Bessie Smith; or Elizabeth Catlett, or Katherine Dunham, either — brings me to the title of this essay, "In Search of Our Mothers' Gardens," which is a personal account that is yet shared, in its theme and its meaning, by all of us. I found, while thinking about the far-reaching world of creative black woman, that often the truest answer to a question that really matters can be found very close.

In the late 1920s my mother ran away from home to marry my father. Marriage, if not running away, was expected of seventeen-year-old girls. By the time she was twenty, she had two children and was pregnant with a third. Five children later, I was born. And this is how I came to know my mother: She seemed a large, soft, loving-eyed woman who was rarely impatient in our home. Her quick, violent temper was on view only a few times a year, when she battled with the white landlord who had the misfortune to suggest to her that her children did not need to go to school.

She made all the clothes we wore, even my brothers' overalls. She made all the towels and sheets we used. She spent the summers canning vegetables and fruits. She spent the winter evenings making quilts enough to cover our beds. 30

During the "working" day, she labored beside — not behind — my father in the fields. Her day began before sunup, and did not end until late at night. There was never a moment for her to sit down, undisturbed, to unravel her own private thoughts; never a time free from interruption — by work or the noisy inquiries of her many children. And yet, it is to my mother — and all our mothers who were not famous — that I went in search of the secret of what has fed that muzzled and often mutilated, but vibrant, creative spirit that the black woman has inherited, and that pops out in wild and unlikely places to this day.

But when, you will ask, did my overworked mother have time to know or care about feeding the creative spirit?

The answer is so simple that many of us have spent years discovering it. We have constantly looked high, when we should have looked high — and low.

For example: In the Smithsonian Institution in Washington, D.C., there hangs a quilt unlike any other in the world. In fanciful, inspired and yet simple and identifiable figures, it portrays the story of the Crucifixion. It is considered rare, beyond price. Though it follows no known pattern of quilt-making, and though it is made of bits and pieces of worthless rags, it is obviously the work of a person of powerful imagination and deep spiritual feeling. Below this quilt I saw a note that says it was made by "an anonymous Black woman in Alabama, a hundred years ago."

If we could locate this "anonymous" black woman from Alabama, she would turn out to be one of our grandmothers — an artist who left her mark in the only materials she could afford, and in the only medium her position in society allowed her to use. 35

As Virginia Woolf wrote further, in *A Room of One's Own*:

> Yet genius of a sort must have existed among women as it must have existed among the working class. [Change this to "slaves" and "the wives and daughters of sharecroppers."] Now and again an Emily Brontë or a Robert Burns [change this to "a Zora Hurston or a Richard Wright"] blazes out and proves its presence. But certainly it never got itself on to paper. When, however, one reads of a witch being ducked, of a woman possessed by devils [or "Sainthood"], of a wise woman selling herbs [our root work-

ers], or even a very remarkable man who had a mother, then I think we are on the track of a lost novelist, a suppressed poet, or some mute and inglorious Jane Austen. . . . Indeed, I would venture to guess that Anon, who wrote so many poems without signing them, was often a woman. . . .

And so our mothers and grandmothers have, more often than not anonymously, handed on the creative spark, the seed of the flower they themselves never hoped to see: or like a sealed letter they could not plainly read.

And so it is, certainly, with my own mother. Unlike "Ma" Rainey's songs, which retained their creator's name even while blasting forth from Bessie Smith's mouth, no song or poem will bear my mother's name. Yet so many of the stories that I write, that we all write, are my mother's stories. Only recently did I fully realize this: that through years of listening to my mother's stories of her life, I have absorbed not only the stories themselves, but something of the manner in which she spoke, something of the urgency that involves the knowledge that her stories — like her life — must be recorded. It is probably for this reason that so much of what I have written is about characters whose counterparts in real life are so much older than I am.

But the telling of these stories, which came from my mother's lips as naturally as breathing, was not the only way my mother showed herself as an artist. For stories, too, were subject to being distracted, to dying without conclusion. Dinners must be started, and cotton must be gathered before the big rains. The artist that was and is my mother showed itself to me only after many years. This is what I finally noticed:

Like Mem, a character in *The Third Life of Grange Copeland*, [3] my mother   40 adorned with flowers whatever shabby house we were forced to live in. And not just your typical straggly country stand of zinnias, either. She planted ambitious gardens — and still does — with over fifty different varieties of plants that bloom profusely from early March until late November. Before she left home for the fields, she watered her flowers, chopped up the grass, and laid out new beds. When she returned from the fields, she might divide clumps of bulbs, dig a cold pit, uproot and replant roses, or prune branches from her taller bushes or trees — until night came and it was too dark to see.

Whatever she planted grew as if by magic, and her fame as a grower of flowers spread over three counties. Because of her creativity with her flowers, even my memories of poverty are seen through a screen of blooms — sunflowers, petunias, roses, dahlias, forsythia, spirea, delphiniums, verbena . . . and on and on.

And I remember people coming to my mother's yard to be given cuttings from her flowers; I hear again the praise showered on her because

[3] *The Third Life of Grange Copeland*: Walker's first novel, published in 1970.

whatever rocky soil she landed on, she turned into a garden. A garden so brilliant with colors, so original in its design, so magnificent with life and creativity, that to this day people drive by our house in Georgia — perfect strangers and imperfect strangers — and ask to stand or walk among my mother's art.

I notice that it is only when my mother is working in her flowers that she is radiant, almost to the point of being invisible — except as Creator: hand and eye. She is involved in work her soul must have. Ordering the universe in the image of her personal conception of Beauty.

Her face, as she prepares the Art that is her gift, is a legacy of respect she leaves to me, for all that illuminates and cherishes life. She has handed down respect for the possibilities — and the will to grasp them.

For her, so hindered and intruded upon in so many ways, being an artist has still been a daily part of her life. This ability to hold on, even in very simple ways, is work black women have done for a very long time. 45

This poem is not enough, but it is something, for the woman who literally covered the holes in our walls with sunflowers:

> They were women then
> My mama's generation
> Husky of voice — Stout of
> Step
> With fists as well as
> Hands
> How they battered down
> Doors
> And ironed
> Starched white
> Shirts
> How they led
> Armies
> Headragged Generals
> Across mined
> Fields
> Booby-trapped
> Kitchens
> To discover books
> Desks
> A place for us
> How they knew what we
> *Must* know
> Without knowing a page
> Of it
> Themselves

Guided by my heritage of a love of beauty and a respect for strength — in search of my mother's garden, I found my own.

And perhaps in Africa over two hundred years ago, there was just such a mother; perhaps she painted vivid and daring decorations in oranges and yellows and greens on the walls of her hut; perhaps she sang — in a voice like Roberta Flack's — *sweetly* over the compounds of her village; perhaps she wove the most stunning mats or told the most ingenious stories of all the village storytellers. Perhaps she was herself a poet — though only her daughter's name is signed to the poems that we know.

Perhaps Phillis Wheatley's mother was also an artist.

Perhaps in more than Phillis Wheatley's biological life is her mother's 50 signature made clear.

FROM READING TO REREADING

1. Walker titles her essay "In Search of *Our* Mothers' Gardens," not of "*My* Mothers' Garden." What does her mother have in common with all the mothers she writes about? Clearly, not all of these generations of mothers kept gardens. In what sense is Walker using the idea of gardens in this essay?

2. Walker's essay is embedded with quotations. She begins with an epigraph from the noted black male poet and novelist, Jean Toomer, which serves as a point of departure for her characterization of African American women. She quotes, too, from a number of other literary sources, especially from Virginia Woolf. Note how Walker handles quotations, how she doesn't merely insert them into her essay but works closely with them. Consider in what ways her use of quotation contributes to the overall theme of Walker's essay.

3. Walker's quotations, of course, are part of her literary legacy and demonstrate the creative struggles of women who did find a voice. But what of those who didn't? According to Walker, how did these women manage to keep the creative spirit alive? What are some examples of their creations? How do these nonliterary creations also serve as a legacy, and how have they contributed to Walker's own artistic spirit?

VIRGINIA WOOLF

22 Hyde Park Gate

"Happy families are all alike," wrote Leo Tolstoy in the opening lines of Anna
Karenina, *and then added, "every unhappy family is unhappy in its own way."
In "22 Hyde Park Gate," Virginia Woolf describes one such unique, unhappy
family — her own. Their mother dead, their famous father "deaf, eccentric,
absorbed in his work, and entirely shut off from the world," she and her sister
Vanessa spent much of their teenage years in the company of an older half-brother,
George Duckworth, who was a child of their mother's first marriage and who
also lived at 22 Hyde Park Gate. In this autobiographical essay, Virginia Woolf
discloses the shocking details of her relationship with George. The essay was read
aloud sometime during 1920–21 to a small circle of family and friends who
frequently gathered together to share each other's intimate memories. Calling
themselves "The Memoir Club," the group insisted upon "absolute frankness."
The essay was not intended for publication and thus opens with a casual reference
to previous discussions. The events in the essay take place around the turn of the
century, when Virginia Woolf was eighteen and George Duckworth thirty-two.*

A S I HAVE SAID, the drawing room at Hyde Park Gate was divided by
black folding doors picked out with thin lines of raspberry red. We
were still much under the influence of Titian. Mounds of plush Watts'[1]
portraits, busts shrined in crimson velvet, enriched the gloom of a room
naturally dark and thickly shaded in summer by showers of Virginia Creeper.
But it is of the folding doors that I wish to speak. How could family
life have been carried on without them? As soon dispense with water-closets
or bathrooms as with folding doors in a family of nine men and women, one
of whom into the bargain was an idiot. Suddenly there would be a crisis —
a servant dismissed, a lover rejected, pass books opened, or poor Mrs Tyndall
who had lately poisoned her husband by mistake come for consolation. On
one side of the door Cousin Adeline, Duchess of Bedford, perhaps would be
on her knees — the Duke had died tragically at Woburn; Mrs Dolmetsch
would be telling how she had found her husband in bed with the parlour-
maid or Lisa Stillman would be sobbing that Walter Headlam had chalked
her nose with a billiard cue — "which", she cried, "is what comes of smoking
a pipe before gentlemen" — and my mother had much ado to persuade her

---

[1] *Titian . . . Watts*: Titian (ca. 1477–1576), famous Venetian painter; George Frederick
Watts (1817–1904), British painter known for his portraits and allegorical works; he was
married to the English actress, Ellen Terry (see Virginia Woolf's essay on Terry in Part 3).

that life had still to be faced, and the flower of virginity was still unplucked in spite of a chalk mark on the nose.

Though dark and agitated on one side, the other side of the door, especially on Sunday afternoons, was cheerful enough. There round the oval tea table with its pink china shell full of spice buns would be found old General Beadle, talking of the Indian Mutiny; or Mr Haldane, or Sir Frederick Pollock — talking of all things under the sun; or old C. B. Clarke, whose name is given to three excessively rare Himalayan ferns; and Professor Wolstenholme, capable, if you interrupted him, of spouting two columns of tea not unmixed with sultanas through his nostrils; after which he would relapse into a drowsy ursine torpor, the result of eating opium to which he had been driven by the unkindness of his wife and the untimely death of his son Oliver who was eaten, somewhere off the coast of Coromandel, by a shark. These gentlemen came and came again; and they were often reinforced by Mr Frederick Gibbs, sometime tutor to the Prince of Wales, whose imperturbable common sense and fund of information about the colonies in general and Canada in particular were a perpetual irritation to my father who used to wonder whether a brain fever at college in the year 1863 had not something to do with it. These old gentlemen were generally to be found, eating very slowly, staying very late and making themselves agreeable at Christmas-time with curious presents of Indian silver work, and hand bags made form the skin of the ornithorhynchus — as I seem to remember.

The tea table however was also fertilized by a ravishing stream of female beauty — the three Miss Lushingtons, the three Miss Stillmans, and the three Miss Montgomeries — all triplets, all ravishing, but of the nine the paragon for wit, grace, charm, and distinction was undoubtedly the lovely Kitty Lushington — now Mrs Leo Maxse. (Their engagement under the jackmanii in the Love Corner at St Ives was my first introduction to the passion of love.) At the time I speak of she was in process of disengaging herself from Lord Morpeth, and had, I suspect, to explain her motives to my mother, a martinet in such matters, for first promising to marry a man and then breaking it off. My mother believed that all men required an infinity of care. She laid all the blame, I feel sure, upon Kitty. At any rate I have a picture of her as she issued from the secret side of the folding doors bearing on her delicate pink cheeks two perfectly formed pear-shaped crystal tears. They neither fell nor in the least dimmed the lustre of her eyes. She at once became the life and soul of the tea table — perhaps Leo Maxse was there — perhaps Ronny Norman — perhaps Esmé Howard — perhaps Arthur Studd, for the gentlemen were not all old, or all professors by any means — and when my father groaned beneath his breath but very audibly, "Oh Gibbs, what a bore you are!" it was Kitty whom my mother instantly threw into the breach. "Kitty wants to tell you how much she loved your lecture", my mother would cry, and Kitty still with the tears on her cheeks would improvise with the utmost gallantry some compliment or opinion which pacified my father who was extremely sensitive to female charm and largely depended upon female praise. Repenting of his irritation he would press poor Gibbs warmly by the hand and beg him to come soon again — which needless to say, poor Gibbs did.

And then there would come dancing into the room rubbing his hands, wrinkling his forehead, the most remarkable figure, as I sometimes think, that our household contained. I have alluded to a grisly relic of another age which we used to disinter from the nursery wardrobe — Herbert Duckworth's wig. (Herbert Duckworth had been a barrister.) Herbert Duckworth's son — George Herbert — was by no means grisly. His hair curled naturally in dark crisp ringlets; he was six foot high; he had been in the Eton Eleven; he was now cramming at Scoones' in the hope of passing the Foreign Office examination. When Miss Willett of Brighton saw him 'throwing off his ulster' in the middle of her drawing room she was moved to write an Ode Comparing George Duckworth to the Hermes of Praxiteles [2] — which Ode my mother kept in her writing table drawer, along with a little Italian medal that George had won for saving a peasant from drowning. Miss Willett was reminded of the Hermes; but if you looked at him closely you noticed that one of his ears was pointed; and the other round; you also noticed that though he had the curls of a God and the ears of a faun he had unmistakably the eyes of a pig. So strange a compound can seldom have existed. And in the days I speak of, God, faun and pig were all in all alive, all in opposition, and in their conflicts producing the most astonishing eruptions.

To begin with the God — well, he was only a plaster cast perhaps of Miss Willett's Hermes, but I cannot deny that the benign figure of George Duckworth teaching his small half-brothers and sisters by the hour on a strip of coco-nut matting to play forward with a perfectly straight bat had something Christlike about it. He was certainly Christian rather than Pagan in his divinity, for it soon became clear that this particular forward stroke to be applied to every ball indifferently, was a symbol of moral rectitude, and that one could neither slog nor bowl a sneak without paltering rather dangerously (as poor Gerald Duckworth used to do) with the ideals of a sportsman and an English gentleman. Then, he would run miles to fetch cushions; he was always shutting doors and opening windows; it was always George who said the tactful thing, and broke bad news, and braved my father's irritation, and read aloud to us when we had the whooping cough, and remembered the birthdays of aunts, and sent turtle soup to the invalids, and attended funerals, and took children to the pantomime — oh yes, whatever else George might be he was certainly a saint.

But then there was the faun. Now this animal was at once sportive and

[2] *Hermes of Praxiteles*: Praxiteles, who flourished in the fourth century B.C., was one of the most influential sculptors of the classical era; Hermes is the messenger god of Greek mythology.

demonstrative and thus often at variance with the self-sacrificing nature of the God. It was quite a common thing to come into the drawing room and find George on his knees with his arms extended, addressing my mother, who might be adding up the weekly books, in tones of fervent adoration. Perhaps he had been staying with the Chamberlains for the week-end. But he lavished caresses, endearments, enquiries and embraces as if, after forty years in the Australian bush, he had at last returned to the home of his youth and found an aged mother still alive to welcome him. Meanwhile we gathered round — the dinner bell had already rung — awkward, but appreciative. Few families, we felt, could exhibit such a scene as this. Tears rushed to his eyes with equal abandonment. For example when he had a tooth out he flung himself into the cook's arms in a paroxysm of weeping. When Judith Blunt refused him he sat at the head of the table sobbing loudly, but continuing to eat. He cried when he was vaccinated. He was fond of sending telegrams which began "My darling mother" and went on to say that he would be dining out. (I copied this style of his, I regret to say, with disastrous results on one celebrated occasion. "She is an angel" I wired, on hearing that Flora Russell had accepted him, and signed my nickname 'Goat'. "She is an aged Goat" was the version that arrived, at Islay, and had something to do, George said, with Flora's reluctance to ally herself with the Stephen family.) But all this exuberance of emotion was felt to be wholly to George's credit. It proved not only how deep and warm his feelings were, but how marvellously he had kept the open heart and simple manners of a child.

But when nature refused him two pointed ears and gave him only one she knew, I think, what she was about. In his wildest paroxysms of emotion, when he bellowed with grief, or danced round the room, leaping like a kid, and flung himself on his knees before the Dowager Lady Carnarvon there was always something self conscious, a little uneasy about him, as though he were not quite sure of the effect — as though the sprightly faun had somehow been hobbled together with a timid and conventional old sheep.

It is true that he was abnormally stupid. He passed the simplest examinations with incredible difficulty. For years he was crammed by Mr Scoones; and again and again he failed to pass the Foreign Office examination. He had existed all his life upon jobs found for him by his friends. His small brown eyes seemed perpetually to be boring into something too hard for them to penetrate. But when one compares them to the eyes of a pig, one is alluding not merely to their stupidity, or to their greed — George, I have been told, had the reputation of being the greediest young man in London ball-rooms — but to something obstinate and pertinacious in their expression as if the pig were grouting for truffles with his snout and would by sheer persistency succeed in unearthing them. Never shall I forget the pertinacity with which he learnt "Love in the Valley" by heart in order to impress Flora Russell; or the determination with which he mastered the first volume of *Middlemarch* [3] for the same purpose; and how immensely he was relieved when he left the second volume in a train and got my father, whose set was ruined, to declare that in his opinion one volume of *Middlemarch* was enough. Had his obstinacy been directed solely to self-improvement there would have been no call for us to complain. I myself might even have been of use to him. But it gradually became clear that he was muddling out a scheme, a plan of campaign, a system of life — I scarcely know what to call it — and then we had every reason to feel the earth tremble beneath our feet and the heavens darken. For George Duckworth had become after my mother's death, for all practical purposes, the head of the family. My father was deaf, eccentric, absorbed in his work, and entirely shut off from the world. The management of affairs fell upon George. It was usually said that he was father and mother, sister and brother in one — and all the old ladies of Kensington and Belgravia added with one accord that Heaven had blessed those poor Stephen girls beyond belief and it remained for them to prove that they were worthy of such devotion.

But what was George Duckworth thinking and what was there alarming   10 in the sight of him as he sat in the red leather arm-chair after dinner, mechanically stroking the dachshund Schuster, and lugubriously glancing at the pages of George Eliot? Well, he might be thinking about the crest on the post office notepaper, and how nice it would look picked out in red (he was now Austen Chamberlain's private secretary) or he might be thinking how the Duchess of St Albans had given up using fish knives at dinner; or how Mrs Grenfell had asked him to stay and he had created as he thought a good impression by refusing; at the same time he was revolving in the slow whirlpool of his brain schemes of the utmost thoughtfulness — plans for sending us for treats; for providing us with riding lessons; for finding jobs for some of poor Augusta Croft's innumerable penniless children. But the alarming thing was that he looked not merely muddled and emotional but obstinate. He looked as if he had made up his mind about something and would refuse to budge an inch. At the time it was extremely difficult to say what he had made up his mind to, but after the lapse of many years I think it may be said brutally and baldly, that George had made up his mind to rise in the social scale. He had a curious inborn reverence for the British aristocracy; the beauty of our great aunts had allied us in the middle of the nineteenth century with, I think I am right in saying, two dukes and quite a number of earls and countesses. They naturally showed no particular wish to remember the connection but George did his best to live up to it. His reverence for the symbols of greatness now that he was attached to a Cabinet Minister had fuller scope. His talk was all of ivory buttons that the coachmen

[3] *Middlemarch*: George Eliot (the pen name of Mary Ann Evans) published the multivolume classic novel *Middlemarch* in 1872.

of Cabinet Ministers wear in their coats; of having the entrée at Court; of baronies descending in the female line; of countesses secreting the diamonds of Marie Antoinette in black boxes under their beds. His secret dreams as he sat in the red leather chair stroking Schuster were all of marrying a wife with diamonds, and having a coachman with a button, and having the entrée at Court. But the danger was that his dreams were secret even to himself. Had you told him — and I think Vanessa did once — that he was a snob, he would have burst into tears. What he liked, he explained, was to know 'nice people'; Lady Jeune was nice; so were Lady Sligo, Lady Carnarvon and Lady Leitrim. Poor Mrs Clifford, on the other hand, was not; nor was old Mr Wolstenholme; of all our old friends, Kitty Maxse, who might have been Lady Morpeth, came nearest to his ideal. It was not a question of birth or wealth; it was — and then if you pressed him further he would seize you in his arms and cry out that he refused to argue with those he loved. "Kiss me, kiss me, you beloved", he would vociferate; and the argument was drowned in kisses. Everything was drowned in kisses. He lived in the thickest emotional haze, and as his passions increased and his desires became more vehement — he lived, Jack Hills assured me, in complete chastity until his marriage — one felt like an unfortunate minnow shut up in the same tank with an unwieldy and turbulent whale.

Nothing stood in the way of his advancement. He was a bachelor of prepossessing appearance though inclined to fat, aged about thirty years, with an independent income of something over a thousand a year. As private secretary to Austen Chamberlain he was as a matter of course invited to all the great parties of all the great peers. Hostesses had no time to remember, if they had ever known, that the Duckworths had made their money in cotton, or coal, not a hundred years ago, and did not really rank, as George made out, among the ancient families of Somersetshire. For I have it on the best authority that when the original Duckworth acquired Orchardleigh about the year 1810 he filled it with casts from the Greek to which he had attached not merely fig leaves for the Gods but aprons for the Goddesses — much to the amusement of the Lords of Longleat who never forgot that old Duckworth had sold cotton by the yard and probably bought his aprons cheap. George, as I say, could have mounted alone to the highest pinnacles of London society. His mantelpiece was a gallery of invitation cards from every house in London. Why then did he insist upon cumbering himself with a couple of half-sisters who were more than likely to drag him down? It is probably useless to enquire. George's mind swam and steamed like a cauldron of rich Irish stew. He believed that aristocratic society was possessed of all the virtues and all the graces. He believed that his family had been entrusted to his care. He believed that it was his sacred duty — but when he reached that point his emotions overcame him; he began to sob; he flung himself on his knees; he seized Vanessa in his arms; he implored her in the name of her mother, of her grandmother, by all that was sacred in the female sex and holy in the traditions of our family to accept Lady Arthur Russell's invitation to dinner, to spend the week-end with the Chamberlains at Highbury.

I cannot conceal my own opinion that Vanessa was to blame; not indeed that she could help herself, but if, I sometimes think, she had been born with one shoulder higher than another, with a limp, with a squint, with a large mole on her left cheek, both our lives would have been changed for the better. As it was, George had a good deal of reason on his side. It was plain that Vanessa in her white satin dress made by Mrs Young, wearing a single flawless amethyst round her neck, and a blue enamel butterfly in her hair — the gifts, of course, of George himself — beautiful, motherless, aged only eighteen, was a touching spectacle, an ornament for any dinner table, a potential peeress, anything might be made of such precious material as she was — outwardly at least; and to be seen hovering round her, providing her with jewels, and Arab horses, and expensive clothes, whispering encouragement, lavishing embraces which were not entirely concealed from the eyes of strangers, redounded to the credit of George himself and invested his figure with a pathos which it would not otherwise have had in the eyes of the dowagers of Mayfair. [4] Unfortunately, what was inside Vanessa did not altogether correspond with what was outside. Underneath the necklaces and the enamel butterflies was one passionate desire — for paint and turpentine, for turpentine and paint. But poor George was no psychologist. His perceptions were obtuse. He never saw within. He was completely at a loss when Vanessa said she did not wish to stay with the Chamberlains at Highbury; and would not dine with Lady Arthur Russell — a rude, tyrannical old woman, with a bloodstained complexion and the manners of a turkey cock. He argued, he wept, he complained to Aunt Mary Fisher, who said that she could not believe her ears. Every battery was turned upon Vanessa. She was told that she was selfish, unwomanly, callous and incredibly ungrateful considering the treasures of affection that had been lavished upon her — the Arab horse she rode and the slabs of bright blue enamel which she wore. Still she persisted. She did not wish to dine with Lady Arthur Russell. As the season wore on, every morning brought its card of invitation for Mr Duckworth and Miss Stephen; and every evening witnessed a battle between them. For the first year or so George, I suppose, was usually the victor. Off they went, in the hansom cab of those days and late at night Vanessa would come into my room complaining that she had been dragged from party to party, where she knew no one, and had been bored to death by the civilities of young men from the Foreign Office and the condescensions of old ladies of title. The more Vanessa resisted, the more George's natural obstinacy persisted. At last there was a crisis. Lady Arthur Russell was giving a series of select parties on Thursday evenings in South Audley Street. Vanessa had sat through one entire evening without opening her lips. George insisted

---

[4] *Mayfair*: A fashionable residential district of London.

that she must go next week and make amends, or he said, "Lady Arthur will never ask you to her house again." They argued until it was getting too late to dress. At last Vanessa, more in desperation than in concession, rushed upstairs, flung on her clothes and announced that she was ready to go. Off they went. What happened in the cab will never be known. But whenever they reached 2 South Audley Street — and they reached it several times in the course of the evening — one or the other was incapable of getting out. George refused to enter with Vanessa in such a passion; and Vanessa refused to enter with George in tears. So the cabman had to be told to drive once more round the Park. Whether they ever managed to alight I do not know.

But next morning as I was sitting spelling out my Greek George came into my room carrying in his hand a small velvet box. He presented me with the jewel it contained — a Jews' harp made of enamel with a pinkish blob of matter swinging in the centre which I regret to say only fetched a few shillings when I sold it the other day. But his face showed that he had come upon a different errand. His face was sallow and scored with innumerable wrinkles, for his skin was as loose and flexible as a pug dog's, and he would express his anguish in the most poignant manner by puckering lines, folds, and creases from forehead to chin. His manner was stern. His bearing rigid. If Miss Willett of Brighton could have seen him then she would certainly have compared him to Christ on the cross. After giving me the Jews' harp he stood before the fire in complete silence. Then, as I expected, he began to tell me his version of the preceding night — wrinkling his forehead more than ever, but speaking with a restraint that was at once bitter and manly. Never, never again, he said, would he ask Vanessa to go out with him. He had seen a look in her eyes which positively frightened him. It should never be said of him that he made her do what she did not wish to do. Here he quivered, but checked himself. Then he went on to say that he had only done what he knew my mother would have wished him to do. His two sisters were the most precious things that remained to him. His home had always meant more to him — more than he could say, and here he became agitated, struggled for composure, and then burst into a statement which was at once dark and extremely lurid. We were driving Gerald from the house, he cried — when a young man was not happy at home — he himself had always been content — but if his sisters — if Vanessa refused to go out with him — if he could not bring his friends to the house — in short, it was clear that the chaste, the immaculate George Duckworth would be forced into the arms of whores. Needless to say he did not put it like that; and I could only conjure up in my virgin consciousness, dimly irradiated by having read the "Symposium" with Miss Case, horrible visions of the vices to which young men were driven whose sisters did not make them happy at home. So we went on talking for an hour or two. The end of it was that he begged me, and I agreed, to go a few nights later to the Dowager Marchioness of Sligo's ball. I had already been to May Week at Cambridge, and my recollections of gallopading round the room with Hawtrey, or sitting on the stairs and quizzing the dancers with Clive, [5] were such as to make me wonder why Vanessa found dances in London so utterly detestable. A few nights later I discovered for myself. After two hours of standing about in Lady Sligo's ball-room, of waiting to be introduced to strange young men, of dancing a round with Conrad Russell or with Esmé Howard, of dancing very badly, of being left without a partner, of being told by George that I looked lovely but must hold myself upright, I retired to an ante-room and hoped that a curtain concealed me. For some time it did. At length old Lady Sligo discovered me, judged the situation for herself and being a kind old peeress with a face like a rubicund sow's carried me off to the dining room, cut me a large slice of iced cake, and left me to devour it by myself in a corner.

On that occasion George was lenient. We left about two o'clock, and on the way home he praised me warmly, and assured me that I only needed practice to be a great social success. A few days later he told me that the Dowager Countess of Carnarvon particularly wished to make my acquaintance, and had invited me to dinner. As we drove across the Park he stroked my hand, and told me how he hoped that I should make friends with Elsie — for so both he and Vanessa had called her for some time at her own request — how I must not be frightened — how though she had been vice-reine of Canada and vice-reine of Ireland she was simplicity itself — always since the death of her husband dressed in black — refused to wear any of her jewels though she had inherited the diamonds of Marie Antoinette — and was the one woman, he said, with a man's sense of honour. The portrait he drew was of great distinction and bereavement. There would also be present her sister, Mrs Popham of Littlecote, a lady also of distinction and also bereaved, for her husband, Dick Popham of Littlecote, came of an ancient unhappy race, cursed in the reign of Henry the Eighth, since which time the property had never descended from father to son. Sure enough Mary Popham was childless, and Dick Popham was in a lunatic asylum. I felt that I was approaching a house of grandeur and desolation, and was not a little impressed. But I could see nothing alarming either in Elsie Carnarvon or in Mrs Popham of Littlecote. They were a couple of spare prim little women, soberly dressed in high black dresses, with grey hair strained off their foreheads, rather prominent blue eyes, and slightly protruding front teeth. We sat down to dinner.

The conversation was mild and kindly. Indeed I soon felt that I could 15 not only reply to their questions — was I fond of painting? — was I fond of reading? — did I help my father in his work? — but could initiate remarks of my own. George had always complained of Vanessa's silence. I would prove that I could talk. So off I started. Heaven knows what devil prompted me — or why to Lady Carnarvon and Mrs Popham of Littlecote of all people

[5] *Hawtrey . . . Clive*: Ralph Hawtrey and Clive Bell, friends of the Woolf sisters.

in the world I, a chit of eighteen, should have chosen to discourse upon the need of expressing the emotions! That, I said, was the great lack of modern life. The ancients, I said, discussed everything in common. Had Lady Carnarvon ever read the dialogues of Plato? "We — both men and women — " once launched it was difficult to stop, nor was I sure that my audacity was not holding them spell-bound with admiration. I felt that I was earning George's gratitude for ever. Suddenly a twitch, a shiver, a convulsion of amazing expressiveness, shook the Countess by my side; her diamonds, of which she wore a chaste selection, flashed in my eyes; and stopping, I saw George Duckworth blushing crimson on the other side of the table. I realised that I had committed some unspeakable impropriety. Lady Carnarvon and Mrs Popham began at once to talk of something entirely different; and directly dinner was over George, pretending to help me on with my cloak, whispered in my ear in a voice of agony, "They're not used to young women saying <u>anything</u> — ." And then as if to apologize to Lady Carnarvon for my ill breeding, I saw him withdraw with her behind a pillar in the hall, and though Mrs Popham of Littlecote tried to attract my attention to a fine specimen of Moorish metal work which hung on the wall, we both distinctly heard them kiss. But the evening was not over. Lady Carnarvon had taken tickets for the French actors, who were then appearing in some play whose name I have forgotten. We had stalls of course, and filed soberly to our places in the very centre of the crowded theatre. The curtain went up. Snubbed, shy, indignant, and uncomfortable, I paid little attention to the play. But after a time I noticed that Lady Carnarvon on one side of me, and Mrs Popham on the other, were both agitated by the same sort of convulsive twitching which had taken them at dinner. What could be the matter? They were positively squirming in their seats. I looked at the stage. The hero and heroine were pouring forth a flood of voluble French which I could not disentangle. Then they stopped. To my great astonishment the lady leapt over the back of a sofa; the gentleman followed her. Round and round the stage they dashed, the lady shrieking, the man groaning and grunting in pursuit. It was a fine piece of realistic acting. As the pursuit continued, the ladies beside me held to the arms of their stalls with claws of iron. Suddenly, the actress dropped exhausted upon the sofa, and the man with a howl of gratification, loosening his clothes quite visibly, leapt on top of her. The curtain fell. Lady Carnarvon, Mrs Popham of Littlecote and George Duckworth rose simultaneously. Not a word was said. Out we filed. And as our procession made its way down the stalls I saw Arthur Cane leap up in his seat like a jack-in-the-box, amazed and considerably amused that George Duckworth and Lady Carnarvon of all people should have taken a girl of eighteen to see the French actors copulate upon the stage.

The brougham was waiting, and Mrs Popham of Littlecote, without speaking a word or even looking at me, immediately secreted herself inside it. Nor could Lady Carnarvon bring herself to face me. She took my hand,

and said in a tremulous voice — her elderly cheeks were flushed with emotion
— "I do hope, Miss Stephen, that the evening has not tired you very much."
Then she stepped into the carriage, and the two bereaved ladies returned to
Bruton Street. George meanwhile had secured a cab. He was much confused,
and yet very angry. I could see that my remarks at dinner upon the dialogues
of Plato rankled bitterly in his mind. And he told the cabman to go, not back
to Hyde Park Gate as I hoped, but on to Melbury Road.

"It's quite early still", he said in his most huffy manner as he sat down.
"And I think you want a little practice in how to behave to strangers. It's
not your fault of course, but you have been out much less than most girls of
your age." So it appeared that my education was to be continued, and that
I was about to have another lesson in the art of behaviour at the house of
Mrs Holman Hunt. She was giving a large evening party. Melbury Road was
lined with hansoms, four-wheelers, hired flies, and an occasional carriage
drawn by a couple of respectable family horses. "A very *dritte* crowd", said
George disdainfully as we took our place in the queue. Indeed all our old
family friends were gathered together in the Moorish Hall, and directly I
came in I recognised the Stillmans, the Lushingtons, the Montgomeries, the
Morrises, the Burne-Joneses — Mr Gibbs, Professor Wolstenholme, and General Beadle would certainly have been there too had they not all been sleeping
for many years beneath the sod. The effect of the Moorish Hall, after Bruton
Street, was garish, a little eccentric, and certainly very dowdy. The ladies
were intense and untidy; the gentlemen had fine foreheads and short evening
trousers, in some cases revealing a pair of bright red Pre-Raphaelite socks.
George stepped among them like a Prince in disguise. I soon attached myself
to a little covey of Kensington ladies who were being conveyed by Gladys
Holman Hunt across the Moorish Hall to the studio. There we found old
Holman Hunt [6] himself dressed in a long Jaeger dressing gown, holding forth
to a large gathering about the ideas which had inspired him in painting "The
Light of the World", a copy of which stood upon an easel. He sipped cocoa
and stroked his flowing beard as he talked, and we sipped cocoa and shifted
our shawls — for the room was chilly — as we listened. Occasionally some
of us strayed off to examine with reverent murmurs other bright pictures
upon other easels, but the tone of the assembly was devout, high-minded,
and to me after the tremendous experiences of the evening, soothingly and
almost childishly simple. George was never lacking in respect for old men of
recognised genius, and he now advanced with his opera hat pressed beneath
his arm; drew his feet together, and made a profound bow over Holman

[6] *Holman Hunt*: William Holman Hunt (1827–1910), an English painter who specialized in
religious subjects, was one of the founders of the Pre-Raphaelites, an art movement
committed to the ideals of beauty that had inspired early Italian painting. His most
celebrated work, *The Light of the World*, was painted in 1854, nearly fifty years before the
scene Woolf describes here. To Woolf's amusement, Hunt is still pontificating about that
work.

Hunt's hand. Holman Hunt had no notion who he was, or indeed who any of us were; but went on sipping his cocoa, stroking his beard, and explaining what ideas had inspired him in painting "The Light of the World", until we left.

At last — at last — the evening was over.

I went up to my room, took off my beautiful white satin dress, and unfastened the three pink carnations which had been pinned to my breast by the Jews' harp. Was it really possible that tomorrow I should open my Greek dictionary and go on spelling out the dialogues of Plato with Miss Case? I felt I knew much more about the dialogues of Plato than Miss Case could ever do. I felt old and experienced and disillusioned and angry, amused and excited, full of mystery, alarm and bewilderment. In a confused whirlpool of sensation I stood slipping off my petticoats, withdrew my long white gloves, and hung my white silk stockings over the back of a chair. Many different things were whirling round in my mind — diamonds and countesses, copulations, the dialogues of Plato, Mad Dick Popham, and "The Light of the World". Ah, how pleasant it would be to stretch out in bed, fall asleep and forget them all!

Sleep had almost come to me. The room was dark. The house silent. 20 Then, creaking stealthily, the door opened; treading gingerly, someone entered. "Who?" I cried. "Don't be frightened", George whispered. "And don't turn on the light, oh beloved. Beloved — " and he flung himself on my bed, and took me in his arms.

Yes, the old ladies of Kensington and Belgravia never knew that George Duckworth was not only father and mother, brother and sister to those poor Stephen girls; he was their lover also.

FROM READING TO REREADING

1. Virginia Woolf opens her essay with a reference to "black folding doors." Consider the significance of this image: What do the doors suggest about life at 22 Hyde Park Gate? You might want to read through the essay again, this time noting the many occurrences of doors. How does this imagery (a) help to establish a dominant mood and (b) reinforce the point Woolf makes about her family life?

2. The essay ends with a sudden and surprising disclosure. But Virginia Woolf provides a number of clues along the way that subtly prepare us for her shocking revelation. In drama, such clues are known as "foreshadowing" — the author presents information in ways that allow us to anticipate later events. Consider how foreshadowing works in this essay. What methods does Virginia Woolf use to prepare us for what's to come?

3. It's important to keep in mind the special context of this essay: it was written to be read aloud in front of a small group of family and friends, and not to be published. Some of the people listening to the essay — such as Woolf's sister, Vanessa

— are mentioned *in* the essay. Most of Woolf's audience would have personally known (or known of) all the people mentioned. Consider how the connection between an author and an audience can affect how something is written. In this case, how might Virginia Woolf's awareness of her audience influence the way she presents her story? How, for example, might it affect her concern for the facts and the truth?

From Reading to Writing

1. No two essays in this chapter evoke a stronger sense of domestic space than those by Joan Didion and Virginia Woolf. And yet, the presentation of physical detail is conditioned in no small degree by the thematic concerns of each writer. Reread these essays paying close attention to the ways that Didion and Woolf choose to include some details and leave others out. Then, explain in a few paragraphs how the inclusion (or exclusion) of a particular detail or set of details in one of the essays aids the reader in coming to grasp the central themes of the work in question.

2. The essays by Cynthia Ozick and Alice Walker portray daughters engaged in the act of defining themselves in relation to their mothers. Moreover, they attempt to do so by considering their own artistic expression in the light of their mothers' efforts, conscious or unconscious, to express themselves. In a short essay, explore the different forms of expression attributed to these women by their daughters. Consider how the conditions of each woman's life shaped her creativity. Be sure to note similarities as well as differences between the legacies each daughter inherited from her mother or mothers. In a short essay examine your own relationship to the parent, grandparent, or other relative who has most helped to foster your creativity. How did they express their own creativity? How did they influence your own?

3. Both E. B. White's "Aunt Poo" and James Baldwin's "Notes of a Native Son" deal with the knowledge we have of family members. Though White never met his wife's aunt, he feels he knows her fairly well through her private writings and family stories. Baldwin, on the other hand, though he grew up with his father, feels that he never really knew him. In a short personal essay describe as best you can a member of your own family that you either never met or never truly got to know.

3

Heroes and Heroines

JOAN DIDION
John Wayne: A Love Song

Anyone who reads today's magazines is familiar with the celebrity profile. Often a cover story, usually focusing on a popular performer, and almost always tied to the promotion of a new film or record album, the celebrity piece has become the staple of the magazine industry. Most of these articles are written for instant consumption, but in the hands of a talented writer, the conventional celebrity profile can be raised to a higher literary level. In "John Wayne: A Love Song," for example, Joan Didion uses all the familiar strategies of celebrity journalism — the interview, the snatches of background information, the shoptalk of production sets, and so on — but rearranges these into something that resembles a personal essay more than it does a celebrity article. Her technique can perhaps best be seen in the way she underplays the interview. "I am bad at interviewing people," she writes: "I avoid situations in which I have to talk to anyone's press agent." The essay, which originally appeared in The Saturday Evening Post *in 1965, fourteen years before John Wayne's death, was collected in Didion's first volume of essays,* Slouching Towards Bethlehem.

IN THE SUMMER of 1943 I was eight, and my father and mother and small brother and I were in Peterson Field in Colorado Springs. A hot wind blew through that summer, blew until it seemed that before August broke, all the dust in Kansas would be in Colorado, would have drifted over the tar-paper barracks and the temporary strip and stopped only when it hit Pikes Peak. There was not much to do, a summer like that: there was the day they brought in the first B-29, an event to remember but scarcely a vacation program. There was an Officers' Club, but no swimming pool; all the Officers' Club had of interest was artificial blue rain behind the bar. The rain interested me a good deal, but I could not spend the summer watching it, and so we went, my brother and I, to the movies.

We went three and four afternoons a week, sat on folding chairs in the darkened Quonset hut which served as a theater, and it was there, that summer of 1943 while the hot wind blew outside, that I first saw John Wayne. Saw the walk, heard the voice. Heard him tell the girl in a picture called *War of the Wildcats* that he would build her a house, "at the bend in the river where the cottonwoods grow." As it happened I did not grow up to be the kind of woman who is the heroine in a Western, and although the men I have known have many virtues and have taken me to live in many places I have come to love, they have never been John Wayne, and they have never taken me to that bend in the river where the cottonwoods grow. Deep in that part of my heart where the artificial rain forever falls, that is still the line I wait to hear.

I tell you this neither in a spirit of self-revelation nor as an exercise in total recall, but simply to demonstrate that when John Wayne rode through my childhood, and perhaps through yours, he determined forever the shape of certain of our dreams. It did not seem possible that such a man could fall ill, could carry within him that most inexplicable and ungovernable of diseases. The rumor struck some obscure anxiety, threw our very childhoods into question. In John Wayne's world, John Wayne was supposed to give the orders. "Let's ride," he said, and "Saddle up." "Forward *ho*," and "A man's gotta do what he's gotta do." "Hello, there," he said when he first saw the girl, in a construction camp or on a train or just standing around on the front porch waiting for somebody to ride up through the tall grass. When John Wayne spoke, there was no mistaking his intentions; he had a sexual authority so strong that even a child could perceive it. And in a world we understood early to be characterized by venality and doubt and paralyzing ambiguities, he suggested another world, one which may or may not have existed ever but in any case existed no more: a place where a man could move free, could make his own code and live by it; a world in which, if a man did what he had to do, he could one day take the girl and go riding through the draw and find himself home free, not in a hospital with something wrong inside, not in a high bed with the flowers and the drugs and the forced smiles, but there at the bend in the bright river, the cottonwoods shimmering in the early morning sun.

"Hello, there." Where did he come from, before the tall grass? Even his history seemed right, for it was no history at all, nothing to intrude upon the dream. Born Marion Morrison in Winterset, Iowa, the son of a druggist. Moved as a child to Lancaster, California, part of the migration to that promised land sometimes called "the west coast of Iowa." Not that Lancaster was the promise fulfilled; Lancaster was a town on the Mojave where the dust blew through. But Lancaster was still California, and it was only a year from there to Glendale, where the desolation had a different flavor: antimacassars among the orange groves, a middle-class prelude to Forest Lawn. Imagine Marion Morrison in Glendale. A Boy Scout, then a student at Glendale High. A tackle for U.S.C., a Sigma Chi. Summer vacations, a job moving props on the old Fox lot. There, a meeting with John Ford, [1] one of the several directors who were to sense that into this perfect mold might be poured the inarticulate longings of a nation wondering at just what pass the trail had been lost. "Dammit," said Raoul Walsh [2] later, "the son of a bitch looked like a man." And so after a while the boy from Glendale became a

---

[1] *John Ford* (1895–1973): Director of many classic western films.

[2] *Raoul Walsh* (1887–1980): Prolific director whose career spanned many decades.

star. He did not become an actor, as he has always been careful to point out to interviewers ("How many times do I gotta tell you, I don't act at all, I *re-act*"), but a star, and the star called John Wayne would spend most of the rest of his life with one or another of those directors, out on some forsaken location, in search of the dream.

> Out where the skies are a trifle bluer
> Out where friendship's a little truer
> That's where the West begins

Nothing very bad could happen in the dream, nothing a man could not   5 face down. But something did. There it was, the rumor, and after a while the headlines. "I licked the Big C," John Wayne announced, as John Wayne would, reducing those outlaw cells to the level of any other outlaws, but even so we all sensed that this would be the one unpredictable confrontation, the one shootout Wayne could lose. I have as much trouble as the next person with illusion and reality, and I did not much want to see John Wayne when he must be (or so I thought) having some trouble with it himself, but I did, and it was down in Mexico when he was making the picture his illness had so long delayed, down in the very country of the dream.

It was John Wayne's 165th picture. It was Henry Hathaway's 84th. It was number 34 for Dean Martin, who was working off an old contract to Hal Wallis, for whom it was independent production number 65. It was called *The Sons of Katie Elder*, and it was a Western, and after the three-month delay they had finally shot the exteriors up in Durango, and now they were in the waning days of interior shooting at Estudio Churubusco outside Mexico City, and the sun was hot and the air was clear and it was lunchtime. Out under the pepper trees the boys from the Mexican crew sat around sucking cara-mels, and down the road some of the technical men sat around a place which served a stuffed lobster and a glass of tequila for one dollar American, but it was inside the cavernous empty commissary where the talent sat around, the reasons for the exercise, all sitting around the big table picking at *huevos con queso* [3] and Carta Blanca beer. Dean Martin, unshaven. Mack Gray, who goes where Martin goes. Bob Goodfried, who was in charge of Paramount publicity and who had flown down to arrange for a trailer and who had a delicate stomach. "Tea and toast," he warned repeatedly. "That's the ticket. You can't trust the lettuce." And Henry Hathaway, the director, who did not seem to be listening to Goodfried. And John Wayne, who did not seem to be listening to anyone.

"This week's gone slow," Dean Martin said, for the third time.

"How can you say that?" Mack Gray demanded.

"*This . . . week's . . . gone . . . slow*, that's how I can say it."

---

[3] *huevos con queso*: Eggs with cheese.

"You don't mean you want it to end." 10

"I'll say it right out, Mack, I want it to *end*. Tomorrow night I shave this beard, I head for the airport, I say *adiós amigos!* Bye-bye *muchachos!*"

Henry Hathaway lit a cigar and patted Martin's arm fondly. "Not tomorrow, Dino."

"Henry, what are you planning to add? A World War?"

Hathaway patted Martin's arm again and gazed into the middle distance. At the end of the table someone mentioned a man who, some years before, had tried unsuccessfully to blow up an airplane.

"He's still in jail," Hathaway said suddenly. 15

"In jail?" Martin was momentarily distracted from the question whether to send his golf clubs back with Bob Goodfried or consign them to Mack Gray. "What's he in jail for if nobody got killed?"

"Attempted murder, Dino," Hathaway said gently. "A felony."

"You mean some guy just *tried* to kill me he'd end up in jail?"

Hathaway removed the cigar from his mouth and looked across the table. "Some guy just tried to kill *me* he wouldn't end up in jail. How about you, Duke?"

Very slowly, the object of Hathaway's query wiped his mouth, pushed 20 back his chair, and stood up. It was the real thing, the authentic article, the move which had climaxed a thousand scenes on 165 flickering frontiers and phantasmagoric battlefields before, and it was about to climax this one, in the commissary at Estudio Churubusco outside Mexico City. "Right," John Wayne drawled. "I'd kill him."

Almost all the cast of *Katie Elder* had gone home, that last week; only the principals were left, Wayne, and Martin, and Earl Holliman, and Michael Anderson, Jr., and Martha Hyer. Martha Hyer was not around much, but every now and then someone referred to her, usually as "the girl." They had all been together nine weeks, six of them in Durango. Mexico City was not quite Durango; wives like to come along to places like Mexico City, like to shop for handbags, go to parties at Merle Oberon Pagliai's, like to look at her paintings. But Durango. The very name hallucinates. Man's country. Out where the West begins. There had been ahuehuete trees in Durango; a waterfall, rattlesnakes. There had been weather, nights so cold that they had postponed one or two exteriors until they could shoot inside at Churubusco. "It was the girl," they explained. "You couldn't keep the girl out in cold like that." Henry Hathaway had cooked in Durango, *gazpacho* and ribs and the steaks that Dean Martin had ordered flown down from the Sands; he had wanted to cook in Mexico City, but the management of the Hotel Bamer refused to let him set up a brick barbecue in his room. "You really missed something, *Durango*," they would say, sometimes joking and sometimes not, until it became a refrain, Eden lost.

But if Mexico City was not Durango, neither was it Beverly Hills. No one else was using Churubusco that week, and there inside the big sound stage that said LOS HIJOS DE KATIE ELDER on the door, there with the pepper trees and the bright sun outside, they could still, for just so long as the picture lasted, maintain a world peculiar to men who like to make Westerns, a world of loyalties and fond raillery, of sentiment and shared cigars, of interminable desultory recollections; campfire talk, its only point to keep a human voice raised against the night, the wind, the rustlings in the brush.

"Stuntman got hit accidentally on a picture of mine once," Hathaway would say between takes of an elaborately choreographed fight scene. "What was his name, married Estelle Taylor, met her down in Arizona."

The circle would close around him, the cigars would be fingered. The delicate art of the staged fight was to be contemplated.

"I only hit one guy in my life," Wayne would say. "Accidentally, I mean. That was Mike Mazurki."   25

"Some guy. Hey, Duke says he only hit one guy in his life, Mike Mazurki."

"Some choice." Murmurings, assent.

"It wasn't a choice, it was an accident."

"I can believe it."

"You bet."   30

"Oh boy. Mike Mazurki."

And so it would go. There was Web Overlander, Wayne's makeup man for twenty years, hunched in a blue Windbreaker, passing out sticks of Juicy Fruit. "*Insect* spray," he would say. "Don't tell us about insect spray. We saw insect spray in Africa, all right. Remember Africa?" Or, "*Steamer* clams. Don't tell us about steamer clams. We got our fill of steamer clams all right, on the *Hatari!*[4] appearance tour. Remember Bookbinder's?" There was Ralph Volkie, Wayne's trainer for eleven years, wearing a red baseball cap and carrying around a clipping from Hedda Hopper,[5] a tribute to Wayne. "This Hopper's some lady," he would say again and again. "Not like some of these guys, all they write is sick, sick, sick, how can you call that guy *sick*, when he's got pains, coughs, works all day, *never complains*. That guy's got the best hook since Dempsey, not *sick*."

And there was Wayne himself, fighting through number 165. There was Wayne, in his thirty-three-year-old spurs, his dusty neckerchief, his blue shirt. "You don't have too many worries about what to wear in these things," he said. "You can wear a blue shirt, or, if you're down in Monument Valley, you can wear a yellow shirt." There was Wayne, in a relatively new hat, a

[4] *Hatari!*: 1962 John Wayne movie filmed in Tanganyika; the title means "Danger!" in Swahili.

[5] *Hedda Hopper* (1890–1966). Hollywood gossip columnist.

hat which made him look curiously like William S. Hart. [6] "I had this old cavalry hat I loved, but I lent it to Sammy Davis. I got it back, it was unwearable. I think they all pushed it down on his head and said *O.K., John Wayne* — you know, a joke."

There was Wayne, working too soon, finishing the picture with a bad cold and a racking cough, so tired by late afternoon that he kept an oxygen inhalator on the set. And still nothing mattered but the Code. "That guy," he muttered of a reporter who had incurred his displeasure. "I admit I'm balding. I admit I got a tire around my middle. What man fifty-seven doesn't? Big news. Anyway, that guy."

He paused, about to expose the heart of the matter, the root of the distaste, the fracture of the rules that bothered him more than the alleged misquotations, more than the intimation that he was no longer the Ringo Kidd. "He comes down, uninvited, but I ask him over anyway. So we're sitting around drinking mescal out of a water jug."

He paused again and looked meaningfully at Hathaway, readying him for the unthinkable denouement. "He had to be *assisted* to his room."

They argued about the virtues of various prizefighters, they argued about the price of J & B in pesos. They argued about dialogue.

"As rough a guy as he is, Henry, I still don't think he'd raffle off his mother's *Bible*."

"I like a shocker, Duke."

They exchanged endless training-table jokes. "You know why they call this memory sauce?" Martin asked, holding up a bowl of chili.

"Why?"

"Because you *remember it in the morning*."

"Hear that, Duke? Hear why they call this memory sauce?"

They delighted one another by blocking out minute variations in the free-for-all fight which is a set piece in Wayne pictures; motivated or totally gratuitous, the fight sequence has to be in the picture, because they so enjoy making it. "Listen — this'll really be funny. Duke picks up the kid, see, and then it takes both Dino and Earl to throw him out the door — *how's that?*"

They communicated by sharing old jokes; they sealed their camaraderie by making gentle, old-fashioned fun of wives, those civilizers, those tamers. "So Señora Wayne takes it into her head to stay up and have one brandy. So for the rest of the night it's 'Yes, Pilar, you're right, dear. I'm a bully, Pilar, you're right, I'm impossible.'"

"You hear that? Duke says Pilar threw a table at him."

"Hey, Duke, here's something funny. That finger you hurt today, get the Doc to bandage it up, go home tonight, show it to Pilar, tell her she did

---

[6] *William S. Hart* (1870–1946): Star of many silent westerns.

it when she threw the table. You know, make her think she was really cutting up."

They treated the oldest among them respectfully; they treated the youngest fondly. "You see that kid?" they said of Michael Anderson, Jr. "What a kid."

"He don't act, it's right from the heart," said Hathaway, patting his heart.

"Hey kid," Martin said. "You're gonna be in my next picture. We'll 50 have the whole thing, no beards. The striped shirts, the girls, the hi-fi, the eye lights."

They ordered Michael Anderson his own chair, with "BIG MIKE" tooled on the back. When it arrived on the set, Hathaway hugged him. "You see that?" Anderson asked Wayne, suddenly too shy to look him in the eye. Wayne gave him the smile, the nod, the final accolade. "I saw it, kid."

On the morning of the day they were to finish *Katie Elder*, Web Overlander showed up not in his Windbreaker but in a blue blazer. "Home, Mama," he said, passing out the last of his Juicy Fruit. "I got on my getaway clothes." But he was subdued. At noon, Henry Hathaway's wife dropped by the commissary to tell him that she might fly over to Acapulco. "Go ahead," he told her. "I get through here, all I'm gonna do is take Seconal to a point just this side of suicide." They were all subdued. After Mrs. Hathaway left, there were desultory attempts at reminiscing, but man's country was receding fast; they were already halfway home, and all they could call up was the 1961 Bel Air fire, during which Henry Hathaway had ordered the Los Angeles Fire Department off his property and saved the place himself by, among other measures, throwing everything flammable into the swimming pool. "Those fire guys might've just given it up," Wayne said. "Just let it burn." In fact this was a good story, and one incorporating several of their favorite themes, but a Bel Air story was still not a Durango story.

In the early afternoon they began the last scene, and although they spent as much time as possible setting it up, the moment finally came when there was nothing to do but shoot it. "Second team out, first team in, *doors closed*," the assistant director shouted one last time. The stand-ins walked off the set, John Wayne and Martha Hyer walked on. "All right, boys, *silencio*, this is a picture." They took it twice. Twice the girl offered John Wayne the tattered Bible. Twice John Wayne told her that "there's a lot of places I go where that wouldn't fit in." Everyone was very still. And at 2:30 that Friday afternoon Henry Hathaway turned away from the camera, and in the hush that followed he ground out his cigar in a sand bucket. "O.K.," he said. "That's it."

Since that summer of 1943 I had thought of John Wayne in a number of ways. I had thought of him driving cattle up from Texas, and bringing airplanes in on a single engine, thought of him telling the girl at the Alamo that "Republic is a beautiful word." I had never thought of him having dinner with his family and with me and my husband in an expensive restaurant in Chapultepec Park, but time brings odd mutations, and there we were, one night that last week in Mexico. For a while it was only a nice evening, an evening anywhere. We had a lot of drinks and I lost the sense that the face across the table was in certain ways more familiar than my husband's.

And then something happened. Suddenly the room seemed suffused   55
with the dream, and I could not think why. Three men appeared out of nowhere, playing guitars. Pilar Wayne leaned slightly forward, and John Wayne lifted his glass almost imperceptibly toward her. "We'll need some Pouilly-Fuissé for the rest of the table," he said, "and some red Bordeaux for the Duke." We all smiled, and drank the Pouilly-Fuissé for the rest of the table and the red Bordeaux for the Duke, and all the while the men with the guitars kept playing, until finally I realized what they had been playing all along: "The Red River Valley" and the theme from *The High and the Mighty.* [7] They did not quite get the beat right, but even now I can hear them, in another country and a long time later, even as I tell you this.

[7] "*The Red River Valley*": Theme song from *Red River,* a 1948 John Wayne western, considered a film classic; *The High and the Mighty,* forerunner of airline disaster films, featured Wayne with an all-star cast. Both films had award-winning musical scores.

FROM READING AND REREADING

1.   Joan Didion claims that she is "bad at interviewing people." Do you think her self-criticism is accurate? What might she have done differently had she been a "better" interviewer? Can you distinguish quotations she apparently received from John Wayne directly from those she received indirectly? In what ways does her reluctance to conduct a structured interview contribute to the strength of the essay?

2.   "John Wayne: A Love Song" is in some ways as much about Joan Didion as it is about its subject. How does Didion establish her presence in the essay? How does she link her own life to Wayne's career? Why does she begin with her childhood? What reasons does she give for being on the set of John Wayne's film?

3.   Notice how much of the essay's dialogue is given over to the people working with Wayne on the set. Why do you think Didion does this? How does it affect our perception of John Wayne? Note that Wayne says relatively little: in your estimation, does his silence make him more or less of a hero to Didion?

ANNIE DILLARD
The Stunt Pilot

Our heroes and heroines are not always celebrities; sometimes they are people who impress us with their mastery of difficult skills. Not many people have heard of the late Dave Rahm, though he had an international reputation as a magnificent stunt pilot and was a noted American geologist. For Annie Dillard, Rahm was both artist and hero in the sense that his daring aerobatic stunts reached remarkable aesthetic proportions. Though "The Stunt Pilot" appeared in Esquire *and contains elements of the magazine profile/interview, it is important to note that the essay was originally written as an integral, untitled chapter of a book called* The Writing Life. *In the opening sentence of that book, Dillard introduces the image of the "line": "When you write, you lay out a line of words." The term "line," of course, is appropriate to art, music, dance, and writing, and it's an image that figures significantly in "The Stunt Pilot."*

DAVE RAHM lived in Bellingham, Washington, north of Seattle. Bellingham, a harbor town, lies between the alpine North Cascade Mountains and the San Juan Islands in Haro Strait above Puget Sound. The latitude is that of Newfoundland. Dave Rahm was a stunt pilot, the air's own genius.

In 1975, with a newcomer's willingness to try anything once, I attended the Bellingham Air Show. The Bellingham airport was a wide clearing in a forest of tall Douglas firs; its runways suited small planes. It was June. People wearing blue or tan zipped jackets stood loosely on the concrete walkways and runways outside the coffee shop. At that latitude in June, you stayed outside because you could, even most of the night, if you could think up something to do. The sky did not darken until ten o'clock or so, and it never got very dark. Your life parted and opened in the sunlight. You tossed your dark winter routines, thought up mad projects, and improvised everything from hour to hour. Being a stunt pilot seemed the most reasonable thing in the world; you could wave your arms in the air all day and all night, and sleep next winter.

I saw from the ground a dozen stunt pilots; the air show scheduled them one after the other, for an hour of aerobatics. Each pilot took up his or her plane and performed a batch of tricks. They were precise and impressive. They flew upside down, and straightened out; they did barrel rolls, and straightened out; they drilled through dives and spins, and landed gently on a far runway.

For the end of the day, separated from all other performances of every

sort, the air show director had scheduled a program titled "Dave Rahm."
The leaflet said that Rahm was a geologist who taught at Western Washington
University. He had flown for King Hussein in Jordan. A tall man in the crowd
told me Hussein had seen Rahm fly on a visit the king made to the United
States; he had invited him to Jordan to perform at ceremonies. Hussein was
a pilot, too. "Hussein thought he was the greatest thing in the world."

Idly, paying scant attention, I saw a medium-sized, rugged man dressed   5
in brown leather, all begoggled, climb in a black biplane's open cockpit. The
plane was a Bücker Jungman, built in the thirties. I saw a tall, dark-haired
woman seize a propeller tip at the plane's nose and yank it down till the
engine caught. He was off; he climbed high over the airport in his biplane,
very high until he was barely visible as a mote, and then seemed to fall down
the air, diving headlong, and streaming beauty in spirals behind him.

The black plane dropped spinning, and flattened out spinning the
other way; it began to carve the air into forms that built wildly and musically
on each other and never ended. Reluctantly, I started paying attention. Rahm
drew high above the world an inexhaustibly glorious line; it piled over our
heads in loops and arabesques. It was like a Saul Steinberg[1] fantasy; the
plane was the pen. Like Steinberg's contracting and billowing pen line, the
line Rahm spun moved to form new, punning shapes from the edges of the
old. Like a Klee[2] line, it smattered the sky with landscapes and systems.

The air show announcer hushed. He had been squawking all day, and
now he quit. The crowd stilled. Even the children watched dumbstruck as
the slow, black biplane buzzed its way around the air. Rahm made beauty
with his whole body; it was pure pattern, and you could watch it happen.
The plane moved every way a line can move, and it controlled three dimensions, so the line carved massive and subtle slits in the air like sculptures.
The plane looped the loop, seeming to arch its back like a gymnast; it stalled,
dropped, and spun out of it climbing; it spiraled and knifed west on one
side's wings and back east on another; it turned cartwheels, which must be
physically impossible; it played with its own line like a cat with yarn. How
did the pilot know where in the air he was? If he got lost, the ground would
swat him.

Rahm did everything his plane could do: tailspins, four-point rolls, flat
spins, figure eights, snap rolls, and hammerheads. He did pirouettes on the
plane's tail. The other pilots could do these stunts too, skillfully, one at a
time. But Rahm used the plane inexhaustibly, like a brush marking thin air.

His was pure energy and naked spirit. I have thought about it for years.

[1] *Saul Steinberg*: Contemporary artist (b. 1914) whose drawings often appeared on the cover
of *The New Yorker* magazine.

[2] *Klee*: Paul Klee (1879–1940), influential Swiss abstract painter considered one of the
twentieth century's finest artists.

Rahm's line unrolled in time. Like music, it split the bulging rim of the future along its seam. It pried out the present. We watchers waited for the split-second curve of beauty in the present to reveal itself. The human pilot, Dave Rahm, worked in the cockpit right at the plane's nose; his very body tore into the future for us and reeled it down upon us like a curling peel.

Like any fine artist, he controlled the tension of the audience's longing. 10
You desired, unwittingly, a certain kind of roll or climb, or a return to a certain portion of the air, and he fulfilled your hope slantingly, like a poet, or evaded it until you thought you would burst, and then fulfilled it surprisingly, so you gasped and cried out.

The oddest, most exhilarating and exhausting thing was this: he never quit. The music had no periods, no rests or endings; the poetry's beautiful sentence never ended; the line had no finish; the sculptured forms piled overhead, one into another without surcease. Who could breathe, in a world where rhythm itself had no periods?

It had taken me several minutes to understand what an extraordinary thing I was seeing. Rahm kept all that embellished space in mind at once. For another twenty minutes I watched the beauty unroll and grow more fantastic and unlikely before my eyes. Now Rahm brought the plane down slidingly, and just in time, for I thought I would snap from the effort to compass and remember the line's long intelligence; I could not add another curve. He brought the plane down on a far runway. After a pause, I saw him step out, an ordinary man, and make his way back to the terminal.

The show was over. It was late. Just as I turned from the runway, something caught my eye and made me laugh. It was a swallow, a blue-green swallow, having its own air show, apparently inspired by Rahm. The swallow climbed high over the runway, held its wings oddly, tipped them, and rolled down the air in loops. The inspired swallow. I always want to paint, too, after I see the Rembrandts: The blue-green swallow tumbled precisely, and caught itself and flew up again as if excited, and looped down again, the way swallows do, but tensely, holding its body carefully still. It was a stunt swallow.

I went home and thought about Rahm's performance that night, and the next day, and the next.

I had thought I knew my way around beauty a little bit. I knew I had 15 devoted a good part of my life to it, memorizing poetry and focusing my attention on complexity of rhythm in particular, on force, movement, repetition, and surprise, in both poetry and prose. Now I had stood among dandelions between two asphalt runways in Bellingham, Washington, and begun learning about beauty. Even the Boston Museum of Fine Arts was never more inspiriting than this small northwestern airport on this time-killing Sunday afternoon in June. Nothing on earth is more gladdening than knowing we must roll up our sleeves and move back the boundaries of the humanly possible once more.

Later I flew with Dave Rahm; he took me up. A generous geographer, Dick Smith, at Western Washington University, arranged it, and came along. Rahm and Dick Smith were colleagues at the university. In geology, Rahm had published two books and many articles. Rahm was handsome in a dull sort of way, blunt-featured, wide-jawed, wind-burned, keen-eyed, and taciturn. As anyone would expect. He was forty. He wanted to show me the Cascade Mountains; these enormous peaks, only fifty miles from the coast, rise over nine thousand feet; they are heavily glaciated. Whatcom County has more glaciers than the lower forty-eight states combined; the Cascades make the Rocky Mountains look like hills. Mount Baker is volcanic, like most Cascade peaks. That year, Mount Baker was acting up. Even from my house at the shore I could see, early in the morning on clear days, volcanic vapor rise near its peak. Often the vapor made a cloud that swelled all morning and hid the snows. Every day the newspapers reported on Baker's activity: Would it blow? (A few years later, Mount St. Helens did blow.)

Rahm was not flying his trick biplane that day, but a faster, enclosed plane, a single-engine Cessna. We flew from a bumpy grass airstrip near my house, out over the coast and inland. There was coastal plain down there, but we could not see it for clouds. We were over the clouds at five hundred feet and inside them too, heading for an abrupt line of peaks we could not see. I gave up on everything, the way you do in airplanes; it was out of my hands. Every once in a while Rahm saw a peephole in the clouds and buzzed over for a look. "That's Larsen's pea farm," he said, or "That's Nooksack Road," and he changed our course with a heave.

When we got to the mountains, he slid us along Mount Baker's flanks sideways.

Our plane swiped at the mountain with a roar. I glimpsed a windshield view of dirty snow traveling fast. Our shaking, swooping belly seemed to graze the snow. The wings shuddered; we peeled away and the mountain fell back and the engines whined. We felt flung, because we were in fact flung; parts of our faces and internal organs trailed pressingly behind on the curves. We came back for another pass at the mountain, and another. We dove at the snow headlong like suicides; we jerked up, down, or away at the last second, so late we left our hearts, stomachs, and lungs behind. If I forced myself to hold my heavy head up against the G's,[3] and to raise my eyelids, heavy as barbells, and to notice what I saw, I could see the wrinkled green crevasses cracking the glaciers' snow.

Pitching snow filled all the windows, and shapes of dark rock. I had no notion which way was up. Everything was black or gray or white except   20

---

[3] *G's*: Units of gravitational force applied to a body when accelerated.

the fatal crevasses; everything made noise and shook. I felt my face smashed sideways and saw rushing abstractions of snow in the windshield. Patches of cloud obscured the snow fleetingly. We straightened out, turned, and dashed at the mountainside for another pass, which we made, apparently, on our ear, an inch or two away from the slope. Icefalls and cornices jumbled and fell away. If a commercial plane's black box, such as the FAA[4] painstakingly recovers from crash sites, could store videotapes as well as pilots' last words, some videotapes would look like this: a mountainside coming up at the windows from all directions, ice and snow and rock filling the screen up close and screaming by.

Rahm was just being polite. His geographer colleague wanted to see the fissure on Mount Baker from which steam escaped. Everybody in Bellingham wanted to see that sooty fissure, as did every geologist in the country; no one on earth could fly so close to it as Rahm. He knew the mountain by familiar love and feel, like a face; he knew what the plane could do and what he dared to do.

When Mount Baker inexplicably let us go, he jammed us into cloud again and soon tilted. "The Sisters!" someone shouted, and I saw the windshield fill with red rock. This mountain looked infernal, a drear and sheer plane of lifeless rock. It was red and sharp; its gritty blades cut through the clouds at random. The mountain was quiet. It was in shade. Careening, we made sideways passes at these brittle peaks too steep for snow. Their rock was full of iron, somebody shouted at me then or later; the iron had rusted, so they were red. Later, when I was back on the ground, I recalled that, from a distance, the two jagged peaks called the Twin Sisters looked translucent against the sky; they were sharp, tapered, and fragile as arrowheads.

I talked to Rahm. He was flying us out to the islands now. The islands were fifty or sixty miles away. Like many other people, I had picked Bellingham, Washington, by looking at an atlas. It was clear from the atlas that you could row in the salt water and see snow-covered mountains; you could scale a glaciated mountainside with an ice ax in August, skirting green crevasses two hundred feet deep, and look out on the islands in the sea. Now, in the air, the clouds had risen over us; dark forms lay on the glinting water. There was almost no color to the day, just blackened green and some yellow. I knew the islands were forested in dark Douglas firs the size of skyscrapers. Bald eagles scavenged on the beaches; robins the size of herring gulls sang in the clearings. We made our way out to the islands through the layer of air between the curving planet and its held, thick clouds.

"When I started trying to figure out what I was going to do with my life, I decided to become an expert on mountains. It wasn't much to be, it wasn't everything, but it was something. I was going to know everything about mountains from every point of view. So I started out in geography."

---

[4] *FAA*: Federal Aviation Administration.

Geography proved too pedestrian for Rahm, too concerned with "how many bushels of wheat an acre." So he ended up in geology. Smith had told me that geology departments throughout the country used Rahm's photographic slides — close-ups of geologic features from the air.

"I used to climb mountains. But you know, you can get a better feel   25 for a mountain's power flying around it, flying all around it, than you can from climbing it tied to its side like a flea."

He talked about his flying performances. He thought of the air as a line, he said. "This end of the line, that end of the line — like a rope." He improvised. "I get a rhythm going and stick with it." While he was performing in a show, he paid attention, he said, to the lighting. He didn't play against the sun. That was all he said about what he did.

In aerobatic maneuvers, pilots pull about seven positive G's on some stunts and six negative G's on others. Some gyrations push; others pull. Pilots alternate the pressures carefully, so they do not gray out or black out.

Later I learned that some stunt pilots tune up by wearing gravity boots. These are boots made to hook over a doorway; wearing them, you hang in the doorway upside down. It must startle a pilot's children to run into their father or mother in the course of their home wanderings — the parents hanging wide-eyed, upside down in the doorway like a bat.

We were landing; here was the airstrip on Stuart Island — that island to which Ferrar Burn was dragged by the tide. We put down, climbed out of the plane, and walked. We wandered a dirt track through fields to a lee shore where yellow sandstone ledges slid into the sea. The salt chuck, people there called salt water. The sun came out. I caught a snake in the salt chuck; the snake, eighteen inches long, was swimming in the green shallows.

I had a survivor's elation. Rahm had found Mount Baker in the clouds   30 before Mount Baker found the plane. He had wiped it with the fast plane like a cloth and we had lived. When we took off from Stuart Island and gained altitude, I asked if we could turn over — could we do a barrel roll? The plane was making a lot of noise, and Dick Smith did not hear any of this, I learned later. "Why not?" Rahm said, and added surprisingly, "It won't hurt the plane." Without ado he leaned on the wheel and the wing went down and we went somersaulting over it. We upended with a roar. We stuck to the plane's sides like flung paint. All the blood in my body bulged on my face; it piled between my skull and skin. Vaguely I could see the chrome sea twirling over Rahm's head like a baton, and the dark islands sliding down the skies like rain.

The G's slammed me into my seat like thugs and pinned me while my heart pounded and the plane turned over slowly and compacted each organ in turn. My eyeballs were newly spherical and full of heartbeats. I seemed to hear a crescendo; the wing rolled shuddering down the last 90 degrees and settled on the flat. There were the islands, admirably below us, and the clouds, admirably above. When I could breathe, I asked if we could do it again, and we did. He rolled the other way. The brilliant line of the sea slid up the side window bearing its heavy islands. Through the shriek of my blood and the plane's shakes I glimpsed the line of the sea over the windshield, thin as a spear. How in performance did Rahm keep track while his brain blurred and blood roared in his ears without ceasing? Every performance was a tour de force and a show of will, a *Machtspruch*. [5] I had seen the other stunt pilots straighten out after a trick or two; their blood could drop back and the planet simmer down. An Olympic gymnast, at peak form, strings out a line of spins ten stunts long across a mat, and is hard put to keep his footing at the end. Rahm endured much greater pressure on his faster spins using the plane's power, and he could spin in three dimensions and keep twirling till he ran out of sky room or luck.

When we straightened out, and had flown straightforwardly for ten minutes toward home, Dick Smith, clearing his throat, brought himself to speak. "What was that we did out there?"

"The barrel rolls?" Rahm said. "They were barrel rolls." He said nothing else. I looked at the back of his head; I could see the serious line of his cheek and jaw. He was in shirtsleeves, tanned, strong-wristed. I could not imagine loving him under any circumstance; he was alien to me, unfazed. He looked like GI Joe. He flew with that matter-of-fact, bored gesture pilots use. They click overhead switches and turn dials as if only their magnificent strength makes such dullness endurable. The half circle of wheel in their big hands looks like a toy they plan to crush in a minute; the wiggly stick the wheel mounts seems barely attached.

A crop-duster pilot in Wyoming told me the life expectancy of a crop-duster pilot is five years. They fly too low. They hit buildings and power lines. They have no space to fly out of trouble, and no space to recover from a stall. We were in Cody, Wyoming, out on the north fork of the Shoshone River. The crop duster had wakened me that morning flying over the ranch house and clearing my bedroom roof by half an inch. I saw the bolts on the wheel assembly a few feet from my face. He was spraying with pesticide the plain old grass. Over breakfast I asked him how long he had been dusting crops. "Four years," he said, and the figure stalled in the air between us for a moment. "You know you're going to die at it someday," he added. "We all know it. We accept that; it's part of it." I think now that, since the crop duster was in his twenties, he accepted only that he had to say such stuff; privately he counted on skewing the curve.

I suppose Rahm knew the fact too. I do not know how he felt about it. "It's worth it," said the early French aviator Mermoz. He was Antoine de Saint-Exupéry's friend. "It's worth the final smashup."

[5] *Machtspruch*: Literally, "power speech" in German.

Rahm smashed up in front of King Hussein, in Jordan, during a performance. The plane spun down and never came out of it; it nosedived into the ground and exploded. He bought the farm. I was living then with my husband out on that remote island in the San Juans, cut off from everything. Battery radios picked up the Canadian Broadcasting Company out of Toronto, half a continent away; island people would, in theory, learn if the United States blew up, but not much else. There were no newspapers. One friend got the Sunday *New York Times* by mail boat on the following Friday. He saved it until Sunday and had a party, every week; we all read the Sunday *Times* and no one mentioned that it was last week's.

One day, Paul Glenn's brother flew out from Bellingham to visit; he had a seaplane. He landed in the water in front of the cabin and tied up to our mooring. He came in for coffee, and he gave out news of this and that, and — Say, did we know that stunt pilot Dave Rahm had cracked up? In Jordan, during a performance: he never came out of a dive. He just dove right down into the ground, and his wife was there watching. "I saw it on CBS News last night." And then — with a sudden sharp look at my filling eyes — "What, did you know him?" But no, I did not know him. He took me up once. Several years ago. I admired his flying. I had thought that danger was the safest thing in the world, if you went about it right.

Later I found a newspaper. Rahm was living in Jordan that year; King Hussein invited him to train the aerobatics team, the Royal Jordanian Falcons. He was also visiting professor of geology at the University of Jordan. In Amman that day he had been flying a Pitt Special, a plane he knew well. Katy Rahm, his wife of six months, was sitting beside Hussein in the viewing stands, with her daughter. Rahm died performing a Lomcevak combined with a tail slide and hammerhead. In a Lomcevak, the pilot brings the plane up on a slant and pirouettes. I had seen Rahm do this: the falling plane twirled slowly like a leaf. Like a ballerina, the plane seemed to hold its head back stiff in concentration at the music's slow, painful beauty. It was one of Rahm's favorite routines. Next the pilot flies straight up, stalls the plane, and slides down the air on his tail. He brings the nose down — the hammerhead — kicks the engine, and finishes with a low loop.

It is a dangerous maneuver at any altitude, and Rahm was doing it low. He hit the ground on the loop; the tail slide had left him no height. When Rahm went down, King Hussein dashed to the burning plane to pull him out, but he was already dead.

A few months after the air show, and a month after I had flown with Rahm, I was working at my desk near Bellingham, where I lived, when I heard a sound so odd it finally penetrated my concentration. It was the buzz of an airplane, but it rose and fell musically, and it never quit; the plane never flew out of earshot. I walked out on the porch and looked up: it was Rahm in the black and gold biplane, looping all over the air. I had been 40 wondering about his performance flight: Could it really have been so beautiful? It was, for here it was again. The little plane twisted all over the air like a vine. It trailed a line like a very long mathematical proof you could follow only so far, and then it lost you in its complexity. I saw Rahm flying high over the Douglas firs, and out over the water, and back over farms. The air was a fluid, and Rahm was an eel.

It was as if Mozart could move his body through his notes, and you could walk out on the porch, look up, and see him in periwig and breeches, flying around in the sky. You could hear the music as he dove through it; it streamed after him like a contrail.

I lost myself; standing on the firm porch, I lost my direction and reeled. My neck and spine rose and turned, so I followed the plane's line kinesthetically. In his open-cockpit black plane, Rahm demonstrated curved space. He slid down ramps of air, he vaulted and wheeled. He piled loops in heaps and praised height. He unrolled the scroll of the air, extended it, and bent it into Möbius strips; he furled line in a thousand new ways, as if he were inventing a script and writing it in one infinitely recurring utterance until I thought the bounds of beauty must break.

From inside, the looping plane had sounded tinny, like a kazoo. Outside, the buzz rose and fell to the Doppler effect as the plane looped near or away. Rahm cleaved the sky like a prow and tossed out time left and right in his wake. He performed for forty minutes; then he headed the plane, as small as a wasp, back to the airport inland. Later I learned Rahm often practiced acrobatic flights over this shore. His idea was that if he lost control and was going to go down, he could ditch in the salt chuck, where no one else would get hurt.

If I had not turned two barrel rolls in an airplane, I might have fancied Rahm felt good up there, and playful. Maybe Jackson Pollock felt a sort of playfulness, in addition to the artist's usual deliberate and intelligent care. In my limited experience, painting, unlike writing, pleases the senses while you do it, and more while you do it than after it is done. Drawing lines with an airplane, unfortunately, tortures the senses. Jet bomber pilots black out. I knew Rahm felt as if his brain were bursting his eardrums, felt that if he let his jaws close as tight as centrifugal force pressed them, he would bite through his lungs.

"All virtue is a form of acting," Yeats said. Rahm deliberately turned   45 himself into a figure. Sitting invisible at the controls of a distant airplane, he became the agent and the instrument of art and invention. He did not tell me how he felt when we spoke of his performance flying; he told me instead that he paid attention to how his plane and its line looked to the audience against the lighted sky. If he had noticed how he felt, he could not have done the work. Robed in his airplane, he was as featureless as a priest. He was lost in his figural aspect like an actor or a king. Of his flying, he had said only, "I get a rhythm and stick with it." In its reticence, this statement reminded me of Veronese's "Given a large canvas, I enhanced it as I saw fit." But Veronese was ironic, and Rahm was not; he was as literal as an astronaut; the machine gave him tongue.

When Rahm flew, he sat down in the middle of art and strapped himself in. He spun it all around him. He could not see it himself. If he never saw it on film, he never saw it at all — as if Beethoven could not hear his final symphonies not because he was deaf but because he was inside the paper on which he wrote. Rahm must have felt it happen, that fusion of vision and metal, motion and idea. I think of this man as a figure, a college professor with a Ph.D. upside down in the loud band of beauty. What are we here for? *Propter chorum*, the monks say: for the sake of the choir.

"Purity does not lie in separation from but in deeper penetration into the universe," Teilhard de Chardin [6] wrote. It is hard to imagine a deeper penetration into the universe than Rahm's last dive in his plane, or than his inexpressible wordless, selfless line's inscribing the air and dissolving. Any other art may be permanent. I cannot recall one Rahm sequence. He improvised. If Christo [7] wraps a building or dyes a harbor, we join his poignant and fierce awareness that the work will be gone in days. Rahm's plane shed a ribbon in space, a ribbon whose end unraveled in memory while its beginning unfurled as surprise. He may have acknowledged that what he did could be called art, but it would have been, I think, only in the common misusage, which holds art to be the last extreme of skill. Rahm rode the point of the line to the possible; he discovered it and wound it down to show. He made his dazzling probe on the run. "The world is filled, and filled with the Absolute," Teilhard de Chardin wrote. "To see this is to be made free."

---

[6] *Teilhard de Chardin*: Pierre Teilhard de Chardin (1881–1955), a Catholic priest and paleontologist who tried in his writings (most notably in *The Phenomenon of Man*) to fuse scientific views with religious faith. Another of the essayists in this book, Stephen Jay Gould, has written extensively on Teilhard.

[7] *Christo*: Contemporary artist who has done many large-scale environmental works. For another example of Christo's work, see Joan Didion's "Miami" in Part 5.

FROM READING TO REREADING

1. "The Stunt Pilot" skillfully blends two kinds of writing: it works as a profile of an interesting, adventurous flyer and at the same time it manages to convey a philosophical view of artistic performance. How does Dillard accomplish this? Which elements of her essay appear to be dependent on interview? which on perception?

2. At the heart of Dillard's essay is what critics call a controlling metaphor, an extended resemblance that connects two areas of thought and that helps organize an essay around a central comparison. Writers often use a controlling metaphor to discuss one subject in terms of another or to invite us to visualize one subject in terms of

another. What is Dillard's controlling metaphor in this essay? What is stunt flying like? When is the metaphor first introduced? How does the resemblance help shape her entire essay?

3. Consider Dave Rahm as a hero. In what ways does Dillard find him heroic? In what ways does she find him ordinary? Why do you think she says of him that "he was as literal as an astronaut"? What does that suggest about his place in her controlling metaphor? What does his personality suggest about the relation of the artist to his or her art?

E. B. WHITE
Will Strunk

As a satirist and skeptic, E. B. White was a writer with few heroes and heroines. In fact, throughout most of his work — especially in his popular children's books — he distrusted the heroic mode, preferring instead to view life from a deliberately mundane and humorous perspective. Perhaps that is why White's main heroes — Montaigne and Thoreau — were essayists who focused with loving attention on life's everyday details. It should come as no surprise, then, that another of White's heroes was an apparently unheroic individual, a bespectacled Cornell English professor whose main claim to fame was a forty-three-page, privately printed rulebook for composition called The Elements of Style. *Will Strunk was White's writing teacher and mentor. In 1957, some ten years after Strunk's death, the "little book" came once again into White's hands and became the occasion for one of his* New Yorker *essays. The essay, in turn, inspired a publisher to ask White, who was by then considered one of the nation's preeminent stylists, to prepare an enlarged edition of the book. Strunk and White's* The Elements of Style *appeared in 1962 and, astonishingly for a composition rulebook, made the best-seller list. The "little book" is still going strong.*

Turtle Bay, July 15, 1957

MOSQUITOES HAVE ARRIVED with the warm nights, and our bedchamber is their theater under the stars. I have been up and down all night, swinging at them with a face towel dampened at one end to give it authority. This morning I suffer from the lightheadedness that comes from no sleep — a sort of drunkenness, very good for writing because all sense of responsibility for what the words say is gone. Yesterday evening my wife showed up with a few yards of netting, and together we knelt and covered the fireplace with an illusion veil. It looks like a bride. (One of our many theories is that mosquitoes come down chimneys.) I bought a couple of adjustable screens at the hardware store on Third Avenue and they are in place in the windows; but the window sashes in this building are so old and irregular that any mosquito except one suffering from elephantiasis has no difficulty walking into the room through the space between sash and screen. (And then there is the even larger opening between upper sash and lower sash when the lower sash is raised to receive the screen — a space that hardly ever occurs to an apartment dweller but must occur to all mosquitoes.) I also bought a very old air-conditioning machine for twenty-five dollars, a great bargain, and

I like this machine. It has almost no effect on the atmosphere of the room, merely chipping the edge off the heat, and it makes a loud grinding noise reminiscent of the subway, so that I can snap off the lights, close my eyes, holding the damp towel at the ready, and imagine, with the first stab, that I am riding in the underground and being pricked by pins wielded by angry girls.

Another theory of mine about the Turtle Bay mosquito is that he is swept into one's bedroom through the air conditioner, riding the cool indraft as an eagle rides a warm updraft. It is a feeble theory, but a man has to entertain theories if he is to while away the hours of sleeplessness. I wanted to buy some old-fashioned bug spray, and went to the store for that purpose, but when I asked the clerk for a Flit gun and some Flit, he gave me a queer look, as though wondering where I had been keeping myself all these years. "We got something a lot stronger than that," he said, producing a can of stuff that contained chlordane and several other unmentionable chemicals. I told him I couldn't use it because I was hypersensitive to chlordane. "Gets me right in the liver," I said, throwing a wild glance at him.

The mornings are the pleasantest times in the apartment, exhaustion having set in, the sated mosquitoes at rest on ceiling and walls, sleeping it off, the room a swirl of tortured bedclothes and abandoned garments, the vines in their full leafiness filtering the hard light of day, the air conditioner silent at last, like the mosquitoes. From Third Avenue comes the sound of the mad builders — American cicadas, out in the noonday sun. In the garden the sparrow chants — a desultory second courtship, a subdued passion, in keeping with the great heat, love in summertime, relaxed and languorous. I shall miss this apartment when it is gone; we are quitting it come fall, to turn ourselves out to pasture. Every so often I make an attempt to simplify my life, burning my books behind me, selling the occasional chair, discarding the accumulated miscellany. I have noticed, though, that these purifications of mine — to which my wife submits with cautious grace — have usually led to even greater complexity in the long pull, and I have no doubt this one will, too, for I don't trust myself in a situation of this sort and suspect that my first act as an old horse will be to set to work improving the pasture. I may even join a pasture-improvement society. The last time I tried to purify myself by fire, I managed to acquire a zoo in the process and am still supporting it and carrying heavy pails of water to the animals, a task that is sometimes beyond my strength.

A book I have decided not to get rid of is a small one that arrived in the mail not long ago, a gift from a friend in Ithaca. It is *The Elements of Style*, by the late William Strunk, Jr., and it was known on the Cornell campus in my day as "the little book," with the stress on the word "little." I must have once owned a copy, for I took English 8 under Professor Strunk in 1919 and the book was required reading, but my copy presumably failed to survive an

early purge. I'd not laid eyes on it in thirty-eight years. Am now delighted
to study it again and rediscover its rich deposits of gold.

   The Elements of Style was Will Strunk's *parvum opus*, [1] his attempt to cut   5
the vast tangle of English rhetoric down to size and write its rules and
principles on the head of a pin. Will himself hung the title "little" on the
book: he referred to it sardonically and with secret pride as "the *little* book,"
always giving the word "little" a special twist, as though he were putting a
spin on a ball. The title page reveals that the book was privately printed
(Ithaca, N.Y.) and that it was copyrighted in 1918 by the author. It is a forty-
three-page summation of the case for cleanliness, accuracy, and brevity in
the use of English. Its vigor is unimpaired, and for sheer pith I think it
probably sets a record that is not likely to be broken. The Cornell University
Library has one copy. It had two, but my friend pried one loose and mailed
it to me.

   The book consists of a short introduction, eight rules of usage, ten
principles of composition, a few matters of form, a list of words and expressions commonly misused, a list of words commonly misspelled. That's all
there is. The rules and principles are in the form of direct commands,
Sergeant Strunk snapping orders to his platoon. "Do not join independent
clauses with a comma." (Rule 5.) "Do not break sentences in two." (Rule
6.) "Use the active voice." (Rule 11.) "Omit needless words." (Rule 13.)
"Avoid a succession of loose sentences." (Rule 14.) "In summaries, keep to
one tense." (Rule 17.) Each rule or principle is followed by a short hortatory
essay, and the exhortation is followed by, or interlarded with, examples in
parallel columns — the true vs. the false, the right vs. the wrong, the timid
vs. the bold, the ragged vs. the trim. From every line there peers out at me
the puckish face of my professor, his short hair parted neatly in the middle
and combed down over his forehead, his eyes blinking incessantly behind
steel-rimmed spectacles as though he had just emerged into strong light, his
lips nibbling each other like nervous horses, his smile shuttling to and fro in
a carefully edged mustache.

   "Omit needless words!" cries the author on page 21, and into that
imperative Will Strunk really put his heart and soul. In the days when I was
sitting in his class, he omitted so many needless words, and omitted them
so forcibly and with such eagerness and obvious relish, that he often seemed
in the position of having short-changed himself, a man left with nothing
more to say yet with time to fill, a radio prophet who had outdistanced the
clock. Will Strunk got out of this predicament by a simple trick: he uttered
every sentence three times. When he delivered his oration on brevity to the
class, he leaned forward over his desk, grasped his coat lapels in his hands,
and in a husky, conspiratorial voice said, "Rule Thirteen. Omit needless
words! Omit needless words! Omit needless words!"

---

[1] *parvum opus*: Literally, "small work" in Latin.

He was a memorable man, friendly and funny. Under the remembered sting of his kindly lash, I have been trying to omit needless words since 1919, and although there are still many words that cry for omission and the huge task will never be accomplished, it is exciting to me to reread the masterly Strunkian elaboration of this noble theme. It goes:

> Vigorous writing is concise. A sentence should contain no unnecessary words, a paragraph no unnecessary sentences, for the same reason that a drawing should have no unnecessary lines and a machine no unnecessary parts. This requires not that the writer make all his sentences short, or that he avoid all detail and treat his subjects only in outline, but that every word tell.

There you have a short, valuable essay on the nature and beauty of brevity — sixty-three words that could change the world. Having recovered from his adventure in prolixity (sixty-three words were a lot of words in the tight world of William Strunk, Jr.), the Professor proceeds to give a few quick lessons in pruning. The student learns to cut the deadwood from "This is a subject which . . . ," reducing it to "This subject . . . ," a gain of three words. He learns to trim " . . . used for fuel purposes" down to "used for fuel." He learns that he is being a chatterbox when he says "The question as to whether" and that he should just say "Whether" — a gain of four words out of a possible five.

The Professor devotes a special paragraph to the vile expression "the fact that," a phrase that causes him to quiver with revulsion. The expression, he says, should be "revised out of every sentence in which it occurs." But a shadow of gloom seems to hang over the page, and you feel that he knows how hopeless his cause is. I suppose I have written "the fact that" a thousand times in the heat of composition, revised it out maybe five hundred times in the cool aftermath. To be batting only .500 this late in the season, to fail half the time to connect with this fat pitch, saddens me, for it seems a betrayal of the man who showed me how to swing at it and made the swinging seem worthwhile. 10

I treasure *The Elements of Style* for its sharp advice, but I treasure it even more for the audacity and self-confidence of its author. Will knew where he stood. He was so sure of where he stood, and made his position so clear and so plausible, that his peculiar stance has continued to invigorate me — and, I am sure, thousands of other ex-students — during the years that have intervened since our first encounter. He had a number of likes and dislikes that were almost as whimsical as the choice of a necktie, yet he made them seem utterly convincing. He disliked the word "forceful" and advised us to use "forcible" instead. He felt that the word "clever" was greatly overused; "it is best restricted to ingenuity displayed in small matters." He despised the expression "student body," which he termed gruesome, and made a special trip downtown to the *Alumni News* office one day to protest the expression and suggest that "studentry" be substituted, a coinage of his own which he felt was similar to "citizenry." I am told that the *News* editor was so charmed by the visit, if not by the word, that he ordered the student body buried, never to rise again. "Studentry" has taken its place. It's not much of an improvement, but it does sound less cadaverous, and it made Will Strunk quite happy.

A few weeks ago I noticed a headline in the *Times* about Bonnie Prince Charlie: "CHARLES' TONSILS OUT." Immediately Rule 1 leapt to mind.

> 1. Form the possessive singular of nouns with 's. Follow this rule whatever the final consonant. Thus write,
>> Charles's friend
>> Burns's poems
>> the witch's malice.

Clearly Will Strunk had foreseen, as far back as 1918, the dangerous tonsil-lectomy of a Prince, in which the surgeon removes the tonsils and the *Times* copy desk removes the final "s." He started his book with it. I commend Rule 1 to the *Times* and I trust that Charles's throat, not Charles' throat, is mended.

Style rules of this sort are, of course, somewhat a matter of individual preference, and even the established rules of grammar are open to challenge. Professor Strunk, although one of the most inflexible and choosy of men, was quick to acknowledge the fallacy of inflexibility and the danger of doctrine.

"It is an old observation," he wrote, "that the best writers sometimes disregard the rules of rhetoric. When they do so, however, the reader will usually find in the sentence some compensating merit, attained at the cost of the violation. Unless he is certain of doing as well, he will probably do best to follow the rules."

It is encouraging to see how perfectly a book, even a dusty rulebook, 15 perpetuates and extends the spirit of a man. Will Strunk loved the clear, the brief, the bold, and his book is clear, brief, bold. Boldness is perhaps its chief distinguishing mark. On page 24, explaining one of his parallels, he says, "The left-hand version gives the impression that the writer is undecided or timid; he seems unable or afraid to choose one form of expression and hold to it." And his Rule 12 is "Make definite assertions." That was Will all over. He scorned the vague, the tame, the colorless, the irresolute. He felt it was worse to be irresolute than to be wrong. I remember a day in class when he leaned far forward in his characteristic pose — the pose of a man about to impart a secret — and croaked, "If you don't know how to pronounce a word, say it loud! If you don't know how to pronounce a word, say it loud!" This comical piece of advice struck me as sound at the time, and I still respect it. Why compound ignorance with inaudibility? Why run and hide?

All through *The Elements of Style* one finds evidences of the author's deep sympathy for the reader. Will felt that the reader was in serious trouble most of the time, a man floundering in a swamp, and that it was the duty of anyone attempting to write English to drain this swamp quickly and get his man up on dry ground, or at least throw him a rope.

"The little book" has long since passed into disuse. Will died in 1946, and he had retired from teaching several years before that. Longer, lower textbooks are in use in English classes nowadays, I daresay — books with upswept tail fins and automatic verbs. I hope some of them manage to compress as much wisdom into as small a space, manage to come to the point as quickly and illuminate it as amusingly. I think, though, that if I suddenly found myself in the, to me, unthinkable position of facing a class in English usage and style, I would simply lean far out over the desk, clutch my lapels, blink my eyes, and say, "Get the *little* book! Get the *little* book! Get the *little* book!"

P.S. (April 1962). Soon after this piece about Professor Strunk appeared in *The New Yorker*, a publisher asked me to revise and amplify *The Elements of Style* in order that it might be reissued. I agreed to do this, and did it; but the job, which should have taken about a month's time, took me a year. I discovered that for all my fine talk I was no match for the parts of speech — was, in fact, over my depth and in trouble. Not only that, I felt uneasy at posing as an expert on rhetoric, when the truth is I write by ear, always with difficulty and seldom with any exact notion of what is taking place under the hood. Some of the material in the Strunk book proved too much for me, and two or three times during my strange period of confinement I was forced to turn for help to a friend who is a grammarian and could set me straight.

When the book came out, it managed to get on the best-seller list, where it stayed for a while. The appearance of a style book on hallowed ground was considered a freak of publishing, and a couple of newspapers ran editorials about it, asking what was happening to the world, that people should show interest in English usage. I was as surprised as the next man, but I think I now understand what happened. The Strunk book, which is a "right and wrong" book, arrived on the scene at a time when a wave of reaction was setting in against the permissive school of rhetoric, the Anything Goes school where right and wrong do not exist and there is no foundation all down the line. The little book climbed on this handy wave and rode it in.

It was during the permissive years that the third edition of Webster's 20 *New International Dictionary* was being put together, along new lines of lexicography, and it was Dr. Gove, the head man, who perhaps expressed the whole thing most succinctly when he remarked that a dictionary "should have no traffic with . . . artificial notions of correctness or superiority. It must be descriptive and not prescriptive." This approach struck many people as chaotic and degenerative, and that's the way it strikes me. Strunk was a fundamentalist; he believed in right and wrong, and so, in the main, do I. Unless someone is willing to entertain notions of superiority, the English language disintegrates, just as a home disintegrates unless someone in the family sets standards of good taste, good conduct, and simple justice.

One parting note: readers of the first edition of the book were overjoyed to discover that the phrase "the fact that" had slid by me again, landing solidly in the middle of one of my learned dissertations. It has since disappeared, but it had its little day.

FROM READING TO REREADING

1. Note how slowly White gets into his subject. Why do you think he opens with a description of his New York City apartment and its bothersome mosquitoes? Can you think of any relevance the first three paragraphs bear to the essay as a whole? Why didn't White begin directly with a description of the essay's subject — Will Strunk?

2. For many people, the rules of composition recommended by Will Strunk are trivial, arbitrary, or downright silly. Why does White find them important? What qualities does he most admire in his mentor, Will Strunk? In what ways can these qualities be said to be heroic?

3. Notice that White offers us very few details from Strunk's life — we find out nothing about his religious or political views, we don't know what other writing he might have done, whether he had a family, and so on. What effect does this have on our sense of Strunk's character? Why do you think White focuses primarily on the book? What connection does he see between the book and the person?

STEPHEN JAY GOULD

The Streak of Streaks [1]

As one of America's leading writers on science, Stephen Jay Gould has written about a number of his scientific heroes, especially Charles Darwin. But in this essay he shows a different side of himself: his great affection for baseball. Though an enthusiastic fan of the game, Gould nevertheless brings to his love of baseball an uncompromising love of scientific fact (Gould would, of course, see no opposition between these two passions). In "The Streak of Streaks," he looks at one of his less scientific childhood heroes, Joe DiMaggio, and shows why the hall-of-fame Yankee outfielder's 56-game hitting streak in 1941 is "both the greatest factual achievement in the history of baseball and a principal icon of American mythology." In examining this "central item of our cultural history," Gould also demonstrates some of the larger issues at stake, issues that reach far beyond sports statistics and lead to a subtle assessment of human perception, intuition, and prejudice.

M Y FATHER was a court stenographer. At his less than princely salary, we watched Yankee games from the bleachers or high in the third deck. But one of the judges had season tickets, so we occasionally sat in the lower boxes when hizzoner couldn't attend. One afternoon, while DiMaggio was going 0 for 4 against, of all people, the lowly St. Louis Browns, the great man fouled one in our direction. "Catch it, Dad," I screamed. "You never get them," he replied, but stuck up his hand like the Statue of Liberty — and the ball fell right in. I mailed it to DiMaggio, and, bless him, he actually sent the ball back, signed and in a box marked "insured." Insured, that is, to make me the envy of the neighborhood, and DiMaggio the model and hero of my life.

I met DiMaggio a few years ago on a small playing field at the Presidio of San Francisco. My son, wearing DiMaggio's old number 5 on his Little League jersey, accompanied me, exactly one generation after my father caught that ball. DiMaggio gave him a pointer or two on batting and then signed a baseball for him. One generation passeth away, and another generation cometh: But the earth abideth forever.

My son, uncoached by Dad, and given the chance that comes but once

[1] This essay originally appeared in the *New York Review of Books* as a review of Michael Seidel's *Streak: Joe DiMaggio and the Summer of 1941* (New York: McGraw-Hill, 1988). I have excised the references to Seidel's book in order to forge a more general essay, but I thank him both for the impetus and for writing such a fine book. [Gould's note]

in a lifetime, asked DiMaggio as his only query about life and career: "Suppose you had walked every time up during one game of your 56-game hitting streak? Would the streak have been over?" DiMaggio replied that, under 1941 rules, the streak would have ended, but that this unfair statute has since been revised, and such a game would not count today.

My son's choice for a single question tells us something vital about the nature of legend. A man may labor for a professional lifetime, especially in sport or in battle, but posterity needs a single transcendant event to fix him in permanent memory. Every hero must be a Wellington on the right side of his personal Waterloo; [2] generality of excellence is too diffuse. The un-ambiguous factuality of a single achievement is adamantine. Detractors can argue forever about the general tenor of your life and works, but they can never erase a great event.

In 1941, as I gestated in my mother's womb, Joe DiMaggio got at least one hit in each of 56 successive games. Most records are only incrementally superior to runners-up; Roger Maris hit 61 homers in 1961, but Babe Ruth hit 60 in 1927 and 59 in 1921, while Hank Greenberg (1938) and Jimmy Foxx (1932) both hit 58. But DiMaggio's 56-game hitting streak is ridiculously, almost unreachably far from all challengers (Wee Willie Keeler and Pete Rose, both with 44, come second). Among sabermetricians (a happy neologism based on an acronym for members of the Society for American Baseball Research, and referring to the statistical mavens of the sport) — a contentious lot not known for agreement about anything — we find virtual consensus that DiMaggio's 56-game hitting streak is the greatest accomplishment in the history of baseball, if not all modern sport.

The reasons for this respect are not far to seek. Single moments of unexpected supremacy — Johnny Vander Meer's back-to-back no-hitters in 1938, Don Larsen's perfect game in the 1956 World Series — can occur at any time to almost anybody, and have an irreducibly capricious character. Achievements of a full season — such as Maris's 61 homers in 1961 and Ted Williams's batting average of .406, also posted in 1941 and not equaled since — have a certain overall majesty, but they don't demand unfailing consistency every single day; you can slump for a while, so long as your average holds. But a streak must be absolutely exceptionless; you are not allowed a single day of subpar play, or even bad luck. You bat only four or five times in an average game. Sometimes two or three of these efforts yield walks, and you get only one or two shots at a hit. Moreover, as tension mounts and notice increases, your life becomes unbearable. Reporters dog your every step; fans are even more intrusive than usual (one stole DiMaggio's favorite bat right in the middle of his streak). You cannot make a single mistake.

Thus Joe DiMaggio's 56-game hitting streak is both the greatest factual

[2] *Every hero must be* . . . : In one of history's most decisive battles, the British general Arthur Wellesley Wellington defeated Napolean at Waterloo (a town now in Belgium) in 1815.

achievement in the history of baseball and a principal icon of American mythology. What shall we do with such a central item of our cultural history?

Statistics and mythology may strike us as the most unlikely of bedfellows. How can we quantify Caruso or measure *Middlemarch*?[3] But if God could mete out heaven with the span (Isaiah 40:12), perhaps we can say something useful about hitting streaks. The statistics of "runs," defined as continuous series of good or bad results (including baseball's streaks and slumps), is a well-developed branch of the profession, and can yield clear — but wildly counterintuitive — results. (The fact that we find these conclusions so surprising is the key to appreciating DiMaggio's achievement, the point of this article, and the gateway to an important insight about the human mind.)

Start with a phenomenon that nearly everyone both accepts and considers well understood — "hot hands" in basketball. Now and then, someone just gets hot, and can't be stopped. Basket after basket falls in — or out as with "cold hands," when a man can't buy a bucket for love or money (choose your cliché). The reason for this phenomenon is clear enough: It lies embodied in the maxim, "When you're hot, you're hot; and when you're not, you're not." You get that touch, build confidence; all nervousness fades, you find your rhythm; *swish, swish, swish.* Or you miss a few, get rattled, endure the booing, experience despair; hands start shaking and you realize that you shoulda stood in bed.

Everybody knows about hot hands. The only problem is that no such phenomenon exists. Stanford psychologist Amos Tversky studied every basket made by the Philadelphia 76ers for more than a season. He found, first of all, that the probability of making a second basket did not rise following a successful shot. Moreover, the number of "runs," or baskets in succession, was no greater than what a standard random, or coin-tossing, model would predict. (If the chance of making each basket is 0.5, for example, a reasonable value for good shooters, five hits in a row will occur, on average, once in 32 sequences — just as you can expect to toss five successive heads about once in 32 times, or 0.5^5.)

Of course Larry Bird, the great forward of the Boston Celtics, will have more sequences of five than Joe Airball — but not because he has greater will or gets in that magic rhythm more often. Larry has longer runs because his average success rate is so much higher, and random models predict more frequent and longer sequences. If Larry shoots field goals at 0.6 probability of success, he will get five in a row about once every 13 sequences (0.6^5). If Joe, by contrast, shoots only 0.3, he will get his five straight only about once in 412 times. In other words, we need no special explanation for the apparent pattern of long runs. There is no ineffable "causality of circumstance" (to

10

---

[3] *How can we . . . ?*: Gould is referring to the artistic performances of the great Italian opera singer Enrico Caruso and of George Eliot in her major novel, *Middlemarch* (1872).

coin a phrase), no definite reason born of the particulars that make for heroic myths — courage in the clinch, strength in adversity, etc. You only have to know a person's ordinary play in order to predict his sequences. (I rather suspect that we are convinced of the contrary not only because we need myths so badly, but also because we remember the successes and simply allow the failures to fade from memory. More on this later.) But how does this revisionist pessimism work for baseball?

My colleague Ed Purcell, Nobel laureate in physics but, for purposes of this subject, just another baseball fan, has done a comprehensive study of all baseball streak and slump records. His firm conclusion is easily and swiftly summarized. Nothing ever happened in baseball above and beyond the frequency predicted by coin-tossing models. The longest runs of wins or losses are as long as they should be, and occur about as often as they ought to. Even the hapless Orioles, at 0 and 21 to start the 1988 season, only fell victim to the laws of probability (and not to the vengeful God of racism, out to punish major league baseball's only black manager). [4]

But "treasure your exceptions," as the old motto goes. Purcell's rule has but one major exception, one sequence so many standard deviations above the expected distribution that it should never have occurred at all: Joe DiMaggio's 56-game hitting streak in 1941. The intuition of baseball aficionados has been vindicated. Purcell calculated that to make it likely (probability greater than 50 percent) that a run of even 50 games will occur once in the history of baseball up to now (and 56 is a lot more than 50 in this kind of league), baseball's rosters would have to include either four lifetime .400 batters or 52 lifetime .350 batters over careers of 1,000 games. In actuality, only three men have lifetime batting averages in excess of .350, and no one is anywhere near .400 (Ty Cobb at .367, Rogers Hornsby at .358, and Shoeless Joe Jackson at .356). DiMaggio's streak is the most extraordinary thing that ever happened in American sports. He sits on the shoulders of two bearers — mythology and science. For Joe DiMaggio accomplished what no other ballplayer has done. He beat the hardest taskmaster of all, a woman who makes Nolan Ryan's fastball look like a cantaloupe in slow motion — Lady Luck.

A larger issue lies behind basic documentation and simple appreciation. For we don't understand the truly special character of DiMaggio's record because we are so poorly equipped, whether by habits of culture or by our modes of cognition, to grasp the workings of random processes and patterning in nature.

Omar Khayyám, the old Persian tentmaker, understood the quandary [15] of our lives (*Rubaiyat of Omar Khayyám*, Edward Fitzgerald, trans.):

---

[4] When I wrote this essay, Frank Robinson, the Baltimore skipper, was the only black man at the helm of a major league team. For more on the stats of Baltimore's slump, see my article "Winning and Losing: It's All in the Game," *Rotunda*, Spring 1989. [Gould's note]

Into this Universe, and Why not knowing,
Nor Whence, like Water willy-nilly flowing;
And out of it, as Wind along the Waste,
I know not Whither, willy-nilly blowing.

But we cannot bear it. We must have comforting answers. We see pattern, for pattern surely exists, even in a purely random world. (Only a highly nonrandom universe could possibly cancel out the clumping that we perceive as pattern. We think we see constellations because stars are dispersed at random in the heavens, and therefore clump in our sight — see Essay 17.) Our error lies not in the perception of pattern but in automatically imbuing pattern with meaning, especially with meaning that can bring us comfort, or dispel confusion. Again, Omar took the more honest approach:

Ah, love! could you and I with Fate conspire
To grasp this sorry Scheme of Things entire,
Would not we shatter it to bits — and then
Re-mould it nearer to the Heart's Desire!

We, instead, have tried to impose that "heart's desire" upon the actual earth and its largely random patterns (Alexander Pope, *Essay on Man*, end of Epistle 1):

All Nature is but Art, unknown to thee;
All Chance, Direction, which thou canst not see;
All Discord, Harmony not understood:
All partial Evil, universal Good.

Sorry to wax so poetic and tendentious about something that leads back to DiMaggio's hitting streak, but this broader setting forms the source of our misinterpretation. We believe in "hot hands" because we must impart meaning to a pattern — and we like meanings that tell stories about heroism, valor, and excellence. We believe that long streaks and slumps must have direct causes internal to the sequence itself, and we have no feel for the frequency and length of sequences in random data. Thus, while we understand that DiMaggio's hitting streak was the longest ever, we don't appreciate its truly special character because we view all the others as equally patterned by cause, only a little shorter. We distinguish DiMaggio's feat merely by quantity along a continuum of courage; we should, instead, view his 56-game hitting streak as a unique assault upon the otherwise unblemished record of Dame Probability.

Amos Tversky, who studied "hot hands," has performed, with Daniel Kahneman, a series of elegant psychological experiments. These long-term studies have provided our finest insight into "natural reasoning" and its curious departure from logical truth. To cite an example, they construct a fictional description of a young woman: "Linda is 31 years old, single, outspoken, and very bright. She majored in philosophy. As a student, she was deeply concerned with issues of discrimination and social justice, and also participated in anti-nuclear demonstrations." Subjects are then given a list of hypothetical statements about Linda: They must rank these in order of presumed likelihood, most to least probable. Tversky and Kahneman list eight statements, but five are a blind, and only three make up the true experiment:

> Linda is active in the feminist movement;
> Linda is a bank teller;
> Linda is a bank teller and is active in the feminist movement.

Now it simply must be true that the third statement is least likely, since any conjunction has to be less probable than either of its parts considered separately. Everybody can understand this when the principle is explained explicitly and patiently. But all groups of subjects, sophisticated students who have pondered logic and probability as well as folks off the street corner, rank the last statement as more probable than the second. (I am particularly fond of this example because I know that the third statement is least probable, yet a little homunculus in my head continues to jump up and down, shouting at me — "but she can't just be a bank teller; read the description.")

Why do we so consistently make this simple logical error? Tversky and Kahneman argue, correctly I think, that our minds are not built (for whatever reason) to work by the rules of probability, though these rules clearly govern our universe. We do something else that usually serves us well, but fails in crucial instances: We "match to type." We abstract what we consider the "essence" of an entity, and then arrange our judgments by their degree of similarity to this assumed type. Since we are given a "type" for Linda that implies feminism, but definitely not a bank job, we rank any statement matching the type as more probable than another that only contains material contrary to the type. This propensity may help us to understand an entire range of human preferences, from Plato's theory of form to modern stereotyping of race or gender.

We might also understand the world better, and free ourselves of unseemly prejudice, if we properly grasped the workings of probability and its inexorable hold, through laws of logic, upon much of nature's pattern. "Matching to type" is one common error; failure to understand random patterning in streaks and slumps is another — hence Tversky's study of both the fictional Linda and the 76ers' baskets. Our failure to appreciate the uniqueness of DiMaggio's streak derives from the same unnatural and uncomfortable relationship that we maintain with probability. (If we knew Lady Luck better, Las Vegas might still be a roadstop in the desert.)

My favorite illustration of this basic misunderstanding, as applied to DiMaggio's hitting streak, appeared in a recent article by baseball writer John Holway, "A Little Help from His Friends," and subtitled "Hits or Hype in '41" (*Sports Heritage*, 1987). Holway points out that five of DiMaggio's successes were narrow escapes and lucky breaks. He received two benefits-of-the-doubt from official scorers on plays that might have been judged as errors. In each of two games, his only hit was a cheapie. In game 16, a ball dropped untouched in the outfield and had to be called a hit, even though the ball had been misjudged and could have been caught; in game 54, DiMaggio dribbled one down the third-base line, easily beating the throw because the third baseman, expecting the usual, was playing far back. The fifth incident is an oft-told tale, perhaps the most interesting story of the streak. In game 38, DiMaggio was 0 for 3 going into the last inning. Scheduled to bat fourth, he might have been denied a chance to hit at all. Johnny Sturm popped up to begin the inning, but Red Rolfe then walked. Slugger Tommy Henrich, up next, was suddenly swept with a premonitory fear: Suppose I ground into a double play and end the inning? An elegant solution immediately occurred to him: Why not bunt (an odd strategy for a power hitter). Henrich laid down a beauty; DiMaggio, up next, promptly drilled a double to left.

I enjoyed Holway's account, but his premise is entirely, almost preciously, wrong. First of all, none of the five incidents represents an egregious miscall. The two hits were less than elegant, but undoubtedly legitimate; the two boosts from official scorers were close calls on judgment plays, not gifts. As for Henrich, I can only repeat manager Joe McCarthy's comment when Tommy asked him for permission to bunt: "Yeah, that's a good idea." Not a terrible strategy either — to put a man into scoring position for an insurance run when you're up 3–1.

But these details do not touch the main point: Holway's premise is false because he accepts the conventional mythology about long sequences. He believes that streaks are unbroken runs of causal courage — so that any prolongation by hook-or-crook becomes an outrage against the deep meaning of the phenomenon. But extended sequences are not pure exercises in valor. Long streaks always are, and must be, a matter of extraordinary luck imposed upon great skill. Please don't make the vulgar mistake of thinking that Purcell or Tversky or I or anyone else would attribute a long streak to "just luck" — as though everyone's chances are exactly the same, and streaks represent nothing more than the lucky atom that kept moving in one direction. Long hitting streaks happen to the greatest players — Sisler, Keeler, DiMaggio, Rose — because their general chance of getting a hit is so much higher than average. Just as Joe Airball cannot match Larry Bird for runs of baskets, Joe's cousin Bill Ofer, with a lifetime batting average of .184, will never have a streak to match DiMaggio's with a lifetime average of .325. The statistics show something else, and something fascinating: There is no "causality of circumstance," no "extra" that the great can draw from the soul of their valor to extend a streak beyond the ordinary expectation of coin-tossing models for a series of unconnected events, each occurring with a characteristic probability for that particular player. Good players have higher characteristic probabilities, hence longer streaks.

Of course DiMaggio had a little luck during his streak. That's what streaks are all about. No long sequence has ever been entirely sustained in any other way (the Orioles almost won several of those 21 games). DiMaggio's remarkable achievement — its uniqueness, in the unvarnished literal sense of that word — lies in whatever he did to extend his success well beyond the reasonable expectations of random models that have governed every other streak or slump in the history of baseball.

Probability does pervade the universe — and in this sense, the old chestnut about baseball imitating life really has validity. The statistics of streaks and slumps, properly understood, do teach an important lesson about epistemology, and life in general. The history of a species, or any natural phenomenon that requires unbroken continuity in a world of trouble, works like a batting streak. All are games of a gambler playing with a limited stake against a house with infinite resources. The gambler must eventually go bust. His aim can only be to stick around as long as possible, to have some fun while he's at it, and, if he happens to be a moral agent as well, to worry about staying the course with honor. The best of us will try to live by a few simple rules: Do justly, love mercy, walk humbly with thy God, and never draw to an inside straight.

DiMaggio's hitting streak is the finest of legitimate legends because it   25 embodies the essence of the battle that truly defines our lives. DiMaggio activated the greatest and most unattainable dream of all humanity, the hope and chimera of all sages and shamans: He cheated death, at least for a while.

FROM READING TO REREADING

1. Gould argues that we cannot bear "a purely random world," and therefore err not only in finding a pattern in things or events but in "imbuing pattern with meaning." How does Gould's principle apply to the lesson of DiMaggio's hitting streak?

2. What does Gould mean when he criticizes a baseball historian for accepting "the conventional mythology about long sequences"? What is that mythology? Why doesn't a rejection of this mythology then diminish DiMaggio's heroism?

3. Note Gould's rather surprising conclusion. In what way does DiMaggio become a legendary hero? What does death have to do with his achievement? In what sense did DiMaggio cheat death?

VIRGINIA WOOLF
Ellen Terry

When our heroes or heroines are very famous people, we rarely meet them in person, as Joan Didion did John Wayne. Most of us get to know a celebrity we admire only through indirect sources, through articles, interviews, public appearances, or biographies. Many movie stars, moreover, write (or have someone ghostwrite) an autobiography in which they usually attempt to offer the reader an intimate view of the private person behind the public persona. Such autobiographies go back to around the turn of the century; one of the early examples of the genre was The Story of My Life, *written in 1908 (and reprinted in 1933) by Ellen Terry (1847–1928), the most celebrated stage actress of her time. It is this book that Virginia Woolf examines as she tries to discover the "real" person behind an extremely "mutable" woman. Though Woolf is trying to understand an exceptionally articulate Shakespearean actress, her frustrations with Ellen Terry's book are not very different from those we might experience in reading any Hollywood autobiography on today's best-seller list.*

W HEN SHE CAME on to the stage as Lady Cicely in *Captain Brassbound's Conversion*,[1] the stage collapsed like a house of cards and all the limelights were extinguished. When she spoke it was as if someone drew a bow over a ripe, richly seasoned 'cello; it grated, it glowed, and it growled. Then she stopped speaking. She put on her glasses. She gazed intently at the back of a settee. She had forgotten her part. But did it matter? Speaking or silent, she was Lady Cicely — or was it Ellen Terry? At any rate, she filled the stage and all the other actors were put out, as electric lights are put out in the sun.

Yet this pause when she forgot what Lady Cicely said next was significant. It was a sign not that she was losing her memory and past her prime, as some said. It was a sign that Lady Cicely was not a part that suited her. Her son, Gordon Craig, insists that she only forgot her part when there was something uncongenial in the words, when some speck of grit had got into the marvellous machine of her genius. When the part was congenial, when she was Shakespeare's Portia, Desdemona, Ophelia, every word, every comma was consumed. Even her eyelashes acted. Her body lost its weight. Her son, a mere boy, could lift her in his arms. "I am not myself," she said. "Something comes upon me. . . . I am always-in-the-air, light and bodiless."

[1] *When she came on stage . . .* : Nobel prize–winning English dramatist George Bernard Shaw (1856–1950) wrote *Captain Brassbound's Conversion* in 1900 especially for Ellen Terry.

We, who can only remember her as Lady Cicely on the little stage at the Court Theatre, only remember what, compared with her Ophelia or her Portia, was as a picture postcard compared with the great Velasquez[2] in the gallery.

It is the fate of actors to leave only picture postcards behind them. Every night when the curtain goes down the beautiful coloured canvas is rubbed out. What remains is at best only a wavering, insubstantial phantom — a verbal life on the lips of the living. Ellen Terry was well aware of it. She tried herself, overcome by the greatness of Irving[3] as Hamlet and indignant at the caricatures of his detractors, to describe what she remembered. It was in vain. She dropped her pen in despair. "Oh God, that I were a writer!" she cried. "Surely a *writer* could not string words together about Henry Irving's Hamlet and say *nothing, nothing.*" It never struck her, humble as she was, and obsessed by her lack of book learning, that she was, among other things, a writer. It never occurred to her when she wrote her autobiography, or scribbled page after page to Bernard Shaw late at night, dead tired after a rehearsal, that she was "writing." The words in her beautiful rapid hand bubbled off her pen. With dashes and notes of exclamation she tried to give them the very tone and stress of the spoken word. It is true, she could not build a house with words, one room opening out of another, and a staircase connecting the whole. But whatever she took up became in her warm, sensitive grasp a tool. If it was a rolling-pin, she made perfect pastry. If it was a carving knife, perfect slices fell from the leg of mutton. If it were a pen, words peeled off, some broken, some suspended in mid-air, but all far more expressive than the tappings of the professional typewriter.

With her pen then at odds and ends of time she has painted a self-portrait. It is not an Academy portrait, glazed, framed, complete. It is rather a bundle of loose leaves upon each of which she has dashed off a sketch for a portrait — here a nose, here an arm, here a foot, and there a mere scribble in the margin. The sketches done in different moods, from different angles, sometimes contradict each other. The nose cannot belong to the eyes; the arm is out of all proportion to the foot. It is difficult to assemble them. And there are blank pages, too. Some very important features are left out. There was a self she did not know, a gap she could not fill. Did she not take Walt Whitman's words for a motto? "Why, even I myself, I often think, know little or nothing of my real life. Only a few hints — a few diffused faint clues and indirections. . . . I seek . . . to trace out here."

Nevertheless, the first sketch is definite enough. It is the sketch of her ⁵ childhood. She was born to the stage. The stage was her cradle, her nursery.

---

[2] *Velasquez* (1599–1660): Spanish Baroque artist considered one of the world's finest portrait painters.

[3] *Irving:* Actor Henry Irving (1838–1905) and his partner Ellen Terry (1847–1928) were the dominant forces in British theater for decades.

When other little girls were being taught sums and pothooks she was being cuffed and buffeted into the practice of her profession. Her ears were boxed, her muscles suppled. All day she was hard at work on the boards. Late at night when other children were safe in bed she was stumbling along the dark streets wrapped in her father's cloak. And the dark street with its curtained windows was nothing but a sham to that little professional actress, and the rough and tumble life on the boards was her home, her reality. "It's all such sham there," she wrote — meaning by "there" what she called "life lived in houses" — "sham — cold — hard — pretending. It's not sham here in our theatre — here all is real, warm and kind — we live a lovely spiritual life here."

That is the first sketch. But turn to the next page. The child born to the stage has become a wife. She is married at sixteen to an elderly famous painter. The theatre has gone; its lights are out and in its place is a quiet studio in a garden. In its place is a world full of pictures and "gentle artistic people with quiet voices and elegant manners." She sits mum in her corner while the famous elderly people talk over her head in quiet voices. She is content to wash her husband's brushes; to sit to him; to play her simple tunes on the piano to him while he paints. In the evening she wanders over the Downs with the great poet, Tennyson. "I was in Heaven," she wrote. "I never had one single pang of regret for the theatre." If only it could have lasted! But somehow — here a blank page intervenes — she was an incongruous element in that quiet studio. She was too young, too vigorous, too vital, perhaps. At any rate, the marriage was a failure.

And so, skipping a page or two, we come to the next sketch. She is a mother now. Two adorable children claim all her devotion. She is living in the depths of the country, in the heart of domesticity. She is up at six. She scrubs, she cooks, she sews. She teaches the children. She harnesses the pony. She fetches the milk. And again she is perfectly happy. To live with children in a cottage, driving her little cart about the lanes, going to church on Sunday in blue and white cotton — that is the ideal life! She asks no more than that it shall go on like that for ever and ever. But one day the wheel comes off the pony cart. Huntsmen in pink leap over the hedge. One of them dismounts and offers help. He looks at the girl in a blue frock and exclaims: "Good God! It's Nelly!" She looks at the huntsman in pink and cries, "Charles Reade!" [4] And so, all in a jiffy, back she goes to the stage, and to forty pounds a week. For — that is the reason she gives — the bailiffs are in the house. She must make money.

At this point a very blank page confronts us. There is a gulf which we can only cross at a venture. Two sketches face each other; Ellen Terry in blue cotton among the hens; Ellen Terry robed and crowned as Lady Macbeth on the stage of the Lyceum. The two sketches are contradictory yet

---

[4] *"Charles Reade!"*: English novelist (1814–1884) whose work focused on social reform.

they are both of the same woman. She hates the stage; yet she adores it. She worships her children; yet she forsakes them. She would like to live for ever among pigs and ducks in the open air; yet she spends the rest of her life among actors and actresses in the limelight. Her own attempt to explain the discrepancy is hardly convincing. "I have always been more woman than artist," she says. Irving put the theatre first. "He had none of what I may call my bourgeois qualities — the love of being in love, the love of a home, the dislike of solitude." She tries to persuade us that she was an ordinary woman enough; a better hand at pastry than most; an adept at keeping house; with an eye for colour, a taste for furniture, and a positive passion for washing children's heads. If she went back to the stage it was because — well, what else could she do when the baliffs were in the house?

This is the little sketch that she offers us to fill in the gap between the two Ellen Terrys — Ellen the mother, and Ellen the actress. But here we remember her warning: "Why, even I myself know little or nothing of my real life." There was something in her that she did not understand; something that came surging up from the depths and swept her away in its clutches. The voice she heard in the lane was not the voice of Charles Reade; nor was it the voice of the bailiffs. It was the voice of her genius; the urgent call of something that she could not define, could not suppress, and must obey. So she left her children and followed the voice back to the stage, back to the Lyceum, back to a long life of incessant toil, anguish, and glory.

But, having gazed at the full-length portrait of Ellen Terry as Sargent[5] painted her, robed and crowned as Lady Macbeth, turn to the next page. It is done from another angle. Pen in hand, she is seated at her desk. A volume of Shakespeare lies before her. It is open at *Cymbeline*, and she is making careful notes in the margin. The part of Imogen presents great problems. She is, she says, "on the rack" about her interpretation. Perhaps Bernard Shaw can throw light upon the question? A letter from the brilliant young critic of the *Saturday Review* lies beside Shakespeare. She has never met him, but for years they have written to each other, intimately, ardently, disputatiously, some of the best letters in the language. He says the most outrageous things. He compares dear Henry to an ogre, and Ellen to a captive chained in his cage. But Ellen Terry is quite capable of holding her own against Bernard Shaw. She scolds him, laughs at him, fondles him, and contradicts him. She has a curious sympathy for the advanced views that Henry Irving abominated. But what suggestions has the brilliant critic to make about Imogen? None apparently that she has not already thought for herself. She is as close and critical a student of Shakespeare as he is. She has studied every line, weighed the meaning of every word; experimented with every gesture. Each of those golden moments when she becomes bodiless, not herself, is the result of months of minute and careful study. "Art," 10

[5] *Sargent*: John Singer Sargent (1856–1925), one of America's greatest portrait painters.

she quotes, "needs that which we can give her, I assure you." In fact this mutable woman, all instinct, sympathy, and sensation, is as painstaking a student and as careful of the dignity of her art as Flaubert [6] himself.

But once more the expression on that serious face changes. She works like a slave — none harder. But she is quick to tell Mr. Shaw that she does not work with her brain only. She is not in the least clever. Indeed, she is happy she tells him, "*not to be clever*." She stresses the point with a jab of her pen. "You clever people," as she calls him and his friends, miss so much, mar so much. As for education, she never had a day's schooling in her life. As far as she can see, but the problem baffles her, the main spring of her art is imagination. Visit mad-houses, if you like; take notes; observe; study endlessly. But first, imagine. And so she takes her part away from the books out into the woods. Rambling down grassy rides, she lives her part until she is it. If a word jars or grates, she must re-think it, re-write it. Then when every phrase is her own, and every gesture spontaneous, out she comes onto the stage and is Imogen, Ophelia, Desdemona.

But is she, even when the great moments are on her, a great actress? She doubts it. "I cared more for love and life," she says. Her face, too, has been no help to her. She cannot sustain emotion. Certainly she is not a great tragic actress. Now and again, perhaps, she has acted some comic part to perfection. But even while she analyses herself, as one artist to another, the sun slants upon an old kitchen chair. "Thank the Lord for my eyes!" she exclaims. What a world of joy her eyes have brought her! Gazing at the old "rush-bottomed, sturdy-legged, and wavy-backed" chair, the stage is gone, the limelights are out, the famous actress is forgotten.

Which, then, of all these women is the real Ellen Terry? How are we to put the scattered sketches together? Is she mother, wife, cook, critic, actress, or should she have been, after all, a painter? Each part seems the right part until she throws it aside and plays another. Something of Ellen Terry it seems overflowed every part and remained unacted. Shakespeare could not fit her; not Ibsen; nor Shaw. The stage could not hold her; nor the nursery. But there is, after all, a greater dramatist than Shakespeare, Ibsen, or Shaw. There is Nature. Hers is so vast a stage, and so innumerable a company of actors, that for the most part she fobs them off with a tag or two. They come on and they go off without breaking the ranks. But now and again Nature creates a new part, an original part. The actors who act that part always defy our attempts to name them. They will not act the stock parts — they forget the words, they improvise others of their own. But when they come on the stage falls like a pack of cards and the limelights are extinguished. That was Ellen Terry's fate — to act a new part. And thus

---

[6] *Flaubert*: Gustave Flaubert (1821–1880), French novelist and author of *Madame Bovary* (1857); he was deeply committed to the aesthetic quality of fiction.

while other actors are remembered because they were Hamlet, Phèdre, or Cleopatra, Ellen Terry is remembered because she was Ellen Terry.

FROM READING TO REREADING

1. Note that Woolf begins with an embarrassing incident from Ellen Terry's career — a moment in which she forgot her lines. Why do you think Woolf chose such an incident to begin her examination of the actress's character? What does that incident allow Woolf to do?

2. Like Woolf's essay that appeared in Part 1, "The Moment: Summer's Night," this essay, too, was collected in a volume called *The Moment and Other Essays*. Can you find any resemblances between these two essays? In what ways does the idea of a "moment" play a significant part in each essay?

3. Throughout the essay, Woolf discusses Ellen Terry's writing and compares the actress's life to a book ("here a blank page intervenes"). At other times, she focuses on Terry as a subject of painting or photography. What effect does this aesthetic emphasis have upon our sense of who Ellen Terry was? Why do you think Woolf approached her subject in this fashion?

ALICE WALKER
Looking for Zora

What if our heroes or heroines are people we think ought to be more famous than they are? In "Looking for Zora," Alice Walker — hungry for information about a seriously neglected black woman writer, Zora Neale Hurston — travels to Eatonville, Florida, in search of Hurston's hometown and unmarked grave. The trip becomes a ritualistic journey, as Walker slowly pieces together scraps of information and conflicting stories about Hurston (herself an anthropologist and story-collector) and rather unceremoniously manages to provide her literary heroine with an appropriate headstone. Walker's essay originally appeared in Ms *magazine in 1975, fifteen years after Hurston had died, destitute and lonely, in a Florida Welfare Home. Today, Zora Neale Hurston is far better known, thanks largely to the efforts of Alice Walker, who has discussed her work in several essays and has also edited a* Zora Neale Hurston Reader.

> On January 16, 1959, Zora Neale Hurston, suffering from the effects of a stroke and writing painfully in longhand, composed a letter to the "editorial department" of Harper & Brothers inquiring if they would be interested in seeing "the book I am laboring upon at present — a life of Herod the Great." One year and twelve days later, Zora Neale Hurston died without funds to provide for her burial, a resident of the St. Lucie County, Florida, Welfare Home. She lies today in an unmarked grave in a segregated cemetery in Fort Pierce, Florida, a resting place generally symbolic of the black writer's fate in America.
>
> Zora Neale Hurston is one of the most significant unread authors in America, the author of two minor classics and four other major books.
>
> — Robert Hemenway,
> "Zora Hurston and the Eatonville Anthropology,"
> in *The Harlem Renaissance Remembered*

O N AUGUST 15, 1973, I wake up just as the plane is lowering over Sanford, Florida, which means I am also looking down on Eatonville, Zora Neale Hurston's birthplace. I recognize it from Zora's description in *Mules and Men*: [1] "the city of five lakes, three croquet courts, three hundred brown skins, three hundred good swimmers, plenty guavas, two schools, and no jailhouse." Of course I cannot see the guavas, but the five lakes are still there, and it is the lakes I count as the plane prepares to land in Orlando.

---

[1] *Mules and Men*: Hurston's 1935 collection of stories about voodoo that she gathered while doing anthropological research among southern blacks.

From the air, Florida looks completely flat, and as we near the ground this impression does not change. This is the first time I have seen the interior of the state, which Zora wrote about so well, but there are the acres of orange groves, the sand, mangrove trees, and scrub pine that I know from her books. Getting off the plane I walk through the humid air of midday into the tacky but air-conditioned airport. I search for Charlotte Hunt, my companion on the Zora Hurston expedition. She lives in Winter Park, Florida, very near Eatonville, and is writing her graduate dissertation on Zora. I see her waving — a large, pleasant-faced woman in dark glasses. We have written to each other for several weeks, swapping our latest finds (mostly hers) on Zora, and trying to make sense out of the mass of information obtained (often erroneous or simply confusing) from Zora herself — through her stories and autobiography — and from people who wrote about her.

Eatonville has lived for such a long time in my imagination that I can hardly believe it will be found existing in its own right. But after twenty minutes on the expressway, Charlotte turns off and I see a small settlement of houses and stores set with no particular pattern in the sandy soil off the road. We stop in front of a neat gray building that has two fascinating signs: EATONVILLE POST OFFICE and EATONVILLE CITY HALL.

Inside the Eatonville City Hall half of the building, a slender, dark-brown-skin woman sits looking through letters on a desk. When she hears we are searching for anyone who might have known Zora Neale Hurston, she leans back in thought. Because I don't wish to inspire foot-dragging in people who might know something about Zora they're not sure they should tell, I have decided on a simple, but I feel profoundly *useful*, lie.

"I am Miss Hurston's niece," I prompt the young woman, who brings   5
her head down with a smile.

"I think Mrs. Moseley is about the only one still living who might remember her," she says.

"Do you mean *Mathilda* Moseley, the woman who tells those 'woman-is-smarter-than-man' lies in Zora's book?"

"Yes," says the young woman. "Mrs. Moseley is real old now, of course. But this time of day, she should be at home."

I stand at the counter looking down on her, the first Eatonville resident I have spoken to. Because of Zora's books, I feel I know something about her; at least I know what the town she grew up in was like years before she was born.

"Tell me something," I say. "Do the schools teach Zora's books here?"   10

"No," she says, "they don't. I don't think most people know anything about Zora Neale Hurston, or know about any of the great things she did. She was a fine lady. I've real all of her books myself, but I don't think many other folks in Eatonville have."

"Many of the church people around here, as I understand it," says

Charlotte in a murmured aside, "thought Zora was pretty loose. I don't think they appreciated her writing about them."

"Well," I say to the young woman, "thank you for your help." She clarifies her directions to Mrs. Moseley's house and smiles as Charlotte and I turn to go.

> The letter to Harper's does not expose a publisher's rejection of an un-known masterpiece, but it does reveal how the bright promise of the Harlem Renaissance deteriorated for many of the writers who shared in its exuberance. It also indicates the personal tragedy of Zora Neale Hurston: Barnard graduate, author of four novels, two books of folklore, one volume of autobiography, the most important collector of Afro-American folklore in America, reduced by poverty and circumstance to seek a publisher by unsolicited mail.
>
> — Robert Hemenway
>
> Zora Hurston was born in 1901, 1902, or 1903 — depending on how old she felt herself to be at the time someone asked.
>
> — Librarian, Beinecke Library,
> Yale University

The Moseley house is small and white and snug, its tiny yard nearly swallowed up by oleanders and hibiscus bushes. Charlotte and I knock on the door. I call out. But there is no answer. This strikes us as peculiar. We have had time to figure out an age for Mrs. Moseley — not dates or a number, just old. I am thinking of a quivery, bedridden invalid when we hear the car. We look behind us to see an old black-and-white Buick — paint peeling and grillwork rusty — pulling into the drive. A neat old lady in a purple dress and with white hair is straining at the wheel. She is frowning because Charlotte's car is in the way.

Mrs. Moseley looks at us suspiciously. "Yes, I knew Zora Neale," she 15 says, unsmilingly and with a rather cold stare at Charlotte (who, I imagine, feels very *white* at that moment), "but that was a long time ago, and I don't want to talk about it."

"Yes, ma'am," I murmur, bringing all my sympathy to bear on the situation.

"Not only that," Mrs. Moseley continues, "I've been sick. Been in the hospital for an operation. Ruptured artery. The doctors didn't believe I was going to live, but you see me alive, don't you?"

"Looking well, too," I comment.

Mrs. Moseley is out of her car. A thin, sprightly woman with nice gold-studded false teeth, uppers and lowers. I like her because she stands there *straight* beside her car, with a hand on her hip and her straw pocketbook on her arm. She wears white T-strap shoes with heels that show off her well-shaped legs.

"I'm eighty-two years old, you know," she says. "And I just can't 20
remember things the way I used to. Anyhow, Zora Neale left here to go to
school and she never really came back to live. She'd come here for material
for her books, but that was all. She spent most of her time down in South
Florida."

"You know, Mrs. Moseley, I saw your name in one of Zora's books."

"You did?" She looks at me with only slightly more interest. "I read
some of her books a long time ago, but then people got to borrowing and
borrowing and they borrowed them all away."

"I could send you a copy of everything that's been reprinted," I offer.
"Would you like me to do that?"

"No," says Mrs. Moseley promptly. "I don't read much any more.
Besides, all of that was *so* long ago. . . . "

Charlotte and I settle back against the car in the sun. Mrs. Moseley 25
tells us at length and with exact recall every step in her recent operation,
ending with: "What those doctors didn't know — when they were expecting
me to die (and they didn't even think I'd live long enough for them to have
to take out my stitches!) — is that Jesus is the best doctor, and if *He* says
for you to get well, that's all that counts."

With this philosophy, Charlotte and I murmur quick assent: being
Southerners and church bred, we have heard that belief before. But what
we learn from Mrs. Moseley is that she does not remember much beyond
the year 1938. She shows us a picture of her father and mother and says that
her father was Joe Clarke's brother. Joe Clarke, as every Zora Hurston reader
knows, was the first mayor of Eatonville; his fictional counterpart is Jody
Starks of *Their Eyes Were Watching God*. [2] We also get directions to where Joe
Clarke's store *was* — where Club Eaton is now. Club Eaton, a long orange-
beige nightspot we had seen on the main road, is apparently famous for the
good times in it regularly had by all. It is, perhaps, the modern equivalent
of the store porch, where all the men of Zora's childhood came to tell "lies,"
that is, black folk tales, that were "made and used on the spot," to take a
line from Zora. As for Zora's exact birthplace, Mrs. Moseley has no idea.

After I have commented on the healthy growth of her hibiscus bushes,
she becomes more talkative. She mentions how much she *loved* to dance,
when she was a young woman, and talks about how good her husband was.
When he was alive, she says, she was completely happy because he allowed
her to be completely free. "I was so free I had to pinch myself sometimes
to tell if I was a married woman."

Relaxed now, she tells us about going to school with Zora "Zora and I
went to the same school. It's called Hungerford High now. It *was* only to
the eighth grade. But our teachers were so good that by the time you left

[2] *Their Eyes Were Watching God*: One of Hurston's most famous works, this 1935 novel is set
in the Eatonville community.

you knew college subjects. When I went to Morris Brown in Atlanta, the teachers there were just teaching me the same things I had already learned right in Eatonville. I wrote Mama and told her I was going to come home and help her with her babies. I wasn't learning anything new."

"Tell me something, Mrs. Moseley," I ask. "Why do you suppose Zora was against integration? I read somewhere that she was against school desegregation because she felt it was an insult to black teachers."

"Oh, one of them [white people] came around asking me about integration. One day I was doing my shopping. I heard 'em over there talking about it in the store, about the schools. And I got on out of the way because I knew if they asked me, they wouldn't like what I was going to tell 'em. But they came up and asked me anyhow. 'What do you think about this integration?' one of them said. I acted like I had heard wrong. 'You're asking *me* what *I* think about integration?' I said. 'Well, as you can see, I'm just an old colored woman' — I was seventy-five or seventy-six then — 'and this is the first time anybody ever asked me about integration. And nobody asked my grandmother what she thought, either, but her daddy was one of you all.'" Mrs. Moseley seems satisfied with this memory of her rejoinder. She looks at Charlotte. "I have the blood of three races in my veins," she says belligerently, "white, black, and Indian, and nobody asked me *anything* before." 30

"Do you think living in Eatonville made integration less appealing to you?"

"Well, I can tell you this: I have lived in Eatonville all my life, and I've been in the governing of this town. I've been everything but mayor and I've been *assistant* mayor. Eatonville was and is an all-black town. We have our own police department, post office, and town hall. Our own school and good teachers. Do I need integration?

"They took over Goldsboro, because the black people who lived there never incorporated, like we did. And now I don't even know if any black folks live there. They built big houses up there around the lakes. But we didn't let that happen in Eatonville, and we don't sell land to just anybody. And you see, we're still here."

When we leave, Mrs. Moseley is standing by her car, waving. I think of the letter Roy Wilkins [3] wrote to a black newspaper blasting Zora Neale for her lack of enthusiasm about the integration of schools. I wonder if he knew the experience of Eatonville she was coming from. Not many black people in America have come from a self-contained, all-black community where loyalty and unity are taken for granted. A place where black pride is nothing new.

There is, however, one thing Mrs. Moseley said that bothered me. 35

---

[3] *Roy Wilkins*: Civil rights leader Roy Wilkins was executive director of the National Association for the Advancement of Colored People (NAACP) between 1965 and 1977.

"Tell me, Mrs. Moseley," I had asked, "why is it that thirteen years after Zora's death, no marker has been put on her grave?"

And Mrs. Moseley answered: "The reason she doesn't have a stone is because she wasn't buried here. She was buried down in South Florida somewhere. I don't think anybody really knew where she was."

> Only to reach a wider audience, need she ever write books — because she is a perfect book of entertainment in herself. In her youth she was always getting scholarships and things from wealthy white people, some of whom simply paid her just to sit around and represent the Negro race for them, she did it in such a racy fashion. She was full of sidesplitting anecdotes, humorous tales, and tragicomic stories, remembered out of her life in the South as a daughter of a traveling minister of God. She could make you laugh one minute and cry the next. To many of her white friends, no doubt, she was a perfect "darkie," in the nice meaning they give the term — that is, a naïve, childlike, sweet, humorous, and highly colored Negro.
>
> But Miss Hurston was clever, too — a student who didn't let college give her a broad "a" and who had great scorn for all pretensions, academic or otherwise. That is why she was such a fine folklore collector, able to go among the people and never act as if she had been to school at all. Almost nobody else could stop the average Harlemite on Lenox Avenue and measure his head with a strange-looking, anthropological device and not get bawled out for the attempt, except Zora, who used to stop anyone whose head looked interesting, and measure it.
>
> — Langston Hughes,
> *The Big Sea*

What does it matter what white folks must have thought about her?

— Student, black women writers class
Wellesley College

Mrs. Sarah Peek Patterson is a handsome, red-haired woman in her late forties, wearing orange slacks and gold earrings. She is the director of Lee-Peek Mortuary in Fort Pierce, the establishment that handled Zora's burial. Unlike most black funeral homes in Southern towns that sit like palaces among the general poverty, Lee-Peek has a run-down, *small* look. Perhaps this is because it is painted purple and white, as are its Cadillac chariots. These colors do not age well. The rooms are cluttered and grimy, and the bathroom is a tiny, stale-smelling prison, with a bottle of black hair dye (apparently used to touch up the hair of the corpses) dripping into the face bowl. Two pine burial boxes are resting in the bathtub.

Mrs. Patterson herself is pleasant and helpful.

"As I told you over the phone, Mrs. Patterson," I begin, shaking her hand and looking into her penny-brown eyes, "I am Zora Neale Hurston's niece, and I would like to have a marker put on her grave. You said, when I called you last week, that you could tell me where the grave is." 40

By this time I am, of course, completely into being Zora's niece, and the lie comes with perfect naturalness to my lips. Besides, as far as I'm concerned, she *is* my aunt — and that of all black people as well.

"She was buried in 1960," exclaims Mrs. Patterson. "That was when my father was running this funeral home. He's sick now or I'd let you talk to him. But I know where she's buried. She's in the old cemetery, the Garden of the Heavenly Rest, on Seventeenth Street. Just when you go in the gate there's a circle, and she's buried right in the middle of it. Hers is the only grave in that circle — because people don't bury in that cemetery any more."

She turns to a stocky, black-skinned woman in her thirties, wearing a green polo shirt and white jeans cut off at the knee. "This lady will show you where it is," she says.

"I can't tell you how much I appreciate this," I say to Mrs. Patterson, as I rise to go. "And could you tell me something else? You see, I never met my aunt. When she died, I was still a junior in high school. But could you tell me what she died of, and what kind of funeral she had?"

"I don't know exactly what she died of," Mrs. Patterson says. "I know   45
she didn't have any money. Folks took up a collection to bury her. . . . I believe she died of malnutrition."

"*Malnutrition?*"

Outside, in the blistering sun, I lean my head against Charlotte's even more blistering car top. The sting of the hot metal only intensifies my anger. "*Malnutrition,*" I manage to mutter. "Hell, our condition hasn't changed *any* since Phillis Wheatley's [4] time. *She* died of malnutrition!"

"Really?" says Charlotte. "I didn't know that."

One cannot overemphasize the extent of her commitment. It was so great that her marriage in the spring of 1927 to Herbert Sheen was short-lived. Although divorce did not come officially until 1931, the two separated amicably after only a few months, Hurston to continue her collecting, Sheen to attend Medical School. Hurston never married again.

— Robert Hemenway

"What is your name?" I ask the woman who has climbed into the back seat.

"Rosalee," she says. She has a rough, pleasant voice, as if she is a   50
singer who also smokes a lot. She is homely, and has an air of ready indifference.

"Another woman came by here wanting to see the grave," she says, lighting up a cigarette. "She was a little short, dumpty white lady from one of these Florida schools. Orlando or Daytona. But let me tell you something before we gets started. All I know is where the cemetery is. I don't know

[4] *Phillis Wheatley:* A Boston slave who was America's first black published poet (ca. 1754–1784) and who, like Hurston, died in poverty and obscurity. See Alice Walker's "In Search of Our Mothers' Gardens" in Part 2.

one thing about that grave. You better go back in and ask her to draw you a map."

A few moments later, with Mrs. Patterson's diagram of where the grave is, we head for the cemetery.

We drive past blocks of small, pastel-colored houses and turn right onto Seventeenth Street. At the very end, we reach a tall curving gate, with the words "Garden of the Heavenly Rest" fading into the stone. I expected, from Mrs. Patterson's small drawing, to find a small circle — which would have placed Zora's grave five or ten paces from the road. But the "circle" is over an acre large and looks more like an abandoned field. Tall weeds choke the dirt road and scrape against the sides of the car. It doesn't help either that I step out into an active ant hill.

"I don't know about y'all," I say, "but I don't even believe this." I am used to the haphazard cemetery-keeping that is traditional in most Southern black communities, but this neglect is staggering. As far as I can see there is nothing but bushes and weeds, some as tall as my waist. One grave is near the road, and Charlotte elects to investigate it. It is fairly clean, and belongs to someone who died in 1963.

Rosalee and I plunge into the weeds; I pull my long dress up to my hips. The weeds scratch my knees, and the insects have a feast. Looking back, I see Charlotte standing resolutely near the road.

"Aren't you coming?" I call.

"No," she calls back. "I'm from these parts and I know what's out there." She means snakes.

"Shit," I say, my whole life and the people I love flashing melodramatically before my eyes. Rosalee is a few yards to my right.

"How're you going to find anything out here?" she asks. And I stand still a few seconds, looking at the weeds. Some of them are quite pretty, with tiny yellow flowers. They are thick and healthy, but dead weeds under them have formed a thick gray carpet on the ground. A snake could be lying six inches from my big toe and I wouldn't see it. We move slowly, very slowly, our eyes alert, our legs trembly. It is hard to tell where the center of the circle is since the circle is not really round, but more like half of something round. There are things crackling and hissing in the grass. Sandspurs are sticking to the inside of my skirt. Sand and ants cover my feet. I look toward the road and notice that there are, indeed, *two* large curving stones, making an entrance and exit to the cemetery. I take my bearings from them and try to navigate to exact center. But the center of anything can be very large, and a grave is not a pinpoint. Finding the grave seems positively hopeless. There is only one thing to do:

"Zora!" I yell, as loud as I can (causing Rosalee to jump). "Are you out here?"

"If she is, I sho hope she don't answer you. If she do, I'm gone."

"Zora!" I call again. "I'm here. Are you?"

"If she is," grumbles Rosalee, "I hope she'll keep it to herself."

55

60

"Zora!" Then I start fussing with her. "I hope you don't think I'm going to stand out here all day, with these snakes watching me and these ants having a field day. In fact, I'm going to call you just one or two more times." On a clump of dried grass, near a small bushy tree, my eye falls on one of the largest bugs I have ever seen. It is on its back, and is as large as three of my fingers. I walk toward it, and yell "Zo-ra!" and my foot sinks into a hole. I look down. I am standing in a sunken rectangle that is about six feet long and about three or four feet wide. I look up to see where the two gates are.

"Well," I say, "this is the center, or approximately anyhow. It's also   65 the only sunken spot we've found. Doesn't this look like a grave to you?"

"For the sake of not going no farther through these bushes," Rosalee growls, "yes, it do."

"Wait a minute," I say, "I have to look around some more to be sure this is the only spot that resembles a grave. But you don't have to come."

Rosalee smiles — a grin, really — beautiful and tough.

"Naw," she says, "I feels sorry for you. If one of these snakes got ahold of you out here by yourself I'd feel *real* bad." She laughs. "I done come this far, I'll go on with you."

"Thank you, Rosalee," I say. "Zora thanks you too."   70

"Just as long as she don't try to tell me in person," she says, and together we walk down the field.

The gusto and flavor of Zora Neal[e] Hurston's storytelling, for example, long before the yarns were published in "Mules and Men" and other books, became a local legend which might . . . have spread further under different conditions. A tiny shift in the center of gravity could have made them best-sellers.

— Arna Bontemps,
Personals

Bitter over the rejection of her folklore's value, especially in the black community, frustrated by what she felt was her failure to convert the Afro-American world view into the forms of prose fiction, Hurston finally gave up.

— Robert Hemenway

When Charlotte and I drive up to the Merritt Monument Company, I immediately see the headstone I want.

"How much is this one?" I ask the young woman in charge, pointing to a tall black stone. It looks as majestic as Zora herself must have been when she was learning voodoo from those root doctors down in New Orleans.

"Oh, *that* one," she says, "that's our finest. That's Ebony Mist."

"Well, how much is it?"   75

"I don't know. But wait," she says, looking around in relief, "here comes somebody who'll know."

A small, sunburned man with squinty green eyes comes up. He must be the engraver, I think, because his eyes are contracted into slits, as if he has been keeping stone dust out of them for years.

"That's Ebony Mist," he says. "That's our best."

"How much is it?" I ask, beginning to realize I probably *can't* afford it.

He gives me a price that would feed a dozen Sahelian drought victims 80 for three years. I realize I must honor the dead, but between the dead great and the living starving, there is no choice.

"I have a lot of letters to be engraved," I say, standing by the plain gray marker I have chosen. It is pale and ordinary, not at all like Zora, and makes me momentarily angry that I am not rich.

We go into his office and I hand him a sheet of paper that has:

ZORA NEALE HURSTON
"A GENIUS OF THE SOUTH"
NOVELIST   FOLKLORIST
ANTHROPOLOGIST
1901   1960

"A genius of the South" is from one of Jean Toomer's[5] poems.

"Where is this grave?" the monument man asks. "If it's in a new cemetery, the stone has to be flat."

"Well, it's not a new cemetery and Zora — my aunt — doesn't need 85 anything flat, because with the weeds out there, you'd never be able to see it. You'll have to go out there with me."

He grunts.

"And take a long pole and 'sound' the spot," I add. "Because there's no way of telling it's a grave, except that it's sunken."

"Well," he says, after taking my money and writing up a receipt, in the full awareness that he's the only monument dealer for miles, "you take this flag" (he hands me a four-foot-long pole with a red-metal marker on top) "and take it out to the cemetery and put it where you think the grave is. It'll take us about three weeks to get the stone out there."

I wonder if he knows he is sending me to another confrontation with the snakes. He probably does. Charlotte has told me she will cut my leg and suck out the blood if I am bit.

"At least send me a photograph when it's done, won't you?" 90
He says he will.

Hurston's return to her folklore-collecting in December of 1927 was made possible by Mrs. R. Osgood Mason, an elderly white patron of the arts, who at various times also helped Langston Hughes, Alain Locke, Rich-

---

[5] *Jean Toomer* (1894–1967): Black poet and novelist who was one of the leading figures of the Harlem Renaissance.

mond Barthe, and Miguel Covarrubias. Hurston apparently came to her attention through the intercession of Locke, who frequently served as a kind of liaison between the young black talent and Mrs. Mason. The entire relationship between this woman and the Harlem Renaissance deserves extended study, for it represents much of the ambiguity involved in white patronage of black artists. All her artists were instructed to call her "God-mother"; there was a decided emphasis on the "primitive" aspects of black culture, apparently a holdover from Mrs. Mason's interest in the Plains Indians. In Hurston's case there were special restrictions imposed by her patron: although she was to be paid a handsome salary for her folklore collecting, she was to limit her correspondence and publish nothing of her research without prior approval.

— Robert Hemenway

You have to read the chapters Zora *left out* of her autobiography.

— Student, Special Collections Room
Beinecke Library, Yale University

Dr. Benton, a friend of Zora's and a practicing M.D. in Fort Pierce, is one of those old, good-looking men whom I always have trouble not liking. (It no longer bothers me that I may be constantly searching for father figures; by this time, I have found several and dearly enjoyed knowing them all.) He is shrewd, with steady brown eyes under hair that is almost white. He is probably in his seventies, but doesn't look it. He carries himself with dignity, and has cause to be proud of the new clinic where he now practices medicine. His nurse looks at us with suspicion, but Dr. Benton's eyes have the penetration of a scalpel cutting through skin. I guess right away that if he knows anything at all about Zora Hurston, he will not believe I am her niece.

"Eatonville?" Dr. Benton says, leaning forward in his chair, looking first at me, then at Charlotte. "Yes, I know Eatonville; I grew up not far from there. I knew the whole bunch of Zora's family." (He looks at the shape of my cheekbones, the size of my eyes, and the nappiness of my hair.) "I knew her daddy. The old man. He was a hard-working, Christian man. Did the best he could for his family. He was the mayor of Eatonville for a while, you know.

"My father was the mayor of Goldsboro. You probably never heard of it. It never incorporated like Eatonville did, and has just about disappeared. But Eatonville is still all black."

He pauses and looks at me. "And you're Zora's niece," he says wonderingly.

"Well," I say with shy dignity, yet with some tinge, I hope, of a   95
nineteenth-century blush, "I'm illegitimate. That's why I never knew Aunt Zora."

I love him for the way he comes to my rescue. "You're *not* illegitimate!" he cries, his eyes resting on me fondly. "All of us are God's children! Don't you even *think* such a thing!"

And I hate myself for lying to him. Still, I ask myself, would I have gotten this far toward getting the headstone and finding out about Zora Hurston's last days without telling my lie? Actually, I probably would have. But I don't like taking chances that could get me stranded in central Florida.

"Zora didn't get along with her family. I don't know why. Did you read her autobiography, *Dust Tracks on a Road?*" [6]

"Yes, I did," I say. "It pained me to see Zora pretending to be naïve and grateful about the old white 'Godmother' who helped finance her research, but I loved the part where she ran off from home after falling out with her brother's wife."

Dr. Benton nods. "When she got sick, I tried to get her to go back to   100 her family, but she refused. There wasn't any real hatred; they just never had gotten along and Zora wouldn't go to them. She didn't want to go to the county home, either, but she had to, because she couldn't do a thing for herself."

"I was surprised to learn she died of malnutrition."

Dr. Benton seems startled. "Zora *didn't* die of malnutrition," he says indignantly. "Where did you get that story from? She had a stroke and she died in the welfare home." He seems peculiarly upset, distressed, but sits back reflectively in his chair. "She was an incredible woman," he muses. "Sometimes when I closed my office, I'd go by her house and just talk to her for an hour or two. She was a well-read, well-traveled woman and always had her own ideas about what was going on. . . ."

"I never knew her, you know. Only some of Carl Van Vechten's [7] photographs and some newspaper photographs. . . . What did she look like?"

"When I knew her, in the fifties, she was a big woman, *erect.* Not quite as light as I am [Dr. Benton is dark beige], and about five foot, seven inches, and she weighed about two hundred pounds. Probably more. She . . ."

"What! Zora was *fat!* She wasn't, in Van Vechten's pictures!"   105

"Zora loved to eat," Dr. Benton says complacently. "She could sit down with a mound of ice cream and just eat and talk till it was all gone."

While Dr. Benton is talking, I recall that the Van Vechten pictures were taken when Zora was still a young woman. In them she appears tall, tan, and healthy. In later newspaper photographs — when she was in her forties — I remembered that she seemed heavier and several shades lighter. I reasoned that the earlier photographs were taken while she was busy collecting folklore materials in the hot Florida sun.

"She had high blood pressure. Her health wasn't good. . . . She used to live in one of my houses — on School Court Street. It's a block house.

[6] *Dust Tracks on a Road*: Hurston's autobiography, published in 1942.

[7] *Carl Van Vechten* (1880–1964): American novelist and critic who wrote about Harlem life.

. . . I don't recall the number. But my wife and I used to invite her over to the house for dinner. *She always ate well,*" he says emphatically.

"That's comforting to know," I say, wondering where Zora ate when she wasn't with the Bentons.

"Sometimes she would run out of groceries — after she got sick — and 110 she'd call me. 'Come over here and see 'bout me,' she'd say. And I'd take her shopping and buy her groceries.

"She was always studying. Her mind — before the stroke — just worked all the time. She was always going somewhere, too. She once went to Honduras to study something. And when she died, she was working on that book about Herod the Great. She was so intelligent! And really had perfect expressions. Her English was beautiful." (I suspect this is a clever way to let me know Zora herself didn't speak in the "black English" her characters used.)

"I used to read all of her books," Dr. Benton continues, "but it was a long time ago. I remember one about . . . it was called, I think, 'The Children of God' [*Their Eyes Were Watching God*], and I remember Janie and Teapot [Teacake] and the mad dog riding on the cow in that hurricane and bit old Teapot on the cheek. . . ."

I am delighted that he remembers even this much of the story, even if the names are wrong, but seeing his affection for Zora I feel I must ask him about her burial. "Did she *really* have a pauper's funeral?"

"She *didn't* have a pauper's funeral!" he says with great heat. "Everybody around here *loved* Zora."

"We just came back from ordering a headstone," I say quietly, because 115 he *is* an old man and the color is coming and going on his face, "but to tell the truth, I can't be positive what I found is the grave. All I know is the spot I found was the only grave-size hole in the area."

"I remember it wasn't near the road," says Dr. Benton, more calmly. "Some other lady came by here and we went out looking for the grave and I took a long iron stick and poked all over that part of the cemetery but we didn't find anything. She took some pictures of the general area. Do the weeds still come up to your knees?"

"And beyond," I murmur. This time there isn't any doubt. Dr. Benton feels ashamed.

As he walks us to our car, he continues to talk about Zora. "She couldn't really write much near the end. She had the stroke and it left her weak; her mind was affected. She couldn't think about anything for long.

"She came here from Daytona, I think. She owned a houseboat over there. When she came here, she sold it. She lived on that money, then she worked as a maid — for an article on maids she was writing — and she worked for the *Chronicle* writing the horoscope column.

"I think black people here in Florida got mad at her because she was for some politician they were against. She said this politician *built* schools for blacks while the one they wanted just talked about it. And although Zora wasn't egotistical, what she thought, she thought; and generally what she thought, she said."

When we leave Dr. Benton's office, I realize I have missed my plane back home to Jackson, Mississippi. That being so, Charlotte and I decide to find the house Zora lived in before she was taken to the county welfare home to die. From among her many notes, Charlotte locates a letter of Zora's she has copied that carries the address: 1734 School Court Street. We ask several people for directions. Finally, two old gentlemen in a dusty gray Plymouth offer to lead us there. School Court Street is not paved, and the road is full of mud puddles. It is dismal and squalid, redeemed only by the brightness of the late afternoon sun. Now I can understand what a "block" house is. It is a house shaped like a block, for one thing, surrounded by others just like it. Some houses are blue and some are green or yellow. Zora's is light green. They are tiny — about fifty by fifty feet, squatty with flat roofs. The house Zora lived in looks worse than the others, but that is its only distinction. It also has three ragged and dirty children sitting on the steps.

"Is this where y'all live?" I ask, aiming my camera.

"No, ma'am," they say in unison, looking at me earnestly. "We live over yonder. This Miss So-and-So's house; but she in the horspital."

We chatter inconsequentially while I take more pictures. A car drives up with a young black couple in it. They scowl fiercely at Charlotte and don't look at me with friendliness, either. They get out and stand in their doorway across the street. I go up to them to explain. "Did you know Zora Hurston used to live right across from you?" I ask.

"Who?" They stare at me blankly, then become curiously attentive, as if they think I made the name up. They are both Afroed and he is somberly dashikied. 125

I suddenly feel frail and exhausted. "It's too long a story," I say, "but tell me something: is there anybody on this street who's lived here for more than thirteen years?"

"That old man down there," the young man says, pointing. Sure enough, there is a man sitting on his steps three houses down. He has graying hair and is very neat, but there is a weakness about him. He reminds me of Mrs. Turner's husband in *Their Eyes Were Watching God*. He's rather "vanishing"-looking, as if his features have been sanded down. In the old days, before black was beautiful, he was probably considered attractive, because he has wavy hair and light-brown skin; but now, well, light skin has ceased to be its own reward.

After the preliminaries, there is only one thing I want to know: "Tell me something," I begin, looking down at Zora's house. "Did Zora like flowers?"

He looks at me queerly. "As a matter of fact," he says, looking regretfully at the bare, rough yard that surrounds her former house, "she was crazy about them. And she was a great gardener. She loved azaleas, and that running and blooming vine [morning-glories], and she really loved that night-smelling flower [gardenia]. She kept a vegetable garden year-round, too. She raised collards and tomatoes and things like that.

"Everyone in this community thought well of Miss Hurston. When she   130
died, people all up and down this street took up a collection for her burial. We put her away nice."

"Why didn't somebody put up a headstone?"

"Well, you know, one was never requested. Her and her family didn't get along. They didn't even come to the funeral."

"And did she live down there by herself?"

"Yes, until they took her away. She lived with — just her and her companion, Sport."

My ears perk up. "Who?"   135

"Sport, you know, her dog. He was her only companion. He was a big brown-and-white dog."

When I walk back to the car, Charlotte is talking to the young couple on the porch. They are relaxed and smiling.

"I told them about the famous lady who used to live across the street from them," says Charlotte as we drive off. "Of course they had no idea Zora ever lived, let alone that she lived across the street. I think I'll send some of her books to them."

"That's real kind of you," I say.

> I am not tragically colored. There is no great sorrow dammed up in my soul, nor lurking behind my eyes. I do not mind at all. I do not belong to the sobbing school of Negrohood who hold that nature somehow has given them a lowdown dirty deal and whose feelings are all hurt about it. . . . No, I do not weep at the world — I am too busy sharpening my oyster knife.
>
> — Zora Neale Hurston,
> "How It Feels To Be Colored Me,"
> *World Tomorrow*, 1928

There are times — and finding Zora Hurston's grave was one of them   140
— when normal responses of grief, horror, and so on do not make sense because they bear no real relation to the depth of the emotion one feels. It was impossible for me to cry when I saw the field full of weeds where Zora is. Partly this is because I have come to know Zora through her books and she was not a teary sort of person herself; but partly, too, it is because there is a point at which even grief feels absurd. And at this point, laughter gushes up to retrieve sanity.

It is only later, when the pain is not so direct a threat to one's own existence, that what was learned in that moment of comical lunacy is understood. Such moments rob us of both youth and vanity. But perhaps they are also times when greater disciplines are born.

FROM READING AND REREADING

1. Walker has interspersed her narrative with various critical comments about Zora Neale Hurston. Why do you think she shaped her essay this way? Of what importance is the opening comment from Robert Hemenway? What do these comments provide the reader that her narrative does not? How do they serve as a kind of counterpoint to the rhythm of her essay?

2. Notice how often Walker chooses to interview people in this essay. What interview techniques does she use to get people to talk? In what ways is her "lie" an important part of the process? In what ways does it seem integral to the tone and atmosphere of the entire essay?

3. Zora Neale Hurston's political views went against the grain of the civil rights movement of the fifties and sixties. She held opinions that today might not be considered "politically correct." What are some of these opinions and how does Alice Walker handle them?

From Reading to Writing

1. Both Joan Didion and Stephen Jay Gould actually meet their respective heroes, if only briefly. Have you ever met a celebrity (or someone you consider famous, such as a politician or a professional athlete) in person? Consider your meeting and write an essay describing it. Did you learn anything about the person that you might not have otherwise?

2. In attempting to reconstruct the personalities of their heroines, Virginia Woolf and Alice Walker are entirely dependent upon information derived from others. Write an essay in which you discuss how each writer uses her sources. How does each writer decide which sources are most reliable and which least? To what extent do they trust the personal writings of their respective subjects? In what ways do Woolf's and Walker's methods of interpretation differ? In what ways are they similar?

3. Annie Dillard and E. B. White each offers a character description of someone they knew and admired, someone they learned something important from. Consider a similar person in your own life who has achieved some degree of prominence — a teacher, a coach, a religious instructor, or some other leader — and write a personal essay in which you vividly describe both the person and what that person taught you.

4

Teaching and Learning

GEORGE ORWELL
St. Cyprian's

Part 1, "Moments of Insight," contains the first section of George Orwell's "Such, Such Were the Joys," his bitter reminiscence of St. Cyprian's, the snobbish private prep school Orwell attended between 1911 and 1916. In the second section of this long, autobiographical essay, Orwell describes the type of education he received there. As one of the poorer scholarship students, who were expected to be a credit to the school, Orwell was subjected to a rigorous course of study that emphasized a rote mastery of history and the classics at the expense of other subjects. Orwell never forgot his experiences at St. Cyprian's and retained a lifelong hatred for its educational methods and for its dictatorial headmaster and his wife, a couple the students nicknamed Sambo and Flip.

S T CYPRIAN's was an expensive and snobbish school which was in process of becoming more snobbish, and, I imagine, more expensive. The public school with which it had special connections was Harrow, but during my time an increasing proportion of the boys went on to Eton. Most of them were the children of rich parents, but on the whole they were the un-aristocratic rich, the sort of people who live in huge shrubberied houses in Bournemouth or Richmond, and who have cars and butlers but not country estates. There were a few exotics among them — some South American boys, sons of Argentine beef barons, one or two Russians, and even a Siamese prince, or someone who was described as a prince.

Sambo had two great ambitions. One was to attract titled boys to the school, and the other was to train up pupils to win scholarships at public schools, above all at Eton. He did, towards the end of my time, succeed in getting hold of two boys with real English titles. One of them, I remember, was a wretched drivelling little creature, almost an albino, peering upwards out of weak eyes, with a long nose at the end of which a dewdrop always seemed to be trembling. Sambo always gave these boys their titles when mentioning them to a third person, and for their first few days he actually addressed them to their faces as "Lord So-and-so." Needless to say he found ways of drawing attention to them when any visitor was being shown round the school. Once, I remember, the little fair-haired boy had a choking fit at dinner, and a stream of snot ran out of his nose on to his plate in a way horrible to see. Any lesser person would have been called a dirty little beast and ordered out of the room instantly: but Sambo and Flip laughed it off in a "boys will be boys" spirit.

All the very rich boys were more or less undisguisedly favoured. The school still had a faint suggestion of the Victorian "private academy" with its "parlour boarders," and when I later read about that kind of school in Thackeray I immediately saw the resemblance. The rich boys had milk and biscuits in the middle of the morning, they were given riding lessons once or twice a week, Flip mothered them and called them by their Christian names, and above all they were never caned. Apart from the South Americans, whose parents were safely distant, I doubt whether Sambo ever caned any boy whose father's income was much above £2,000 a year. But he was sometimes willing to sacrifice financial profit to scholastic prestige. Occasionally, by special arrangement, he would take at greatly reduced fees some boy who seemed likely to win scholarships and thus bring credit on the school. It was on these terms that I was at St Cyprian's myself: otherwise my parents could not have afforded to send me to so expensive a school.

I did not at first understand that I was being taken at reduced fees; it was only when I was about eleven that Flip and Sambo began throwing the fact in my teeth. For my first two or three years I went through the ordinary educational mill: then, soon after I had started Greek (one started Latin at eight, Greek at ten), I moved into the scholarship class, which was taught, so far as classics went, largely by Sambo himself. Over a period of two or three years the scholarship boys were crammed with learning as cynically as a goose is crammed for Christmas. And with what learning! This business of making a gifted boy's career depend on a competitive examination, taken when he is only twelve or thirteen, is an evil thing at best, but there do appear to be preparatory schools which send scholars to Eton, Winchester, etc. without teaching them to see everything in terms of marks. At St Cyprian's the whole process was frankly a preparation for a sort of confidence trick. Your job was to learn exactly those things that would give an examiner the impression that you knew more than you did know, and as far as possible to avoid burdening your brain with anything else. Subjects which lacked examination-value, such as geography, were almost completely neglected, mathematics was also neglected if you were a "classical," science was not taught in any form — indeed it was so despised that even an interest in natural history was discouraged — and even the books you were encouraged to read in your spare time were chosen with one eye on the "English paper." Latin and Greek, the main scholarship subjects, were what counted, but even these were deliberately taught in a flashy, unsound way. We never, for example, read right through even a single book of a Greek or Latin author: we merely read short passages which were picked out because they were the kind of thing likely to be set as an "unseen translation." During the last year or so before we went up for our scholarships, most of our time was spent in simply working our way through the scholarship papers of previous years. Sambo had sheaves of these in his possession, from every one of the major public schools. But the greatest outrage of all was the teaching of history.

There was in those days a piece of nonsense called the Harrow History 5
Prize, an annual competition for which many preparatory schools entered. It
was a tradition for St Cyprian's to win it every year, as well we might, for
we had mugged up every paper that had been set since the competition
started, and the supply of possible questions was not inexhaustible. They
were the kind of stupid question that is answered by rapping out a name or
a quotation. Who plundered the Begams? Who was beheaded in an open
boat? Who caught the Whigs bathing and ran away with their clothes? Almost
all our historical teaching was on this level. History was a series of unrelated,
unintelligible but — in some way that was never explained to us — important
facts with resounding phrases tied to them. Disraeli brought peace with
honour. Clive was astonished at his moderation. Pitt called in the New World
to redress the balance of the Old. And the dates, and the mnemonic devices!
(Did you know, for example, that the initial letters of "A black Negress was
my aunt: there's her house behind the barn" are also the initial letters of the
battles in the Wars of the Roses?) Flip, who "took" the higher forms in
history, revelled in this kind of thing. I recall positive orgies of dates, with
the keener boys leaping up and down in their places in their eagerness to
shout out the right answers, and at the same time not feeling the faintest
interest in the meaning of the mysterious events they were naming.
    "1587?"
    "Massacre of St Bartholomew!"
    "1707?"
    "Death of Aurangzeeb!"
    "1713?"
    "Treaty of Utrecht!"
    "1773?"
    "Boston Tea Party!"
    "1520?"
    "Oo, Mum, please Mum — " 15
    "Please, Mum, please, Mum! Let me tell him, Mum!"
    "Well! 1520?"
    "Field of the Cloth of Gold!"
    And so on.
But history and such secondary subjects were not bad fun. It was in 20
"classics" that the real strain came. Looking back, I realise that I then worked
harder than I have ever done since, and yet at the time it never seemed
possible to make quite the effort that was demanded of one. We would sit
round the long, shiny table, made of some very pale-coloured hard wood,
with Sambo goading, threatening, exhorting, sometimes joking, very occasionally praising, but always prodding, prodding away at one's mind to keep
it up to the right pitch of concentration, as one might keep a sleepy person
awake by sticking pins into him.
    "Go on, you little slacker! Go on, you idle, worthless little boy! The

whole trouble with you is that you're bone and horn idle. You eat too much, that's why. You wolf down enormous meals, and then when you come here you're half asleep. Go on, now, put your back into it. You're not *thinking*. Your brain doesn't sweat."

He would tap away at one's skull with his silver pencil, which, in my memory, seems to have been about the size of a banana, and which certainly was heavy enough to raise a bump: or he would pull the short hairs round one's ears, or, occasionally, reach out under the table and kick one's shin. On some days nothing seemed to go right, and then it would be: "All right, then, I know what you want. You've been asking for it the whole morning. Come along, you useless little slacker. Come into the study." And then whack, whack, whack, whack, and back one would come, red-wealed and smarting — in later years Sambo had abandoned his riding-crop in favour of a thin rattan cane which hurt very much more — to settle down to work again. This did not happen very often, but I do remember, more than once, being led out of the room in the middle of a Latin sentence, receiving a beating and then going straight ahead with the same sentence, just like that. It is a mistake to think such methods do not work. They work very well for their special purpose. Indeed, I doubt whether classical education ever has been or can be successfully carried on without corporal punishment. The boys themselves believed in its efficacy. There was a boy named Beacham, with no brains to speak of, but evidently in acute need of a scholarship. Sambo was flogging him towards the goal as one might do with a foundered horse. He went up for a scholarship at Uppingham, came back with a consciousness of having done badly, and a day or two later received a severe beating for idleness. "I wish I'd had that caning before I went up for the exam," he said sadly — a remark which I felt to be contemptible, but which I perfectly well understood.

The boys of the scholarship class were not all treated alike. If a boy were the son of rich parents to whom the saving of fees was not all-important, Sambo would goad him along in a comparatively fatherly way, with jokes and digs in the ribs and perhaps an occasional tap with the pencil, but no hair-pulling and no caning. It was the poor but "clever" boys who suffered. Our brains were a gold-mine in which he had sunk money, and the dividends must be squeezed out of us. Long before I had grasped the nature of my financial relationship with Sambo, I had been made to understand that I was not on the same footing as most of the other boys. In effect there were three castes in the school. There was the minority with an aristocratic or millionaire background, there were the children of the ordinary suburban rich, who made up the bulk of the school, and there were a few underlings like myself, the sons of clergyman, Indian civil servants, struggling widows and the like. These poorer ones were discouraged from going in for "extras" such as shooting and carpentry, and were humiliated over clothes and petty possessions. I never, for instance, succeeded in getting a cricket bat of my own, because "Your parents wouldn't be able to afford it." This phrase pursued me throughout my schooldays. At St Cyprian's we were not allowed to keep the money we brought back with us, but had to "give it in" on the first day of term, and then from time to time were allowed to spend it under supervision. I and similarly placed boys were always choked off from buying expensive toys like model aeroplanes, even if the necessary money stood to our credit. Flip, in particular, seemed to aim consciously at inculcating a humble outlook in the poorer boys. "Do you think that's the sort of thing a boy like you should buy?" I remember her saying to somebody — and she said this in front of the whole school: "You know you're not going to grow up with money, don't you? Your people aren't rich. You must learn to be sensible. Don't get above yourself!" There was also the weekly pocket-money, which we took out in sweets, dispensed by Flip from a large table. The millionaires had sixpence a week, but the normal sum was threepence. I and one or two others were only allowed twopence. My parents had not given instructions to this effect, and the saving of a penny a week could not conceivably have made any difference to them: it was a mark of status. Worse yet was the detail of the birthday cakes. It was usual for each boy, on his birthday, to have a large iced cake with candles, which was shared out at tea between the whole school. It was provided as a matter of routine and went on his parents' bill. I never had such a cake, though my parents would have paid for it readily enough. Year after year, never daring to ask, I would miserably hope that this year a cake would appear. Once or twice I even rashly pretended to my companions that this time I *was* going to have a cake. Then came tea-time, and no cake, which did not make me more popular.

Very early it was impressed upon me that I had no chance of a decent future unless I won a scholarship at a public school. Either I won my scholarship, or I must leave school at fourteen and become, in Sambo's favourite phrase "a little office boy at forty pounds a year." In my circumstances it was natural that I should believe this. Indeed, it was universally taken for granted at St Cyprian's that unless you went to a "good" public school (and only about fifteen schools came under this heading) you were ruined for life. It is not easy to convey to a grown-up person the sense of strain, of nerving oneself for some terrible, all-deciding combat, as the date of the examination crept nearer — eleven years old, twelve years old, then thirteen, the fatal year itself! Over a period of about two years, I do not think there was ever a day when "the exam," as I called it, was quite out of my waking thoughts. In my prayers it figured invariably: and whenever I got the bigger portion of a wishbone, or picked up a horseshoe, or bowed seven times to the new moon, or succeeded in passing through a wishing-gate without touching the sides, then the wish I earned by doing so went on "the exam" as a matter of course. And yet curiously enough I was also tormented by an almost irresistible impulse *not* to work. There were days when my heart sickened at the labours ahead of me, and I stood stupid as an animal before the elementary difficulties. In the holidays, also, I could not work. Some of the scholarship boys received extra tuition from a certain Mr Batchelor, a likeable, very hairy man who wore shaggy suits and lived in a typical bachelor's "den" — book-lined walls, overwhelming stench of tobacco — somewhere in the town. During the holidays Mr Batchelor used to send us extracts from Latin authors to translate, and we were supposed to send back a wad of work once a week. Somehow I could not do it. The empty paper and the black Latin dictionary lying on the table, the consciousness of a plain duty shirked, poisoned my leisure, but somehow I could not start, and by the end of the holidays I would only have sent Mr Batchelor fifty or a hundred lines. Undoubtedly part of the reason was that Sambo and his cane were far away. But in term-time, also, I would go through periods of idleness and stupidity when I would sink deeper and deeper into disgrace and even achieve a sort of feeble, snivelling defiance, fully conscious of my guilt and yet unable or unwilling — I could not be sure which — to do any better. Then Sambo or Flip would send for me, and this time it would not even be a caning.

Flip would search me with her baleful eyes. (What colour were those 25 eyes, I wonder? I remember them as green, but actually no human being has green eyes. Perhaps they were hazel.) She would start off in her peculiar, wheedling, bullying style, which never failed to get right through one's guard and score a hit on one's better nature.

"I don't think it's awfully decent of you to behave like this, is it? Do you think it's quite playing the game by your mother and father to go on idling your time away, week after week, month after month? Do you *want* to throw all your chances away? You know your people aren't rich, don't you? You know they can't afford the same things as other boys' parents. How are they to send you to a public school if you don't win a scholarship? I know how proud your mother is of you. Do you *want* to let her down?"

"I don't think he wants to go to a public school any longer," Sambo would say, addressing himself to Flip with a pretence that I was not there. "I think he's given up that idea. He wants to be a little office boy at forty pounds a year."

The horrible sensation of tears — a swelling in the breast, a tickling behind the nose — would already have assailed me. Flip would bring out her ace of trumps:

"And do you think it's quite fair to *us*, the way you're behaving? After all we've done for you? You *do* know what we've done for you, don't you?" Her eyes would pierce deep into me, and though she never said it straight out, I did know. "We've had you here all these years — we even had you here for a week in the holidays so that Mr Batchelor could coach you. We don't *want* to have to send you away, you know, but we can't keep a boy here just to eat up our food, term after term. *I* don't think it's very straight, the way you're behaving. Do you?"

I never had any answer except a miserable "No, Mum," or "Yes, 30 Mum," as the case might be. Evidently it was *not* straight, the way I was behaving. And at some point or other the unwanted tear would always force its way out of the corner of my eye, roll down my nose, and splash.

Flip never said in plain words that I was a non-paying pupil, no doubt because vague phrases like "all we've done for you" had a deeper emotional appeal. Sambo, who did not aspire to be loved by his pupils, put it more brutally, though, as was usual with him, in pompous language. "You are living on my bounty" was his favourite phrase in this context. At least once I listened to these words between blows of the cane. I must say that these scenes were not frequent, and except on one occasion they did not take place in the presence of other boys. In public I was reminded that I was poor and that my parents "wouldn't be able to afford" this or that, but I was not actually reminded of my dependent position. It was a final unanswerable argument, to be brought forth like an instrument of torture when my work became exceptionally bad.

To grasp the effect of this kind of thing on a child of ten or twelve, one has to remember that the child has little sense of proportion or probability. A child may be a mass of egoism and rebelliousness, but it has no accumulated experience to give it confidence in its own judgements. On the whole it will accept what it is told, and it will believe in the most fantastic way in the knowledge and powers of the adults surrounding it. Here is an example.

I have said that at St Cyprian's we were not allowed to keep our own money. However, it was possible to hold back a shilling or two, and sometimes I used furtively to buy sweets which I kept hidden in the loose ivy on the playing-field wall. One day when I had been sent on an errand I went into a sweet-shop a mile or more from the school and bought some chocolates. As I came out of the shop I saw on the opposite pavement a small sharp-faced man who seemed to be staring very hard at my school cap. Instantly a horrible fear went through me. There could be no doubt as to who the man was. He was a spy placed there by Sambo! I turned away unconcernedly, and then, as though my legs were doing it of their own accord, broke into a clumsy run. But when I got round the next corner I forced myself to walk again, for to run was a sign of guilt, and obviously there would be other spies posted here and there about the town. All that day and the next I waited for the summons to the study, and was surprised when it did not come. It did not seem to me strange that the headmaster of a private school should dispose of an army of informers, and I did not even imagine that he would have to pay them. I assumed that any adult, inside the school or outside, would collaborate voluntarily in preventing us from breaking the rules. Sambo was all-powerful; it was natural that his agents should be everywhere. When this episode happened I do not think I can have been less than twelve years old.

I hated Sambo and Flip, with a sort of shamefaced, remorseful hatred, but it did not occur to me to doubt their judgement. When they told me that I must either win a public-school scholarship or become an office boy at fourteen, I believed that those were the unavoidable alternatives before me. And above all, I believed Sambo and Flip when they told me they were my benefactors. I see now, of course, that from Sambo's point of view I was a good speculation. He sank money in me, and he looked to get it back in the form of prestige. If I had "gone off," as promising boys sometimes do, I imagine that he would have got rid of me swiftly. As it was I won him two scholarships when the time came, and no doubt he made full use of them in his prospectuses. But it is difficult for a child to realise that a school is primarily a commercial venture. A child believes that the school exists to educate and that the schoolmaster disciplines him either for his own good, or from a love of bullying. Flip and Sambo had chosen to befriend me, and their friendship included canings, reproaches and humiliations, which were good for me and saved me from an office stool. That was their version, and I believed in it. It was therefore clear that I owed them a vast debt of gratitude. But I was *not* grateful, as I very well knew. On the contrary, I hated both of them. I could not control my subjective feelings, and I could not conceal them from myself. But it is wicked, is it not, to hate your benefactors? So I was taught, and so I believed. A child accepts the codes of behaviour that are presented to it, even when it breaks them. From the age of eight, or even earlier, the consciousness of sin was never far away from me. If I contrived to seem callous and defiant, it was only a thin cover over a mass of shame and dismay. All through my boyhood I had a profound conviction that I was no good, that I was wasting my time, wrecking my talents, behaving with monstrous folly and wickedness and ingratitude — and all this, it seemed, was inescapable, because I lived among laws which were absolute, like the law of gravity, but which it was not possible for me to keep.

FROM READING TO REREADING

1. In a later section of "Such, Such Were the Joys," Orwell claims that "Whoever writes about his childhood must beware of exaggeration and self-pity." Orwell is clearly someone who wants to avoid both of these autobiographical pitfalls. How does he try to do this? To what extent do you think he succeeds?

2. Orwell was clearly a successful student and performed precisely as St. Cyprian's hoped he would — he eventually won two scholarships. Why doesn't he take pride in this fact? Can you find any traces of boastfulness or self-congratulation in the selection?

3. Of the subjects taught at St. Cyprian's, Orwell focuses most on history. What does he object to about the way it is taught? Look again at the question and answer dialogue introduced by paragraph 5. What point is Orwell making by using this dialogue? How do you think Orwell prefers that history be taught?

CYNTHIA OZICK
Washington Square, 1946

One's first day at college is always a memorable event. In the following autobiographical essay, Cynthia Ozick recalls her first trip to New York University (which is in the section of Greenwich Village known as Washington Square) on the opening day of spring term in February 1946. Seventeen and a half years old, she was entering college just after the Second World War, along with scores of veterans who had been admitted as part of the G.I. Bill, legislation that enabled thousands of American men and women to obtain a college degree. The essay was first published in 1985 as "The First Day of School: Washington Square 1946" in Harper's *magazine.*

> . . . this portion of New York appears to many persons the most delectable. It has a kind of established repose which is not of frequent occurrence in other quarters of the long, shrill city; it has a riper, richer, more honorable look than any of the upper ramifications of the great longitudinal thoroughfare — the look of having had something of a social history.
>
> — Henry James, *Washington Square*

I FIRST CAME down to Washington Square on a colorless February morning in 1946. I was seventeen and a half years old and was carrying my lunch in a brown paper bag, just as I had carried it to high school only a month before. It was — I thought it was — the opening day of spring term at Washington Square College, my initiation into my freshman year at New York University. All I knew of N.Y.U. then was that my science-minded brother had gone there; he had written from the Army that I ought to go there too. With master-of-ceremonies zest he described the Browsing Room on the second floor of the Main Building as a paradisal chamber whose bookish loungers leafed languidly through magazines and exchanged high-principled witticisms between classes. It had the sound of a carpeted Olympian club in Oliver Wendell Holmes's Boston, Hub of the Universe, strewn with leather chairs and delectable old copies of *The Yellow Book*.[1]

On that day I had never heard of Oliver Wendell Holmes or *The Yellow Book*, and Washington Square was a faraway bower where wounded birds fell out of trees. My brother had once brought home from Washington Square

---

[1] *Oliver Wendell Holmes* (1809–1894): Physician, Harvard professor, poet, and one of the most popular American essayists of his time; *The Yellow Book*: A fashionable nineteenth-century British literary quarterly.

173

Park a baby sparrow with a broken leg, to be nurtured back to flight. It died instead, emitting in its last hours melancholy faint cheeps, and leaving behind a dense recognition of the minute explicitness of mortality. All the same, in the February grayness Washington Square had the allure of the celestial unknown. A sparrow might die, but my own life was luminously new: I felt my youth like a nimbus.

Which dissolves into the dun gauze of a low and sullen city sky. And here I am flying out of the Lexington Avenue subway at Astor Place, just a few yards from Wanamaker's, here I am turning the corner past a secondhand bookstore and a union hall; already late, I begin walking very fast toward the park. The air is smoky with New York winter grit, and on clogged Broadway a mob of trucks shifts squawking gears. But there, just ahead, crisscrossed by paths under high branches, is Washington Square; and on a single side-walk, three clear omens; or call them riddles, intricate and redolent. These I will disclose in a moment, but before that you must push open the heavy brass-and-glass doors of the Main Building, and come with me, at a hard and panting pace, into the lobby of Washington Square College on the earliest morning of the freshman year.

On the left, a bank of elevators. Straight ahead, a long burnished corridor, spooky as a lit tunnel. And empty, all empty. I can hear my solitary footsteps reverberate, as in a radio mystery drama: they lead me up a short staircase into a big dark ghost-town cafeteria. My brother's letter, along with an account of the physics and chemistry laboratories (I will never see them), has already explained that this place is called Commons — and here my heart will learn to shake with the merciless newness of life. But not today; today there is nothing. Tables and chairs squat in dead silhouette. I race back through a silent maze of halls and stairways to the brass-and-glass doors — there stands a lonely guard. From the pocket of my coat I retrieve a scrap with a classroom number on it and ask the way. The guard announces in a sly croak that the first day of school is not yet; come back tomorrow, he says.

A dumb bad joke: I'm humiliated. I've journeyed the whole way down 5 from the end of the line — Pelham Bay, in the northeast Bronx — to find myself in desolation, all because of a muddle: Tuesday isn't Wednesday. The nimbus of expectation fades off. The lunch bag in my fist takes on a greasy sadness. I'm not ready to dive back into the subway — I'll have a look around.

Across the street from the Main Building, the three omens. First, a pretzel man with a cart. He's wearing a sweater, a cap that keeps him faceless — he's nothing but the shadows of his creases — and wool gloves with the fingertips cut off. He never moves; he might as well be made of papier-mâché, set up and left out in the open since spring. There are now almost no pretzels for sale, and this gives me a chance to inspect the construction of his bare pretzel poles. The pretzels are hooked over a column of gray cardboard cylinders, themselves looped around a stick, the way horseshoes drop around a post. The cardboard cylinders are the insides of toilet paper rolls.

The pretzel man is rooted between a Chock Full o' Nuts (that's the second omen) and a newsstand (that's the third).

The Chock Full: the doors are like fans, whirling remnants of conversation. *She will marry him. She will not marry him.* Fragrance of coffee and hot chocolate. *We can prove that the senses are partial and unreliable vehicles of information, but who is to say that reason is not equally the product of human limitation?* Powdered doughnut sugar on their lips.

Attached to a candy store, the newsstand. Copies of *Partisan Review:* the table of the gods. Jean Stafford, Mary McCarthy, Elizabeth Hardwick, Irving Howe, Delmore Schwartz, Alfred Kazin, Clement Greenberg, Stephen Spender, William Phillips, John Berryman, Saul Bellow, Philip Rahv, Richard Chase, Randall Jarrell, Simone de Beauvoir, Karl Shapiro, George Orwell! I don't know a single one of these names, but I feel their small conflagration flaming in the gray street: the succulent hotness of their promise. I mean to penetrate every one of them. Since all the money I have is my subway fare — two nickels — I don't buy a copy (the price of *Partisan* in 1946 is fifty cents); I pass on.

I pass on to the row of houses on the north side of the Square. Henry   10
James was born in one of these, but I don't know that either. Still, they are plainly old, though no longer aristocratic: haughty last-century shabbies with shut eyelids, built of rosy-ripe respectable brick, down on their luck. Across the park bulks Judson Church, with its squat squarish bell tower; by the end of the week I will be languishing at the margins of a basketball game in its basement, forlorn in my blue left-over-from-high-school gym suit and mooning over Emily Dickinson:

There's a certain Slant of light,
Winter Afternoons —
That oppresses, like the Heft
Of Cathedral Tunes —

There is more I don't know. I don't know that W. H. Auden lives just down *there,* and might at any moment be seen striding toward home under his tall, rumpled hunch; I don't know that Marianne Moore is only up the block, her doffed tricorn resting on her bedroom dresser. It's Greenwich Village — I know *that* — no more than twenty years after Edna St. Vincent Millay[2] has sent the music of her name (her best, perhaps her only, poem) into the bohemian streets: bohemia, the honey pot of poets.

On that first day in the tea-leafed cup of the town I am ignorant,

[2] *W.H. Auden, Marianne Moore, and Edna St. Vincent Millay:* A few of the famous poets who lived in Greenwich Village.

ignorant! But the three riddle-omens are soon to erupt, and all of them together will illumine Washington Square.

Begin with the benches in the Park. Here, side by side with students and their loose-leafs, lean or lie the shadows of the pretzel man, his creased ghosts or doubles: all those pitiables, half-women and half-men, neither awake nor asleep, the discountable, the repudiated, the unseen. No more notice is taken of any of them than of a scudding fragment of newspaper in the path. Even then, even so long ago, the benches of Washington Square are pimpled with this hell-tossed crew, these Mad Margarets and Cokey Joes, these volcanic coughers, shakers, groaners, tremblers, droolers, blasphemers, these public urinators with vomitous breath and rusted teeth-stumps, dead-eyed and self-abandoned, dragging their makeshift junkyard shoes, their buttonless layers of raggedy ratfur. The pretzel man with his toilet paper rolls conjures and spews them all — he is a loftier brother to these citizens of the lower pox, he is guardian of the garden of the jettisoned. They rattle along all the seams of Washington Square. They are the pickled City, the true and universal City-below-Cities, the wolfish vinegar-Babylon that dogs the spittled skirts of bohemia. The toilet paper rolls are the temple-columns of this sacred grove.

Next, the whirling doors of Chock Full o' Nuts. Here is the market-place of Washington Square, its bazaar, its roiling gossip parlor, its match-maker's office and arena — the outermost wing, so to speak, evolved from the Commons. On a day like today, when the Commons is closed, the Chock Full is thronged with extra power, a cello making up for a missing viola. Until now, the fire of my vitals has been for the imperious tragedians of the *Aeneid;* I have lived in the narrow throat of poetry. Another year or so of this oblivion, until at last I am hammer-struck with the shock of Europe's skull, the bled planet of death camp and war. Eleanor Roosevelt has not yet written her famous column announcing the discovery of Anne Frank's diary. The term "cold war" is new. The Commons, like the college itself, is over-crowded, veterans in their pragmatic thirties mingling with the reluctant dreamy young. And the Commons is convulsed with politics: a march to the docks is organized, no one knows by whom, to protest the arrival of Walter Gieseking, the German musician who flourished among Nazis. The Com-munists — two or three readily recognizable cantankerous zealots — stomp through with their daily leaflets and sneers. There is even a Monarchist, a small poker-faced rectangle of a man with secretive tireless eyes who, when approached for his views, always demands, in perfect Bronx tones, the restoration of his king. The engaged girls — how many of them there seem to be! — flash their rings and tangle their ankles in their long New Look skirts. There is no feminism and no feminists; I am, I think, the only one. The Commons is a tide: it washes up the cold war, it washes up the engaged girls' rings, it washes up the several philosophers and the numerous poets.

The philosophers are all Existentialists; the poets are all influenced by "The Waste Land." When the Commons overflows, the engaged girls cross the street to show their rings at the Chock Full.

Call it density, call it intensity, call it continuity: call it, finally, society. 15
The Commons belongs to the satirists. Here, one afternoon, is Alfred Chester, holding up a hair, a single strand, before a crowd. (He will one day write stories and novels. He will die young.) "What is that hair?" I innocently ask, having come late on the scene. "A pubic hair," he replies, and I feel as Virginia Woolf did when she declared human nature to have "changed in or about December 1910" — soon after her sister Vanessa explained away a spot on her dress as "semen."

In or about February 1946 human nature does not change; it keeps on. On my bedroom wall I tack — cut out from *Life* magazine — the wildest Picasso I can find: a face that is also a belly. Mr. George E. Mutch, a lyrical young English teacher twenty-seven years old, writes on the blackboard: "When lilacs last in the dooryard bloom'd," and "Bare, ruined choirs, where late the sweet birds sang," and "A green thought in a green shade"; he tells us to burn, like Pater, [3] with a hard, gemlike flame. Another English teacher — his name is Emerson — compares Walt Whitman to a plumber; next year he will shoot himself in a wood. The initial letters of Washington Square College are a device to recall three of the Seven Deadly Sins: Wantonness, Sloth, Covetousness. In Commons they argue the efficacy of the orgone box. Eda Lou Walton, sprightly as a bird, knows all the Village bards, and is a Village bard herself. Sidney Hook is an intellectual rumble in the logical middle distance. Homer Watt, chairman of the English Department, is the very soul who, in a far-off time of bewitchment, hired Thomas Wolfe. [4]

And so, in February 1946, I make my first purchase of a "real" book — which is to say, not for the classroom. It is displayed in the window of the secondhand bookstore between the Astor Place subway station and the union hall, and for weeks I have been coveting it: *Of Time and the River.* I am transfigured; I am pierced through with rapture; skipping gym, I sit among morning mists on a windy bench a foot from the stench of Mad Margaret, sinking into that cascading syrup: "Man's youth is a wonderful thing: It is so full of anguish and of magic and he never comes to know it as it is, until it is gone from him forever. . . . And what is the essence of that strange and bitter miracle of life which we feel so poignantly, so unutterably, with such a bitter pain and joy, when we are young?" Thomas Wolfe, lost, and by the wind grieved, ghost, come back again! In Washington Square I

---

[3] *Pater:* Walter Pater (1839–1894), English critic and essayist noted for his aesthetic philosophy and literary style.

[4] *Thomas Wolfe* (1900–1938): American novelist who wrote *Look Homeward, Angel* (1929) and *Of Time and the River* (1935). His once-enormous reputation has severely declined.

am appareled in the "numb exultant secrecies of fog, fog-numb air filled with solemn joy of nameless and impending prophecy, an ancient yellow light, the old smoke-ochre of the morning. . . ."

The smoke-ochre of the morning. Ah, you who have flung Thomas Wolfe, along with your strange and magical youth, onto the ash heap of juvenilia and excess, myself among you, isn't this a lovely phrase still? It rises out of the old pavements of Washington Square as delicately colored as an eggshell.

The veterans in their pragmatic thirties are nailed to Need; they have families and futures to attend to. When Mr. George E. Mutch exhorts them to burn with a hard, gemlike flame, [5] and writes across the blackboard the line that reveals his own name,

> The world is too much with us; late and soon,
> Getting and spending, we lay waste our powers, [6]

one of the veterans heckles, "What about getting a Buick, what about spending a buck?" Chester, at sixteen, is a whole year younger than I; he has transparent eyes and a rosebud mouth, and is in love with a poet named Diana. He has already found his way to the Village bars, and keeps in his wallet Truman Capote's secret telephone number. We tie our scarves tight against the cold and walk up and down Fourth Avenue, winding in and out of the rows of secondhand bookshops crammed one against the other. The proprietors sit reading their wares and never look up. The books in all their thousands smell sleepily of cellar. Our envy of them is speckled with longing; our longing is sick with envy. We are the sorrowful literary young.

Every day, month after month, I hang around the newsstand near the candy store, drilling through the enigmatic pages of *Partisan Review*. I still haven't bought a copy; I still can't understand a word. I don't know what "cold war" means. Who is Trotsky? I haven't read *Ulysses;* my adolescent phantoms are rowing in the ablative absolute with *pius* Aeneas. I'm in my mind's cradle, veiled by the exultant secrecies of fog.

Washington Square will wake me. In a lecture room in the Main Building, Dylan Thomas will cry his webwork syllables. Afterward he'll warm himself at the White Horse Tavern. Across the corridor I will see Sidney Hook plain. I will read the Bhagavad Gita and Catullus and Lessing, and, in Hebrew, a novel eerily called *Whither?* It will be years and years before I am smart enough, worldly enough, to read Alfred Kazin and Mary McCarthy.

In the spring, all of worldly Washington Square will wake up to the luster of little green leaves.

[5] *gemlike flame*: An allusion to one of Walter Pater's (see footnote 3) famous quotations.

[6] *The world* . . . : The opening lines of William Wordsworth's sonnet, "The World Is Too Much With Us."

FROM READING TO REREADING

1. An interesting aspect of Ozick's essay is the way she is always careful to separate what she knows now from what she knew then. Why is this an important consideration in autobiography? How does it affect your assessment of Ozick's reliability as a narrator?

2. Note that Ozick doesn't mention New York University in her title but refers only to Washington Square. Of what significance to the essay is it that she showed up for classes on the wrong day? How does that fact shape the emphasis of the essay?

3. In the sixth paragraph Ozick introduces "the three omens." What are they and why does she call them "omens"? They are certainly enigmatic; what interpretation can you give them? What are they omens *of?* How do they affect the mood of the essay?

JAMES BALDWIN

1963

A Talk to Teachers

Lectures or talks are often occasions for essays. Nearly all of Ralph Waldo Emerson's essays, for example, began as lectures. The lecturer usually addresses a specific audience and usually employs certain rhetorical conventions (such as parallelism and repetition) in order to be clearly understood. Sometimes the writer in revising the lecture as an essay will eliminate many of the oral devices, since such devices are often less desirable in writing than in speech. But in "A Talk to Teachers," James Baldwin, an experienced speaker with a gift for oratory, decided to retain the oral qualities of his original lecture. The result is a less polished prose than Baldwin ordinarily published; but, on the other hand, his language comes across with a sense of passion and urgency that might otherwise be lost in a meticulous revision. The talk is an angry one; Baldwin apparently did not want to appear "composed." It was delivered in 1963 as "The Negro Child — His Self-Image," and though many of Baldwin's references may seem dated (the references to Khrushchev and the cold war, for example), its concern with minority education and a truly democratic curriculum are as relevant today as they were some thirty years ago at the height of the civil rights movement.

L ET'S BEGIN by saying that we are living through a very dangerous time. Everyone in this room is in one way or another aware of that. We are in a revolutionary situation, no matter how unpopular that word has become in this country. The society in which we live is desperately menaced, not by Khrushchev, but from within. So any citizen of this country who figures himself as responsible — and particularly those of you who deal with the minds and hearts of young people — must be prepared to "go for broke." Or to put it another way, you must understand that in the attempt to correct so many generations of bad faith and cruelty, when it is operating not only in the classroom but in society, you will meet the most fantastic, the most brutal, and the most determined resistance. There is no point in pretending that this won't happen.

Since I am talking to schoolteachers and I am not a teacher myself, and in some ways am fairly easily intimidated, I beg you to let me leave that and go back to what I think to be the entire purpose of education in the first place. It would seem to me that when a child is born, if I'm the child's parent, it is my obligation and my high duty to civilize that child. Man is a social animal. He cannot exist without a society. A society, in turn, depends on certain things which everyone within that society takes for granted. Now, the crucial paradox which confronts us here is that the whole process of education occurs within a social framework and is designed to perpetuate the aims of society. Thus, for example, the boys and girls who were born during the era of the Third Reich, when educated to the purposes of the Third Reich, became barbarians. The paradox of education is precisely this — that as one begins to become conscious one begins to examine the society in which he is being educated. The purpose of education, finally, is to create in a person the ability to look at the world for himself, to make his own decisions, to say to himself this is black or this is white, to decide for himself whether there is a God in heaven or not. To ask questions of the universe, and then learn to live with those questions, is the way he achieves his own identity. But no society is really anxious to have that kind of person around. What societies really, ideally, want is a citizenry which will simply obey the rules of society. If a society succeeds in this, that society is about to perish. The obligation of anyone who thinks of himself as responsible is to examine society and try to change it and to fight it — at no matter what risk. This is the only hope society has. This is the only way societies change.

Now, if what I have tried to sketch has any validity, it becomes thoroughly clear, at least to me, that any Negro who is born in this country and undergoes the American educational system runs the risk of becoming schizophrenic. On the one hand he is born in the shadow of the stars and stripes and he is assured it represents a nation which has never lost a war. He pledges allegiance to that flag which guarantees "liberty and justice for all." He is part of a country in which anyone can become president, and so forth. But on the other hand he is also assured by his country and his countrymen that he has never contributed anything to civilization — that his past is nothing more than a record of humiliations gladly endured. He is assured by the republic that he, his father, his mother, and his ancestors were happy, shiftless, watermelon-eating darkies who loved Mr. Charlie and Miss Ann, that the value he has as a black man is proven by one thing only — his devotion to white people. If you think I am exaggerating, examine the myths which proliferate in this country about Negroes.

All this enters the child's consciousness much sooner than we as adults would like to think it does. As adults, we are easily fooled because we are so anxious to be fooled. But children are very different. Children, not yet aware that it is dangerous to look too deeply at anything, look at everything, look at each other, and draw their own conclusions. They don't have the vocabulary to express what they see, and we, their elders, know how to intimidate them very easily and very soon. But a black child, looking at the world around him, though he cannot know quite what to make of it, is aware that there is a reason why his mother works so hard, why his father is always on edge. He is aware that there is some reason why, if he sits down in the front of the bus, his father or mother slaps him and drags him to the back of the bus. He is aware that there is some terrible weight on his parents' shoulders which menaces him. And it isn't long — in fact it begins when he is in school — before he discovers the shape of his oppression.

Let us say that the child is seven years old and I am his father, and I 5 decide to take him to the zoo, or to Madison Square Garden, or to the U.N. Building, or to any of the tremendous monuments we find all over New York. We get into a bus and we go from where I live on 131st Street and Seventh Avenue downtown through the park and we get into New York City, which is not Harlem. Now, where the boy lives — even if it is a housing project — is in an undesirable neighborhood. If he lives in one of those housing projects of which everyone in New York is so proud, he has at the front door, if not closer, the pimps, the whores, the junkies — in a word, the danger of life in the ghetto. And the child knows this, though he doesn't know why.

I still remember my first sight of New York. It was really another city when I was born — where I was born. We looked down over the Park Avenue streetcar tracks. It was Park Avenue, but I didn't know what Park Avenue meant *downtown*. The Park Avenue I grew up on, which is still standing, is dark and dirty. No one would dream of opening a Tiffany's on that Park Avenue, and when you go downtown you discover that you are literally in the white world. It is rich — or at least it looks rich. It is clean — because they collect garbage downtown. There are doormen. People walk about as though they owned where they are — and indeed they do. And it's a great shock. It's very hard to relate yourself to this. You don't know what it means. You know — you know instinctively — that none of this is for you. You know this before you are told. And who is it for and who is paying for it? And why isn't it for you?

Later on when you become a grocery boy or messenger and you try to enter one of those buildings a man says, "Go to the back door." Still later, if you happen by some odd chance to have a friend in one of those buildings, the man says, "Where's your package?" Now this by no means is the core of the matter. What I'm trying to get at is that by this time the Negro child has had, effectively, almost all the doors of opportunity slammed in his face, and there are very few things he can do about it. He can more or less accept it with an absolutely inarticulate and dangerous rage inside — all the more dangerous because it is never expressed. It is precisely those silent people whom white people see every day of their lives — I mean your porter and your maid, who never say anything more than "Yes, Sir" and "No, Ma'am." They will tell you it's raining if that is what you want to hear, and they will tell you the sun is shining if *that* is what you want to hear. They really hate you — really hate you because in their eyes (and they're right) you stand between them and life. I want to come back to that in a moment. It is the most sinister of the facts, I think, which we now face.

There is something else the Negro child can do, too. Every street boy — and I was a street boy, so I know — looking at the society which has produced him, looking at the standards of that society which are not honored by anybody, looking at your churches and the government and the politicians, understands that this structure is operated for someone else's benefit — not for his. And there's no reason in it for him. If he is really cunning, really ruthless, really strong — and many of us are — he becomes a kind of criminal. He becomes a kind of criminal because that's the only way he can live. Harlem and every ghetto in this city — every ghetto in this country — is full of people who live outside the law. They wouldn't dream of calling a policeman. They wouldn't, for a moment, listen to any of those professions of which we are so proud on the Fourth of July. They have turned away from this country forever and totally. They live by their wits and really long to see the day when the entire structure comes down.

The point of all this is that black men were brought here as a source of cheap labor. They were indispensable to the economy. In order to justify the fact that men were treated as though they were animals, the white republic had to brainwash itself into believing that they were, indeed, animals and *deserved* to be treated like animals. Therefore it is almost impossible for any Negro child to discover anything about his actual history. The reason is that this "animal," once he suspects his own worth, once he starts believing that he is a man, has begun to attack the entire power structure. This is why America has spent such a long time keeping the Negro in his place. What I am trying to suggest to you is that it was not an accident, it was not an act of God, it was not done by well-meaning people muddling into something which they didn't understand. It was a deliberate policy hammered into place in order to make money from black flesh. And now, in 1963, because we have never faced this fact, we are in intolerable trouble.

The Reconstruction, as I read the evidence, was a bargain between the North and South to this effect: "We've liberated them from the land — and delivered them to the bosses." When we left Mississippi to come North we did not come to freedom. We came to the bottom of the labor market, and we are still there. Even the Depression of the 1930s failed to make a dent in Negroes' relationship to white workers in the labor unions. Even today, so brainwashed is this republic that people seriously ask in what they suppose to be good faith, "What does the Negro want?" I've heard a great many asinine questions in my life, but that is perhaps the most asinine and perhaps the most insulting. But the point here is that people who ask that question, thinking that they ask it in good faith, are really the victims of this conspiracy to make Negroes believe they are less than human.

In order for me to live, I decided very early that some mistake had been made somewhere. I was not a "nigger" even though you called me one. But if I was a "nigger" in your eyes, there was something about *you* — there was something *you* needed. I had to realize when I was very young that I was none of those things I was told I was. I was not, for example, happy. I never touched a watermelon for all kinds of reasons that had been invented by white people, and I knew enough about life by this time to understand that whatever you invent, whatever you project, is you! So where we are now is that a whole country of people believe I'm a "nigger," and I *don't,* and the battle's on! Because if I am not what I've been told I am, then it means that *you're* not what you thought *you* were *either*! And that is the crisis.

It is not really a "Negro revolution" that is upsetting the country. What is upsetting the country is a sense of its own identity. If, for example, one managed to change the curriculum in all the schools so that Negroes learned more about themselves and their real contributions to this culture, you would be liberating not only Negroes, you'd be liberating white people who know nothing about their own history. And the reason is that if you are compelled to lie about one aspect of anybody's history, you must lie about it all. If you have to lie about my real role here, if you have to pretend that I hoed all that cotton just because I loved you, then you have done something to yourself. You are mad.

Now let's go back a minute. I talked earlier about those silent people — the porter and the maid — who, as I said, don't look up at the sky if you ask them if it is raining, but look into your face. My ancestors and I were very well trained. We understood very early that this was not a Christian nation. It didn't matter what you said or how often you went to church. My father and my mother and my grandfather and my grandmother knew that Christians didn't act this way. It was as simple as that. And if that was so there was no point in dealing with white people in terms of their own moral professions, for they were not going to honor them. What one did was to turn away, smiling all the time, and tell white people what they wanted to hear. But people always accuse you of reckless talk when you say this.

All this means that there are in this country tremendous reservoirs of bitterness which have never been able to find an outlet, but may find an outlet soon. It means that well-meaning white liberals place themselves in great danger when they try to deal with Negroes as though they were missionaries. It means, in brief, that a great price is demanded to liberate all those silent people so that they can breathe for the first time and *tell* you what they think of you. And a price is demanded to liberate all those white children — some of them near forty — who have never grown up, and who never will grow up, because they have no sense of their identity.

What passes for identity in America is a series of myths about one's 15 heroic ancestors. It's astounding to me, for example, that so many people really appear to believe that the country was founded by a band of heroes who wanted to be free. That happens not to be true. What happened was that some people left Europe because they couldn't stay there any longer and had to go someplace else to make it. That's all. They were hungry, they were poor, they were convicts. Those who were making it in England, for example, did not get on the *Mayflower.* That's how the country was settled. Not by Gary Cooper. Yet we have a whole race of people, a whole republic, who believe the myths to the point where even today they select political representatives, as far as I can tell, by how closely they resemble Gary Cooper. Now this is dangerously infantile, and it shows in every level of national life. When I was living in Europe, for example, one of the worst revelations to me was the way Americans walked around Europe buying this and buying that and insulting everybody — not even out of malice, just because they didn't know any better. Well, that is the way they have always treated me. They weren't cruel, they just didn't know you were alive. They didn't know you had any feelings.

What I am trying to suggest here is that in the doing of all this for 100 years or more, it is the American white man who has long since lost his grip on reality. In some peculiar way, having created this myth about Negroes, and the myth about his own history, he created myths about the world so that, for example, he was astounded that some people could prefer Castro, astounded that there are people in the world who don't go into hiding when they hear the word "Communism," astounded that Communism is one of the realities of the twentieth century which we will not overcome by pretending that it does not exist. The political level in this country now, on the part of the people who should know better, is abysmal.

The Bible says somewhere that where there is no vision the people perish. I don't think anyone can doubt that in this country today we are menaced — intolerably menaced — by a lack of vision.

It is inconceivable that a sovereign people should continue, as we do so abjectly, to say, "I can't do anything about it. It's the government." The government is the creation of the people. It is responsible to the people. And the people are responsible for it. No American has the right to allow the present government to say, when Negro children are being bombed and hosed and shot and beaten all over the Deep South, that there is nothing we can do about it. There must have been a day in this country's life when the bombing of the children in Sunday School would have created a public uproar and endangered the life of a Governor Wallace. It happened here and there was no public uproar.

I began by saying that one of the paradoxes of education was that precisely at the point when you begin to develop a conscience, you must find yourself at war with your society. It is your responsibility to change society if you think of yourself as an educated person. And on the basis of the evidence — the moral and political evidence — one is compelled to say that this is a backward society. Now if I were a teacher in this school, or any Negro school, and I was dealing with Negro children, who were in my care only a few hours of every day and would then return to their homes and to the streets, children who have an apprehension of their future which with every hour grows grimmer and darker, I would try to teach them — I would try to make them know — that those streets, those houses, those dangers, those agonies by which they are surrounded, are criminal. I would try to make each child know that these things are the results of a criminal conspiracy to destroy him. I would teach him that if he intends to get to be a man, he must at once decide that he is stronger than this conspiracy and that he must never make his peace with it. And that one of his weapons for refusing to make his peace with it and for destroying it depends on what he decides he is worth. I would teach him that there are currently very few standards in this country which are worth a man's respect. That it is up to him to begin to change these standards for the sake of the life and the health of the country. I would suggest to him that the popular culture — as represented, for example, on television and in comic books and in movies — is based on fantasies created by very ill people, and he must be aware that these are fantasies that have nothing to do with reality. I would teach him that the press he reads is not as free as it says it is — and that he can do something about that, too. I would try to make him know that just as American history is longer, larger, more various, more beautiful, and more terrible than anything anyone has ever said about it, so is the world larger, more daring, more beautiful and more terrible, but principally larger — and that it belongs to him. I would teach him that he doesn't have to be bound by the expediencies of any given administration, any given policy, any given morality; that he has the right and the necessity to examine everything. I would try to show him that one has not learned anything about Castro when one says, "He is a Communist." This is a way of his learning something about Castro, something about Cuba, something, in time, about the world. I would suggest to him that he is living, at the moment, in an enormous province. America is not the world and if America is going to become a nation, she must find a way — and this child must help her to find a way to use the tremendous potential and tremendous energy which this child represents. If this country does not find a way to use that energy, it will be destroyed by that energy.

FROM READING TO REREADING

1. Baldwin uses many expressions that are more appropriate to a speech or talk than to a written essay. Go through the essay and identify these expressions. How do they affect your response? What happens if you eliminate them or rewrite them?

2. Baldwin begins his "Talk" by admitting that he is "fairly easily intimidated." Yet his speech — angry and threatening — hardly sounds like that of an intimidated person. How do you explain this?

3. Like George Orwell in the opening selection of this part, Baldwin is concerned with the way history is taught. In what ways are their objections similar? What connection does Baldwin find between history and identity? In his opinion, how has the teaching of American history distorted our national identity?

LEWIS THOMAS
How to Fix the Premedical Curriculum

What would happen if colleges scrapped their premed programs and medical schools began to base their admissions on a knowledge of Latin, Greek, literature, philosophy, and foreign language? We'd have better doctors, better colleges, and a better all-around curriculum, argues Lewis Thomas in this provocative essay. As a physician and a professor of medicine, Dr. Thomas, in his best-selling essay collections, adroitly balances a specialist's grasp of biomedical topics with a humanistic knowledge of classical languages, music, and literature. "How to Fix the Premedical Curriculum" first appeared in 1979.

THE INFLUENCE of the modern medical school on liberal-arts education in this country over the last decade has been baleful and malign, nothing less. The admission policies of the medical schools are at the root of the trouble. If something is not done quickly to change these, all the joy of going to college will have been destroyed, not just for that growing majority of undergraduate students who draw breath only to become doctors, but for everyone else, all the students, and all the faculty as well.

The medical schools used to say they wanted applicants as broadly educated as possible, and they used to mean it. The first two years of medical school were given over entirely to the basic biomedical sciences, and almost all entering students got their first close glimpse of science in those years. Three chemistry courses, physics, and some sort of biology were all that were required from the colleges. Students were encouraged by the rhetoric of medical-school catalogues to major in such nonscience disciplines as history, English, philosophy. Not many did so; almost all premedical students in recent generations have had their majors in chemistry or biology. But anyway, they were authorized to spread around in other fields if they wished.

There is still some talk in medical deans' offices about the need for general culture, but nobody really means it, and certainly the premedical students don't believe it. They concentrate on science.

They concentrate on science with a fury, and they live for grades. If there are courses in the humanities that can be taken without risk to class standing they will line up for these, but they will not get into anything tough except science. The so-called social sciences have become extremely popular as stand-ins for traditional learning.

The atmosphere of the liberal-arts college is being poisoned by premed- 5

187

ical students. It is not the fault of the students, who do not start out as a necessarily bad lot. They behave as they do in the firm belief that if they behave any otherwise they won't get into medical school.

I have a suggestion, requiring for its implementation the following announcement from the deans of all the medical schools: henceforth, any applicant who is self-labeled as a "premed," distinguishable by his course selection from his classmates, will have his dossier placed in the third stack of three. Membership in a "premedical society" will, by itself, be grounds for rejection. Any college possessing something called a "premedical curriculum," or maintaining offices for people called "premedical advisers," will be excluded from recognition by the medical schools.

Now as to grades and class standing. There is obviously no way of ignoring these as criteria for acceptance, but it is the grades *in general* that should be weighed. And, since so much of the medical-school curriculum is, or ought to be, narrowly concerned with biomedical science, more attention should be paid to the success of students in other, nonscience disciplines before they are admitted, in order to assure the scope of intellect needed for a physician's work.

Hence, if there are to be MCAT tests, the science part ought to be made the briefest, and weigh the least. A knowledge of literature and languages ought to be the major test, and the scariest. History should be tested, with rigor.

The best thing would be to get rid of the MCATs, once and for all, and rely instead, wholly, on the judgment of the college faculties.

You could do this if there were some central, core discipline, universal within the curricula of all the colleges, which could be used for evaluating the free range of a student's mind, his tenacity and resolve, his innate capacity for the understanding of human beings, and his affection for the human condition. For this purpose, I propose that classical Greek be restored as the centerpiece of undergraduate education. The loss of Homeric and Attic[1] Greek from American college life was one of this century's disasters. Putting it back where it once was would quickly make up for the dispiriting impact which generations of spotty Greek in translation have inflicted on modern thought. The capacity to read Homer's language closely enough to sense the terrifying poetry in some of the lines could serve as a shrewd test for the qualities of mind and character needed in a physician.

If everyone had to master Greek, the college students aspiring to medical school would be placed on the same footing as everyone else, and their identifiability as a separate group would be blurred, to everyone's advantage. Moreover, the currently depressing drift on some campuses toward special courses for prelaw students, and even prebusiness students, might be inhibited before more damage is done.

Latin should be put back as well, but not if it is handled, as it ought

[1] *Homeric and Attic*: Two historical periods of ancient Greek civilization.

to be, by the secondary schools. If Horace[2] has been absorbed prior to college, so much for Latin. But Greek is a proper discipline for the college mind.

English, history, the literature of at least two foreign languages, and philosophy should come near the top of the list, just below Classics, as basic requirements, and applicants for medical school should be told that their grades in these courses will count more than anything else.

Students should know that if they take summer work as volunteers in the local community hospital, as ward aides or laboratory assistants, this will not necessarily be held against them, but neither will it help.

Finally, the colleges should have much more of a say about who goes on to medical school. If they know, as they should, the students who are typically bright and also respected, this judgment should carry the heaviest weight for admission. If they elect to use criteria other than numerical class standing for recommending applicants, this evaluation should hold.

The first and most obvious beneficiaries of this new policy would be the college students themselves. There would no longer be, anywhere where they could be recognized as a coherent group, the "premeds," that most detestable of all cliques eating away at the heart of the college. Next to benefit would be the college faculties, once again in possession of the destiny of their own curriculum, for better or worse. And next in line, but perhaps benefiting the most of all, are the basic-science faculties of the medical schools, who would once again be facing classrooms of students who are ready to be startled and excited by a totally new and unfamiliar body of knowledge, eager to learn, unpreoccupied by the notions of relevance that are paralyzing the minds of today's first-year medical students already so surfeited by science that they want to start practicing psychiatry in the first trimester of the first year.

Society would be the ultimate beneficiary. We could look forward to a generation of doctors who have learned as much as anyone can learn, in our colleges and universities, about how human beings have always lived out their lives. Over the bedrock of knowledge about our civilization, the medical schools could then construct as solid a structure of medical science as can be built, but the bedrock would always be there, holding everything else upright.

[2] *Horace* (65–8 B.C.): Latin poet considered one of the world's greatest lyric poets.

FROM READING TO REREADING

1. Lewis Thomas has nothing good to say about premed programs. Why does he dislike them? Why does he think they are harmful not just to premed students but to the university as a whole?

2. Thomas clearly finds a relation between the study of classics and the performance of medicine. What is it? Why does he think his proposed curriculum would lead to better doctors?

3. Do you think Dr. Thomas's proposal would ever be implemented? What academic and professional resistance would it encounter? Does Thomas anticipate such resistance? Given the enormous obstacles Thomas's proposal would be met with, one might argue that his essay is mainly wishful thinking. How serious do you think he is?

STEPHEN JAY GOULD

The Dinosaur Rip-off

As an essayist, Stephen Jay Gould is a master at changing directions: he can start an essay on one topic and then surprise us by suddenly transforming it into another topic, one that at first appears unrelated but turns out to be amazingly connected. "The Dinosaur Rip-off" is a good example of Gould's structural ingenuity: it starts off with a humorous account of a fashionable children's trend — all those dinosaur games, puzzles, T-shirts, cereals, and countless other items — but concludes with a serious critique of American education. The essay first appeared in Natural History *magazine in 1989.*

W E LOVE occasional reversals of established order, both to defuse the tension of inequity and to infuse a bit of variety into our lives. Consider the medieval feast of fools (where slaves could be masters, in jest and only for a moment), Sadie Hawkins Day, and the genre of quiz that supplies the answer and asks a contestant to reconstruct the question. I begin this essay in such a spirit by giving my answer to a question that has surpassed all others (except, perhaps, "Where is human evolution going?") in my catalogue of inquiries from people who love natural history. My answer, unfortunately, must be: "Damned if I know" — which won't help you much in trying to guess the question. So I'll reveal the question without further ado: "What's behind the great dinosaur mania that's been sweeping the country during the past few years?"

Readers will scarcely need my words to document the phenomenon, for we are all surrounded by dinosaur tote bags, lunch boxes, pens and pencils, underpants, ties, and T-shirts that say "bossosaurus" or "secretary-osaurus," as the case may be. You can buy dinosaur-egg soap to encourage your kids to take a bath, a rocking stegosaurus for indoor recreation (a mere 800 bucks from F.A.O. Schwarz), a brontosaurus bank to encourage thrift, or a dinosaur growth chart to hang on the wall and measure your tyke's progress toward the N.B.A. In Key West, where dinosaurs have edged out flamingos as icons of kitsch, I even saw dinosaur toilet paper with a different creature on each perforated segment — providing quite a sense of power, I suppose, when used for its customary purpose. (This reminded me of the best attempt I ever encountered for defusing the Irish situation. I once stayed in a small motel in Eire where the bathrooms had two rolls of toilet paper — one green, the other orange.)

I offer no definitive answer to the cause of this mania, but I can at least document a fact strongly relevant to the solution. Perhaps dinosaur

Where the wild things are?

Max

not normal; can't see powerful   imagination

mania is intrinsic and endemic, a necessary and permanent fact of life (once the fossils had been discovered and properly characterized); perhaps dinosaurs act as the trigger for a deep Jungian archetype [1] of the soul; perhaps they rank as incarnations of primal fears and fascinations, programmed into our brains as the dragons of Eden. But these highfalutin suggestions cannot suffice for the simple reason that dinosaurs have been well documented throughout our century, while few people granted them more than passing notice before the recent craze hit.

Dinosaur trading cards

I can testify to the previous status of dinosaurs among the arcana of our culture, for I was a kiddie dinosaur nut in the late 1940s when nobody gave a damn. I fell in love with the great skeletons at the American Museum of Natural History and then, with all the passion of youth, sought collateral material with thoroughness and avidity. I would pounce on any reinforcement of my greatest interest — a Sinclair Oil logo or a hokey concrete tyrannosaur bestriding (like a colossus) Hole 15 at the local miniature golf course. There sure wasn't much to find — a few overpriced brass figures and a book or two by Roy Chapman Andrews and Ned Colbert, all hard to get anywhere outside the Museum shop. Representations in pop culture were equally scarce, ranging little beyond King Kong versus the pteranodon and Alley Oop riding a brontosaurus.

Always portrayed together on T.V.

One story will indicate both the frustration of a young adept in a world   5
of ignorance and the depth of that ignorance itself. At age nine or so, in the Catskills at one of those innumerable summer camps with an Indian name, I got into a furious argument with a bunkmate over the old issue of whether humans and dinosaurs ever inhabited the earth together. We agreed — bad, bad mistake — to abide by the judgment of the first adult claiming to know the answer, and we bet the camp currency, a chocolate bar, on the outcome. We asked all the counselors and staff, but none had ever heard of a brontosaurus. At parents' weekend, his came and mine didn't. We asked his father, who assured us that of course dinosaurs and people lived together; just look at Alley Oop. I paid — and seethed — and still seethe. This could not happen today. Anyone — a few "scientific creationists" excepted — would both know the answer and give you the latest rundown on theories for the extinction of dinosaurs. [2]

All this I tell for humor, but a part of the story isn't so funny. Kiddie culture can be cruel and fiercely anti-intellectual. I survived because I wasn't hopeless at punchball, and I won some respect for my knowledge of baseball

---

[1] *archetype*: Psychologist Carl Jung introduced the concept of archetypes — unconscious "primordial images" that are often expressed in myths, literature, and dreams.

[2] I was too optimistic. Never overestimate the depth of our anti-intellectual traditions! A week after I published this essay, results of a comprehensive survey showed that about 30 percent of American adults accept the probable contemporaneity of humans and dinosaurs. Still, our times are better than before. Seventy percent of that camp could have answered our inquiry before parental arrival. [Gould's note]

stats. But any kid with a passionate interest in science was a wonk, a square, a dweeb, a doofus, or a geek (I don't remember what word held sway at the time, but one item in that particular litany of cruelty is always in vogue). I was taunted by many classmates as peculiar. I was called "fossil face" on the playground. It hurt.

I once asked my colleague Shep White, a leading child psychologist, why kids were so interested in dinosaurs. He gave an answer both elegant and succinct: "Big, fierce, and extinct." I love this response, but it can't resolve the question that prompted this essay. Dinosaurs were also big, fierce, and extinct twenty years ago, but few kids or adults gave a damn about them. And so I return to the original question: What started the current dinosaur craze?

The optimistic answer for any intellectual must be that public taste follows scientific discovery. The past twenty years have been a heyday for new findings and fundamental revisions in our view of dinosaurs. The drab, lumbering, slow-witted, inefficient beasts of old interpretations have been replaced with smooth, sleek, colorful, well-oiled, and at least adequately intelligent revised versions. The changes have been most significant in three subjects: anatomy, behavior, and extinction. All three have provided a more congenial and more interesting perspective on dinosaurs. For anatomy, a herd of brontosauruses charging through the desert inspires more awe than a few behemoths so encumbered by their own weight that they must live in ponds. For behavior, the images of the newly christened *Maiasauria,* the good mother lizard, brooding her young, or a herd of migrating ornithopods, with vulnerable juveniles in the center and strong adults at the peripheries, inspire more sympathy than a dumb stegosaur laying her eggs and immediately abandoning them by instinct and ignorance. For extinction, crashing comets and global dust clouds surely inspire more attention than gradually changing sea levels or solar outputs.

I wish that I could locate the current craze in these exciting intellectual developments. But a moment's thought must convince anyone that this good reason cannot provide the right answer. Dinosaurs might not have been quite so jazzy and sexy twenty years ago, but the brontosaurs weren't any smaller back then, the tyrannosaurs were just as fierce, and the whole clan was every bit as extinct (my camp friend's father notwithstanding). You may accept or reject Shep White's three categories, but choose any alternate criteria and dinosaurs surely had the capacity to inspire a craze at any time — twenty years ago as well as today. (At least two mini-crazes of earlier years — in England after Waterhouse Hawkins displayed his life-sized models at the Crystal Palace in the 1850s, and in America after Sinclair promoted a dinosaur exhibit at the New York World's Fair in 1939 — illustrate this permanent potential.) We must conclude, I think, that dinosaurs have never lacked the seeds of appeal, that the missing ingredient must be adequate publicity, and that the key to "why now?" resides in promotion, not new knowledge.

I must therefore assume that the solution lies in that great and dubious 10
driving force of American society — marketing. At some definable point,
some smart entrepreneur recognized an enormous and largely unexploited
potential for profit. What craze is any different? Did goldfish reach an optimal
size and tastiness for swallowing in the early 1940s? Did a breakthrough in
yo-yo technology spawn the great passion that swept the streets of New York
in my youth? Did hula hoops fit some particular social niche and need
uniquely confined to a few months during the 1950s?

I don't doubt that a few more general factors may form part of the
story. Perhaps the initial entrepreneurs developed their own interest and
insight by reading about new discoveries. Perhaps the vast expansion of
museum gift shops — a dubious trend (in my view), with more to lament in
skewed priorities than to praise in heightened availability of worthy paraphernalia — gave an essential boost in providing an initial arena for sales.
Still, most crazes get started for odd and unpredictable reasons and then
propagate by a kind of mass intoxication and social conformity. If I am right
in arguing that the current dinosaur craze could have occurred long ago and
owes both its origin and initial spread to a marketing opportunity seized by
a few diligent entrepreneurs (with later diffusion by odd mechanisms of
crowd psychology that engender chain reactions beyond a critical mass), then
the source of this phenomenon may not be a social trend or a new discovery,
but the cleverness of a person or persons unknown (with a product or products
unrecognized). As this craze is no minor item in twentieth-century American
cultural history, I would love to identify the instigators and the insights. If
anyone knows, please tell me.

I do confess to some cynical dubiety about the inundation of kiddie
culture with dinosaurs in every cute, furry, and profitable venue that any
marketing agent can devise. I don't, of course, advocate a return to the
ignorance and unavailability of information during my youth, but a dinosaur
on every T-shirt and milk carton does foreclose any sense of mystery or joy
of discovery — and certain forms of marketing do inexorably lead to trivial-
ization. Interest in dinosaurs becomes one of those ephemeral episodes —
somewhere between policeman and fireman — in the canonical sequence of
childhood interests. Something to burn brightly in its appointed season and
then, all too often, to die — utterly and without memory.

As intellectuals, we acknowledge and accept a minority status in our
culture (since hope, virtue, and reality rarely coincide). We therefore know
that we must seize our advantages by noting popular trends and trying to
divert some of their energy into rivulets that might benefit learning and
education. The dinosaur craze should be a blessing for us, since the source
material is a rip-off of our efforts — the labor of paleontologists, the great
skeletons mounted in our museums. Indeed, we have done well — damned
well, as things go. Lurking in and around the book covers and shopping bags
are a pretty fair number of mighty good books, films, puzzles, games, and
other items of — dare I say it — decent intellectual and educational content.

It is now time to segue, via a respectable transition, into the second part of this essay. (But before we do, and while I'm throwing out requests for enlightenment, can anyone tell me how this fairly obscure Italian term from my musical education managed its recent entry into trendy American speech?)

We all acknowledge the sorry state of primary and secondary education in America, both by contrast with the success of other nations and by any absolute standard of educational need in an increasingly complex world. We also recognize that the crisis is particularly acute for the teaching of science. Well, being of an optimistic nature, I survey the dinosaur craze and wonder why science suffers so badly within our schools. The dinosaur craze has generated, amidst a supersaurus-sized pile of kitsch and crap, a remarkable range of worthy material that kids seem to like and use. Kids love science so long as fine teaching and good material grace the presentation. If the dinosaur craze of pop culture has been adequately subverted for educational ends, why can't we capitalize on this benevolent spin-off? Why can't we sustain the interest, rather than letting it wither like the flower of grass, as soon as a child moves on to his next stage? Why can't we infuse some of this excitement into our schools and use it to boost and expand interest in all of science? Think of the aggregate mental power vested in 10 million five-year-olds, each with an average of twenty monstrous Latin dinosaur names committed to memory with the effortless joy and awesome talent of human beings at the height of their powers for rote learning. Can't we transfer this skill to all the other domains — arithmetic, spelling, and foreign languages, in particular — that benefit so greatly from rote learning in primary school years? (Let no adult disparage the value of rote because we lose both the ability and the joy in later years.)

Why is the teaching of science in such trouble in our nation's public schools? Why is the shortage of science teachers so desperate that hundreds of high schools have dropped physics entirely, while about half of all science courses still on the books are now being taught by people without formal training in science? To understand this lamentable situation, we must first dispel the silly and hurtful myth that science is simply too hard for preadults. (Supporters of this excuse argue that we succeeded in the past only because science was much simpler before the great explosion of modern knowledge.)

This claim cannot be sustained for two basic reasons. First, science uses and requires no special mental equipment beyond the scope of a standard school curriculum. The subject matter may be different but the cerebral tools are common to all learning. Science probes the factual state of the world; religion and ethics deal with moral reasoning; art and literature treat aesthetic and social judgment.

Second, we may put aside all abstract arguments and rely on the empirical fact that other nations have had great success in science education. If their kids can handle the material, so can ours, with proper motivation and instruction. Korea has made great strides in education, particularly in mathematics and the physical sciences. And if you attempt to take refuge in the cruel and fallacious argument that Orientals are genetically built to excel in such subjects, I simply point out that European nations, filled with people more like most of us, have been just as successful. The sciences are well taught and appreciated in the Soviet Union, for example, where the major popular bookstores on Leninsky Prospekt are stocked with technical books both browsed and purchased in large numbers. Moreover, we proved the point to ourselves in the late 1950s, when the Soviet Sputnik inspired cold war fears of Russian technological takeover, and we responded, for once, with adequate cash, expertise, and enthusiasm by launching a major effort to improve secondary education in science. But that effort, begun for the wrong reasons, soon petered out into renewed mediocrity (graced, as always, with pinpoints of excellence here and there, whenever a great teacher and adequate resources coincide).

We live in a profoundly nonintellectual culture, made all the worse by a passive hedonism abetted by the spread of wealth and its dissipation into countless electronic devices that impart the latest in entertainment and supposed information — all in short (and loud) doses of "easy listening." The kiddie culture, or playground, version of this nonintellectualism can be even more strident and more one-dimensional, but the fault must lie entirely with adults — for our kids are only enhancing a role model read all too clearly.

I'm beginning to sound like an aging Miniver Cheevy, or like the chief reprobate on Ko-Ko's little list "of society offenders who might well be underground" — and he means dead and buried, not romantically in opposition: "the idiot who praises with enthusiastic tone, all centuries but this and every country but his own." I want to make an opposite and curiously optimistic point about our current mores: We are a profoundly nonintellectual culture, but we are not committed to this attitude; in fact, we are scarcely committed to anything. We may be the most labile culture in all history, capable of rapid and massive shifts of prevailing opinions, all imposed from above by concerted media effort. Passivity and nonintellectual judgment are the greatest spurs to such lability. Everything comes to us in fifteen-second sound bites and photo opportunities. All possibility for ambiguity — the most precious trait of any adequate analysis — is erased. He wins who looks best or shouts loudest. We are so fearful of making judgments ourselves that we must wait until the TV commentators have spoken before deciding whether Bush or Dukakis won the debate.

We are therefore maximally subject to imposition from above. Nonetheless, this dangerous trait can be subverted for good. A few years ago, in the wake of an unparalleled media blitz, drugs rose from insignificance to a strong number one on the list of serious American problems in that most mercurial court of public opinion as revealed by polling. Surely we can provoke the same immediate recognition for poor education. Talk about "wasted minds." Which cause would you pick as the greater enemy, quantitatively speaking, in America: crack or lousy education abetted by conformity and peer pressure in an anti-intellectual culture?

We live in a capitalist economy, and I have no particular objection to honorable self-interest. We cannot hope to make the needed, drastic improvement in primary and secondary education without a dramatic restructuring of salaries. In my opinion, you cannot pay a good teacher enough money to recompense the value of talent applied to the education of young children. I teach an hour or two a day to tolerably well-behaved near-adults — and come home exhausted. By what possible argument are my services worth more in salary than those of a secondary-school teacher with six classes a day, little prestige, less support, massive problems of discipline, and a fundamental role in shaping minds. (In comparison, I only tinker with intellects already largely formed.) Why are salaries so low, and attendant prestige so limited, for the most important job in America? How can our priorities be so skewed that when we wish to raise the status of science teachers, we take the media route and try to place a member of the profession into orbit (with disastrous consequences, as it happened), rather than boosting salaries on earth? (The crisis in science teaching stems directly from this crucial issue of compensation. Science graduates can begin in a variety of industrial jobs at twice the salary of almost any teaching position; potential teachers in the arts and humanities often lack these well-paid alternatives and enter the public schools *faute de mieux*.) [3]

We are now at a crux of opportunity, and the situation may not persist if we fail to exploit it. If I were king, I would believe Gorbachev, realize that the cold war is a happenstance of history — not a necessary and permanent state of world politics — make some agreements, slash the military budget, and use just a fraction of the savings to double the salary of every teacher in American public schools. I suspect that a shift in prestige, and the consequent attractiveness of teaching to those with excellence and talent, would follow.

I don't regard these suggestions as pipe dreams, but having been born before yesterday, I don't expect their immediate implementation either. I also acknowledge, of course, that reforms are not imposed from above without vast and coordinated efforts of lobbying and pressuring from below. Thus, as we work toward a larger and more coordinated solution, and as a small contribution to the people's lobby, could we not immediately subvert more of the dinosaur craze from crass commercialism to educational value?

Dinosaur names can become the model for rote learning. Dinosaur facts and figures can inspire visceral interest and lead to greater wonder about science. Dinosaur theories and reconstructions can illustrate the rudiments of scientific reasoning. But I'd like to end with a more modest suggestion. Nothing makes me sadder than the peer pressure that enforces conformity 25

[3] *faute de mieux*: French: "for lack of anything better."

and erases wonder. Countless Americans have been permanently deprived of the joys of singing because a thoughtless teacher once told them not to sing, but only to mouth the words at the school assembly because they were "off-key." Once told, twice shy and perpetually fearful. Countless others had the light of intellectual wonder extinguished because a thoughtless and swaggering fellow student called them nerds on the playground. Don't point to the obsessives — I was one — who will persist and succeed despite these petty cruelties of youth. For each of us, a hundred are lost — more timid and fearful, but just as capable. We must rage against the dying of the light — and although Dylan Thomas spoke of bodily death in his famous line, we may also apply his words to the extinction of wonder in the mind, by pressures of conformity in an anti-intellectual culture.

The *New York Times,* in an article on science education in Korea, interviewed a nine-year-old girl and inquired after her personal hero. She replied: Stephen Hawking. [4] Believe me, I have absolutely nothing against Larry Bird or Michael Jordan, but wouldn't it be lovely if even one American kid in 10,000 gave such an answer. The article went on to say that science whizzes are class heroes in Korean schools, not isolated and ostracized dweebs.

English wars may have been won on the playing fields of Eton, but American careers in science are destroyed on the playgrounds of Shady Oaks Elementary School. Can we not invoke dinosaur power to alleviate these unspoken tragedies? Can't dinosaurs be the great levelers and integrators — the joint passion of the class rowdy and the class intellectual? I will know that we are on our way when the kid who names *Chasmosaurus* as his personal hero also earns the epithet of Mr. Cool.

[4] *Stephen Hawking* (b. 1942): Brilliant British scientist who has written extensively on the origins of the universe.

FROM READING TO REREADING

1. Notice how Gould moves into his essay by alluding to the popular quiz show, *Jeopardy.* What does the show have to do with his topic? How does it prepare us for the overall tone and style of his essay?

2. Gould's hope in this essay is that the dinosaur craze could be rechanneled into an important educational opportunity. How would this happen? What benefits would it lead to?

3. In reading essays, one of the things to pay close attention to is the author's use of pronouns. Gould begins his essay with the word "We." Who is this "we"? At one point, Gould writes "As intellectuals, we acknowledge and accept a minority status in our culture. . . ." And at another point, he says "We are so fearful of making

judgments ourselves that we must wait until the TV commentators have spoken. . . ." Are these two uses of "we" identical? Where does the reader fit in?

From Reading to Writing

1. George Orwell and Cynthia Ozick write personally about their education. Choose a moment in your own education — a first day of school, a confrontation with a teacher, an important exam, or some other event — and describe it in an essay. Be sure, as Orwell and Ozick do, to consider the differences between yourself at the time and yourself now.

2. Both James Baldwin and Lewis Thomas are concerned about changing the basic curriculum. Consider your own relation to the range of courses you need to take. Write an essay in which you offer a well-thought-out reform of either the high-school or college curriculum and explain why you think your ideas will improve educational standards in general.

3. In his essay, Stephen Jay Gould invites speculation about the reasons behind the recent dinosaur craze. Take him up on his invitation. You may have some firsthand experiences in this area; you may even have had a few dinosaur products that would be worth contributing to his list. How do you personally explain the dinosaur craze?

5

Journeys Near and Far

voyeur - peeping tom
people think in privacy,
but being watched
by visitors

CYNTHIA OZICK
The Shock of Teapots

*What makes travel a special kind of experience? In "The Shock of Teapots,"
Cynthia Ozick uses a trip to Stockholm as a way of exploring, not the Swedish
capital, but the nature of travel itself. Travel sharpens our perceptions; it returns
us to the fresh vision of childhood. Part of the pleasure of a journey is the way
it can transform a familiar object like a teapot into something extraordinary.
This brief, though lavishly written, essay first appeared in 1985 as "Enchant-
ments at First Encounter" in the travel supplement of the* New York Times
Magazine.

O NE MORNING in Stockholm, after rain and just before November, a
mysteriously translucent shadow began to paint itself across the top of
the city. It skimmed high over people's heads, a gauzy brass net, keeping
well above the streets, skirting everything fabricated by human arts — though
one or two steeples were allowed to dip into it, like pens filling their nibs
with palest ink. It made a sort of watermark over Stockholm, as if a faintly
luminous river ran overhead, yet with no more weight or gravity than a vapor.

This glorious strangeness — a kind of crystalline wash — was the
sunlight of a Swedish autumn. The sun looked *new*: it had a lucidity, a
texture, a tincture, a position across the sky that my New York gape had
never before taken in. The horizontal ladder of light hung high up, higher
than any sunlight I had ever seen, and the quality of its glow seemed thinner,
wanner, more tentatively morning-brushed; or else like gold leaf beaten
gossamer as tissue — a lambent skin laid over the spired marrow of the town.

"Ah yes, the sun *does* look a bit different this time of year," say the
Stockholmers in their perfect English (English as a second first language),
but with a touch of ennui. Whereas I, under the electrified rays of my
whitening hair, stand drawn upward to the startling sky, restored to the clarity
of childhood. The Swedes have known a Swedish autumn before; I have
not.

Travel returns us in just this way to sharpness of notice; and to be
saturated in the sight of what is entirely new — the sun at an unaccustomed
slope, stretched across the northland, separate from the infiltrating dusk that
always seems about to fall through clear gray Stockholm — is to revisit the
enigmatically lit puppet-stage outlines of childhood: those mental photographs and dreaming woodcuts or engravings that we retain from our earliest
years. What we remember from childhood we remember forever — perma-

nent ghosts, stamped, imprinted, eternally seen. Travelers regain this ghost-
seizing brightness, eeriness, firstness.

They regain it because they have cut themselves loose from their own   5
society, from every society; they are, for a while, floating vagabonds, like
astronauts out for a space walk on a long free line. They are subject to
preternatural exhilarations, absurd horizons, unexpected forms and trans-
mutations: the matter-of-fact (a battered old stoop, say, or the shape of a
door) appears beautiful; or a stone that at home would not merit the blink
of your eye here arrests you with its absolute particularity — just because it
is what your hand already intimately knows. You think: a stone, a stone!
They have stones here too! And you think: how uncannily the planet is
girdled, as stone-speckled in Sweden as in New York. For the vagabond-
voyeur (and for travelers voyeurism is irresistible), nothing is not for notice,
nothing is banal, nothing is ordinary: not a rock, not the shoulder of a
passerby, not a teapot.

Plenitude assaults; replication invades. Everything known has its
spooky shadow and Doppelgänger. [1] On my first trip anywhere — it was 1957
and I landed in Edinburgh with the roaring of the plane's four mammoth
propellers for days afterward embedded in my ears — I rode in a red airport
bus to the middle of the city, out of which ascended its great castle. It is a
fairy-book castle, dreamlike, Arthurian, secured in the long-ago. But the
shuddery red bus — hadn't I been bounced along in an old bus before,
perhaps not so terrifically red as this one? — the red bus was not within
reach of plain sense. Every inch of its interior streamed with unearthliness,
with an undivulged and consummate witchery. It put me in the grip of a
wild Elsewhere. This unexceptional vehicle, with its bright forward snout,
was all at once eclipsed by a rush of the abnormal, the unfathomably Martian.
It was the bus, not the phantasmagorical castle, that clouded over and
bewildered our reasoned humanity. The red bus was what I intimately knew:
only I had never seen it before. A reflected flicker of the actual. A looking-
glass bus. A Scottish ghost.

This is what travelers discover: that when you sever the links of nor-
mality and its claims, when you break off from the quotidian, it is the teapots
that truly shock. Nothing is so awesomely unfamiliar as the familiar that
discloses itself at the end of a journey. Nothing shakes the heart so much as
meeting — far, far away — what you last met at home. Some say that
travelers are informal anthropologists. But it is ontology — the investigation
of the nature of being — that travelers do. Call it the flooding-in of the real.

There is, besides, the flooding-in of character. Here one enters not
landscape or streetlit night scenes, but fragments of drama: splinters of
euphoria that catch you up when you are least deserving. Sometimes it is a
jump into a pop-up book, as when a cockney cabdriver, of whom you have

[1] *Doppelgänger:* Ghostly, invisible counterpart or double that haunts a person (German).

asked directions while leaning out from the curb, gives his native wink of blithe goodwill. Sometimes it is a mazy stroll into a toy theater, as when, in a museum, you suddenly come on the intense little band following the lecturer on Mesopotamia, or the lecturer on genre painting, and the muse of civilization alights on these rapt few. What you are struck with then — one of those mental photographs that go on sticking to the retina — is not what lies somnolently in the glass case or hangs romantically on the wall, but the enchantment of a minutely idiosyncratic face shot into your vision with indelible singularity, delivered over forever by your own fertile gaze. When travelers stare at heads and ears and necks and beads and mustaches, they are — in the encapsuled force of the selection — making art: portraits, voice sonatinas, the quick haiku of a strictly triangular nostril.

Traveling is seeing; it is the implicit that we travel by. Travelers are fantasists, conjurers, seers — and what they finally discover is that every round object everywhere is a crystal ball: stone, teapot, the marvelous globe of the human eye.

FROM READING TO REREADING

1. Though this is largely a reflective essay on travel in general, notice that Ozick opens with a specific moment. Why would she begin this way and not with a more general statement? What point do her opening paragraphs establish?

2. Look closely at the opening sentence of the fourth paragraph. You will observe that it is quite long and contains nearly every possible kind of punctuation. What is the effect of this sentence? How does it show the movement of Ozick's thought?

3. On first reading, you may not notice how often the word "ghost" appears in the essay. Reread the essay, concentrating on the image of ghosts and its related concepts ("eeriness," "spooky," etc.). Why do you think Ozick has introduced this web of related imagery? How does it inform her idea of travel?

ALICE WALKER
Journey to Nine Miles

Essayists have long written about their visits to the birth and burial places of famous people. In "Journey to Nine Miles," Alice Walker (who wrote about her trip to Zora Neale Hurston's grave in "Looking for Zora") travels to Jamaica to visit the isolated place where the world famous reggae singer Bob Marley was born and is buried (he died in 1981). She finds Marley's mausoleum, but she finds also a "ravaged land." Walker's essay originally appeared in Mother Jones *in 1986 under the title "Redemption Day."*

BY FIVE O'CLOCK we were awake, listening to the soothing slapping of the surf, and watching the sky redden over the ocean. By six we were dressed and knocking on my daughter's door. She and her friend Kevin were going with us (Robert and me) to visit Nine Miles, the birthplace of someone we all loved, Bob Marley. It was Christmas Day, bright, sunny, and very warm and the traditional day of thanksgiving for the birth of someone sacred.

I missed Bob Marley when his body was alive, and I have often wondered how that could possibly be. It happened, though, because when he was singing all over the world, I was living in Mississippi, being political, digging into my own his/herstory, writing books, having a baby — and listening to local music, B. B. King, and the Beatles. I liked dreadlocks, but only because I am an Aquarian; I was unwilling to look beyond the sexism of Rastafarianism. [1] The music stayed outside my consciousness. It didn't help either that the most political and spiritual of reggae music was suppressed in the United States, so that "Stir It Up," and not "Natty Dread" or "Lively Up Yourself" or "Exodus," was what one heard. And then, of course, there *was* disco, a music so blatantly soulless as to be frightening, and impossible to do anything to but exercise.

I first really *heard* Bob Marley when I was in the throes of writing a draft of the screenplay for *The Color Purple*. Each Monday I drove up to my studio in the country, a taxing three-hour drive, worked steadily until Friday, drove back to the city, and tried to be two parents to my daughter on weekends. We kept in touch by phone during the week, and I had the impression that she was late for school every day and living on chocolates. (No *way*! She always smiled innocently.)

My friends Jan and Chris, a white couple nearby, seeing my stress,

---

[1] *Rastafarianism:* Jamaican religion that considers Africa the promised land and Haile Selassie I (1892–1975), former emperor of Ethiopia, the messiah.

offered their help, which I accepted in the form of dinner at their house every night after a day's work on the script. One night after yet another sumptuous meal, we pushed back the table and, in our frustration at the pain that rides on the seat next to joy in life (cancer, pollution, invasions, the bomb), began dancing to reggae records: UB-40, Black Uhuru . . . Bob Marley. I was transfixed. It was hard to believe the beauty of the soul I heard in "No Woman No Cry," "Coming In from the Cold," "Could You Be Loved?," "Three Little Birds," and "Redemption Song." Here was a man who loved his roots, even after he'd been nearly assassinated in his own country, and knew they extended to the ends of the earth. Here was a soul who loved Jamaica and loved Jamaicans and loved *being* a Jamaican (nobody got more pleasure out of the history, myths, traditions, and language of Jamaica than Bob Marley) but who knew it was not meant to limit itself, or even could, to an island of any sort. Here was the radical peasant-class, working-class consciousness that fearlessly denounced the Wasichus (the greedy and destructive) and did it with such grace you could dance to it. Here was a man of extraordinary sensitivity, political acumen, spiritual power, and sexual wildness; a free spirit if ever there was one. Here, I felt, was my brother. It was as if there had been a great and gorgeous light on all over the world, and somehow I'd missed it. Every night for the next two months I listened to Bob Marley. I danced with his spirit — so much more alive still than many people walking around. I felt my own dreadlocks begin to grow.

Over time, the draft of the script I was writing was finished. My 5 evenings with my friends came to an end. My love of Marley spread easily over my family, and it was as neophyte rastas, [2] having decided that "rasta" for us meant a commitment to a religion of attentiveness and joy, that we appeared when we visited Jamaica in 1984.

What we saw is a ravaged land, a place where people, often rastas, eat out of garbage cans and where, one afternoon in a beach café during a rainstorm, I overheard a thirteen-year-old boy offer, along with some Jamaican pot, his eleven-year-old sister (whose grownup's earrings looked larger, almost, than her face) to a large, hirsute American white man (who blushingly declined).

The car we rented, from a harried, hostile dealer who didn't even seem to want to tell us where to buy gas, had already had two flats. On the way to Nine Miles it had three more. Eventually, however, after an agonizing seven hours from Negril, where we were staying, blessing the car at every bump in the road, to encourage it to live through the trip, we arrived.

Nine Miles, because it is nine miles from the nearest village of any size, is one of the stillest and most isolated spots on the face of the earth. It is only several houses, spread out around the top of a hill. There are small, poor farms, with bananas appearing to be the predominant crop.

[2] *rastas:* Followers of Rastafarianism.

Several men and many children come down the hill to meet our car. They know we've come to visit Bob. They walk with us up the hill where Bob Marley's body is entombed in a small mausoleum with stained-glass windows; the nicest building in Nine Miles. Next to it is a small one-room house where Bob and his wife, Rita, lived briefly during their marriage. I think of how much energy Bob Marley had to generate to project himself into the world beyond this materially impoverished place; and of how exhausted, in so many of his later photographs, he looked. On the other hand, it is easy to understand — listening to the deep stillness that makes a jet soaring overhead sound like the buzzing of a fly — why he wanted to be brought back to his home village, back to Nine Miles, to rest. We see the tomb from a distance of about fifty feet, because we cannot pass through, or climb over, an immense chain-link fence that has recently been erected to keep the too eager (and apparently destructive and kleptomaniacal) tourists at bay. One thing that I like very much: built into the hill facing Bob's tomb is a permanent stage. On his birthday, February 6, someone tells us, people from all over the world come to Nine Miles to sing to him.

The villagers around us are obviously sorry about the fence. Perhaps 10 we were not the ones intended to be kept out? Their faces seem to say as much. They are all men and boys. No women or girls among them. On a front porch below the hill I see some women and girls, studiously avoiding us.

One young man, the caretaker, tells us that, though we can't go in, there *is* a way we can get closer to Bob. I almost tell him I could hardly *be* any closer to Bob and still be alive, but I don't want to try to explain. He points out a path that climbs the side of the hill, and we — assisted by half a dozen of the more agile villagers — take it. It passes through bananas and weeds, flowers, past goats tethered out of the sun, past chickens. Past the home, one says, of Bob Marley's cousin, a broken but gallant-looking man in his fifties, nearly toothless, and with a gentle and generous smile. He sits in his tiny, bare house and watches us. His face is radiant with the pride of relationship.

From within the compound now we hear singing. Bob's songs come from the lips of the caretaker, who says he and Bob were friends. That he loved Bob. Loved his music. He sings terribly. But perhaps this is only because he is, though about the age Bob would have been now, early forties, lacking his front teeth. He is very dark, and quite handsome, teeth or no. And it is his humble, terrible singing — as he moves proprietarily about the yard where his friend is enshrined — that makes him so. It is as if he sings Bob's songs *for* Bob, in an attempt to animate the tomb. The little children are all about us, nearly underfoot. Beautiful children. One little boy is right beside me. He is about six, of browner skin than the rest — who are nearer to black — with curlier hair. He looks like Bob.

I ask his name. He tells me. I have since forgotten it. As we linger by the fence, our fingers touch. For a while we hold hands. I notice that over the door to the tomb someone has plastered a bumper sticker with the name of Rita Marley's latest album. It reads: "Good Girls Culture." I am offended by it; there are so many possible meanings. For a moment I try to imagine the sticker plastered across Bob's forehead. It drops off immediately, washed away by his sweat (as he sings and dances in the shamanistic trance I so love) and his spirit's inability to be possessed by anyone other than itself, and Jah. [3] The caretaker says Rita erected the fence. I understand the necessity.

Soon it is time to go. We clamber back down the hill to the car. On the way down the little boy who looks like Bob asks for money. Thinking of our hands together and how he is so like Bob must have been at his age, I don't want to give him money. But what else can I give him, I wonder.

I consult "the elders," the little band of adults who've gathered about us.   15

"The children are asking for money," I say. "What should we do?"

"You should give it" is the prompt reply. So swift and unstudied is the answer, in fact, that suddenly the question seems absurd.

"They ask because they have none. There is nothing here."

"Would Bob approve?" I ask. Then I think, Probably. The man has had himself planted here to fund the village.

"Yes" is the reply. "Because he would understand."   20

Starting with the children, but by no means stopping there, because the grownups look as expectant as they, we part with some of our "tourist" dollars, realizing that tourism is a dead thing, a thing of the past; that no one can be a tourist anymore, and that, like Bob, all of us can find our deepest rest at home.

It is a long, hot, anxious drive that we have ahead of us. We make our usual supplications to our little tin car and its four shiny tires. But even when we have another flat, bringing us to our fourth for the trip, it hardly touches us. Jamaica is a poor country reduced to selling its living and its dead while much of the world thinks of it as "real estate" and a great place to lie in the sun; but Jamaicans as a people have been seen in all their imperfections and beauty by one of their own and fiercely affirmed, even from the grave, and loved. There is no poverty, only richness in this. We sing "Redemption Song" as we change the tire; feeling very Jamaica, very Bob, very rasta, very *no woman no cry.*

[3] *Jah:* God, from the Hebrew *Jahweh.*

FROM READING TO REREADING

1. Walker opens her essay on a religious note: "It was Christmas Day, bright, sunny, and very warm and the traditional day of thanksgiving for the birth of someone

sacred." How does Walker's choice of details reinforce the idea of a religious pilgrimage? How, for example, is the rented car brought into the overall religious context?

2. Walker notes that she resisted reggae music at first because she was "unwilling to look beyond the sexism of Rastafarianism" (the Jamaican religion that inspired Marley). Why and how does she eventually deal with this conflict between her feminism and Marley's religious background?

3. When writing of foreign cultures we admire, there is a tendency to sentimentalize them or to portray them only in a favorable light. This tendency, of course, plays a large part in conventional travel writing, which is largely published to promote tourism. How does Walker avoid this? What details does she introduce that keep her essay from being a mere promotional piece?

E. B. WHITE
Walden

Throughout his long career as an essayist, E. B. White held one writer and one book in deep esteem. The writer was Henry David Thoreau; the book was Thoreau's Walden. *Published in 1854,* Walden; or, Life in the Woods *is Thoreau's meditative account of two years spent in a small cabin he built for himself at the edge of Walden Pond in his hometown of Concord, Massachusetts. Though now a recognized American classic, the book was not well received at first, and it was not until the 1930s that critics began paying it the attention it warranted. White's essay, published in 1939 in his monthly* Harper's *column, was one of several essays he wrote on Thoreau. The essay is, appropriately enough, an account of a brief journey — the kind both White and Thoreau relished. Those who have read* Walden *(or parts of it) will notice how often White echoes Thoreau's style and language.*

MISS NIMS, take a letter to Henry David Thoreau. Dear Henry: I thought of you the other afternoon as I was approaching Concord doing fifty on Route 62. That is a high speed at which to hold a philosopher in one's mind, but in this century we are a nimble bunch.

On one of the lawns in the outskirts of the village a woman was cutting the grass with a motorized lawn mower. What made me think of you was that the machine had rather got away from her, although she was game enough, and in the brief glimpse I had of the scene it appeared to me that the lawn was mowing the lady. She kept a tight grip on the handles, which throbbed violently with every explosion of the one-cylinder motor, and as she sheered around bushes and lurched along at a reluctant trot behind her impetuous servant, she looked like a puppy who had grabbed something that was too much for him. Concord hasn't changed much, Henry; the farm implements and the animals still have the upper hand.

I may as well admit that I was journeying to Concord with the deliberate intention of visiting your woods; for although I have never knelt at the grave of a philosopher nor placed wreaths on moldy poets, and have often gone a mile out of my way to avoid some place of historical interest, I have always wanted to see Walden Pond. The account that you left of your sojourn there is, you will be amused to learn, a document of increasing pertinence; each year it seems to gain a little headway, as the world loses ground. We may all be transcendental yet, whether we like it or not. As our common complexities increase, any tale of individual simplicity (and yours is the best written and the cockiest) acquires a new fascination; as our goods accumulate, but not our well-being, your report of an existence without material adornment takes on a certain awkward credibility.

My purpose in going to Walden Pond, like yours, was not to live cheaply or to live dearly there, but to transact some private business with the fewest obstacles. Approaching Concord, doing forty, doing forty-five, doing fifty, the steering wheel held snug in my palms, the highway held grimly in my vision, the crown of the road now serving me (on the righthand curves), now defeating me (on the lefthand curves), I began to rouse myself from the stupefaction that a day's motor journey induces. It was a delicious evening, Henry, when the whole body is one sense, and imbibes delight through every pore, if I may coin a phrase. Fields were richly brown where the harrow, drawn by the stripped Ford, had lately sunk its teeth; pastures were green; and overhead the sky had that same everlasting great look which you will find on Page 144 of the Oxford pocket edition. I could feel the road entering me, through tire, wheel, spring, and cushion; shall I not have intelligence with earth too? Am I not partly leaves and vegetable mold myself? — a man of infinite horsepower, yet partly leaves.

Stay with me on 62 and it will take you into Concord. As I say, it was a delicious evening. The snake had come forth to die in a bloody S on the highway, the wheel upon its head, its bowels flat now and exposed. The turtle had come up too to cross the road and die in the attempt, its hard shell smashed under the rubber blow, its intestinal yearning (for the other side of the road) forever squashed. There was a sign by the wayside which announced that the road had a "cotton surface." You wouldn't know what that is, but neither, for that matter, did I. There is a cryptic ingredient in many of our modern improvements — we are awed and pleased without knowing quite what we are enjoying. It is something to be traveling on a road with a cotton surface.

The civilization round Concord today is an odd distillation of city, village, farm, and manor. The houses, yards, fields look not quite suburban, not quite rural. Under the bronze beech and the blue spruce of the departed baron grazes the milch goat of the heirs. Under the porte-cochère stands the reconditioned station wagon; under the grape arbor sit the puppies for sale. (But why do men degenerate ever? What makes families run out?)

It was June and everywhere June was publishing her immemorial stanza; in the lilacs, in the syringa, in the freshly edged paths and the sweetness of moist beloved gardens, and the little wire wickets that preserve the tulips' front. Farmers were already moving the fruits of their toil into their yards, arranging the rhubarb, the asparagus, the strictly fresh eggs on the painted stands under the little shed roofs with the patent shingles. And though it was almost a hundred years since you had taken your ax and started cutting out your home on Walden Pond, I was interested to observe that the philosophical spirit was still alive in Massachusetts: in the center of a vacant lot some boys were assembling the framework of the rude shelter, their whole mind and skill concentrated in the rather inauspicious helter-skeleton of studs and rafters. They too were escaping from town, to live naturally, in a rich blend of savagery and philosophy.

That evening, after supper at the inn, I strolled out into the twilight to dream my shapeless transcendental dreams and see that the car was locked up for the night (first open the right front door, then reach over, straining, and pull up the handles of the left rear and the left front till you hear the click, then the handle of the right rear, then shut the right front but open it again, remembering that the key is still in the ignition switch, remove the key, shut the right front again with a bang, push the tiny keyhole cover to one side, insert key, turn, and withdraw). It is what we all do, Henry. It is called locking the car. It is said to confuse thieves and keep them from making off with the laprobe. Four doors to lock behind one robe. The driver himself never uses a laprobe, the free movement of his legs being vital to the operation of the vehicle; so that when he locks the car it is a pure and unselfish act. I have in my life gained very little essential heat from laprobes, yet I have ever been at pains to lock them up.

The evening was full of sounds, some of which would have stirred your memory. The robins still love the elms of New England villages at sundown. There is enough of the thrush in them to make song inevitable at the end of day, and enough of the tramp to make them hang round the dwellings of men. A robin, like many another American, dearly loves a white house with green blinds. Concord is still full of them.

Your fellow-townsmen were stirring abroad — not many afoot, most of them in their cars; and the sound that they made in Concord at evening was a rustling and a whispering. The sound lacks steadfastness and is wholly unlike that of a train. A train, as you know who lived so near the Fitchburg line, whistles once or twice sadly and is gone, trailing a memory in smoke, soothing to ear and mind. Automobiles, skirting a village green, are like flies that have gained the inner ear — they buzz, cease, pause, start, shift, stop, halt, brake, and the whole effect is a nervous polytone curiously disturbing.

As I wandered along, the toc toc of ping pong balls drifted from an attic window. In front of the Reuben Brown house a Buick was drawn up. At the wheel, motionless, his hat upon his head, a man sat, listening to Amos and Andy on the radio (it is a drama of many scenes and without an end). The deep voice of Andrew Brown, emerging from the car, although it originated more than two hundred miles away, was unstrained by distance. When you used to sit on the shore of your pond on Sunday morning, listening to the church bells of Acton and Concord, you were aware of the excellent filter of the intervening atmosphere. Science has attended to that, and sound now maintains its intensity without regard for distance. Properly sponsored, it goes on forever.

A fire engine, out for a trial spin, roared past Emerson's house, hot with readiness for public duty. Over the barn roofs the martins dipped and chittered. A swarthy daughter of an asparagus grower, in culottes, shirt, and bandanna, pedalled past on her bicycle. It was indeed a delicious evening, and I returned to the inn (I believe it was your house once) to rock with the old ladies on the concrete veranda.

Next morning early I started afoot for Walden, out Main Street and down Thoreau, past the depot and the Minuteman Chevrolet Company. The morning was fresh, and in a bean field along the way I flushed an agriculturalist, quietly studying his beans. Thoreau Street soon joined Number 126, an artery of the State. We number our highways nowadays, our speed being so great we can remember little of their quality or character and are lucky to remember their number. (Men have an indistinct notion that if they keep up this activity long enough all will at length ride somewhere, in next to no time.) Your pond is on 126.

I knew I must be nearing your woodland retreat when the Golden Pheasant lunchroom came into view — Sealtest ice cream, toasted sandwiches, hot frankfurters, waffles, tonics, and lunches. Were I the proprietor, I should add rice, Indian meal, and molasses — just for old time's sake. The Pheasant, incidentally, is for sale: a chance for some nature lover who wishes to set himself up beside a pond in the Concord atmosphere and live deliberately, fronting only the essential facts of life on Number 126. Beyond the Pheasant was a place called Walden Breezes, an oasis whose porch pillars were made of old green shutters sawed into lengths. On the porch was a distorting mirror, to give the traveler a comical image of himself, who had miraculously learned to gaze in an ordinary glass without smiling. Behind the Breezes, in a sun-parched clearing, dwelt your philosophical descendants in their trailers, each trailer the size of your hut, but all grouped together for the sake of congeniality. Trailer people leave the city, as you did, to discover solitude and in any weather, at any hour of the day or night, to improve the nick of time; but they soon collect in villages and get bogged deeper in the mud than ever. The camp behind Walden Breezes was just rousing itself to the morning. The ground was packed hard under the heel, and the sun came through the clearing to bake the soil and enlarge the wry smell of cramped housekeeping. Cushman's bakery truck had stopped to deliver an early basket of rolls. A camp dog, seeing me in the road, barked petulantly. A man emerged from one of the trailers and set forth with a bucket to draw water from some forest tap.

Leaving the highway I turned off into the woods toward the pond, 15 which was apparent through the foliage. The floor of the forest was strewn with dried old oak leaves and *Transcripts*. [1] From beneath the flattened

[1] *Transcripts:* A Boston newspaper.

popcorn wrapper (*granum explosum*)[2] peeped the frail violet. I followed a footpath and descended to the water's edge. The pond lay clear and blue in the morning light, as you have seen it so many times. In the shallows a man's waterlogged shirt undulated gently. A few flies came out to greet me and convoy me to your cove, past the No Bathing signs on which the fellows and the girls had scrawled their names. I felt strangely excited suddenly to be snooping around your premises, tiptoing along watchfully, as though not to tread by mistake upon the intervening century. Before I got to the cove I heard something that seemed to me quite wonderful: I heard your frog, a full, clear *troonk*, guiding me, still hoarse and solemn, bridging the years as the robins had bridged them in the sweetness of the village evening. But he soon quit, and I came on a couple of young boys throwing stones at him.

Your front yard is marked by a bronze tablet set in a stone. Four small granite posts, a few feet away, show where the house was. On top of the tablet was a pair of faded blue bathing trunks with a white stripe. Back of it is a pile of stones, a sort of cairn, left by your visitors as a tribute I suppose. It is a rather ugly little heap of stones, Henry. In fact the hillside itself seems faded, browbeaten; a few tall skinny pines, bare of lower limbs, a smattering of young maples in suitable green, some birches and oaks, and a number of trees felled by the last big wind. It was from the bole of one of these fallen pines, torn up by the roots, that I extracted the stone that I added to the cairn — a sentimental act in which I was interrupted by a small terrier from a nearby picnic group, who confronted me and wanted to know about the stone.

I sat down for a while on one of the posts of your house to listen to the bluebottles and the dragonflies. The invaded glade sprawled shabby and mean at my feet, but the flies were tuned to the old vibration. There were the remains of a fire in your ruins, but I doubt that it was yours; also two beer bottles trodden into the soil and become part of the earth. A young oak had taken root in your house, and two or three ferns, unrolling like the ticklers at a banquet. The only other furnishings were a DuBarry pattern sheet, a page torn from a picture magazine, and some crusts in wax paper.

Before I quit I walked clear round the pond and found the place where you used to sit on the northeast side to get the sun in the fall, and the beach where you got sand for scrubbing your floor. On the eastern side of the pond, where the highway borders it, the State has built dressing rooms for swimmers, a float with diving towers, drinking fountains of porcelain, and rowboats for hire. The pond is in fact a State Preserve, and carries a twenty-dollar fine for picking wild flowers, a decree signed in all solemnity by your fellow-citizens Walter C. Wardwell, Erson B. Barlow, and Nathaniel I. Bowditch. There was a smell of creosote where they had been building a wide wooden

---

[2] *granum explosum:* Exploding grain (Latin). A naturalist, Thoreau often used the Latin terms for botanical species. White is having fun giving a similar name to popcorn.

stairway to the road and the parking area. Swimmers and boaters were arriving; bodies plunged vigorously into the water and emerged wet and beautiful in the bright air. As I left, a boatload of town boys were splashing about in mid-pond, kidding and fooling, the young fellows singing at the tops of their lungs in a wild chorus:

> *Amer-ica, Amer-ica, God shed his grace on thee,*
> *And crown thy good with brotherhood —*
> *From sea to shi-ning sea!*

I walked back to town along the railroad, following your custom. The rails were expanding noisily in the hot sun, and on the slope of the roadbed the wild grape and the blackberry sent up their creepers to the track.

The expense of my brief sojourn in Concord was: [3]   20

Canvas shoes............................	$1.95	
Baseball bat.................................	.25 ⎫	gifts to take back
Left-handed fielder's glove	1.25 ⎭	to a boy
Hotel and meals..........................	4.25	
In all	$7.70	

As you see, this amount was almost what you spent for food for eight months. I cannot defend the shoes or the expenditure for shelter and food: they reveal a meanness and grossness in my nature which you would find contemptible. The baseball equipment, however, is the kind of impediment with which you were never on even terms. You must remember that the house where you practiced the sort of economy that I respect was haunted only by mice and squirrels. You never had to cope with a shortstop.

[3] *The expense . . . .:* In the chapter of *Walden* titled "Economy," Thoreau included itemized lists of the expenses he incurred in building his cabin. White playfully alludes to these.

FROM READING TO REREADING

1. Instead of simply writing a travel piece on Walden Pond, White instead pretends to write a letter to Thoreau about the place. Why do you think he gives his essay that twist? What effect does it have? Why does he call Thoreau by his first name? What does a letter allow him to do that a conventionally written essay would not?

2. White begins his essay with an account of himself "doing fifty on Route 62." As you reread the essay, notice how large a role automobiles (and transportation in general) play. White was an extremely deliberate writer: What do you think his purpose was in calling so much attention to vehicles and transportation? For example, why does he introduce a lengthy, detailed account of locking his car?

3. In the third sentence in paragraph 14 White introduces a few of Thoreau's words. In the well-known second chapter of *Walden*, "Where I Lived, and What I

Lived For," Thoreau wrote: "I went to the woods because I wished to live deliberately, to front only the essential facts of life, and see if I could not learn what it had to teach, and not, when I came to die, discover that I had not lived." How does White incorporate these words? Why doesn't he use quotation marks? Why isn't his use considered plagiarism? What effect does he want to achieve?

parallel John Thoreau

difference   now people
              contraction
              state present
              summary
              litter now / not natural

Imagining what it would be like for Thoreau
    to come back for a visit.

kindred spirits

Makes difference w/ short stop
    new information at end
    give something new to
        think about at
            the end

ANNIE DILLARD

In the Jungle

Travel advertisements frequently tout "out-of-the-way places." But "out-of-the-way" of what, Annie Dillard wonders, while visiting one such place, the Napo River in the Ecuadorian jungle. As in most of her essays about place (see "Total Eclipse"), Dillard tries to bring us deep "inside" the natural environment. Once inside such places, we realize that — though they may be far away — they are hardly remote. The Napo River, Dillard concludes, is "not out of the way. It is in the way. . . ." *The essay was collected in her 1982 book,* Teaching a Stone to Talk.

L IKE ANY OUT-OF-THE-WAY PLACE, the Napo River in the Ecuadorian jungle seems real enough when you are there, even central. Out of the way of *what?* I was sitting on a stump at the edge of a bankside palm-thatch village, in the middle of the night, on the headwaters of the Amazon. Out of the way of human life, tenderness, or the glance of heaven?

A nightjar in deep-leaved shadow called three long notes, and hushed. The men with me talked softly in clumps: three North Americans, four Ecuadorians who were showing us the jungle. We were holding cool drinks and idly watching a hand-sized tarantula seize moths that came to the lone bulb on the generator shed beside us.

It was February, the middle of summer. Green fireflies spattered lights across the air and illumined for seconds, now here, now there, the pale trunks of enormous, solitary trees. Beneath us the brown Napo River was rising, in all silence; it coiled up the sandy bank and tangled its foam in vines that trailed from the forest and roots that looped the shore.

Each breath of night smelled sweet, more moistened and sweet than any kitchen, or garden, or cradle. Each star in Orion seemed to tremble and stir with my breath. All at once, in the thatch house across the clearing behind us, one of the village's Jesuit priests began playing an alto recorder, playing a wordless song, lyric, in a minor key, that twined over the village clearing, that caught in the big trees' canopies, muted our talk on the bankside, and wandered over the river, dissolving downstream.

This will do, I thought. This will do, for a weekend, or a season, or a home. 5

Later that night I loosed my hair from its braids and combed it smooth — not for myself, but so the village girls could play with it in the morning.

We had disembarked at the village that afternoon, and I had slumped

218

on some shaded steps, wishing I knew some Spanish or some Quechua so I could speak with the ring of little girls who were alternately staring at me and smiling at their toes. I spoke anyway, and fooled with my hair, which they were obviously dying to get their hands on, and laughed, and soon they were all braiding my hair, all five of them, all fifty fingers, all my hair, even my bangs. And then they took it apart and did it again, laughing, and teaching me Spanish nouns, and meeting my eyes and each other's with open delight, while their small brothers in blue jeans climbed down from the trees and began kicking a volleyball around with one of the North American men.

Now, as I combed my hair in the little tent, another of the men, a free-lance writer from Manhattan, was talking quietly. He was telling us the tale of his life, describing his work in Hollywood, his apartment in Manhattan, his house in Paris. . . . "It makes me wonder," he said, "what I'm doing in a tent under a tree in the village of Pompeya, on the Napo River, in the jungle of Ecuador." After a pause he added, "It makes me wonder why I'm going *back*."

The point of going somewhere like the Napo River in Ecuador is not to see the most spectacular anything. It is simply to see what is there. We are here on the planet only once, and might as well get a feel for the place. We might as well get a feel for the fringes and hollows in which life is lived, for the Amazon basin, which covers half a continent, and for the life that — there, like anywhere else — is always and necessarily lived in detail: on the tributaries, in the riverside villages, sucking this particular white-fleshed guava in this particular pattern of shade.

What is there is interesting. The Napo River itself is wide (I mean   10
wider than the Mississippi at Davenport) and brown, opaque, and smeared with floating foam and logs and branches from the jungle. White egrets hunch on shoreline deadfalls and parrots in flocks dart in and out of the light. Under the water in the river, unseen, are anacondas — which are reputed to take a few village toddlers every year — and water boas, stingrays, crocodiles, manatees, and sweet-meated fish.

Low water bares gray strips of sandbar on which the natives build tiny palm-thatch shelters, arched, the size of pup tents, for overnight fishing trips. You see these extraordinarily clean people (who bathe twice a day in the river, and whose straight black hair is always freshly washed) paddling down the river in dugout canoes, hugging the banks.

Some of the Indians of this region, earlier in the century, used to sleep naked in hammocks. The nights are cold. Gordon MacCreach, an American explorer in these Amazon tributaries, reported that he was startled to hear the Indians get up at three in the morning. He was even more startled, night after night, to hear them walk down to the river slowly, half asleep, and bathe in the water. Only later did he learn what they were doing: they were getting warm. The cold woke them; they warmed their skins in the river, which was always ninety degrees; then they returned to their hammocks and slept through the rest of the night.

The riverbanks are low, and from the river you see an unbroken wall of dark forest in every direction, from the Andes to the Atlantic. You get a taste for looking at trees: trees hung with the swinging nests of yellow troupials, trees from which ant nests the size of grain sacks hang like black goiters, trees from which seven-colored tanagers flutter, coral trees, teak, balsa and breadfruit, enormous emergent silk-cotton trees, and the pale-barked *samona* palms.

When you are inside the jungle, away from the river, the trees vault out of sight. It is hard to remember to look up the long trunks and see the fans, strips, fronds, and sprays of glossy leaves. Inside the jungle you are more likely to notice the snarl of climbers and creepers round the trees' boles, the flowering bromeliads and epiphytes in every bough's crook, and the fantastic silk-cotton tree trunks thirty or forty feet across, trunks buttressed in flanges of wood whose curves can make three high walls of a room — a shady, loamy-aired room where you would gladly live, or die. Butterflies, iridescent blue, striped, or clear-winged, thread the jungle paths at eye level. And at your feet is a swath of ants bearing triangular bits of green leaf. The ants with their leaves look like a wide fleet of sailing dinghies — but they don't quit. In either direction they wobble over the jungle floor as far as the eye can see. I followed them off the path as far as I dared, and never saw an end to ants or to those luffing chips of green they bore.

Unseen in the jungle, but present, are tapirs, jaguars, many species of snake and lizard, ocelots, armadillos, marmosets, howler monkeys, toucans and macaws and a hundred other birds, deer, bats, peccaries, capybaras, agoutis, and sloths. Also present in this jungle, but variously distant, are Texaco derricks and pipelines, and some of the wildest Indians in the world, blowgun-using Indians, who killed missionaries in 1956 and ate them.

Long lakes shine in the jungle. We traveled one of these in dugout canoes, canoes with two inches of freeboard, canoes paddled with machete-hewn oars chopped from buttresses of silk-cotton trees, or poled in the shallows with peeled cane or bamboo. Our part-Indian guide had cleared the path to the lake the day before; when we walked the path we saw where he had impaled the lopped head of a boa, open-mouthed, on a pointed stick by the canoes, for decoration.

This lake was wonderful. Herons, egrets, and ibises plodded the sawgrass shores, kingfishers and cuckoos clattered from sunlight to shade, great turkeylike birds fussed in dead branches, and hawks lolled overhead. There was all the time in the world. A turtle slid into the water. The boy in the bow of my canoe slapped stones at birds with a simple sling, a rubber thong and leather pad. He aimed brilliantly at moving targets, always, and always missed; the birds were out of range. He stuffed his sling back in his shirt. I looked around.

The lake and river waters are as opaque as rain-forest leaves; they are veils, blinds, painted screens. You see things only by their effects. I saw the shoreline water roil and the sawgrass heave above a thrashing *paichi*, an enormous black fish of these waters; one had been caught the previous week weighing 430 pounds. Piranha fish live in the lakes, and electric eels. I dangled my fingers in the water, figuring it would be worth it.

We would eat chicken that night in the village, and rice, yucca, onions, beets, and heaps of fruit. The sun would ring down, pulling darkness after it like a curtain. Twilight is short, and the unseen birds of twilight wistful, uncanny, catching the heart. The two nuns in their dazzling white habits — the beautiful-boned young nun and the warm-faced old — would glide to the open cane-and-thatch schoolroom in darkness, and start the children singing. The children would sing in piping Spanish, high-pitched and pure; they would sing "Nearer My God to Thee" in Quechua, very fast. (To reciprocate, we sang for them "Old MacDonald Had a Farm"; I thought they might recognize the animal sounds. Of course they thought we were out of our minds.) As the children became excited by their own singing, they left their log benches and swarmed around the nuns, hopping, smiling at us, everyone smiling, the nuns' faces bursting in their cowls, and the clear-voiced children still singing, and the palm-leafed roofing stirred.

The Napo River: it is not out of the way. It is *in* the way, catching sunlight the way a cup catches poured water; it is a bowl of sweet air, a basin of greenness, and of grace, and, it would seem, of peace.

20

Answers question

FROM READING TO REREADING

1. Though she doesn't explicitly state it, Dillard distills into this brief essay a philosophy of travel. How would you describe her philosophy?

2. Good travelers usually feel a need to learn the "language" of the land they are visiting. How does Dillard's choice of words show her awareness of the Napo River environment?

3. Note Dillard's final scene. It is not of the Napo River but of the singing schoolchildren. Why do you think she concludes her description of the place with this account? What point is she making?

Opposites

JAMES BALDWIN
Equal in Paris

One of a traveler's nightmares is to be arrested and imprisoned in a foreign country as a result of a misunderstanding. In 1949, an impoverished, twenty-five-year-old James Baldwin, who had moved to Paris a year earlier to escape the racism of Harlem and who was trying to launch his career as a writer, experienced a part of France that most tourists never see: its prison system. In "Equal in Paris," a chance encounter with another American sets off a sequence of events that, in Baldwin's terms, has all the elements of a "comic-opera." The essay originally appeared in Commentary *in 1955 and was collected in Baldwin's* Notes of a Native Son.

O N THE NINETEENTH of December, in 1949, when I had been living in Paris for a little over a year, I was arrested as a receiver of stolen goods and spent eight days in prison. My arrest came about through an American tourist whom I had met twice in New York, who had been given my name and address and told to look me up. I was then living on the top floor of a ludicrously grim hotel on the rue du Bac, one of those enormous dark, cold, and hideous establishments in which Paris abounds that seem to breathe forth, in their airless, humid, stone-cold halls, the weak light, scurrying chambermaids, and creaking stairs, an odor of gentility long long dead. The place was run by an ancient Frenchman dressed in an elegant black suit which was green with age, who cannot properly be described as bewildered or even as being in a state of shock, since he had really stopped breathing around 1910. There he sat at his desk in the weirdly lit, fantastically furnished lobby, day in and day out, greeting each one of his extremely impoverished and *louche* [1] lodgers with a stately inclination of the head that he had no doubt been taught in some impossibly remote time was the proper way for a *propriétaire* [2] to greet his guests. If it had not been for his daughter, an extremely hardheaded *tricoteuse* [3] — the inclination of *her* head was chilling and abrupt, like the downbeat of an ax — the hotel would certainly have gone bankrupt long before. It was said that this old man had not gone farther than the door of his hotel for thirty years, which was not at all difficult to believe. He looked as though the daylight would have killed him.

I did not, of course, spend much of my time in this palace. The moment I began living in French hotels I understood the necessity of French cafés.

[1] *louche:* Shady; suspicious (French).

[2] *propriétaire:* Hotel proprietor (French).

[3] *tricoteuse:* A knitter; the sense here is of a knitting machine (French).

This made it rather difficult to look me up, for as soon as I was out of bed I hopefully took notebook and fountain pen off to the upstairs room of the Flore, where I consumed rather a lot of coffee and, as evening approached, rather a lot of alcohol, but did not get much writing done. But one night, in one of the cafés of Saint Germain des Prés, I was discovered by this New Yorker and only because we found ourselves in Paris we immediately established the illusion that we had been fast friends back in the good old U.S.A. This illusion proved itself too thin to support an evening's drinking, but by that time it was too late. I had committed myself to getting him a room in my hotel the next day, for he was living in one of the nest of hotels near the Gare Saint Lazare, where, he said, the *propriétaire* was a thief, his wife a repressed nymphomaniac, the chambermaids "pigs," and the rent a crime. Americans are always talking this way about the French and so it did not occur to me that he meant what he said or that he would take into his own hands the means of avenging himself on the French Republic. It did not occur to me, either, that the means which he *did* take could possibly have brought about such dire results, results which were not less dire for being also comic-opera.

It came as the last of a series of disasters which had perhaps been made inevitable by the fact that I had come to Paris originally with a little over forty dollars in my pockets, nothing in the bank, and no grasp whatever of the French language. It developed, shortly, that I had no grasp of the French character either. I considered the French an ancient, intelligent, and cultured race, which indeed they are. I did not know, however, that ancient glories imply, at least in the middle of the present century, present fatigue and, quite probably, paranoia; that there is a limit to the role of the intelligence in human affairs; and that no people come into possession of a culture without having paid a heavy price for it. This price they cannot, of course, assess, but it is revealed in their personalities and in their institutions. The very word "institutions," from my side of the ocean, where, it seemed to me, we suffered so cruelly from the lack of them, had a pleasant ring, as of safety and order and common sense; one had to come into contact with these institutions in order to understand that they were also outmoded, exasperating, completely impersonal, and very often cruel. Similarly, the personality which had seemed from a distance to be so large and free had to be dealt with before one could see that, if it was large, it was also inflexible and, for the foreigner, full of strange, high, dusty rooms which could not be inhabited. One had, in short, to come into contact with an alien culture in order to understand that a culture was not a community basket-weaving project, nor yet an act of God; was something neither desirable nor undesirable in itself, being inevitable, being nothing more or less than the recorded and visible effects on a body of people of the vicissitudes with which they had been forced to deal. And their great men are revealed as simply another of these vicissitudes, even if, quite against their will, the brief battle of their great men with them has left them richer.

When my American friend left his hotel to move to mine, he took with him, out of pique, a bedsheet belonging to the hotel and put it in his suitcase. When he arrived at my hotel I borrowed the sheet, since my own were filthy and the chambermaid showed no sign of bringing me any clean ones, and put it on my bed. The sheets belonging to *my* hotel I put out in the hall, congratulating myself on having thus forced on the attention of the Grand Hôtel du Bac the unpleasant state of its linen. Thereafter, since, as it turned out, we kept very different hours — I got up at noon, when, as I gathered by meeting him on the stairs one day, he was only just getting in — my new-found friend and I saw very little of each other.

On the evening of the nineteenth I was sitting thinking melancholy 5 thoughts about Christmas and staring at the walls of my room. I imagine that I had sold something or that someone had sent me a Christmas present, for I remember that I had a little money. In those days in Paris, though I floated, so to speak, on a sea of acquaintances, I knew almost no one. Many people were eliminated from my orbit by virtue of the fact that they had more money than I did, which placed me, in my own eyes, in the humiliating role of a free-loader; and other people were eliminated by virtue of the fact that they enjoyed their poverty, shrilly insisting that this wretched round of hotel rooms, bad food, humiliating concierges, and unpaid bills was the Great Adventure. It couldn't, however, for me, end soon enough, this Great Adventure; there was a real question in my mind as to which would end soonest, the Great Adventure or me. This meant, however, that there were many evenings when I sat in my room, knowing that I couldn't work there, and not knowing what to do, or whom to see. On this particular evening I went down and knocked on the American's door.

There were two Frenchmen standing in the room, who immediately introduced themselves to me as policemen; which did not worry me. I had got used to policemen in Paris bobbing up at the most improbable times and places, asking to see one's *carte d'identité*. [4] These policemen, however, showed very little interest in my papers. They were looking for something else. I could not imagine what this would be and, since I knew I certainly didn't have it, I scarcely followed the conversation they were having with my friend. I gathered that they were looking for some kind of gangster and since I wasn't a gangster and knew that gangsterism was not, insofar as he had one, my friend's style, I was sure that the two policemen would presently bow and say *Merci, messieurs,* and leave. For by this time, I remember very clearly, I was dying to have a drink and go to dinner.

I did not have a drink or go to dinner for many days after this, and when I did my outraged stomach promptly heaved everything up again. For now one of the policemen began to exhibit the most vivid interest in me and asked, very politely, if he might see my room. To which we mounted,

---

[4] *carte d'identité:* Identity papers or I.D. (French).

making, I remember, the most civilized small talk on the way and even continuing it for some moments after we were in the room in which there was certainly nothing to be seen but the familiar poverty and disorder of that precarious group of people of whatever age, race, country, calling, or intention which Paris recognizes as *les étudiants*[5] and sometimes, more ironically and precisely, as *les nonconformistes*. Then he moved to my bed, and in a terrible flash, not quite an instant before he lifted the bedspread, I understood what he was looking for. We looked at the sheet, on which I read, for the first time, lettered in the most brilliant scarlet I have ever seen, the name of the hotel from which it had been stolen. It was the first time the word *stolen* entered my mind. I had certainly seen the hotel monogram the day I put the sheet on the bed. It had simply meant nothing to me. In New York I had seen hotel monograms on everything from silver to soap and towels. Taking things from New York hotels was practically a custom, though, I suddenly realized, I had never known anyone to take a *sheet*. Sadly, and without a word to me, the inspector took the sheet from the bed, folded it under his arm, and we started back downstairs. I understood that I was under arrest.

And so we passed through the lobby, four of us, two of us very clearly criminal, under the eyes of the old man and his daughter, neither of whom said a word, into the streets where a light rain was falling. And I asked, in French, "But is this very serious?"

For I was thinking, it is, after all, only a sheet, not even new.

"No," said one of them. "It's not serious."

"It's nothing at all," said the other. 10

I took this to mean that we would receive a reprimand at the police station and be allowed to go to dinner. Later on I concluded that they were not being hypocritical or even trying to comfort us. They meant exactly what they said. It was only that they spoke another language.

In Paris everything is very slow. Also, when dealing with the bureaucracy, the man you are talking to is never the man you have to see. The man you have to see has just gone off to Belgium, or is busy with his family, or has just discovered that he is a cuckold; he will be in next Tuesday at three o'clock, or sometime in the course of the afternoon, or possibly tomorrow, or, possibly, in the next five minutes. But if he is coming in the next five minutes he will be far too busy to be able to see you today. So that I suppose I was not really astonished to learn at the commissariat that nothing could possibly be done about us before The Man arrived in the morning. But no, we could not go off and have dinner and come back in the morning. Of course he knew that we *would* come back — that was not the question. Indeed, there was no question: we would simply have to stay there for the night. We were placed in a cell which rather resembled a chicken coop. It

[5] *les étudiants:* College students (French).

was now about seven in the evening and I relinquished the thought of dinner and began to think of lunch.

I discouraged the chatter of my New York friend and this left me alone with my thoughts. I was beginning to be frightened and I bent all my energies, therefore, to keeping my panic under control. I began to realize that I was in a country I knew nothing about, in the hands of a people I did not understand at all. In a similar situation in New York I would have had some idea of what to do because I would have had some idea of what to expect. I am not speaking now of legality which, like most of the poor, I had never for an instant trusted, but of the temperament of the people with whom I had to deal. I had become very accomplished in New York at guessing and, therefore, to a limited extent manipulating to my advantage the reactions of the white world. But this was not New York. None of my old weapons could serve me here. I did not know what they saw when they looked at me. I knew very well what Americans saw when they looked at me and this allowed me to play endless and sinister variations on the role which they had assigned me; since I knew that it was, for them, of the utmost importance that they never be confronted with what, in their own personalities, made this role so necessary and gratifying to them, I knew that they could never call my hand or, indeed, afford to know what I was doing; so that I moved into every crucial situation with the deadly and rather desperate advantages of bitterly accumulated perception, of pride and contempt. This is an awful sword and shield to carry through the world, and the discovery that, in the game I was playing, I did myself a violence of which the world, at its most ferocious, would scarcely have been capable, was what had driven me out of New York. It was a strange feeling, in this situation, after a year in Paris, to discover that my weapons would never again serve me as they had.

It was quite clear to me that the Frenchmen in whose hands I found myself were no better or worse than their American counterparts. Certainly their uniforms frightened me quite as much, and their impersonality, and the threat, always very keenly felt by the poor, of violence, was as present in that commissariat as it had ever been for me in any police station. And I had seen, for example, what Paris policemen could do to Arab peanut vendors. The only difference here was that I did not understand these people, did not know what techniques their cruelty took, did not know enough about their personalities to see danger coming, to ward it off, did not know on what ground to meet it. That evening in the commissariat I was not a despised black man. They would simply have laughed at me if I had behaved like one. For them, I was an American. And here it was they who had the advantage, for that word, *Américain*, gave them some idea, far from inaccurate, of what to expect from me. In order to corroborate none of their ironical expectations I said nothing and did nothing — which was not the way any Frenchman, white or black, would have reacted. The question thrusting up from the bottom of my mind was not *what* I was, but *who*. And this question, since a *what* can get by with skill but a *who* demands resources, was my first real intimation of what humility must mean.

In the morning it was still raining. Between nine and ten o'clock a black Citroën took us off to the Ile de la Cité, to the great, gray Préfecture. I realize now that the questions I put to the various policemen who escorted us were always answered in such a way as to corroborate what I wished to hear. This was not out of politeness, but simply out of indifference — or, possibly, an ironical pity — since each of the policemen knew very well that nothing would speed or halt the machine in which I had become entangled. They knew I did not know this and there was certainly no point in their telling me. In one way or another I would certainly come out at the other side — for they also knew that being found with a stolen bedsheet in one's possession was not a crime punishable by the guillotine. (They had the advantage over me there, too, for there were certainly moments later on when I was not so sure.) If I did *not* come out at the other side — well, that was just too bad. So, to my question, put while we were in the Citroën — "Will it be over today?" — I received a "*Oui, bien sûr.*" [6] He was not lying. As it turned out, the *procès-verbal* [7] was over that day. Trying to be realistic, I dismissed, in the Citroën, all thoughts of lunch and pushed my mind ahead to dinner.

At the Préfecture we were first placed in a tiny cell, in which it was almost impossible either to sit or to lie down. After a couple of hours of this we were taken down to an office, where, for the first time, I encountered the owner of the bedsheet and where the *procès-verbal* took place. This was simply an interrogation, quite chillingly clipped and efficient (so that there was, shortly, no doubt in one's own mind that one *should* be treated as a criminal), which was recorded by a secretary. When it was over, this report was given to us to sign. One had, of course, no choice but to sign it, even though my mastery of written French was very far from certain. We were being held, according to the law in France, incommunicado, and all my angry demands to be allowed to speak to my embassy or to see a lawyer met with a stony "*Oui, oui. Plus tard.*" [8] The *procès-verbal* over, we were taken back to the cell, before which, shortly, passed the owner of the bedsheet. He said he hoped we had slept well, gave a vindictive wink, and disappeared.

By this time there was only one thing clear: that we had no way of controlling the sequence of events and could not possibly guess what this sequence would be. It seemed to me, since what I regarded as the high point — the *procès-verbal* — had been passed and since the hotel-keeper was once again in possession of his sheet, that we might reasonably expect to be released from police custody in a matter of hours. We had been detained

[6] *Oui, bien sûr:* "Yes, of course." (French).

[7] *procès-verbal:* Statement (French).

[8] *Oui, oui. Plus tard:* "Yes, yes. Later." (French).

now for what would soon be twenty-four hours, during which time I had learned only that the official charge against me was *receleur*. [9] My mental shifting, between lunch and dinner, to say nothing of the physical lack of either of these delights, was beginning to make me dizzy. The steady chatter of my friend from New York, who was determined to keep my spirits up, made me feel murderous; I was praying that some power would release us from this freezing pile of stone before the impulse became the act. And I was beginning to wonder what was happening in that beautiful city, Paris, which lived outside these walls. I wondered how long it would take before anyone casually asked, "But where's Jimmy? He hasn't been around" — and realized, knowing the people I knew, that it would take several days.

Quite late in the afternoon we were taken from our cells; handcuffed, each to a separate officer; led through a maze of steps and corridors to the top of the building; fingerprinted; photographed. As in movies I had seen, I was placed against a wall, facing an old-fashioned camera, behind which stood one of the most completely cruel and indifferent faces I had ever seen, while someone next to me and, therefore, just outside my line of vision, read off in a voice from which all human feeling, even feeling of the most base description, had long since fled, what must be called my public characteristics — which, at that time and in that place, seemed anything but that. He might have been roaring to the hostile world secrets which I could barely, in the privacy of midnight, utter to myself. But he was only reading off my height, my features, my approximate weight, my color — that color which, in the United States, had often, odd as it may sound, been my salvation — the color of my hair, my age, my nationality. A light then flashed, the photographer and I staring at each other as though there was murder in our hearts, and then it was over. Handcuffed again, I was led downstairs to the bottom of the building, into a great enclosed shed in which had been gathered the very scrapings off the Paris streets. Old, old men, so ruined and old that life in them seemed really to prove the miracle of the quickening power of the Holy Ghost — for clearly their life was no longer their affair, it was no longer even their burden, they were simply the clay which had once been touched. And men not so old, with faces the color of lead and the consistency of oatmeal, eyes that made me think of stale *café-au-lait* spiked with arsenic, bodies which could take in food and water — any food and water — and pass it out, but which could not do anything more, except possibly, at midnight, along the riverbank where rats scurried, rape. And young men, harder and crueler than the Paris stones, older by far than I, their chronological senior by some five to seven years. And North Africans, old and young, who seemed the only living people in this place because they yet retained the grace to be bewildered. But they were not bewildered by being in this shed: they were simply bewildered because they were no longer

[9] *receleur:* Receiver of stolen goods (French).

in North Africa. There was a great hole in the center of this shed which was the common toilet. Near it, though it was impossible to get very far from it, stood an old man with white hair, eating a piece of camembert. It was at this point, probably, that thought, for me, stopped, that physiology, if one may say so, took over. I found myself incapable of saying a word, not because I was afraid I would cry but because I was afraid I would vomit. And I did not think any longer of the city of Paris but my mind flew back to that home from which I had fled. I was sure that I would never see it any more. And it must have seemed to me that my flight from home was the cruelest trick I had ever played on myself, since it had led me here, down to a lower point than any I could ever in my life have imagined — lower, far, than anything I had seen in that Harlem which I had so hated and so loved, the escape from which had soon become the greatest direction of my life. After we had been here an hour or so a functionary came and opened the door and called out our names. And I was sure that *this* was my release. But I was handcuffed again and led out of the Préfecture into the streets — it was dark now, it was still raining — and before the steps of the Préfecture stood the great police wagon, doors facing me, wide open. The handcuffs were taken off, I entered the wagon, which was peculiarly constructed. It was divided by a narrow aisle, and on each side of the aisle was a series of narrow doors. These doors opened on a narrow cubicle, beyond which was a door which opened onto another narrow cubicle: three or four cubicles, each private, with a locking door. I was placed in one of them; I remember there was a small vent just above my head which let in a little light. The door of my cubicle was locked from the outside. I had no idea where this wagon was taking me and, as it began to move, I began to cry. I suppose I cried all the way to prison, the prison called Fresnes, which is twelve kilometers outside of Paris.

For reasons I have no way at all of understanding, prisoners whose last 20 initial is A, B, or C are always sent to Fresnes; everybody else is sent to a prison called, rather cynically it seems to me, La Santé. I will, obviously, never be allowed to enter La Santé, but I was told by people who certainly seemed to know that it was infinitely more unbearable than Fresnes. This arouses in me, until today, a positive storm of curiosity concerning what I promptly began to think of as The Other Prison. My colleague in crime, occurring lower in the alphabet, had been sent there and I confess that the minute he was gone I missed him. I missed him because he was not French and because he was the only person in the world who knew that the story I told was true.

For, once locked in, divested of shoelaces, belt, watch, money, papers, nailfile, in a freezing cell in which both the window and the toilet were broken, with six other adventurers, the story I told of *l'affaire du drap de lit* [10] elicited only the wildest amusement or the most suspicious disbelief.

[10] *l'affaire du . . . lit:* The affair of the bedsheet (French).

Among the people who shared my cell the first three days no one, it is true, had been arrested for anything much more serious — or, at least, not serious in my eyes. I remember that there was a boy who had stolen a knitted sweater from a *monoprix*, [11] who would probably, it was agreed, receive a six-month sentence. There was an older man there who had been arrested for some kind of petty larceny. There were two North Africans, vivid, brutish, and beautiful, who alternated between gaiety and fury, not at the fact of their arrest but at the state of the cell. None poured as much emotional energy into the fact of their arrest as I did; they took it, as I would have liked to take it, as simply another unlucky happening in a very dirty world. For, though I had grown accustomed to thinking of myself as looking upon the world with a hard, penetrating eye, the truth was that they were far more realistic about the world than I, and more nearly right about it. The gap between us, which only a gesture I made could have bridged, grew steadily, during thirty-six hours, wider. I could not make any gesture simply because they frightened me. I was unable to accept my imprisonment as a fact, even as a temporary fact. I could not, even for a moment, accept my present companions as *my* companions. And they, of course, felt this and put it down, with perfect justice, to the fact that I was an American.

There was nothing to do all day long. It appeared that we would one day come to trial but no one knew when. We were awakened at seven-thirty by a rapping on what I believe is called the Judas, that small opening in the door of the cell which allows the guards to survey the prisoners. At this rapping we rose from the floor — we slept on straw pallets and each of us was covered with one thin blanket — and moved to the door of the cell. We peered through the opening into the center of the prison, which was, as I remember, three tiers high, all gray stone and gunmetal steel, precisely that prison I had seen in movies, except that, in the movies, I had not known that it was cold in prison. I had not known that when one's shoelaces and belt have been removed one is, in the strangest way, demoralized. The necessity of shuffling and the necessity of holding up one's trousers with one hand turn one into a rag doll. And the movies fail, of course, to give one any idea of what prison food is like. Along the corridor, at seven-thirty, came three men, each pushing before him a great garbage can, mounted on wheels. In the garbage can of the first was the bread — this was passed to one through the small opening in the door. In the can of the second was the coffee. In the can of the third was what was always called *la soupe*, a pallid paste of potatoes which had certainly been bubbling on the back of the prison stove long before that first, so momentous revolution. Naturally, it was cold by this time and, starving as I was, I could not eat it. I drank the coffee — which was not coffee — because it was hot, and spent the rest of the day, huddled in my blanket, munching on the bread. It was not the French bread

[11] *monoprix:* Inexpensive department store (French).

one bought in bakeries. In the evening the same procession returned. At ten-thirty the lights went out. I had a recurring dream, each night, a nightmare which always involved my mother's fried chicken. At the moment I was about to eat it came the rapping at the door. Silence is really all I remember of those first three days, silence and the color gray.

I am not sure now whether it was on the third or the fourth day that I was taken to trial for the first time. The days had nothing, obviously, to distinguish them from one another. I remember that I was very much aware that Christmas Day was approaching and I wondered if I was really going to spend Christmas Day in prison. And I remember that the first trial came the day before Christmas Eve.

On the morning of the first trial I was awakened by hearing my name called. I was told, hanging in a kind of void between my mother's fried chicken and the cold prison floor, "*Vous préparez. Vous êtes extrait*" [12] — which simply terrified me, since I did not know what interpretation to put on the word "*extrait*," and since my cellmates had been amusing themselves with me by telling terrible stories about the inefficiency of French prisons, an inefficiency so extreme that it had often happened that someone who was supposed to be taken out and tried found himself on the wrong line and was guillotined instead. The best way of putting my reaction to this is to say that, though I knew they were teasing me, it was simply not possible for me to totally *dis*believe them. As far as I was concerned, once in the hands of the law in France, anything could happen. I shuffled along with the others who were *extrait* to the center of the prison, trying, rather, to linger in the office, which seemed the only warm spot in the whole world, and found myself again in that dreadful wagon, and was carried again to the Ile de la Cité, this time to the Palais de Justice. The entire day, except for ten minutes, was spent in one of the cells, first waiting to be tried, then waiting to be taken back to prison.

For I was *not* tried that day. By and by I was handcuffed and led through the halls, upstairs to the courtroom where I found my New York friend. We were placed together, both stage-whisperingly certain that this was the end of our ordeal. Nevertheless, while I waited for our case to be called, my eyes searched the courtroom, looking for a face I knew, hoping, anyway, that there was someone there who knew *me*, who would carry to someone outside the news that I was in trouble. But there was no one I knew there and I had had time to realize that there was probably only one man in Paris who could help me, an American patent attorney for whom I had worked as an office boy. He could have helped me because he had a quite solid position and some prestige and would have testified that, while working for him, I had handled large sums of money regularly, which made it rather unlikely that I would stoop to trafficking in bedsheets. However,

[12] *Vous préparez . . . extrait:* "Get ready. You are taken out." (French).

he was somewhere in Paris, probably at this very moment enjoying a snack and a glass of wine and as far as the possibility of reaching him was concerned, he might as well have been on Mars. I tried to watch the proceedings and to make my mind a blank. But the proceedings were not reassuring. The boy, for example, who had stolen the sweater *did* receive a six-month sentence. It seemed to me that all the sentences meted out that day were excessive; though, again, it seemed that all the people who were sentenced that day had made, or clearly were going to make, crime their career. This seemed to be the opinion of the judge, who scarcely looked at the prisoners or listened to them; it seemed to be the opinion of the prisoners, who scarcely bothered to speak in their own behalf; it seemed to be the opinion of the lawyers, state lawyers for the most part, who were defending them. The great impulse of the courtroom seemed to be to put these people where they could not be seen — and not because they were offended at the crimes, unless, indeed, they were offended that the crimes were so petty, but because they did not wish to know that their society could be counted on to produce, probably in greater and greater numbers, a whole body of people for whom crime was the only possible career. Any society inevitably produces its criminals, but a society at once rigid and unstable can do nothing whatever to alleviate the poverty of its lowest members, cannot present to the hypothetical young man at the crucial moment that so-well-advertised right path. And the fact, perhaps, that the French are the earth's least sentimental people and must also be numbered among the most proud aggravates the plight of their lowest, youngest, and unluckiest members, for it means that the idea of rehabilitation is scarcely real to them. I confess that this attitude on their part raises in me sentiments of exasperation, admiration, and despair, revealing as it does, in both the best and the worst sense, their renowned and spectacular hard-headedness.

Finally our case was called and we rose. We gave our names. At the point that it developed that we were American the proceedings ceased, a hurried consultation took place between the judge and what I took to be several lawyers. Someone called out for an interpreter. The arresting officer had forgotten to mention our nationalities and there was, therefore, no interpreter in the court. Even if our French had been better than it was we would not have been allowed to stand trial without an interpreter. Before I clearly understood what was happening, I was handcuffed again and led out of the courtroom. The trial had been set back for the twenty-seventh of December.

I have sometimes wondered if I would *ever* have got out of prison if it had not been for the older man who had been arrested for the mysterious petty larceny. He was acquitted that day and when he returned to the cell — for he could not be released until morning — he found me sitting numbly on the floor, having just been prevented, by the sight of a man, all blood, being carried back to *his* cell on a stretcher, from seizing the bars and screaming until they let me out. The sight of the man on the stretcher proved, however, that screaming would not do much for me. The petty-larceny man went around asking if he could do anything in the world outside for those he was leaving behind. When he came to me I, at first, responded, "No, nothing" — for I suppose I had by now retreated into the attitude, the earliest I remember, that of my father, which was simply (since I had lost his God) that nothing could help me. And I suppose I will remember with gratitude until I die the fact that the man now insisted: "*Mais, êtes-vous sûr?*" [13] Then it swept over me that he was going *outside* and he instantly became my first contact since the Lord alone knew how long with the outside world. At the same time, I remember, I did not really believe that he would help me. There was no reason why he should. But I gave him the phone number of my attorney friend and my own name.

So, in the middle of the next day, Christmas Eve, I shuffled downstairs again, to meet my visitor. He looked extremely well fed and sane and clean. He told me I had nothing to worry about any more. Only not even he could do anything to make the mill of justice grind any faster. He would, however, send me a lawyer of his acquaintance who would defend me on the 27th, and he would himself, along with several other people, appear as a character witness. He gave me a package of Lucky Strikes (which the turnkey took from me on the way upstairs) and said that, though it was doubtful that there would be any celebration in the prison, he would see to it that I got a fine Christmas dinner when I got out. And this, somehow, seemed very funny. I remember being astonished at the discovery that I was actually laughing. I was, too, I imagine, also rather disappointed that my hair had not turned white, that my face was clearly not going to bear any marks of tragedy, disappointed at bottom, no doubt, to realize, facing him in that room, that far worse things had happened to most people and that, indeed, to paraphrase my mother, if this was the worst thing that ever happened to me I could consider myself among the luckiest people ever to be born. He injected — my visitor — into my solitary nightmare common sense, the world, and the hint of blacker things to come.

The next day, Christmas, unable to endure my cell, and feeling that, after all, the day demanded a gesture, I asked to be allowed to go to Mass, hoping to hear some music. But I found myself, for a freezing hour and a half, locked in exactly the same kind of cubicle as in the wagon which had first brought me to prison, peering through a slot placed at the level of the eye at an old Frenchman, hatted, overcoated, muffled, and gloved, preaching in this language which I did not understand, to this row of wooden boxes, the story of Jesus Christ's love for men.

The next day, the twenty-sixth, I spent learning a peculiar kind of game, played with matchsticks, with my cellmates. For, since I no longer felt that I would stay in this cell forever, I was beginning to be able to make

30

---

[13] *Mais . . . sûr?:* "But, are you certain?" (French).

peace with it for a time. On the twenty-seventh I went again to trial and, as had been predicted, the case against us was dismissed. The story of the *drap de lit*, [14] finally told, caused great merriment in the courtroom, whereupon my friend decided that the French were "great." I was chilled by their merriment, even though it was meant to warm me. It could only remind me of the laughter I had often heard at home, laughter which I had sometimes deliberately elicited. This laughter is the laughter of those who consider themselves to be at a safe remove from all the wretched, for whom the pain of the living is not real. I had heard it so often in my native land that I had resolved to find a place where I would never hear it any more. In some deep, black, stony, and liberating way, my life, in my own eyes, began during that first year in Paris, when it was borne in on me that this laughter is universal and never can be stilled.

[14] *drap de lit:* Bedsheet (French).

FROM READING TO REREADING

1. Consider Baldwin's title within the context of the entire essay. What do you think he means by "equal"? To whom does the word apply?

2. Baldwin uses the term "comic-opera" to describe a certain aspect of his experience. How does Baldwin introduce comic elements into the essay? In what sense does Baldwin find his own experience to be humorous?

3. Baldwin claims that his experience ended with an illumination. What does he learn about the French and about life in general? What does he learn about himself from his encounter with the French legal system?

JOAN DIDION
Miami

Joan Didion has a reputation for being one of the most astute observers of place among contemporary American writers. In her essays and nonfiction books she has written about, among other places, Hawaii, El Salvador, New York, and Los Angeles. Unlike many American essayists who seem more at home in rural than urban landscapes, Didion has a remarkable talent for assessing the material and moral fabric of a major city. The following selection, though not originally published as an essay, is a self-contained vignette from her 1987 book, Miami. *It shows Didion doing what she does best: painting a large picture with just a few well-placed strokes.*

DURING THE SPRING when I began visiting Miami all of Florida was reported to be in drought, with dropping water tables and unfilled aquifers and SAVE WATER signs, but drought, in a part of the world which would be in its natural state a shelf of porous oolitic limestone covered most of the year by a shallow sheet flow of fresh water, proved relative. During this drought the city of Coral Gables continued, as it had every night since 1924, to empty and refill its Venetian Pool with fresh unchlorinated water, 820,000 gallons a day out of the water supply and into the storm sewer. There was less water than there might have been in the Biscayne Aquifer but there was water everywhere above it. There were rains so hard that windshield wipers stopped working and cars got swamped and stalled on I-95. There was water roiling and bubbling over the underwater lights in decorative pools. There was water sluicing off the six-story canted window at the Omni, a hotel from which it was possible to see, in the Third World way, both the slums of Overtown and those island houses with the Unusual Security and Ready Access to the Ocean, equally wet. Water plashed off banana palms, water puddled on flat roofs, water streamed down the CARNE U.S. GOOD & U.S. STANDARD signs on Flagler Street. Water rocked the impounded drug boats which lined the Miami River and water lapped against the causeways on the bay. I got used to the smell of incipient mildew in my clothes. I stuffed Kleenex in wet shoes and stopped expecting them to dry.

A certain liquidity suffused everything about the place. Causeways and bridges and even Brickell Avenue did not stay put but rose and fell, allowing the masts of ships to glide among the marble and glass facades of the unleased office buildings. The buildings themselves seemed to swim free against the sky: there had grown up in Miami during the recent money years an architecture which appeared to have slipped its moorings, a not inappropriate style for a terrain with only a provisional claim on being land at all. Surfaces were reflective, opalescent. Angles were oblique, intersecting to disorienting effect. The Arquitectonica office, which produced the celebrated glass condominium on Brickell Avenue with the fifty-foot cube cut from its center, the frequently photographed "sky patio" in which there floated a palm tree, a Jacuzzi, and a lipstick-red spiral staircase, accompanied its elevations with crayon sketches, all moons and starry skies and airborne maidens, as in a Chagall. [1] Skidmore, Owings and Merrill managed, in its Southeast Financial Center, the considerable feat of rendering fifty-five stories of polished gray granite incorporeal, a sky-blue illusion.

Nothing about Miami was exactly fixed, or hard. Hard consonants were missing from the local speech patterns, in English as well as in Spanish. Local money tended to move on hydraulic verbs: when it was not being washed it was being diverted, or channeled through Mexico, or turned off in Washington. Local stories tended to turn on underwater plot points, submerged snappers: on unsoundable extradition proceedings in the Bahamas, say, or fluid connections with the Banco Nacional de Colombia. I recall trying to touch the bottom of one such story in the *Herald*, about six hand grenades which had just been dug up in the bay-front backyard of a Biscayne Boulevard pawnbroker who had been killed in his own bed a few years before, shot at close range with a .25-caliber automatic pistol.

There were some other details on the surface of this story, for example the wife who fired the .25-caliber automatic pistol and the nineteen-year-old daughter who was up on federal weapons charges and the flight attendant who rented the garage apartment and said that the pawnbroker had collected "just basic things like rockets, just defused things," but the underwater narrative included, at last sounding, the Central Intelligence Agency (with which the pawnbroker was said to have been associated), the British intelligence agency M16 (with which the pawnbroker was also said to have been associated), the late Anastasio Somoza Debayle (whose family the pawnbroker was said to have spirited into Miami shortly before the regime fell in Managua), the late shah of Iran (whose presence in Panama was said to have queered an arms deal about which the pawnbroker had been told), Dr. Josef Mengele [2] (for whom the pawnbroker was said to be searching), and a Pompano Beach resident last seen cruising Miami in a cinnamon-colored Cadillac Sedan de Ville and looking to buy, he said for the Salvadoran

[1] *Chagall*: Marc Chagall (1887–1985), Russian-born French artist known for his dreamlike paintings.

[2] *Dr. Josef Mengele* (1911–1979): Notorious Nazi concentration camp doctor who sent over four hundred thousand victims to the gas chambers and conducted horrific "medical" experiments on prisoners. Mengele was the most elusive of the Nazi war criminals.

insurgents, a million rounds of ammunition, thirteen thousand assault rifles, and "at least a couple" of jeep-mounted machine guns.

In this mood Miami seemed not a city at all but a tale, a romance of 5 the tropics, a kind of waking dream in which any possibility could and would be accommodated. The most ordinary morning, say at the courthouse, could open onto the distinctly lurid. "I don't think he came out with me, that's all," I recall hearing someone say one day in an elevator at the Miami federal courthouse. His voice had kept rising. "What happened to all that stuff about how next time, he gets twenty keys, he could run wherever-it-is Idaho, now he says he wouldn't know what to do with five keys, what is this shit?" His companion had shrugged. We had continued in silence to the main floor. Outside one courtroom that day a group of Colombians, the women in silk shirts and Chanel necklaces and Charles Jourdan suede pumps, the children in appliquéd dresses from Baby Dior, had been waiting for the decision in a pretrial detention hearing, one in which the government was contending that the two defendants, who between them lived in houses in which eighty-three kilos of cocaine and a million-three in cash had been found, failed to qualify as good bail risks.

"That doesn't make him a longtime drug dealer," one of the two defense lawyers, both of whom were Anglo and one of whom drove a Mercedes 380 SEL with the license plate DEFENSE, had argued about the million-three in cash. "That could be one transaction." Across the hall that day closing arguments were being heard in a boat case, a "boat case" being one in which a merchant or fishing vessel has been boarded and drugs seized and eight or ten Colombian crew members arrested, the kind of case in which pleas were typically entered so that one of the Colombians would get eighteen months and the others deported. There were never any women in Chanel necklaces around a boat case, and the lawyers (who were usually hired and paid for not by the defendants but by the unnamed owner of the "load," or shipment) tended to be Cuban. "You had the great argument, you got to give me some good ideas," one of the eight Cuban defense lawyers on this case joked with the prosecutor during a recess. "But you haven't heard my argument yet," another of the defense lawyers said. "The stuff about communism. Fabulous closing argument."

Just as any morning could turn lurid, any moment could turn final, again as in a dream. "I heard a loud, short noise and then there was jsut a plain moment of dullness," the witness to a shooting in a Miami Beach supermarket parking lot told the *Herald*. "There was no one around except me and two bagboys." I happened to be in the coroner's office one morning when autopsies were being performed on the bodies of two Mariels, shot and apparently pushed from a car on I-95 about nine the evening before, another plain moment of dullness. The story had been on television an hour or two after it happened: I had seen the crime site on the eleven o'clock news, and had not expected to see the victims in the morning. "When he came here in Mariel he stayed at our house but he didn't get along with my mom," a young girl was saying in the anteroom to one of the detectives working the case. "These two guys were killed together," the detective had pressed. "They probably knew each other."

"For sure," the young girl had said, agreeably. Inside the autopsy room the hands of the two young men were encased in the brown paper bags which indicated that the police had not yet taken what they needed for laboratory studies. Their flesh had the marbleized yellow look of the recently dead. There were other bodies in the room, in various stages of autopsy, and a young woman in a white coat taking eyes, for the eye bank. "Who are we going to start on next?" one of the assistant medical examiners was saying. "The fat guy? Let's do the fat guy."

It was even possible to enter the waking dream without leaving the house, just by reading the *Herald*. A Mariel named Jose "Coca-Cola" Yero gets arrested, with nine acquaintances, in a case involving 1,664 pounds of cocaine, a thirty-seven-foot Cigarette boat named *The Connection*, two Lamborghinis, a million-six in cash, a Mercedes 500 SEL with another $350,000 in cash in the trunk, one dozen Rolex watches color-coordinated to match Jose "Coca-Cola" Yero's wardrobe, and various houses in Dade and Palm Beach counties, a search of one of which turns up not just a photograph of Jose "Coca-Cola" Yero face down in a pile of white powder but also a framed poster of Al Pacino as Tony Montana, the Mariel who appears at a dramatic moment in *Scarface* face down in a pile of white powder. "They got swept up in the fast lane," a Metro-Dade narcotics detective advises the *Herald*. "The fast lane is what put this whole group in jail." A young woman in South Palm Beach goes out to the parking lot of her parents' condominium and gets into her 1979 Pontiac Firebird, opens the T-top, starts the ignition and loses four toes when the bomb goes off. "She definitely knows someone is trying to kill her," the sheriff's investigator tells the *Herald*. "She knew they were coming, but she didn't know when."

Surfaces tended to dissolve here. Clear days ended less so. I recall an 10 October Sunday when my husband and I were taken, by Gene Miller, a *Herald* editor who had won two Pulitzer Prizes for investigative reporting and who had access to season tickets exactly on the fifty-yard line at the Orange Bowl, to see the Miami Dolphins beat the Pittsburgh Steelers, 21–17. In a row below us the former Dolphin quarterback Earl Morrall signed autographs for the children who wriggled over seats to slip him their programs and steal surreptitious glances at his Super Bowl ring. A few rows back an Anglo teenager in sandals and shorts and a black T-shirt smoked a marijuana cigarette in full view of the Hispanic police officer behind him. Hot dogs were passed, and Coca-Cola spilled. Sony Watchmans were compared, for the definition on the instant replay. The NBC cameras dollied along the sidelines and the Dolphin cheerleaders kneeled on their white pom-poms and there was a good deal of talk about red dogging and weak secondaries and who would be seen and what would be eaten in New Orleans, come Super Bowl weekend.

The Miami on display in the Orange Bowl that Sunday afternoon would have seemed another Miami altogether, one with less weather and harder, more American surfaces, but by dinner we were slipping back into the tropical: in a virtually empty restaurant on top of a virtually empty condominium off Biscayne Boulevard, with six people at the table, one of whom was Gene Miller and one of whom was Martin Dardis, who as the chief investigator for the state attorney's office in Miami had led Carl Bernstein [3] through the local angles on Watergate and who remained a walking data bank on CDs at the Biscayne Bank and on who called who on what payoff and on how to follow a money chain, we sat and we talked and we watched a storm break over Biscayne Bay. Sheets of warm rain washed down the big windows. Lightning began to fork somewhere around Bal Harbour. Gene Miller mentioned the Alberto Duque trial, then entering its fourth week at the federal courthouse, the biggest bank fraud case ever tried in the United States. Martin Dardis mentioned the ESM Government Securities collapse, just then breaking into a fraud case maybe bigger than the Duque.

The lightning was no longer forking now but illuminating the entire sky, flashing a dead strobe white, turning the bay fluorescent and the islands black, as if in negative. I sat and I listened to Gene Miller and Martin Dardis discuss these old and new turns in the underwater narrative and I watched the lightning backlight the islands. During the time I had spent in Miami many people had mentioned, always as something extraordinary, something I should have seen if I wanted to understand Miami, the *Surrounded Islands* project executed in Biscayne Bay in 1983 by the Bulgarian artist Christo. *Surrounded Islands*, which had involved surrounding eleven islands with two-hundred-foot petals, or skirts, of pink polypropylene fabric, had been mentioned both by people who were knowledgeable about conceptual art and by people who had not before heard and could not then recall the name of the man who had surrounded the islands. All had agreed. It seemed that the pink had shimmered in the water. It seemed that the pink had kept changing color, fading and reemerging with the movement of the water and the clouds and the sun and the night lights. It seemed that this period when the pink was in the water had for many people exactly defined, as the backlit islands and the fluorescent water and the voices at the table were that night defining for me, Miami.

[3] *Carl Bernstein*: One of the *Washington Post* reporters who broke the Watergate scandal that led to President Nixon's resignation.

FROM READING TO REREADING

1. The selection begins with literal references to drought and water. How do those references take on metaphorical significance? How do they help establish an image of the city?

2. Didion works into her description many brief quotations, several of them overheard remarks. What effect do these comments have on your overall impression of Miami?

3. Didion ends her description with a reference to *Surrounded Islands,* an art work by the Bulgarian artist Christo. Why do people think that Christo's work helps one understand Miami? How does it contribute to Didion's definition of Miami?

From Reading to Writing

1. Both Alice Walker and E. B. White write about visits to sites in which they pay homage to the memory of someone they admire. Consider similar journeys you may have taken — to a historical monument, to a national or local landmark, or to a commemorative event. Write an essay in which you describe your journey and what you found there. (You may even want to imitate E. B. White and style your essay in the form of a letter.)

2. The essays of Cynthia Ozick and Annie Dillard contain what may be called a philosophy of travel. Both deal with travel and perception; both attempt to describe the particularity of place. Using their essays as examples, write an essay in which you develop your own philosophy of travel. What do you think travelers should be alert to? Do you make any distinction between travelers and tourists?

3. Both James Baldwin and Joan Didion write about some of the sinister and criminal aspects of large cities. What have been your experiences in visiting a new city, either at home or abroad? Write an essay describing such a visit. Can you capture or "define" the mood of the city in a few well-selected details? Did the city take on any frightening qualities?

6

Other Creatures

LEWIS THOMAS
The Tucson Zoo

When the French writer Michel de Montaigne set the essay on its modern course some four hundred years ago, he not only gave the genre its name and its personality but he also established a range of themes that future essayists would return to again and again. One of these recurring themes is what Montaigne referred to as "the animals that live among us." In his earliest work, Montaigne wrote that "there is more difference between a given man and a given man than between a given animal and a given man." An avid reader of Montaigne, Lewis Thomas has often written about other creatures, especially those of microscopic size. In "The Tucson Zoo," with its sensitivity to animal life, its skepticism about rationality, and its sudden jumps in thought, Thomas clearly shows his indebtedness to Montaigne's still influential style of writing and thinking.

S CIENCE GETS MOST of its information by the process of reductionism, exploring the details, then the details of the details, until all the smallest bits of the structure, or the smallest parts of the mechanism, are laid out for counting and scrutiny. Only when this is done can the investigation be extended to encompass the whole organism or the entire system. So we say.

Sometimes it seems that we take a loss, working this way. Much of today's public anxiety about science is the apprehension that we may forever be overlooking the whole by an endless, obsessive preoccupation with the parts. I had a brief, personal experience of this misgiving one afternoon in Tucson, where I had time on my hands and visited the zoo, just outside the city. The designers there have cut a deep pathway between two small artificial ponds, walled by clear glass, so when you stand in the center of the path you can look into the depths of each pool, and at the same time you can regard the surface. In one pool, on the right side of the path, is a family of otters; on the other side, a family of beavers. Within just a few feet from your face, on either side, beavers and otters are at play, underwater and on the surface, swimming toward your face and then away, more filled with life than any creatures I have ever seen before, in all my days. Except for the glass, you could reach across and touch them.

I was transfixed. As I now recall it, there was only one sensation in my head: pure elation mixed with amazement at such perfection. Swept off my feet, I floated from one side to the other, swiveling my brain, staring astounded at the beavers, then at the otters. I could hear shouts across my corpus callosum, from one hemisphere to the other. I remember thinking, with what was left in charge of my consciousness, that I wanted no part of the science of beavers and otters; I wanted never to know how they performed their marvels; I wished for no news about the physiology of their breathing, the coordination of their muscles, their vision, their endocrine systems, their digestive tracts. I hoped never to have to think of them as collections of cells. All I asked for was the full hairy complexity, then in front of my eyes, of whole, intact beavers and otters in motion.

It lasted, I regret to say, for only a few minutes, and then I was back in the late twentieth century, reductionist as ever, wondering about the details by force of habit, but not, this time, the details of otters and beavers. Instead, me. Something worth remembering had happened in my mind. I was certain of that; I would have put it somewhere in the brain stem; maybe this was my limbic system at work. I became a behavioral scientist, an experimental psychologist, an ethologist, and in the instant I lost all the wonder and the sense of being overwhelmed. I was flattened.

But I came away from the zoo with something, a piece of news about myself: I am coded, somehow, for otters and beavers. I exhibit instinctive behavior in their presence, when they are displayed close at hand behind glass, simultaneously below water and at the surface. I have receptors for this display. Beavers and otters possess a "releaser" for me, in the terminology of ethology, and the releasing was my experience. What was released? Behavior. What behavior? Standing, swiveling flabbergasted, feeling exultation and a rush of friendship. I could not, as the result of the transaction, tell you anything more about beavers and otters than you already know. I learned nothing new about them. Only about me, and I suspect also about you, maybe about human beings at large: we are endowed with genes which code out our reaction to beavers and otters, maybe our reaction to each other as well. We are stamped with stereotyped, unalterable patterns of response, ready to be released. And the behavior released in us, by such confrontations, is, essentially, a surprised affection. It is compulsory behavior and we can avoid it only by straining with the full power of our conscious minds, making up conscious excuses all the way. Left to ourselves, mechanistic and autonomic, we hanker for friends.

Everyone says, stay away from ants. They have no lessons for us; they are crazy little instruments, inhuman, incapable of controlling themselves, lacking manners, lacking souls. When they are massed together, all touching, exchanging bits of information held in their jaws like memoranda, they become a single animal. Look out for that. It is debasement, a loss of individuality, a violation of human nature, an unnatural act.

Sometimes people argue this point of view seriously and with deep thought. Be individuals, solitary and selfish, is the message. Altruism, a jargon word for what used to be called love, is worse than weakness, it is sin, a violation of nature. Be separate. Do not be a social animal. But this is a hard argument to make convincingly when you have to depend on language

to make it. You have to print up leaflets or publish books and get them
bought and sent around, you have to turn up on television and catch the
attention of millions of other human beings all at once, and then you have
to say to all of them, all at once, all collected and paying attention: be
solitary; do not depend on each other. You can't do this and keep a straight
face.

Maybe altruism is our most primitive attribute, out of reach, beyond
our control. Or perhaps it is immediately at hand, waiting to be released,
disguised now, in our kind of civilization, as affection or friendship or attachment. I don't see why it should be unreasonable for all human beings to
have strands of DNA coiled up in chromosomes, coding out instincts for
usefulness and helpfulness. Usefulness may turn out to be the hardest test
of fitness for survival, more important than aggression, more effective, in the
long run, than grabbiness. If this is the sort of information biological science
holds for the future, applying to us as well as to ants, then I am all for
science.

One thing I'd like to know most of all: When those ants have made
the Hill, and are all there, touching and and exchanging, and the whole mass
begins to behave like a single huge creature, and *thinks*, what on earth is that
thought? And while you're at it, I'd like to know a second thing: When it
happens, does any single ant know about it? Does his hair stand on end?

FROM READING TO REREADING

1. The level of diction, or word choice, we use in our essays often determines
our overall tone and self-image: Do we sound formal, informal, chatty, slangy, or
stuffy? Notice that Lewis Thomas juxtaposes two levels of diction — one scientific,
the other colloquial — as he moves through his essay. Make a rough classification of
words from each level. How does this mixture help Thomas make his point?

2. Notice that in paragraph 5, Thomas moves from "I" to "we." What is the
significance of this jump? Do you think it is justified?

3. In the sixth paragraph, Thomas suddenly jumps to a consideration of ants,
with no conventional paragraph transition. The sudden jump is, of course, deliberate.
Why do you think Thomas violates normal compositional usage at this point?

ANNIE DILLARD
Living Like Weasels

"Living Like Weasels" seems to pick up where the preceding esssay left off: How do other creatures think? *Is it possible to know? What would it be like to enter the mind of an otter, or an ant, or a weasel? Stimulated by a sudden moment of intense contact with a weasel, Annie Dillard wonders about the way her own mind works and offers a meditation on how life might be lived if we learned "something in mindlessness" and the "purity of living in the physical senses." When Dillard assembled a set of essays for inclusion in her 1982 collection* Teaching a Stone to Talk, *she opened the volume with this one.*

A WEASEL IS WILD. Who knows what he thinks? He sleeps in his underground den, his tail draped over his nose. Sometimes he lives in his den for two days without leaving. Outside, he stalks rabbits, mice, muskrats, and birds, killing more bodies than he can eat warm, and often dragging the carcasses home. Obedient to instinct, he bites his prey at the neck, either splitting the jugular vein at the throat or crunching the brain at the base of the skull, and he does not let go. One naturalist refused to kill a weasel who was socketed into his hand deeply as a rattlesnake. The man could in no way pry the tiny weasel off, and he had to walk half a mile to water, the weasel dangling from his palm, and soak him off like a stubborn label.

And once, says Ernest Thompson Seton [1] — once, a man shot an eagle out of the sky. He examined the eagle and found the dry skull of a weasel fixed by the jaws to his throat. The supposition is that the eagle had pounced on the weasel and the weasel swiveled and bit as instinct taught him, tooth to neck, and nearly won. I would like to have seen that eagle from the air a few weeks or months before he was shot: Was the whole weasel still attached to his feathered throat, a fur pendant? Or did the eagle eat what he could reach, gutting the living weasel with his talons before his breast, bending his beak, cleaning the beautiful airborne bones?

I have been reading about weasels because I saw one last week. I startled a weasel who startled me, and we exchanged a long glance.

Twenty minutes from my house, through the woods by the quarry and across the highway, is Hollins Pond, a remarkable piece of shallowness, where

---

[1] *Ernest Thompson Seton* (1860–1946): American author and naturalist who founded the wildlife organization upon which the Boy Scout movement was later patterned.

I like to go at sunset and sit on a tree trunk. Hollins Pond is also called Murray's Pond; it covers two acres of bottomland near Tinker Creek with six inches of water and six thousand lily pads. In winter, brown-and-white steers stand in the middle of it, merely dampening their hooves; from the distant shore they look like miracle itself, complete with miracle's nonchalance. Now, in summer, the steers are gone. The water lilies have blossomed and spread to a green horizontal plane that is terra firma to plodding blackbirds, and tremulous ceiling to black leeches, crayfish, and carp.

This is, mind you, suburbia. It is a five-minute walk in three directions 5 to rows of houses, though none is visible here. There's a 55 mph highway at one end of the pond, and a nesting pair of wood ducks at the other. Under every bush is a muskrat hole or a beer can. The far end is an alternating series of fields and woods, fields and woods, threaded everywhere with motorcycle tracks — in whose bare clay wild turtles lay eggs.

So. I had crossed the highway, stepped over two low barbed-wire fences, and traced the motorcycle path in all gratitude through the wild rose and poison ivy of the pond's shoreline up into high grassy fields. Then I cut down through the woods to the mossy fallen tree where I sit. This tree is excellent. It makes a dry, upholstered bench at the upper, marshy end of the pond, a plush jetty raised from the thorny shore between a shallow blue body of water and a deep blue body of sky.

The sun had just set. I was relaxed on the tree trunk, ensconced in the lap of lichen, watching the lily pads at my feet tremble and part dreamily over the thrusting path of a carp. A yellow bird appeared to my right and flew behind me. It caught my eye; I swiveled around — and the next instant, inexplicably, I was looking down at a weasel, who was looking up at me.

Weasel! I'd never seen one wild before. He was ten inches long, thin as a curve, a muscled ribbon, brown as fruitwood, soft-furred, alert. His face was fierce, small and pointed as a lizard's; he would have made a good arrowhead. There was just a dot of chin, maybe two brown hairs' worth, and then the pure white fur began that spread down his underside. He had two black eyes I didn't see, any more than you see a window.

The weasel was stunned into stillness as he was emerging from beneath an enormous shaggy wild rose bush four feet away. I was stunned into stillness twisted backward on the tree trunk. Our eyes locked, and someone threw away the key.

Our look was as if two lovers, or deadly enemies, met unexpectedly 10 on an overgrown path when each had been thinking of something else: a clearing blow to the gut. It was also a bright blow to the brain, or a sudden beating of brains, with all the charge and intimate grate of rubbed balloons. It emptied our lungs. It felled the forest, moved the fields, and drained the pond; the world dismantled and tumbled into that black hole of eyes. If you and I looked at each other that way, our skulls would split and drop to our shoulders. But we don't. We keep our skulls. So.

He disappeared. This was only last week, and already I don't remember what shattered the enchantment. I think I blinked, I think I retrieved my brain from the weasel's brain, and tried to memorize what I was seeing, and the weasel felt the yank of separation, the careening splashdown into real life and the urgent current of instinct. He vanished under the wild rose. I waited motionless, my mind suddenly full of data and my spirit with pleadings, but he didn't return.

Please do not tell me about "approach-avoidance conflicts." I tell you I've been in that weasel's brain for sixty seconds, and he was in mine. Brains are private places, muttering through unique and secret tapes — but the weasel and I both plugged into another tape simultaneously, for a sweet and shocking time. Can I help it if it was a blank?

What goes on in his brain the rest of the time? What does a weasel think about? He won't say. His journal is tracks in clay, a spray of feathers, mouse blood and bone: uncollected, unconnected, loose-leaf, and blown.

I would like to learn, or remember, how to live. I come to Hollins Pond not so much to learn how to live as, frankly, to forget about it. That is, I don't think I can learn from a wild animal how to live in particular — shall I suck warm blood, hold my tail high, walk with my footprints precisely over the prints of my hands? — but I might learn something of mindlessness, something of purity of living in the physical senses and the dignity of living without bias or motive. The weasel lives in necessity and we live in choice, hating necessity and dying at the last ignobly in its talons. I would like to live as I should, as the weasel lives as he should. And I suspect that for me the way is like the weasel's: open to time and death painlessly, noticing everything, remembering nothing, choosing the given with a fierce and pointed will.

I missed my chance. I should have gone for the throat. I should have   15
lunged for that streak of white under the weasel's chin and held on, held on through mud and into the wild rose, held on for a dearer life. We could live under the wild rose wild as weasels, mute and uncomprehending. I could very calmly go wild. I could live two days in the den, curled, leaning on mouse fur, sniffing bird bones, blinking, licking, breathing musk, my hair tangled in the roots of grasses. Down is a good place to go, where the mind is single. Down is out, out of your ever-loving mind and back to your careless senses. I remember muteness as a prolonged and giddy fast, where every moment is a feast of utterance received. Time and events are merely poured, unremarked, and ingested directly, like blood pulsed into my gut through a jugular vein. Could two live that way? Could two live under the wild rose,

and explore by the pond, so that the smooth mind of each is as everywhere present to the other, and as received and as unchallenged, as falling snow? We could, you know. We can live any way we want. People take vows of poverty, chastity, and obedience — even of silence — by choice. The thing is to stalk your calling in a certain skilled and supple way, to locate the most tender and live spot and plug into that pulse. This is yielding, not fighting. A weasel doesn't "attack" anything; a weasel lives as he's meant to, yielding at every moment to the perfect freedom of single necessity.

I think it would be well, and proper, and obedient, and pure, to grasp your one necessity and not let it go, to dangle from it limp wherever it takes you. Then even death, where you're going no matter how you live, cannot you part. Seize it and let it seize you up aloft even, till your eyes burn out and drop; let your musky flesh fall off in shreds, and let your very bones unhinge and scatter, loosened over fields, over fields and woods, lightly, thoughtless, from any height at all, from as high as eagles.

FROM READING AND REREADING

1. Dillard begins her essay with two documented accounts of weasels, presumably drawn from her reading. What do these accounts have in common? How do they establish the dominant characteristic of weasels and the theme of the essay?

2. "Our eyes locked," Dillard says in describing her encounter with the weasel. Why is this an appropriate image? How does the idea of "locking" run through the essay?

3. Toward the end of her essay, Dillard contrasts the weasel's life of "necessity" to the human life of "choice." What does she mean by this contrast and how does the essay illustrate it? Why does she prefer the life of necessity?

E. B. WHITE
Death of a Pig

In the 1930s, E. B. White moved from New York City, where he served on the staff of The New Yorker, *to a saltwater farm in Maine. White loved the rural isolation and the everyday life of a working farm. He raised hens, sheep, and livestock and fattened pigs for slaughter. Farm life provided not only food for the table but food for thought. White enjoyed reading and ruminating about the ways of animals and he put them to imaginative use in his popular fiction for children —* Charlotte's Web, Stuart Little, *and* The Trumpet of the Swan. *His experiences on the farm also served as the basis for some of his most widely anthologized essays, one of which is "Death of a Pig."*

I SPENT several days and nights in mid-September with an ailing pig, and I feel driven to account for this stretch of time, more particularly since the pig died at last, and I lived, and things might easily have gone the other way round and none left to do the accounting. Even now, so close to the event, I cannot recall the hours sharply and am not ready to say whether death came on the third night or the fourth night. This uncertainty afflicts me with a sense of personal deterioration; if I were in decent health I would know how many nights I had sat up with a pig.

The scheme of buying a spring pig in blossomtime, feeding it through summer and fall, and butchering it when the solid cold weather arrives is a familiar scheme to me and follows an antique pattern. It is a tragedy enacted on most farms with perfect fidelity to the original script. The murder, being premeditated, is in the first degree but is quick and skillful, and the smoked bacon and ham provide a ceremonial ending whose fitness is seldom questioned.

Once in a while something slips — one of the actors goes up in his lines and the whole performance stumbles and halts. My pig simply failed to show up for a meal. The alarm spread rapidly. The classic outline of the tragedy was lost. I found myself cast suddenly in the role of pig's friend and physician — a farcical character with an enema bag for a prop. I had a presentiment, the very first afternoon, that the play would never regain its balance and that my sympathies were now wholly with the pig. This was slapstick — the sort of dramatic treatment that instantly appealed to my old dachshund, Fred, who joined the vigil, held the bag, and, when all was over, presided at the interment. When we slid the body into the grave, we both were shaken to the core. The loss we felt was not the loss of ham but the loss of pig. He had evidently become precious to me, not that he represented a distant nourishment in a hungry time, but that he had suffered in a suffering world. But I'm running ahead of my story and shall have to go back.

My pigpen is at the bottom of an old orchard below the house. The pigs I have raised have lived in a faded building that once was an icehouse. There is a pleasant yard to move about in, shaded by an apple tree that overhangs the low rail fence. A pig couldn't ask for anything better — or none has, at any rate. The sawdust in the icehouse makes a comfortable bottom in which to root, and a warm bed. This sawdust, however, came under suspicion when the pig took sick. One of my neighbors said he thought the pig would have done better on new ground — the same principle that applies in planting potatoes. He said there might be something unhealthy about that sawdust, that he never thought well of sawdust.

It was about four o'clock in the afternoon when I first noticed that there was something wrong with the pig. He failed to appear at the trough for his supper, and when a pig (or a child) refuses supper a chill wave of fear runs through any household, or ice-household. After examining my pig, who was stretched out in the sawdust inside the building, I went to the phone and cranked it four times. Mr. Dameron answered, "What's good for a sick pig?" I asked. (There is never any identification needed on a country phone; the person on the other end knows who is talking by the sound of the voice and by the character of the question.)

"I don't know, I never had a sick pig," said Mr. Dameron, "but I can find out quick enough. You hang up and I'll call Henry."

Mr. Dameron was back on the line again in five minutes. "Henry says roll him over on his back and give him two ounces of castor oil or sweet oil, and if that doesn't do the trick give him an injection of soapy water. He says he's almost sure the pig's plugged up, and even if he's wrong, it can't do any harm."

I thanked Mr. Dameron. I didn't go right down to the pig, though. I sank into a chair and sat still for a few minutes to think about my troubles, and then I got up and went to the barn, catching up on some odds and ends that needed tending to. Unconsciously I held off, for an hour, the deed by which I would officially recognize the collapse of the performance of raising a pig; I wanted no interruption in the regularity of feeding, the steadiness of growth, the even succession of days. I wanted no interruption, wanted no oil, no deviation. I just wanted to keep on raising a pig, full meal after full meal, spring into summer into fall. I didn't even know whether there were two ounces of castor oil on the place.

Shortly after five o'clock I remembered that we had been invited out to dinner that night and realized that if I were to dose a pig there was no time to lose. The dinner date seemed a familiar conflict: I move in a desultory society and often a week or two will roll by without my going to anybody's house to dinner or anyone's coming to mine, but when an occasion does arise, and I am summoned, something usually turns up (an hour or two in advanced) to make all human intercourse seem vastly inappropriate. I have come to believe that there is in hostesses a special power of divination, and that they deliberately arrange dinners to coincide with pig failure or some other sort of failure. At any rate, it was after five o'clock and I knew I could put off no longer the evil hour.

When my son and I arrived at the pigyard, armed with a small bottle 10 of castor oil and a length of clothesline, the pig had emerged from his house and was standing in the middle of his yard, listlessly. He gave us a slim greeting. I could see that he felt uncomfortable and uncertain. I had brought the clothesline thinking I'd have to tie him (the pig weighed more than a hundred pounds), but we never used it. My son reached down, grabbed both front legs, upset him quickly, and when he opened his mouth to scream I turned the oil into his throat — a pink, corrugated area I had never seen before. I had just time to read the label while the neck of the bottle was in his mouth. It said Puretest. The screams, slightly muffled by oil, were pitched in the hysterically high range of pig-sound, as though torture were being carried out, but they didn't last long: it was all over rather suddenly, and, his legs released, the pig righted himself.

In the upset position the corners of his mouth had been turned down, giving him a frowning expression. Back on his feet again, he regained the set smile that a pig wears even in sickness. He stood his ground, sucking slightly at the residue of oil; a few drops leaked out of his lips while his wicked eyes, shaded by their coy little lashes, turned on me in disgust and hatred. I scratched him gently with oily fingers and he remained quiet, as though trying to recall the satisfaction of being scratched when in health, and seeming to rehearse in his mind the indignity to which he had just been subjected. I noticed, as I stood there, four or five small dark spots on his back near the tail end, reddish brown in color, each about the size of a housefly. I could not make out what they were. They did not look troublesome but at the same time they did not look like mere surface bruises or chafe marks. Rather they seemed blemishes of internal origin. His stiff white bristles almost completely hid them and I had to part the bristles with my fingers to get a good look.

Several hours later, a few minutes before midnight, having dined well and at someone else's expense, I returned to the pighouse with a flashlight. The patient was asleep. Kneeling, I felt his ears (as you might put your hand on the forehead of a child) and they seemed cool, and then with the light made a careful examination of the yard and the house for sign that the oil had worked. I found none and went to bed.

We had been having an unseasonable spell of weather — hot, close days, with the fog shutting in every night, scaling for a few hours in midday, then creeping back again at dark, drifting in first over the trees on the point, then suddenly blowing across the fields, blotting out the world and taking possession of houses, men, and animals. Everyone kept hoping for a break, but the break failed to come. Next day was another hot one. I visited the pig before breakfast and tried to tempt him with a little milk in his trough. He just stared at it, while I made a sucking sound through my teeth to remind him of past pleasures of the feast. With very small, timid pigs, weanlings, this ruse is often quite successful and will encourage them to eat; but with a large, sick pig the ruse is senseless and the sound I made must have made him feel, if anything, more miserable. He not only did not crave food, he felt a positive revulsion to it. I found a place under the apple tree where he had vomited in the night.

At this point, although a depression had settled over me, I didn't suppose that I was going to lose my pig. From the lustiness of a healthy pig a man derives a feeling of personal lustiness; the stuff that goes into the trough and is received with such enthusiasm is an earnest of some later feast of his own, and when this suddenly comes to an end and the food lies stale and untouched, souring in the sun, the pig's imbalance becomes the man's, vicariously, and life seems insecure, displaced, transitory.

As my own spirits declined, along with the pig's, the spirits of my vile 15 old dachshund rose. The frequency of our trips down the footpath through the orchard to the pigyard delighted him, although he suffers greatly from arthritis, moves with difficulty, and would be bedridden if he could find anyone willing to serve him meals on a tray.

He never missed a chance to visit the pig with me, and he made many professional calls on his own. You could see him down there at all hours, his white face parting the grass along the fence as he wobbled and stumbled about, his stethoscope dangling — a happy quack, writing his villainous prescriptions and grinning his corrosive grin. When the enema bag appeared, and the bucket of warm suds, his happiness was complete, and he managed to squeeze his enormous body between the two lowest rails of the yard and then assumed full charge of the irrigation. Once, when I lowered the bag to check the flow, he reached in and hurriedly drank a few mouthfuls of the suds to test their potency. I have noticed that Fred will feverishly consume any substance that is associated with trouble — the bitter flavor is to his liking. When the bag was above reach, he concentrated on the pig and was everywhere at once, a tower of strength and inconvenience. The pig, curiously enough, stood rather quietly through this colonic carnival, and the enema, though ineffective, was not as difficult as I had anticipated.

I discovered, though, that once having given a pig an enema there is no turning back, no chance of resuming one of life's more stereotyped roles. The pig's lot and mine were inextricably bound now, as though the rubber tube were the silver cord. From then until the time of his death I held the pig steadily in the bowl of my mind; the task of trying to deliver him from his misery became a strong obsession. His suffering soon became the embodiment of all earthly wretchedness. Along toward the end of the afternoon, defeated in physicking, I phoned the veterinary twenty miles away and placed the case formally in his hands. He was full of questions, and when I casually mentioned the dark spots on the pig's back, his voice changed its tone.

"I don't want to scare you," he said, "but when there are spots, erysipelas has to be considered."

Together we considered erysipelas, with frequent interruptions from the telephone operator, who wasn't sure the connection had been established.

"If a pig has erysipelas can he give it to a person?" I asked.   20

"Yes, he can," replied the vet.

"Have they answered?" asked the operator.

"Yes, they have," I said. Then I addressed the vet again. "You better come over here and examine this pig right away."

"I can't come myself," said the vet, "but McFarland can come this evening if that's all right. Mac knows more about pigs than I do anyway. You needn't worry too much about the spots. To indicate erysipelas they would have to be deep hemorrhagic infarcts."

"Deep hemorrhagic what?" I asked.   25

"Infarcts," said the vet.

"Have they answered?" asked the operator.

"Well," I said, "I don't know what you'd call these spots, except they're about the size of a housefly. If the pig has erysipelas I guess I have it, too, by this time, because we've been very close lately."

"McFarland will be over," said the vet.

I hung up. My throat felt dry and I went to the cupboard and got a   30 bottle of whiskey. Deep hemorrhagic infarcts — the phrase began fastening its hooks in my head. I had assumed that there could be nothing much wrong with a pig during the months it was being groomed for murder; my confidence in the essential health and endurance of pigs had been strong and deep, particularly in the health of pigs that belonged to me and that were part of my proud scheme. The awakening had been violent, and I minded it all the more because I knew that what could be true of my pig could be true also of the rest of my tidy world. I tried to put this distasteful idea from me, but it kept recurring. I took a short drink of the whiskey and then, although I wanted to go down to the yard and look for fresh signs, I was scared to. I was certain I had erysipelas.

It was long after dark and the supper dishes had been put away when a car drove in and McFarland got out. He had a girl with him. I could just make her out in the darkness — she seemed young and pretty. "This is Miss Owen," he said. "We've been having a picnic supper on the shore, that's why I'm late."

McFarland stood in the driveway and stripped off his jacket, then his shirt. His stocky arms and capable hands showed up in my flashlight's gleam as I helped him find his coverall and get zipped up. The rear seat of his car contained an astonishing amount of paraphernalia, which he soon overhauled, selecting a chain, a syringe, a bottle of oil, a rubber tube, and some other things I couldn't identify. Miss Owen said she'd go along with us and see the pig. I led the way down the warm slope of the orchard, my light picking out the path for them, and we all three climbed the fence, entered the pighouse, and squatted by the pig while McFarland took a rectal reading. My flashlight picked up the glitter of an engagement ring on the girl's hand.

"No elevation," said McFarland, twisting the thermometer in the light. "You needn't worry about erysipelas." He ran his hand slowly over the pig's stomach and at one point the pig cried out in pain.

"Poor piggledy-wiggledy!" said Miss Owen.

The treatment I had been giving the pig for two days was then repeated, somewhat more expertly, by the doctor, Miss Owen and I handing him things as he needed them — holding the chain that he had looped around the pig's upper jaw, holding the syringe, holding the bottle stopper, the end of the tube, all of us working in darkness and in comfort, working with the instinctive teamwork induced by emergency conditions, the pig unprotesting, the house shadowy, protecting, intimate. I went to bed tired but with a feeling of relief that I had turned over part of the responsibility of the case to a licensed doctor. I was beginning to think, though, that the pig was not going to live.

He died twenty-four hours later, or it might have been forty-eight — there is a blur in time here, and I may have lost or picked up a day in the telling and the pig one in the dying. At intervals during the last day I took cool fresh water down to him, and at such times as he found the strength to get to his feet he would stand with head in the pail and snuffle his snout around. He drank a few sips but no more; yet it seemed to comfort him to dip his nose in water and bobble it about, sucking in and blowing out through his teeth. Much of the time, now, he lay indoors half buried in sawdust. Once, near the last, while I was attending him I saw him try to make a bed for himself but he lacked the strength, and when he set his snout into the dust he was unable to plow even the little furrow he needed to lie down in.

He came out of the house to die. When I went down, before going to bed, he lay stretched in the yard a few feet from the door. I knelt, saw that he was dead, and left him there: his face had a mild look, expressive neither of deep peace nor of deep suffering, although I think he had suffered a good deal. I went back up to the house and to bed, and cried internally — deep hemorrhagic intears. I didn't wake till nearly eight the next morning, and when I looked out the open window the grave was already being dug, down beyond the dump under a wild apple. I could hear the spade strike against the small rocks that blocked the way. Never send to know for whom the grave is dug, I said to myself, it's dug for thee. Fred, I well knew, was supervising the work of digging, so I ate breakfast slowly.

It was a Saturday morning. The thicket in which I found the gravediggers at work was dark and warm, the sky overcast. Here, among alders and young hackmatacks, at the foot of the apple tree, Lennie had dug a beautiful hole, five feet long, three feet wide, three feet deep. He was standing in it, removing the last spadefuls of earth while Fred patrolled the brink in simple but impressive circles, disturbing the loose earth of the mound so that it trickled back in. There had been no rain in weeks and the soil, even three feet down, was dry and powdery. As I stood and stared, an enormous earthworm which had been partially exposed by the spade at the bottom dug itself deeper and made a slow withdrawal, seeking even remoter moistures at even lonelier depths. And just as Lennie stepped out and rested his spade against the tree and lit a cigarette, a small green apple separated itself from a branch overhead and fell into the hole. Everything about this last scene seemed overwritten — the dismal sky, the shabby woods, the imminence of rain, the worm (legendary bedfellow of the dead), the apple (conventional garnish of a pig).

But even so, there was a directness and dispatch about animal burial, I thought, that made it a more decent affair than human burial: there was no stopover in the undertaker's foul parlor, no wreath nor spray; and when we hitched a line to the pig's hind legs and dragged him swiftly from his yard, throwing our weight into the harness and leaving a wake of crushed grass and smoothed rubble over the dump, ours was a businesslike procession, with Fred, the dishonorable pallbearer, staggering along in the rear, his perverse bereavement showing in every seam in his face; and the post mortem performed handily and swiftly right at the edge of the grave, so that the inwards that had caused the pig's death preceded him into the ground and he lay at last resting squarely on the cause of his own undoing.

I threw in the first shovelful, and then we worked rapidly and without 40
talk, until the job was complete. I picked up the rope, made it fast to Fred's collar (he is a notorious ghoul), and we all three filed back up the path to the house, Fred bringing up the rear and holding back every inch of the way, feigning unusual stiffness. I noticed that although he weighed far less than the pig, he was harder to drag, being possessed of the vital spark.

The news of the death of my pig travelled fast and far, and I received many expressions of sympathy from friends and neighbors, for no one took the event lightly and the premature expiration of a pig is, I soon discovered, a departure which the community marks solemnly on its calendar, a sorrow in which it feels fully involved. I have written this account in penitence and in grief, as a man who failed to raise his pig, and to explain my deviation from the classic course of so many raised pigs. The grave in the woods is unmarked, but Fred can direct the mourner to it unerringly and with immense good will, and I know he and I shall often revisit it, singly and together, in seasons of reflection and despair, on flagless memorial days of our own choosing.

FROM READING TO REREADING

1. Note that White opens and closes his essay by directly stating his motive for writing it. What is that motive? What troubles him most about the entire incident? Is it the death of his pig?

2. In the second paragraph, White introduces his "scheme." Why is this term important to understanding the problems White experiences in the course of the essay? Note, too, the theatrical imagery he uses in this paragraph. Of what importance is this to White's essay? Where else in the essay does it appear?

3. White mentions several times that he lost track of time during the pig's illness. Why is this detail so important to him? As you reread the essay, pay close attention to the passage of time. How many days can you account for? If you were White and in the midst of writing the essay, how might you have established more accurately what happened on what day? Why doesn't White do this?

GEORGE ORWELL
Shooting an Elephant

"Most of the good memories of my childhood, and up to the age of about twenty,"
Orwell writes in Such, Such Were the Joys, *"are in some way connected with*
animals." In fact, a British critic who knew Orwell pointed out that Orwell
"found it easier to present animals than human beings in a sympathetic light."
There is some question whether the incident reported in this essay ever happened.
If Orwell did shoot an elephant, he probably did it toward the end of his stint
as a police officer in Burma, where, after Eton, he had gone instead of to college.
At the time of the event, which would have occurred in 1926 or 1927, Orwell
was in his midtwenties; he wrote the essay, which has since become one of the
classic essays of the twentieth century, in 1936. Orwell would later take up the
connection of animals and politics in one of his most popular books, Animal
Farm *(1945).*

IN MOULMEIN, in Lower Burma, I was hated by large numbers of people
— the only time in my life that I have been important enough for this to
happen to me. I was sub-divisional police officer of the town, and in an
aimless, petty kind of way anti-European feeling was very bitter. No one
had the guts to raise a riot, but if a European woman went through the
bazaars alone somebody would probably spit betel juice over her dress. As a
police officer I was an obvious target and was baited whenever it seemed
safe to do so. When a nimble Burman tripped me up on the football field
and the referee (another Burman) looked the other way, the crowd yelled
with hideous laughter. This happened more than once. In the end the
sneering yellow faces of young men that met me everywhere, the insults
hooted after me when I was at a safe distance, got badly on my nerves. The
young Buddhist priests were the worst of all. There were several thousands
of them in the town and none of them seemed to have anything to do except
stand on street corners and jeer at Europeans.

All this was perplexing and upsetting. For at that time I had already
made up my mind that imperialism was an evil thing and the sooner I chucked
up my job and got out of it the better. Theoretically — and secretly, of
course — I was all for the Burmese and all against their oppressors, the
British. As for the job I was doing, I hated it more bitterly than I can perhaps
make clear. In a job like that you see the dirty work of Empire at close
quarters. The wretched prisoners huddling in the stinking cages of the lock-
ups, the grey, cowed faces of the long-term convicts, the scarred buttocks of
the men who had been flogged with bamboos — all these oppressed me with

an intolerable sense of guilt. But I could get nothing into perspective. I was young and ill-educated and I had had to think out my problems in the utter silence that is imposed on every Englishman in the East. I did not even know that the British Empire is dying, still less did I know that it is a great deal better than the younger empires that are going to supplant it. All I knew was that I was stuck between my hatred of the empire I served and my rage against the evil-spirited little beasts who tried to make my job impossible. With one part of my mind I thought of the British Raj[1] as an unbreakable tyranny, as something clamped down, in *saecula saeculorum*,[2] upon the will of prostrate peoples; with another part I thought that the greatest joy in the world would be to drive a bayonet into a Buddhist priest's guts. Feelings like these are the normal by-products of imperialism; ask any Anglo-Indian official, if you can catch him off duty.

One day something happened which in a roundabout way was enlightening. It was a tiny incident in itself, but it gave me a better glimpse than I had had before of the real nature of imperialism — the real motives for which despotic governments act. Early one morning the sub-inspector at a police station the other end of the town rang me up on the 'phone and said that an elephant was ravaging the bazaar. Would I please come and do something about it? I did not know what I could do, but I wanted to see what was happening and I got on to a pony and started out. I took my rifle, an old .44 Winchester and much too small to kill an elephant, but I thought the noise might be useful *in terrorem*.[3] Various Burmans stopped me on the way and told me about the elephant's doings. It was not, of course, a wild elephant, but a tame one which had gone "must."[4] It had been chained up, as tame elephants always are when their attack of "must" is due, but on the previous night it had broken its chain and escaped. Its mahout,[5] the only person who could manage it when it was in that state, had set out in pursuit, but had taken the wrong direction and was now twelve hours' journey away, and in the morning the elephant had suddenly reappeared in the town. The Burmese population had no weapons and were quite helpless against it. It had already destroyed somebody's bamboo hut, killed a cow and raided some fruit-stalls and devoured the stock; also it had met the municipal rubbish van and, when the driver jumped out and took to his heels, had turned the van over and inflicted violences upon it.

The Burmese sub-inspector and some Indian constables were waiting for me in the quarter where the elephant had been seen. It was a very poor

[1] *Raj*: The British adminstration.
[2] *saecula saeculorum*: Forever and ever (Latin).
[3] *in terrorem*: As a warning (Latin).
[4] *"must"*: Sexual arousal.
[5] *mahout*: Keeper (Hindi).

quarter, a labyrinth of squalid bamboo huts, thatched with palm-leaf, winding all over a steep hillside. I remember that it was a cloudy, stuffy morning at the beginning of the rains. We began questioning the people as to where the elephant had gone and, as usual, failed to get any definite information. That is invariably the case in the East; a story always sounds clear enough at a distance, but the nearer you get to the scene of events the vaguer it becomes. Some of the people said that the elephant had gone in one direction, some said that he had gone in another, some professed not even to have heard of any elephant. I had almost made up my mind that the whole story was a pack of lies, when we heard yells a little distance away. There was a loud, scandalized cry of "Go away, child! Go away this instant!" and an old woman with a switch in her hand came round the corner of a hut, violently shooing away a crowd of naked children. Some more women followed, clicking their tongues and exclaiming; evidently there was something that the children ought not to have seen. I rounded the hut and saw a man's dead body sprawling in the mud. He was an Indian, a black Dravidian [6] coolie, almost naked, and he could not have been dead many minutes. The people said that the elephant had come suddenly upon him round the corner of the hut, caught him with its trunk, put its foot on his back and ground him into the earth. This was the rainy season and the ground was soft, and his face had scored a trench a foot deep and a couple of yards long. He was lying on his belly with arms crucified and head sharply twisted to one side. His face was coated with mud, the eyes wide open, the teeth bared and grinning with an expression of unendurable agony. (Never tell me, by the way, that the dead look peaceful. Most of the corpses I have seen looked devilish.) The friction of the great beast's foot had stripped the skin from his back as neatly as one skins a rabbit. As soon as I saw the dead man I sent an orderly to a friend's house nearby to borrow an elephant rifle. I had already sent back the pony, not wanting it to go mad with fright and throw me if it smelt the elephant.

The orderly came back in a few minutes with a rifle and five cartridges, 5 and meanwhile some Burmans had arrived and told us that the elephant was in the paddy fields below, only a few hundred yards away. As I started forward practically the whole population of the quarter flocked out of the houses and followed me. They had seen the rifle and were all shouting excitedly that I was going to shoot the elephant. They had not shown much interest in the elephant when he was merely ravaging their homes, but it was different now that he was going to be shot. It was a bit of fun to them, as it would be to an English crowd; besides they wanted the meat. It made me vaguely uneasy. I had no intention of shooting the elephant — I had merely sent for the rifle to defend myself if necessary — and it is always unnerving to have a crowd following you. I marched down the hill, looking and feeling a fool, with the rifle over my shoulder and an ever-growing army

[6] *Dravidian*: A populous Indian group.

of people jostling at my heels. At the bottom, when you got away from the huts, there was a metalled road and beyond that a miry waste of paddy fields a thousand yards across, not yet ploughed but soggy from the first rains and dotted with coarse grass. The elephant was standing eight yards from the road, his left side towards us. He took not the slightest notice of the crowd's approach. He was tearing up bunches of grass, beating them against his knees to clean them and stuffing them into his mouth.

I had halted on the road. As soon as I saw the elephant I knew with perfect certainty that I ought not to shoot him. It is a serious matter to shoot a working elephant — it is comparable to destroying a huge and costly piece of machinery — and obviously one ought not to do it if it can possibly be avoided. And at that distance, peacefully eating, the elephant looked no more dangerous than a cow. I thought then and I think now that his attack of "must" was already passing off; in which case he would merely wander harmlessly about until the mahout came back and caught him. Moreover, I did not in the least want to shoot him. I decided that I would watch him for a little while to make sure that he did not turn savage again, and then go home.

But at that moment I glanced round at the crowd that had followed me. It was an immense crowd, two thousand at the least and growing every minute. It blocked the road for a long distance on either side. I looked at the sea of yellow faces above the garish clothes — faces all happy and excited over this bit of fun, all certain that the elephant was going to be shot. They were watching me as they would watch a conjurer about to perform a trick. They did not like me, but with the magical rifle in my hands I was momentarily worth watching. And suddenly I realized that I should have to shoot the elephant after all. The people expected it of me and I had got to do it; I could feel their two thousand wills pressing me forward, irresistibly. And it was at this moment, as I stood there with the rifle in my hands, that I first grasped the hollowness, the futility of the white man's dominion in the East. Here was I, the white man with his gun, standing in front of the unarmed native crowd — seemingly the leading actor of the piece; but in reality I was only an absurd puppet pushed to and fro by the will of those yellow faces behind. I perceived in this moment that when the white man turns tyrant it is his own freedom that he destroys. He becomes a sort of hollow, posing dummy, the conventionalized figure of a sahib. For it is the condition of his rule that he shall spend his life in trying to impress the "natives," and so in every crisis he has got to do what the "natives" expect of him. He wears a mask, and his face grows to fit it. I had got to shoot the elephant. I had committed myself to doing it when I sent for the rifle. A sahib has got to act like a sahib; he has got to appear resolute, to know his own mind and do definite things. To come all that way, rifle in hand, with two thousand people marching at my heels, and then to trail feebly away, having done nothing — no, that was impossible. The crowd would laugh at me. And my whole life, every white man's life in the East, was one long struggle not to be laughed at.

But I did not want to shoot the elephant. I watched him beating his bunch of grass against his knees, with that preoccupied grandmotherly air that elephants have. It seemed to me that it would be murder to shoot him. At that age I was not squeamish about killing animals, but I had never shot an elephant and never wanted to. (Somehow it always seems worse to kill a *large* animal.) Besides, there was the beast's owner to be considered. Alive, the elephant was worth at least a hundred pounds; dead, he would only be worth the value of his tusks, five pounds, possibly. But I had got to act quickly. I turned to some experienced-looking Burmans who had been there when we arrived, and asked them how the elephant had been behaving. They all said the same thing: he took no notice of you if you left him alone, but he might charge if you went too close to him.

It was perfectly clear to me what I ought to do. I ought to walk up to within, say, twenty-five yards of the elephant and test his behavior. If he charged, I could shoot; if he took no notice of me, it would be safe to leave him until the mahout came back. But also I knew that I was going to do no such thing. I was a poor shot with a rifle and the ground was soft mud into which one would sink at every step. If the elephant charged and I missed him, I should have about as much chance as a toad under a steam-roller. But even then I was not thinking particularly of my own skin, only of the watchful yellow faces behind. For at that moment, with the crowd watching me, I was not afraid in the ordinary sense, as I would have been if I had been alone. A white man mustn't be frightened in front of "natives"; and so, in general, he isn't frightened. The sole thought in my mind was that if anything went wrong those two thousand Burmans would see me pursued, caught, trampled on and reduced to a grinning corpse like that Indian up the hill. And if that happened it was quite probable that some of them would laugh. That would never do. There was only one alternative. I shoved the cartridges into the magazine and lay down on the road to get a better aim.

The crowd grew very still, and a deep, low, happy sigh, as of people who see the theatre curtain go up at last, breathed from innumerable throats. They were going to have their bit of fun after all. The rifle was a beautiful German thing with cross-hair sights. I did not then know that in shooting an elephant one should shoot to cut an imaginary bar running from ear-hole to ear-hole. I ought, therefore, as the elephant was sideways on, to have aimed straight at his ear-hole; actually I aimed several inches in front of this, thinking the brain would be further forward.

When I pulled the trigger I did not hear the bang or feel the kick — one never does when a shot goes home — but I heard the devilish roar of glee that went up from the crowd. In that instant, in too short a time, one would have thought, even for the bullet to get there, a mysterious, terrible change had come over the elephant. He neither stirred nor fell, but every line of his body had altered. He looked suddenly stricken, shrunken, immensely old, as though the frightful impact of the bullet had paralysed him without knocking him down. At last, after what seemed a long time — it might have been five seconds, I dare say — he sagged flabbily to his knees. His mouth slobbered. An enormous senility seemed to have settled upon him. One could have imagined him thousands of years old. I fired again into the same spot. At the second shot he did not collapse but climbed with desperate slowness to his feet and stood weakly upright, with legs sagging and head drooping. I fired a third time. That was the shot that did for him. You could see the agony of it jolt his whole body and knock the last remnant of strength from his legs. But in falling he seemed for a moment to rise, for as his hind legs collapsed beneath him he seemed to tower upward like a huge rock toppling, his trunk reaching skywards like a tree. He trumpeted, for the first and only time. And then down he came, his belly towards me, with a crash that seemed to shake the ground even where I lay.

I got up. The Burmans were already racing past me across the mud. It was obvious that the elephant would never rise again, but he was not dead. He was breathing very rhythmically with long rattling gasps, his great mound of a side painfully rising and falling. His mouth was wide open — I could see far down into caverns of pale pink throat. I waited a long time for him to die, but his breathing did not weaken. Finally I fired my two remaining shots into the spot where I thought his heart must be. The thick blood welled out of him like red velvet, but still he did not die. His body did not even jerk when the shots hit him, the tortured breathing continued without a pause. He was dying, very slowly and in great agony, but in some world remote from me where not even a bullet could damage him further. I felt that I had got to put an end to that dreadful noise. It seemed dreadful to see the great beast lying there, powerless to move and yet powerless to die, and not even to be able to finish him. I sent back for my small rifle and poured shot after shot into his heart and down his throat. They seemed to make no impression. The tortured gasps continued as steadily as the ticking of a clock.

In the end I could not stand it any longer and went away. I heard later that it took him half an hour to die. Burmans were bringing dahs [7] and baskets even before I left, and I was told they had stripped his body almost to the bones by the afternoon.

Afterwards, of course, there were endless discussions about the shooting of the elephant. The owner was furious, but he was only an Indian and could do nothing. Besides, legally I had done the right thing, for a mad elephant has to be killed, like a mad dog, if its owner fails to control it. Among the Europeans opinion was divided. The older men said I was right, the younger men said it was a damn shame to shoot an elephant for killing

---

[7] *dahs*: Large knives.

a coolie, because an elephant was worth more than any damn Coringhee coolie. And afterwards I was very glad that the coolie had been killed; it put me legally in the right and it gave me a sufficient pretext for shooting the elephant. I often wondered whether any of the others grasped that I had done it solely to avoid looking a fool.

FROM READING TO REREADING

1. A form of literature with a long tradition is the animal fable — a tale that uses animals to point out a moral. Aesop's *Fables* are perhaps the best known of this genre; also well known is Orwell's antitotalitarian *Animal Farm*, a book still popular in our high schools. What elements of the moral fable can you find in "Shooting an Elephant"?

2. At the center of Orwell's essay is an ideological conflict. How would you express this conflict? Why can't it be expressed in simple terms, by saying which side or position Orwell favored? How does he complicate matters?

3. Several critics have doubted that this incident ever took place; there is no historical record or corroborative documentation. How does Orwell try to convince you that he really did shoot an elephant? Are there any elements *inside* the essay that make you distrust him? Suppose you could prove that the incident never happened. How would that affect your response to the work? Would it still be an essay, or would you consider it a short story?

VIRGINIA WOOLF
The Death of the Moth

In one of her best-known essays, Virginia Woolf finds herself suddenly preoccupied by a tiny moth (exactly what sort she doesn't say) dancing desperately against the windowpane of her study. The moth's agitated rhythms begin to elicit her sympathies, and she enters into its fluttering life with the same attention she bestows on all types of shimmering movement, from the surge of waves at sea to the stream of human consciousness. As the essay progresses, the tiny, insignificant moth becomes an emblem for Woolf of the way energy dominates the world, ebbing and flowing, creating and destroying. The essay appeared in The Death of the Moth and Other Essays, *a collection published in 1942, a year after her own death.*

MOTHS THAT FLY by day are not properly to be called moths; they do not excite that pleasant sense of dark autumn nights and ivy-blossom which the commonest yellow-underwing asleep in the shadow of the curtain never fails to rouse in us. They are hybrid creatures, neither gay like butterflies nor somber like their own species. Nevertheless the present specimen, with his narrow hay-colored wings, fringed with a tassel of the same color, seemed to be content with life. It was a pleasant morning, mid-September, mild, benignant, yet with a keener breath than that of the summer months. The plough was already scoring the field opposite the window, and where the share had been, the earth was pressed flat and gleamed with moisture. Such vigor came rolling in from the fields and the down beyond that it was difficult to keep the eyes strictly turned upon the book. The rooks too were keeping one of their annual festivities; soaring round the tree tops until it looked as if a vast net with thousands of black knots in it had been cast up into the air; which, after a few moments sank slowly down upon the trees until every twig seemed to have a knot at the end of it. Then, suddenly, the net would be thrown into the air again in a wider circle this time, with the utmost clamor and vociferation, as though to be thrown into the air and settle slowly down upon the tree tops were a tremendously exciting experience.

The same energy which inspired the rooks, the ploughmen, the horses, and even, it seemed, the lean bare-backed downs, sent the moth fluttering from side to side of his square of the windowpane. One could not help watching him. One, was, indeed, conscious of a queer feeling of pity for him. The possibilities of pleasure seemed that morning so enormous and so various that to have only a moth's part in life, and a day moth's at that, appeared a hard fate, and his zest in enjoying his meager opportunities to the full, pathetic. He flew vigorously to one corner of his compartment, and, after waiting there a second, flew across to the other. What remained for him but to fly to a third corner and then to a fourth? That was all he could do, in spite of the size of the downs, the width of the sky, the far-off smoke of houses, and the romantic voice, now and then, of a steamer out at sea. What he could do he did. Watching him, it seemed as if a fiber, very thin but pure, of the enormous energy of the world had been thrust into his frail and diminutive body. As often as he crossed the pane, I could fancy that a thread of vital light became visible. He was little or nothing but life.

Yet, because he was so small, and so simple a form of the energy that was rolling in at the open window and driving its way through so many narrow and intricate corridors in my own brain and in those of other human beings, there was something marvelous as well as pathetic about him. It was as if someone had taken a tiny bead of pure life and decking it as lightly as possible with down and feathers, had set it dancing and zigzagging to show us the true nature of life. Thus displayed one could not get over the strangeness of it. One is apt to forget all about life, seeing it humped and bossed and garnished and cumbered so that it has to move with the greatest circumspection and dignity. Again, the thought of all that life might have been had he been born in any other shape caused one to view his simple activities with a kind of pity.

After a time, tired by his dancing apparently, he settled on the window ledge in the sun, and, the queer spectacle being at an end, I forgot about him. Then, looking up, my eye was caught by him. He was trying to resume his dancing, but seemed either so stiff or so awkward that he could only flutter to the bottom of the windowpane; and when he tried to fly across it he failed. Being intent on other matters I watched these futile attempts for a time without thinking, unconsciously waiting for him to resume his flight, as one waits for a machine, that has stopped momentarily, to start again without considering the reason of its failure. After perhaps a seventh attempt he slipped from the wooden ledge and fell, fluttering his wings, on to his back on the windowsill. The helplessness of his attitude roused me. It flashed upon me that he was in difficulties; he could no longer raise himself; his legs struggled vainly. But, as I stretched out a pencil, meaning to help him to right himself, it came over me that the failure and awkwardness were the approach of death. I laid the pencil down again.

The legs agitated themselves once more. I looked as if for the enemy 5 against which he struggled. I looked out of doors. What had happened there? Presumably it was midday, and work in the fields had stopped. Stillness and quiet had replaced the previous animation. The birds had taken themselves off to feed in the brooks. The horses stood still. Yet the power was there all the same, massed outside, indifferent, impersonal, not attending to anything in particular. Somehow it was opposed to the little hay-colored moth. It was useless to try to do anything. One could only watch the extraordinary efforts made by those tiny legs against an oncoming doom which could, had it chosen, have submerged an entire city, not merely a city, but masses of human beings; nothing, I knew had any chance against death. Nevertheless after a pause of exhaustion the legs fluttered again. It was superb this last protest, and so frantic that he succeeded at last in righting himself. One's sympathies, of course, were all on the side of life. Also, when there was nobody to care or to know, this gigantic effort on the part of an insignificant little moth, against a power of such magnitude, to retain what no one else valued or desired to keep, moved one strangely. Again, somehow, one saw life, a pure bead. I lifted the pencil again, useless though I knew it to be. But even as I did so, the unmistakable tokens of death showed themselves. The body relaxed, and instantly grew stiff. The struggle was over. The insignificant little creature now knew death. As I looked at the dead moth, this minute wayside triumph of so great a force over so mean an antagonist filled me with wonder. Just as life had been strange a few minutes before, so death was now as strange. The moth having righted himself now lay most decently and uncomplainingly composed. O yes, he seemed to say, death is stronger than I am.

FROM READING TO REREADING

1. Note that Woolf calls her essay "The Death of *the* Moth," whereas White called his "Death of *a* Pig." What difference do these articles make? How do they affect your response? Why didn't Woolf call her essay "The Death of a Moth"? What quality does the definite article add?

2. "He was little or nothing but life," Woolf says of the tiny moth. What does she mean by this statement? What does "life" mean in the context of this essay?

3. Though we learn a great deal about the moth's activities in the essay, we see little of Woolf herself. What is she apparently doing? In what ways is her condition similar to the moth's? Note the several times a "pencil" appears in the essay. What connections can you find between the life and death of the moth and the writing of the essay?

From Reading to Writing

1. In the essays by Lewis Thomas and Annie Dillard, each writer wonders about the thought processes of other creatures. Obviously, such

processes are a mystery and the best we can do is imagine them. Select a creature that fascinates you (like a pet or an animal you've studied, or observed) and try to describe that creature's mental processes. How close do you think it is to your own? How different?

2. Both E. B. White and George Orwell offer personal accounts of the way another creature affected their own lives. Compare their two essays. In what ways do the writers present themselves as similar? In what ways are they interested in establishing a motive for writing? Each writer clearly expects his readers to believe that the incident he describes really happened. What do they do specifically to try to convince you of this? How do they succeed?

3. Consider Virginia Woolf's "The Death of the Moth." Write an essay in which you examine not the role of the moth but the role of the writer. In what ways does the essay illustrate the processes of composition?

7

Men and Women

ALICE WALKER

Brothers and Sisters

Who teaches us the "facts of life"? Our mothers? Our fathers? And how can the way we learn those "facts" shape our ideas not only about sexual realities but about men and women in general? In "Brothers and Sisters," Alice Walker describes what she and her brothers and sisters learned about sex and the sexes from growing up on a farm in the South in the fifties. "On a farm it is important not to be conscious of sex," she observes, recalling how her father encouraged the boys to watch the mating of animals and how her mother discouraged the girls from knowing such things. The essay first appeared in Ms. *magazine in 1975 with the title "Can I Be My Brother's Sister?" For its publication then, Walker used the pseudonym Straight Pine. The essay was later collected in Walker's* In Search of Our Mothers' Gardens.

W E LIVED ON A FARM in the South in the fifties, and my brothers, the four of them I knew (the fifth had left home when I was three years old), were allowed to watch animals being mated. This was not unusual; nor was it considered unusual that my older sister and I were frowned upon if we even asked, innocently, what was going on. One of my brothers explained the mating one day, using words my father had given him: "The bull is getting a little something on his stick," he said. And he laughed. "What stick?" I wanted to know. "Where did he get it? How did he pick it up? Where did he put it?" All my brothers laughed.

I believe my mother's theory about raising a large family of five boys and three girls was that the father should teach the boys and the mother teach the girls the facts, as one says, of life. So my father went around talking about bulls getting something on their sticks and she went around saying girls did not need to know about such things. They were "womanish" (a very bad way to be in those days) if they asked.

The thing was, watching the matings filled my brothers with an aimless sort of lust, as dangerous as it was unintentional. They knew enough to know that cows, months after mating, produced calves, but they were not bright enough to make the same connection between women and their offspring.

Sometimes, when I think of my childhood, it seems to me a particularly hard one. But in reality, everything awful that happened to me didn't seem to happen to *me* at all, but to my older sister. Through some incredible power to negate my presence around people I did not like, which produced invisibility (as well as an ability to appear mentally vacant when I was nothing of

270

the kind), I was spared the humiliation she was subjected to, though at the same time, I felt every bit of it. It was as if she suffered for my benefit, and I vowed early in my life that none of the things that made existence so miserable for her would happen to me.

The fact that she was not allowed at official matings did not mean she never saw any. While my brothers followed my father to the mating pens on the other side of the road near the barn, she stationed herself near the pigpen, or followed our many dogs until they were in a mating mood, or, failing to witness something there, she watched the chickens. On a farm it is impossible *not* to be conscious of sex, to wonder about it, to dream . . . but to whom was she to speak of her feelings? Not to my father, who thought all young women perverse. Not to my mother, who pretended all her children grew out of stumps she magically found in the forest. Not to me, who never found anything wrong with this lie.

When my sister menstruated she wore a thick packet of clean rags between her legs. It stuck out in front like a penis. The boys laughed at her as she served them at the table. Not knowing any better, and because our parents did not dream of actually *discussing* what was going on, she would giggle nervously at herself. I hated her for giggling, and it was at those times I would think of her as dim-witted. She never complained, but she began to have strange fainting fits whenever she had her period. Her head felt as if it were splitting, she said, and everything she ate came up again. And her cramps were so severe she could not stand. She was forced to spend several days of each month in bed.

My father expected all of his sons to have sex with women. "Like bulls," he said, "a man *needs* to get a little something on his stick." And so, on Saturday nights, into town they went, chasing the girls. My sister was rarely allowed into town alone, and if the dress she wore fit too snugly at the waist, or if her cleavage dipped too far below her collarbone, she was made to stay home.

"But why can't I go too," she would cry, her face screwed up with the effort not to wail.

"They're boys, your brothers, *that's* why they can go."

Naturally, when she got the chance, she responded eagerly to boys. But when this was discovered she was whipped and locked up in her room.

I would go in to visit her.

"Straight Pine," she would say, "you don't know what it *feels* like to want to be loved by a man."

"And if this is what you get for feeling like it I never will," I said, with — I hoped — the right combination of sympathy and disgust.

"Men smell so good," she would whisper ecstatically. "And when they look into your eyes, you just melt."

Since they were so hard to catch, naturally she thought almost any of them terrific.

"Oh, that Alfred!" she would moon over some mediocre, square-headed boy, "he's so *sweet!*" And she would take his ugly picture out of her bosom and kiss it.

My father was always warning her not to come home if she ever found herself pregnant. My mother constantly reminded her that abortion was a sin. Later, although she never became pregnant, her period would not come for months at a time. The painful symptoms, however, never varied or ceased. She fell for the first man who loved her enough to beat her for looking at someone else, and when I was still in high school, she married him.

My fifth brother, the one I never knew, was said to be different from the rest. He had not liked matings. He would not watch them. He thought the cows should be given a choice. My father had disliked him because he was soft. My mother took up for him. "Jason is just tender-hearted," she would say in a way that made me know he was her favorite; "he takes after me." It was true that my mother cried about almost anything.

Who was this oldest brother? I wondered.

"Well," said my mother, "he was someone who always loved you. Of   20 course he was a great big boy when you were born and out working on his own. He worked on a road gang building roads. Every morning before he left he would come in the room where you were and pick you up and give you the biggest kisses. He used to look at you and just smile. It's a pity you don't remember him."

I agreed.

At my father's funeral I finally "met" my oldest brother. He is tall and black with thick gray hair above a young-looking face. I watched my sister cry over my father until she blacked out from grief. I saw my brothers sobbing, reminding each other of what a great father he had been. My oldest brother and I did not shed a tear between us. When I left my father's grave he came up and introduced himself. "You don't ever have to walk alone," he said, and put his arms around me.

One out of five ain't *too* bad, I thought, snuggling up.

But I didn't discover until recently his true uniqueness: He is the only one of my brothers who assumes responsibility for all his children. The other four all fathered children during those Saturday-night chases of twenty years ago. Children — my nieces and nephews whom I will probably never know — they neither acknowledge as their own, provide for, or even see.

It was not until I became a student of women's liberation ideology that   25 I could understand and forgive my father. I needed an ideology that would define his behavior in context. The black movement had given me an ideology that helped explain his colorism (he *did* fall in love with my mother partly because she was so light; he never denied it). Feminism helped explain his sexism. I was relieved to know his sexist behavior was not something uniquely his own, but, rather, an imitation of the behavior of the society around us.

All partisan movements add to the fullness of our understanding of society as a whole. They never detract; or, in any case, one must not allow them to do so. Experience adds to experience. "The more things the better," as O'Connor and Welty [1] both have said, speaking, one of marriage, the other of Catholicism.

I desperately needed my father and brothers to give me male models I could respect, because white men (for example; being particularly handy in this sort of comparison) — whether in films or in person — offered man as dominator, as killer, and always as hypocrite.

My father failed because he copied the hypocrisy. And my brothers — except for one — never understood they must represent half the world to me, as I must represent the other half to them. [2]

[1] *O'Connor . . . Welty:* Flannery O'Connor (1925–1964), Eudora Welty (b. 1909): two prominent Southern fiction writers.

[2] Since this essay was written, my brothers have offered their name, acknowledgment, and some support to all their children. [Walker's note]

FROM READING TO REREADING

1. This is a tough-minded essay, not simply in the way it deals with the so-called facts of life but also in the way Alice Walker deals with her immediate family. How does she present the various members of her family and what does she have against them? What, for example, does she appear to dislike most about four of her brothers?

2. When Walker discusses the difficulties of her childhood, she says something strange: "But in reality, everything awful that happened to me didn't seem to happen to *me* at all, but to my older sister." How do you interpret this statement? To what extent does she approve and disapprove of her older sister?

3. Walker intends her title to be read in two ways: "brothers and sisters" refers both to her actual siblings and, by extension, to black men and women in general. Consider the essay's overall meaning. What point is Walker making about differences in gender?

VIRGINIA WOOLF
Thoughts on Peace in an Air Raid

The context of this essay is important to its understanding. Virginia Woolf wrote it for an American symposium on women in 1940, before the United States had declared war on Nazi Germany and allied itself with Great Britain. This helps explain the "we" she is addressing, and the reference to America in the final paragraph. At the time Woolf was writing, the German air force had undertaken nightly bombing raids of Britain, raids that resulted in an enormous loss of lives and property. One of Woolf's last essays (she died a year after), "Thoughts on Peace in an Air Raid" was collected in the posthumous volume, The Death of the Moth and Other Essays.

T HE GERMANS were over this house last night and the night before that. Here they are again. It is a queer experience, lying in the dark and listening to the zoom of a hornet, which may at any moment sting you to death. It is a sound that interrupts cool and consecutive thinking about peace. Yet it is a sound — far more than prayers and anthems — that should compel one to think about peace. Unless we can think peace into existence we — not this one body in this one bed but millions of bodies yet to be born — will lie in the same darkness and hear the same death rattle overhead. Let us think what we can do to create the only efficient air-raid shelter while the guns on the hill go pop pop pop and the searchlights finger the clouds and now and then, sometimes close at hand, sometimes far away, a bomb drops.

Up there in the sky young Englishmen and young German men are fighting each other. The defenders are men, the attackers men. Arms are not given to Englishwomen either to fight the enemy or to defend herself. She must lie weaponless tonight. Yet if she believes that the fight going on up in the sky is a fight by the English to protect freedom, by the Germans to destroy freedom, she must fight, so far as she can, on the side of the English. How far can she fight for freedom without firearms? By making arms, or clothes or food. But there is another way of fighting for freedom without arms; we can fight with the mind. We can make ideas that will help the young Englishman who is fighting up in the sky to defeat the enemy.

But to make ideas effective, we must be able to fire them off. We must put them into action. And the hornet in the sky rouses another hornet in the mind. There was one zooming in the *Times* this morning — a woman's voice saying, "Women have not a word to say in politics." There is no woman in the Cabinet; nor in any responsible post. All the idea-makers who are in a position to make ideas effective are men. That is a thought that damps thinking, and encourages irresponsibility. Why not bury the head in the pillow, plug the ears, and cease this futile activity of idea-making? Because there are other tables besides officer tables and conference tables. Are we not leaving the young Englishman without a weapon that might be of value to him if we give up private thinking, tea-table thinking, because it seems useless? Are we not stressing our disability because our ability exposes us perhaps to abuse, perhaps to contempt? "I will not cease from mental fight," Blake [1] wrote. Mental fight means thinking against the current, not with it.

That current flows fast and furious. It issues in a spate of words from the loudspeakers and the politicians. Every day they tell us that we are a free people, fighting to defend freedom. That is the current that has whirled the young airman up into the sky and keeps him circling there among the clouds. Down here, with a roof to cover us and a gas-mask handy, it is our business to puncture gas-bags and discover seeds of truth. It is not true that we are free. We are both prisoners tonight — he boxed up in his machine with a gun handy; we lying in the dark with a gas-mask handy. If we were free we should be out in the open, dancing, at the play, or sitting at the window talking together. What is it that prevents us? "Hitler!" the loudspeakers cry with one voice. Who is Hitler? What is he? Aggressiveness, tyranny, the insane love of power made manifest, they reply. Destroy that, and you will be free.

The drone of the planes is now like the sawing of a branch overhead.   5 Round and round it goes, sawing and sawing at a branch directly above the house. Another sound begins sawing its way in the brain. "Women of ability" — it was Lady Astor [2] speaking in the *Times* this morning — "are held down because of a subconscious Hitlerism in the hearts of men." Certainly we are held down. We are equally prisoners tonight — the Englishmen in their planes, the Englishwomen in their beds. But if he stops to think he may be killed; and we too. So let us think for him. Let us try to drag up into consciousness the subconscious Hitlerism that holds us down. It is the desire for aggression; the desire to dominate and enslave. Even in the darkness we can see that made visible. We can see shop windows blazing; and women gazing; painted women; dressed-up women; women with crimson lips and crimson fingernails. They are slaves who are trying to enslave. If we could free ourselves from slavery we should free men from tyranny. Hitlers are bred by slaves.

A bomb drops. All the windows rattle. The anti-aircraft guns are getting active. Up there on the hill under a net tagged with strips of green and

[1] *Blake*: William Blake (1757–1827), English poet.

[2] *Lady Astor*: American-born Nancy Witcher (Langhorne), Viscountess Astor (1879–1964), was the first woman elected to the House of Commons, where she served from 1919 to 1945. A political Conservative, she nevertheless advocated many social reforms, including women's rights. In the 1930s, however, she also proposed an appeasement policy toward Nazi Germany.

brown stuff to imitate the hues of autumn leaves guns are concealed. Now they all fire at once. On the nine o'clock radio we shall be told "Forty-four enemy planes were shot down during the night, ten of them by anti-aircraft fire." And one of the terms of peace, the loudspeakers say, is to be disarmament. There are to be no more guns, no army, no navy, no air force in the future. No more young men will be trained to fight with arms. That rouses another mind-hornet in the chambers of the brain — another quotation. "To fight against a real enemy, to earn undying honour and glory by shooting total strangers, and to come home with my breast covered with medals and decorations, that was the summit of my hope. . . . It was for this that my whole life so far had been dedicated, my education, training, everything. . . ."

Those were the words of a young Englishman who fought in the last war. In the face of them, do the current thinkers honestly believe that by writing "Disarmament" on a sheet of paper at a conference table they will have done all that is needful? Othello's [3] occupation will be gone; but he will remain Othello. The young airman up in the sky is driven not only by the voices of loudspeakers; he is driven by voices in himself — ancient instincts, instincts fostered and cherished by education and tradition. Is he to be blamed for those instincts? Could we switch off the maternal instinct at the command of a table full of politicians? Suppose that imperative among the peace terms was: "Child-bearing is to be restricted to a very small class of specially selected women," would we submit? Should we not say, "The maternal instinct is a woman's glory. It was for this that my whole life has been dedicated, my education, training, everything. . . ." But if it were necessary, for the sake of humanity, for the peace of the world, that child-bearing should be restricted, the maternal instinct subdued; women would attempt it. Men would help them. They would honour them for their refusal to bear children. They would give them other openings for their creative power. That too must make part of our fight for freedom. We must help the young Englishmen to root out from themselves the love of medals and decorations. We must create more honourable activities for those who try to conquer in themselves their fighting instinct, their subconscious Hitlerism. We must compensate the man for the loss of his gun.

The sound of sawing overhead has increased. All the searchlights are erect. They point at a spot exactly above this roof. At any moment a bomb may fall on this very room. One, two, three, four, five, six . . . the seconds pass. The bomb did not fall. But during those seconds of suspense all thinking stopped. All feeling, save one dull dread, ceased. A nail fixed the whole being to one hard board. The emotion of fear and of hate is therefore sterile, unfertile. Directly that fear passes, the mind reaches out and instinctively revives itself by trying to create. Since the room is dark it can create

[3] *Othello:* Shakespeare's tragic character Othello was a military leader.

only from memory. It reaches out to the memory of other Augusts — in Bayreuth, listening to Wagner; in Rome, walking over the Campagna; in London. Friends' voices come back. Scraps of poetry return. Each of those thoughts, even in memory, was far more positive, reviving, healing, and creative than the dull dread made of fear and hate. Therefore if we are to compensate the young man for the loss of his glory and of his gun, we must give him access to the creative feelings. We must make happiness. We must free him from the machine. We must bring him out of his prison into the open air. But what is the use of freeing the young Englishman if the young German and the young Italian remain slaves?

The searchlights, wavering across the flat, have picked up the plane now. From this window one can see a little silver insect turning and twisting in the light. The guns go pop pop pop. Then they cease. Probably the raider was brought down behind the hill. One of the pilots landed safe in a field near here the other day. He said to his captors, speaking fairly good English, "How glad I am that the fight is over!" Then an Englishman gave him a cigarette, and an Englishwoman made him a cup of tea. That would seem to show that if you can free the man from the machine, the seed does not fall upon altogether stony ground. The seed may be fertile.

At last all the guns have stopped firing. All the searchlights have been   10 extinguished. The natural darkness of a summer's night returns. The innocent sounds of the country are heard again. An apple thuds to the ground. An owl hoots, winging its way from tree to tree. And some half-forgotten words of an old English writer come to mind: "The huntsmen are up in America. . . ." Let us send these fragmentary notes to the huntsmen who are up in America, to the men and women whose sleep has not yet been broken by machine-gun fire, in the belief that they will rethink them generously and charitably, perhaps shape them into something serviceable. And now, in the shadowed half of the world, to sleep.

FROM READING TO REREADING

1. The word *Thoughts* in the title is deliberately chosen. How does it refer to both the essay's structure and its content? What, for example, does Woolf mean when she says, "Unless we can think peace into existence . . ."?

2. Note the numerous references to sound and noise in the essay. As you reread the piece, try focusing on Woolf's continual allusions to hearing. Why are these references appropriate? How are they related to thinking?

3. Though the essay ties together issues of feminism and militarism, Woolf's political position is never clearly and directly stated. What ideas and ideals do you think Woolf is arguing for? What does she want women to do? What does she want men to do?

JAMES BALDWIN
Here Be Dragons

The noted literary critic, Harold Bloom, thought the final statement of this essay to be "Baldwin's most poignant, ever." Written in the last years of his life, the essay explores several of the themes that preoccupied Baldwin throughout his career — the problem of identity, the idea of manhood, the vicious effects of racism. And, like most of his work, the essay is also intensely autobiographical, even confessional, as Baldwin examines his own homosexuality, his abused childhood, his debilitating poverty. The essay originally appeared in Playboy *(parts of it appear to have been responses to editorial questions from that magazine) as "Freaks and the American Ideal of Manhood" in 1985, and was collected later that year without revision as the final essay in Baldwin's* The Price of the Ticket.

TO BE ANDROGYNOUS, *Webster's* informs us, is to have both male and female characteristics. This means that there is a man in every woman and a woman in every man. Sometimes this is recognized only when the chips are, brutally, down — when there is no longer any way to avoid this recognition. But love between a man and a woman, or love between any two human beings, would not be possible did we not have available to us the spiritual resources of both sexes.

To be androgynous does not imply both male and female sexual equipment, which is the state, uncommon, of the hermaphrodite. However, the existence of the hermaphrodite reveals, in intimidating exaggeration, the truth concerning every human being — which is why the hermaphrodite is called a freak. The human being does not, in general, enjoy being intimidated by what he/she finds in the mirror.

The hermaphrodite, therefore, may make his/her living in side shows or brothels, whereas the merely androgynous are running banks or filling stations or maternity wards, churches, armies or countries.

The last time you had a drink, whether you were alone or with another, you were having a drink with an androgynous human being; and this is true for the last time you broke bread or, as I have tried to suggest, the last time you made love.

There seems to be a vast amount of confusion in the Western world 5 concerning these matters, but love and sexual activity are not synonymous: only by becoming inhuman can the human being pretend that they are. The mare is not obliged to love the stallion, nor is the bull required to love the cow. They are doing what comes naturally.

But this by no means sums up the state or the possibilities of the human being in whom the awakening of desire fuels imagination and in whom imagination fuels desire. In other words, it is not possible for the human being to be as simple as a stallion or a mare, because the human imagination is perpetually required to examine, control, and redefine reality, of which we must assume ourselves to be the center and the key. Nature and revelation are perpetually challenging each other; this relentless tension is one of the keys to human history and to what is known as the human condition.

Now, I can speak only of the Western world and must rely on my own experience, but the simple truth of this universal duality, this perpetual possibility of communion and completion, seems so alarming that I have watched it lead to addiction, despair, death, and madness. Nowhere have I seen this panic more vividly than in my country and in my generation.

The American idea of sexuality appears to be rooted in the American idea of masculinity. Idea may not be the precise word, for the idea of one's sexuality can only with great violence be divorced or distanced from the idea of the self. Yet something resembling this rupture has certainly occurred (and is occurring) in American life, and violence has been the American daily bread since we have heard of America. This violence, furthermore, is not merely literal and actual but appears to be admired and lusted after, and the key to the American imagination.

All countries or groups make of their trials a legend or, as in the case of Europe, a dubious romance called "history." But no other country has ever made so successful and glamorous a romance out of genocide and slavery; therefore, perhaps the word I am searching for is not idea but ideal.

The American *ideal*, then, of sexuality appears to be rooted in the American ideal of masculinity. This ideal has created cowboys and Indians, good guys and bad guys, punks and studs, tough guys and softies, butch and faggot, black and white. It is an ideal so paralytically infantile that it is virtually forbidden — as an unpatriotic act — that the American boy evolve into the complexity of manhood. 10

The exigencies created by the triumph of the Industrial Revolution — or, in other terms, the rise of Europe to global dominance — had, among many mighty effects, that of commercializing the roles of men and women. Men became the propagators, or perpetrators, of property, and women became the means by which that property was protected and handed down. One may say that this was nothing more than the ancient and universal division of labor — women nurtured the tribe, men battled for it — but the concept of property had undergone a change. This change was vast and deep and sinister.

For the first time in human history, a man was reduced not merely to a thing but to a thing the value of which was determined, absolutely, by that thing's commercial value. That this pragmatic principle dictated the slaughter of the native American, the enslavement of the black and the monumental rape of Africa — to say nothing of creating the wealth of the Western world — no one, I suppose, will now attempt to deny.

But this principle also raped and starved Ireland, for example, as well as Latin America, and it controlled the pens of the men who signed the Declaration of Independence — a document more clearly commercial than moral. This is how, and why, the American Constitution was able to define the slave as three-fifths of a man, from which legal and commercial definition it legally followed that a black man "had no rights a white man was bound to respect."

Ancient maps of the world — when the world was flat — inform us, concerning that void where America was waiting to be discovered, HERE BE DRAGONS. Dragons may not have been here then, but they are certainly here now, breathing fire, belching smoke; or, to be less literary and biblical about it, attempting to intimidate the mores, morals, and morality of this particular and peculiar time and place. Nor, since this country is the issue of the entire globe and is also the most powerful nation currently to be found on it, are we speaking only of this time and place. And it can be said that the monumental struggles being waged in our time and not only in this place resemble, in awesome ways, the ancient struggle between those who insisted that the world was flat and those who apprehended that it was round.

Of course, I cannot possibly imagine what it can be like to have both male and female sexual equipment. That's a load of family jewels to be hauling about, and it seems to me that it must make choice incessant or impossible — or, in terms unavailable to me, unnecessary. Yet, not to be frivolous concerning what I know I cannot — or, more probably, dare not — imagine, I hazard that the physically androgynous state must create an all-but-intolerable loneliness, since we all exist, after all, and crucially, in the eye of the beholder. We all react to and, to whatever extent, become what that eye sees. This judgment begins in the eyes of one's parents (the crucial, the definitive, the all-but-everlasting judgment), and so we move, in the vast and claustrophobic gallery of Others, on up or down the line, to the eye of one's enemy or one's friend or one's lover.

It is virtually impossible to trust one's human value without the collaboration or corroboration of that eye — which is to say that no one can live without it. One can, of course, instruct that eye as to what to see, but this effort, which is nothing less than ruthless intimidation, is wounding and exhausting: while it can keep humiliation at bay, it confirms the fact that humiliation is the central danger of one's life. And since one cannot risk love without risking humiliation, love becomes impossible.

I hit the streets when I was about six or seven, like most black kids of my generation, running errands, doing odd jobs. This was in the black world — my turf — which means that I felt protected. I think that I really was,

15

though poverty is poverty and we were, if I may say so, among the truly needy, in spite of the tins of corned beef we got from home relief every week, along with prunes. (Catsup had not yet become a vegetable; indeed, I don't think we had ever heard of it.) My mother fried corned beef, she boiled it, she baked it, she put potatoes in it, she put rice in it, she disguised it in corn bread, she boiled it in soup(!), she wrapped it in cloth, she beat it with a hammer, she banged it against the wall, she threw it onto the ceiling. Finally, she gave up, for nothing could make us eat it anymore, and the tins reproachfully piled up on the shelf above the bathtub — along with the prunes, which we also couldn't eat anymore. While I won't speak for my brothers and sisters, I can't bear corned-beef hash or prunes even today.

Poverty. I remember one afternoon when someone dropped a dime in front of the subway station at 125th Street and Lenox Avenue and I and a man of about forty both scrambled for it. The man won, giving me a cheerful goodbye as he sauntered down the subway steps. I was bitterly disappointed, a dime being a dime, but I laughed, too.

The truly needy. Once, my father gave me a dime — the last dime in the house, though I didn't know that — to go to the store for kerosene for the stove, and I fell on the icy streets and dropped the dime and lost it. My father beat me with an iron cord from the kitchen to the back room and back again, until I lay, half-conscious, on my belly on the floor.

Yet — strange though it is to realize this, looking back — I never felt threatened in those years, when I was growing up in Harlem, my home town. I think this may be because it was familiar; the white people who lived there then were as poor as we, and there was no TV setting our teeth on edge with exhortations to buy what we could never hope to afford.

On the other hand, I was certainly unbelievably unhappy and pathologically shy, but that, I felt, was nobody's fault but mine. My father kept me in short pants longer than he should have, and I had been told, and I believed, that I was ugly. This meant that the idea of myself as a sexual possibility, or target, as a creature capable of desire, had never entered my mind. And it entered my mind, finally, by means of the rent made in my short boy-scout pants by a man who had lured me into a hallway, saying that he wanted to send me to the store. That was the very last time I agreed to run an errand for any stranger.

Yet I was, in peculiar truth, a very lucky boy. Shortly after I turned sixteen, a Harlem racketeer, a man of about thirty-eight, fell in love with me, and I will be grateful to that man until the day I die. I showed him all my poetry, because I had no one else in Harlem to show it to, and even now, I sometimes wonder what on earth his friends could have been thinking, confronted with stingy-brimmed, mustachioed, razor-toting Poppa and skinny, popeyed Me when he walked me (rarely) into various shady joints, I drinking ginger ale, he drinking brandy. I think I was supposed to be his nephew, some nonsense like that, though he was Spanish and Irish, with curly black hair. But I knew that he was showing me off and wanted his friends to be happy for him — which, indeed, if the way they treated me can be taken as a barometer, they were. They seemed to feel that this was his business — that he would be in trouble if it became *their* business.

And though I loved him, too — in my way, a boy's way — I was mightily tormented, for I was still a child evangelist, which everybody knew, Lord. My soul looks back and wonders.

For what this really means is that all of the American categories of male and female, straight or not, black or white, were shattered, thank heaven, very early in my life. Not without anguish, certainly; but once you have discerned the meaning of a label, it may seem to define you for others, but it does not have the power to define you to yourself.

This prepared me for my life downtown, where I quickly discovered that my existence was the punch line of a dirty joke.   25

The condition that is now called gay was then called queer. The operative word was *faggot* and, later, pussy, but those epithets really had nothing to do with the question of sexual preference: you were being told simply that you had no balls.

I certainly had no desire to harm anyone, nor did I understand how anyone could look at me and suppose me physically capable of *causing* any harm. But boys and men chased me, saying I was a danger to their sisters. I was thrown out of cafeterias and rooming houses because I was "bad" for the neighborhood.

The cops watched all this with a smile, never making the faintest motion to protect me or to disperse my attackers; in fact, I was even more afraid of the cops than I was of the populace.

By the time I was nineteen, I was working in the Garment Center. I was getting on very badly at home and delayed going home after work as long as possible. At the end of the workday, I would wander east, to the Forty-second Street Library. Sometimes, I would sit in Bryant Park — but I discovered that I could not sit there long. I fled, to the movies, and so discovered Forty-second Street. Today that street is exactly what it was when I was an adolescent: it has simply become more blatant.

There were no X-rated movies then, but there were, so to speak, X-   30
rated audiences. For example, I went in complete innocence to the Apollo, on Forty-second Street, because foreign films were shown there — *The Lower Depths, Childhood of Maxim Gorky, La Bête Humaine* — and I walked out as untouched (by human hands) as I had been when I walked in. There were the stores, mainly on Sixth Avenue, that sold "girlie" magazines. These magazines were usually to be found at the back of the store, and I don't so much remember them as I remember the silent men who stood there. They stood, it seemed, for hours, with the magazines in their hands and a kind of

miasma in their eyes. There were all kinds of men, mostly young and, in those days, almost exclusively white. Also, for what it's worth, they were heterosexual, since the images they studied, at crotch level, were those of women.

Actually, I guess I hit Forty-second Street twice and have very nearly blotted the first time out. I was not at the mercy of the street the first time, for, though I may have dreaded *going* home, I hadn't *left* home yet. Then, I spent a lot of time in the library, and I stole odds and ends out of Woolworth's — with no compunction at all, due to the way they treated us in Harlem. When I went to the movies, I imagine that a combination of innocence and terror prevented me from too clearly apprehending the action taking place in the darkness of the Apollo — though I understood it well enough to remain standing a great deal of the time. This cunning stratagem failed when, one afternoon, the young boy I was standing behind put his hand behind him and grabbed my cock at the very same moment that a young boy came up behind me and put his cock against my hand: ignobly enough, I fled, though I doubt that I was missed. The men in the men's room frightened me, so I moved in and out as quickly as possible, and I also dimly felt, I remember, that I didn't want to "fool around" and so risk hurting the feelings of my uptown friend.

But if I was paralyzed by guilt and terror, I cannot be judged or judge myself too harshly, for I remember the faces of the men. These men, so far from being or resembling faggots, looked and sounded like the vigilantes who banded together on weekends to beat faggots up. (And I was around long enough, suffered enough, and learned enough to be forced to realize that this was very often true. I might not have learned this if I had been a white boy; but sometimes a white man will tell a black boy anything, everything, weeping briny tears. He knows that the black boy can never betray him, for no one will believe his testimony.)

These men looked like cops, football players, soldiers, sailors, Marines or bank presidents, admen, boxers, construction workers; they had wives, mistresses, and children. I sometimes saw them in other settings — in, as it were, the daytime. Sometimes they spoke to me, sometimes not, for anguish has many days and styles. But I had first seen them in the men's room, sometimes on their knees, peering up into the stalls, or standing at the urinal stroking themselves, staring at another man, stroking, and with this miasma in their eyes. Sometimes, eventually, inevitably, I would find myself in bed with one of these men, a despairing and dreadful conjunction, since their need was as relentless as quicksand and as impersonal, and sexual rumor concerning blacks had preceded me. As for sexual roles, these were created by the imagination and limited only by one's stamina.

At bottom, what I had learned was that the male desire for a male roams everywhere, avid, desperate, unimaginably lonely, culminating often in drugs, piety, madness or death. It was also dreadfully like watching myself at the end of a long, slow-moving line: soon I would be next. All of this was very frightening. It was lonely and impersonal and demeaning. I could not believe — after all, I was only nineteen — that I could have been driven to the lonesome place where these men and I met each other so soon, to stay.

The American idea of masculinity: There are few things under heaven 35 more difficult to understand or, when I was younger, to forgive.

During the Second World War (the first one having failed to make the world safe for democracy) and some time after the Civil War (which had failed, unaccountably, to liberate the slave), life for niggers was fairly rough in Greenwich Village. There were only about three of us, if I remember correctly, when I first hit those streets, and I was the youngest, the most visible, and the most vulnerable.

On every street corner, I was called a faggot. This meant that I was despised, and, however horrible this is, it is clear. What was *not* clear at that time of my life was what motivated the men and boys who mocked and chased me; for, if they found me when they were alone, they spoke to me very differently — frightening me, I must say, into a stunned and speechless paralysis. For when they were alone, they spoke very gently and wanted me to take them home and make love. (They could not take *me* home; they lived with their families.) The bafflement and the pain this caused in me remain beyond description. I was far too terrified to be able to accept their propositions, which could only result, it seemed to me, in making myself a candidate for gang rape. At the same time, I was moved by their loneliness, their halting, nearly speechless need. But I did not understand it.

One evening, for example, I was standing at the bottom of the steps to the Waverly Place subway station, saying goodbye to some friends who were about to take the subway. A gang of boys stood at the top of the steps and cried, in high, feminine voices, "Is this where the fags meet?"

Well. This meant that I certainly could not go back upstairs but would have to take the subway with my friends and get off at another station and maneuver my way home. But one of the gang saw me and, without missing a beat or saying a word to his friends, called my name and came down the steps, throwing one arm around me and asking where I'd been. He had let me know, some time before, that he wanted me to take him home — but I was surprised that he could be so open before his friends, who for their part seemed to find nothing astonishing in this encounter and disappeared, probably in search of other faggots.

The boys who are left of that time and place are all my age or older. 40 But many of them are dead, and I remember how some of them died — some in the streets, some in the Army, some on the needle, some in jail. Many years later, we managed, without ever becoming friends — it was too late for that — to be friendly with one another. One of these men and I had a very brief, intense affair shortly before he died. He was on drugs and knew that he could not live long. "What a waste," he said, and he was right.

One of them said, "My God, Jimmy, you were moving so fast in those years, you never stopped to talk to me."

I said, "That's right, baby; I didn't stop because I didn't want you to think that I was trying to seduce you."

"Man," he said, indescribably, "why didn't you?"

But the queer — not yet gay — world was an even more intimidating area of this hall of mirrors. I knew that I was in the hall and present at this company — but the mirrors threw back only brief and distorted fragments of myself.

In the first place, as I have said, there were very few black people in 45 the Village in those years, and of that handful, I was decidedly the most improbable. Perhaps, as they say in the theater, I was a hard type to cast; yet I was eager, vulnerable, and lonely. I was terribly shy, but boys *are* shy. I am saying that I don't think I felt absolutely, irredeemably grotesque — nothing that a friendly wave of the wand couldn't alter — but I was miserable. I moved through that world very quickly; I have described it as "my season in hell," for I was never able to make my peace with it.

It wasn't only that I didn't wish to seem or sound like a woman, for it was this detail that most harshly first struck my eye and ear. I am sure that I was afraid that I already seemed and sounded too much like a woman. In my childhood, at least until my adolescence, my playmates had called me a sissy. It seemed to me that many of the people I met were making fun of women, and I didn't see why. *I* certainly needed all the friends I could get, male *or* female, and women had nothing to do with whatever my trouble might prove to be.

At the same time, I had already been sexually involved with a couple of white women in the Village. There were virtually no black women there when I hit those streets, and none who needed or could have afforded to risk herself with an odd, raggedy-assed black boy who clearly had no future. (The first black girl I met who dug me I fell in love with, lived with and almost married. But I met her, though I was only twenty-two, many light-years too late.)

The white girls I had known or been involved with — different categories — had paralyzed me, because I simply did not know what, apart from my sex, they wanted. Sometimes it was great, sometimes it was just moaning and groaning, but, ultimately, I found myself at the mercy of a double fear. The fear of the world was bearable until it entered the bedroom. But it sometimes entered the bedroom by means of the motives of the girl, who intended to civilize you into becoming an appendage or who had found a black boy to sleep with because she wanted to humiliate her parents. Not an easy scene to play, in any case, since it can bring out the worst in both parties, and more than one white girl had already made me know that her color was more powerful than my dick.

Which had nothing to do with how I found myself in the gay world. I would have found myself there anyway, but perhaps the very last thing this black boy needed were clouds of imitation white women and speculations concerning the size of his organ; speculations sometimes accompanied by an attempt at the laying on of hands. "*Ooo!* Look at him! He's cute — he doesn't like you to touch him there!"

In short, I was black in that world, and I was used that way, and by   50 people who truly meant me no harm.

And they could *not* have meant me any harm, because they did not see me. There were exceptions, of course, for I also met some beautiful people. Yet even today, it seems to me (possibly because I am black) very dangerous to model one's opposition to the arbitrary definition, the imposed ordeal, merely on the example supplied by one's oppressor.

The object of one's hatred is never, alas, conveniently outside but is seated in one's lap, stirring in one's bowels and dictating the beat of one's heart. And if one does not know this, one risks becoming an imitation — and, therefore, a continuation — of principles one imagines oneself to despise.

I, in any case, had endured far too much debasement willingly to debase myself. I had absolutely no fantasies about making love to the last cop or hoodlum who had beaten the shit out of me. I did not find it amusing, in any way whatever, to act out the role of the darky.

So I moved on out of there.

In fact, I found a friend — more accurately, a friend found *me* — an   55 Italian, about five years older than I, who helped my morale greatly in those years. I was told that he had threatened to kill anyone who touched me. I don't know about that, but people stopped beating me up. Our relationship never seemed to worry him or his friends or his women.

My situation in the Village stabilized itself to the extent that I began working as a waiter in a black West Indian restaurant, The Calypso, on MacDougal Street. This led, by no means incidentally, to the desegregation of the San Remo, an Italian bar and restaurant on the corner of MacDougal and Bleecker. Every time I entered the San Remo, they threw me out. I had to pass it all the time on my way to and from work, which is, no doubt, why the insult rankled.

I had won the Saxton Fellowship, which was administered by Harper & Brothers, and I knew Frank S. MacGregor, the president of Harper's. One night, when he asked me where we should have dinner, I suggested, spontaneously, the San Remo.

We entered, and they seated us and we were served. I went back to

MacGregor's house for a drink and then went straight back to the San Remo, sitting on a bar stool in the window. The San Remo thus began to attract a varied clientele, indeed — so much so that Allen Ginsberg[1] and company arrived there the year I left New York for Paris.

As for the people who ran and worked at the San Remo, they never bothered me again. Indeed, the Italian community never bothered me again — or rarely and, as it were, by accident. But the Village was full of white tourists, and one night, when a mob gathered before the San Remo, demanding that I come out, the owners closed the joint and turned the lights out and we sat in the back room, in the dark, for a couple of hours, until they judged it safe to drive me home.

This was a strange, great and bewildering time in my life. Once I was in the San Remo, for example, I was *in*, and anybody who messed with me was *out* — that was all there was to it, and it happened more than once. And no one seemed to remember a time when I had not been there. 60

I could not quite get it together, but it seemed to me that I was no longer black for them and they had ceased to be white for me, for they sometimes introduced me to their families with every appearance of affection and pride and exhibited not the remotest interest in whatever my sexual proclivities chanced to be.

They had fought me very hard to prevent this moment, but perhaps we were all much relieved to have got beyond the obscenity of color.

Matters were equally bewildering, though in a different way, at The Calypso. All kinds of people came into our joint — I am now referring to white people — and one of their most vivid aspects, for me, was the cruelty of their alienation. They appeared to have no antecedents nor any real connections.

"Do you really *like* your mother?" someone asked me, seeming to be astounded, totally disbelieving the possibility.

I was astounded by the question. Certainly, my mother and I did not 65 agree about everything, and I knew that she was very worried about the dangers of the life I lived, but that was normal, since I was a boy and she was a woman. Of course she was worried about me: she was my *mother*. But she knew I wasn't crazy and that I would certainly never do anything, deliberately, to hurt her. Or my tribe, my brothers and sisters, who were probably worried about me, too.

My family was a part of my life. I could not imagine life without them, might never have been able to reconcile myself to life without them. And certainly one of the reasons I was breaking my ass in the Village had to do with my need to try to move us out of our dangerous situation. I was perfectly

[1] *Allen Ginsberg* (b. 1926): American poet who was one of the leaders of the Beat movement in the 1950s; he published his long poem *Howl* in 1956.

aware of the odds — my father had made that very clear — but he had also given me my assignment. "Do you really *like* your mother?" did not cause me to wonder about my mother or myself but about the person asking the question.

And perhaps because of such questions, I was not even remotely tempted by the possibilities of psychiatry or psychoanalysis. For one thing, there were too many schools — Freud, Horney, Jung, Reich (to suggest merely the tip of that iceberg) — and, for another, it seemed to me that anyone who thought seriously that I had any desire to be "adjusted" to this society had to be ill; too ill, certainly, as time was to prove, to be trusted.

I sensed, then — without being able to articulate it — that this dependence on a formula for safety, for that is what it was, signaled a desperate moral abdication. People went to the shrink in order to find justification for the empty lives they led and the meaningless work they did. Many turned, helplessly, hopefully, to Wilhelm Reich [2] and perished in orgone boxes.

I seem to have strayed a long way from our subject, but our subject is social and historical — and continuous. The people who leaped into orgone boxes in search of the perfect orgasm were later to turn to acid. The people so dependent on psychiatric formulas were unable to give their children any sense of right or wrong — indeed, this sense was in themselves so fragile that during the McCarthy era, more than one shrink made a lot of money by convincing his patients, or clients, that their psychic health demanded that they inform on their friends. (Some of these people, after their surrender, attempted to absolve themselves in the civil rights movement.)

What happened to the children, therefore, is not even remotely astonishing. The flower children — who became the Weather Underground, the Symbionese Liberation Army, the Manson Family — are creatures from this howling inner space. 70

I am not certain, therefore, that the present sexual revolution is either sexual or a revolution. It strikes me as a reaction to the spiritual famine of American life. The present androgynous "craze" — to underestimate it — strikes me as an attempt to be honest concerning one's nature, and it is instructive, I think, to note that there is virtually no emphasis on overt sexual activity. There is nothing more boring, anyway, than sexual activity as an end in itself, and a great many people who came out of the closet should reconsider.

Such figures as Boy George do not disturb me nearly so much as do those relentlessly hetero (sexual?) keepers of the keys and seals, those who

---

[2] *Wilhelm Reich* (1897–1957): Influential psychoanalyst and pioneer in sexual therapy; explored negative body images, especially as they affected the sexual lives of his patients. Orgone boxes were a part of his therapy.

know what the world needs in the way of order and who are ready and willing to supply that order.

This rage for order can result in chaos, and in this country, chaos connects with color. During the height of my involvement in the civil rights movement, for example, I was subjected to hate mail of a terrifying precision. Volumes concerning what my sisters, to say nothing of my mother, were capable of doing; to say nothing of my brothers; to say nothing of the monumental size of *my* organ and what I did with it. Someone described, in utterly riveting detail, a scene he swore he had witnessed (I *think* it was a *he* — such mail is rarely signed) on the steps of houses in Baltimore of niggers fucking their dogs.

At the same time, I was also on the mailing list of one of the more elegant of the KKK societies, and I still have some of that mail in my files. Someone, of course, eventually realized that the organization should not be sending that mail to this particular citizen, and it stopped coming — but not before I had had time to be struck by the similarity of tone between the hate mail and the mail of the society, and not before the society had informed me, by means of a parody of an Audubon Society postcard, what it felt and expected me to feel concerning a certain "Red-breasted" Martin Luther King, Jr.

The Michael Jackson cacophony is fascinating in that it is not about 75 Jackson at all. I hope he has the good sense to know it and the good fortune to snatch his life out of the jaws of a carnivorous success. He will not swiftly be forgiven for having turned so many tables, for he damn sure grabbed the brass ring, and the man who broke the bank at Monte Carlo has nothing on Michael. All that noise is about America, as the dishonest custodian of black life and wealth; the blacks, especially males, in America; and the burning, buried American guilt; and sex and sexual roles and sexual panic; money, success and despair — to all of which may now be added the bitter need to find a head on which to place the crown of Miss America.

Freaks are called freaks and are treated as they are treated — in the main, abominably — because they are human beings who cause to echo, deep within us, our most profound terrors and desires.

Most of us, however, do not appear to be freaks — though we are rarely what we appear to be. We are, for the most part, visibly male or female, our social roles defined by our sexual equipment.

But we are all androgynous, not only because we are all born of a woman impregnated by the seed of a man but because each of us, helplessly and forever, contains the other — male in female, female in male, white in black and black in white. We are a part of each other. Many of my countrymen appear to find this fact exceedingly inconvenient and even unfair, and so, very often, do I. But none of us can do anything about it.

FROM READING TO REREADING

1. Baldwin opens and closes his essay by considering androgyny. Why is androgyny important to him? What does he see as its current relevance? What does it have to do with American men and manhood?

2. Baldwin uses as his title a legend from ancient maps. Of what relevance are those maps to his essay? What do the dragons stand for today? What is their connection to Baldwin's subject?

3. Of Baldwin's final three paragraphs, Harold Bloom writes: "Baldwin is most prophetic, and most persuasive, when his voice is as subdued as it is here. What gives the rhetorical effect of self-subdual is the precise use of plural pronouns throughout." Consider these final paragraphs carefully. What does Bloom mean by Baldwin's subdued voice and how is it achieved by his use of pronouns?

LEWIS THOMAS
Scabies, Scrapie

As a writer and medical researcher, Lewis Thomas is equally at home with the technical article and the informal essay. He has written many of each. In this oddly titled essay, he begins with his interest in an arcane medical subject but soon switches to his main point: the differences between the sexes. His tone throughout is easygoing, somewhat social and somewhat scientific: "I am, in short, swept off my feet by women, and I do not think they have yet been assigned the place in the world's affairs that they are biologically made for." The piece appeared in Thomas's essayistic memoir, The Youngest Science *(1983).*

M Y WIFE SAID: "How can you possibly spend four hours talking about scabies?" This was just before I got into a London cab on my way to a seminar in 1981. Not scabies, I said, *scrapie,* but then the door closed and I had lost the chance to explain scrapie and the remarkable properties of the slow viruses of brain disease which infect today and may not produce symptoms of brain damage until twenty-five years from now, and the overwhelming interest everyone, including my wife, ought to have in forms of life that can replicate themselves without, so far as has yet been discovered, any DNA or RNA at all, one of the greatest puzzles in biology today. Halfway along on the London streets it occurred to me that maybe the virus of scrapie is simply a switched-on, normal gene, and the presumably protein agent that causes the disease may not be alive after all, only a signal to switch on a gene in brain cells which is supposed to be kept off. The notion swamped my mind for most of the cab ride, still does, and I couldn't wait until I got home to explain all this to my wife.

But later in the day, Beryl had her inning. She was reading several books at once, as usual: one by a Cambridge University visiting professor from Poland, with whom we had dined several evenings earlier, on the history of law and religion in the ancient East. Did I know that the Black Stone in Mecca long antedated Islam and that it was supposed to have been pure white originally? Did I know about the Four Dogs of Genghis Khan? Would I like to hear about a fourteenth-century political philosopher named Ibn Khaldun? I would. We went on with it, scrapie from my side of the net, Mesopotamian river basins and their cultural centers from hers.

Thinking back over forty years of marriage, I estimate that I have learned more from her, although she has acquired, for better or worse, for richer or poorer, some of my obsessive concerns, including all of Montaigne, lots of Wallace Stevens, some schoolboy Homer. She probably knows more about endotoxin and the Shwartzman reaction than any academic wife in our acquaintance, although I'm afraid it comes up as a lively topic for conversation only from time to time. I, by contrast, have learned all sorts of things I wouldn't have picked up by myself. Beryl not only reads everything, she remembers everything she reads, and likes to tell me about items as she goes along. I would never have started my way through Jane Austen without this subtle guiding and goading. At one time I bobbed along in her wake, getting partway but never all the way into Proust. Next month I shall start George Eliot, or sometime soon anyway, having watched her elation across the room, evenings, through one novel after another. It was only when I heard her hooting with laughter in the middle of Michael Frayn that I realized what I'd been missing. Some places I've not been able to go: Anthony Powell and all those books of conversation, all the Paul Scott, medieval cathedral architecture, any number of the English detective stories she collects like porcelain, Scottish history, French history, English history, David Cecil's *Melbourne* (a favorite of hers), the Restoration poets. I rely on her for knowing what colors go with what other colors, and when a particular shade of rose or green in a curtain or a rug or a painting is a particularly good color. I am not color-blind but color-deaf.

I am a skilled gramophone player, better at Bach, I think, and I like to fill the house with the Beethoven late quartets, late nights, full blast. I went through a time when I couldn't have enough of Bartók and Elliott Carter quartets, played over and over again at high volume. A while back I bought a Sony Walkman, an electronic marvel on which I can play cassettes in loud stereo inaudible beyond my ears, but Beryl is not fond of this instrument, preferring me to make music openly and honestly even when — as I suspect — she might like the silence better.

Living together has been like an extended, engrossing, educational 5 game. We have been exchanging bits of information, tastes, preferences, insights for so long a time that our minds seem to work together. My firm impression is that I've come out ahead so far, in the sense that I've been taught more surprising things by her than I've ever stored up to teach in return. But, even asymmetrically, it has continued to work both ways.

On balance, I believe this kind of family education is something women are better at than men. It is surely better accomplished by women for the children of a family. All the old stories, the myths, the poems comprehended most acutely by young children, the poking and nudging and pinching of very young minds, the waking up of very small children, the learning what smiles and laughter are all about, the vast pleasure of explanation, are by and large the gifts of women to civilization. It is the women who remember and pass along the solid underpinnings of culture, not usually the men. The men may come in later with their everyday practical knowledge of what they see as the great world, sometimes with the necessary ambiguities and abstractions, but they cannot fit their contributions into expanding, exploding young minds unless the women — the mothers and wives, the aunts and grandmothers, the elder sisters — have done their work first. I'm not even sure that a child can discover what fun is, and how to have it, without first being led by the hand into fun by a woman.

While I am at it, I might as well tell the whole truth about the sexes, giving away the whole game. It is my belief, based partly on personal experience but partly also arrived at by looking around at others, that childhood lasts considerably longer in the males of our species than in the females. There is somewhere a deep center of immaturity built into the male brain, always needing steadying and redirection, designed to be reconstructed and instructed, perhaps analogous to the left-brain center for male birdsong, which goes to pieces seasonally and requires the reassembling of neurons to function properly when spring comes. Women keep changing the upper, outer parts of their minds all the time, like shifting the furniture or changing their handbags, but the center tends to hold as a steadier, more solid place.

I am, in short, swept off my feet by women, and I do not think they have yet been assigned the place in the world's affairs that they are biologically made for. Somewhere in that other X chromosome are coils of nucleic acid containing information for a qualitatively different sort of behavior from the instructions in an average Y chromosome. The difference is there, I think, for the long-term needs of the species, and it has something to do with spotting things of great importance. To be sure, most women tend to fret more than most men over the small details of life and the rules of behavior, they tend to worry more about how things look, they are more afflicted by the fear of missing trains or losing one glove, they cry more readily. But on the very big matters, the times requiring exactly the right hunch, the occasions when the survival of human beings is in question, I would trust that X chromosome and worry about the Y.

This brings me to a proposal. Taking all in all, the history of human governments suggests to me that the men of the earth have had a long enough run at running things; their record of folly is now so detailed and documented as to make anyone fear the future in their hands. It is time for a change. Put the women in charge, I say. Let us go for a century without men voting, with women's suffrage as the only suffrage. Try it out, anyway. Write into the law, if you like, a provision that men can begin voting again after a hundred years, if they still want to at that time, but in the meantime, place the single greatest issue in the brief span of human existence, the question whether to use or get rid of thermonuclear weapons of war, squarely in the laps of the world's women. I haven't any doubt at all what they will do with this issue, possessing as they do some extra genes for understanding and appreciating children. I do not trust men in this matter. If it is left in their charge, someone, somewhere, answering some crazy signal from a Y chromosome, will start them going off, and we will be done as a species.

Also, another matter. The world has become crowded with knowledge, 10
and there is more to come. The fair redistribution of knowledge will be a
more important problem in the century ahead than at any time in the past.
Women have not had much hand in this up to now. The full education of
children, up through adolescence into early adult life, will soon become the
great challenge for humanity, once we have become free of the threat of
bombs. All the more reason, I should think, to put the women, born teachers
all of them, in charge. Send the men, for the time being anyway (the time
being a hundred years), off to the showers, for the long, long bath they have
earned.

FROM READING TO REREADING

1. In the first two paragraphs, Thomas establishes some of the differences
between his wife's interests and his own. What are these differences? Are they simply
a matter of science versus humanities? How do these differences help characterize
each person?

2. "This brings me to a proposal," Thomas says in his next-to-last paragraph.
What is that proposal and how seriously do you take it? What are the chances that
societies will implement it?

3. Once we begin looking at the differences between men and women, it's
easy to start constructing vast generalities. Do you think Thomas exaggerates differences in gender? Do you think he indulges in any stereotypes of male/female behavior?
How might he answer such charges?

STEPHEN JAY GOULD
Women's Brains

Besides biology and geology, Stephen Jay Gould also teaches courses in the history of science. One of his special interests is nineteenth-century anthropometry, the scientific attempt to use physical measurements such as skull dimensions and physiognomnic data to understand human differences. In his important book, The Mismeasure of Man, *Gould pointed out the social and political biases that make up the foundation of such sciences and examined many forms of mismeasurement, from Victorian phrenology to today's intelligence tests. "Women's Brains" originally appeared in* Natural History *magazine and was collected in Gould's* The Panda's Thumb *under the category "Science and Politics of Human Differences."*

I N THE PRELUDE to *Middlemarch*, [1] George Eliot lamented the unfulfilled lives of talented women:

> Some have felt that these blundering lives are due to the inconvenient indefiniteness with which the Supreme Power has fashioned the natures of women: if there were one level of feminine incompetence as strict as the ability to count three and no more, the social lot of women might be treated with scientific certitude.

Eliot goes on to discount the idea of innate limitation, but while she wrote in 1872, the leaders of European anthropometry were trying to measure "with scientific certitude" the inferiority of women. Anthropometry, or measurement of the human body, is not so fashionable a field these days, but it dominated the human sciences for much of the nineteenth century and remained popular until intelligence testing replaced skull measurement as a favored device for making invidious comparisons among races, classes, and sexes. Craniometry, or measurement of the skull, commanded the most attention and respect. Its unquestioned leader, Paul Broca (1824–80), professor of clinical surgery at the Faculty of Medicine in Paris, gathered a school of disciples and imitators around himself. Their work, so meticulous and apparently irrefutable, exerted great influence and won high esteem as a jewel of nineteenth-century science.

Broca's work seemed particularly invulnerable to refutation. Had he

---

[1] *Middlemarch*: George Eliot was the pen name of the English novelist Mary Ann Evans (1819–1880); her novel *Middlemarch*, which is considered her best work, was published in 1872.

not measured with the most scrupulous care and accuracy? (Indeed, he had.
I have the greatest respect for Broca's meticulous procedure. His numbers
are sound. But science is an inferential exercise, not a catalog of facts.
Numbers, by themselves, specify nothing. All depends upon what you do
with them.) Broca depicted himself as an apostle of objectivity, a man who
bowed before facts and cast aside superstition and sentimentality. He declared that "there is no faith, however respectable, no interest, however
legitimate, which must not accommodate itself to the progress of human
knowledge and bend before truth." Women, like it or not, had smaller brains
than men and, therefore, could not equal them in intelligence. This fact,
Broca argued, may reinforce a common prejudice in male society, but it is
also a scientific truth. L. Manouvrier, a black sheep in Broca's fold, rejected
the inferiority of women and wrote with feeling about the burden imposed
upon them by Broca's numbers:

> Women displayed their talents and their diplomas. They also invoked
> philosophical authorities. But they were opposed by *numbers* unknown to
> Condorcet or to John Stuart Mill. [2] These numbers fell upon poor women
> like a sledge hammer, and they were accompanied by commentaries and
> sarcasms more ferocious than the most misogynist imprecations of certain
> church fathers. The theologians had asked if women had a soul. Several
> centuries later, some scientists were ready to refuse them a human intel-
> ligence.

Broca's argument rested upon two sets of data: the larger brains of men
in modern societies, and a supposed increase in male superiority through
time. His most extensive data came from autopsies performed personally in
four Parisian hospitals. For 292 male brains, he calculated an average weight
of 1,325 grams; 140 female brains averaged 1,144 grams for a difference of
181 grams, or 14 percent of the male weight. Broca understood, of course,
that part of this difference could be attributed to the greater height of males.
Yet he made no attempt to measure the effect of size alone and actually
stated that it cannot account for the entire difference because we know, a
priori, that women are not as intelligent as men (a premise that the data were
supposed to test, not rest upon):

> We might ask if the small size of the female brain depends exclusively
> upon the small size of her body. Tiedemann has proposed this explanation.
> But we must not forget that women are, on the average, a little less
> intelligent than men, a difference which we should not exaggerate but
> which is, nonetheless, real. We are therefore permitted to suppose that

[2] *Condorcet . . . John Stuart Mill*: The Marquis de Condorcet (1743–1794), eighteenth-
century French mathematician and philosopher influential in the development of sociology
as a quantifiable science; John Stuart Mill (1806–1873), nineteenth-century English economist, philosopher, and social reformer.

the relatively small size of the female brain depends in part upon her physical inferiority and in part upon her intellectual inferiority.

In 1873, the year after Eliot published *Middlemarch*, Broca measured the cranial capacities of prehistoric skulls from L'Homme Mort cave. Here he found a difference of only 99.5 cubic centimeters between males and females, while modern populations range from 129.5 to 220.7. Topinard, Broca's chief disciple, explained the increasing discrepancy through time as a result of differing evolutionary pressures upon dominant men and passive women:

> The man who fights for two or more in the struggle for existence, who has all the responsibility and the cares of tomorrow, who is constantly active in combating the environment and human rivals, needs more brain than the woman whom he must protect and nourish, the sedentary woman, lacking any interior occupations, whose role is to raise children, love, and be passive.

In 1879, Gustave Le Bon, chief misogynist of Broca's school, used these data to publish what must be the most vicious attack upon women in modern scientific literature (no one can top Aristotle). I do not claim his views were representative of Broca's school, but they were published in France's most respected anthropological journal. Le Bon concluded:

> In the most intelligent races, as among the Parisians, there are a large number of women whose brains are closer in size to those of gorillas than to the most developed male brains. This inferiority is so obvious that no one can contest it for a moment; only its degree is worth discussion. All psychologists who have studied the intelligence of women, as well as poets and novelists, recognize today that they represent the most inferior forms of human evolution and that they are closer to children and savages than to an adult, civilized man. They excel in fickleness, inconstancy, absence of thought and logic, and incapacity to reason. Without doubt there exist some distinguished women, very superior to the average man, but they are as exceptional as the birth of any monstrosity, as, for example, of a gorilla with two heads; consequently, we may neglect them entirely.

Nor did Le Bon shrink from the social implications of his views. He was horrified by the proposal of some American reformers to grant women higher education on the same basis as men:

> A desire to give them the same education, and, as a consequence, to propose the same goals for them, is a dangerous chimera. . . . The day when, misunderstanding the inferior occupations which nature has given her, women leave the home and take part in our battles; on this day a social revolution will begin, and everything that maintains the sacred ties of the family will disappear.

Sound familiar? [3]

I have reexamined Broca's data, the basis for all this derivative pronouncement, and I find his numbers sound but his interpretation ill-founded, to say the least. The data supporting his claim for increased difference through time can be easily dismissed. Broca based his contention on the samples from L'Homme Mort alone — only seven male and six female skulls in all. Never have so little data yielded such far-ranging conclusions.

In 1888, Topinard published Broca's more extensive data on the Parisian hospitals. Since Broca recorded height and age as well as brain size, we may use modern statistics to remove their effect. Brain weight decreases with age, and Broca's women were, on average, considerably older than his men. Brain weight increases with height, and his average man was almost half a foot taller than his average woman. I used multiple regression, a technique that allowed me to assess simultaneously the influence of height and age upon brain size. In an analysis of the data for women, I found that, at average male height and age, a woman's brain would weigh 1,212 grams. Correction for height and age reduces Broca's measured difference of 181 grams by more than a third, to 113 grams.

I don't know what to make of this remaining difference because I cannot assess other factors known to influence brain size in a major way. Cause of death has an important effect: degenerative disease often entails a substantial diminution of brain size. (This effect is separate from the decrease attributed to age alone.) Eugene Schreider, also working with Broca's data, found that men killed in accidents had brains weighing, on average, 60 grams more than men dying of infectious diseases. The best modern data I can find (from American hospitals) records a full 100-gram difference between death by degenerative arteriosclerosis and by violence or accident. Since so many of Broca's subjects were very elderly women, we may assume that lengthy degenerative disease was more common among them than among the men.

More importantly, modern students of brain size still have not agreed on a proper measure for eliminating the powerful effect of body size. Height is partly adequate, but men and women of the same height do not share the same body build. Weight is even worse than height, because most of its variation reflects nutrition rather than intrinsic size — fat versus skinny exerts little influence upon the brain. Manouvrier took up this subject in the 1880s and argued that muscular mass and force should be used. He tried to measure this elusive property in various ways and found a marked difference in favor of men, even in men and women of the same height. When he corrected for

10

---

[3] When I wrote this essay, I assumed that Le Bon was a marginal, if colorful, figure. I have since learned that he was a leading scientist, one of the founders of social psychology, and best known for a seminal study on crowd behavior, still cited today (*La psychologie des foules*, 1895), and for his work on unconscious motivation. [Gould's note]

what he called "sexual mass," women actually came out slightly ahead in brain size.

Thus, the corrected 113-gram difference is surely too large; the true figure is probably close to zero and may as well favor women as men. And 113 grams, by the way, is exactly the average difference between a 5 foot 4 inch and a 6 foot 4 inch male in Broca's data. We would not (especially us short folks) want to ascribe greater intelligence to tall men. In short, who knows what to do with Broca's data? They certainly don't permit any confident claim that men have bigger brains than women.

To appreciate the social role of Broca and his school, we must recognize that his statements about the brains of women do not reflect an isolated prejudice toward a single disadvantaged group. They must be weighed in the context of a general theory that supported contemporary social distinctions as biologically ordained. Women, blacks, and poor people suffered the same disparagement, but women bore the brunt of Broca's argument because he had easier access to data on women's brains. Women were singularly denigrated but they also stood as surrogates for other disenfranchised groups. As one of Broca's disciples wrote in 1881: "Men of the black races have a brain scarcely heavier than that of white women." This juxtaposition extended into many other realms of anthropological argument, particularly to claims that, anatomically and emotionally, both women and blacks were like white children — and that white children, by the theory of recapitulation, represented an ancestral (primitive) adult stage of human evolution. I do not regard as empty rhetoric the claim that women's battles are for all of us.

Maria Montessori[4] did not confine her activities to educational reform for young children. She lectured on anthropology for several years at the University of Rome, and wrote an influential book entitled *Pedagogical Anthropology* (English edition, 1913). Montessori was no egalitarian. She supported most of Broca's work and the theory of innate criminality proposed by her compatriot Cesare Lombroso. She measured the circumference of children's heads in her schools and inferred that the best prospects had bigger brains. But she had no use for Broca's conclusions about women. She discussed Manouvrier's work at length and made much of his tentative claim that women, after proper correction of the data, had slightly larger brains than men. Women, she concluded, were intellectually superior, but men had prevailed heretofore by dint of physical force. Since technology has abolished force as an instrument of power, the era of women may soon be upon us: "In such an epoch there will really be superior human beings, there will really be men strong in morality and in sentiment. Perhaps in this way the reign of women is approaching, when the enigma of her anthropological

---

[4] *Maria Montessori* (1870–1952): Italian physician and educator internationally known for her progressive methods of early schooling.

superiority will be deciphered. Woman was always the custodian of human sentiment, morality and honor."

This represents one possible antidote to "scientific" claims for the   15
constitutional inferiority of certain groups. One may affirm the validity of biological distinctions but argue that the data have been misinterpreted by prejudiced men with a stake in the outcome, and that disadvantaged groups are truly superior. In recent years, Elaine Morgan has followed this strategy in her *Descent of Woman*, a speculative reconstruction of human prehistory from the woman's point of view — and as farcical as more famous tall tales by and for men.

I prefer another strategy. Montessori and Morgan followed Broca's philosophy to reach a more congenial conclusion. I would rather label the whole enterprise of setting a biological value upon groups for what it is: irrelevant and highly injurious. George Eliot well appreciated the special tragedy that biological labeling imposed upon members of disadvantaged groups. She expressed it for people like herself — women of extraordinary talent. I would apply it more widely — not only to those whose dreams are flouted but also to those who never realize that they may dream — but I cannot match her prose. In conclusion, then, the rest of Eliot's prelude to *Middlemarch*:

> The limits of variation are really much wider than anyone would imagine from the sameness of women's coiffure and the favorite love stories in prose and verse. Here and there a cygnet is reared uneasily among the ducklings in the brown pond, and never finds the living stream in fellowship with its own oary-footed kind. Here and there is born a Saint Theresa, foundress of nothing, whose loving heartbeats and sobs after an unattained goodness tremble off and are dispersed among hindrances instead of centering in some long-recognizable deed.

FROM READING TO REREADING

1. Note that Gould, a scientist, opens and closes his essay with quotations from *Middlemarch*, the famous Victorian novel by George Eliot (whose real name was Mary Ann Evans). Why do you think he uses *Middlemarch* in his essay? In what way does it establish an appropriate context for him?

2. Though Gould accepts Broca's measurements, he doesn't accept the conclusions Broca drew from them. Yet, Gould can't explain the discrepancy that exists in the measurements even after he corrects for other factors. As a scientist and statistician, how does Gould deal with this problem? Do you think any of his own political predispositions come into play? What might these predispositions be?

3. One way to deal with corrections to Broca's data, as Gould shows, is to form a conclusion opposite to that of Broca's: to argue that the data really prove women's

superiority. What does Gould think about this strategy? How does *Middlemarch* reinforce his position?

From Reading to Writing

1. Both Virginia Woolf and Lewis Thomas base their essays on what has by now become a conventional view of women: that they are less militaristic and more peace-loving than men. Consider this view carefully. Do you agree with it? What are the grounds for believing it? Do you consider it stereotypical? Write an essay in which you discuss this view and where you stand in relation to it.

2. Alice Walker's and James Baldwin's essays explore the ways that the experiences of our childhood and youth can influence our views about sexual preferences and gender. In a personal essay, explore your own influences. How did you learn the "facts of life"? How did early experiences affect the way you now think of sexual or gender differences? How reliable were your models?

3. Here's an ambitious project involving some research and some scientific investigation. Stephen Jay Gould acknowledges that he cannot explain the differences in Broca's male and female brain weights even after he has corrected for the factors known to influence such weights. Look up in your school library all you can find about Broca and his anthropometric school. Then consider Gould's factored data. In an essay provide an explanation of your own that you think will account for the discrepancy.

8

The Power of Language

LEWIS THOMAS
Neanderthals, Cro-Magnons, etc.

"As far back as I can remember," writes Lewis Thomas, "dictionaries have been part of the furniture in our house." For Thomas, a physician, medical researcher, and essayist, the life of words rather resembles the lives of the cells he so often writes about. Alive, capable of surprising mutations, and encoded with the past, words can be a delightful and adventurous form of study. Thomas admits to being an amateur in the field of etymology. He writes in the introduction to Et Cetera, Et Cetera: Notes of a Word-Watcher, *the 1990 book in which the following essay appeared: "My sole qualification for writing these essays on (mostly) Indo-European roots is that I've been enchanted and obsessed by them for over twenty years, and have convinced myself that these antique words continue to hold their old meanings long after almost vanishing into the worlds of modern English." In "Neanderthals, Cro-Magnons, etc." Thomas does not examine the origins of individual words but instead looks at the development and importance of language itself.*

O UR IMMEDIATE PREDECESSORS,[1] perhaps our forebears, more likely distant cousins, were the Neanderthals, first appearing around one hundred twenty thousand years ago, in sparse settlements in Germany's Neander Valley. Most specimens postdate seventy-five thousand years and the last Neanderthals existed around forty thousand years ago. No evidence can be found of a genuine culture beyond crude hand stone tools (no handles or hafts), and signs of the use of fire and burial of their dead. They had bigger brains than ours, but no likelihood of language. Perhaps a larger brain needs editing, as occurs in all human embryos. A larger birth canal in Neanderthal does suggest large newborn brains, which in the circumstance could be a disadvantage. In the modern human embryo, great numbers of cells, neurons and their circuits are put in place, partially interwired, then ruthlessly edited away, on a massive scale, and replaced by others in accordance with the new genetic instructions. The survivor cells at the end of the process may actually be sparser than the populations destroyed in the course of redesigning and rewiring. Neanderthal's adult brain may have been too gross, unpruned, overwired, thus still speechless and muscle-bound.

Also, early childhood, the time when our proper species is at its brightest and best for learning language, may have been a very different and

---

[1] Randall White, *Dark Caves, Bright Visions: Life in Ice Age Europe* (New York: The American Museum of Natural History and W. W. Norton & Co., 1986). [Thomas's note]

probably shorter period for Neanderthal. It has been estimated from measurements of the birth canal (based on the structure of pelvic bones), that gestation was much longer, twelve or thirteen months, and the size of the newborn brain correspondingly larger. This could mean that less time was available for further development and expansion of the brain. The Neanderthal central nervous system may have been more elaborately fixed in place prenatally, leaving a significantly shorter postnatal period for further growth and remodeling, not sufficiently flexible for new masses of cells or new diagrams of wiring. The early months of infancy may thus have lacked time for environmental stimuli to have their effect on the neural adaptation required for speech and the comprehension of speech.

Never mind, for the moment, the more ancient evolutionary leaps and the questions they raise: which gorilla-like or chimpanzee-like or baboon-like (or human-like) is our likeliest (or most likable) ancestor? Only one huge evolutionary event, earthshaking as it was to turn out, concerns us here: the transition from a sort-of-human species like Neanderthal, unable to speak in today's meaning of language, to a talking, comprehending, totally new nervous creature possessed of words and grammar.

Neanderthal was hardly what you might expect in a species destined to dominate a whole planet, and as it turned out he did not. But just to look at him, in his museum reconstructions, standing in front of the cave, his chances would have seemed considerably better than ours. He had enormous shoulders, huge muscles, heavy bones, a cavernous skull case. But he missed, lasted only eighty thousand years, then vanished into time. What did he lack? Not, as has been suggested, the *physical* capacity for speech — it has been an old, accepted notion that Neanderthal's brain was big enough for language but he had the wrong set of pharyngeal and laryngeal structures, preventing the enunciating of all the consonants and vowels at our disposal. This is nonsense; we have speechless people today, deaf, mute, discussing the world eloquently with only their hands for sign language. Anyway, the anatomical defect is not the explanation, according to a recent archaeological group which studied, with close care, a typical Neanderthal dating back around forty thousand years, well-preserved. [2] This ancient man's hyoid bone, a technical necessity for the human larynx, was precisely the same structure, in the same location, as our modern speech organ, as were the other bony points for the attachment of all the muscles needed for the articulation of words, any words. In short, Neanderthal could have spoken at length, if he'd known how to speak or what to say. His brain, big as it was, did not yet contain the needed wiring instructions for making language. And because of this lack, Neanderthal lost his way and vanished in the ice and snows of forty millennia ago.

[2] B. Arensburg et al. "A Middle Paleolithic Human Hyoid Bone." *Nature*, 338 (1989):758–760. [Thomas's note]

Then we came up, naked, hairless, clawless, near toothless for preda- 5
tion, vulnerable, even innocent-looking when viewed close-up. But the pure
sound of the strings of words we could make set us up for survival, then
dominance.

Language is what preserved us. Not because it does real damage to
any other species, but because we can use it together. It binds us, unites us,
can join hundreds, thousands, now billions of us together to make a single
tremendous creature: a social species.

The gift of speech led straight on to another outcome, the added gift
of friendship, even affection.

Left to ourselves, untroubled by the anomalous few among us who
have tended inexplicably and unluckily to become our leaders, folly after
folly, we do indeed like each other, often enough *love* each other. It is a
biological necessity, looked at objectively, if you hope to work your way
through evolution as a social species. We haven't found our way yet to this
kind of safety, but give us a few more centuries.

Cro-Magnon man was a new phenomenon in nature, so separate and
different from Neanderthal as to seem a new species.

Anatomically indistinguishable from today's human being, the new 10
people were spectacularly (and aesthetically) an improvement. New, inventive tools with handles were produced and then steadily improved. Weaving,
rope-making, tailored clothes of a sort (from fabric and skins) appeared, along
with fishhooks, fishline, sinkers. Harpoons, spears, bows and arrows.

They left the signs of long-distance travel, probably trade. Certainly,
there was much more success in population and survival, more dense communities, more niches occupied, whole continents occupied; watercraft was
a certainty. Exploration and colonization thrived. South America, long believed to have been inhabited by humans only eleven thousand years ago,
now displays some evidence indicating settlements as far back as thirty-five
thousand years.

Art arrived in the human mind with the Cro-Magnons, leaving its
evidence in rock paintings, ornaments, jewels, sculpture and musical instruments (flutes, rattles). They had a long run at life, surviving to sixty or more.
This must have affected biological success and improved the survival of
whole populations. Older citizens can be assets for survival, providing a
steady cohort of experienced, savvy minds. And better survival for the old
also means, almost inevitably, better survival all round and therefore more
children. It is hard to imagine the sudden emergence of all these social
activities, especially the evidences of art, without imagining language as well
to make the rest possible. Once we learned this, we could spread around.

And spread we did indeed. In only thirty-six thousand–odd years (many
of them very odd, and very cold) we have occupied every part of the earth's
surface, hostile or not, increased from a few hundred thousand to five billion
and still counting. No such biological explosion has ever happened before

— not even the distinguished, all extinct trilobites, [3] unaccountably almost everywhere, can match the spread of humanity. We are still swarming, talking and talking.

[3] *trilobites*: Fossils of an extinct marine animal that resembles a modern woodlouse.

FROM READING TO REREADING

1. The value of Thomas's argument depends on establishing that Neanderthals had no language. How can we know this? Does Thomas prove it?

2. In introducing the advent of Cro-Magnons, Thomas uses the expression the "gift of speech." How do you interpret this? In what sense was speech a gift? What does the term presuppose?

3. Toward the end of his essay, Thomas makes connections between language and biology. What are some of these connections? What is he suggesting about evolution? How has language increased chances for survival?

GEORGE ORWELL
Politics and the English Language

Throughout his career, George Orwell maintained a keen interest in the social and political dimensions of language. He wrote numerous columns and several essays (one on the formation of new words), and readers of his most famous book, 1984, will recall Orwell's invention of Newspeak, *the repressive language devised to ensure totalitarian control. Orwell wrote "Politics and the English Language" for* Horizon *magazine in 1946, the same year he began work on* 1984. *The essay — one of Orwell's most widely reprinted and quoted — is still relevant today, in England or America, as anyone who listens to political, economic, academic, or corporate speeches can readily testify.*

MOST PEOPLE who bother with the matter at all would admit that the English language is in a bad way, but it is generally assumed that we cannot by conscious action do anything about it. Our civilization is decadent and our language — so the argument runs — must inevitably share in the general collapse. It follows that any struggle against the abuse of language is a sentimental archaism, like preferring candles to electric light or hansom cabs to aeroplanes. Underneath this lies the half-conscious belief that language is a natural growth and not an instrument which we shape for our own purposes.

Now, it is clear that the decline of a language must ultimately have political and economic causes: it is not due simply to the bad influence of this or that individual writer. But an effect can become a cause, reinforcing the original cause and producing the same effect in an intensified form, and so on indefinitely. A man may take to drink because he feels himself to be a failure, and then fail all the more completely because he drinks. It is rather the same thing that is happening to the English language. It becomes ugly and inaccurate because our thoughts are foolish, but the slovenliness of our language makes it easier for us to have foolish thoughts. The point is that the process is reversible. Modern English, especially written English, is full of bad habits which spread by imitation and which can be avoided if one is willing to take the necessary trouble. If one gets rid of these habits one can think more clearly, and to think clearly is a necessary first step towards political regeneration: so that the fight against bad English is not frivolous and is not the exclusive concern of professional writers. I will come back to this presently, and I hope that by that time the meaning of what I have said here will have become clearer. Meanwhile, here are five specimens of the English language as it is now habitually written.

These five passages have not been picked out because they are especially bad — I could have quoted far worse if I had chosen — but because they illustrate various of the mental vices from which we now suffer. They are a little below the average, but are fairly representative samples. I number them so that I can refer back to them when necessary:

(1) I am not, indeed, sure whether it is not true to say that the Milton who once seemed not unlike a seventeenth-century Shelley had not become, out of an experience ever more bitter in each year, more alien [*sic*] to the founder of that Jesuit sect which nothing could induce him to tolerate.

— Professor Harold Laski
(Essay in *Freedom of Expression*).

(2) Above all, we cannot play ducks and drakes with a native battery of idioms which prescribes such egregious collocations of vocables as the Basic *put up with* for *tolerate* or *put at a loss* for *bewilder*.

— Professor Lancelot Hogben (*Interglossa*)

(3) On the one side we have the free personality: by definition it is not neurotic, for it has neither conflict nor dream. Its desires, such as they are, are transparent, for they are just what institutional approval keeps in the forefront of consciousness; another institutional pattern would alter their number and intensity; there is little in them that is natural, irreducible, or culturally dangerous. But *on the other side*, the social bond itself is nothing but the mutual reflection of these self-secure integrities. Recall the definition of love. Is not this the very picture of a small academic? Where is there a place in this hall of mirrors for either personality or fraternity?

— Essay on psychology in *Politics* (New York)

(4) All the "best people" from the gentlemen's clubs, and all the frantic fascist captains, united in common hatred of Socialism and bestial horror of the rising tide of the mass revolutionary movement, have turned to acts of provocation, to foul incendiarism, to medieval legends of poisoned wells, to legalize their own destruction of proletarian organizations, and rouse the agitated petty-bourgeoisie to chauvinistic fervor on behalf of the fight against the revolutionary way out of the crisis.

— Communist pamphlet

(5) If a new spirit *is* to be infused into this old country, there is one thorny and contentious reform which must be tackled, and that is the humanization and galvanization of the B.B.C. Timidity here will bespeak canker and atrophy of the soul. The heart of Britain may be sound and of strong beat, for instance, but the British lion's roar at present is like that of Bottom in Shakespeare's *Midsummer Night's Dream* — as gentle as any sucking dove. A virile new Britain cannot continue indefinitely to be

traduced in the eyes, or rather ears, of the world by the effete languors of Langham Place, brazenly masquerading as "standard English." When the Voice of Britain is heard at nine o'clock, better far and infinitely less ludicrous to hear aitches honestly dropped than the present priggish, inflated, inhibited, school-ma'amish arch braying of blameless bashful mewing maidens!

— Letter in *Tribune*

Each of these passages has faults of its own, but, quite apart from avoidable ugliness, two qualities are common to all of them. The first is staleness of imagery; the other is lack of precision. The writer either had a meaning and cannot express it, or he inadvertently says something else, or he is almost indifferent as to whether his words mean anything or not. This mixture of vagueness and sheer incompetence is the most marked characteristic of modern English prose, and especially of any kind of political writing. As soon as certain topics are raised, the concrete melts into the abstract and no one seems able to think of terms of speech that are not hackneyed: prose consists less and less of *words* chosen for the sake of their meaning, and more and more of *phrases* tacked together like the sections of a prefabricated henhouse. I list below, with notes and examples, various of the tricks by means of which the work of prose-construction is habitually dodged:

DYING METAPHORS.   A newly invented metaphor assists thought by   5
evoking a visual image, while on the other hand a metaphor which is technically "dead" (e.g., *iron resolution*) has in effect reverted to being an ordinary word and can generally be used without loss of vividness. But in between these two classes there is a huge dump of worn-out metaphors which have lost all evocative power and are merely used because they save people the trouble of inventing phrases for themselves. Examples are: *Ring the changes on, take up the cudgels for, toe the line, ride roughshod over, stand shoulder to shoulder with, play into the hands of, no axe to grind, grist to the mill, fishing in troubled waters, on the order of the day, Achilles' heel, swan song, hotbed*. Many of these are used without knowledge of their meaning (what is a "rift," for instance?), and incompatible metaphors are frequently mixed, a sure sign that the writer is not interested in what he is saying. Some metaphors now current have been twisted out of their original meaning without those who use them even being aware of the fact. For example, *toe the line* is sometimes written *tow the line*. Another example is *the hammer and the anvil*, now always used with the implication that the anvil gets the worst of it. In real life it is always the anvil that breaks the hammer, never the other way about: a writer who stopped to think what he was saying would be aware of this, and would avoid perverting the original phrase.

OPERATORS OR VERBAL FALSE LIMBS.   These save the trouble of picking out appropriate verbs and nouns, and at the same time pad each sentence with extra syllables which give it an appearance of symmetry. Characteristic phrases are *render inoperative, militate against, make contact with, be subjected to, give rise to, give grounds for, have the effect of, play a leading part (role) in, make itself felt, take effect, exhibit a tendency to, serve the purpose of, etc., etc.* The keynote is the elimination of simple verbs. Instead of being a single word, such as *break, stop, spoil, mend, kill,* a verb becomes a *phrase,* made up of a noun or adjective tacked on to some general-purposes verb such as *prove, serve, form, play, render.* In addition, the passive voice is wherever possible used in preference to the active, and noun constructions are used instead of gerunds (*by examination of* instead of *by examining*). The range of verbs is further cut down by means of the *-ize* and *de-* formations, and the banal statements are given an appearance of profundity by means of the *not un-* formation. Simple conjunctions and prepositions are replaced by such phrases as *with respect to, having regard to, the fact that, by dint of, in view of, in the interests of, on the hypothesis that;* and the ends of sentences are saved from anticlimax by such resounding commonplaces as *greatly to be desired, cannot be left out of account, a development to be expected in the near future, deserving of serious consideration, brought to a satisfactory conclusion,* and so on and so forth.

PRETENTIOUS DICTION. Words like *phenomenon, element, individual* (as noun), *objective, categorical, effective, virtual, basic, primary, promote, constitute, exhibit, exploit, utilize, eliminate, liquidate* are used to dress up simple statement and give an air of scientific impartiality to biased judgments. Adjectives like *epoch-making, epic, historic, unforgettable, triumphant, age-old, inevitable, inexorable, veritable,* are used to dignify the sordid processes of international politics, while writing that aims at glorifying war usually takes on an archaic color, its characteristic words being: *realm, throne, chariot, mailed fist, trident, sword, shield, buckler, banner, jackboot, clarion.* Foreign words and expressions such as *cul de sac, ancien régime, deus ex machina, mutatis mutandis, status quo, gleichschaltung, weltanschauung,* are used to give an air of culture and elegance. Except for the useful abbreviations *i.e., e.g.,* and *etc.,* there is no real need for any of the hundreds of foreign phrases now current in English. Bad writers, and especially scientific, political and sociological writers, are nearly always haunted by the notion that Latin or Greek words are grander than Saxon ones, and unnecessary words like *expedite, ameliorate, predict, extraneous, deracinated, clandestine, subaqueous* and hundreds of others constantly gain ground from their Anglo-Saxon opposite numbers. [1] The jargon peculiar to Marxist writing (*hyena, hangman, cannibal, petty bourgeois, these gentry, lacquey, flunkey, mad dog, White Guard,* etc.) consists largely of

---

[1] An interesting illustration of this is the way in which the English flower names which were in use till very recently are being ousted by Greek ones, *snapdragon* becoming *antirrhinum, forget-me-not* becoming *myosotis,* etc. It is hard to see any practical reason for this change of fashion: it is probably due to an instinctive turning-away from the more homely word and a vague feeling that the Greek word is scientific. [Orwell's note]

words and phrases translated from Russian, German or French; but the normal way of coining a new word is to use a Latin or Greek root with the appropriate affix and, where necessary, the *-ize* formation. It is often easier to make up words of this kind (*deregionalize, impermissible, extramarital, non-fragmentary* and so forth) than to think up the English words that will cover one's meaning. The result, in general, is an increase in slovenliness and vagueness.

MEANINGLESS WORDS.   In certain kinds of writing, particularly in art criticism and literary criticism, it is normal to come across long passages which are almost completely lacking in meaning. [2] Words like *romantic, plastic, values, human, dead, sentimental, natural, vitality,* as used in art criticism, are strictly meaningless, in the sense that they not only do not point to any discoverable object, but are hardly ever expected to do so by the reader. When one critic writes, "The outstanding feature of Mr. X's work is its living quality," while another writes, "The immediately striking thing about Mr. X's work is its peculiar deadness," the reader accepts this as a simple difference of opinion. If words like *black* and *white* were involved, instead of the jargon words *dead* and *living,* he would see at once that language was being used in an improper way. Many political words are similarly abused. The word *Fascism* has now no meaning except in so far as it signifies "something not desirable." The words *democracy, socialism, freedom, patriotic, realistic, justice,* have each of them several different meanings which cannot be reconciled with one another. In the case of a word like *democracy,* not only is there no agreed definition, but the attempt to make one is resisted from all sides. It is almost universally felt that when we call a country democratic we are praising it: consequently the defenders of every kind of régime claim that it is a democracy, and fear that they might have to stop using the word if it were tied down to any one meaning. Words of this kind are often used in a consciously dishonest way. That is, the person who uses them has his own private definition, but allows his hearer to think he means something quite different. Statements like *Marshal Pétain* [3] *was a true patriot, The Soviet Press is the freest in the world, The Catholic Church is opposed to persecution,* are almost always made with intent to deceive. Other words used in variable

---

[2] Example: "Comfort's catholicity of perception and image, strangely Whitmanesque in range, almost the exact opposite in aesthetic compulsion, continues to evoke that trembling atmospheric accumulative hinting at a cruel, an inexorably serene timelessness. . . . Wrey Gardiner scores by aiming at simple bull's-eyes with precision. Only they are not so simple, and through this contented sadness runs more than the surface bitter-sweet of resignation." [Orwell's note]

[3] *Marshal Pétain*: Henri Phillipe Pétain (1856–1951), chief of state in France from 1940 to 1945, after France surrendered to Germany. A controversial figure, Pétain was regarded by some to be a patriot who had sacrificed himself for his country, while others considered him to be a traitor. He was sentenced to life imprisonment in 1945, the year before Orwell wrote this essay.

314 The Power of Language

meanings, in most cases more or less dishonestly, are: *class, totalitarian, science, progressive, reactionary, bourgeois, equality.*

Now that I have made this catalogue of swindles and perversions, let me give another example of the kind of writing that they lead to. This time it must of its nature be an imaginary one. I am going to translate a passage of good English into modern English of the worst sort. Here is a well-known verse from *Ecclesiastes*:

> I returned and saw under the sun, that the race is not to the swift, nor the battle to the strong, neither yet bread to the wise, nor yet riches to men of understanding, nor yet favour to men of skill; but time and chance happeneth to them all.

Here it is in modern English: 10

> Objective consideration of contemporary phenomena compels the conclusion that success or failure in competitive activities exhibits no tendency to be commensurate with innate capacity, but that a considerable element of the unpredictable must invariably be taken into account.

This is a parody, but not a very gross one. Exhibit (3), above, for instance, contains several patches of the same kind of English. It will be seen that I have not made a full translation. The beginning and ending of the sentence follow the original meaning fairly closely, but in the middle the concrete illustrations — race, battle, bread — dissolve into the vague phrase "success or failure in competitive activities." This had to be so, because no modern writer of the kind I am discussing — no one capable of using phrases like "objective consideration of contemporary phenomena" — would ever tabulate his thoughts in that precise and detailed way. The whole tendency of modern prose is away from concreteness. Now analyse these two sentences a little more closely. The first contains forty-nine words but only sixty syllables, and all its words are those of everyday life. The second contains thirty-eight words of ninety syllables: eighteen of its words are from Latin roots, and one from Greek. The first sentence contains six vivid images, and only one phrase ("time and chance") that could be called vague. The second contains not a single fresh, arresting phrase, and in spite of its ninety syllables it gives only a shortened version of the meaning contained in the first. Yet without a doubt it is the second kind of sentence that is gaining ground in modern English. I do not want to exaggerate. This kind of writing is not yet universal, and outcrops of simplicity will occur here and there in the worst-written page. Still, if you or I were to write a few lines on the uncertainty of human fortunes, we should probably come much nearer to my imaginary sentence than to the one from *Ecclesiastes*.

As I have tried to show, modern writing at its worst does not consist in picking out words for the sake of their meaning and inventing images in order to make the meaning clearer. It consists in gumming together long strips of words which have already been set in order by someone else, and making the results presentable by sheer humbug. The attraction of this way of writing is that it is easy. It is easier — even quicker, once you have the habit — to say *In my opinion it is not an unjustifiable assumption that* than to say *I think.* If you use readymade phrases, you not only don't have to hunt about for words; you also don't have to bother with the rhythms of your sentences, since these phrases are generally so arranged as to be more or less euphonious. When you are composing in a hurry — when you are dictating to a stenographer, for instance, or making a public speech — it is natural to fall into a pretentious, Latinized style. Tags like *a consideration which we should do well to bear in mind* or *a conclusion to which all of us would readily assent* will save many a sentence from coming down with a bump. By using stale metaphors, similes and idioms, you save much mental effort, at the cost of leaving your meaning vague, not only for your reader but for yourself. This is the significance of mixed metaphors. The sole aim of a metaphor is to call up a visual image. When these images clash — as in *The Fascist octopus has sung its swan song, the jackboot is thrown into the melting pot* — it can be taken as certain that the writer is not seeing a mental image of the objects he is naming; in other words he is not really thinking. Look again at the examples I gave at the beginning of this essay. Professor Laski (1) uses five negatives in fifty-three words. One of these is superfluous, making nonsense of the whole passage, and in addition there is the slip *alien* for akin, making further nonsense, and several avoidable pieces of clumsiness which increase the general vagueness. Professor Hogben (2) plays ducks and drakes with a battery which is able to write prescriptions, and, while disapproving of the everyday phrase *put up with,* is unwilling to look *egregious* up in the dictionary and see what it means; (3), if one takes an uncharitable attitude towards it, is simply meaningless: probably one could work out its intended meaning by reading the whole of the article in which it occurs. In (4), the writer knows more or less what he wants to say, but an accumulation of stale phrases chokes him like tea leaves blocking a sink. In (5), words and meaning have almost parted company. People who write in this manner usually have a general emotional meaning — they dislike one thing and want to express solidarity with another — but they are not interested in the detail of what they are saying. A scrupulous writer, in every sentence that he writes, will ask himself at least four questions, thus: What am I trying to say? What words will express it? What image or idiom will make it clearer? Is this image fresh enough to have an effect? And he will probably ask himself two more: Could I put it more shortly? Have I said anything that is avoidably ugly? But you are not obliged to go to all this trouble. You can shirk it by simply throwing your mind open and letting the ready-made phrases come crowding in. They will construct your sentences for you — even think your thoughts for you, to a certain extent — and at need they will perform the important service of partially concealing your meaning even from yourself. It is at this point that the special connection between politics and the debasement of language becomes clear.

In our time it is broadly true that political writing is bad writing. Where it is not true, it will generally be found that the writer is some kind of rebel, expressing his private opinions and not a "party line." Orthodoxy, of whatever color, seems to demand a lifeless, imitative style. The political dialects to be found in pamphlets, leading articles, manifestos, White Papers and the speeches of under-secretaries do, of course, vary from party to party, but they are all alike in that one almost never finds in them a fresh, vivid, home-made turn of speech. When one watches some tired hack on the platform mechanically repeating the familiar phrases — *bestial atrocities, iron heel, bloodstained tyranny, free peoples of the world, stand shoulder to shoulder* — one often has a curious feeling that one is not watching a live human being but some kind of dummy: a feeling which suddenly becomes stronger at moments when the light catches the speaker's spectacles and turns them into blank discs which seem to have no eyes behind them. And this is not altogether fanciful. A speaker who uses that kind of phraseology has gone some distance towards turning himself into a machine. The appropriate noises are coming out of his larynx, but his brain is not involved as it would be if he were choosing his words for himself. If the speech he is making is one that he is accustomed to make over and over again, he may be almost unconscious of what he is saying, as one is when one utters the responses in church. And this reduced state of consciousness, if not indispensable, is at any rate favorable to political conformity.

In our time, political speech and writing are largely the defence of the indefensible. Things like the continuance of British rule in India, the Russian purges and deportations, the dropping of the atom bombs on Japan, can indeed be defended, but only by arguments which are too brutal for most people to face, and which do not square with the professed aims of political parties. Thus political language has to consist largely of euphemism, ques-tion-begging and sheer cloudy vagueness. Defenceless villages are bom-barded from the air, the inhabitants driven out into the countryside, the cattle machine-gunned, the huts set on fire with incendiary bullets: this is called *pacification*. Millions of peasants are robbed of their farms and sent trudging along the roads with no more than they can carry: this is called *transfer of population* or *rectification of frontiers*. People are imprisoned for years without trial, or shot in the back of the neck or sent to die of scurvy in Arctic lumber camps: [4] this is called *elimination of unreliable elements*. Such phraseol-ogy is needed if one wants to name things without calling up mental pictures of them. Consider for instance some comfortable English professor defending Russian totalitarianism. He cannot say outright, "I believe in killing off your

---

[4] *People . . . camps*: Though Orwell is decrying all totalitarian abuse of language, his examples are mainly pointed at the Soviet purges under Stalin.

opponents when you can get good results by doing so." Probably, therefore, he will say something like this:

> While freely conceding that the Soviet régime exhibits certain features which the humanitarian may be inclined to deplore, we must, I think, agree that a certain curtailment of the right to political opposition is an unavoidable concomitant of transitional periods, and that the rigors which the Russian people have been called upon to undergo have been amply justified in the sphere of concrete achievement.

The inflated style is itself a kind of euphemism. A mass of Latin words 15 falls upon the facts like soft snow, blurring the outlines and covering up all the details. The great enemy of clear language is insincerity. When there is a gap between one's real and one's declared aims, one turns as it were instinctively to long words and exhausted idioms, like a cuttlefish squirting out ink. In our age there is no such thing as "keeping out of politics." All issues are political issues, and politics itself is a mass of lies, evasions, folly, hatred and schizophrenia. When the general atmosphere is bad, language must suffer. I should expect to find — this is a guess which I have not sufficient knowledge to verify — that the German, Russian and Italian languages have all deteriorated in the last ten or fifteen years, as a result of dictatorship.

But if thought corrupts language, language can also corrupt thought. A bad usage can spread by tradition and imitation, even among people who should and do know better. The debased language that I have been discussing is in some ways very convenient. Phrases like *a not unjustifiable assumption, leaves much to be desired, would serve no good purpose, a consideration which we should do well to bear in mind,* are a continuous temptation, a packet of aspirins always at one's elbow. Look back through this essay, and for certain you will find that I have again and again committed the very faults I am protesting against. By this morning's post I have received a pamphlet dealing with conditions in Germany. The author tells me that he "felt impelled" to write it. I open it at random, and here is almost the first sentence that I see: "[The Allies] have an opportunity not only of achieving a radical transformation of Germany's social and political structure in such a way as to avoid a nationalistic reaction in Germany itself, but at the same time of laying the foundations of a cooperative and unified Europe." You see, he "feels impelled" to write — feels, presumably, that he has something new to say — and yet his words, like cavalry horses answering the bugle, group themselves automatically into the familiar dreary pattern. This invasion of one's mind by ready-made phrases (*lay the foundations, achieve a radical transformation*) can only be prevented if one is constantly on guard against them, and every such phrase anaesthetizes a portion of one's brain.

I said earlier that the decadence of our language is probably curable. Those who deny this would argue, if they produced an argument at all, that language merely reflects existing social conditions, and that we cannot influence its development by any direct tinkering with words and constructions. So far as the general tone or spirit of a language goes, this may be true, but it is not true in detail. Silly words and expressions have often disappeared, not through any evolutionary process but owing to the conscious action of a minority. Two recent examples were *explore every avenue* and *leave no stone unturned*, which were killed by the jeers of a few journalists. There is a long list of flyblown metaphors which could similarly be got rid of if enough people would interest themselves in the job; and it should also be possible to laugh the *not un-* formation out of existence, [5] to reduce the amount of Latin and Greek in the average sentence, to drive out foreign phrases and strayed scientific words, and, in general, to make pretentiousness unfashionable. But all these are minor points. The defence of the English language implies more than this, and perhaps it is best to start by saying what it does *not* imply.

To begin with it has nothing to do with archaism, with the salvaging of obsolete words and turns of speech, or with the setting up of a "standard English" which must never be departed from. On the contrary, it is especially concerned with the scrapping of every word or idiom which has outworn its usefulness. It has nothing to do with correct grammar and syntax, which are of no importance so long as one makes one's meaning clear, or with the avoidance of Americanisms, or with having what is called a "good prose style." On the other hand it is not concerned with fake simplicity and the attempt to make written English colloquial. Nor does it even imply in every case preferring the Saxon word to the Latin one, though it does imply using the fewest and shortest words that will cover one's meaning. What is above all needed is to let the meaning choose the word, and not the other way about. In prose, the worst thing one can do with words is to surrender to them. When you think of a concrete object, you think wordlessly, and then, if you want to describe the thing you have been visualizing you probably hunt about till you find the exact words that seem to fit it. When you think of something abstract you are more inclined to use words from the start, and unless you make a conscious effort to prevent it, the existing dialect will come rushing in and do the job for you, at the expense of blurring or even changing your meaning. Probably it is better to put off using words as long as possible and get one's meaning as clear as one can through pictures or sensations. Afterwards one can choose — not simply *accept* — the phrases that will best cover the meaning, and then switch round and decide what impression one's words are likely to make on another person. This last effort of the mind cuts out all stale or mixed images, all prefabricated phrases, needless repetitions, and humbug and vagueness generally. But one can often be in doubt about the effect of a word or a phrase, and one needs rules

[5] One can cure oneself of the *not un-* formation by memorizing this sentence: *A not unblack dog was chasing a not unsmall rabbit across a not ungreen field.* [Orwell's note]

that one can rely on when instinct fails. I think the following rules will cover most cases:

i. Never use a metaphor, simile or other figure of speech which you are used to seeing in print.
ii. Never use a long word where a short one will do.
iii. If it is possible to cut a word out, always cut it out.
iv. Never use the passive where you can use the active.
v. Never use a foreign phrase, a scientific word or a jargon word if you can think of an everyday English equivalent.
vi. Break any of these rules sooner than say anything outright barbarous.

These rules sound elementary, and so they are, but they demand a deep change in attitude in anyone who has grown used to writing in the style now fashionable. One could keep all of them and still write bad English, but one could not write the kind of stuff that I quoted in those five specimens at the beginning of this article.

I have not here been considering the literary use of language, but merely language as an instrument for expressing and not for concealing or preventing thought. Stuart Chase and others have come near to claiming that all abstract words are meaningless, and have used this as a pretext for advocating a kind of political quietism. Since you don't know what Fascism is, how can you struggle against Fascism? One need not swallow such absurdities as this, but one ought to recognize that the present political chaos is connected with the decay of language, and that one can probably bring about some improvement by starting at the verbal end. If you simplify your English, you are freed from the worst follies of orthodoxy. You cannot speak any of the necessary dialects, and when you make a stupid remark its stupidity will be obvious, even to yourself. Political language — and with variations this is true of all political parties, from Conservatives to Anarchists — is designed to make lies sound truthful and murder respectable, and to give an appearance of solidity to pure wind. One cannot change this all in a moment, but one can at least change one's own habits, and from time to time one can even, if one jeers loudly enough, send some worn-out and useless phrase — some *jackboot, Achilles' heel, hotbed, melting pot, acid test, veritable inferno* or other lump of verbal refuse — into the dustbin where it belongs.

FROM READING TO REREADING

1. There is, Orwell argues, a "special connection between politics and the debasement of language." What is this connection, and how does Orwell establish it? Is the political misuse of language deliberate or inadvertent?

2. Orwell seems to link bad English with all political parties — Conservatives

to Anarchists. Why do you think this is so? His indictment of political language raises an important question: Is it possible to support a political position or party and still write well? Notice that Orwell does not provide positive examples of political expression. How do you account for this? Is Orwell saying that good, competent political writing is impossible?

3. When Orwell offers a parody of a well-known biblical verse from Ecclesiastes, he is making fun of what we now call "bureaucratese" — the vague, padded, impersonal language associated with institutions and administrations. Try doing what Orwell did: choose a well-known adage or expression that is vivid and clear and transform it into the pretentious abstractions of "modern English."

JAMES BALDWIN

If Black English Isn't a Language, Then Tell Me, What Is?

In this brief essay fired off to the New York Times *opinion page in 1979, James Baldwin was responding to a debate that was raging among critics and academicians at the time (and is still going on): Is what we call Black English a dialect or a separate language? Our point of view on the issue, of course, will determine whether we regard the English as spoken by black Americans as a deviation from standard English (as the British might regard American or Australian English) or as an independent language with its own set of rules. Not a professional linguist, Baldwin from the start of his essay examines the argument as "having nothing to do with language itself but with the* role *of language." His essay is an impassioned argument not only for Black English but for the status of African-American culture and experience.*

T HE ARGUMENT concerning the use, or the status, or the reality, of black English is rooted in American history and has absolutely nothing to do with the question the argument supposes itself to be posing. The argument has nothing to do with language itself but with the *role* of language. Language, incontestably, reveals the speaker. Language, also, far more dubiously, is meant to define the other — and, in this case, the other is refusing to be defined by a language that has never been able to recognize him.

People evolve a language in order to describe and thus control their circumstances, or in order not to be submerged by a reality that they cannot articulate. (And, if they cannot articulate it, they *are* submerged.) A Frenchman living in Paris speaks a subtly and crucially different language from that of the man living in Marseilles; neither sounds very much like a man living in Quebec; and they would all have great difficulty in apprehending what the man from Guadeloupe, or Martinique, is saying, to say nothing of the man from Senegal — although the "common" language of all these areas is French. But each has paid, and is paying, a different price for this "common" language, in which, as it turns out, they are not saying, and cannot be saying, the same things: they each have very different realities to articulate, or control.

What joins all languages, and all men, is the necessity to confront life, in order, not inconceivably, to outwit death: the price for this is the acceptance, and achievement, of one's temporal identity. So that, for example, though it is not taught in the schools (and this has the potential of becoming a political issue) the south of France still clings to its ancient and musical Provençal, which resists being described as a "dialect." And much of the tension in the Basque countries, and in Wales, is due to the Basque and Welsh determination not to allow their languages to be destroyed. This determination also feeds the flames in Ireland for among the many indignities the Irish have been forced to undergo at English hands is the English contempt for their language.

It goes without saying, then, that language is also a political instrument, means, and proof of power. It is the most vivid and crucial key to identity: it reveals the private identity, and connects one with, or divorces one from, the larger, public, or communal identity. There have been, and are, times, and places, when to speak a certain language could be dangerous, even fatal. Or, one may speak the same language, but in such a way that one's antecedents are revealed, or (one hopes) hidden. This is true in France, and is absolutely true in England: the range (and reign) of accents on that damp little island make England coherent for the English and totally incomprehensible for everyone else. To open your mouth in England is (if I may use black English) to "put your business in the street": You have confessed your parents, your youth, your school, your salary, your self-esteem, and alas, your future.

Now, I do not know what white Americans would sound like if there 5 had never been any black people in the United States, but they would not sound the way they sound. *Jazz*, for example, is a very specific sexual term, as in *jazz me, baby*, but white people purified it into the Jazz Age. *Sock it to me*, which means, roughly, the same thing, has been adopted by Nathaniel Hawthorne's descendants with no qualms or hesitations at all, along with *let it all hang out* and *right on! Beat to his socks*, which was once the black's most total and despairing image of poverty, was transformed into a thing called the Beat Generation, which phenomenon was, largely, composed of *uptight*, middle-class white people, imitating poverty, trying to *get down*, to get *with it*, doing their *thing*, doing their despairing best to be *funky*, which we, the blacks, never dreamed of doing — we *were* funky, baby, like *funk* was going out of style.

Now, no one can eat his cake, and have it, too, and it is late in the day to attempt to penalize black people for having created a language that permits the nation its only glimpse of reality, a language without which the nation would be even more *whipped* than it is.

I say that this present skirmish is rooted in American history, and it is. Black English is the creation of the black diaspora. Blacks came to the United States chained to each other, but from different tribes: neither could speak the other's language. If two black people, at that bitter hour of the world's history, had been able to speak to each other, the institution of chattel slavery could never have lasted as long as it did. Subsequently, the slave was given, under the eye, and the gun, of his master, Congo Square, and the Bible —

or, in other words, and under these conditions, the slave began the formation of the black church, and it is within this unprecedented tabernacle that black English began to be formed. This was not, merely, as in the European example, the adoption of a foreign tongue, but an alchemy that transformed ancient elements into a new language: *A language comes into existence by means of brutal necessity, and the rules of the language are dictated by what the language must convey.*

There was a moment, in time, and in this place, when my brother, or my mother, or my father, or my sister, had to convey to me, for example, the danger in which I was standing from the white man standing just behind me, and to convey this with a speed, and in a language, that the white man could not possibly understand, and that, indeed, he cannot understand, until today. He cannot afford to understand it. This understanding would reveal to him too much about himself, and smash that mirror before which he has been frozen for so long.

Now, if this passion, this skill, this (to quote Toni Morrison [1]) "sheer intelligence," this incredible music, the mighty achievement of having brought a people utterly unknown to, or despised by "history" — to have brought this people to their present, troubled, troubling, and unassailable and unanswerable place — if this absolutely unprecedented journey does not indicate that black English is a language, I am curious to know what definition of language is to be trusted.

A people at the center of the Western world, and in the midst of so 10 hostile a population, has not endured and transcended by means of what is patronizingly called a "dialect." We, the blacks, are in trouble, certainly, but we are not doomed, and we are not inarticulate because we are not compelled to defend a morality that we know to be a lie.

The brutal truth is that the bulk of the white people in America never had any interest in educating black people, except as this could serve white purposes. It is not the black child's language that is in question, it is not his language that is despised: it is his experience. A child cannot be taught by anyone who despises him, and a child cannot afford to be fooled. A child cannot be taught by anyone whose demand, essentially, is that the child repudiate his experience, and all that gives him sustenance, and enter a limbo in which he will no longer be black, and in which he knows that he can never become white. Black people have lost too many black children that way.

And, after all, finally, in a country with standards so untrustworthy, a country that makes heroes of so many criminal mediocrities, a country unable to face why so many of the nonwhite are in prison, or on the needle, or standing, futureless, in the streets — it may very well be that both the child,

[1] *Toni Morrison* (b. 1931): African American novelist, author of *Song of Solomon* and *Tar Baby.*

and his elder, have concluded that they have nothing whatever to learn from the people of a country that has managed to learn so little.

FROM READING TO REREADING

1. Baldwin makes a distinction between a mere dialect and a language. What is this distinction and why is it important to his argument? What does he believe will be gained if Black English is recognized as a genuine language?

2. Though Baldwin introduces some words and expressions from Black English in his essay, you will notice that he wrote the essay — as he wrote all of his essays — in what we might call standard educated English. Why do you think he did this? Do you think it weakens his argument or strengthens it?

3. For Baldwin the main issue concerning Black English does not seem to be language at all. Note his concluding paragraphs. How has his topic changed? What to his mind is the question of Black English truly about?

JOAN DIDION

Insider Baseball

"Insider Baseball" isn't really an essay about the national pastime, except only as it shows how a presidential candidate would use baseball to try to enhance his public image. The essay — like George Orwell's — is about language and politics or, to be more precise, rhetoric and politics. In following the 1988 Bush–Dukakis presidential campaign, Didion noticed to what extent American politics has become an insider's game, played by a closely connected and often self-congratulatory network of politicians, pundits, pollsters, consultants, policy advisers, and the news media, all of whom are inside the "process," speak a common language, and have only a minimal connection with the nation. Didion's main idea is reinforced by her technique of using numerous quotations from and references to "inside" sources. For example, Didion's opening quotation from Tom Hayden is pointed. A 1960s leader of the antiwar movement and once politically prominent "outsider," Hayden — after marrying the actress Jane Fonda and settling down in California — soon entered mainstream politics and is now one of the notable insiders. Didion refers to many such insiders; to identify all of them would be distracting and cumbersome as well as unnecessary for a reader's understanding of the essay.

"Insider Baseball" originally appeared in the New York Review of Books *in 1988 and was selected for* The Best American Essays 1989.

1

IT OCCURRED to me, in California in June and in Atlanta in July and in New Orleans in August, in the course of watching first the California primary and then the Democratic and Republican national conventions, that it had not been by accident that the people with whom I had preferred to spend time in high school had, on the whole, hung out in gas stations. They had not run for student body office. They had not gone on to Yale or Swarthmore or DePauw, nor had they even applied. They had gotten drafted, gone through basic at Fort Ord. They had knocked up girls, and married them, had begun what they called the first night of the rest of their lives with a midnight drive to Carson City and a five-dollar ceremony performed by a justice still in his pajamas. They got jobs at the places that had laid off their uncles. They paid their bills or did not pay their bills, made down payments on tract houses, led lives on that social and economic edge referred to, in Washington and among those whose preferred locus is Washington, as "out there." They were never destined to be, in other words, communicants in what we have come to call, when we want to indicate the traditional ways in which power is exchanged and the status quo maintained in the United States, "the process."

"The process today gives everyone a chance to participate," Tom Hayden, by way of explaining "the difference" between 1968 and 1988, said to Bryant Gumbel on NBC at 7:50 A.M. on the day after Jesse Jackson spoke at the Democratic convention in Atlanta. This statement was, at a convention which had as its controlling principle the notably nonparticipatory idea of "unity," demonstrably not true, but people inside the process, constituting as they do a self-created and self-referring class, a new kind of managerial elite, tend to speak of the world not necessarily as it is but as they want people out there to believe it is. They tend to prefer the theoretical to the observable, and to dismiss that which might be learned empirically as "anecdotal." They tend to speak a language common in Washington but not specifically shared by the rest of us. They talk about "programs," and "policy," and how to "implement" them or it, about "trade-offs" and constituencies and positioning the candidate and distancing the candidate, about the "story," and how it will "play." They speak of a candidate's performance, by which they usually mean his skill at circumventing questions, not as citizens but as professional insiders, attuned to signals pitched beyond the range of normal hearing: "I hear he did all right this afternoon," they were saying to one another in the press section of the Louisiana Superdome in New Orleans on the evening Dan Quayle was or was not to be nominated for the vice presidency. "I hear he did O.K. with Brinkley." By the time the balloons fell that night the narrative had changed: "Quayle, zip," the professionals were saying as they brushed the confetti off their laptops.

These are people who speak of the process as an end in itself, connected only nominally, and vestigially, to the electorate and its possible concerns. "She used to be an issues person but now she's involved in the process," a prominent conservative said to me in New Orleans, by way of suggesting why an acquaintance who believed Jack Kemp was "speaking directly to what people out there want" had nonetheless backed George Bush. "Anything that brings the process closer to the people is all to the good," George Bush declared in his 1987 autobiography, *Looking Forward*, accepting as given this relatively recent notion that the people and the process need not automatically be on convergent tracks.

When we talk about the process, then, we are talking, increasingly, not about "the democratic process," or the general mechanism affording the citizens of a state a voice in its affairs, but the reverse: a mechanism seen as so specialized that access to it is correctly limited to its own professionals, to those who manage policy and those who report on it, to those who run the polls and those who quote them, to those who ask and those who answer the questions on the Sunday shows, to the media consultants, to the columnists, to the issues advisers, to those who give the off-the-record breakfasts and to those who attend them; to that handful of insiders who invent, year in and year out, the narrative of public life. "I didn't realize you were a political junkie," Marty Kaplan, the former *Washington Post* reporter and Mondale speechwriter who is now married to Susan Estrich, the manager of the Dukakis campaign, said when I mentioned that I planned to write about the campaign; the assumption here, that the narrative should be not just written only by its own specialists but also legible only to its own specialists, is why, finally, an American presidential campaign raises questions that go so vertiginously to the heart of the structure.

What strikes one most vividly about such a campaign is precisely its 5 remoteness from the actual life of the country. The figures are well known, and suggest a national indifference usually construed, by those inside the process, as ignorance, or "apathy," in any case a defect not in themselves but in the clay they have been given to mold. Only slightly more than half of those eligible to vote in the United States did vote in the 1984 presidential election. An average 18.5 percent of what Nielsen Media Research calls the "television households" in the United States tuned in to network coverage of the 1988 Republican convention in New Orleans, meaning 81.5 percent did not. An average 20.2 percent of these "television households" tuned in to network coverage of the 1988 Democratic convention in Atlanta, meaning 79.8 percent did not. The decision to tune in or out ran along predictable lines: "The demography is good even if the households are low," a programming executive at Bozell, Jacobs, Kenyon & Eckhardt told the *New York Times* in July about the agency's decision to buy "campaign event" time for Merrill Lynch on both CBS and CNN. "The ratings are about 9 percent off 1984," an NBC marketing vice president allowed, again to the *New York Times,* "but the upscale target audience is there."

When I read this piece I recalled standing, the day before the California primary, in a dusty central California schoolyard to which the surviving Democratic candidate had come to speak one more time about what kind of president he wanted to be. The crowd was listless, restless. There were gray thunderclouds overhead. A little rain fell. "We welcome you to Silicon Valley," an official had said by way of greeting the candidate, but this was not in fact Silicon Valley: this was San Jose, and a part of San Jose particularly untouched by technological prosperity, a neighborhood in which the lowering of two-toned Impalas remained a central activity.

"I want to be a candidate who brings people together," the candidate was saying at the exact moment a man began shouldering his way past me and through a group of women with children in their arms. This was not a solid citizen, not a member of the upscale target audience. This was a man wearing a down vest and a camouflage hat, a man with a definite little glitter in his eyes, a member not of the 18.5 percent and not of the 20.2 percent but of the 81.5 percent, the 79.8 percent. "I've got to see the next president," he muttered repeatedly. "I've got something to tell him."

". . . Because that's what this party is all about," the candidate said.

"Where is he?" the man said, confused. "Who is he?"

"Get lost," someone said.   10

". . . Because that's what this country is all about," the candidate said.

Here we had the last true conflict of cultures in America, that between the empirical and the theoretical. On the empirical evidence this country was about two-toned Impalas and people with camouflage hats and a little glitter in their eyes, but this had not been, among people inclined to the theoretical, the preferred assessment. Nor had it even been, despite the fact that we had all stood together on the same dusty asphalt, under the same plane trees, the general assessment: this was how Joe Klein, writing a few weeks later in *New York* magazine, had described those last days before the California primary:

> Breezing across California on his way to the nomination last week, Michael Dukakis crossed a curious American threshold. . . . The crowds were larger, more excited now; they seemed to be searching for reasons to love him. They cheered eagerly, almost without provocation. People reached out to touch him — not to shake hands, just to touch him . . . Dukakis seemed to be making an almost subliminal passage in the public mind: he was becoming presidential.

Those June days on which Michael Dukakis did or did not cross a curious American threshold had in fact been instructive. The day that ended in the schoolyard in San Jose had at first seemed, given that it was the eve of the California primary, underscheduled, pointless, three essentially meaningless events separated by plane flights. At Taft High School in Woodland Hills that morning there had been little girls waving red and gold pompoms in front of the cameras; "Hold That Tiger," the band had played. "Dream . . . maker," the choir had crooned. "Governor Dukakis . . . this is . . . Taft High," the student council president had said. "I understand this is the first time a presidential candidate has come to Taft High," Governor Dukakis had said. "Is there any doubt . . . under those circumstances . . . who you should support?"

"Jackson," a group of Chicano boys on the back sidewalk had shouted in unison.

"That's what it's all about," Governor Dukakis had said, and "health care," and "good teachers and good teaching."

This event had been abandoned, and another materialized: a lunchtime   15 "rally" in a downtown San Diego office plaza through which many people were passing on their way to lunch, a borrowed crowd but a less than attentive one. The cameras focused on the balloons. The sound techs picked up "La Bamba." "We're going to take child-support enforcement seriously in this country," Governor Dukakis had said, and "tough drug enforcement here and abroad." "Tough choices," he had said, and "we're going to make teaching a valued profession in this country."

Nothing said in any venue that day had seemed to have much connection with anybody listening ("I want to work with you and with working people all over this country," the candidate had said in San Diego, but people who work in San Diego do not think of themselves as "working people"), and late that afternoon, on the bus to the San Jose airport, I had asked a reporter who had traveled through the spring with the various campaigns (among those who moved from plane to plane it was agreed, by June, that the Bush campaign had the worst access to the candidate and the best food, that the Dukakis plane had average access and average food, and that the Jackson plane had full access and no time to eat) if the candidate's appearances that day did not seem a little off the point.

"Not really," the reporter said. "He covered three major markets."

Among those who traveled regularly with the campaigns, in other words, it was taken for granted that these "events" they were covering, and on which they were in fact filing, were not merely meaningless but deliberately so: occasions on which film could be shot and no mistakes made ("They hope he won't make any big mistakes," the NBC correspondent covering George Bush kept saying the evening of the September 25 debate at Wake Forest University, and, an hour and a half later, "He didn't make any big mistakes"), events designed only to provide settings for those unpaid television spots which in this case were appearing, even as we spoke, on the local news in California's three major media markets. "On the fishing trip, there was no way for television crews to get videotapes out," the *Los Angeles Times* noted a few weeks later in a piece about how "poorly designed and executed" events had interfered with coverage of a Bush campaign "environmental" swing through the Pacific Northwest. "At the lumber mill, Bush's advance team arranged camera angles so poorly that in one setup only his legs could get on camera." A Bush adviser had been quoted: "There is no reason for camera angles not being provided for. We're going to sit down and talk about these things at length."

Any traveling campaign, then, was a set, moved at considerable expense from location to location. The employer of each reporter on the Dukakis plane the day before the California primary was billed, for a total flying time of under three hours, $1,129.51; the billing to each reporter who happened, on the morning during the Democratic convention when Michael Dukakis and Lloyd Bentsen met with Jesse Jackson, to ride along on the Dukakis bus from the Hyatt Regency to the World Congress Center, a distance of perhaps ten blocks, was $217.18. There was the hierarchy of the set: there were actors, there were directors, there were script supervisors, there were grips. There was the isolation of the set, and the arrogance, the contempt for outsiders. I recall pink-cheeked young aides on the Dukakis campaign referring to themselves, innocent of irony and therefore of history, as "the best and the brightest." On the morning after the September 25 debate, Michael Oreskes of the *New York Times* gave us this memorable account of Bush aides crossing the Wake Forest campus:

> The Bush campaign measured exactly how long it would take its spokesman to walk briskly from the room in which they were watching the debate to the center where reporters were filing their articles. The answer was three-and-a-half minutes — too long for Mr. Bush's strategists, Lee Atwater, Robert Teeter and Mr. Darman. They ran the course instead as young aides cleared students and other onlookers from their path.

There was the tedium of the set: the time spent waiting for the shots to be set up, the time spent waiting for the bus to join the motorcade, the time spent waiting for telephones on which to file, the time spent waiting for the Secret Service ("the agents," they were called on the traveling campaigns, never the Secret Service, just "the agents," or "this detail," or "this rotation") to sweep the plane.

It was a routine that encouraged a certain passivity. There was the   20 plane, or the bus, and one got on it. There was the schedule, and one followed it. There was time to file, or there was not. "We should have had a page-one story," a *Boston Globe* reporter complained to the *Los Angeles Times* after the Bush campaign had failed to provide the advance text of a Seattle "environment" speech scheduled to end only twenty minutes before the departure of the plane for California. "There are times when you sit up and moan, 'Where is Michael Deaver when you need him,'" an ABC producer said to the *Times* on this point.

A final victory, for the staff and the press on a traveling campaign, would mean not a new production but only a new location: the particular setups and shots of the campaign day (the walk on the beach, the meet-and-greet at the housing project) would fade imperceptibly, the isolation and the arrogance and the tedium all intact, into the South Lawns, the Oval Office signings, the arrivals and departures of the administration day. There would still be the "young aides." There would still be "onlookers" to be cleared from the path. Another location, another standup: "We already shot a tarmac departure," they say on the campaign planes. "This schedule has two Rose Gardens," they say in the White House press room. Ronald Reagan, when asked by David Frost how his life in the Oval Office had differed from his expectations of it, said this: ". . . I was surprised at how familiar the whole routine was — the fact that the night before I would get a schedule telling me what I'm going to do all day the next day and so forth."

American reporters "like" covering a presidential campaign (it gets them out on the road, it has balloons, it has music, it is viewed as a big story, one that leads to the respect of one's peers, to the Sunday shows, to lecture fees, and often to Washington), which is one reason why there has developed among those who do it so arresting an enthusiasm for overlooking the contradictions inherent in reporting that which occurs only in order to be reported. They are willing, in exchange for "access," to transmit the images their sources wish transmitted. They are even willing, in exchange for certain colorful details around which a "reconstruction" can be built (the "kitchen table" at which the Dukakis campaign conferred on the night Lloyd Bentsen was added to the Democratic ticket, the "slips of paper" on which key members of the Bush campaign, aboard Air Force Two on their way to New Orleans, wrote down their own guesses for vice president), to present these images not as a story the campaign wants told but as fact. This was *Time*, reporting from New Orleans:

> Bush never wavered in support of the man he had lifted so high. "How's Danny doing?" he asked several times. But the Vice President never felt the compulsion to question Quayle face to face [after Quayle ran into difficulties]. The awkward investigation was left to Baker. Around noon, Quayle grew restive about answering further questions. "Let's go," he urged, but Baker pressed to know more. By early afternoon, the mood began to brighten in the Bush bunker. There were no new revelations: the media hurricane had for the moment blown out to sea.

This was Sandy Grady, reporting from Atlanta:

> Ten minutes before he was to face the biggest audience of his life, Mike Dukakis got a hug from his 84-year-old mother, Euterpe, who chided him, "You'd better be good, Michael." Dukakis grinned and said, "I'll do my best, Ma."

"Appeal to the media by exposing the [Bush campaign's] heavy-handed spin-doctoring," William Safire advised the Dukakis campaign on September 8. "We hate to be seen being manipulated."

"Periodically," the *New York Times* reported last March, "Martin Plissner, the political editor of CBS News, and Susan Morrison, a television producer and former political aide, organize gatherings of the politically connected at their home in Washington. At such parties, they organize secret ballots asking the assembled experts who will win. . . . By November 1, 1987, the results of Mr. Dole's organizing failures were apparent in a new Plissner–Morrison poll. . . ." The symbiosis here was complete, and the only outsider was the increasingly hypothetical voter, who was seen as responsive not to actual issues but to their adroit presentation: "At the moment the Republican message is simpler and more clear than ours," the Democratic chairman for California, Peter Kelly, said to the *Los Angeles Times* on August 31, complaining, on the matter of what was called the Pledge of Allegiance issue, not that it was a false issue but that Bush had seized the initiative, or "the symbolism."

"BUSH GAINING IN BATTLE OF TV IMAGES," the *Washington Post* head-lined a page-one story on September 10, and quoted Jeff Greenfield, now an ABC News political reporter: "George Bush is almost always outdoors, coatless, sometimes with his sleeves rolled up, and looks ebullient and Happy Warrior-ish. Mike Dukakis is almost always indoors, with his jacket on, and almost always behind a lectern." The Bush campaign, according to that week's issue of *Newsweek*, was, because it had the superior gift for getting film shot in "dramatic settings — like Boston Harbor," winning "the all-important battle of the backdrops." A CBS producer covering the Dukakis campaign was quoted, complaining about an occasion when Governor Du-kakis, speaking to students on a California beach, had faced the students instead of the camera. "The only reason Dukakis was out there on the ocean was to get his picture taken," the producer had said. "So you might as well see his face." Pictures, *Newsweek* had concluded, "often speak louder than words."

This "battle of the backdrops" story appeared on page 24 of the issue 25 dated September 12, 1988. On pages 22 and 23 of the same issue there appeared, as illustrations for the lead National Affairs story ("Getting Down and Dirty: As the mudslinging campaign moves into full gear, Bush stays on the offensive — and Dukakis calls back his main street-fighting man"), two half-page color photographs, one of each candidate, which seemed to address the very concerns expressed on page 24 and in the *Post*. The photograph of Vice President Bush showed him indoors, with his jacket on, and behind a lectern. That of Governor Dukakis showed him outdoors, coatless, with his sleeves rolled up, looking ebullient, about to throw a baseball on an airport tarmac: something had been learned from Jeff Greenfield, or something had been told to Jeff Greenfield. "We talk to the press, and things take on a life of their own," Mark Siegel, a Democratic political consultant, said recently to Elizabeth Drew.

About this baseball on the tarmac. On the day that Michael Dukakis appeared at the high school in Woodland Hills and at the rally in San Diego and in the schoolyard in San Jose, there was, although it did not appear on the schedule, a fourth event, what was referred to among the television crews as a "tarmac arrival with ball tossing." This event had taken place in late morning, on the tarmac at the San Diego airport, just after the chartered 737 had rolled to a stop and the candidate had emerged. There had been a moment of hesitation. Then baseball mitts had been produced, and Jack Weeks, the traveling press secretary, had tossed a ball to the candidate. The candidate had tossed the ball back. The rest of us had stood in the sun and given this our full attention, undeflected even by the arrival of an Alaska 767: some forty adults standing on a tarmac watching a diminutive figure in shirtsleeves and a red tie toss a ball to his press secretary.

"Just a regular guy," one of the cameramen had said, his inflection that of the union official who confided, in an early Dukakis commercial aimed at blue-collar voters, that he had known "Mike" a long time, and backed him despite his not being "your shot-and-beer kind of guy."

"I'd say he was a regular guy," another cameraman had said. "Definitely."

"I'd sit around with him," the first cameraman had said.

Kara Dukakis, one of the candidate's daughters, had at that moment   30
emerged from the 737.

"You'd have a beer with him?"

Jack Weeks had tossed the ball to Kara Dukakis.

"I'd have a beer with him."

Kara Dukakis had tossed the ball to her father. Her father had caught the ball and tossed it back to her.

"O.K.," one of the cameramen had said. "We got the daughter. Nice.   35
That's enough. Nice."

The CNN producer then on the Dukakis campaign told me, later in the day, that the first recorded ball tossing on the Dukakis campaign had been outside a bowling alley somewhere in Ohio. CNN had shot it. When the campaign realized that only one camera had it, they had restaged it.

"We have a lot of things like the ball tossing," the producer said. "We have the Greek dancing, for example."

I asked if she still bothered to shoot it.

"I get it," she said, "but I don't call in anymore and say, 'Hey, hold it, I've got him dancing.'"

This sounded about right (the candidate might, after all, bean a citizen   40
during the ball tossing, and CNN would need film), and not until I read Joe Klein's version of these days in California did it occur to me that this eerily contrived moment on the tarmac at San Diego could become, at least provisionally, history. "The Duke seemed downright jaunty," Joe Klein reported. "He tossed a baseball with aides. He was flagrantly multilingual. He danced Greek dances." In the July 25 issue of *U.S. News and World Report*, Michael Kramer opened his cover story, "Is Dukakis Tough Enough?" with a more developed version of the ball tossing:

> The thermometer read 101 degrees, but the locals guessed 115 on the broiling airport tarmac in Phoenix. After all, it was under a noonday sun in the desert that Michael Dukakis was indulging his truly favorite campaign ritual — a game of catch with his aide Jack Weeks. "These days," he had said, "throwing the ball around when we land somewhere is about the only exercise I get." For 16 minutes, Dukakis shagged flies and threw strikes. Halfway through, he rolled up his sleeves, but he never loosened his tie. Finally, mercifully, it was over and time to pitch the obvious tongue-in-cheek question: "Governor, what does throwing a ball around in this heat say about your mental stability?" Without missing a beat, and without

a trace of a smile, Dukakis echoed a sentiment he has articulated repeatedly in recent months: "What it means is that I'm tough."

Nor was this the last word. On July 31 in the *Washington Post,* David S. Broder, who had also been with the Dukakis campaign in Phoenix, gave us a third, and, by virtue of his seniority in the process, perhaps the official version of the ball tossing:

> Dukakis called out to Jack Weeks, the handsome, curly-haired Welshman who good-naturedly shepherds us wayward pressmen through the daily vagaries of the campaign schedule. Weeks dutifully produced two gloves and a baseball, and there on the tarmac, with its surface temperature just below the boiling point, the governor loosened up his arm and got the kinks out of his back by tossing a couple hundred 90-foot pegs to Weeks.

What we had in the tarmac arrival with ball tossing, then, was an understanding: a repeated moment witnessed by many people, all of whom believed it to be a setup and yet most of whom believed that only an outsider, only someone too "naive" to know the rules of the game, would so describe it.

2

The narrative is made up of many such understandings, tacit agreements, small and large, to overlook the observable in the interests of obtaining a dramatic story line. It was understood, for example, that the first night of the Republican National Convention in New Orleans should be for Ronald Reagan "the last hurrah." "REAGAN ELECTRIFIES GOP" was the headline the next morning on page one of *New York Newsday;* in fact the Reagan appearance, which was rhetorically pitched not to a live audience but to the more intimate demands of the camera, was, inside the Superdome, barely registered. It was understood, similarly, that Michael Dukakis's acceptance speech on the last night of the Democratic National Convention in Atlanta should be the occasion on which his "passion," or "leadership," emerged. "Could the no-nonsense nominee reach within himself to discover the language of leadership?" *Time* had asked. "Could he go beyond the pedestrian promises of 'good jobs at good wages' to give voice to a new Democratic vision?"

The correct answer, since the forward flow of the narrative here demanded the appearance of a genuine contender (a contender who could be seventeen points "up," so that George Bush could be seventeen points "down," a position from which he could rise to "claim" his own convention), was yes: "The best speech of his life," David Broder reported. Sandy Grady found it "superb," evoking "Kennedyesque echoes" and showing "unexpected craft and fire." *Newsweek* had witnessed Governor Dukakis "electrifying the convention with his intensely personal acceptance speech." In fact the convention that evening had been electrified, not by the speech, which was the same series of nonsequential clauses Governor Dukakis had em-

ployed during the primary campaign ("My friends . . . it's what the Democratic party is all about"), but because the floor had been darkened, swept
with laser beams, and flooded with "Coming to America," played at concert
volume with the bass turned up.

It is understood that this invented narrative will turn on certain familiar
elements. There is the continuing story line of the "horse race," the reliable
daily drama of one candidate falling behind as another pulls ahead. There is
the surprise of the new poll, the glamour of the one-on-one colloquy on the
midnight plane, a plot point (the nation sleeps while the candidate and his
confidant hammer out its fate) pioneered by Theodore H. White. There is
the abiding if unexamined faith in the campaign as personal odyssey, and in
the spiritual benefits accruing to those who undertake it. There is, in the
presented history of the candidate, the crucible event, the day that "changed
the life."

Robert Dole's life was understood to have changed when he was injured
in Italy in 1945. George Bush's life is understood to have changed when he
and his wife decided to "get out and make it on our own" (his words, or
rather the speechwriter Peggy Noonan's, from the "lived the dream" acceptance speech, suggesting action, shirtsleeves, privilege cast aside) in west
Texas. For Bruce Babbitt, "the dam just kind of broke" during a student
summer in Bolivia. For Michael Dukakis, the dam is understood to have
broken not during his student summer in Peru but after his 1978 defeat in
Massachusetts; his tragic flaw, we have read repeatedly, is neither his evident
sulkiness at losing that election nor what many since have seen as a rather
dissociated self-satisfaction ("We're two people very proud of what we've
done," he said on NBC in Atlanta, falling into a favorite speech pattern,
"very proud of each other, actually . . . and very proud that a couple of guys
named Dukakis and Jackson have come this far"), but the more attractive
"hubris."

The narrative requires broad strokes. Michael Dukakis was physically
small and had associations with Harvard, which suggested that he might be
an "intellectual"; the "immigrant factor," on the other hand, could make
him tough (as in "What it means is that I'm tough"), a "streetfighter." "He's
cool, shrewd and still trying to prove he's tough," the July 25 cover of *U.S.
News and World Report* said about Dukakis. "Toughness is what it's all about,"
one of his advisers is quoted as having said in the cover story. "People need
to feel that a candidate is tough enough to be president. It is the threshold
perception."

George Bush had presented a more tortured narrative problem. The
tellers of the story had not understood, or had not responded, to the essential
Bush style, which was complex, ironic, the diffident edge of the northeastern
elite. This was what was at first identified as "the wimp factor," which was
replaced not by a more complicated view of the personality but by its reverse:

45

George Bush was by late August no longer a "wimp" but someone who had "thrown it over," "struck out" to make his own way: no longer a product of the effete Northeast but someone who had thrived in Texas, and was therefore "tough enough to be president."

That George Bush might have thrived in Texas not in spite of but precisely because he was a member of the northeastern elite was a shading which had no part in the narrative: "He was considered back at the time one of the most charismatic people ever elected to public office in the history of Texas," Congressman Bill Archer of Houston has said. "That charisma, people talked about it over and over again." People talked about it, probably, because Andover and Yale and the inheritable tax avoidance they suggested were, during the years George Bush lived in Texas, the exact ideals toward which the Houston and Dallas establishment aspired, but the narrative called for a less ambiguous version: "Lived in a little shotgun house, one room for the three of us," as Bush, or Peggy Noonan, had put it in the celebrated no-subject-pronoun cadences of the "lived the dream" acceptance speech. "Worked in the oil business, started my own. . . . Moved from the shotgun to a duplex apartment to a house. Lived the dream — high school football on Friday night, Little League, neighborhood barbecue . . . pushing into unknown territory with kids and a dog and a car."

All stories, of course, depend for their popular interest upon the invention of personality, or "character," but in the political narrative, designed as it is to maintain the illusion of "consensus" by obscuring rather than addressing actual issues, this invention served a further purpose. It was by 1988 generally, if unspecifically, agreed that the United States faced certain social and economic realities which, if not intractable, did not entirely lend themselves to the kinds of policy fixes people who run for elected office, on whatever ticket, were likely to undertake. We had not yet accommodated the industrialization of parts of the third world. We had not yet adjusted to the economic realignment of a world in which the United States was no longer the principal catalyst for change. "We really are in an age of transition," Brent Scowcroft, Bush's leading foreign policy adviser, recently told Robert Scheer of the *Los Angeles Times*, "from a postwar world where the Soviets were the enemy, where the United States was a superpower and trying to build up both its allies and its former enemies and help the Third World transition to independence. That whole world and all of those things are coming to an end or have ended, and we are now entering a new and different world that will be complex and much less unambiguous than the old one."

What continued to dominate the rhetoric of the campaign, however, was not this awareness of a new and different world but nostalgia for an old one, and coded assurance that symptoms of ambiguity or change, of what George Bush called the "deterioration of values," would be summarily dealt with by increased social control. It was not by accident that the word "en-

forcement," devoid of any apparent awareness that it had been tried before, kept coming up in this campaign. A problem named seemed, for both campaigns, a problem solved. Michael Dukakis had promised, by way of achieving his goal of "no safe haven for dope dealers and drug profits anywhere on this earth," to "double the number" of Drug Enforcement Administration agents, not a promising approach. George Bush, for his part, had repeatedly promised the death penalty, and not only the Pledge of Allegiance but prayer, or "moments of silence," in the schools. "We have to change this whole culture," he said in the Wake Forest debate; the polls indicated that the electorate wanted "change," and this wish for change had been translated, by both campaigns, into the wish for a "change back," a change to that "gentler nation" of which Vice President Bush repeatedly spoke.

To the extent that there were differences between the candidates,   50 these differences lay in just where on the time scale this gentler America could be found. The Dukakis campaign was oriented to "programs," and the programs it proposed were similar to those that had worked (the encouragement of private sector involvement in low-cost housing, say) in the boom years after World War II. The Bush campaign was oriented to "values," and the values to which it referred were not postwar but prewar. In neither case did "ideas" play a part: "This election isn't about ideology, it's about competence," Michael Dukakis had said in Atlanta. "First and foremost, it's a choice between two persons," one of his senior advisers, Thomas Kiley, had told the *Wall Street Journal*. "What it all comes down to, after all the shouting and the cheers, is the man at the desk," George Bush had said in New Orleans. In other words, what it was "about," what it came "down to," what was wrong or right with America, was not a historical shift largely unaffected by the actions of individual citizens but "character," and if "character" could be seen to count, then every citizen — since everyone was a judge of character, an expert in the field of personality — could be seen to count. This notion, that the citizen's choice among determinedly centrist candidates makes a "difference," is in fact the narrative's most central element, and also its most fictive.

3

The Democratic National Convention of 1968, during which the process was put to a popular vote on the streets of Chicago and after which it was decided that what had occurred could not be allowed to recur, is generally agreed to have prompted the multiplication of primaries, and the concomitant coverage of those primaries, which led to the end of the national party convention as a more than ceremonial occasion. A year and a half ago, as the primary campaigns got under way for the 1988 election, David S. Broder, in the *Washington Post*, offered this analysis of the power these "reforms" in the nominating procedure had vested not in the party leadership, which is where this power of choice ultimately resides, but in "the existing communications system," by which he meant the press, or the medium through which the party leadership sells its choice:

> Once the campaign explodes to 18 states, as it will the day after New Hampshire, when the focus shifts to a super-primary across the nation, the existing communications system simply will not accommodate more than two or three candidates in each party. Neither the television networks, nor newspapers nor magazines, have the resources of people, space and time to describe and analyze the dynamics of two simultaneous half-national elections among Republicans and Democrats. That task is simply beyond us. Since we cannot reduce the number of states voting on Super Tuesday, we have to reduce the number of candidates treated as serious contenders. Those news judgments will be arbitrary — but not subject to appeal. Those who finish first or second in Iowa and New Hampshire will get tickets from the mass media to play in the next big round. Those who don't, won't. A minor exception may be made for the two reverends, Jesse L. Jackson and Marion G. (Pat) Robertson, who have their own church-based communications and support networks and are less dependent on mass-media attention. But no one else.

By the time the existing communications system set itself up in Atlanta and New Orleans the priorities were clear. "NOTICE NOTICE NOTICE," read the typed note given to some print reporters when they picked up their credentials in Atlanta. "Because the National Democratic Convention Committee permitted the electronic media to exceed specifications for their broadcast booths, your assigned seat's sightline to the podium and the convention floor was obliterated." The network skyboxes, in other words, had been built in front of the sections originally assigned to the periodical press. "This is a place that was chosen to be, for all intents and purposes, a large TV studio, to be able to project our message to the American people and a national audience," Paul Kirk, the chairman of the DNC, said by way of explaining why the podium and the skyboxes had so reduced the size of the Omni Coliseum in Atlanta that some thousand delegates and alternates and guests had been, on the evening Jesse Jackson spoke, locked out.

Mayor Andrew Young of Atlanta apologized for the lockout, but said that it would be the same on nights to follow: "The 150 million people in this country who are going to vote have got to be our major target." Still, convention delegates were seen to have a real role: "The folks in the hall are so important for how it looks," Lane Venardos, senior producer in charge of convention coverage for CBS News, said to the *New York Times* about the Republican convention. The delegates, in other words, could be seen as dress extras.

During those eight summer evenings this year, four in Atlanta and four in New Orleans, when roughly 80 percent of the television sets "out there" were tuned somewhere else, the entire attention of those inside the process was directed toward the invention of this story in which they themselves were the principal players, and for which they themselves were the principal audience. The great arenas in which the conventions were held became worlds all their own, constantly transmitting their own images back to themselves, connected by skywalks to interchangeable structures composed not of floors but of "levels," mysteriously separated by fountains and glass elevators and escalators that did not quite connect.

In the Louisiana Superdome in New Orleans as in the Omni Coliseum 55 in Atlanta, the grids of lights blazed and dimmed hypnotically. Men with rifles patrolled the high catwalks. The nets packed with thousands of balloons swung gently overhead, poised for that instant known as the "money shot," the moment, or "window," when everything was working and no network had cut to a commercial. The minicams trawled the floor, fishing in Atlanta for Rob Lowe, in New Orleans for Donald Trump. In the NBC skybox Tom Brokaw floated over the floor, adjusting his tie, putting on his jacket, leaning to speak to John Chancellor. In the CNN skybox Mary Alice Williams sat bathed in white light, the blond madonna of the skyboxes. On the television screens in the press section the images reappeared, but from another angle: Tom Brokaw and Mary Alice Williams again, broadcasting not just above us but also to us, the circle closed.

At the end of prime time, when the skyboxes went dark, the action moved across the skywalks and into the levels, into the lobbies, into one or another Hyatt or Marriott or Hilton or Westin. In the portage from lobby to lobby, level to level, the same people kept materializing in slightly altered roles. On a level of the Hyatt in Atlanta I saw Ann Lewis in her role as a Jackson adviser. On a level of the Hyatt in New Orleans I saw Ann Lewis in her role as a correspondent for *Ms.* Some pictures were vivid: "I've been around this process a while, and one thing I've noticed, it's the people who write the checks who get treated as if they have a certain amount of power," I recall Nadine Hack, the chairman of Dukakis's New York Finance Council, saying in a suite at the Hyatt in Atlanta: here was a willowy woman with long blond hair who was standing barefoot on a table and trying to explain how to buy into the action. "The great thing about those evenings was you could even see Michael Harrington there," I recall Richard Viguerie saying to me at a party in New Orleans: here was the man who manages the action for the American right trying to explain the early sixties, and evenings we had both spent on Washington Square.

There was in Atlanta, according to the Democratic National Committee, "twice the media presence" that there had been at the 1984 convention. There were in New Orleans "media workspaces" assigned not only to 117 newspapers and news services and to the American television and radio industry in full strength but to 52 foreign networks. On every corner one turned in New Orleans someone was doing a stand-up. There were telephone numbers to be called for quotes: "Republican State and Local Officials" or "Pat Robertson Campaign" or "Richard Wirthlin, Reagan's Pollster." Newspapers came with teams of thirty, forty, fifty. In every lobby there were stacks of fresh newspapers, the *Atlanta Constitution*, the *New Orleans Times-Picayune*, the *Washington Post*, the *Miami Herald*, the *Los Angeles Times*. In Atlanta these papers were collected in bins and "recycled": made into thirty thousand posters, which were in turn distributed to the press in New Orleans.

This perfect recycling tended to present itself, in the narcosis of the event, as a model for the rest: like American political life itself, and like the printed and transmitted images on which that life depended, this was a world with no half-life. It was understood that what was said here would go on the wire and vanish. Garrison Keillor and his cute kids would vanish. Ann Richards and her peppery ripostes would vanish. Phyllis Schlafly and Olympia Snowe would vanish. All the opinions and all the rumors and all the housemaid Spanish spoken in both Atlanta and New Orleans would vanish, all the quotes would vanish, and all that would remain would be the huge arenas themselves, the arenas and the lobbies and levels and skywalks to which they connected, the incorporeal heart of the process itself, the agora, the symbolic marketplace in which the narrative was not only written but immediately, efficiently, entirely, consumed.

A certain time lag exists between this world of the arenas and the world as we know it. One evening in New York between the Democratic and Republican conventions I happened to go down to Lafayette Street, to the Public Theatre, to look at clips from documentaries on which the English-born filmmaker Richard Leacock had worked during his fifty years in America. We saw folk singers in Virginia in 1941 and oil riggers in Louisiana in 1946 (this was *Louisiana Story*, which Leacock had shot for Robert Flaherty) and tent performers in the corn belt in 1954; we saw Eddy Sachs preparing for the Indianapolis 500 in 1960 and Piri Thomas in Spanish Harlem in 1961. We saw parades, we saw baton twirlers. We saw quints in South Dakota in 1963.

There on the screen at the Public Theatre that evening were images   60
and attitudes from an America that had largely vanished, and what was striking was this: these were the very images and attitudes on which "the campaign" of 1988 was predicated. That "unknown territory" into which George Bush had pushed "with the kids and a dog and a car" had existed in this vanished America, and long since been subdivided, cut up for those tract houses on which the people who were not part of the process had made down payments. Michael Dukakis's "snow blower," and both the amusing frugality and the admirable husbandry of resources it was meant to suggest, derived from some half-remembered idea of what citizens of this vanished America had laughed at and admired. "The Pledge" was an issue from that

world. "A drug-free America" had perhaps seemed in that world an achievable ideal, as had "better schools."

I recall listening in Atlanta to Dukakis's foreign policy expert, Madeleine Albright, as she conjured up, in the course of arguing against a "no first use" minority plan in the Democratic platform, a scenario in which "Soviet forces overrun Europe" and the United States has, by promising no first use of nuclear weapons, crippled its ability to act: she was talking about a world that had not turned since 1948. What was at work here seemed on the one hand a grave, although in many ways a comfortable, miscalculation of what people in America might have as their deepest concerns in 1988; it seemed on the other hand just another understanding, another of those agreements to overlook the observable.

4

It was into this sedative fantasy of a fixable imperial America that Jesse Jackson rode, on a Trailways bus. "You've never heard a sense of panic sweep the party as it has in the last few days," David Garth had told the *New York Times* during those perilous spring weeks when there seemed a real possibility that a black candidate with no experience in elected office, a candidate believed to be so profoundly unelectable that he could take the entire Democratic party down with him, might go to Atlanta with more delegates than any other Democratic candidate. "The party is up against an extraordinary end-game," the pollster Paul Maslin had said. "I don't know where this leaves us," Robert S. Strauss had said. One superdelegate then still uncommitted, the *New York Times* had reported, "said the Dukakis campaign had changed its message since Mr. Dukakis lost the Illinois primary. Mr. Dukakis is no longer the candidate of 'inevitability' but the candidate of order, he said. 'They're not doing the train's leaving the station and you better be on it routine anymore,' this official said. 'They're now saying that the station's about to be blown up by terrorists and we're the only ones who can defuse the bomb.'"

The threat, or the possibility, presented by Jesse Jackson, the "historic" (as people liked to say after it became certain he would not have the numbers) part of his candidacy, derived from something other than the fact that he was black, a circumstance which had before been and could be again compartmentalized. For example: "Next week, when we launch our black radio buys, when we start doing our black media stuff, Jesse Jackson needs to be on the air in the black community on our behalf," Donna Brazile of the Dukakis campaign said to the *New York Times* on September 8, by way of emphasizing how much the Dukakis campaign "sought to make peace" with Jackson.

"Black," in other words, could be useful, and even a moral force, a way for white Americans to attain more perfect attitudes: "His color is an enormous plus. . . . How moving it is, and how important, to see a black candidate meet and overcome the racism that lurks in virtually all of us white Americans," Anthony Lewis had noted in a March column explaining why the notion that Jesse Jackson could win was nonetheless "a romantic delusion" of the kind that had "repeatedly undermined" the Democratic party. "You look at what Jesse Jackson has done, you have to wonder what a Tom Bradley of Los Angeles could have done, what an Andy Young of Atlanta could have done," I heard someone say on one of the Sunday shows after the Jackson campaign had entered its "historic" (or, in the candidate's word, its "endless") phase.

"Black," then, by itself and in the right context — the "right context" 65 being a reasonable constituency composed exclusively of blacks and supportive liberal whites — could be accommodated by the process. Something less traditional, and also less manageable, was at work in the 1988 Jackson candidacy. I recall having dinner, the weekend before the California primary, at the Pebble Beach house of the chairman of a large American corporation. There were sixteen people at the table, all white, all well off, all well dressed, all well educated, and all socially conservative. During the course of the evening it came to my attention that six of the sixteen, or every one of the registered Democrats present, intended to vote on Tuesday for Jesse Jackson. Their reasons were unspecific, but definite. "I heard him, he didn't sound like a politician," one said. "He's talking about right now," another said. "You get outside the gate here, take a look around, you have to know we've got some problems, and he's talking about them."

What made the 1988 Jackson candidacy a bomb that had to be defused, then, was not that blacks were supporting a black candidate, but that significant numbers of whites were supporting — not only supporting but in many cases overcoming deep emotional and economic conflicts of their own in order to support — a candidate who was attractive to them not because but in spite of the fact that he was black, a candidate whose most potent attraction was that he "didn't sound like a politician." "Character" seemed not to be, among these voters, the point-of-sale issue the narrative made it out to be: a number of white Jackson supporters to whom I talked would quite serenely describe their candidate as a "con man," or even as, in George Bush's word, a "hustler."

"And yet . . ." they would say. What "and yet" turned out to mean, almost without variation, was that they were willing to walk off the edge of the known political map for a candidate who was running against, as he repeatedly said, "politics as usual," against what he called "consensualist centrist politics"; against what had come to be the very premise of the process, the notion that the winning and the maintaining of public office warranted the invention of a public narrative based only tangentially on observable reality.

In other words they were not idealists, these white Jackson voters, but empiricists. By the time Jesse Jackson got to California, where he would eventually get 25 percent of the entire white vote and 49 percent of the total vote from voters between the demographically key ages of thirty to forty-five, the idealists had rallied behind the sole surviving alternative, who was, accordingly, just then being declared "presidential." In Los Angeles, during May and early June, those Democrats who had not fallen in line behind Dukakis were described as "self-indulgent," or as "immature"; they were even described, in a dispiriting phrase that prefigured the tenor of the campaign to come, as "issues wimps." I recall talking to a rich and politically well-connected Californian who had been, through the primary campaign there, virtually the only prominent Democrat on the famously liberal west side of Los Angeles who was backing Jackson. He said that he could afford "the luxury of being more interested in issues than in process," but that he would pay for it: "When I want something, I'll have a hard time getting people to pick up the phone. I recognize that. I made the choice."

On the June night in Los Angeles when Michael Dukakis was declared the winner of the California Democratic primary, and the bomb officially defused, there took place in the Crystal Room of the Biltmore Hotel a "victory party" that was less a celebration than a ratification by the professionals, a ritual convergence of those California Democrats for whom the phones would continue to get picked up. Charles Manatt was there. John Van de Kamp was there. Leo McCarthy was there. Robert Shrum was there. All the custom-made suits and monogrammed shirts in Los Angeles that night were there, met in the wide corridors of the Biltmore in order to murmur assurances to one another. The ballroom in fact had been cordoned as if to repel late invaders, roped off in such a way that once the Secret Service, the traveling press, the local press, the visiting national press, the staff, and the candidate had assembled, there would be room for only a controllable handful of celebrants, over whom the cameras would dutifully pan.

In fact the actual "celebrants" that evening were not at the Biltmore at all, but a few blocks away at the Los Angeles Hilton, dancing under the mirrored ceiling of the ballroom in which the Jackson campaign had gathered, its energy level in defeat notably higher than that of other campaigns in victory. Jackson parties tended to spill out of ballrooms onto several levels of whatever hotel they were in, and to last until three or four in the morning: anyone who wanted to be at a Jackson party was welcome at a Jackson party, which was unusual among the campaigns, and tended to reinforce the populist spirit that had given this one its extraordinary animation.

Of that evening at the Los Angeles Hilton I recall a pretty woman in a gold lamé dress, dancing with a baby in her arms. I recall empty beer bottles, Corona and Excalibur and Budweiser, sitting around the loops of television cables. I recall the candidate himself, dancing on the stage, and, on this June evening when the long shot had not come in, this evening when the campaign was effectively over, giving the women in the traveling press the little parody wave they liked to give him, "the press chicks' wave," the stiff-armed palm movement they called "the Nancy Reagan wave"; then taking off his tie and throwing it into the crowd, like a rock star. This was of course a narrative of its own, but a relatively current one, and one which had, because it seemed at some point grounded in the recognizable, a powerful glamour for those estranged from the purposeful nostalgia of the traditional narrative.

In the end the predictable decision was made to go with the process, with predictable, if equivocal, results. On the last afternoon of the Republican convention in New Orleans I walked from the hotel in the Quarter where I was staying over to look at 544 Camp Street, a local point of interest not noted on the points-of-interest maps distributed at the convention but one that figures large in the literature of American conspiracy. "544 Camp Street" was the address stamped on the leaflets Lee Harvey Oswald was distributing around New Orleans between May and September of 1963, the "Fair Play for Cuba Committee" leaflets that, in the years after Lee Harvey Oswald assassinated John F. Kennedy, suggested to some that he had been acting for Fidel Castro and to others that he had been set up to appear to have been acting for Fidel Castro. Guy Banister had his detective agency at 544 Camp. David Ferrie and Jack Martin frequented the coffee shop on the ground floor at 544 Camp. The Cuban Revolutionary Council rented an office at 544 Camp. People had taken the American political narrative seriously at 544 Camp. They had argued about it, fallen out over it, had hit each other over the head with pistol butts over it.

When I went to look for 544 Camp that afternoon twenty-five years later there was, it turned out, no more such address: the small building had been bought and torn down in order to construct a new federal courthouse. Across the street in Lafayette Square that day there had been a loudspeaker, and a young man on a makeshift platform talking about abortion, and unwanted babies being put down the Disposall and "clogging the main sewer drains of New Orleans," but no one had been there to listen. "Satan — you're the liar," the young woman with him on the platform had sung, lip-syncing a tape originally made, she told me, by a woman who sings with an Alabama traveling ministry, the Ministry of the Happy Hunters. "There's one thing you can't deny . . . you're the father of every lie." The young woman had been wearing a black cape, and was made up to portray Satan, or Death, I was unclear which, and it had not seemed a distinction worth pursuing.

Still, there were clouds off the Gulf that day and the air was wet and there was about the melancholy of Camp Street a certain sense of abandoned historic moment, heightened, quite soon, by something unusual: the New Orleans police began lining Camp Street, blocking every intersection from Canal Street south. I noticed a man in uniform on a roof. Before long there were Secret Service agents, with wires in their ears. The candidates, it seemed, would be traveling north on Camp Street on their way from the Republican National Committee Finance Committee Gala (Invitation Only) at the Convention Center to the Ohio Caucus Rally (Media Invited) at the Hilton. I stood for a while on Camp Street, on this corner which might be construed as one of those occasional accidental intersections where the remote narrative had collided with the actual life of the country, and waited until the motorcade itself, entirely and perfectly insulated, a mechanism dedicated like the process for which it stood only to the maintenance of itself, had passed, and then I walked to the Superdome. "I hear he did O.K. with Brinkley," they said that night in the Superdome, and then, as the confetti fell, "Quayle, zip."

FROM READING TO REREADING

1. Look carefully at Didion's opening paragraph. Note how much she accomplishes right at the start. How does she establish (a) the difference between outsiders and insiders; (b) her own sympathies and affiliations; and (c) her sensitivity to language?

2. Didion argues that the insiders "invent, year in and year out, the narrative of public life." In what sense is Didion using the word "narrative" here? What is the narrative? In what ways is it based on deceit? How do the insiders invent it? How does the idea of this narrative run throughout Didion's essay?

3. Notice how often Didion places words in quotation marks. Go through the essay and make a list of recurring terms that are quoted ("process," for example). Look at the many fuller quotations. What do they have in common? What is Didion doing and why? What general effect does she want the quoted terms and the longer quotations to have?

CYNTHIA OZICK

The Question of Our Speech:
The Return to Aural Culture

In 1905 the prominent American novelist Henry James gave the commencement address at Bryn Mawr College. His talk, a reaction to what he thought was a rapidly deteriorating style of speech and idiom in America, was published soon after as "The Question of Our Speech." Some eighty years later, Cynthia Ozick would closely question James's speech in an attempt to understand what has happened to American literacy and a reading culture that once seemed so formidable. In her examination of what happened to "the era of print supremacy," Ozick not only offers a thoroughly reasoned explanation for its demise, but she also vividly (and somewhat humorously) introduces us to the way she herself learned to speak. The essay was first published in the Fiftieth Anniversary Issue of The Partisan Review *(1984–1985).*

W HEN I WAS a thirteen-year-old New Yorker, a trio of women from the provinces took up, relentlessly and extravagantly, the question of my speech. Their names were Miss Evangeline Trolander, Mrs. Olive Birch Davis, and Mrs. Ruby S. Papp (pronounced *pop*). It was Mrs. Papp's specialty to explain how to "breathe from the diaphragm." She would place her fingers tip-to-tip on the unyielding hard shell of her midriff, hugely inhaling: how astonishing then to see how the mighty action of her lungs caused her fingertips to spring apart! This demonstration was for the repair of the New York voice. What the New York voice, situated notoriously "in the throat," required above everything was to descend, pumping air, to this nether site, so that "Young Lochinvar came out of the WEST" [1] might come bellowing out of the pubescent breast.

The New York palate, meanwhile, was consonantally in neglect. *T*'s, *d*'s, and *l*'s were being beaten out against the teeth, European-fashion — this was called "dentalization" — while the homeless *r* and *n* went wandering in the perilous trough behind the front incisors. There were corrective exercises for these transgressions, the chief one being a liturgical recitation of "Tillie the Toiler took Tommy Tucker to tea," with the tongue anxiously flying up above the teeth to strike precisely on the lower ridge of the upper palate.

---

[1] *Young . . . WEST*: First line of a Sir Walter Scott (1771–1832) poem frequently used for recitation in American classrooms.

The diaphragm; the upper palate; and finally the arena in the cave of the mouth where the vowels were prepared. A New Yorker could not say a proper *a,* as in "paper" — this indispensable vibration was manufactured somewhere back near the nasal passage, whereas civility demanded the *a* to emerge frontally, directly from the lips' vestibule. The New York *i* was worst of all: how Mrs. Davis, Mrs. Papp, and Miss Trolander mimicked and ridiculed the New York *i*! "Oi loik oice cream," they mocked.

All these emendations, as it happened, were being applied to the entire population of a high school for girls in a modest Gothic pile [2] on East Sixty-eighth Street in the 1940s, and no one who emerged from that pile after four years of daily speech training ever sounded the same again. On the eve of graduation, Mrs. Olive Birch Davis turned to Mrs. Ruby S. Papp and said: "Do you remember the *ugliness* of her *diction* when she came to us?" She meant me; I was about to deliver the Class Speech. I had not yet encountered Shaw's *Pygmalion,* and its popular recrudescence in the form of *My Fair Lady* [3] was still to occur; all the same, that night, rehearsing for commencement, I caught in Mrs. Davis and Mrs. Papp something of Professor Higgins's victory, and in myself something of Eliza's humiliation.

Our teachers had, like young Lochinvar, come out of the West, but I   5 had come out of the northeast Bronx. Called on to enunciate publicly for the first time, I responded with the diffidence of secret pleasure; I liked to read aloud, and thought myself not bad at it. Instead, I was marked down as a malfeasance in need of overhaul. The revisions and transformations that followed were not unlike an evangelical conversion. One had to be willing to be born again; one had to be willing to repudiate wholesale one's former defective self. It could not be accomplished without faith and shame: faith in what one might newly become, shame in the degrading process itself — the dedicated repetition of mantras. "Tillie the Toiler took Tommy Tucker to tea," "Oh! young LOCHinvar has come out of the WEST, Through all the wide BORder HIS steed was the BEST." All the while pneumatically shooting out one's diaphragm, and keeping one's eye (never one's *oi*) peeled for the niggardly approval of Miss Evangeline Trolander.

In this way I was, at an early age, effectively made over. Like a multitude of other graduates of my high school, I now own a sort of robot's speech — it has no obvious native county. At least not to most ears, though a well-tutored listener will hear that the vowels hang on, and the cadence of every sentence has a certain laggardly northeast Bronx drag. Brooklyn, by contrast, is divided between very fast and very slow. Irish New York has its

---

[2] *pile*: A lofty building.

[3] *Pygmalion . . . My Fair Lady*: The Broadway musical *My Fair Lady* was based on George Bernard Shaw's 1912 drama *Pygmalion.* The play is about a professor of phonetics (Henry Higgins) who wagers that he can turn a cockney flower girl (Eliza Doolittle) into a duchess simply by correcting her "atrocious" accent.

own sound, Italian New York another; and a refined ear can distinguish between Bronx and Brooklyn Irish and Bronx and Brooklyn Jewish: four separate accents, with the differences to be found not simply in vowels and consonants, but in speed and inflection. Nor is it so much a matter of ancestry as of neighborhood. If, instead of clinging to the green-fronded edge of Pelham Bay Park, my family had settled three miles west, in a denser "section" called Pelham Parkway, I would have spoken Bronx Jewish. Encountering City Island, Bronx Jewish said Ciddy Oilen. In Pelham Bay, where Bronx Irish was almost exclusively spoken in those days, it was Ciddy Allen. When Terence Cooke became cardinal of New York, my heart leaped up: Throggs Neck! I had assimilated those sounds long ago on a pebbly beach. No one had ever put the cardinal into the wringer of speech repair. I knew him through and through. He was my childhood's brother, and restored my orphaned ear.

Effectively made over: these noises that come out of me are not an overlay. They do not vanish during the free play of dreams or screams. I do not, cannot, "revert." This may be because Trolander, Davis, and Papp caught me early; or because I was so passionate a devotee of their dogma.

Years later I tried to figure it all out. What did these women have up their sleeves? An aesthetic ideal, perhaps: Standard American English. But behind the ideal — and Trolander, Davis, and Papp were the strictest and most indefatigable idealists — there must have been an ideology; and behind the ideology, whatever form it might take, a repugnance. The speech of New York streets and households soiled them: you could see in their proud pained meticulous frowns. They were intent on our elevation. Though they were dead set on annihilating Yiddish-derived "dentalization," they could not be said to be anti-Semites, since they were just as set on erasing the tumbling consonants of Virginia Greene's Alexander Avenue Irish Bronx; and besides, in our different styles, we *all* dentalized. Was it, then, the Melting Pot that inspired Trolander, Davis, and Papp? But not one of us was an "immigrant"; we were all fully Americanized, and our parents before us, except for the handful of foreign-born "German refugees." These were marched off to a special Speech Clinic for segregated training; their r's drew Mrs. Davis's eyes toward heaven, and I privately recognized that the refugees were almost all of them hopeless cases. A girl named Hedwig said that she *didn't care*, which made me conclude that she was frivolous, trivialized, not serious; wasn't it ignominious enough (like a kind of cheese) to be called "Hedwig"?

Only the refugees were bona fide foreigners. The rest of us were garden-variety subway-riding New Yorkers. Trolander, Davis, and Papp saw us nevertheless as tainted with foreignness, and it was the remnants of that foreignness they meant to wipe away: the last stages of the great turn-of-the-century alien flood. Or perhaps they intended that, like Shaw's Eliza, we should have the wherewithal to rise to a higher station. Yet, looking back on their dress and manner, I do not think Trolander, Davis, and Papp at all sought out or even understood "class"; they were reliably American, and class was nothing they were capable of believing in.

What, then, did these ferrywomen imagine we would find on the farther shore, once we left behind, through artifice and practice, our native speech? Was it a kind of "manners," was it what they might have called "breeding"? They thought of themselves as democratic noblewomen (nor did they suppose this to be a contradiction in terms), and they expected of us, if not the same, then at least a recognition of the category. They trusted in the power of models. They gave us the astonishing maneuvers of their teeth, their tongues, their lungs, and drilled us in imitation of those maneuvers. In the process, they managed — this was their highest feat — to break down embarrassment, to deny the shaming theatricality of the ludicrous. We lost every delicacy and dignity in acting like freaks or fools while trying out the new accent. Contrived consonants began freely to address feigned vowels: a world of parroting and parody. And what came of it all?

What came of it was that they caused us — and here was a category *they* had no recognition of — they caused us to exchange one regionalism for another. New York gave way to Midwest. We were cured of Atlantic Seaboard, a disease that encompassed north, middle, and south; and yet only the middle, and of that middle only New York, was considered to be on the critical list. It was New York that carried the hottest and sickest inflammation. In no other hollow of the country was such an effort mounted, on such a scale, to eliminate regionalism. The South might have specialized in Elocution, but the South was not ashamed of its idiosyncratic vowels; neither was New England; and no one sent missionaries.

Of course this was exactly what our democratic noblewomen were: missionaries. They restored, if not our souls, then surely and emphatically our *r*'s — those *r*'s that are missing in the end syllables of New Yorkers, who call themselves Noo Yawkizz and nowadays worry about muggizz. From Boston to New York to Atlanta, the Easterner is an Eastinna, his mother is a mutha, his father a fahtha, and the most difficult stretch of anything is the hahd paht; and so fawth. But only in New York is the absent *r* — i.e., the absent *aw* — an offense to good mannizz. To be sure, our missionaries did not dream that they imposed a parochialism of their own. And perhaps they were right not to dream it, since by the forties of this century the radio was having its leveling effect, and Midwest speech, colonizing by means of "announcers," had ascended to the rank of standard speech.

Still, only forty years earlier, Henry James, visiting from England after a considerable period away, was freshly noticing and acidly deploring the pervasively conquering *r*:

> . . . the letter, I grant, gets terribly little rest among those great masses of our population that strike us, in the boundless West especially, as, under

some strange impulse received toward consonantal recovery of balance, making it present even in words from which it is absent, bringing it in everywhere as with the small vulgar effect of a sort of morose grinding of the back teeth. There are, you see, sounds of a mysterious intrinsic meanness, and there are sounds of a mysterious intrinsic frankness and sweetness; and I think the recurrent note I have indicated — fatherr and motherr and otherr, waterr and matterr and scatterr, harrd and barrd, parrt, starrt, and (dreadful to say) arrt (the repetition it is that drives home the ugliness), are signal specimens of what becomes of a custom of utterance out of which the principle of taste has dropped.

In 1905, to drop the *r* was to drop, for the cultivated ear, a principle of taste; but for our democratic noblewomen four decades on, exactly the reverse was true. James's New York/Boston expectations, reinforced by southern England, assumed that Eastern American speech, tied as it was to the cultural reign of London, had a right to rule and to rule out. The history and sociolinguistics governing this reversal is less pressing to examine than the question of "standard speech" itself. James thought that "the voice *plus* the way it is employed" determined "positively the history of the national character, almost the history of the people." His views on all this, his alarms and anxieties, he compressed into a fluid little talk ("The Question of Our Speech") he gave at the Bryn Mawr College commencement of June 8, 1905 — exactly one year and two days before my mother, nine years old, having passed through Castle Garden, [4] stood on the corner of Battery Park, waiting to board the horsecar for Madison Street on the Lower East Side.

James was in great fear of the child waiting for the horsecar. "Keep in sight," he warned, "the so interesting historical truth that no language, so far back as our acquaintance with history goes, has known any such ordeal, any such stress or strain, as was to await the English in this huge new community it was to help, at first, to father and mother. It came *over*, as the phrase is, came over originally without fear and without guile — but to find itself transplanted to spaces it had never dreamed, in its comparative humility, of covering, to conditions it had never dreamed, in its comparative innocence, of meeting." He spoke of English as an "unfriended heroine," "our transported medium, our unrescued Andromeda, [5] our medium of utterance, . . . disjoined from all the associations, the other presences, that had attended her, that had watched for her and with her, that had helped to form her manners and her voice, her taste and her genius."

And if English, orphaned as it was and cut off from its "ancestral circle," did not have enough to contend with in its own immigrant situation, arriving "without fear and without guile" only to be ambushed by "a social

[4] *Castle Garden*: A New York City immigration station.

[5] *Andromeda*: In Greek mythology, a beautiful Ethiopian princess who was left as a sacrifice to a sea monster but was rescued by Perseus who then married her.

and political order that was both without previous precedent and example and incalculably expansive," including also the expansiveness of a diligent public school network and "the mighty maniac" of journalism — if all this was not threatening enough, there was the special danger my nine-year-old mother posed. She represented an unstable new ingredient. She represented violation, a kind of linguistic Armageddon. She stood for disorder and promiscuity. "I am perfectly aware," James said at Bryn Mawr,

> that the common school and the newspaper are influences that shall often have been named to you, exactly, as favorable, as positively and actively contributive, to the prosperity of our idiom; the answer to which is that the matter depends, distinctively, on what is meant by prosperity. It is prosperity, of a sort, that a hundred million people, a few years hence, will be unanimously, loudly — above all loudly, I think! — speaking it, and that, moreover, many of these millions will have been artfully wooed and weaned from the Dutch, from the Spanish, from the German, from the Italian, from the Norse, from the Finnish, from the Yiddish even, strange to say, and (stranger still to say), even from the English, for the sweet sake, or the sublime consciousness, as we may perhaps put it, of speaking, of talking, for the first time in their lives, *really* at their ease. There are many things our now so profusely important and, as is claimed, quickly assimilated foreign brothers and sisters may do at their ease in this country, and at two minutes' notice, and without asking any one else's leave or taking any circumstance whatever into account — any save an infinite uplifting sense of freedom and facility; but the thing they may best do is play, to their heart's content, with the English language, or, in other words, dump their mountain of promiscuous material into the foundation of the American.

"All the while we sleep," he continued, "the vast contingent of aliens whom we make welcome, and whose main contention, as I say, is that, from the moment of their arrival, they have just as much property in our speech as we have, and just as good a right to do what they choose with it . . . all the while we sleep the innumerable aliens are sitting up (*they* don't sleep!) to work their will on their new inheritance." And he compared the immigrants' use of English to oilcloth — "highly convenient . . . durable, tough, cheap."

James's thesis in his address to his audience of young aristocrats was not precisely focused. On the one hand, in describing the depredations of the innumerable sleepless aliens, in protesting "the common schools and the 'daily paper,'" he appeared to admit defeat — "the forces of looseness are in possession of the field." Yet in asking the graduates to see to the perfection of their own speech, he had, he confessed, no models to offer them. Imitate, he advised — but whom? Parents and teachers were themselves not watchful. "I am at a loss to name you particular and unmistakable, edifying and illuminating groups or classes," he said, and recommended, in the most general way, the hope of "encountering, blessedly, here and there, articulate individuals, torch-bearers, as we may rightly describe them, guardians of the sacred flame."

As it turned out, James not only had no solution; he had not even put the right question. These young women of good family whom he was exhorting to excellence were well situated in society to do exactly what James had described the immigrants as doing: speaking "*really* at their ease," playing, "to their heart's content, with the English language" in "an infinite uplifting sense of freedom and facility." Whereas the "aliens," hard-pressed by the scramblings of poverty and cultural confusions, had no notion at all of linguistic "freedom and facility," took no writing license with the English tongue, and felt no remotest ownership in the language they hoped merely to earn their wretched bread by. If they did not sleep, it was because of long hours in the sweatshops and similar places of employment; they were no more in a position to "play" with English than they were to acquire bona fide *Mayflower* ancestry. Ease, content, facility — these were not the lot of the unsleeping aliens.

To the young people of Bryn Mawr James could offer nothing more sanguine, nothing less gossamer, than the merest metaphor — "guardians of the sacred flame." Whom then should they imitate but himself, the most "articulate individual" of them all? We have no record of the graduates' response to James's extravagant "later style" as profusely exhibited in this address: whatever it was, they could not have accepted it for standard American. James's English had become, by this time, an invention of his own fashioning, so shaded, so leafy, so imbricated, so brachiate, so filigreed, as to cast a thousand momentary ornamental obscurities, like the effect of the drill-holes in the spiraled stone hair of an imperial Roman portrait bust. He was the most eminent torchbearer in sight, the purest of all possible guardians of the flame — but a model he could not have been for anyone's everyday speech, no more than the Romans talked like the Odes of Horace. [6] Not that he failed to recognize the exigencies of an active language, "a living organism, fed by the very breath of those who employ it, whoever these may happen to be," a language able "to respond, from its core, to the constant appeal of time, perpetually demanding new tricks, new experiments, new amusements." He saw American English as the flexible servant "of those who carry it with them, on their long road, as their specific experience grows larger and more complex, and who need it to help them to meet this expansion." And at the same time he excluded from these widened possibilities its slangy young native speakers and the very immigrants whose educated children would enrich and reanimate the American language (eight decades later we may judge how vividly), as well as master and augment its literature.

Its literature. It is striking beyond anything that James left out, in the course of this lecture, any reference to reading. Certainly it was not overtly 20

[6] *Horace* (65–8 B.C.): Latin poet whose Odes rank among the world's classics.

his subject. He was concerned with enunciation and with idiom, with syllables, with vowels and consonants, with tone and inflection, with *sound* —
but he linked the American voice to such "underlying things" as "proprieties
and values, perfect possessions of the educated spirit, clear humanities," as
well as "the imparting of a coherent culture." Implicit was his conviction
that speech affects literature, as, in the case of native speakers, it inevitably
does: naturalism in the dialogue of a novel, say, is itself always a kind of
dialect of a particular place and time. But in a newly roiling society of
immigrant speakers, James could not see ahead (and why should he have
seen ahead? Castle Garden was unprecedented in all human history) to the
idea that a national literature can create a national speech. The immigrants
who learned to read learned to speak. Those who only learned to speak did
not, in effect, learn to speak.

In supposing the overriding opposite — that quality of speech creates
culture, rather than culture quality of speech — James in "The Question of
Our Speech" slighted the one formulation most pertinent to his complaints:
the uses of literature. Pressing for "civility of utterance," warning against
"influences round about us that make for . . . the confused, the ugly, the
flat, the thin, the mean, the helpless, that reduce articulation to an easy and
ignoble minimum, and so keep it as little distinct as possible from the
grunting, the squealing, the barking or roaring of animals," James thought it
overwhelmingly an issue of the imitation of oral models, an issue of "the
influence of *observation*," above all an issue of manners —- "for that," he
insisted, "is indissolubly involved." How like Mrs. Olive Birch Davis he is
when, at Bryn Mawr, he hopes to inflame his listeners to aspiration! "At first
dimly, but then more and more distinctly, you will find yourselves noting,
comparing, preferring, at last positively emulating and imitating." Bryn
Mawr, of course, was the knowing occasion, not the guilty target, of this
admonition — he was speaking of the young voices he had been hearing in
the street and in the parlors of friends, and he ended with a sacred charge
for the graduates themselves: "you may, sounding the clearer note of intercourse as only women can, become yourselves models and missionaries [*sic*],
perhaps even a little martyrs, of the good cause."

But why did he address himself to this thesis exclusively in America?
Could he not, even more emphatically, have made the same declarations,
uttered the same dooms, in his adopted England? No doubt it would not
have been seemly; no doubt he would have condemned any appearance of
ingratitude toward his welcoming hosts. All true, but this was hardly the
reason the lecture at Bryn Mawr would not have done for Girton College. [7]
In Britain, regionalisms are the soul of ordinary English speech, and in
James's time more than in our own. Even now one can move from hamlet

---

[7] *Girton College*: English women's college founded in 1869 that is affiliated with Cambridge
University.

to hamlet and hear the vowels chime charmingly with a different tone in each village. Hull, England, is a city farther from London in speech — though in distance only 140 miles to the north — than Hull, Massachusetts, is from San Francisco, 3,000 miles to the west. Of England, it is clear, James had only the expectations of class, and a single class set the standard for cultivated speech. Back home in America, diversity was without enchantment, and James demanded a uniform sound. He would not have dreamed of requiring a uniform British sound: English diversity was *English* diversity, earned, native, beaten out over generations of the "ancestral circle" — while American diversity meant a proliferating concatenation of the innumerable sleepless aliens and the half-educated slangy young. With regard to England, James knew whence the standard derived. It was a quality — an emanation, even — of those who, for generations, had been privileged in their education. As Virginia Woolf acknowledged in connection with another complaint, the standard was Oxbridge. [8] To raise the question of "our" speech in England would have been a superfluity: both the question and the answer were self-evident. In England the question, if anyone bothered to put it at all, was: Who sets the standard? And the answer, if anyone bothered to give it at all, was: Those who have been through the great public schools, those who have been through either of the great pair of ancient universities — in short, those who run things.

This was perhaps what led James, in his American reflections, to trip over the issues, and to miss getting at the better question, the right and pertinent question: *the* question, in fact, concerning American speech. In Britain, and in the smaller America of his boyhood that strained to be a mirror of the cousinly English culture, it remained to the point to ask who sets the standard. And the rejoinder was simple enough: the people at the top. To risk the identical question in the America of 1905, with my mother about to emerge from Castle Garden to stand waiting for the horsecar on the corner of Battery Park, was unavoidably to hurtle to the very answer James most dreaded and then desperately conceded: the people at the bottom.

The right and pertinent question for America was something else. If, in politics, America's Enlightenment cry before the world was to be "a nation of laws, not of men," then it was natural for culture to apply in its own jurisdiction the same measure: unassailable institutions are preferable to models or heroes. To look for aristocratic models for common speech in the America of 1905 was to end exactly where James *did* end: "I am at a loss to name you particular and unmistakably edifying and illuminating groups or classes." It could not be done. As long as James believed — together with Trolander, Davis, and Papp, his immediate though paradoxical heirs: paradoxical because their ideal was democratic and his was the-people-at-the-top — as long as he believed in the premise of "edifying and illuminating"

[8] *Oxbridge*: Short for Oxford and Cambridge universities.

models, his analysis could go nowhere. Or, rather, it could go only into the rhapsody of vaporous hope that is the conclusion of "The Question of Our Speech" — "become yourselves models and missionaries, even a little martyrs, of the good cause." Holy and resplendent words I recognize on the instant, having learned them — especially the injunction to martyrdom — at the feet of Trolander, Davis, and Papp.

No, it was the wrong question for America, this emphasis on *who;* the wrong note for a campus (however homogeneous, however elite) just outside Philadelphia, that Enlightenment citadel, whose cracked though mighty Bell was engraved with a rendering of the majestic Hebrew word *dror*: a word my nine-year-old mother, on her way to Madison Street, would have been able to read in the original, though presumably James could not — a deprivation of literacy my mother might have marked him down for. "All life," James asserted on that brilliant June day (my mother's life was that day still under the yoke of the Czar; the Kishinev pogrom, with its massacre and its maimings, had occurred only two years earlier), "all life comes back to the question of our speech, the medium through which we communicate with each other; for all life comes back to the question of our relations with each other." And: "A care for tone is part of a care for many things besides; for the fact, for the value, of good breeding, above all, as to which tone unites with various other personal, social signs to bear testimony. The idea of good breeding . . . is one of the most precious conquests of civilization, the very core of our social heritage."

Speech, then, was *who;* it was breeding; it was "relations"; it was manners; and manners, in this view, make culture. As a novelist, and particularly as a celebrated practitioner of "the novel of manners" (though to reduce James merely to this is to diminish him radically as a recorder of evil and to silence his full moral genius), it was requisite, it was the soul of vitality itself, for James to analyze in the mode of *who*. But for a social theorist — and in his lecture social theory was what James was pressing toward — it was a failing and an error. The absence of models was not simply an embarrassment; it should have been a hint. It should have hinted at the necessary relinquishment of *who* in favor of *what*: not who appoints the national speech, but what creates the standard.

If, still sticking to his formulation, James had dared to give his private answer, he might have announced: "Young women, I, Henry James, am that august Who who fixes the firmament of our national speech. Follow me, and you follow excellence." But how had this vast substantial Who that was Henry James come to be fashioned? It was not Who *he* followed. It was instead a great cumulative corporeal What, the voluminous and manifold heritage of Literature he had been saturated in since childhood. In short, he *read*: he was a reader, he had always read, reading was not so much his passion or his possession as it was his bread, and not so much his bread as it was the primordial fountain of his life. Ludicrous it is to say of Henry James that he read, he was a reader! As much say of Vesuvius that it erupted, or of Olympus that it kept the gods. But reading — just that, *what is read* — is the whole, the intricate, secret of his exemplum.

The vulgarity of the low press James could see for himself. On the other hand, he had never set foot in an American public school (his education was, to say the least, Americanly untypical), and he had no inkling of any representative curriculum. Nevertheless it was this public but meticulous curriculum that was to set the standard; and it was a curriculum not far different from what James might have found for himself, exploring on his own among his father's shelves.

A year or so after my mother stepped off the horsecar into Madison Street, she was given Sir Walter Scott's "The Lady of the Lake" [9] to read as a school assignment. She never forgot it. She spoke of it all her life. Mastering it was the triumph of her childhood, and though, like every little girl of her generation, she read *Pollyanna*, [10] and in the last months of her eighty-third year every word of Willa Cather, [11] it was "The Lady of the Lake" that enduringly typified achievement, education, culture.

Some seventy-odd years after my mother studied it at P.S. 131 on the Lower East Side, I open "The Lady of the Lake" and take in lines I have never looked on before: [30]

Not thus, in ancient days of Caledon,
    Was thy voice mute amid the festal crowd,
When lay of hopeless love, or glory won,
    Aroused the fearful, or subdued the proud.
At each according pause was heard aloud
    Thine ardent symphony sublime and high!
Fair dames and crested chiefs attention bowed;
    For still the burden of thy minstrelsy
Was Knighthood's dauntless deed, and Beauty's matchless eye.

O wake once more! how rude soe'er the hand
    That ventures o'er thy magic maze to stray;
O wake once more! though scarce my skill command
    Some feeble echoing of thine earlier lay;
Though harsh and faint, and soon to die away,
    And all unworthy of thy nobler strain,
Yet if one heart throb higher at its sway,
    The wizard note has not been touched in vain.
Then silent be no more! Enchantress, wake again!

---

[9] *The Lady of the Lake*: Published in 1810, *The Lady of the Lake* is a long, romantic, narrative poem with many interpolated songs and lyrics.

[10] *Pollyanna*: Popular American novel by Eleanor Porter (1868–1920).

[11] *Willa Cather* (1873–1947): American novelist; her many well-known books include *My Ántonia* and *Death Comes for the Archbishop*.

My mother was an immigrant child, the poorest of the poor. She had come in steerage; she knew not a word of English when she stepped off the horsecar into Madison Street; she was one of the innumerable unsleeping aliens. Her teachers were the entirely ordinary daughters of the Irish immigration (as my own teachers still were, a generation on), and had no special genius, and assuredly no special training (a certain Miss Walsh was in fact ferociously hostile), for the initiation of a Russian Jewish child into the astoundingly distant and incomprehensible premises of such poetry. And yet it was accomplished, and within the briefest period after the voyage in steerage.

What was accomplished was not merely that my mother "learned" this sort of poetry — i.e., could read and understand it. She learned what it represented in the widest sense — not only the legendary heritage implicit in each and every word and phrase (to a child from Hlusk, where the wooden sidewalks sank into mud and the peasants carried water buckets dangling from shoulder yokes, what was "minstrelsy," what was "Knighthood's dauntless deed," what on earth was a "wizard note"?), but what it represented in the American social and tribal code. The quickest means of stitching all this down is to say that what "The Lady of the Lake" stood for, in the robes and tapestries of its particular English, was the received tradition exemplified by Bryn Mawr in 1905, including James's presence there as commencement speaker.

The American standard derived from an American institution: the public school, free, democratic, open, urgent, pressing on the young a program of reading not so much for its "literary value," though this counted too, as for the stamp of Heritage. All this James overlooked. He had no firsthand sense of it. He was himself the grandson of an ambitiously money-making Irish immigrant; but his father, arranging his affluent life as a metaphysician, had separated himself from public institutions — from any practical idea, in fact, of institutions *per se* — and dunked his numerous children in and out of school on two continents, like a nomad in search of the wettest oasis of all. It was hardly a wonder that James, raised in a self-enclosed clan, asserted the ascendancy of manners over institutions, or that he ascribed to personal speech "positively the history of the national character, almost the history of the people," or that he spoke of the "ancestral circle" as if kinship were the only means to transmit that national character and history.

It was as if James, who could imagine nearly everything, had in this instance neglected imagination itself: kinship as construct and covenant, kinship imagined — and what are institutions if not invented kinship circles: society as contract? In the self-generating Enlightenment society of the American founding philosophers, it was uniquely the power of institutions to imagine, to create, kinship and community. The Constitution, itself a kind of covenant or imaginatively established "ancestral circle," created peoplehood out of an idea, and the public schools, begotten and proliferated by that idea, implemented the Constitution; and more than the Constitution. They implemented and transmitted the old cultural mesh. Where there was so much diversity, the institution substituted for the clan, and discovered — through a kind of civic magnetism — that it could transmit, almost as effectively as the kinship clan itself, "the very core of our social heritage."

To name all this the principle of the Melting Pot is not quite right, and overwhelmingly insufficient. The Melting Pot called for imitation. Imagination, which is at the heart of institutionalized covenants, promotes what is intrinsic. I find on my shelves two old textbooks used widely in the "common schools" James deplored. The first is *A Practical English Grammar*, dated 1880, the work of one Albert N. Raub, A.M., Ph.D. ("Author of 'Raub's Readers,' 'Raub's Arithmetics,' 'Plain Educational Talks, Etc.'"). It is a relentless volume, thorough, determined, with no loopholes; every permutation of the language is scrutinized, analyzed, accounted for. It is also a commonplace book replete with morally instructive quotations, some splendidly familiar. Each explanatory chapter is followed by "Remarks," "Cautions," and "Exercises," and every Exercise includes a high-minded hoard of literary Remarks and Cautions. For instance, under Personal Pronouns:

> Though the mills of God grind slowly,
>   yet they grind exceedingly small;
> Though with patience He stands waiting,
>   with exactness grinds He all.

> This above all, to thine own self be true,
> And it must follow, as the night the day,
> Thou canst not then be false to any man.

> These are thy glorious works, Parent of good,
>   Almighty! Thine this universal frame.

> Alas! they had been friends in youth,
> But whispering tongues can poison truth;
> And constancy lives in realms above,
>   And life is thorny, and youth is vain;
> And to be wroth with one we love
>   Doth work like madness on the brain.

So much for Longfellow, Shakespeare, Milton, and Coleridge. But also Addison, Cowper, Pope, Ossian, Scott, Ruskin, Thomson, Wordsworth, Trollope, Gray, Byron, Whittier, Lowell, Holmes, Moore, Collins, Hood, Goldsmith, Bryant, Dickens, Bacon, Franklin, Locke, the Bible — these appear throughout, in the form of addenda to Participles, Parsing, Irregular Verbs, and the rule of the Nominative Independent; in addition, a handful of lost presences: Bushnell, H. Wise, Wayland, Dwight, Blair, Mrs. Welby (nearly the only woman in the lot), and Anon. The *content* of this volume is not its subject matter, neither its syntactic lesson nor its poetic maxims. It is the voice of a language; rather, of language itself, language as texture, gesture, innateness. To read from beginning to end of a schoolbook of this sort is to recognize at once that James had it backwards and upside down: it is not that manners lead culture; it is culture that leads manners. What shapes culture — this is not a tautology or a redundancy — is culture. "Who makes the country?" was the latent question James was prodding and poking, all gingerly; and it was the wrong — because unanswerable — one. "What kind of country shall we have?" was Albert N. Raub's question, and it *was* answerable. The answer lay in the reading given to the children in the schoolhouses: the institutionalization, so to say, of our common speech at its noblest.

My second text is even more striking: *The Etymological Reader*, edited by Epes Sargent and Amasa May, dated 1872. "We here offer to the schools of the United States," begins the Preface, "the first systematic attempt to associate the study of etymology with exercises in reading." What follows is a blitz of "vocabulary," Latin roots, Saxon roots, prefixes, and suffixes, but these quickly subside, and nine tenths of this inventive book is an anthology engaging in its richness, range, and ambition. "Lochinvar" is here; so are the Declaration of Independence and selections from Shakespeare; so is Shelley's "To a Skylark"; so is the whole "Star-Spangled Banner." But also: "Description of a Bee Hunt," "Creation a Continuous Work," "The Sahara," "Anglo-Saxon and Norman French," "Conversation," "Progress of Civilization," "Effects of Machinery," "On the Choice of Books," "Our Indebtedness to the Greeks," "Animal Heat," "Corruptions of Language," "Jerusalem from the Mount of Olives," "On the Act of Habeas Corpus," "Individual Character," "Going Up in a Balloon," and dozens of other essays. Among the writers: Dickens, Macaulay, Wordsworth, Irving, Mark Twain, Emerson, Channing, John Stuart Mill, Carlyle, De Quincey, Tennyson, Mirabeau, and so on and so on.

It would be foolish to consider *The Etymological Reader* merely charming, a period piece, "Americana" — it is too immediately useful, too uncompromising, and, for the most part, too enduring to be dismissed with condescension.

> It was one of those heads which Guido has often painted — mild, pale, penetrating, free from all commonplace ideas of fat, contented ignorance, looking downward upon the earth; it looked forward, but looked as if it looked at something beyond this world. How one of his order came by it, Heaven above, who let it fall upon a monk's shoulders, best knows; but it would have suited a Brahmin, and had I met it upon the plains of Hindostan, I had reverenced it.

To come upon Sterne, [12] just like this, all of a sudden, for the first time, pressed between Southey's sigh ("How beautiful is night!") and Byron's "And the might of the Gentile, unsmote by the sword, / Hath melted like snow in the glance of the Lord" — to come upon Sterne, just like that, is to come upon an unexpected human fact. Such textbooks filled vessels more fundamental than the Melting Pot — blood vessels, one might venture. Virtuous, elevated, striving and stirring, the best that has been thought and said: thus the voice of the common schools. A fraction of their offerings had a heroic, or monumental, quality, on the style perhaps of George Washington's head. They stood for the power of civics. But the rest were the purest belles-lettres: [13] and it was belles-lettres that were expected to be the fountainhead of American civilization, including civility. Belles-lettres provided style, vocabulary, speech itself; and also the themes of Victorian seriousness: conscience and work. Elevated literature was the model for an educated tongue. Sentences, like conscience and work, were demanding.

What did these demanding sentences do in and for society? First, they demanded to be studied. Second, they demanded sharpness and cadence in writing. They promoted, in short, literacy — and not merely literacy, but a vigorous and manifold recognition of literature as a *force*. They promoted an educated class. Not a hereditarily educated class, but one that had been introduced to the initiating and shaping texts early in life, almost like the hereditarily educated class itself.

All that, we know, is gone. Where once the *Odyssey* was read in the schools, in a jeweled and mandarin translation, Holden Caulfield [14] takes his stand. He is winning and truthful, but he is not demanding. His sentences reach no higher than his gaze. The idea of belles-lettres, when we knock our unaccustomed knees against it, looks archaic and bizarre: rusted away, like an old car chassis. The content of belles-lettres is the property of a segregated caste or the dissipated recollections of the very old.

Belles-lettres in the schools fashioned both speech and the art of punc-   40 tuation — the sound and the look of nuance. Who spoke well pointed well; who pointed well spoke well. One was the skill of the other. No one now punctuates for nuance — or, rather, whoever punctuates for nuance is "corrected." Copy editors do not know the whole stippled range of the colon or the semicolon, do not know that "O" is not "oh," do not know that not all juxtaposed adjectives are coordinate adjectives; and so forth. The degener-

[12] *Sterne*: Laurence Sterne (1713–1768), English novelist and author of the nine-volume novel, *The Life and Opinions of Tristram Shandy.*

[13] *belles-lettres*: Literally "fine letters" (French); the term, now considered old-fashioned, was often used to refer to literature as a fine art. Some libraries still catalogue essays and general critical works under this heading.

[14] *Holden Caulfield*: Main character of J. D. Salinger's popular 1951 novel, *Catcher in the Rye.*

ation of punctuation and word-by-word literacy is pandemic among English speakers: this includes most poets and novelists. To glimpse a typical original manuscript undoctored by a copy editor is to suffer a shock at the sight of ignorant imprecision; and to examine a densely literate manuscript after it has passed through the leveling hands of a copy editor is again to suffer a shock at the sight of ignorant imprecision.

In 1930 none of this was so. The relentlessly gradual return of aural culture, beginning with the telephone (a farewell to letter-writing), the radio, the motion picture, and the phonograph, speeded up by the television set, the tape recorder, and lately the video recorder, has by now, after half a century's worth of technology, restored us to the pre-literate status of face-to-face speech. And mass literacy itself is the fixity of no more than a century, starting with the advancing reforms following the industrial revolution — reforms introducing, in England, the notion of severely limited leisure to the classes that formerly had labored with no leisure at all. Into that small new recreational space fell what we now call the "nineteenth-century novel," in both its supreme and its lesser versions. The act of reading — the *work*, in fact, of the act of reading — appeared to complicate and intensify the most ordinary intelligence. The silent physiological translation of letters into sounds, the leaping eye encoding, the transmigration of blotches on a page into the story of, say, Dorothea Brooke, [15] must surely count among the most intricate of biological and transcendent designs. In 1930 the so-called shop-girl, with her pulp romance, is habitually engaged in this electrifying web-work of eye and mind. In 1980 she reverts, via electronics, to the simple speaking face. And then it is all over, by and large, for mass literacy. High literacy has been the province of an elite class since Sumer; [16] there is nothing novel in having a caste of princely readers. But the culture of mass literacy, in its narrow period from 1830 to 1930, was something else: Gutenberg's [17] revolution did not take effect in a popular sense — did not properly begin — until the rise of the middle class at the time, approximately, of the English Reform Act of 1832. Addison's *Spectator*, [18] with its Latin epigraphs, was read by gentlemen, but Dickens was read by nearly everyone. The almost universal habit of reading for recreation or excitement conferred the greatest complexity on the greatest number, and the thinnest sliver of history expressed it: no more than a single century. It flashed by between aural culture

---

[15] *Dorothea Brooke*: Heroine of George Eliot's 1872 novel *Middlemarch*.

[16] *Sumer*: Ancient Mesopotamian city (now in Iraq) considered to be among the earliest sites of Western civilization.

[17] *Gutenberg*: Johann Gutenberg (1400?–1468?), German printer credited with the invention of moveable type, which revolutionized publishing.

[18] *Spectator*: Joseph Addison (1672–1719) began collaborating in 1711 on *The Spectator Papers*, one of the landmarks in the development of the English essay.

and aural culture, no longer-lived than a lightning bug. The world of the VCR is closer to the pre-literate society of traveling mummers than it is to that of the young Scott Fitzgerald's readership in 1920.

When James read out "The Question of Our Speech" in 1905, the era of print supremacy was still in force, unquestioned; the typewriter and the electric light had arrived to strengthen it, and the telephone was greeted only as a convenience, not a substitute. The telephone was particularly welcome — not much was lost that ought not to have been lost in the omission of letters agreeing to meet the 8:42 on Tuesday night on the east platform. Since then, the telephone has abetted more serious losses: exchanges between artists and thinkers; documents of family and business relations; quarrels and cabals among politicians; everything that in the past tended to be preserved for biographers and cultural historians. The advent of the computer used as word processor similarly points toward the wiping out of any *progressive* record of thought; the grain of a life can lie in the illumination of the crossed-out word.

But James, in the remoteness of post-Victorian technology, spoke unshadowed by these threatened disintegrations among the community of the literate; he spoke in the very interior of what seemed then to be a permanently post-aural culture. He read from a manuscript; later that year, Houghton, Mifflin published it together with another lecture, this one far more famous, "The Lesson of Balzac." We cannot hear his voice on a phonograph record, as we can hear his fellow self-exile T. S. Eliot's; and this, it might be said, is another kind of loss. If we cherish photographs of Henry James's extraordinarily striking head with its lantern eyes, we can regret the loss of a filmed interview of the kind that nowadays captures and delivers into the future Norman Mailer and John Updike. The return to an aural culture is, obviously, not *all* a question of loss; only of the most significant loss of all: the widespread nurture by portable print; print as water, and sometimes wine. It was, in its small heyday (we must now begin to say *was*), the most glorious work of the eye-linked brain.

And in the heyday of that glorious work, James made a false analysis. In asking for living models, his analysis belonged to the old aural culture, and he did not imagine its risks. In the old aural culture, speech *was* manner, manner *was* manners, manners *did* teach the tone of the civilized world. In the new aural culture, speech remains manner, manner becomes manners, manners go on teaching the tone of the world. The difference is that the new aural culture, based, as James urged, on emulation, is governed from below. Emulation as a principle cannot control its sources. To seize on only two blatancies: the guerrilla toy of the urban underclass, the huge and hugely loud portable radio — the "ghetto blaster" — is adopted by affluent middle-class white adolescents; so is the locution "Hey, man," which now crosses both class and gender. James worried about the replacement in America of "Yes" by "Yeah" (and further by the comedic "Yep"), but its source was the drawl endemic to the gilt-and-plush parlors of the upper middle class. "Yeah" did not come out of the street; it went into the street. But it is also fairly certain that the "Yeah"-sayers, whatever their place in society, could not have been strong readers, even given the fissure that lies between reading and the style of one's talk. The more attached one is to the community of readers, the narrower the fissure. In a society where belles-lettres are central to education of the young, what controls speech is the degree of absorption in print. Reading governs speech, governs tone, governs manner and manners and civilization. "It is easier to overlook any question of speech than to trouble about it," James complained, "but then it is also easier to snort or neigh, to growl or 'meaow,' than to articulate and intonate."

And yet he overlooked the primacy of the high act of reading. No one 45
who, in the age of conscience and work, submitted to "The Lady of the Lake," or parsed under the aegis of Albert N. Raub, or sent down a bucket into *The Etymological Reader*, was likely to snort or neigh or emit the cry of the tabby. Agreed, it was a more publicly formal and socially encrusted age than ours, and James was more publicly formal and socially encrusted than many of his contemporaries: he was an old-fashioned gentleman. He had come of age during the Civil War. His clothes were laid out by a manservant. His standard was uncompromising. All the same, he missed how and where his own standard ruled. He failed to discover it in the schoolhouses, to which it had migrated after the attenuation of the old aural culture. To be sure, the school texts, however aspiring, could not promise to the children of the poor, or to the children of the immigrants, or to the children of working men, any hope of a manservant; but they *did* promise a habit of speech, more mobilizing and organizing, even, than a valet. The key to American speech was under James's nose. It was at that very moment being turned in a thousand locks. It was opening gate after gate. Those who could read according to an elevated standard could write sufficiently accomplished sentences, and those who could write such sentences could "articulate and intonate."

"Read, read! Read yourself through all the stages of the masters of the language," James might have exhorted the graduates. Instead, he told them to seek "contact and communication, a beneficent contagion," in order to "bring about the happy state — the state of sensibility to tone." It offended him, he confessed, that there were "forces assembled to make you believe that no form of speech is provably better than another." Forty years on, Trolander, Davis, and Papp set their own formidable forces against the forces of relativism in enunciation. Like James, they were zealous to impose their own parochialisms. James did not pronounce the *r* in "mother"; it was, therefore, vulgar to let it be heard. Our Midwestern teachers *did* pronounce the *r*; it was, therefore, vulgar *not* to let it be heard. How, then, one concludes, *is* any form of speech "provably better than another"? In a relativist era, the forces representing relativism in enunciation have for the moment won the argument, it seems; yet James has had his way all the same. With the exception of the South and parts of the East Coast, there is very nearly a uniform *vox Americana*. [19] And we have everywhere a uniform "tone." It is in the streets and in the supermarkets, on the radio and on television; and it is low, low, low. In music, in speech, in manner, the upper has learned to imitate the lower. Cheapened imprecise speech is the triumph of James's tribute to emulation; it is the only possible legacy that could have come of the principle of emulation.

Then why did James plead for vocal imitation instead of reading? He lived in a sea of reading, at the highest tide of literacy, in the time of the crashing of its billows. He did not dream that the sea would shrink, that it was impermanent, that we would return, through the most refined technologies, to the aural culture. He had had his own dealings with a continuing branch of the aural culture — the theater. He had written for it as if for a body of accomplished readers, and it turned on him with contempt. "Forget not," he warned in the wake of his humiliation as a playwright, "that you write for the stupid — that is, your maximum of refinement must meet the minimum of intelligence of the audience — the intelligence, in other words, of the biggest ass it may conceivably contain. It is a most unholy trade!" He was judging, in this outcry, all those forms that arrange for the verbal to bypass the eye and enter solely through the ear. The ear is, for subtlety of interpretation, a coarser organ than the eye; it follows that nearly all verbal culture designed for the ear is broader, brighter, larger, louder, simpler, less intimate, more insistent — more *theatrical* — than any page of any book.

For the population in general, the unholy trades — they are now tremendously in the plural, having proliferated — have rendered reading nearly obsolete, except as a source of data and as a means of record-keeping — "warehousing information." For this the computer is an admittedly startling advance over Pharaoh's indefatigably meticulous scribes, notwithstanding the lofty liturgical poetry that adorned the ancient records, offering a tendril of beauty among the granary lists. Pragmatic reading cannot die, of course, but as the experience that feeds *Homo ridens*, [20] reading is already close to moribund. In the new aural culture of America, intellectuals habitually define "film" as "art" in the most solemn sense, as a counterpart of the literary novel, and ridicule survivors of the age of "movies" as naïfs incapable of making the transition from an old form of popular entertainment to a new form of serious expression meriting a sober equation with written art — as if the issue had anything to do with what is inherently complex in the medium, rather than with what is inherently complex in the recipient of the medium. Undoubtedly any movie is more "complicated" than any book; and also more

[19] *vox Americana*: American voice (Latin).

[20] *Homo ridens*: Laughing man (Latin). A reference to the philosopher Henri Bergson's notion that man is the only animal that laughs.

limited by the apparatus of the "real." As James noted, the maker of aural culture brings to his medium a "maximum of refinement" — i.e., he does the best he can with what he has to work with; sometimes he is even Shakespeare. But the job of sitting in a theater or in a movie house or at home in front of a television set is not so reciprocally complex as the wheels-within-wheels job of reading almost anything at all (including the comics). Reading is an act of imaginative conversion. That specks on a paper can turn into a tale or philosophy is as deep a marvel as alchemy or wizardry. A secret brush construes phantom portraits. In the proscenium or the VCR everything is imagined *for* one: there is nothing to do but see and hear, and what's there is what is literally there. When film is "poetic," it is almost never because of language, but rather because of the resemblance to paintings or engravings — one thinks of the knight on a horse in a field of flowers in Bergman's *The Virgin Spring.* [21] When film is most art, it is least a novelty.

The new aural culture is prone to appliance-novelty — a while ago who could have predicted the video recorder or the hand-held miniature television set, and who now knows what variations and inventions lie ahead? At the same time there is a rigidity to the products of the aural culture — like those static Egyptian sculptures, stylistically unaltered for three millennia, that are brilliantly executed but limited in imaginative intent.

In the new aural culture there is no prevalent belles-lettres curriculum to stimulate novel imaginative intent, that "wizard note" of the awakened Enchantress; what there is is replication — not a reverberation or an echo, but a copy. The Back to Basics movement in education, which on the surface looks as if it is calling for revivification of a belles-lettres syllabus, is not so much reactionary as lost in literalism, or *trompe l'oeil*: [22] another example of the replication impulse of the new aural culture, the culture of theater. Only in a *trompe l'oeil* society would it occur to anyone to "bring back the old values" through bringing back the McGuffey Reader [23] — a scenic designer's idea, and still another instance of the muddle encouraged by the notion of "emulation." The celebration of the McGuffey Reader can happen only in an atmosphere where "film," a copyist's medium, is taken as seriously as a book.

A book is not a "medium" at all; it is far spookier than that, one of the few things-in-themselves that we can be sure of, a Platonic form that can inhabit a virtual infinity of experimental incarnations: any idea, any story, any body of poetry, any incantation, in any language. Above all, a book is the riverbank for the river of language. Language without the riverbank is only television talk — a free fall, a loose splash, a spill. And that is what an

[21] *The Virgin Spring*: The 1959 film by Swedish director Ingmar Bergman.

[22] *trompe l'oeil*: "A trick of the eye" (French); the term is used to describe paintings of objects that look exactly like the objects themselves.

[23] *McGuffey Reader*: Popular nineteenth-century textbook series.

aural society, following a time of complex literacy, finally admits to: spill and more spill. James had nothing to complain of: he flourished in a period when whoever read well could speak well; the rest was provincialism — or call it, in kindness, regional exclusiveness. Still, the river of language — to cling to the old metaphor — ran most forcefully when confined to the banks that governed its course. But we who come after the hundred-year hegemony of the ordinary reader, we who see around us, in all these heaps of appliances (each one a plausible "electronic miracle"), the dying heaves of the caste-free passion for letters, should know how profoundly — and possibly how irreversibly — the mummers have claimed us.

FROM READING TO REREADING

1. Notice how Cynthia Ozick juxtaposes James's commencement address with her mother's arrival in America. What is the effect of this juxtaposition? How does Ozick use it in her argument?

2. Ozick points out that James omitted one element in his address: the importance of literature to speech. Why does she think James, one of America's most literary individuals, overlooked this matter? Why does Ozick believe that literature is so important to speech?

3. *Belles-lettres* is the French expression for fine literature. It is a literary term that's now out of fashion; in fact, the term is now almost always used in a derogatory way. But notice that Ozick uses the word more positively. Of what importance is *belles-lettres* to speech? How has it been dropped from schools' curricula and why? Do you think that restoring the type of literary material Ozick recommends will improve our language?

From Reading to Writing

1. Both George Orwell's and Joan Didion's essays are about the connections between politics and language. Examine the way both essayists use examples of political language they disapprove of. In an essay, use George Orwell's objections to political language to critique Didion's examples. How do the quotations she uses from the 1988 campaign relate to Orwell's illustrations of sloppy English?

2. Lewis Thomas argues that language is what preserved us as a species: it binds us and unites us. Yet James Baldwin's essay is about the divisiveness of language. Write an essay in which you consider the role of language in human society. Do you agree with Thomas or with Baldwin? Do

you think language promotes social harmony or dissension? Base your argument on both your thoughts and your personal experience.

3. Cynthia Ozick recalls the training she received in speech and how it influenced her life. How did you learn to speak? Who were your main models: were they parents, friends, television, movies, teachers? What models of speech were rewarded in your home or social groups? Write an essay in which you describe as accurately as you can why you talk the way you do.

9

Science and the Imagination

GEORGE ORWELL
What Is Science?

Handwritten annotations in top margin: "What you teach and how you teach person to think" / "Different ways of thinking"

Much of George Orwell's nonfiction consists of newspaper and magazine columns, short opinion pieces, and reviews that he himself regarded more as journalism than as literary essays. The following is one such column, written for the Tribune, *a British Socialist weekly to which Orwell contributed regularly in the 1940s. Though not as fully developed as his more personal and critical essays, "What Is Science?" nevertheless shows Orwell in his characteristic mode: rational, skeptical, humane. The column was written in the fall of 1945; the specific occasion for Orwell's thoughts about science was America's use of atomic weapons against Japan a few months earlier. The week before this piece was published, Orwell had contributed an essay to the same paper titled "You and the Atom Bomb."*

I N LAST week's *Tribune*, there was an interesting letter from Mr J. Stewart Cook, in which he suggested that the best way of avoiding the danger of a "scientific hierarchy" would be to see to it that every member of the general public was, as far as possible, scientifically educated. At the same time, scientists should be brought out of their isolation and encouraged to take a greater part in politics and administration.

As a general statement, I think most of us would agree with this, but I notice that, as usual, Mr Cook does not define science, and merely implies in passing that it means certain exact sciences whose experiments can be made under laboratory conditions. Thus, adult education tends "to neglect scientific studies in favour of literary, economic and social subjects," economics and sociology not being regarded as branches of science, apparently. This point is of great importance. For the word *science* is at present used in at least two meanings, and the whole question of scientific education is obscured by the current tendency to dodge from one meaning to the other.

Science is generally taken as meaning either (a) the exact sciences, such as chemistry, physics, etc, or (b) a method of thought which obtains verifiable results by reasoning logically from observed fact.

If you ask any scientist, or indeed almost any educated person, "What is science?" you are likely to get an answer approximating to (b). In everyday life, however, both in speaking and in writing, when people say "science" they mean (a). Science means something that happens in a laboratory: the very word calls up a picture of graphs, test-tubes, balances, Bunsen burners, microscopes. A biologist, an astronomer, perhaps a psychologist or a mathematician, is described as a "man of science": no one would think of applying

371

this term to a statesman, a poet, a journalist or even a philosopher. And those who tell us that the young must be scientifically educated mean, almost invariably, that they should be taught more about radioactivity, or the stars, or the physiology of their own bodies, rather than that they should be taught to think more exactly.

This confusion of meaning, which is partly deliberate, has in it a great danger. Implied in the demand for more scientific education is the claim that if one has been scientifically trained one's approach to *all* subjects will be more intelligent than if one had had no such training. A scientist's political opinions, it is assumed, his opinions on sociological questions, on morals, on philosophy, perhaps even on the arts, will be more valuable than those of a layman. The world, in other words, would be a better place if the scientists were in control of it. But a "scientist," as we have just seen, means in practice a specialist in one of the exact sciences. It follows that a chemist or a physicist, as such, is politically more intelligent than a poet or a lawyer, as such. And, in fact, there are already millions of people who do believe this.

But is it really true that a "scientist," in this narrower sense, is any likelier than other people to approach nonscientific problems in an objective way? There is not much reason for thinking so. Take one simple test — the ability to withstand nationalism. It is often loosely said that "Science is international," but in practice the scientific workers of all countries line up behind their own governments with fewer scruples than are felt by the writers and the artists. The German scientific community, as a whole, made no resistance to Hitler. Hitler may have ruined the long-term prospects of German science, but there were still plenty of gifted men to do the necessary research on such things as synthetic oil, jet planes, rocket projectiles and the atomic bomb. Without them the German war machine could never have been built up.

On the other hand, what happened to German literature when the Nazis came to power? I believe no exhaustive lists have been published, but I imagine that the number of German scientists — Jews apart — who voluntarily exiled themselves or were persecuted by the régime was much smaller than the number of writers and journalists. More sinister than this, a number of German scientists swallowed the monstrosity of "racial science." You can find some of the statements to which they set their names in Professor Brady's *The Spirit and Structure of German Fascism*.

But, in slightly different forms, it is the same picture everywhere. In England, a large proportion of our leading scientists accept the structure of capitalist society, as can be seen from the comparative freedom with which they are given knighthoods, baronetcies, and even peerages. Since Tennyson, no English writer worth reading — one might, perhaps, make an exception of Sir Max Beerbohm [1]—has been given a title. And those English

---

[1] *Tennyson . . . Beerbohm*: Alfred Lord Tennyson (1809–1892), poet laureate of England for nearly a half century; Sir Max Beerbohm (1872–1956), British humorist and essayist.

scientists who do not simply accept the status quo are frequently Communists, which means that, however intellectually scrupulous they may be in their own line of work, they are ready to be uncritical and even dishonest on certain subjects. The fact is that a mere training in one or more of the exact sciences, even combined with very high gifts, is no guarantee of a humane or sceptical outlook. The physicists of half a dozen great nations, all feverishly and secretly working away at the atomic bomb, are a demonstration of this.

But does all this mean that the general public should *not* be more scientifically educated? On the contrary! All it means is that scientific education for the masses will do little good, and probably a lot of harm, if it simply boils down to more physics, more chemistry, more biology, etc. to the detriment of literature and history. Its probable effect on the average human being would be to narrow the range of his thoughts and make him more than ever contemptuous of such knowledge as he did not possess: and his political reactions would probably be somewhat less intelligent than those of an illiterate peasant who retained a few historical memories and a fairly sound aesthetic sense.

Clearly, scientific education ought to mean the implanting of a rational, sceptical, experimental habit of mind. It ought to mean acquiring a *method* — a method that can be used on any problem that one meets — and not simply piling up a lot of facts. Put it in those words, and the apologist of scientific education will usually agree. Press him further, ask him to particularise, and somehow it always turns out that scientific education means more attention to the exact sciences, in other words — more *facts*. The idea that science means a way of looking at the world, and not simply a body of knowledge, is in practice strongly resisted. I think sheer professional jealousy is part of the reason for this. For if science is simply a method or an attitude, so that anyone whose thought-processes are sufficiently rational can in some sense be described as a scientist — what then becomes of the enormous prestige now enjoyed by the chemist, the physicist, etc. and his claim to be somehow wiser than the rest of us? 10

A hundred years ago, Charles Kingsley[2] described science as "making nasty smells in a laboratory." A year or two ago a young industrial chemist informed me, smugly, that he "could not see what was the use of poetry." So the pendulum swings to and fro, but it does not seem to me that one attitude is any better than the other. At the moment, science is on the upgrade, and so we hear, quite rightly, the claim that the masses should be scientifically educated: we do not hear, as we ought, the counterclaim that the scientists themselves would benefit by a little education. Just before writing this, I saw in an American magazine the statement that a number of British and American physicists refused from the start to do research on the atomic bomb, well knowing what use would be made of it. Here you have

[2] *Charles Kingsley* (1819–1875): English clergyman and historical novelist.

a group of sane men in the middle of a world of lunatics. And though no names were published, I think it would be a safe guess that all of them were people with some kind of general cultural background, some acquaintance with history or literature or the arts — in short, people whose interests were not, in the current sense of the word, purely scientific.

FROM READING TO REREADING

1. Orwell believes that people usually mean two different things when they use the word *science*. He then says that this "confusion of meaning . . . is partly deliberate." What does he mean by this? On whose part and for what reasons would the confusion be deliberate?

2. Orwell doesn't accept the common assumption that the opinions of scientists are more valuable than those of others. What examples does he offer to prove his point? How convincing do you find his examples to be?

3. The main point that Orwell starts with — that the general public should be scientifically educated — is one that is still commonly made and is an educational goal that usually strikes people as reasonable. Yet, why does Orwell dispute it? What exactly does he dispute about it? What precisely does he find wrong with the idea of a scientifically educated public? Is he against scientific education?

LEWIS THOMAS
Humanities and Science

The essays of the first two important writers in the genre, those of Montaigne (1533–1592) and Francis Bacon (1561–1626), consistently promoted an experiential and skeptical view of the world. Both empiricists, Montaigne and (especially) Bacon would establish scientific inquiry as one of the essay's recurring modes. Montaigne's motto, "Que sais-je?" ("What do I know?"), and Bacon's insistence that in the pursuit of knowledge we distrust all of our preconceived ideas, helped set the style and tone of the modern essay. In "Humanities and Science," Lewis Thomas combines Bacon's respect for knowledge with Montaigne's respect for ignorance, and in the best tradition of the scientific essay shows that they are two sides of the same coin. The essay appeared in Late Night Thoughts on Listening to Mahler's Ninth Symphony *(1983).*

LORD KELVIN [1] was one of the great British physicists of the late nineteenth century, an extraordinarily influential figure in his time, and in some ways a paradigm of conventional, established scientific leadership. He did a lot of good and useful things, but once or twice he, like Homer, nodded. The instances are worth recalling today, for we have nodders among our scientific eminences still, from time to time, needing to have their elbows shaken.

On one occasion, Kelvin made a speech on the overarching importance of numbers. He maintained that no observation of nature was worth paying serious attention to unless it could be stated in precisely quantitative terms. The numbers were the final and only test, not only of truth but about meaning as well. He said, "When you can measure what you are speaking about, and express it in numbers, you know something about it. But when you cannot — your knowledge is of a meagre and unsatisfactory kind."

But, as at least one subsequent event showed, Kelvin may have had things exactly the wrong way round. The task of converting observations into numbers is the hardest of all, the last task rather than the first thing to be done, and it can be done only when you have learned, beforehand, a great deal about the observations themselves. You can, to be sure, achieve a very deep understanding of nature by quantitative measurement, but you must know what you are talking about before you can begin applying the numbers for making predictions. In Kelvin's case, the problem at hand was

[1] *Lord Kelvin*: William Thomson (1824–1907), Irish-born mathematician and physicist, as well as professor of natural philosophy.

the age of the earth and solar system. Using what was then known about the sources of energy and the loss of energy from the physics of that day, he calculated that neither the earth nor the sun were older than several hundred million years. This caused a considerable stir in biological and geological circles, especially among the evolutionists. Darwin himself was distressed by the numbers; the time was much too short for the theory of evolution. Kelvin's figures were described by Darwin as one of his "sorest troubles."

T. H. Huxley [2] had long been aware of the risks involved in premature extrapolations from mathematical treatment of biological problems. He said, in an 1869 speech to the Geological Society concerning numbers, "This seems to be one of the many cases in which the admitted accuracy of mathematical processes is allowed to throw a wholly inadmissible appearance of authority over the results obtained by them. . . . As the grandest mill in the world will not extract wheat flour from peascods, so pages of formulas will not get a definite result out of loose data."

The trouble was that the world of physics had not moved fast enough 5 to allow for Kelvin's assumptions. Nuclear fusion and fission had not yet been dreamed of, and the true age of the earth could not even be guessed from the data in hand. It was not yet the time for mathematics in this subject.

There have been other examples, since those days, of the folly of using numbers and calculations uncritically. Kelvin's own strong conviction that science could not be genuine science without measuring things was catching. People in other fields of endeavor, hankering to turn their disciplines into exact sciences, beset by what has since been called "physics envy," set about converting whatever they knew into numbers and thence into equations with predictive pretensions. We have it with us still, in economics, sociology, psychology, history, even, I fear, in English-literature criticism and linguistics, and it frequently works, when it works at all, with indifferent success. The risks of untoward social consequences in work of this kind are considerable. It is as important — and as hard — to learn *when* to use mathematics as *how* to use it, and this matter should remain high on the agenda of consideration for education in the social and behavioral sciences.

Of course, Kelvin's difficulty with the age of the earth was an exceptional, almost isolated instance of failure in quantitative measurement in nineteenth-century physics. The instruments devised for approaching nature by way of physics became increasingly precise and powerful, carrying the field through electromagnetic theory, triumph after triumph, and setting the stage for the great revolution of twentieth-century physics. There is no doubt about it: measurement works when the instruments work, and when you have a fairly clear idea of what it is that is being measured, and when you know what to do with the numbers when they tumble out. The system for

[2] *T. H. Huxley*: Thomas Henry Huxley (1825–1895), English biologist and an important figure in the development of the scientific essay.

gaining information and comprehension about nature works so well, indeed, that it carries another hazard: the risk of convincing yourself that you know everything.

Kelvin himself fell into this trap toward the end of the century. (I don't mean to keep picking on Kelvin, who was a very great scientist; it is just that he happened to say a couple of things I find useful for this discussion.) He stated, in a summary of the achievements of nineteenth-century physics, that it was an almost completed science; virtually everything that needed knowing about the material universe had been learned; there were still a few anomalies and inconsistencies in electromagnetic theory, a few loose ends to be tidied up, but this would be done within the next several years. Physics, in these terms, was not a field any longer likely to attract, as it previously had, the brightest and most imaginative young brains. The most interesting part of the work had already been done. Then, within the next decade, came radiation, Planck, the quantum, Einstein, Rutherford, Bohr, and all the rest — quantum mechanics — and the whole field turned over and became a brand-new sort of human endeavor, still now, in the view of many physicists, almost a full century later, a field only at its beginnings.

But even today, despite the amazements that are turning up in physics each year, despite the jumps taken from the smallest parts of nature — particle physics — to the largest of all — the cosmos itself — the impression of science that the public gains is rather like the impression left in the nineteenth-century public mind by Kelvin. Science, in this view, is first of all a matter of simply getting all the numbers together. The numbers are sitting out there in nature, waiting to be found, sorted and totted up. If only they had enough robots and enough computers, the scientists could go off to the beach and wait for their papers to be written for them. Second of all, what we know about nature today is pretty much the whole story: we are very nearly home and dry. From here on, it is largely a problem of tying up loose ends, tidying nature up, getting the files in order. The only real surprises for the future — and it is about those that the public is becoming more concerned and apprehensive — are the technological applications that the scientists may be cooking up from today's knowledge.

I suggest that the scientific community is to blame. If there are dis- 10 agreements between the world of the humanities and the scientific enterprise as to the place and importance of science in a liberal-arts education, and the role of science in twentieth-century culture, I believe that the scientists are themselves responsible for a general misunderstanding of what they are really up to.

Over the past half century, we have been teaching the sciences as though they were the same academic collection of cut-and-dried subjects as always, and — here is what has really gone wrong — as though they would always be the same. The teaching of today's biology, for example, is pretty much the same kind of exercise as the teaching of Latin was when I was in high school long ago. First of all, the fundamentals, the underlying laws, the essential grammar, and then the reading of texts. Once mastered, that is that: Latin is Latin and forever after will be Latin. And biology is precisely biology, a vast array of hard facts to be learned as fundamentals, followed by a reading of the texts.

Moreover, we have been teaching science as though its facts were somehow superior to the facts in all other scholarly disciplines, more fundamental, more solid, less subject to subjectivism, immutable. English literature is not just one way of thinking, it is all sorts of ways. Poetry is a moving target. The facts that underlie art, architecture, and music are not really hard facts, and you can change them any way you like by arguing about them, but science is treated as an altogether different kind of learning: an unambiguous, unalterable, and endlessly useful display of data needing only to be packaged and installed somewhere in one's temporal lobe in order to achieve a full understanding of the natural world.

And it is, of course, not like this at all. In real life, every field of science that I can think of is incomplete, and most of them — whatever the record of accomplishment over the past two hundred years — are still in the earliest stage of their starting point. In the fields I know best, among the life sciences, it is required that the most expert and sophisticated minds be capable of changing those minds, often with a great lurch, every few years. In some branches of biology the mind-changing is occurring with accelerating velocities. The next week's issue of any scientific journal can turn a whole field upside down, shaking out any number of immutable ideas and installing new bodies of dogma, and this is happening all the time. It is an almost everyday event in physics, in chemistry, in materials research, in neurobiology, in genetics, in immunology. The hard facts tend to soften overnight, melt away, and vanish under the pressure of new hard facts, and the interpretations of what appear to be the most solid aspects of nature are subject to change, now more than at any other time in history. The conclusions reached in science are always, when looked at closely, far more provisional and tentative than are most of the assumptions arrived at by our colleagues in the humanities.

The running battle now in progress between the sociobiologists and the antisociobiologists is a marvel for students to behold, close up. To observe, in open-mouthed astonishment, the polarized extremes, one group of highly intelligent, beautifully trained, knowledgeable, and imaginative scientists maintaining that all sorts of behavior, animal and human, are governed exclusively by genes, and another group of equally talented scientists saying precisely the opposite and asserting that all behavior is set and determined by the environment, or by culture, and both sides brawling in the pages of periodicals such as the *New York Review of Books*, is an educational experience that no college student should be allowed to miss. The essential lesson to be learned has nothing to do with the relative validity of the facts underlying the argument, it is the argument itself that is the education: we do not yet know enough to settle such questions.

It is true that at any given moment there is the appearance of satisfac- 15 tion, even self-satisfaction, within every scientific discipline. On any Tuesday morning, if asked, a good working scientist will gladly tell you that the affairs of the field are nicely in order, that things are finally looking clear and making sense, and all is well. But come back again, on another Tuesday, and he may let you know that the roof has just fallen in on his life's work, that all the old ideas — last week's ideas in some cases — are no longer good ideas, that something strange has happened.

It is the very strangeness of nature that makes science engrossing. That ought to be at the center of science teaching. There are more than seven-times-seven types of ambiguity [3] in science, awaiting analysis. The poetry of Wallace Stevens [4] is crystal-clear alongside the genetic code.

I prefer to turn things around in order to make precisely the opposite case. Science, especially twentieth-century science, has provided us with a glimpse of something we never really knew before, the revelation of human ignorance. We have been used to the belief, down one century after another, that we more or less comprehend everything bar one or two mysteries like the mental processes of our gods. Every age, not just the eighteenth century, regarded itself as the Age of Reason, and we have never lacked for explanations of the world and its ways. Now, we are being brought up short, and this has been the work of science. We have a wilderness of mystery to make our way through in the centuries ahead, and we will need science for this but not science alone. Science will, in its own time, produce the data and some of the meaning in the data, but never the full meaning. For getting a full grasp, for perceiving real significance when significance is at hand, we shall need minds at work from all sorts of brains outside the fields of science, most of all the brains of poets, of course, but also those of artists, musicians, philosophers, historians, writers in general.

It is primarily because of this need that I would press for changes in the way science is taught. There is a need to teach the young people who will be doing the science themselves, but this will always be a small minority among us. There is a deeper need to teach science to those who will be needed for thinking about it, and this means pretty nearly everyone else, in hopes that a few of these people — a much smaller minority than the scientific community and probably a lot harder to find — will, in the thinking, be able to imagine new levels of meaning that are likely to be lost on the rest of us.

In addition, it is time to develop a new group of professional thinkers, perhaps a somewhat larger group than the working scientists, who can create

[3] *seven-times-seven . . . ambiguity*: Reference to *Seven Types of Ambiguity*, an influential book of literary criticism by William Empson.
[4] *Wallace Stevens* (1879–1955): American poet whose verse is often difficult.

a discipline of scientific criticism. We have had good luck so far in the emergence of a few people ranking as philosophers of science and historians and journalists of science, and I hope more of these will be coming along, but we have not yet seen a Ruskin or a Leavis or an Edmund Wilson. [5] Science needs critics of this sort, but the public at large needs them more urgently.

I suggest that the introductory courses in science, at all levels from grade school through college, be radically revised. Leave the fundamentals, the so-called basics, aside for a while, and concentrate the attention of all students on the things that are *not* known. You cannot possibly teach quantum mechanics without mathematics, to be sure, but you can describe the strangeness of the world opened up by quantum theory. Let it be known, early on, that there are deep mysteries, and profound paradoxes, revealed in their distant outlines, by the quantum. Let it be known that these can be approached more closely, and puzzled over, once the language of mathematics has been sufficiently mastered. [20]

Teach at the outset, before any of the fundamentals, the still imponderable puzzles of cosmology. Let it be known, as clearly as possible, by the youngest minds, that there are some things going on in the universe that lie beyond comprehension, and make it plain how little is known.

Do not teach that biology is a useful and perhaps profitable science; that can come later. Teach instead that there are structures squirming inside all our cells, providing all the energy for living, that are essentially foreign creatures, brought in for symbiotic living a billion or so years ago, the lineal descendants of bacteria. Teach that we do not have the ghost of an idea how they got there, where they came from, or how they evolved to their present structure and function. The details of oxidative phosphorylation and photosynthesis can come later.

Teach ecology early on. Let it be understood that the earth's life is a system of interliving, interdependent creatures, and that we do not understand at all how it works. The earth's environment, from the range of atmospheric gases to the chemical constituents of the sea, has been held in an almost unbelievably improbable state of regulated balance since life began, and the regulation of stability and balance is accomplished solely by the life itself, like the internal environment of an immense organism, and we do not know how *that* one works, even less what it means. Teach that.

Go easy, I suggest, on the promises sometimes freely offered by science. Technology relies and depends on science these days, more than ever before, but technology is nothing like the first justification for doing research, nor is it necessarily an essential product to be expected from science. Public decisions about what to have in the way of technology are totally different

---

[5] *Ruskin . . . Leavis . . . Wilson*: John Ruskin (1819–1900), F. R. Leavis (1895–1978), and Edmund Wilson (1895–1972) are major literary critics. Leavis figures prominently in the next essay.

problems from decisions about science, and the two enterprises should not be tangled together. The central task of science is to arrive, stage by stage, at a clearer comprehension of nature, but this does not mean, as it is sometimes claimed to mean, a search for mastery over nature. Science may provide us, one day, with a better understanding of ourselves, but never, I hope, with a set of technologies for doing something or other to improve ourselves. I am made nervous by assertions that human consciousness will someday be unraveled by research, laid out for close scrutiny like the workings of a computer, and then, *and then*! I hope with some fervor that we can learn a lot more than we now know about the human mind, and I see no reason why this strange puzzle should remain forever and entirely beyond us. But I would be deeply disturbed by any prospect that we might use the knowledge in order to begin doing something about it, to improve it, say. This is a different matter from searching for information to use against schizophrenia or dementia, where we are badly in need of technologies, indeed likely one day to be sunk without them. But the ordinary, everyday, more or less normal human mind is too marvelous an instrument ever to be tampered with by anyone, science or no science.

The education of humanists cannot be regarded as complete, or even 25 adequate, without exposure in some depth to where things stand in the various branches of science, and particularly, as I have said, in the areas of our ignorance. This does not mean that I know how to go about doing it, nor am I unaware of the difficulties involved. Physics professors, most of them, look with revulsion on assignments to teach their subject to poets. Biologists, caught up by the enchantment of their new power, armed with flawless instruments to tell the nucleotide sequences of the entire human genome, nearly matching the physicists in the precision of their measurements of living processes, will resist the prospect of broad survey courses; each biology professor will demand that any student in his path must master every fine detail within that professor's research program. The liberal-arts faculties, for their part, will continue to view the scientists with suspicion and apprehension. "What do the scientists want?" asked a Cambridge professor in Francis Cornford's wonderful *Microcosmographia Academica*. "Everything that's going," was the quick answer. That was back in 1912, and universities haven't much changed.

The worst thing that has happened to science education is that the great fun has gone out of it. A very large number of good students look at it as slogging work to be got through on the way to medical school. Others look closely at the premedical students themselves, embattled and bleeding for grades and class standing, and are turned off. Very few see science as the high adventure it really is, the wildest of all explorations ever undertaken by human beings, the chance to catch close views of things never seen before, the shrewdest maneuver for discovering how the world works. Instead, they become baffled early on, and they are misled into thinking that bafflement is simply the result of not having learned all the facts. They are not told, as they should be told, that everyone else — from the professor in his endowed chair down to the platoons of postdoctoral students in the laboratory all night — is baffled as well. Every important scientific advance that has come in looking like an answer has turned, sooner or later — usually sooner — into a question. And the game is just beginning.

An appreciation of what is happening in science today, and of how great a distance lies ahead for exploring, ought to be one of the rewards of a liberal-arts education. It ought to be a good in itself, not something to be acquired on the way to a professional career but part of the cast of thought needed for getting into the kind of century that is now just down the road. Part of the intellectual equipment of an educated person, however his or her time is to be spent, ought to be a feel for the queerness of nature, the inexplicable things.

And maybe, just maybe, a new set of courses dealing systematically with ignorance in science might take hold. The scientists might discover in it a new and subversive technique for catching the attention of students driven by curiosity, delighted and surprised to learn that science is exactly as Bush [6] described it: an "endless frontier." The humanists, for their part, might take considerable satisfaction watching their scientific colleagues confess openly to not knowing everything about everything. And the poets, on whose shoulders the future rests, might, late nights, thinking things over, begin to see some meanings that elude the rest of us. It is worth a try.

[6] *Bush*: Vannevar Bush (1890–1974), electrical engineer, author, and government adviser on science and defense policy.

FROM READING TO REREADING

1. A favorite strategy of essayists is to reverse conventional thinking, to show that something is really the opposite of what it seems. Thomas's strategy of "turn(ing) things around" pervades most of his essay. How does reversal play a part in his case against Lord Kelvin? In his educational proposal?

2. Thomas recommends that there be a "new group of professional thinkers . . . who can create a discipline of scientific criticism." Why does the work of scientists need to be criticized? Do you think Thomas's essay itself is a step in this direction?

3. Although Thomas is critical of science in this essay, he nevertheless enjoys the discipline. What does he like most about it? In what ways is Thomas's enjoyment of science also reflected in his essayistic style? In other words, what similarities can you see between Thomas as a scientist and Thomas as an essayist?

CYNTHIA OZICK

Science and Letters: God's Work — and Ours

In 1959 a British scientist and novelist, C. P. Snow, published a little book that spawned a great debate. The essay-length book called The Two Cultures *made the point that the educated world had become irreparably divided between those who belonged to the realm of arts and humanities and those who belonged to the sciences. Snow argued that the gap between both worlds of endeavor was so great that one group could barely communicate with another — poets had no idea what physicists were talking about, and vice versa. Responses to Snow's argument were intellectually intense and almost seemed to prove Snow's thesis: both worlds argued furiously and neither seemed to understand the other's position. Perhaps the weightiest attack on the "two-culture" doctrine was that of the esteemed Cambridge University literary critic, F. R. Leavis. Leavis didn't accept at all Snow's premise of two cultures, since he didn't believe that scientists even had a culture to begin with. For Leavis, there was only one culture — the culture of arts and letters. Thirty years later, Snow's influential book still provokes debate and is very often cited in essays dealing with the uneasy relations of science and humanities, especially as those relations are felt within the university curriculum. The issue has long occupied the attention of Cynthia Ozick, who has dealt with it in her fiction, and who here examines some new versions of the problem in a short essay written for the* New York Times Book Review *in 1987.*

> For constantly I felt I was moving among two groups — comparable in intelligence, identical in race, not grossly different in social origin, earning about the same incomes, who had almost ceased to communicate at all, who in intellectual, moral and psychological climate had so little in common that . . . one might have crossed an ocean.
> — C. P. Snow, "The Two Cultures and the Scientific Revolution"

D ISRAELI [1] in his novel "Sybil" spoke of "two nations," the rich and the poor. After the progress of more than a century, the phrase (and the reality) remains regrettably apt. But in the less than three decades since C. P. Snow proposed his "two cultures" thesis — the gap of incomprehension between the scientific and literary elites — the conditions of what we still like to call culture have altered so drastically that Snow's arguments are

---

[1] *Disraeli*: Benjamin Disraeli (1804–1881), English prime minister and author.

mostly dissolved into pointlessness. His compatriot and foremost needler, the Cambridge critic F. R. Leavis, had in any case set out to flog Snow's hypothesis from the start. Snow, he said, "rides on an advancing swell of cliché," "doesn't know what literature is" and hasn't "had the advantage of an intellectual discipline of any kind." And besides — here Leavis emitted his final boom — "there is only one culture."

In the long run both were destined to be mistaken — Leavis perhaps more than Snow. In 1959, when Snow published "The Two Cultures," we had already had well over a hundred years to get used to the idea of science as a multidivergent venture — dozens and dozens of disciplines, each one nearly a separate nation with its own governance, psychology, entelechy. It might have been possible to posit, say, a unitary medical culture in the days when barbers were surgeons; but in recent generations we don't expect our dentist to repair a broken kneecap, or our orthopedist to practice cardiology. And nowadays we are learning that an ophthalmologist with an understanding of the cornea is likely to be a bit shaky on the subject of the retina. Engineers are light-years from astrophysicists. Topology is distinct from topography, paleobotany from paleogeology, particle physics from atomic. In reiterating that scientific culture is specialist culture — who doesn't know this? — one risks riding an advancing swell of cliché. Yet science, multiplying, fragmented, in hot pursuit of split ends, is in a way a species of polytheism, or, rather, animism: every grain of matter, every path of conceptualization, has its own ruling spirit, its differentiated lawgiver and traffic director. Investigative diversity and particularizing empiricism have been characteristic of science since — well, since alchemy turned into physical chemistry (and lately into superconductivity); since the teakettle inspired the locomotive; since Icarus took off his wax wings to become Pan Am; since Archimedes stepped out of his tub into Einstein's sea.

Snow was in command of all this, of course — he was pleased to identify himself as an exceptional scientist who wrote novels — and still he chose to make a monolith out of splinters. Why did he do it? In order to have one unanimity confront another. While it may have been a polemical contrivance to present a diversiform scientific culture as unitary, it was patently not wrong, thirty years ago, to speak of literary culture as a single force or presence. That was what was meant by the peaceable word "humanities." And it was what Leavis meant, too, when he growled back at Snow that one culture was all there was worth having. "Don't mistake me," Leavis pressed, "I am not preaching that we should defy, or try to reverse, the accelerating movement of external civilization (the phrase sufficiently explains itself, I hope) that is determined by advancing technology. . . . What I *am* saying is that such a concern is not enough — disastrously not enough." Not enough, he argued, for "a human future . . . in full intelligent possession of its full humanity." For Leavis, technology was the mere outer rind of culture, and the job of literature (the hot core at the heart of culture) was not to oppose science but to humanize it. Only in Snow's wretchedly deprived mind did literature stand apart from science; Snow hardly understood what literature was *for*. And no wonder; Snow's ideas about literary intellectuals came, Leavis sneered, from "the reviewing in the Sunday papers."

It has never been easy to fashion a uniform image of science — which is why we tend to say "the sciences." But until not very long ago one could take it for granted (despite the headlong decline of serious high art) that there was, on the humanities side, a concordant language of sensibility, an embracing impulse toward integration, above all the conviction of human connectedness — even if that conviction occasionally partook of a certain crepuscular nostalgia we might better have done without. Snow pictured literature and science as two angry armies. Leavis announced that there was only one army, with literature as its commander in chief. Yet it was plain that both Leavis and Snow, for all their antagonisms, saw the kingdom of letters as an intact and enduring power.

This feeling for literary culture as a glowing wholeness — it *was* a feeling, a stirring, a flush of idealism — is now altogether dissipated. The fragrant term that encapsulated it — belles-lettres — is nearly archaic and surely effete: it smacks of leather tooling for the moneyed, of posturing. But it was once useful enough. Belles-lettres stood for a binding thread of observation and civilizing emotion. It signified not so much that letters are beautiful as that the house of letters is encompassingly humane and undivisive, no matter how severally its windows are shaped, or who looks out or in. Poets, scholars, journalists, librarians, novelists, playwrights, art critics, philosophers, historians, political theorists and all the rest may have inhabited different rooms, differently furnished, but it was indisputably one house with a single roof and plenty of connecting doors and passageways. And sometimes — so elastic and compressive was the humanist principle — poet, scholar, essayist, philosopher, etc., all lived side by side in the same head. Seamlessness (even if only an illusion) never implied locked and separate cells.

And now? Look around. Now "letters" suggest a thousand enemy camps, "genres" like fortresses, professions isolated by crocodiled moats. The living tissue of intuition and inference that nurtured the commonalty of the humanities is ruptured by an abrupt invasion of specialists. In emulation of the sciences? But we don't often hear of astronomers despising molecular biologists; in science, it may be natural for knowledge to run, like quicksilver, into crannies.

In the ex-community of letters, factions are in fashion, and the business of factions is to despise. Matthew Arnold's[2] mild and venerable dictum, an open-ended, open-armed, definition of literature that clearly intends a nobility of inclusiveness — "the best that is known and thought in the

[2] *Matthew Arnold* (1822–1888): English poet and critic who as an Oxford professor exerted an enormous influence on literary education.

world" — earns latter-day assaults and jeers. What can all that mean now but "canon," and what can a received canon mean but reactionary, racist, sexist, elitist closure? Politics presses against disinterestedness; all categories are suspect, no category is allowed to display its wares without the charge of enslavement by foregone conclusion and vested interest. What Arnold called the play of mind is asked to show its credentials and prove its legitimacy. "Our organs of criticism," Arnold complained in 1864 (a period as uninnocent as our own), "are organs of men and parties having practical ends to serve, and with them those practical ends are the first thing and the play of mind the second."

And so it is with us. The culture of the humanities has split and split and split again, always for reasons of partisan ascendancy and scorn. Once it was not unusual for writers — Dreiser, Stephen Crane, Cather, Hemingway! — to turn to journalism for a taste of the workings of the world. Today novelists and journalists are alien breeds reared apart, as if imagination properly belonged only to the one and never to the other; as if society and instinct were designed for estrangement. The two crafts are contradictory even in method; journalists are urged to tell secrets in the top line; novelists insinuate suspensefully, and wait for the last line to spill the real beans. Dickens, saturated in journalism, excelled at shorthand; was a court reporter; edited topical magazines.

In the literary academy, Jacques Derrida has the authority that Duns Scotus [3] had for medieval scholastics — and it is authority, not literature, that mainly engages faculties. In the guise of maverick or rebel, professors kowtow to dogma. English departments have set off after theory, and use culture as an instrument to illustrate doctrinal principles, whether Marxist or "French Freud." The play of mind gives way to signing up and lining up. College teachers were never so cut off from the heat of poets dead or alive as they are now; only think of the icy distances separating syllables by, say, Marianne Moore, A. R. Ammons, May Swenson or Amy Clampitt from the papers read at last winter's Modern Language Association meeting — viz., "Written Discourse as Dialogic Interaction," "Abduction, Transference, and the Reading Stage," "The Politics of Feminism and the Discourse of Feminist Literary Criticism."

And more: poets trivialize novelists, novelists trivialize poets. Both   10
trivialize critics. Critics trivialize reviewers. Reviewers report that they *are* critics. Short-story writers assert transfigurations unavailable to novelists. Novelists declare the incomparable glories of the long pull. Novelizing es-

---

[3] *Derrida . . . Duns Scotus*: Jacques Derrida (b. 1930), contemporary French philosopher whose writings have shaped much modern critical theory; Duns Scotus (1265?–1308), Scottish theologian and philosopher of the Middle Ages. Both men were interested in the philosophy of language.

theticians, admitting to literature no claims of moral intent, ban novelizing moralists. The moralists condemn the estheticians as precious, barren, solipsist. Few essayists essay fiction. Few novelists hazard essays. Denselanguage writers vilify minimalists. Writers of plain prose ridicule complex sentences. Professors look down on commercial publishers. Fiction writers dread university presses. The so-called provinces envy and despise the provinciality of New York. New York sees sour grapes in California and everywhere else. The so-called mainstream judges which writers are acceptably universal and which are to be exiled as "parochial." The so-called parochial, stung or cowardly or both, fear all particularity and attempt impersonation of the acceptable. "Star" writers — recall the International PEN [4] Congress in New York last year — treat lesser-knowns as invisible, negligible. The lesser-knowns, crushed, disparage the stars.

And even the public library, once the unchallenged repository of the best that is known and thought, begins to split itself off, abandons its mandate and rents out Polaroid cameras and videotapes, like some semiphilanthropic Crazy Eddie. My own local library, appearing to jettison the basic arguments of the age, flaunts shelf after shelf prominently marked Decorating, Consumer Power, How-To, Cookery, Hooray for Hollywood, Accent on You, What Makes Us Laugh and many more such chitchat categories. But there are no placards for Literature, History, Biography; and Snow and Leavis, whom I needed to moon over in order to get started on this essay, were neither one to be had. (I found them finally in the next town, in a much smaller if more traditionally bookish library.)

Though it goes against the grain of respected current belief to say so, literature is really *about* something. It is about us. That may be why we are drawn to think of the kingdom of letters as a unity, at least in potential. Science, teeming and multiform, is about how the earth and the heavens and the microbes and the insects and our mammalian bodies are constructed, but literature is about the meaning of the finished construction. Or, to set afloat a more transcendent vocabulary: science is about God's work; literature is about our work. If our work lies untended (and what is our work but aspiration?), if literary culture falls into a heap of adversarial splinters — into competing contemptuous clamorers for turf and mental dominance — then what will be left to tell us that we are one human presence?

To forward that strenuous telling, Matthew Arnold (himself now among the jettisoned) advised every reader and critic to "try and possess one great literature, at least, besides his own; and the more unlike his own, the better." Not to split off from but to add on to the kingdom of letters: so as to uncover its human face.

An idea which — in a time of ten thousand self-segregating literary technologies — may be unwanted, if not obsolete.

---

[4] *PEN*: International Association of Poets, Playwrights, Editors, Essayists, and Novelists.

FROM READING TO REREADING

1. Cynthia Ozick opens her essay with a summary of the Snow–Leavis debate, even though she believes both writers were mistaken. In what ways does she think they were mistaken? How are their mistakes relevant to her essay?

2. Ozick says that Snow "pictured literature and science as two angry armies." How does this image control much of her word choice? Comment on the effect this has on her tone and style.

3. Despite their differences, Ozick argues that both Leavis and Snow "saw the kingdom of letters as an intact and enduring power." According to Ozick, what conditions helped sustain literature's wholeness and power? What does she see as happening to "the kingdom of letters"? In what way does she view this as a contemporary problem? Why is it a problem?

STEPHEN JAY GOULD
Darwin's Middle Road

Stephen Jay Gould has written extensively on Darwin and is one of our finest explicators of what the theory of natural selection truly means. In "Darwin's Middle Road," however, he examines not so much the meaning of Darwin's still astounding theory as the mental processes by which Darwin reached it. As usual with Gould, one topic becomes a pretext for investigating another, and thus in the course of the essay Gould also provides us with an insight into the dynamics of scientific creativity. "Darwin's Middle Road" first appeared in Natural History *magazine and was collected in Gould's second volume of essays,* The Panda's Thumb *(1980).*

W E BEGAN to sail up the narrow strait lamenting," narrates Odysseus. "For on the one hand lay Scylla, with twelve feet all dangling down; and six necks exceeding long, and on each a hideous head, and therein three rows of teeth set thick and close, full of black death. And on the other mighty Charybdis sucked down the salt sea water. As often as she belched it forth, like a cauldron on a great fire she would seethe up through all her troubled deeps." Odysseus managed to swerve around Charybdis, but Scylla grabbed six of his finest men and devoured them in his sight — "the most pitiful thing mine eyes have seen of all my travail in searching out the paths of the sea." [1]

False lures and dangers often come in pairs in our legends and metaphors — consider the frying pan and the fire, or the devil and the deep blue sea. Prescriptions for avoidance either emphasize a dogged steadiness — the straight and narrow of Christian evangelists — or an averaging between unpleasant alternatives — the golden mean of Aristotle. The idea of steering a course between undesirable extremes emerges as a central prescription for a sensible life.

The nature of scientific creativity is both a perennial topic of discussion and a prime candidate for seeking a golden mean. The two extreme positions have not been directly competing for allegiance of the unwary. They have, rather, replaced each other sequentially, with one now in the ascendency, the other eclipsed.

The first — inductivism — held that great scientists are primarily great observers and patient accumulators of information. For new and significant theory, the inductivists claimed, can only arise from a firm foundation of

[1] *We began. . . . sea:* Gould opens with an episode from Homer's epic poem, the *Odyssey.*

facts. In this architectural view, each fact is a brick in a structure built without blueprints. Any talk or thought about theory (the completed building) is fatuous and premature before the bricks are set. Inductivism once commanded great prestige within science, and even represented an "official" position of sorts, for it touted, however falsely, the utter honesty, complete objectivity, and almost automatic nature of scientific progress toward final and incontrovertible truth.

Yet, as its critics so rightly claimed, inductivism also depicted science   5 as a heartless, almost inhuman discipline offering no legitimate place to quirkiness, intuition, and all the other subjective attributes adhering to our vernacular notion of genius. Great scientists, the critics claimed, are distinguished more by their powers of hunch and synthesis, than their skill in experiment or observation. The criticisms of inductivism are certainly valid and I welcome its dethroning during the past thirty years as a necessary prelude to better understanding. Yet, in attacking it so strongly, some critics have tried to substitute an alternative equally extreme and unproductive in its emphasis on the essential subjectivity of creative thought. In this "eureka" view, creativity is an ineffable something, accessible only to persons of genius. It arises like a bolt of lightning, unanticipated, unpredictable and unanalyzable — but the bolts strike only a few special people. We ordinary mortals must stand in awe and thanks. (The name refers, of course, to the legendary story of Archimedes running naked through the streets of Syracuse shouting *eureka* [I have discovered it] when water displaced by his bathing body washed the scales abruptly from his eyes and suggested a method for measuring volumes.)

I am equally disenchanted by both these opposing extremes. Inductivism reduces genius to dull, rote operations; eurekaism grants it an inaccessible status more in the domain of intrinsic mystery than in a realm where we might understand and learn from it. Might we not marry the good features of each view, and abandon both the elitism of eurekaism and the pedestrian qualities of inductivism. May we not acknowledge the personal and subjective character of creativity, but still comprehend it as a mode of thinking that emphasizes or exaggerates capacities sufficiently common to all of us that we may at least understand if not hope to imitate.

In the hagiography of science, a few men hold such high positions that all arguments must apply to them if they are to have any validity. Charles Darwin, as the principal saint of evolutionary biology, has therefore been presented both as an inductivist and as a primary example of eurekaism. I will attempt to show that these interpretations are equally inadequate, and that recent scholarship on Darwin's own odyssey toward the theory of natural selection supports an intermediate position.

So great was the prestige of inductivism in his own day, that Darwin himself fell under its sway and, as an old man, falsely depicted his youthful accomplishments in its light. In an autobiography, written as a lesson in morality for his children and not intended for publication, he penned some famous lines that misled historians for nearly a hundred years. Describing his path to the theory of natural selection, he claimed: "I worked on true Baconian [2] principles, and without any theory collected facts on a wholesale scale."

The inductivist interpretation focuses on Darwin's five years aboard the *Beagle* and explains his transition from a student for the ministry to the nemesis of preachers as the result of his keen powers of observation applied to the whole world. Thus, the traditional story goes, Darwin's eyes opened wider and wider as he saw, in sequence, the bones of giant South American fossil mammals, the turtles and finches of the Galapagos, and the marsupial fauna of Australia. The truth of evolution and its mechanism of natural selection crept up gradually upon him as he sifted facts in a sieve of utter objectivity.

The inadequacies of this tale are best illustrated by the falsity of its conventional premier example — the so-called Darwin's finches of the Galapagos. We now know that although these birds share a recent and common ancestry on the South American mainland, they have radiated into an impressive array of species on the outlying Galapagos. Few terrestrial species manage to cross the wide oceanic barrier between South America and the Galapagos. But the fortunate migrants often find a sparsely inhabited world devoid of the competitors that limit their opportunities on the crowded mainland. Hence, the finches evolved into roles normally occupied by other birds and developed their famous set of adaptations for feeding — seed crushing, insect eating, even grasping and manipulating a cactus needle to dislodge insects from plants. Isolation — both of the islands from the mainland and among the islands themselves — provided an opportunity for separation, independent adaptation, and speciation.

According to the traditional view, Darwin discovered these finches, correctly inferred their history, and wrote the famous lines in his notebook: "If there is the slightest foundation for these remarks the zoology of Archipelagoes will be worth examining; for such facts would undermine the stability of Species." But, as with so many heroic tales from Washington's cherry tree to the piety of Crusaders, hope rather than truth motivates the common reading. Darwin found the finches to be sure. But he didn't recognize them as variants of a common stock. In fact, he didn't even record the island of discovery for many of them — some of his labels just read "Galapagos Islands." So much for his immediate recognition of the role of isolation in the formation of new species. He reconstructed the evolutionary tale only after his return to London, when a British Museum ornithologist correctly identified all the birds as finches.

---

[2] *Baconian*: Darwin is referring to the scientific principles of Francis Bacon (1561–1616), the English essayist and philosopher who emphasized observation and inductive reasoning.

The famous quotation from his notebook refers to Galapagos tortoises and to the claim of native inhabitants that they can "at once pronounce from which Island any Tortoise may have been brought" from subtle differences in size and shape of body and scales. This is a statement of different, and much reduced, order from the traditional tale of finches. For the finches are true and separate species — a living example of evolution. The subtle differences among tortoises represent minor geographic variation within a species. It is a jump in reasoning, albeit a valid one as we now know, to argue that such small differences can be amplified to produce a new species. All creationists, after all, acknowledged geographic variation (consider human races), but argued that it could not proceed beyond the rigid limits of a created archetype.

I don't wish to downplay the pivotal influence of the *Beagle* voyage on Darwin's career. It gave him space, freedom and endless time to think in his favored mode of independent self-stimulation. (His ambivalence toward university life, and his middling performance there by conventional standards, reflected his unhappiness with a curriculum of received wisdom.) He writes from South America in 1834: "I have not one clear idea about cleavage, stratification, lines of upheaval. I have no books, which tell me much and what they do I cannot apply to what I see. In consequence I draw my own conclusions, and most gloriously ridiculous ones they are." The rocks and plants and animals that he saw did provoke him to the crucial attitude of doubt — midwife of all creativity. Sydney, Australia — 1836. Darwin wonders why a rational God would create so many marsupials on Australia since nothing about its climate or geography suggests any superiority for pouches: "I had been lying on a sunny bank and was reflecting on the strange character of the animals of this country as compared to the rest of the World. An unbeliever in everything beyond his own reason might exclaim, 'Surely two distinct Creators must have been at work.'"

Nonetheless, Darwin returned to London without an evolutionary theory. He suspected the truth of evolution, but had no mechanism to explain it. Natural selection did not arise from any direct reading of the *Beagle*'s facts, but from two subsequent years of thought and struggle as reflected in a series of remarkable notebooks that have been unearthed and published during the past twenty years. In these notebooks, we see Darwin testing and abandoning a number of theories and pursuing a multitude of false leads — so much for his later claim about recording facts with an empty mind. He read philosophers, poets, and economists, always searching for meaning and insight — so much for the notion that natural selection arose inductively from the *Beagle*'s facts. Later, he labeled one notebook as "full of metaphysics on morals."

Yet if this tortuous path belies the Scylla of inductivism, it has engendered an equally simplistic myth — the Charybdis of eurekaism. In his maddeningly misleading autobiography, Darwin does record a eureka and suggests that natural selection struck him as a sudden, serendipitous flash after more than a year of groping frustration:

> In October 1838, that is, fifteen months after I had begun my systematic inquiry, I happened to read for amusement Malthus on Population, [3] and being well prepared to appreciate the struggle for existence which every-where goes on from long-continued observation of the habits of animals and plants, it at once struck me that under these circumstances favorable variations would tend to be preserved, and unfavorable ones to be destroyed. The result of this would be the formation of new species. Here, then, I had at last got a theory by which to work.

Yet, again, the notebooks belie Darwin's later recollections — in this case by their utter failure to record, at the time it happened, any special exultation over his Malthusian insight. He inscribes it as a fairly short and sober entry without a single exclamation point, though he habitually used two or three in moments of excitement. He did not drop everything and reinterpret a confusing world in its light. On the very next day, he wrote an even longer passage on the sexual curiosity of primates.

The theory of natural selection arose neither as a workmanlike induction from nature's facts, nor as a mysterious bolt from Darwin's subconscious, triggered by an accidental reading of Malthus. It emerged instead as the result of a conscious and productive search, proceeding in a ramifying but ordered manner, and utilizing both the facts of natural history and an astonishingly broad range of insights from disparate disciplines far from his own. Darwin trod the middle path between inductivism and eurekaism. His genius is neither pedestrian nor inaccessible.

Darwinian scholarship has exploded since the centennial of the *Origin* in 1959. The publication of Darwin's notebooks and the attention devoted by several scholars to the two crucial years between the *Beagle*'s docking and the demoted Malthusian insight has clinched the argument for a "middle path" theory of Darwin's creativity. Two particularly important works focus on the broadest and narrowest scales. Howard E. Gruber's masterful intellectual and psychological biography of this phase in Darwin's life, *Darwin on Man*, traces all the false leads and turning points in Darwin's search. Gruber shows that Darwin was continually proposing, testing, and abandoning hypotheses, and that he never simply collected facts in a blind way. He began with a fanciful theory involving the idea that new species arise with a prefixed life span, and worked his way gradually, if fitfully, toward an idea of extinction by competition in a world of struggle. He recorded no exultation upon reading Malthus, because the jigsaw puzzle was only missing a piece or two at the time.

Silvan S. Schweber has reconstructed, in detail as minute as the record

---

[3] *Malthus on Population*: Thomas Malthus (1766–1834), English economist who published his *Essay on the Principle of Population* in 1798.

will allow, Darwin's activities during the few weeks before Malthus (The Origin of the *Origin* Revisited, *Journal of the History of Biology*, 1977). He argues that the final pieces arose not from new facts in natural history, but from Darwin's intellectual wanderings in distant fields. In particular, he read a long review of social scientist and philosopher Auguste Comte's[4] most famous work, the *Cours de philosophie positive*. He was particularly struck by Comte's insistence that a proper theory be predictive and at least potentially quantitative. He then turned to Dugald Stewart's *On the Life and Writing of Adam Smith*,[5] and imbibed the basic belief of the Scottish economists that theories of overall social structure must begin by analyzing the unconstrained actions of individuals. (Natural selection is, above all, a theory about the struggle of individual organisms for success in reproduction.) Then, searching for quantification, he read a lengthy analysis of work by the most famous statistician of his time — the Belgian Adolphe Quetelet. In the review of Quetelet, he found, among other things, a forceful statement of Malthus's quantitative claim — that population would grow geometrically and food supplies only arithmetically, thus guaranteeing an intense struggle for existence. In fact, Darwin had read the Malthusian statement several times before; but only now was he prepared to appreciate its significance. Thus, he did not turn to Malthus by accident, and he already knew what it contained. His "amusement," we must assume, consisted only in a desire to read in its original formulation the familiar statement that had so impressed him in Quetelet's secondary account.

In reading Schweber's detailed account of the moments preceding [20] Darwin's formulation of natural selection, I was particularly struck by the absence of deciding influence from his own field of biology. The immediate precipitators were a social scientist, an economist, and a statistician. If genius has any common denominator, I would propose breadth of interest and the ability to construct fruitful analogies between fields.

In fact, I believe that the theory of natural selection should be viewed as an extended analogy — whether conscious or unconscious on Darwin's part I do not know — to the laissez faire economics of Adam Smith. The essence of Smith's argument is a paradox of sorts: if you want an ordered economy providing maximal benefits to all, then let individuals compete and struggle for their own advantages. The result, after appropriate sorting and elimination of the inefficient, will be a stable and harmonious polity. Apparent order arises naturally from the struggle among individuals, not from predestined principles or higher control. Dugald Stewart epitomized Smith's system in the book Darwin read:

[4] *Auguste Comte* (1798–1857): French philosopher and founder of positivism, a philosophy that attempted to coordinate all of the sciences. Comte named what he considered the most important of the sciences "sociology."

[5] *Adam Smith* (1723–1790): Scottish economist and philosopher; published his major work *An Inquiry Into the Nature and Causes of the Wealth of Nations* in 1770.

> The most effective plan for advancing a people . . . is by allowing every man, as long as he observes the rules of justice, to pursue his own interest in his own way, and to bring both his industry and his capital into the freest competition with those of his fellow citizens. Every system of policy which endeavors . . . to draw towards a particular species of industry a greater share of the capital of the society than would naturally go to it . . . is, in reality, subversive of the great purpose which it means to promote.

As Schweber states: "The Scottish analysis of society contends that the combined effect of individual actions results in the institutions upon which society is based, and that such a society is a stable and evolving one and functions without a designing and directing mind."

We know that Darwin's uniqueness does not reside in his support for the idea of evolution — scores of scientists had preceded him in this. His special contribution rests upon his documentation and upon the novel character of his theory about how evolution operates. Previous evolutionists had proposed unworkable schemes based on internal perfecting tendencies and inherent directions. Darwin advocated a natural and testable theory based on immediate interaction among individuals (his opponents considered it heartlessly mechanistic). The theory of natural selection is a creative transfer to biology of Adam Smith's basic argument for a rational economy: the balance and order of nature does not arise from a higher, external (divine) control, or from the existence of laws operating directly upon the whole, but from struggle among individuals for their own benefits (in modern terms, for the transmission of their genes to future generations through differential success in reproduction).

Many people are distressed to hear such an argument. Does it not compromise the integrity of science if some of its primary conclusions originate by analogy from contemporary politics and culture rather than from data of the discipline itself? In a famous letter to Engels, [6] Karl Marx identified the similarities between natural selection and the English social scene:

> It is remarkable how Darwin recognizes among beasts and plants his English society with its division of labor, competition, opening up of new markets, "invention," and the Malthusian "struggle for existence." It is Hobbes' [7] *bellum omnium contra omnes* (the war of all against all).

Yet Marx was a great admirer of Darwin — and in this apparent paradox lies resolution. For reasons involving all the themes I have emphasized here — that inductivism is inadequate, that creativity demands breadth, and that analogy is a profound source of insight — great thinkers cannot be divorced from their social background. But the source of an idea is one thing; its truth

[6] *Engels*: Friedrich Engels (1820–1895), German socialist philosopher who collaborated with Karl Marx in writing the *Communist Manifesto* in 1848.

[7] *Hobbes'*: In *The Leviathan*, English political philosopher Thomas Hobbes (1588–1679) argued that human beings would live in anarchy — the war of all against all — if there were no absolute authority.

or fruitfulness is another. The psychology and utility of discovery are very different subjects indeed. Darwin may have cribbed the idea of natural selection from economics, but it may still be right. As the German socialist Karl Kautsky wrote in 1902: "The fact that an idea emanates from a particular class, or accords with their interests, of course proves nothing as to its truth or falsity." In this case, it is ironic that Adam Smith's system of laissez faire does not work in his own domain of economics, for it leads to oligopoly and revolution, rather than to order and harmony. Struggle among individuals does, however, seem to be the law of nature.

Many people use such arguments about social context to ascribe great insights primarily to the indefinable phenomenon of good luck. Thus, Darwin was lucky to be born rich, lucky to be on the *Beagle*, lucky to live amidst the ideas of his age, lucky to trip over Parson Malthus — essentially little more than a man in the right place at the right time. Yet, when we read of his personal struggle to understand, the breadth of his concerns and study, and the directedness of his search for a mechanism of evolution, we understand why Pasteur[8] made his famous quip that fortune favors the prepared mind.

[8] *Pasteur*: Louis Pasteur (1822–1895), French chemist and microbiologist.

FROM READING TO REREADING

1. Consider Gould's essay from the perspective of C. P. Snow's "two cultures" outlined in the preceding essay. In what ways does Gould appear to bridge the gap between science and literature? How is this bridging reflected in his style and examples? How is it reflected in his assessment of Darwin's thinking itself?

2. Though Gould accepts both the inductive and "eureka" approach, he does not believe that either one taken by itself can sufficiently explain scientific creativity. Why is this? What does each method or approach leave out?

3. Note that Gould's final assessment of Darwin's singular genius puts the emphasis on analogy. What is analogy? How does it pertain to both science and humanities? How does it pertain to writing? How, for example, does Gould's opening paragraph supply us with an instance of analogical thinking?

ANNIE DILLARD
Stalking

This richly textured, mosaic-like essay may at first seem more appropriate to Part 6, "Other Creatures." But in its gradual evolution, the essay reveals more and more a particular kind of scientific imagination, one that sees no intrinsic separation between one's painstaking observations of nature and one's unpredictable rushes of insight. "I am no scientist," Dillard warns her readers elsewhere, offering a more modest account of her activities: "I explore the neighborhood." Whether such exploration is, strictly speaking, science or not, the explorations that make up "Stalking" lead Dillard to considerations that reach directly to the heart of modern scientific thinking. "Stalking" is a chapter from Dillard's Pulitzer Prize–winning nonfiction book, Pilgrim at Tinker Creek *(1974), and contains a few casual references to earlier portions of the book.*

1

SUMMER: I GO DOWN to the creek again, and lead a creek life. I watch and stalk.

The Eskimos' life changes in summer, too. The caribou flee from the inland tundra's mosquitos to the windy shores of the Arctic Ocean, and coastal Eskimos hunt them there. In the old days before they had long-range rifles, the men had to approach the wary animals very closely for a kill. Sometimes, waiting for a favorable change of weather so they could rush in unseen and unscented, the Eskimos would have to follow the fleet herds on foot for days, sleepless.

Also in summer they dredge for herring with nets from shoreline camps. In the open water off the Mackenzie River delta, they hunt the white whale (the beluga) and bearded seal. They paddle their slender kayaks inland to fresh water and hunt muskrats, too, which they used to snare or beat with sticks.

To travel from camp to camp in summer, coastal Eskimos ply the open seas in big umiaks paddled by women. They eat fish, goose or duck eggs, fresh meat, and anything else they can get, including fresh "salad" of greens still raw in a killed caribou's stomach and dressed with the delicate acids of digestion.

On St. Lawrence Island, women and children are in charge of netting little birds. They have devised a cruel and ingenious method: after they net a few birds with great effort and after much stalking, they thread them alive and squawking through their beaks' nostrils, and fly them like living kites at the end of long lines. The birds fly frantically, trying to escape, but they cannot, and their flapping efforts attract others of their kind, curious — and the Eskimos easily net the others.

They used to make a kind of undershirt out of bird skins, which they wore under fur parkas in cold weather, and left on inside the igloos after they'd taken the parkas off. It was an elaborate undertaking, this making of a bird-skin shirt, requiring thousands of tiny stitches. For thread they had the stringy sinew found along a caribou's backbone. The sinew had to be dried, frayed, and twisted into a clumsy thread. Its only advantages were that it swelled in water, making seams more or less waterproof, and it generally contained a minute smear of fat, so if they were starving they could suck their sewing thread and add maybe five minutes to their lives. For needles they had shards of bone, which got thinner and shorter every time they pushed through tough skins, so that an old needle might be little more than a barely enclosed slit. When the Eskimos first met the advanced culture of the south, men and women alike admired it first and foremost for its sturdy sewing needles. For it is understood that without good clothing, you perish. A crewman from a whaler with a paper of needles in his pocket could save many lives, and was welcome everywhere as the rich and powerful always are.

I doubt that they make bird-skin shirts anymore, steel needles or no. They do not do many of the old things at all any more, except in my mind, where they hunt and stitch well, with an animal skill, in silhouette always against white oceans of ice.

Down here, the heat is on. Even a bird-skin shirt would be too much. In the cool of the evening I take to the bridges over the creek. I am prying into secrets again, and taking my chances. I might see anything happen; I might see nothing but light on the water. I walk home exhilarated or becalmed, but always changed, alive. "It scatters and gathers," Heraclitus [1] said, "it comes and goes." And I want to be in the way of its passage, and cooled by its invisible breath.

In summer, I stalk. Summer leaves obscure, heat dazzles, and creatures hide from the red-eyed sun, and me. I have to seek things out. The creatures I seek have several senses and free will; it becomes apparent that they do not wish to be seen. I can stalk them in either of two ways. The first is not what you think of as true stalking, but it is the *Via negativa,* [2] and as fruitful as actual pursuit. When I stalk this way I take my stand on a bridge and wait, emptied. I put myself in the way of the creature's passage, like spring Eskimos at a seal's breathing hole. Something might come; something might

---

[1] *Heraclitus* (c. 540–c. 480 B.C.): Pre-Socratic Greek philosopher who held that everything was continually in flux.

[2] *Via negativa*: The negative way (Latin).

go. I am Newton under the apple tree, Buddha under the bo. Stalking the other way, I forge my own passage seeking the creature. I wander the banks; what I find, I follow, doggedly, like Eskimos haunting the caribou herds. I am Wilson [3] squinting after the traces of electrons in a cloud chamber; I am Jacob at Peniel wrestling with the angel. [4]

Fish are hard to see either way. Although I spend most of the summer   10
stalking muskrats, I think it is fish even more than muskrats that by their very mystery and hiddenness crystalize the quality of my summer life at the creek. A thick spawning of fish, a bedful of fish, is too much, horror; but I walk out of my way in hopes of glimpsing three bluegills bewitched in a pool's depth or rising to floating petals or bubbles.

The very act of trying to see fish makes them almost impossible to see. My eyes are awkward instruments whose casing is clumsily outsized. If I face the sun along a bank I cannot see into the water; instead of fish I see water striders, the reflected undersides of leaves, birds' bellies, clouds and blue sky. So I cross to the opposite bank and put the sun at my back. Then I can see into the water perfectly within the blue shadow made by my body; but as soon as that shadow looms across them, the fish vanish in a flurry of flashing tails.

Occasionally by waiting still on a bridge or by sneaking smoothly into the shade of a bankside tree, I see fish slowly materialize in the shallows, one by one, swimming around and around in a silent circle, each one washed in a blue like the sky's and all as tapered as tears. Or I see them suspended in a line in deep pools, parallel to the life-giving current, literally "stream-lined." Because fish have swim bladders filled with gas that balances their weight in the water, they are actually hanging from their own bodies, as it were, as gondolas hang from balloons. They wait suspended and seemingly motionless in clear water; they look dead, under a spell, or captured in amber. They look like the expressionless parts hung in a mobile, which has apparently suggested itself to mobile designers. Fish! They manage to be so water-colored. Theirs is not the color of the bottom but the color of the light itself, the light dissolved like a powder in the water. They disappear and reappear as if by spontaneous generation: sleight of fish.

I am coming around to fish as spirit. The Greek acronym for some of the names of Christ yields *ichthys*, Christ as fish, and fish as Christ. The more I glimpse the fish in Tinker Creek, the more satisfying the coincidence becomes, the richer the symbol, not only for Christ but for the spirit as well. The people must live. Imagine for a Mediterranean people how much easier it is to haul up free, fed fish in nets than to pasture hungry herds on those

---

[3] *Wilson*: Charles Thomas Rees Wilson (1869–1959), British physicist and 1927 Nobel Prize winner.

[4] *Jacob . . . angel*: Reference to Genesis 32:24–30.

bony hills and feed them through a winter. To say that holiness is a fish is a statement of the abundance of grace; it is the equivalent of affirming in a purely materialistic culture that money does indeed grow on trees. "Not as the world gives do I give to you"; these fish are spirit food. And revelation is a study in stalking: "Cast the net on the right side of the ship, and ye shall find."

Still — of course — there is a risk. More men in all of time have died at fishing than at any other human activity except perhaps the making of war. You go out so far . . . and you are blown, or stove, or swamped, and never seen again. Where are the fish? Out in the underwater gaps, out where the winds are, wary, adept, invisible. You can lure them, net them, troll for them, club them, clutch them, chase them up an inlet, stun them with plant juice, catch them in a wooden wheel that runs all night — and you still might starve. They are there, they are certainly there, free, food, and wholly fleeting. You can see them if you want to; catch them if you can.

It scatters and gathers; it comes and goes. I might see a monstrous carp 15 heave out of the water and disappear in a smack of foam, I might see a trout emerge in a riffle under my dangling hand, or I might see only a flash of back parts fleeing. It is the same all summer long, all year long, no matter what I seek. Lately I have given myself over almost entirely to stalking muskrats — eye food. I found out the hard way that waiting is better than pursuing; now I usually sit on a narrow pedestrian bridge at a spot where the creek is shallow and wide. I sit alone and alert, but stilled in a special way, waiting and watching for a change in the water, for the tremulous ripples rising in intensity that signal the appearance of a living muskrat from the underwater entrance to its den. Muskrats are cautious. Many, many evenings I wait without seeing one. But sometimes it turns out that the focus of my waiting is misdirected, as if Buddha had been expecting the fall of an apple. For when the muskrats don't show, something else does.

I positively ruined the dinner of a green heron on the creek last week. It was fairly young and fairly determined not to fly away, but not to be too foolhardy, either. So it had to keep an eye on me. I watched it for half an hour, during which time it stalked about in the creek moodily, expanding and contracting its incredible, brown-streaked neck. It made only three lightning-quick stabs at strands of slime for food, and all three times occurred when my head was turned slightly away.

The heron was in calm shallows; the deepest water it walked in went two inches up its orange legs. It would go and get something from the cattails on the side, and, when it had eaten it — tossing up its beak and contracting its throat in great gulps — it would plod back to a dry sandbar in the center of the creek which seemed to serve as its observation tower. It wagged its stubby tail up and down; its tail was so short it did not extend beyond its folded wings.

Mostly it just watched me warily, as if I might shoot it, or steal its minnows for my own supper, if it did not stare me down. But my only weapon was stillness, and my only wish its continued presence before my eyes. I knew it would fly away if I made the least false move. In half an hour it got used to me — as though I were a bicycle somebody had abandoned on the bridge, or a branch left by high water. It even suffered me to turn my head slowly, and to stretch my aching legs very slowly. But finally, at the end, some least motion or thought set it off, and it rose, glancing at me with a cry, and winged slowly away upstream, around a bend, and out of sight.

I find it hard to see anything about a bird that it does not want seen. It demands my full attention. Several times waiting for muskrats, however, I have watched insects doing various special things who were, like the mantis laying her eggs, happily oblivious to my presence. Twice I was not certain what I had seen.

Once it was a dragonfly flying low over the creek in an unusual rhythm. 20 I looked closely; it was dipping the tip of its abdomen in the water very quickly, over and over. It was flying in a series of tight circles, just touching the water at the very bottom arc of each circle. The only thing I could imagine it was doing was laying eggs, and this later proved to be the case. I actually saw this, I thought — I actually saw a dragonfly laying her eggs not five feet away.

It is this peculiar stitching motion of the dragonfly's abdomen that earned it the name "darning needle" — parents used to threaten their children by saying that, if the children told lies, dragonflies would hover over their faces as they slept and sew their lips together. Interestingly, I read that only the great speed at which the egg-laying female dragonfly flies over the water prevents her from being "caught by the surface tension and pulled down." And at that same great speed the dragonfly I saw that day whirred away, downstream: a drone, a dot, and then gone.

Another time I saw a water strider behaving oddly. When there is nothing whatsoever to see, I watch the water striders skate over the top of the water, and I watch the six dots of shade — made by their feet dimpling the water's surface — slide dreamily over the bottom silt. Their motion raises tiny ripples or wavelets ahead of them over the water's surface, and I had noticed that when they feel or see these ripples coming towards them, they tend to turn away from the ripples' source. In other words, they avoid each other. I figure this behavior has the effect of distributing them evenly over an area, giving them each a better chance at whatever it is they eat.

But one day I was staring idly at the water when something out of the ordinary triggered my attention. A strider was skating across the creek purposefully instead of randomly. Instead of heading away from ripples made by another insect, it was racing towards them. At the center of the ripples I saw that some sort of small fly had fallen into the water and was struggling to right itself. The strider acted extremely "interested"; it jerked after the fly's frantic efforts, following it across the creek and back again, inching closer and closer like Eskimos stalking caribou. The fly could not escape the surface tension. Its efforts were diminishing to an occasional buzz; it floated against the bank, and the strider pursued it there — but I could not see what happened, because overhanging grasses concealed the spot.

Again, only later did I learn what I had seen. I read that striders are attracted to any light. According to William H. Amos, "Often the attracting light turns out to be the reflections off the ripples set up by an insect trapped on the surface, and it is on such creatures that the striders feed." They suck them dry. Talk about living on jetsam! At any rate, it will be easy enough to watch for this again this summer. I especially want to see if the slow ripples set up by striders themselves reflect less light than the ripples set up by trapped insects — but it might be years before I happen to see another insect fall on the water among striders. I was lucky to have seen it once. Next time I will know what is happening, and if they want to play the last bloody act offstage, I will just part the curtain of grasses and hope I sleep through the night.

2

Learning to stalk muskrats took me several years.   25

I've always known there were muskrats in the creek. Sometimes when I drove late at night my headlights' beam on the water would catch the broad lines of ripples made by a swimming muskrat, a bow wave, converging across the water at the raised dark vee of its head. I would stop the car and get out: nothing. They eat corn and tomatoes from my neighbors' gardens, too, by night, so that my neighbors were always telling me that the creek was full of them. Around here, people call them "mushrats"; Thoreau called them "Musquashes." They are not of course rats at all (let alone squashes). They are more like diminutive beavers, and, like beavers, they exude a scented oil from musk glands under the base of the tail — hence the name. I had read in several respectable sources that muskrats are so wary they are almost impossible to observe. One expert who made a full-time study of large populations, mainly by examining "sign" and performing autopsies on corpses, said he often went for weeks at a time without seeing a single living muskrat.

One hot evening three years ago, I was standing more or less *in* a bush. I was stock-still, looking deep into Tinker Creek from a spot on the bank opposite the house, watching a group of bluegills stare and hang motionless near the bottom of a deep, sunlit pool. I was focused for depth. I had long since lost myself, lost the creek, the day, lost everything but still amber depth. All at once I couldn't see. And then I could: a young muskrat had appeared on top of the water, floating on its back. Its forelegs were folded langorously across its chest; the sun shone on its upturned belly. Its youthfulness and rodent grin, coupled with its ridiculous method of locomotion, which consisted of a lazy wag of the tail assisted by an occasional dabble of a webbed hind foot, made it an enchanting picture of decadence, dissipation, and summer sloth. I forgot all about the fish.

But in my surprise at having the light come on so suddenly, and at having my consciousness returned to me all at once and bearing an inverted muskrat, I must have moved and betrayed myself. The kit — for I know now it was just a young kit — righted itself so that only its head was visible above water, and swam downstream, away from me. I extricated myself from the bush and foolishly pursued it. It dove sleekly, reemerged, and glided for the opposite bank. I ran along the bankside brush, trying to keep it in sight. It kept casting an alarmed look over its shoulder at me. Once again it dove, under a floating mat of brush lodged in the bank, and disappeared. I never saw it again. (Nor have I ever, despite all the muskrats I have seen, again seen a muskrat floating on its back.) But I did not know muskrats then; I waited panting, and watched the shadowed bank. Now I know that I cannot outwait a muskrat who knows I am there. The most I can do is get "there" quietly, while it is still in its hole, so that it never knows, and wait there until it emerges. But then all I knew was that I wanted to see more muskrats.

I began to look for them day and night. Sometimes I would see ripples suddenly start beating from the creek's side, but as I crouched to watch, the ripples would die. Now I know what this means, and have learned to stand perfectly still to make out the muskrat's small, pointed face hidden under overhanging bank vegetation, watching me. That summer I haunted the bridges, I walked up creeks and down, but no muskrats ever appeared. You must just have to be there, I thought. You must have to spend the rest of your life standing in bushes. It was a once-in-a-lifetime thing, and you've had your once.

Then one night I saw another, and my life changed. After that I knew 30
where they were in numbers, and I knew when to look. It was late dusk; I was driving home from a visit with friends. Just on the off chance I parked quietly by the creek, walked out on the narrow bridge over the shallows, and looked upstream. Someday, I had been telling myself for weeks, someday a muskrat is going to swim right through that channel in the cattails, and I am going to see it. That is precisely what happened. I looked up into the channel for a muskrat, and there it came, swimming right toward me. Knock; seek; ask. It seemed to swim with a side-to-side, sculling motion of its vertically flattened tail. It looked bigger than the upside-down muskrat, and its face more reddish. In its mouth it clasped a twig of tulip tree. One thing amazed me: it swam right down the middle of the creek. I thought it would hide in the brush along the edge; instead, it plied the waters as obviously as an aquaplane. I could just look and look.

But I was standing on the bridge, not sitting, and it saw me. It changed its course, veered towards the bank, and disappeared behind an indentation in the rushy shoreline. I felt a rush of such pure energy I thought I would not need to breathe for days.

That innocence of mine is mostly gone now, although I felt almost the same pure rush last night. I have seen many muskrats since I learned to look for them in that part of the creek. But still I seek them out in the cool of the evening, and still I hold my breath when rising ripples surge from under the creek's bank. The great hurrah about wild animals is that they exist at all, and the greater hurrah is the actual moment of seeing them. Because they have a nice dignity, and prefer to have nothing to do with me, not even as the simple objects of my vision. They show me by their very wariness what a prize it is simply to open my eyes and behold.

Muskrats are the bread and butter of the carnivorous food chain. They are like rabbits and mice: if you are big enough to eat mammals, you eat them. Hawks and owls prey on them, and foxes; so do otters. Minks are their special enemies; minks live near large muskrat populations, slinking in and out of their dens and generally hanging around like mantises outside a beehive. Muskrats are also subject to a contagious blood disease that wipes out whole colonies. Sometimes, however, their whole populations explode, just like lemmings', which are their near kin; and they either die by the hundreds or fan out across the land migrating to new creeks and ponds.

Men kill them, too. One Eskimo who hunted muskrats for a few weeks each year strictly as a sideline says that in fourteen years he killed 30,739 muskrats. The pelts sell, and the price is rising. Muskrats are the most important fur animal on the North American continent. I don't know what they bring on the Mackenzie River delta these days, but around here, fur dealers, who paid $2.90 in 1971, now pay $5.00 a pelt. They make the pelts into coats, calling the fur anything but muskrat: "Hudson seal" is typical. In the old days, after they had sold the skins, trappers would sell the meat, too, calling it "marsh rabbit." Many people still stew muskrat.

Keeping ahead of all this slaughter, a female might have as many as five litters a year, and each litter contains six or seven or more muskrats. The nest is high and dry under the bank; only the entrance is under water, usually by several feet, to foil enemies. Here the nests are marked by simple holes in a creek's clay bank; in other parts of the country muskrats build floating, conical winter lodges which are not only watertight, but edible to muskrats.

The very young have a risky life. For one thing, even snakes and raccoons eat them. For another, their mother is easily confused, and may abandon one or two of a big litter here or there, forgetting as it were to count noses. The newborn hanging on their mother's teats may drop off if the mother has to make a sudden dive into the water, and sometimes these drown. The just-weaned young have a rough time, too, because new litters are coming along so hard and fast that they have to be weaned before they really know how to survive. And if the just-weaned young are near starving, they might eat the newborn — if they can get to them. Adult muskrats, including their own mothers, often kill them if they approach too closely. But if they live through all these hazards, they can begin a life of swimming at twilight and munching cattail roots, clover, and an occasional crayfish. Paul Errington, [5] a usually solemn authority, writes, "The muskrat nearing the end of its first month may be thought of as an independent enterprise in a very modest way."

The wonderful thing about muskrats in my book is that they cannot see very well, and are rather dim, to boot. They are extremely wary if they know I am there, and will outwait me every time. But with a modicum of skill and a minimum loss of human dignity, such as it is, I can be right "there," and the breathing fact of my presence will never penetrate their narrow skulls.

What happened last night was not only the ultimate in muskrat dimness, it was also the ultimate in human intrusion, the limit beyond which I am certain I cannot go. I would never have imagined I could go that far, actually to sit beside a feeding muskrat as beside a dinner partner at a crowded table.

What happened was this. Just in the past week I have been frequenting a different place, one of the creek's nameless feeder streams. It is mostly a shallow trickle joining several pools up to three feet deep. Over one of these pools is a tiny pedestrian bridge known locally, if at all, as the troll bridge. I was sitting on the troll bridge about an hour before sunset, looking upstream about eight feet to my right where I know the muskrats have a den. I had just lighted a cigarette when a pulse of ripples appeared at the mouth of the den, and a muskrat emerged. He swam straight toward me and headed under the bridge.

Now the moment a muskrat's eyes disappear from view under a bridge, 40 I go into action. I have about five seconds to switch myself around so that I will be able to see him very well when he emerges on the other side of the bridge. I can easily hang my head over the other side of the bridge, so that when he appears from under me, I will be able to count his eyelashes if I want. The trouble with this maneuver is that, once his beady eyes appear again on the other side, I am stuck. If I move again, the show is over for the evening. I have to remain in whatever insane position I happen to be caught, for as long as I am in his sight, so that I stiffen all my muscles, bruise my ankles on the concrete, and burn my fingers on the cigarette. And if the muskrat goes out on a bank to feed, there I am with my face hanging a foot

[5] *Paul Errington* (190?–196?)· American zoologist who researched food habits of predators; author of *Muskrats and Marsh Management.*

over the water, unable to see anything but crayfish. So I have learned to take it easy on these five-second flings.

When the muskrat went under the bridge, I moved so I could face downstream comfortably. He reappeared, and I had a good look at him. He was eight inches long in the body, and another six in the tail. Muskrat tails are black and scaled, flattened not horizontally, like beavers' tails, but vertically, like a belt stood on edge. In the winter, muskrats' tails sometimes freeze solid, and the animals chew off the frozen parts up to about an inch of the body. They must swim entirely with their hind feet, and have a terrible time steering. This one used his tail as a rudder and only occasionally as a propeller; mostly he swam with a pedaling motion of his hind feet, held very straight and moving down and around, "toeing down" like a bicycle racer. The soles of his hind feet were strangely pale; his toenails were pointed in long cones. He kept his forelegs still, tucked up to his chest.

The muskrat clambered out on the bank across the stream from me, and began feeding. He chomped down on a ten-inch weed, pushing it into his mouth steadily with both forepaws as a carpenter feeds a saw. I could hear his chewing; it sounded like somebody eating celery sticks. Then he slid back into the water with the weed still in his mouth, crossed under the bridge, and, instead of returning to his den, rose erect on a submerged rock and calmly polished off the rest of the weed. He was about four feet away from me. Immediately he swam under the bridge again, hauled himself out on the bank, and unerringly found the same spot on the grass, where he devoured the weed's stump.

All this time I was not only doing an elaborate about-face every time his eyes disappeared under the bridge, but I was also smoking a cigarette. He never noticed that the configuration of the bridge metamorphosed utterly every time he went under it. Many animals are the same way: they can't see a thing unless it's moving. Similarly, every time he turned his head away, I was free to smoke the cigarette, although of course I never knew when he would suddenly turn again and leave me caught in some wretched position. The galling thing was, he was downwind of me and my cigarette: was I really going through all this for a creature without any sense whatsoever?

After the weed stump was gone, the muskrat began ranging over the grass with a nervous motion, chewing off mouthfuls of grass and clover near the base. Soon he had gathered a huge, bushy mouthful; he pushed into the water, crossed under the bridge, swam towards his den, and dove.

When he launched himself again shortly, having apparently cached the grass, he repeated the same routine in a businesslike fashion, and returned with another shock of grass.

Out he came again. I lost him for a minute when he went under the bridge; he did not come out where I expected him. Suddenly to my utter disbelief he appeared on the bank next to me. The troll bridge itself is on a level with the low bank; there I was, and there he was, at my side. I could have touched him with the palm of my hand without straightening my elbow. He was ready to hand.

Foraging beside me he walked very humped up, maybe to save heat loss through evaporation. Generally, whenever he was out of water he assumed the shape of a shmoo, [6] his shoulders were as slender as a kitten's. He used his forepaws to part clumps of grass extremely tidily; I could see the flex in his narrow wrists. He gathered mouthfuls of grass and clover less by actually gnawing than by biting hard near the ground, locking his neck muscles, and pushing up jerkily with his forelegs.

His jaw was underslung, his black eyes close set and glistening, his small ears pointed and furred. I will have to try and see if he can cock them. I could see the water-slicked long hairs of his coat, which gathered in rich brown strands that emphasized the smooth contours of his body, and which parted to reveal the paler, softer hair like rabbit fur underneath. Despite his closeness, I never saw his teeth or belly.

After several minutes of rummaging about in the grass at my side, he eased into the water under the bridge and paddled to his den with the jawful of grass held high, and that was the last I saw of him.

In the forty minutes I watched him, he never saw me, smelled me, or 50 heard me at all. When he was in full view of course I never moved except to breathe. My eyes would move, too, following his, but he never noticed. I even swallowed a couple of times: nothing. The swallowing thing interested me because I had read that, when you are trying to hand-tame wild birds, if you inadvertently swallow, you ruin everything. The bird, according to this theory, thinks you are swallowing in anticipation, and off it goes. The muskrat never twitched. Only once, when he was feeding from the opposite bank about eight feet away from me, did he suddenly rise upright, all alert — and then he immediately resumed foraging. But he never knew I was there.

I never knew I was there, either. For that forty minutes last night I was as purely sensitive and mute as a photographic plate; I received impressions, but I did not print out captions. My own self-awareness had disappeared; it seems now almost as though, had I been wired with electrodes, my EEG would have been flat. I have done this sort of thing so often that I have lost self-consciousness about moving slowly and halting suddenly; it is second nature to me now. And I have often noticed that even a few minutes of this self-forgetfulness is tremendously invigorating. I wonder if we do not waste most of our energy just by spending every waking minute saying hello to ourselves. Martin Buber quotes an old Hasid master who said, "When you walk across the fields with your mind pure and holy, then from all the stones, and all growing things, and all animals, the sparks of their soul come out and cling to you, and then they are purified and become a holy fire in you." This

---

[6] *shmoo:* Reference to cartoon creatures in Al Capp's *L'il Abner* comic strip; shmoos were bottom-heavy, bell-shaped characters.

is one way of describing the energy that comes, using the specialized Kabbalistic vocabulary of Hasidism. [7]

I have tried to show muskrats to other people, but it rarely works. No matter how quiet we are, the muskrats stay hidden. Maybe they sense the tense hum of consciousness, the buzz from two human beings who in the silence cannot help but be aware of each other, and so of themselves. Then too, the other people invariably suffer from a self-consciousness that prevents their stalking well. It used to bother me, too: I just could not bear to lose so much dignity that I would completely alter my whole way of being for a muskrat. So I would move or look around or scratch my nose, and no muskrats would show, leaving me alone with my dignity for days on end, until I decided that it was worth my while to learn — from the muskrats themselves — how to stalk.

The old, classic rule for stalking is, "Stop often 'n' set frequent." The rule cannot be improved upon, but muskrats will permit a little more. If a muskrat's eyes are out of sight, I can practically do a buck-and-wing on his tail, and he'll never notice. A few days ago I approached a muskrat feeding on a bank by the troll bridge simply by taking as many gliding steps toward him as possible while his head was turned. I spread my weight as evenly as I could, so that he wouldn't feel my coming through the ground, and so that no matter when I became visible to him, I could pause motionless until he turned away again without having to balance too awkwardly on one leg.

When I got within ten feet of him, I was sure he would flee, but he continued to browse nearsightedly among the mown clovers and grass. Since I had seen just about everything I was ever going to see, I continued approaching just to see when he would break. To my utter bafflement, he never broke. I broke first. When one of my feet was six inches from his back, I refused to press on. He could see me perfectly well, of course, but I was stock-still except when he lowered his head. There was nothing left to do but kick him. Finally he returned to the water, dove, and vanished. I do not know to this day if he would have permitted me to keep on walking right up his back.

It is not always so easy. Other times I have learned that the only way   55 to approach a feeding muskrat for a good look is to commit myself to a procedure so ridiculous that only a total unselfconsciousness will permit me to live with myself. I have to ditch my hat, line up behind a low boulder, and lay on my belly to inch snake-fashion across twenty feet of bare field until I am behind the boulder itself and able to hazard a slow peek around it. If my head moves from around the boulder when the muskrat's head

---

[7] *Buber. . . . Hasidism*: Martin Buber (1878–1965), Jewish philosopher and theologian; Hasidism, a mystical sect of orthodox Judaism founded in the mid-eighteenth century; Kabbalistic refers to the cabala, a medieval system of theosophy and mysticism.

happens to be turned, then all is well. I can be fixed into position and still by the time he looks around. But if he sees me move my head, then he dives into the water, and the whole belly-crawl routine was in vain. There is no way to tell ahead of time; I just have to chance it and see.

I have read that in the unlikely event that you are caught in a stare-down with a grizzly bear, the best thing to do is talk to him softly and pleasantly. Your voice is supposed to have a soothing effect. I have not yet had occasion to test this out on grizzly bears, but I can attest that it does not work on muskrats. It scares them witless. I have tried time and again. Once I watched a muskrat feeding on a bank ten feet away from me; after I had looked my fill I had nothing to lose, so I offered a convivial greeting. Boom. The terrified muskrat flipped a hundred and eighty degrees in the air, nose-dived into the grass at his feet, and disappeared. The earth swallowed him; his tail shot straight up in the air and then vanished into the ground without a sound. Muskrats make several emergency escape holes along a bank for just this very purpose, and they don't like to feed too far away from them. The entire event was most impressive, and illustrates the relative power in nature of the word and the sneak.

Stalking is a pure form of skill, like pitching or playing chess. Rarely is luck involved. I do it right or I do it wrong; the muskrat will tell me, and that right early. Even more than baseball, stalking is a game played in the actual present. At every second, the muskrat comes, or stays, or goes, depending on my skill.

Can I stay still? How still? It is astonishing how many people cannot, or will not, hold still. I could not, or would not, hold still for thirty minutes inside, but at the creek I slow down, center down, empty. I am not excited; my breathing is slow and regular. In my brain I am not saying, Muskrat! Muskrat! There! I am saying nothing. If I must hold a position, I do not "freeze." If I freeze, locking my muscles, I will tire and break. Instead of going rigid, I go calm. I center down wherever I am; I find a balance and repose. I retreat — not inside myself, but outside myself, so that I am a tissue of senses. Whatever I see is plenty, abundance. I am the skin of water the wind plays over; I am petal, feather, stone.

3

Living this way by the creek, where the light appears and vanishes on the water, where muskrats surface and dive, and redwings scatter, I have come to know a special side of nature. I look to the mountains, and the mountains still slumber, blue and mute and rapt. I say, it gathers; the world abides. But I look to the creek, and I say: it scatters, it comes and goes. When I leave the house the sparrows flee and hush; on the banks of the creek jays scream in alarm, squirrels race for cover, tadpoles dive, frogs leap, snakes freeze, warblers vanish. Why do they hide? I will not hurt them. They simply do not want to be seen. "Nature," said Heraclitus, "is wont to hide herself." A fleeing mockingbird unfurls for a second a dazzling array of white fans . . . and disappears in the leaves. Shane! . . . Shane! [8] Nature flashes the old mighty glance — the come-hither look — drops the hand-kerchief, turns tail, and is gone. The nature I know is old touch-and-go.

I wonder whether what I see and seem to understand about nature is 60 merely one of the accidents of freedom, repeated by chance before my eyes, or whether it has any counterpart in the worlds beyond Tinker Creek. I find in quantum mechanics a world symbolically similar to my world at the creek.

Many of us are still living in the universe of Newtonian physics, and fondly imagine that real, hard scientists have no use for these misty ram-blings, dealing as scientists do with the measurable and known. We think that at least the physical causes of physical events are perfectly knowable, and that, as the results of various experiments keep coming in, we gradually roll back the cloud of unknowing. We remove the veils one by one, pain-stakingly, adding knowledge to knowledge and whisking away veil after veil, until at last we reveal the nub of things, the sparkling equation from whom all blessings flow. Even wildman Emerson [9] accepted the truly pathetic fallacy of the old science when he wrote grudgingly toward the end of his life, "When the microscope is improved, we shall have the cells analysed, and all will be electricity, or somewhat else." All we need to do is perfect our instruments and our methods, and we can collect enough data like birds on a string to predict physical events from physical causes.

But in 1927 Werner Heisenberg [10] pulled out the rug, and our whole understanding of the universe toppled and collapsed. For some reason it has not yet trickled down to the man on the street that some physicists now are a bunch of wild-eyed, raving mystics. For they have perfected their instru-ments and methods just enough to whisk away the crucial veil, and what stands revealed is the Cheshire cat's grin.

The Principle of Indeterminacy, which saw the light in the summer of 1927, says in effect that you cannot know both a particle's velocity and position. You can guess statistically what any batch of electrons might do, but you cannot predict the career of any one particle. They seem to be as free as dragonflies. You can perfect your instruments and your methods till the cows come home, and you will never ever be able to measure this one basic thing. It cannot be done. The electron is a muskrat; it cannot be

---

[8] *Shane*: At the end of *Shane*, a 1953 Western film classic starring Alan Ladd, a young boy poignantly calls out the gunfighter Shane's name as he rides away from the boy's homestead.

[9] *Emerson*: Ralph Waldo Emerson (1803–1882), American essayist.

[10] *Werner Heisenberg* (1901–1976): German physicist and philosopher who was awarded the Nobel Prize in 1932 for his work on quantum mechanics.

perfectly stalked. And nature is a fan dancer born with a fan; you can wrestle her down, throw her on the stage and grapple with her for the fan with all your might, but it will never quit her grip. She comes that way; the fan is attached.

It is not that we lack sufficient information to know both a particle's velocity and its position; that would have been a perfectly ordinary situation well within the understanding of classical physics. Rather, we know now for sure that there is no knowing. You can determine the position, and your figure for the velocity blurs into vagueness; or, you can determine the velocity, but whoops, there goes the position. The use of instruments and the very fact of an observer seem to bollix the observations; as a consequence, physicists are saying that they cannot study nature per se, but only their own investigation of nature. And I can only see bluegills within my own blue shadow, from which they immediately flee.

The Principle of Indeterminacy turned science inside-out. Suddenly 65 determinism goes, causality goes, and we are left with a universe composed of what Eddington calls, "mind-stuff." Listen to these physicists: Sir James Jeans, [11] Eddington's successor, invokes "fate," saying that the future "may rest on the knees of whatever gods there be." Eddington says that "the physical world is entirely abstract and without 'actuality' apart from its linkage to consciousness." Heisenberg himself says, "method and object can no longer be separated. *The scientific world-view has ceased to be a scientific view in the true sense of the word.*" Jeans says that science can no longer remain opposed to the notion of free will. Heisenberg says, "there is a higher power, not influenced by our wishes, which finally decides and judges." Eddington says that our dropping causality as a result of the Principle of Indeterminacy "leaves us with no clear distinction between the Natural and the Supernatural." And so forth.

These physicists are once again mystics, as Kepler [12] was, standing on a rarefied mountain pass, gazing transfixed into an abyss of freedom. And they got there by experimental method and a few wild leaps such as Einstein made. What a pretty pass!

All this means is that the physical world as we understand it now is more like the touch-and-go creek world I see than it is like the abiding world of which the mountains seem to speak. The physicists' particles whiz and shift like rotifers in and out of my microscope's field, and that this valley's ring of granite mountains is an airy haze of those same particles I must

[11] *Eddington . . . Jeans*: Sir Arthur Stanley Eddington (1882–1944), English scientist who made many contributions to astronomy and relativity theory; Sir James Jeans (1877–1946), another highly influential English physicist and astronomer.

[12] *Kepler*: Johannes Kepler (1571–1630), German astronomer who deduced the laws of planetary motion.

believe. The whole universe is a swarm of those wild, wary energies, the sun that glistens from the wet hairs on a muskrat's back and the stars which the mountains obscure on the horizon but which catch from on high in Tinker Creek. It is all touch and go. The heron flaps away; the dragonfly departs at thirty miles an hour; the water strider vanishes under a screen of grass; the muskrat dives, and the ripples roll from the bank, and flatten, and cease altogether.

Moses said to God, "I beseech thee, shew me thy glory." And God said, "Thou canst not see my face: for there shall no man see me, and live." But he added, "There is a place by me, and thou shalt stand upon a rock: and it shall come to pass, while my glory passeth by, that I will put thee in a clift of the rock, and will cover thee with my hand while I pass by: And I will take away mine hand, and thou shalt see my back parts: but my face shall not be seen." So Moses went up on Mount Sinai, waited still in a clift of the rock, and saw the back parts of God. Forty years later he went up on Mount Pisgah, and saw the promised land across the Jordan, which he was to die without ever being permitted to enter.

Just a glimpse, Moses: a clift in the rock here, a mountaintop there, and the rest is denial and longing. You have to stalk everything. Everything scatters and gathers; everything comes and goes like fish under a bridge. You have to stalk the spirit, too. You can wait forgetful anywhere, for anywhere is the way of his fleet passage, and hope to catch him by the tail and shout something in his ear before he wrests away. Or you can pursue him wherever you dare, risking the shrunken sinew in the hollow of the thigh; you can bang at the door all night till the innkeeper relents, if he ever relents; and you can wail till you're hoarse or worse the cry for incarnation always in John Knoepfle's poem: "and christ is red rover . . . and the children are calling/come over come over." I sit on a bridge as on Pisgah or Sinai, and I am both waiting becalmed in a clift of the rock and banging with all my will, calling like a child beating on a door: Come on out! . . . I know you're there.

And then occasionally the mountains part. The tree with the lights in 70 it appears, the mockingbird falls, and time unfurls across space like an oriflamme. Now we rejoice. The news, after all, is not that muskrats are wary, but that they can be seen. The hem of the robe was a Nobel Prize to Heisenberg; he did not go home in disgust. I wait on the bridges and stalk along banks for those moments I cannot predict, when a wave begins to surge under the water, and ripples strengthen and pulse high across the creek and back again in a texture that throbs. It is like the surfacing of an impulse, like the materialization of fish, this rising, this coming to a head, like the ripening of nutmeats still in their husks, ready to split open like buckeyes in a field, shining with newness. "Surely the Lord is in this place; and I knew it not." The fleeing shreds I see, the back parts, are a gift, an abundance. When Moses came down from the clift in Mount Sinai, the people were afraid of him: the very skin on his face shone.

Do the Eskimos' faces shine, too? I lie in bed alert: I am with the Eskimos on the tundra who are running after the click-footed caribou, running sleepless and dazed for days, running spread out in scraggling lines across the glacier-ground hummocks and reindeer moss, in sight of the ocean, under the long-shadowed pale sun, running silent all night long.

FROM READING TO REREADING

1. In her 1987 autobiography, *An American Childhood*, Dillard writes: "Everywhere, things snagged me. The visible world turned me curious to books; the books propelled me reeling back to the world." How is this dynamic between reading and seeing enacted in "Stalking"?

2. Though Dillard often writes in a mood of spiritual intensity, her writing is not without humor — a side of her which is often overlooked. What are the humorous moments in "Stalking"? What elements of humor can you find in her style and diction?

3. The essay shows Dillard stalking several kinds of creatures, but it then concludes with a reflection on a major scientific discovery: Heisenberg's "Principle of Indeterminacy." How did we get here? What happened to the muskrats? What has stalking to do with modern physics?

From Reading to Writing

1. Both George Orwell and Lewis Thomas are concerned about the way science is taught, and each offers some suggestions for rethinking what a scientific education might mean. Consider your own scientific training, both as it is now and as it may be in the future. Do you think it allowed or will allow for creativity, skepticism, and a humane view of life? Which one of Orwell's definitions do you think your scientific training resembles? Write an essay in which you define what you think a scientific education should be.

2. Stephen Jay Gould and Annie Dillard are both interested in the thought processes that lead to scientific creativity. Read each essay carefully and write a critical essay in which you examine the importance of analogy for each author. You should begin by researching the meaning of analogy and the role it plays in our thinking. Your essay should point out how each writer makes use of analogy both as a conceptual tool and as a feature of composition.

3. Cynthia Ozick makes a distinction between science and literature. Each, she argues, is *about* something different: "science is about God's work; literature is about our work." Consider this distinction carefully. What do you think Ozick means? Does her distinction resemble those that Lewis Thomas and George Orwell make between science and humanities? In an essay of your own, comment on Ozick's distinction between these two areas of thought. Discuss whether you think the distinction is valuable or whether you find it misleading. On a personal note, consider how her distinction conforms to your own educational experience in each area.

The Writing Life

GEORGE ORWELL
Why I Write

Essayists have traditionally shuttled between two considerations: a respect for truth and a respect for style. For George Orwell, the tension between these two, often incompatible, elements played a dominant role in his essays and nonfiction. In "Why I Write," Orwell discusses the conflict he frequently felt as he attempted to "tell the whole truth without violating [his] literary instincts." The essay originally appeared in a British periodical in 1946 and so perfectly did it seem to sum up Orwell's motivations and anxieties as a writer that it was used as the introductory selection for a four-volume edition of his essays, journalism, and letters. As the other Orwell selections in this reader clearly show, he was a writer with a highly developed sense of self-criticism. That trait is abundantly evident in this essay.

FROM A VERY EARLY AGE, perhaps the age of five or six, I knew that when I grew up I should be a writer. Between the ages of about seventeen and twenty-four I tried to abandon this idea, but I did so with the consciousness that I was outraging my true nature and that sooner or later I should have to settle down and write books.

I was the middle child of three, but there was a gap of five years on either side, and I barely saw my father before I was eight. For this and other reasons I was somewhat lonely, and I soon developed disagreeable mannerisms which made me unpopular throughout my schooldays. I had the lonely child's habit of making up stories and holding conversations with imaginary persons, and I think from the very start my literary ambitions were mixed up with the feeling of being isolated and undervalued. I knew that I had a facility with words and a power of facing unpleasant facts, and I felt that this created a sort of private world in which I could get my own back for my failure in everyday life. Nevertheless the volume of serious — i.e., seriously intended — writing which I produced all through my childhood and boyhood would not amount to half a dozen pages. I wrote my first poem at the age of four or five, my mother taking it down to dictation. I cannot remember anything about it except that it was about a tiger and the tiger had "chair-like teeth" — a good enough phrase, but I fancy the poem was a plagiarism of Blake's "Tiger, Tiger." At eleven, when the war of 1914–1918 broke out, I wrote a patriotic poem which was printed in the local newspaper, as was another, two years later, on the death of Kitchener. [1] From time to time,

---

[1] *Kitchener*: Horatio Herbert Kitchener (1850–1916), commander-in-chief of the British army in Africa and in India.

when I was a bit older, I wrote bad and usually unfinished "nature poems" in the Georgian style. [2] I also, about twice, attempted a short story which was a ghastly failure. That was the total of the would-be serious work that I actually set down on paper during all those years.

However, throughout this time I did in a sense engage in literary activities. To begin with there was the made-to-order stuff which I produced quickly, easily and without much pleasure to myself. Apart from school work, I wrote *vers d'occasion*, [3] semi-comic poems which I could turn out at what now seems to me astonishing speed — at fourteen I wrote a whole rhyming play, in imitation of Aristophanes, [4] in about a week — and helped to edit school magazines, both printed and in manuscript. These magazines were the most pitiful burlesque stuff that you could imagine, and I took far less trouble with them than I now would with the cheapest journalism. But side by side with all this, for fifteen years or more, I was carrying out a literary exercise of a quite different kind: this was the making up of a continuous "story" about myself, a sort of diary existing only in the mind. I believe this is a common habit of children and adolescents. As a very small child I used to imagine that I was, say, Robin Hood, and picture myself as the hero of thrilling adventures, but quite soon my "story" ceased to be narcissistic in a crude way and became more and more a mere description of what I was doing and the things I saw. For minutes at a time this kind of thing would be running through my head: "He pushed the door open and entered the room. A yellow beam of sunlight, filtering through the muslin curtains, slanted on to the table, where a matchbox, half open, lay beside the inkpot. With his right hand in his pocket he moved across to the window. Down in the street a tortoiseshell cat was chasing a dead leaf," etc., etc. This habit continued till I was about twenty-five, right through my nonliterary years. Although I had to search, and did search, for the right words, I seemed to be making this descriptive effort almost against my will, under a kind of compulsion from outside. The "story" must, I suppose, have reflected the styles of the various writers I admired at different ages, but so far as I remember it always had the same meticulous descriptive quality.

When I was about sixteen I suddenly discovered the joy of mere words, i.e., the sounds and associations of words. The lines from *Paradise Lost* [5] —

So hee with difficulty and labour hard
Moved on: with difficulty and labour hee,

which do not now seem to me so very wonderful, sent shivers down my backbone; and the spelling "hee" for "he" was an added pleasure. As for the

[2] *Georgian style*: Literary style popular in England at the time; it refers to the reign of George V (1910–1936).

[3] *vers d'occasion*: Occasional verse; poetry written for specific events or occasions (French).

[4] *Aristophanes* (c. 448–380 B.C.): Classical Greek comic playwright.

[5] *Paradise Lost*: John Milton's epic poem, published in 1667.

need to describe things, I knew all about it already. So it is clear what kind of books I wanted to write, in so far as I could be said to want to write books at that time. I wanted to write enormous naturalistic novels with unhappy endings, full of detailed descriptions and arresting similes, and also full of purple passages in which words were used partly for the sake of their sound. And in fact my first complete novel, *Burmese Days,* which I wrote when I was thirty but projected much earlier, is rather that kind of book.

I give all this background information because I do not think one can assess a writer's motives without knowing something of his early development. His subject matter will be determined by the age he lives in — at least this is true in tumultuous, revolutionary ages like our own — but before he ever begins to write he will have acquired an emotional attitude from which he will never completely escape. It is his job, no doubt, to discipline his temperament and avoid getting stuck at some immature stage, or in some perverse mood: but if he escapes from his early influences altogether, he will have killed his impulse to write. Putting aside the need to earn a living, I think there are four great motives for writing, at any rate for writing prose. They exist in different degrees in every writer, and in any one writer the proportions will vary from time to time, according to the atmosphere in which he is living. They are:

1. Sheer egoism. Desire to seem clever, to be talked about, to be remembered after death, to get your own back on grownups who snubbed you in childhood, etc., etc. It is humbug to pretend that this is not a motive, and a strong one. Writers share this characteristic with scientists, artists, politicians, lawyers, soldiers, successful businessmen — in short, with the whole top crust of humanity. The great mass of human beings are not acutely selfish. After the age of about thirty they abandon individual ambition — in many cases, indeed, they almost abandon the sense of being individuals at all — and live chiefly for others, or are simply smothered under drudgery. But there is also the minority of gifted, wilful people who are determined to live their own lives to the end, and writers belong to this class. Serious writers, I should say, are on the whole more vain and self-centred than journalists, though less interested in money.

2. Esthetic enthusiasm. Perception of beauty in the external world, or, on the other hand, in words and their right arrangement. Pleasure in the impact of one sound on another, in the firmness of good prose or the rhythm of a good story. Desire to share an experience which one feels is valuable and ought not to be missed. The esthetic motive is very feeble in a lot of writers, but even a pamphleteer or a writer of textbooks will have pet words and phrases which appeal to him for nonutilitarian reasons; or he may feel strongly about typography, width of margins, etc. Above the level of a railway guide, no book is quite free from esthetic considerations.

3. Historical impulse. Desire to see things as they are, to find out true facts and store them up for the use of posterity.

4. Political purpose — using the word "political" in the widest possible

sense. Desire to push the world in a certain direction, to alter other people's idea of the kind of society that they should strive after. Once again, no book is genuinely free from political bias. The opinion that art should have nothing to do with politics is itself a political attitude.

It can be seen how these various impulses must war against one another, 10 and how they must fluctuate from person to person and from time to time. By nature — taking your "nature" to be the state you have attained when you are first adult — I am a person in whom the first three motives would outweigh the fourth. In a peaceful age I might have written ornate or merely descriptive books, and might have remained almost unaware of my political loyalties. As it is I have been forced into becoming a sort of pamphleteer. First I spent five years in an unsuitable profession (the Indian Imperial Police, in Burma), and then I underwent poverty and the sense of failure. This increased my natural hatred of authority and made me for the first time fully aware of the existence of the working classes, and the job in Burma had given me some understanding of the nature of imperialism: but these experiences were not enough to give me an accurate political orientation. Then came Hitler, the Spanish civil war, etc. By the end of 1935 I had still failed to reach a firm decision. I remember a little poem that I wrote at that date, expressing my dilemma:

A happy vicar I might have been
Two hundred years ago,
To preach upon eternal doom
And watch my walnuts grow;

But born, alas, in an evil time,
I missed that pleasant haven,
For the hair has grown on my upper lip
And the clergy are all clean-shaven.

And later still the times were good,
We were so easy to please,
We rocked our troubled thoughts to sleep
On the bosoms of the trees.

All ignorant we dared to own
The joys we now dissemble;
The greenfinch on the apple bough
Could make my enemies tremble.

But girls' bellies and apricots,
Roach in a shaded stream,
Horses, ducks in flight at dawn,
All these are a dream.

It is forbidden to dream again;
We maim our joys and hide them;

Horses are made of chromium steel
And little fat men shall ride them.

I am the worm who never turned,
The eunuch without a harem;
Between the priest and the commissar
I walk like Eugene Aram; [6]

And the commissar is telling my fortune
While the radio plays,
But the priest has promised an Austin Seven, [7]
For Duggie [8] always pays.

I dreamed I dwelt in marble halls,
And woke to find it true;
I wasn't born for an age like this;
Was Smith? Was Jones? Were you?

The Spanish war and other events in 1936–1937 turned the scale and thereafter I knew where I stood. Every line of serious work that I have written since 1936 has been written, directly or indirectly, *against* totalitarianism and *for* democratic socialism, as I understand it. It seems to me nonsense, in a period like our own, to think that one can avoid writing of such subjects. Everyone writes of them in one guise or another. It is simply a question of which side one takes and what approach one follows. And the more one is conscious of one's political bias, the more chance one has of acting politically without sacrificing one's esthetic and intellectual integrity.

What I have most wanted to do throughout the past ten years is to make political writing into an art. My starting point is always a feeling of partisanship, a sense of injustice. When I sit down to write a book, I do not say to myself, "I am going to produce a work of art." I write it because there is some lie that I want to expose, some fact to which I want to draw attention, and my initial concern is to get a hearing. But I could not do the work of writing a book, or even a long magazine article, if it were not also an esthetic experience. Anyone who cares to examine my work will see that even when it is downright propaganda it contains much that a full-time politician would consider irrelevant. I am not able, and I do not want, completely to abandon the world-view that I acquired in childhood. So long as I remain alive and well I shall continue to feel strongly about prose style, to love the surface of the earth, and to take a pleasure in solid objects and scraps of useless information. It is no use trying to suppress that side of myself. The job is to

[6] *Eugene Aram* (1704–1759): English scholar and linguist hanged for the murder of a friend, whose skeleton was found fourteen years after the crime. Aram's story had been retold several times in English poetry and fiction.

[7] *Austin Seven*: British automobile.

[8] *Duggie*: Most probably a reference to Major C. H. Douglas, who believed a reform of the British Monetary System would lead to national prosperity.

reconcile my ingrained likes and dislikes with the essentially public, nonindividual activities that this age forces on all of us.

It is not easy. It raises problems of construction and of language, and it raises in a new way the problem of truthfulness. Let me give just one example of the cruder kind of difficulty that arises. My book about the Spanish civil war, *Homage to Catalonia,* is, of course, a frankly political book, but in the main it is written with a certain detachment and regard for form. I did try very hard in it to tell the whole truth without violating my literary instincts. But among other things it contains a long chapter, full of newspaper quotations and the like, defending the Trotskyists who were accused of plotting with Franco. Clearly such a chapter, which after a year or two would lose its interest for any ordinary reader, must ruin the book. A critic whom I respect read me a lecture about it. "Why did you put in all that stuff?" he said. "You've turned what might have been a good book into journalism." What he said was true, but I could not have done otherwise. I happened to know, what very few people in England had been allowed to know, that innocent men were being falsely accused. If I had not been angry about that I should never have written the book.

In one form or another this problem comes up again. The problem of language is subtler and would take too long to discuss. I will only say that of late years I have tried to write less picturesquely and more exactly. In any case I find that by the time you have perfected any style of writing, you have always outgrown it. *Animal Farm* was the first book in which I tried, with full consciousness of what I was doing, to fuse political purpose and artistic purpose into one whole. I have not written a novel for seven years, but I hope to write another fairly soon. It is bound to be a failure, every book is a failure, but I do know with some clarity what kind of book I want to write.

Looking back through the last page or two, I see that I have made it appear as though my motives in writing were wholly public-spirited. I don't want to leave that as the final impression. All writers are vain, selfish and lazy, and at the very bottom of their motives there lies a mystery. Writing a book is a horrible, exhausting struggle, like a long bout of some painful illness. One would never undertake such a thing if one were not driven on by some demon whom one can neither resist nor understand. For all one knows that demon is simply the same instinct that makes a baby squall for attention. And yet it is also true that one can write nothing readable unless one constantly struggles to efface one's own personality. Good prose is like a window pane. I cannot say with certainty which of my motives are the strongest, but I know which of them deserve to be followed. And looking back through my work, I see that it is invariably where I lacked a *political* purpose that I wrote lifeless books and was betrayed into purple passages, sentences without meaning, decorative adjectives and humbug generally.

FROM READING TO REREADING

1. Orwell tends to make fun of much of his early writing. Note, for example, his account in paragraph 3 of the kind of "story" that often ran through his head. What does he think is wrong with this kind of writing? What effect does his self-criticism have on the reader?

2. "What I have most wanted to do," Orwell says, "is make political writing into an art." Why does he think this is a difficult task? What problems does a writer face in attempting this?

3. After offering "four great motives for writing," Orwell says that "these various impulses must war against one another." How have they warred against one another in Orwell's own career? In rereading the essay, pay close attention to his manner of writing. How are these warring motives reflected in the writing itself?

ANNIE DILLARD
Schedules

Virginia Woolf once said that to be a writer requires a "room of one's own."
Annie Dillard would agree with that, so long as the room was small and without
a view. "Appealing workplaces are to be avoided," Dillard claims, reminding
us of the writer's need for self-discipline. In "Schedules" she takes us close to her
creative process not by describing the how *and* why *of her writing but the* where
and when — *the physical conditions of composition rather than the metaphysical.*
The essay appears in a slightly different form as an untitled chapter in her book
The Writing Life. *The version reprinted here was originally published in the*
magazine Tikkun *and was selected for* The Best American Essays 1989.

> What if man could see Beauty Itself, pure, unalloyed, stripped of mortality
> and all its pollution, stains, and vanities, unchanging, divine, . . . the man
> becoming, in that communion, the friend of God, himself immortal; . . .
> would that be a life to disregard?
>
> — Plato

I HAVE BEEN looking into schedules. Even when we read physics, we
inquire of each least particle, "What then shall I do this morning?" How
we spend our days is, of course, how we spend our lives. What we do with
this hour, and that one, is what we are doing. A schedule defends from chaos
and whim. It is a net for catching days. It is a scaffolding on which a worker
can stand and labor with both hands at sections of time. A schedule is a
mock-up of reason and order — willed, faked, and so brought into being; it
is a peace and a haven set into the wreck of time; it is a lifeboat on which
you find yourself, decades later, still living. Each day is the same, so you
remember the series afterward as a blurred idyll.

The most appealing daily schedule I know is that of a certain turn-of-
the-century Swedish aristocrat. He got up at four and set out on foot to hunt
black grouse, wood grouse, woodcock, and snipe. At eleven he met his
friends who had also been out hunting alone all morning. They converged
"at one of these babbling brooks," he wrote. He outlined the rest of his
schedule. "Take a quick dip, relax with a schnapps and a sandwich, stretch
out, have a smoke, take a nap or just rest, and then sit around and chat until
three. Then I hunt some more until sundown, bathe again, put on white tie
and tails to keep up appearances, eat a huge dinner, smoke a cigar and sleep
like a log until the sun comes up again to redden the eastern sky. This is
living. . . . Could it be more perfect?"

There is no shortage of good days. It is good lives that are hard to come by. A life of good days lived in the senses is not enough. The life of sensation is the life of greed; it requires more and more. The life of the spirit requires less and less; time is ample and its passage sweet. Who would call a day spent reading a good day? But a life spent reading — that is a good life. A day that closely resembles every other day for the past ten or twenty years does not suggest itself as a good one. But who would not call Pasteur's life a good one, or Thomas Mann's? [1]

Wallace Stevens [2] in his forties, living in Hartford, Connecticut, hewed to a productive routine. He rose at six, read for two hours, and walked another hour — three miles — to work. He dictated poems to his secretary. He ate no lunch; at noon he walked for another hour, often to an art gallery. He walked home from work — another hour. After dinner he retired to his study; he went to bed at nine. On Sundays, he walked in the park. I don't know what he did on Saturdays. Perhaps he exchanged a few words with his wife, who posed for the Liberty dime. (One would rather read these people, or lead their lives, than be their wives. When the Swedish aristocrat Wilhelm Dinesen shot birds all day, drank schnapps, napped, and dressed for dinner, he and his wife had three children under three. The middle one was Karen, later known as Isak Dinesen. [3])

Like Stevens, Osip Mandelstam composed poetry on the hoof. So did   5
Dante. Nietzsche, like Emerson, took two long walks a day. "When my creative energy flowed most freely, my muscular activity was always greatest. . . . I might often have been seen dancing; I used to walk through the hills for seven or eight hours on end without a hint of fatigue; I slept well, laughed a good deal — I was perfectly vigorous and patient" (Nietzsche). On the other hand, A. E. Housman, almost predictably, maintained, "I have seldom written poetry unless I was rather out of health." This makes sense, too, because in writing a book you can be too well for your own good.

Jack London claimed to write twenty hours a day. Before he undertook to write, he obtained the University of California course list and all the syllabi; he spent a year reading the textbooks in philosophy and literature. In subsequent years, once he had a book of his own under way, he set his alarm to wake him after four hours of sleep. Often he slept through the alarm, so, by his own account, he rigged it to drop a weight on his head. I cannot say I believe this, though a novel like *The Sea-Wolf* is strong evidence that some sort of weight fell on his head with some sort of frequency —

---

[1] *Pasteur . . . Mann*: Louis Pasteur (1822–1895), French chemist and microbiologist; Thomas Mann (1875–1955), German novelist and essayist.

[2] *Wallace Stevens* (1879–1955): American poet and lawyer who worked as an executive for a Hartford, Connecticut, insurance firm.

[3] *Isak Dinesen* (1885–1962): Danish writer who lived in Kenya and set much of her fiction in Africa.

though you wouldn't think a man would claim credit for it. London maintained that every writer needed experience, a technique, and a philosophical position. Perhaps the position need not be an airtight one; London himself felt comfortable with a weird amalgam of Karl Marx and Herbert Spencer. (Marks & Sparks.) [4]

I write these words in my most recent of many studies — a pine shed on Cape Cod. The pine lumber is unfinished inside the study; the pines outside are finished trees. I see the pines from my two windows. Nuthatches spiral around their long, coarse trunks. Sometimes in June a feeding colony of mixed warblers flies through the pines; the warblers make a racket that draws me out the door. The warblers drift loosely through the stiff pine branches, and I follow through the thin long grass between the trunks.

The study — sold as a prefabricated toolshed — is eight feet by ten feet. Like a plane's cockpit, it is crammed with high-tech equipment. There is no quill pen in sight. There is a computer, a printer, and a photocopying machine. My backless chair, a prie-dieu on which I kneel, slides under the desk; I give it a little kick when I leave. There is an air conditioner, a heater, and an electric kettle. There is a low-tech bookshelf, a shelf of gull and whale bones, and a bed. Under the bed I stow paints — a one-pint can of yellow to touch up the window's trim, and five or six tubes of artists' oils. The study affords ample room for one. One who is supposed to be writing books. You can read in the space of a coffin, and you can write in the space of a toolshed meant for mowers and spades.

I walk up here from the house every morning. The study and its pines, and the old summer cottages nearby, and the new farm just north of me, rise from an old sand dune high over a creeky salt marsh. From the bright lip of the dune I can see oyster farmers working their beds on the tidal flats and sailboats under way in the saltwater bay. After I have warmed myself standing at the crest of the dune, I return under the pines, enter the study, slam the door so the latch catches — and then I cannot see. The green spot in front of my eyes outshines everything in the shade. I lie on the bed and play with a bird bone until I can see it.

Appealing workplaces are to be avoided. One wants a room with no   10
view, so imagination can dance with memory in the dark. When I furnished this study seven years ago, I pushed the long desk against a blank wall, so I could not see from either window. Once, fifteen years ago, I wrote in a cinder-block cell over a parking lot. It overlooked a tar-and-gravel roof. This pine shed under trees is not quite so good as the cinder-block study was, but it will do.

"The beginning of wisdom," according to a West African proverb, "is to get you a roof."

---

[4] *Marks & Sparks*: Slang for the British chain of department stores, Marks & Spencer.

It was on summer nights in Roanoke, Virginia, that I wrote the second half of a book, *Pilgrim at Tinker Creek*. (I wrote the first half in the spring, at home.) Ruefully I noted then that I would possibly look back on those times as an idyll. I vowed to remember the difficulties. I have forgotten them now, however, and I do, in fact, look back on those times as an idyll.

I slept until noon, as did my husband, who was also writing. I wrote once in the afternoon, and once again after our early dinner and a walk. During those months, I subsisted on that dinner, coffee, Coke, chocolate milk, and Vantage cigarettes. I worked till midnight, one, or two. When I came home in the middle of the night I was tired; I longed for a tolerant giant, a person as big as a house, to hold me and rock me. In fact, an exhausted daydream — almost a hallucination — of being rocked and soothed sometimes forced itself upon me, and interrupted me even when I was talking or reading.

I had a room — a study carrel — in the Hollins College library, on the second floor. It was this room that overlooked a tar-and-gravel roof. A plate-glass window, beside me on the left, gave out on a number of objects: the roof, a parking lot, a distant portion of Carvin's Creek, some complicated Virginia sky, and a far hilltop where six cows grazed around a ruined foundation under red cedars.

From my desk I kept an eye out. Intriguing people, people I knew, 15 pulled into the parking lot and climbed from their cars. The cows moved on the hilltop. (I drew the cows, for they were made interestingly; they hung in catenary curves from their skeletons, like two-man tents.) On the flat roof just outside the window, sparrows pecked gravel. One of the sparrows lacked a leg; one was missing a foot. If I stood and peered around, I could see a feeder creek running at the edge of a field. In the creek, even from that great distance, I could see muskrats and snapping turtles. If I saw a snapping turtle, I ran downstairs and out of the library to watch it or poke it.

One afternoon I made a pen drawing of the window and the landscape it framed. I drew the window's aluminum frame and steel hardware; I sketched in the clouds and the far hilltop with its ruined foundation and wandering cows. I outlined the parking lot and its tall row of mercury-vapor lights; I drew the cars, and the graveled rooftop foreground.

If I craned my head, I could see a grassy playing field below. One afternoon I peered around at that field and saw a softball game. Since I happened to have my fielder's glove with me in my study, I thought it would be the generous thing to join the game. On the field, I learned there was a music camp on campus for two weeks. The little boys playing softball were musical whizzes. They could not all play ball, but their patter was a treat. "All right, MacDonald," they jeered when one kid came to bat, "that pizzicato won't help you now." It was slightly better than no softball, so I played with them every day, second base, terrified that I would bust a prodigy's fingers on a throw to first or the plate.

I shut the blinds one day for good. I lowered the venetian blinds and flattened the slats. Then, by lamplight, I taped my drawing to the closed blind. There, on the drawing, was the window's view: cows, parking lot, hilltop, and sky. If I wanted a sense of the world, I could look at the stylized outline drawing. If I had possessed the skill, I would have painted, directly on the slats of the lowered blind, in meticulous colors, a *trompe l'oeil* mural view of all that the blinds hid. Instead, I wrote it.

On the Fourth of July, my husband and our friends drove into the city, Roanoke, to see the fireworks. I begged off; I wanted to keep working. I was working hard, although of course it did not seem hard enough at the time — a finished chapter every few weeks. I castigated myself daily for writing too slowly. Even when passages seemed to come easily, as though I were copying from a folio held open by smiling angels, the manuscript revealed the usual signs of struggle — blood stains, teeth marks, gashes, and burns.

This night, as on most nights, I entered the library at dusk. The 20 building was locked and dark. I had a key. Every night I let myself in, climbed the stairs, found my way between the tall stacks in the dark, located and unlocked my study's door, and turned on the light. I remembered how many stacks I had to hit with my hand in the dark before I turned down the row to my study. Even if I left only to get a drink of water, I felt and counted the stacks with my hand again to find my room. Once in daylight I glanced at a book on a stack's corner, a book I presumably touched every night with my hand. The book was *The World I Live In*, by Helen Keller. I read it at once; it surprised me by its strong and original prose.

When I flicked on my carrel light, there it all was; the bare room with yellow cinder-block walls; the big, flattened venetian blind and my drawing taped to it; two or three quotations taped up on index cards; and on a far table some books, the fielder's mitt, and a yellow bag of chocolate-covered peanuts. There was the long, blond desk and its chair, and on the desk a dozen different-colored pens, some big index cards in careful, splayed piles, and my messy yellow legal pads. As soon as I saw that desktop, I remembered the task: the chapter, its problems, its phrases, its points.

This night I was concentrating on the chapter. The horizon of my consciousness was the contracted circle of yellow light inside my study — the lone lamp in the enormous, dark library. I leaned over the desk, I worked by hand. I doodled deliriously in the legal-pad margins. I fiddled with the index cards. I reread a sentence maybe a hundred times, and if I kept it I changed it seven or eight times, often substantially.

Now a June bug was knocking at my window. I was wrestling inside a sentence. I must have heard it a dozen times before it registered — before

I noticed that I had been hearing a bug knock for half an hour. It made a hollow, bonking sound. Some people call the same fumbling, heavy insects "May beetles." It must have been attracted to my light — what little came between the slats of the blind. I dislike June bugs. Back to work. Knock again, knock again, and finally, to learn what monster of a fat, brown June bug could fly up to a second story and thump so insistently at my window as though it wanted admittance — at last, unthinkingly, I parted the venetian blind slats with my fingers, to look out.

And there were the fireworks, far away. It was the Fourth of July. I had forgotten. They were red and yellow, blue and green and white; they blossomed high in the black sky many miles away. The fireworks seemed as distant as the stars, but I could hear the late banging their bursting made. The sound, those bangs so muffled and out of synch, accompanied at random the silent, far sprays of color widening and raining down. It was the Fourth of July, and I had forgotten all of wide space and all of historical time. I opened the blinds a crack like eyelids, and it all came exploding in on me at once — oh yes, the world.

My working the graveyard shift in Virginia affected the book. It was a 25 nature book full of sunsets; it wholly lacked dawns, and even mornings.

I was reading about Hassidism, [5] among other things. If you stay awake one hundred nights, you get the vision of Elijah. I was not eager for it, although it seemed to be just around the corner. I preferred this: "Rebbe Shmelke of Nickolsburg, it was told, never really heard his teacher, the Maggid of Mezritch, finish a thought because as soon as the latter would say 'and the Lord spoke,' Shmelke would begin shouting in wonderment, 'The Lord spoke, the Lord spoke,' and continue shouting until he had to be carried from the room."

The second floor of the library, where I worked every night, housed the rare book room. It was a wide, carpeted, well-furnished room. On an end table, as if for decoration, stood a wooden chess set.

One night, stuck on an intractable problem in the writing, I wandered the dark library looking for distraction. I flicked on the lights in the rare book room and looked at some of the books. I saw the chess set and moved white's king's pawn. I turned off the light and wandered back to my carrel.

A few nights later, I glanced into the rare book room and walked in, for black's queen's pawn had moved. I moved out my knight.

We were off and running. Every day, my unseen opponent moved. I 30 moved. I never saw anyone anywhere near the rare book room. The college was not in session; almost no one was around. Late at night I heard the night

---

[5] *Hassidism*: Mystical sect of orthodox Judaism that was founded in the mid-eighteenth century.

watchmen clank around downstairs in the dark. The watchmen never came upstairs. There was no one upstairs but me.

When the chess game was ten days old, I entered the rare book room to find black's pieces coming toward me on the carpet. They seemed to be marching, in rows of two. I put them back as they had been and made my move. The next day, the pieces were all pied on the board. I put them back as they had been. The next day, black had moved, rather brilliantly.

Late one night, while all this had been going on, and while the library was dark and locked as it had been all summer and I had accustomed myself to the eeriness of it, I left my carrel to cross the darkness and get a drink of water. I saw a strange chunk of light on the floor between stacks. Passing the stacks, I saw the light spread across the hall. I held my breath. The light was coming from the rare book room; the door was open.

I approached quietly and looked in the room from an angle. There, at the chess table, stood a baby. The baby had blond curls and was wearing only a diaper.

I paused, considering that I had been playing a reasonable game of chess for two weeks with a naked baby. After a while I could make out the sound of voices; I moved closer to the doorway and peered in. There was the young head librarian and his wife, sitting on chairs. I pieced together the rest of it. The librarian stopped by to pick something up. Naturally, he had a key. The couple happened to have the baby along. The baby, just learning to walk, had cruised from the chairs to the table. The baby was holding on to the table, not studying the chess pieces' positions. I greeted the family and played with the baby until they left.

I never did learn who or what was playing chess with me. The game went on until my lunatic opponent scrambled the board so violently the game was over.

During that time, I let all the houseplants die. After the book was finished I noticed them; the plants hung completely black, dead in their pots in the bay window. For I had not only let them die, I had not moved them. During that time, I told all my out-of-town friends they could not visit for a while.

"I understand you're married," a man said to me at a formal lunch in New York that my publisher had arranged. "How do you have time to write a book?"

"Sir?"

"Well," he said, "you have to have a garden, for instance. You have to entertain." And I thought he was foolish, this man in his seventies, who had no idea what you must do. But the fanaticism of my twenties shocks me now. As I feared it would.

FROM READING TO REREADING

1. Throughout the essay Dillard describes her various workplaces and her schedules. These details may strike readers as merely external matters, having little to do with how Dillard writes and — to borrow Orwell's terms — why she writes. Yet how does Dillard manage to give these "external" matters an "internal" importance? How do they reflect the inner-spirit of her writing life?"

2. Note the images of light and dark that appear throughout the essay. How does Dillard use this imagery, especially images of darkness — to create an atmosphere?

3. The strange game of chess that Dillard plays against an unknown opponent is one of the essay's enigmatic, external details that appear to have nothing to do with her writing. But can you detect any connections that Dillard might be making between the chess playing and composition?

JOAN DIDION

On Keeping a Notebook

Writers keep notebooks for all kinds of reasons — to record impressions, to remember factual information, to jot down ideas, to keep a personal history of their consciousness. Though rarely intended for an audience other than one's self, the notebooks of many famous writers (such as Emerson and Thoreau) have been published and make interesting reading in themselves. In the following essay, however, Joan Didion ponders the value of a writer's notebook — in this case, her own. As she reads the notes she jotted down since childhood, she wonders not only about the person she once was but about her notebook entries' significance to anyone but herself. Notebooks, she claims, are filled with "bits of the mind's string too short to use." In "On Keeping a Notebook" she shows how such insignificant bits of string can be neatly tied together to make a very significant essay. The essay first appeared in Holiday *magazine in 1966 and was collected in* Slouching Towards Bethlehem *(1968).*

"THAT WOMAN ESTELLE,'" the note reads, "'is partly the reason why George Sharp and I are separated today.' *Dirty crepe-de-Chine wrapper, hotel bar, Wilmington RR, 9:45 a.m. August Monday morning.*"

Since the note is in my notebook, it presumably has some meaning to me. I study it for a long while. At first I have only the most general notion of what I was doing on an August Monday morning in the bar of the hotel across from the Pennsylvania Railroad station in Wilmington, Delaware (waiting for a train? missing one? 1960? 1961? why Wilmington?), but I do remember being there. The woman in the dirty crepe-de-Chine wrapper had come down from her room for a beer, and the bartender had heard before the reason why George Sharp and she were separated today. "Sure," he said, and went on mopping the floor. "You told me." At the other end of the bar is a girl. She is talking, pointedly, not to the man beside her but to a cat lying in the triangle of sunlight cast through the open door. She is wearing a plaid silk dress from Peck & Peck, and the hem is coming down.

Here is what it is: the girl has been on the Eastern Shore, and now she is going back to the city, leaving the man beside her, and all she can see ahead are the viscous summer sidewalks and the 3 A.M. long-distance calls that will make her lie awake and then sleep drugged through all the steaming mornings left in August (1960? 1961?). Because she must go directly from the train to lunch in New York, she wishes that she had a safety pin for the hem of the plaid silk dress, and she also wishes that she could forget about the hem and the lunch and stay in the cool bar that smells of disinfectant and malt and make friends with the woman in the crepe-de-Chine wrapper. She is afflicted by a little self-pity, and she wants to compare Estelles. That is what that was all about.

Why did I write it down? In order to remember, of course, but exactly what was it I wanted to remember? How much of it actually happened? Did any of it? Why do I keep a notebook at all? It is easy to deceive oneself on all those scores. The impulse to write things down is a peculiarly compulsive one, inexplicable to those who do not share it, useful only accidentally, only secondarily, in the way that any compulsion tries to justify itself. I suppose that it begins or does not begin in the cradle. Although I have felt compelled to write things down since I was five years old, I doubt that my daughter ever will, for she is a singularly blessed and accepting child, delighted with life exactly as life presents itself to her, unafraid to go to sleep and unafraid to wake up. Keepers of private notebooks are a different breed altogether, lonely and resistant rearrangers of things, anxious malcontents, children afflicted apparently at birth with some presentiment of loss.

My first notebook was a Big Five tablet, given to me by my mother   5 with the sensible suggestion that I stop whining and learn to amuse myself by writing down my thoughts. She returned the tablet to me a few years ago; the first entry is an account of a woman who believed herself to be freezing to death in the Arctic night, only to find, when day broke, that she had stumbled onto the Sahara Desert, where she would die of the heat before lunch. I have no idea what turn of a five-year-old's mind could have prompted so insistently "ironic" and exotic a story, but it does reveal a certain predilection for the extreme which has dogged me into adult life; perhaps if I were analytically inclined I would find it a truer story than any I might have told about Donald Johnson's birthday party or the day my cousin Brenda put Kitty Litter in the aquarium.

So the point of my keeping a notebook has never been, nor is it now, to have an accurate factual record of what I have been doing or thinking. That would be a different impulse entirely, an instinct for reality which I sometimes envy but do not possess. At no point have I ever been able successfully to keep a diary; my approach to daily life ranges from the grossly negligent to the merely absent, and on those few occasions when I have tried dutifully to record a day's events, boredom has so overcome me that the results are mysterious at best. What is this business about "shopping, typing piece, dinner with E, depressed"? Shopping for what? Typing what piece? Who is E? Was this "E" depressed, or was I depressed? Who cares?

In fact I have abandoned altogether that kind of pointless entry; instead I tell what some would call lies. "That's simply not true," the members of my family frequently tell me when they come up against my memory of a shared event. "The party was *not* for you, the spider was *not* a black widow, *it wasn't that way at all.*" Very likely they are right, for not only have I always had trouble distinguishing between what happened and what merely might have happened, but I remain unconvinced that the distinction, for my purposes, matters. The cracked crab that I recall having for lunch the day my father came home from Detroit in 1945 must certainly be embroidery, worked into the day's pattern to lend verisimilitude; I was ten years old and would not now remember the cracked crab. The day's events did not turn on cracked crab. And yet it is precisely that fictitious crab that makes me see the afternoon all over again, a home movie run all too often, the father bearing gifts, the child weeping, an exercise in family love and guilt. Or that is what it was to me. Similarly, perhaps it never did snow that August in Vermont; perhaps there never were flurries in the night wind, and maybe no one else felt the ground hardening and summer already dead even as we pretended to bask in it, but that was how it felt to me, and it might as well have snowed, could have snowed, did snow.

How it felt to me: that is getting closer to the truth about a notebook. I sometimes delude myself about why I keep a notebook, imagine that some thrifty virtue derives from preserving everything observed. See enough and write it down, I tell myself, and then some morning when the world seems drained of wonder, some day when I am only going through the motions of doing what I am supposed to do, which is write — on that bankrupt morning I will simply open my notebook and there it will all be, a forgotten account with accumulated interest, paid passage back to the world out there; dialogue overheard in hotels and elevators and at the hatcheck counter in Pavillon (one middle-aged man shows his hat check to another and says, "That's my old football number"); impressions of Bettina Aptheker and Benjamin Sonnenberg and Teddy ("Mr. Acapulco") Stauffer; careful *aperçus* [1] about tennis bums and failed fashion models and Greek shipping heiresses, one of whom taught me a significant lesson (a lesson I could have learned from F. Scott Fitzgerald, but perhaps we all must meet the very rich for ourselves) by asking, when I arrived to interview her in her orchid-filled sitting room on the second day of a paralyzing New York blizzard, whether it was snowing outside.

I imagine, in other words, that the notebook is about other people. But of course it is not. I have no real business with what one stranger said to another at the hatcheck counter in Pavillon; in fact I suspect that the line "That's my old football number" touched not my own imagination at all, but merely some memory of something once read, probably "The Eighty-Yard Run." [2] Nor is my concern with a woman in a dirty crepe-de-Chine wrapper in a Wilmington bar. My stake is always, of course, in the unmentioned girl in the plaid silk dress. *Remember what it was to be me:* that is always the point.

---

[1] *aperçus*: Summarizing glimpse or insight (French).

[2] *"The Eighty-Yard Run"*: Popular short story by Irwin Shaw.

It is a difficult point to admit. We are brought up in the ethic that   10
others, any others, all others, are by definition more interesting than ourselves; taught to be diffident, just this side of self-effacing. ("You're the least
important person in the room and don't forget it," Jessica Mitford's [3] govern-
ess would hiss in her ear on the advent of any social occasion; I copied that
into my notebook because it is only recently that I have been able to enter
a room without hearing some such phrase in my inner ear.) Only the very
young and the very old may recount their dreams at breakfast, dwell upon
self, interrupt with memories of beach picnics and favorite Liberty lawn
dresses and the rainbow trout in a creek near Colorado Springs. The rest of
us are expected, rightly, to affect absorption in other people's favorite dresses,
other people's trout.

And so we do. But our notebooks give us away, for however dutifully
we record what we see around us, the common denominator of all we see is
always, transparently, shamelessly, the implacable "I." We are not talking
here about the kind of notebook that is patently for public consumption, a
structural conceit for binding together a series of graceful *pensées*; [4] we are
talking about something private, about bits of the mind's string too short to
use, an indiscriminate and erratic assemblage with meaning only for its maker.

And sometimes even the maker has difficulty with the meaning. There
does not seem to be, for example, any point in my knowing for the rest of
my life that, during 1964, 720 tons of soot fell on every square mile of New
York City, yet there it is in my notebook, labeled "FACT." Nor do I really
need to remember that Ambrose Bierce liked to spell Leland Stanford's name
"$eland $tanford" [5] or that "smart women almost always wear black in Cuba,"
a fashion hint without much potential for practical application. And does not
the relevance of these notes seem marginal at best?:

> In the basement museum of the Inyo County Courthouse in Independence,
> California, sign pinned to a mandarin coat: "This MANDARIN COAT was
> often worn by Mrs. Minnie S. Brooks when giving lectures on her TEAPOT
> COLLECTION."

> Redhead getting out of car in front of Beverly Wilshire Hotel, chinchilla
> stole, Vuitton bags with tags reading:

> MRS LOU FOX
> HOTEL SAHARA
> VEGAS

---

[3] *Jessica Mitford* (b. 1917): British satirical writer and essayist.

[4] *pensées*: Thoughts or reflections (French).

[5] *Bierce . . . Stanford*: Ambrose Bierce (1842–1914?), American journalist and short story
writer known for his savage wit; Leland Stanford (1824–1893), wealthy railroad builder who
was a governor of California and the founder of Stanford University.

Well, perhaps not entirely marginal. As a matter of fact, Mrs. Minnie S. Brooks and her MANDARIN COAT pull me back into my own childhood, for although I never knew Mrs. Brooks and did not visit Inyo County until I was thirty, I grew up in just such a world, in houses cluttered with Indian relics and bits of gold ore and ambergris and the souvenirs my Aunt Mercy Farnsworth brought back from the Orient. It is a long way from that world to Mrs. Lou Fox's world, where we all live now, and is it not just as well to remember that? Might not Mrs. Minnie S. Brooks help me to remember what I am? Might not Mrs. Lou Fox help me to remember what I am not?

But sometimes the point is harder to discern. What exactly did I have in mind when I noted down that it cost the father of someone I know $650 a month to light the place on the Hudson in which he lived before the Crash? What use was I planning to make of this line by Jimmy Hoffa [6]: "I may have my faults, but being wrong ain't one of them"? And although I think it interesting to know where the girls who travel with the Syndicate have their hair done when they find themselves on the West Coast, will I ever make suitable use of it? Might I not be better off just passing it on to John O'Hara? [7] What is a recipe for sauerkraut doing in my notebook? What kind of magpie keeps this notebook? *"He was born the night the Titanic went down."* That seems a nice enough line, and I even recall who said it, but is it not really a better line in life than it could ever be in fiction?

But of course that is exactly it: not that I should ever use the line, but   15
that I should remember the woman who said it and the afternoon I heard it. We were on her terrace by the sea, and we were finishing the wine left from lunch, trying to get what sun there was, a California winter sun. The woman whose husband was born the night the *Titanic* went down wanted to rent her house, wanted to go back to her children in Paris. I remember wishing that I could afford the house, which cost $1,000 a month. "Someday you will," she said lazily. "Someday it all comes." There in the sun on her terrace it seemed easy to believe in someday, but later I had a low-grade afternoon hangover and ran over a black snake on the way to the supermarket and was flooded with inexplicable fear when I heard the checkout clerk explaining to the man ahead of me why she was finally divorcing her husband. "He left me no choice," she said over and over as she punched the register. "He has a little seven-month-old baby by her, he left me no choice." I would like to believe that my dread then was for the human condition, but of course it was for me, because I wanted a baby and did not then have one and because I wanted to own the house that cost $1,000 a month to rent and because I had a hangover.

[6] *Jimmy Hoffa* (1913–1975?): Controversial leader of the Teamsters Union who disappeared in the mid-seventies.

[7] *John O'Hara* (1905–1970): American novelist who wrote several books about gangsters.

It all comes back. Perhaps it is difficult to see the value in having one's self back in that kind of mood, but I do see it; I think we are well advised to keep on nodding terms with the people we used to be whether we find them attractive company or not. Otherwise they turn up unannounced and surprise us, come hammering on the mind's door at 4 A.M. of a bad night and demand to know who deserted them, who betrayed them, who is going to make amends. We forget all too soon the things we thought we could never forget. We forget the loves and the betrayals alike, forget what we whispered and what we screamed, forget who we were. I have already lost touch with a couple of people I used to be; one of them, a seventeen-year-old, presents little threat, although it would be of some interest to me to know again what it feels like to sit on a river levee drinking vodka-and-orange-juice and listening to Les Paul and Mary Ford[8] and their echoes sing "How High the Moon" on the car radio. (You see I still have the scenes, but I no longer perceive myself among those present, no longer could even improvise the dialogue.) The other one, a twenty-three-year-old, bothers me more. She was always a good deal of trouble, and I suspect she will reappear when I least want to see her, skirts too long, shy to the point of aggravation, always the injured party, full of recriminations and little hurts and stories I do not want to hear again, at once saddening me and angering me with her vulnerability and ignorance, an apparition all the more insistent for being so long banished.

It is a good idea, then, to keep in touch, and I suppose that keeping in touch is what notebooks are all about. And we are all on our own when it comes to keeping those lines open to ourselves: your notebook will never help me, nor mine you. "*So what's new in the whiskey business?*" What could that possibly mean to you? To me it means a blonde in a Pucci bathing suit sitting with a couple of fat men by the pool at the Beverly Hills Hotel. Another man approaches, and they all regard one another in silence for a while. "So what's new in the whiskey business?" one of the fat men finally says by way of welcome, and the blonde stands up, arches one foot and dips it in the pool, looking all the while at the cabaña where Baby Pignatari is talking on the telephone. That is all there is to that, except that several years later I saw the blonde coming out of Saks Fifth Avenue in New York with her California complexion and a voluminous mink coat. In the harsh wind that day she looked old and irrevocably tired to me, and even the skins in the mink coat were not worked the way they were doing them that year, not the way she would have wanted them done, and there is the point of the story. For a while after that I did not like to look in the mirror, and my eyes would skim the newspapers and pick out only the deaths, the cancer victims, the premature coronaries, the suicides, and I stopped riding the

[8] *Les Paul . . . Mary Ford*: Husband-and-wife musical team of the forties and fifties who had many hit records.

Lexington Avenue IRT because I noticed for the first time that all the strangers I had seen for years — the man with the seeing-eye dog, the spinster who read the classified pages every day, the fat girl who always got off with me at Grand Central — looked older than they once had.

It all comes back. Even that recipe for sauerkraut: even that brings it back. I was on Fire Island when I first made that sauerkraut, and it was raining, and we drank a lot of bourbon and ate the sauerkraut and went to bed at ten, and I listened to the rain and the Atlantic and felt safe. I made the sauerkraut again last night and it did not make me feel any safer, but that is, as they say, another story.

FROM READING TO REREADING

1. Didion opens her essay not with a remark about notebooks but with an actual notebook entry. What does the entry sound like? How disorienting is it at first? What effect does she want to convey by starting this way?

2. Didion makes a distinction in paragraph 6 between a notebook and a diary. What is the difference? Why can she keep one and not the other? How is the distinction she makes borne out by her example of a diary entry?

3. Didion's essay presents an interesting case of a writer's audience; the original notebook entries were written for herself, yet she is now making them public. How many levels of audience can you identify in the essay? How does Didion succeed in creating an audience for writing that was never intended to have one? Also, how does she place herself in the position of both the writer and the reader, and how does that affect your role as an audience?

CYNTHIA OZICK
A Drugstore in Winter

What influences go into the making of a writer? Can they be biographically sorted out? How do family, background, neighborhood, and education, reading and daydreams, shape the consciousness of a child who will one day become a writer? In "A Drugstore in Winter," one of America's prominent literary figures attempts to answer this intriguing question by peering into her own past and producing a "summary" of how she came to be where she is now — "and where, God knows, is that?" This autobiographical essay originally appeared in The New York Times Book Review *in 1982 and was collected in* Art & Ardor *(1984).*

T HIS IS ABOUT READING; a drugstore in winter; the gold leaf on the dome of the Boston State House; also loss, panic, and dread.

First, the gold leaf. (This part is a little like a turn-of-the-century pulp tale, though only a little. The ending is a surprise, but there is no plot.) Thirty years ago I burrowed in the Boston Public Library one whole afternoon, to find out — not out of curiosity — how the State House got its gold roof. The answer, like the answer to most Bostonian questions, was Paul Revere. So I put Paul Revere's gold dome into an "article," and took it (though I was just as scared by recklessness then as I am now) to the *Boston Globe*, on Washington Street. The Features Editor had a bare severe head, a closed parenthesis mouth, and silver Dickensian spectacles. He made me wait, standing, at the side of his desk while he read; there was no bone in me that did not rattle. Then he opened a drawer and handed me fifteen dollars. Ah, joy of Homer, joy of Milton! Grub Street[1] bliss!

The very next Sunday, Paul Revere's gold dome saw print. Appetite for more led me to a top-floor chamber in Filene's department store: Window Dressing. But no one was in the least bit dressed — it was a dumbstruck nudist colony up there, a mob of naked frozen enigmatic manikins, tall enameled skinny ladies with bald breasts and skulls, and legs and wrists and necks that horribly unscrewed. Paul Revere's dome paled beside this gold mine! A sight — mute numb Walpurgisnacht[2] — easily worth another fifteen dollars. I had a Master's degree (thesis topic: "Parable in the Later Novels of Henry James")[3] and a job as an advertising copywriter (9 A.M. to 6 P.M.

---

[1] *Grub Street*: London street inhabited by poor and obscure writers trying to make a living; the term is now used to signify hackwork.

[2] *Walpurgisnacht*: In folklore, the day before May 1, when witches supposedly held a sabbath (German).

[3] *James*: The essay is so embedded with references to periodicals and to popular and classical

six days a week, forty dollars per week; if you were male and had no degree at all, sixty dollars.) Filene's Sale Days — Crib Bolsters! Lulla-Buys! Jonnie-Mops! Maternity Skirts with Expanding Invisible Trick Waist! And a company show; gold watches to mark the retirement of elderly Irish salesladies; for me the chance to write song lyrics (to the tune of "On Top of Old Smoky") honoring our Store. But "Mute Numb Walpurgisnacht in Secret Downtown Chamber" never reached the *Globe*. Melancholy and meaning business, the Advertising Director forbade it. Grub Street was bad form, and I had to promise never again to sink to another article. Thus ended my life in journalism.

Next: reading, and certain drugstore winter dusks. These come together. It is an aeon before Filene's, years and years before the Later Novels of Henry James. I am scrunched on my knees at a round glass table near a plate glass door on which is inscribed, in gold leaf Paul Revere never put there, letters that must be read backward: ꙰PARK VIEW PHARMACY   There is an evening smell of late coffee from the fountain, and all the librarians are lined up in a row on the tall stools, sipping and chattering. They have just stepped in from the cold of the Traveling Library, and so have I. The Traveling Library is a big green truck that stops, once every two weeks, on the corner of Continental Avenue, just a little way in from Westchester Avenue, not far from a house that keeps a pig. Other houses fly pigeons from their roofs, other yards have chickens, and down on Mayflower there is even a goat. This is Pelham Bay, the Bronx, in the middle of the Depression, all cattails and weeds, such a lovely place and tender hour! Even though my mother takes me on the subway far, far downtown to buy my winter coat in the frenzy of Klein's on Fourteenth Street, and even though I can recognize the heavy power of a quarter, I don't know it's the Depression. On the trolley on the way to Westchester Square I see the children who live in the boxcar strangely set down in an empty lot some distance from Spy Oak (where a Revolutionary traitor was hanged — served him right for siding with redcoats); the lucky boxcar children dangle their stick-legs from their trainhouse maw and wave; how I envy them! I envy the orphans of the Gould Foundation, who have their own private swings and seesaws. Sometimes I imagine I am an orphan, and my father is an impostor pretending to be my father.

My father writes in his prescription book: *#59330 Dr. O'Flaherty Pow* 5
.60/ #59331 Dr. Mulligan Gtt .65/ #59332 Dr. Thron Tab .90. Ninety cents! A terrifically expensive medicine; someone is really sick. When I deliver a prescription around the corner or down the block, I am offered a nickel tip. I always refuse, out of conscience; I am, after all, the Park View Pharmacy's own daughter, and it wouldn't be seemly. My father grinds and mixes pow-

books that footnotes to all of them would be overwhelming. Ozick's references and allusions are mainly intended to suggest the range and variety of her reading.

ders, weighs them out in tiny snowy heaps on an apothecary scale, folds them into delicate translucent papers or meticulously drops them into gelatin capsules.

In the big front window of the Park View Pharmacy there is a startling display — goldfish bowls, balanced one on the other in amazing pyramids. A German lady enters, one of my father's cronies — his cronies are both women and men. My quiet father's eyes are water-color blue, he wears his small skeptical quiet smile and receives the neighborhood's life-secrets. My father is discreet and inscrutable. The German lady pokes a punchboard with a pin, pushes up a bit of rolled paper, and cries out — she has just won a goldfish bowl, with two swimming goldfish in it! Mr. Jaffe, the salesman from McKesson & Robbins, arrives, trailing two mists: winter steaminess and the animal fog of his cigar, [4] which melts into the coffee smell, the tarpaper smell, the eerie honeyed tangled drugstore smell. Mr. Jaffe and my mother and father are intimates by now, but because it is the 1930s, so long ago, and the old manners still survive, they address one another gravely as Mr. Jaffe, Mrs. Ozick, Mr. Ozick. My mother calls my father Mr. O, even at home, as in a Victorian novel. In the street my father tips his hat to ladies. In the winter his hat is a regular fedora; in the summer it is a straw boater with a black ribbon and a jot of blue feather.

What am I doing at this round glass table, both listening and not listening to my mother and father tell Mr. Jaffe about their struggle with "Tessie," the lion-eyed landlady who has just raised, threefold, in the middle of that Depression I have never heard of, the Park View Pharmacy's devouring rent? My mother, not yet forty, wears bandages on her ankles, covering oozing varicose veins; back and forth she strides, dashes, runs, climbing cellar stairs or ladders; she unpacks cartons, she toils behind drug counters and fountain counters. Like my father, she is on her feet until one in the morning, the Park View's closing hour. My mother and father are in trouble, and I don't know it. I am too happy. I feel the secret center of eternity, nothing will ever alter, no one will ever die. Through the window, past the lit goldfish, the gray oval sky deepens over our neighborhood wood, where all the dirt paths lead down to seagull-specked water. I am familiar with every frog-haunted monument: Pelham Bay Park is thronged with WPA art — statuary, fountains, immense rococo staircases cascading down a hillside, Bacchus-faced stelae — stone Roman glories afterward mysteriously razed by an avenging Robert Moses. [5] One year — how distant it seems now, as if even the climate is past returning — the bay froze so hard that whole

---

[4] Mr. Matthew Bruccoli, another Bronx drugstore child, has written to say that he remembers with certainty that Mr. Jaffe did not smoke. In my memory the cigar is somehow there, so I leave it. [Ozick's note]

[5] *Robert Moses* (1888–1981): Controversial New York City builder and city planner, who was responsible for developing many park, bridge, and highway projects.

families, mine among them, crossed back and forth to City Island, strangers saluting and calling out in the ecstasy of the bright trudge over such a sudden wilderness of ice.

In the Park View Pharmacy, in the winter dusk, the heart in my body is revolving like the goldfish fleet-finned in their clear bowls. The librarians are still warming up over their coffee. They do not recognize me, though only half an hour ago I was scrabbling in the mud around the two heavy boxes from the Traveling Library — oafish crates tossed with a thump to the ground. One box contains magazines — *Boy's Life, The American Girl, Popular Mechanix*. But the other, the other! The other transforms me. It is tumbled with storybooks, with clandestine intimations and transfigurations. In school I am a luckless goosegirl, friendless and forlorn. In P.S. 71 I carry, weighty as a cloak, the ineradicable knowledge of my scandal — I am cross-eyed, dumb, an imbecile at arithmetic; in P.S. 71 I am publicly shamed in Assembly because I am caught not singing Christmas carols; in P.S. 71 I am repeatedly accused of deicide. But in the Park View Pharmacy, in the winter dusk, branches blackening in the park across the road, I am driving in rapture through the Violet Fairy Book and the Yellow Fairy Book, insubstantial chariots snatched from the box in the mud. I have never been *inside* the Traveling Library; only grownups are allowed. The boxes are for the children. No more than two books may be borrowed, so I have picked the fattest ones, to last. All the same, the Violet and the Yellow are melting away. Their pages dwindle. I sit at the round glass table, dreaming, dreaming. Mr. Jaffe is murmuring advice. He tells a joke about Wrong-Way Corrigan. The librarians are buttoning up their coats. A princess, captive of an ogre, receives a letter from her swain and hides it in her bosom. I can visualize her bosom exactly — she clutches it against her chest. It is a tall and shapely vase, with a hand-painted flower on it, like the vase on the secondhand piano at home.

I am incognito. No one knows who I truly am. The teachers in P.S. 71 don't know. Rabbi Meskin, my *cheder* [6] teacher, doesn't know. Tessie the lion-eyed landlady doesn't know. Even Hymie the fountain clerk can't know — though he understands other things better than anyone: how to tighten roller skates with a skatekey, for instance, and how to ride a horse. On Friday afternoons, when the new issue is out, Hymie and my brother fight hard over who gets to see *Life* magazine first. My brother is older than I am, and doesn't like me; he builds radios in his bedroom, he is already W2LOM, and operates his transmitter (*da-di-da-dit, da-da-di-da*) so penetratingly on Sunday mornings that Mrs. Eva Brady, across the way, complains. Mrs. Eva Brady has a subscription to *The Writer;* I fill a closet with her old copies. How to Find a Plot. Narrative and Character, the Writer's Tools. Because my brother has his ham license, I say, "I have a license too." "What kind of license?" my brother asks, falling into the trap. "Poetic license," I reply; my brother hates me, but anyhow his birthday presents are transporting: one

[6] *cheder*: Hebrew school.

year *Alice in Wonderland, Pinocchio* the next, then *Tom Sawyer.* I go after Mark Twain, and find *Joan of Arc* and my first satire, *Christian Science.* My mother surprises me with *Pollyanna,* the admiration of her Lower East Side childhood, along with *The Lady of the Lake.* Mrs. Eva Brady's daughter Jeannie has outgrown her Nancy Drews and Judy Boltons, so on rainy afternoons I cross the street and borrow them, trying not to march away with too many — the child of immigrants, I worry that the Bradys, true and virtuous Americans, will judge me greedy or careless. I wrap the Nancy Drews in paper covers to protect them. Old Mrs. Brady, Jeannie's grandmother, invites me back for more. I am so timid I can hardly speak a word, but I love her dark parlor; I love its black bookcases. Old Mrs. Brady sees me off, embracing books under an umbrella; perhaps she divines who I truly am. My brother doesn't care. My father doesn't notice. I think my mother knows. My mother reads the *Saturday Evening Post* and the *Woman's Home Companion;* sometimes the *Ladies' Home Journal,* but never *Good Housekeeping.* I read all my mother's magazines. My father reads *Drug Topics* and *Der Tog,* the Yiddish daily. In Louie Davidowitz's house (waiting our turn for the rabbi's lesson, he teaches me chess in *cheder*) there is a piece of furniture I am in awe of: a shining circular table that is also a revolving bookshelf holding a complete set of Charles Dickens. I borrow *Oliver Twist.* My cousins turn up with *Gulliver's Travels, Just So Stories, Don Quixote,* Oscar Wilde's *Fairy Tales,* uncannily different from the usual kind. Blindfolded, I reach into a Thanksgiving grabbag and pull out *Mrs. Leicester's School,* Mary Lamb's desolate stories of rejected children. Books spill out of rumor, exchange, miracle. In the Park View Pharmacy's lending library I discover, among the nurse romances, a browning, brittle miracle: *Jane Eyre.* Uncle Morris comes to visit (*his* drugstore is on the other side of the Bronx) and leaves behind, just like that, a three-volume Shakespeare. Peggy and Betty Provan, Scottish sisters around the corner, lend me their *Swiss Family Robinson.* Norma Foti, a whole year older, transmits a rumor about Louisa May Alcott; afterward I read *Little Women* a thousand times. Ten thousand! I am no longer incognito, not even to myself. I am Jo in her "vortex"; not Jo exactly, but some Jo-of-the-future. I am under an enchantment: who I truly am must be deferred, waited for and waited for. My father, silently filling capsules, is grieving over his mother in Moscow. I write letters in Yiddish to my Moscow grandmother, whom I will never know. I will know my Russian aunts, uncles, cousins. In Moscow there is suffering, deprivation, poverty. My mother, threadbare, goes without a new winter coat so that packages can be sent to Moscow. Her fiery justice-eyes are semaphores I cannot decipher.

Someday, when I am free of P.S. 71, I will write stories; meanwhile, 10 in winter dusk, in the Park View, in the secret bliss of the Violet Fairy Book, I both see and do not see how these grains of life will stay forever, papa and mama will live forever, Hymie will always turn my skatekey.

Hymie, after Italy, after the Battle of the Bulge, comes back from the war with a present: *From Here to Eternity.* Then he dies, young. Mama reads

Pride and Prejudice and every single word of Willa Cather. Papa reads, in Yiddish, all of Sholem Aleichem and Peretz. He reads Malamud's *The Assistant* when I ask him to.

Papa and mama, in Staten Island, are under the ground. Some other family sits transfixed in the sun parlor where I read *Jane Eyre* and *Little Women* and, long afterward, *Middlemarch*. The Park View Pharmacy is dismantled, turned into a Hallmark card shop. It doesn't matter! I close my eyes, or else only stare, and everything is in its place again, and everyone.

A writer is dreamed and transfigured into being by spells, wishes, goldfish, silhouettes of trees, boxes of fairy tales dropped in the mud, uncles' and cousins' books, tablets and capsules and powders, papa's Moscow ache, his drugstore jacket with his special fountain pen in the pocket, his beautiful Hebrew paragraphs, his Talmudist's rationalism, his Russian-Gymnasium Latin and German, mama's furnace-heart, her masses of memoirs, her paintings of autumn walks down to the sunny water, her braveries, her reveries, her old, old school hurts.

A writer is buffeted into being by school hurts — Orwell, Forster, Mann! — but after a while other ambushes begin: sorrows, deaths, disappointments, subtle diseases, delays, guilts, the spite of the private haters of the poetry side of life, the snubs of the glamorous, the bitterness of those for whom resentment is a daily gruel, and so on and so on; and then one day you find yourself leaning here, writing at that selfsame round glass table salvaged from the Park View Pharmacy — writing this, an impossibility, a summary of how you came to be where you are now, and where, God knows, is that? Your hair is whitening, you are a well of tears, what you meant to do (beauty and justice) you have not done, papa and mama are under the earth, you live in panic and dread, the future shrinks and darkens, stories are only vapor, your inmost craving is for nothing but an old scarred pen, and what, God knows, is that?

FROM READING TO REREADING

1. Cynthia Ozick begins her essay with an account of writing an "article" for the *Boston Globe*. What is her attitude toward this article? In what ways do you think it differed from "A Drugstore in Winter"?

2. Notice the numerous references Ozick makes to her childhood reading. Try to classify it: What types of books and magazines did she read? What is her attitude toward them? In what ways are they connected to her environment? Of what significance is that connection to Ozick?

3. Notice the pronoun shift in the essay's final paragraph, as Ozick turns from "I" to "you." Who is the "you"? Why would she have made this shift at this point? What effect does it have?

JAMES BALDWIN
Autobiographical Notes

Essayists occasionally use the word "Notes" in a title, thus informing readers ahead of time that a given piece was composed more or less effortlessly and without a deliberate structure. In the following essay, James Baldwin, whose writing often strikes a tone of casual eloquence, extends the idea of "notes" right into the sentence structure of the piece itself, so that at times the essay reads like a spontaneous biographical statement prepared for a book jacket blurb or a magazine profile. The essay was collected in Notes of a Native Son *(1955), but Baldwin did not include it in his 1984 collection of essays and nonfiction,* The Price of the Ticket. *Its exclusion is puzzling since it represents one of the clearest accounts he has given of his motives for writing.*

I WAS BORN in Harlem thirty-one years ago. I began plotting novels at about the time I learned to read. The story of my childhood is the usual bleak fantasy, and we can dismiss it with the restrained observation that I certainly would not consider living it again. In those days my mother was given to the exasperating and mysterious habit of having babies. As they were born, I took them over with one hand and held a book with the other. The children probably suffered, though they have since been kind enough to deny it, and in this way I read *Uncle Tom's Cabin* and *A Tale of Two Cities* over and over and over again; in this way, in fact, I read just about everything I could get my hands on — except the Bible, probably because it was the only book I was encouraged to read. I must also confess that I wrote — a great deal — and my first professional triumph, in any case, the first effort of mine to be seen in print, occurred at the age of twelve or thereabouts, when a short story I had written about the Spanish revolution won some sort of prize in an extremely short-lived church newspaper. I remember the story was censored by the lady editor, though I don't remember why, and I was outraged.

Also wrote plays, and songs, for one of which I received a letter of congratulations from Mayor La Guardia,[1] and poetry, about which the less said, the better. My mother was delighted by all these goings-on, but my father wasn't; he wanted me to be a preacher. When I was fourteen I became a preacher, and when I was seventeen I stopped. Very shortly thereafter I left home. For God knows how long I struggled with the world of commerce

---

[1] *La Guardia;* Fiorella La Guardia (1882–1947), popular New York City mayor who held office from 1934 to 1945.

and industry — I guess they would say they struggled with me — and when I was about twenty-one I had enough done of a novel to get a Saxton Fellowship. When I was twenty-two the fellowship was over, the novel turned out to be unsalable, and I started waiting on tables in a Village restaurant and writing book reviews — mostly, as it turned out, about the Negro problem, [2] concerning which the color of my skin made me automatically an expert. Did another book, in company with photographer Theodore Pelatowski, about the storefront churches in Harlem. This book met exactly the same fate as my first — fellowship, but no sale. (It was a Rosenwald Fellowship.) By the time I was twenty-four I had decided to stop reviewing books about the Negro problem — which, by this time, was only slightly less horrible in print than it was in life — and I packed my bags and went to France, where I finished, God knows how, *Go Tell It on the Mountain*.

Any writer, I suppose, feels that the world into which he was born is nothing less than a conspiracy against the cultivation of his talent — which attitude certainly has a great deal to support it. On the other hand, it is only because the world looks on his talent with such a frightening indifference that the artist is compelled to make his talent important. So that any writer, looking back over even so short a span of time as I am here forced to assess, finds that the things which hurt him and the things which helped him cannot be divorced from each other; he could be helped in a certain way only because he was hurt in a certain way; and his help is simply to be enabled to move from one conundrum to the next — one is tempted to say that he moves from one disaster to the next. When one begins looking for influences one finds them by the score. I haven't thought much about my own, not enough anyway; I hazard that the King James Bible, the rhetoric of the storefront church, something ironic and violent and perpetually understated in Negro speech — and something of Dickens' love for bravura — have something to do with me today; but I wouldn't stake my life on it. Likewise, innumerable people have helped me in many ways; but finally, I suppose the most difficult (and most rewarding) thing in my life has been the fact that I was born a Negro and was forced, therefore, to effect some kind of truce with this reality. (Truce, by the way, is the best one can hope for.)

One of the difficulties about being a Negro writer (and this is not special pleading, since I don't mean to suggest that he has it worse than anybody else) is that the Negro problem is written about so widely. The bookshelves groan under the weight of information, and everyone therefore considers himself informed. And this information, furthermore, operates usually (generally, popularly) to reinforce traditional attitudes. Of traditional attitudes there are only two — For or Against — and I, personally, find it difficult to say which attitude has caused me the most pain. I am speaking

[2] *Negro problem*: The question of how to deal with the injustices suffered by black Americans was for many years termed "the Negro problem."

as a writer; from a social point of view I am perfectly aware that the change from ill-will to good-will, however motivated, however imperfect, however expressed, is better than no change at all.

But it is part of the business of the writer — as I see it — to examine   5
attitudes, to go beneath the surface, to tap the source. From this point of view the Negro problem is nearly inaccessible. It is not only written about so widely; it is written about so badly. It is quite possible to say that the price a Negro pays for becoming articulate is to find himself, at length, with nothing to be articulate about. ("You taught me language," says Caliban to Prospero, "and my profit on't is I know how to curse.")³ Consider: the tremendous social activity that this problem generates imposes on whites and Negroes alike the necessity of looking forward, of working to bring about a better day. This is fine, it keeps the waters troubled; it is all, indeed, that has made possible the Negro's progress. Nevertheless, social affairs are not generally speaking the writer's prime concern, whether they ought to be or not; it is absolutely necessary that he establish between himself and these affairs a distance which will allow, at least, for clarity, so that before he can look forward in any meaningful sense, he must first be allowed to take a long look back. In the context of the Negro problem neither whites nor blacks, for excellent reasons of their own, have the faintest desire to look back; but I think that the past is all that makes the present coherent, and further, that the past will remain horrible for exactly as long as we refuse to assess it honestly.

I know, in any case, that the most crucial time in my own development came when I was forced to recognize that I was a kind of bastard of the West; when I followed the line of my past I did not find myself in Europe but in Africa. And this meant that in some subtle way, in a really profound way, I brought to Shakespeare, Bach, Rembrandt, to the stones of Paris, to the cathedral at Chartres, and to the Empire State Building, a special attitude. These were not really my creations, they did not contain my history; I might search in them in vain forever for any reflection of myself. I was an interloper; this was not my heritage. At the same time I had no other heritage which I could possibly hope to use — I had certainly been unfitted for the jungle or the tribe. I would have to appropriate these white centuries. I would have to make them mine — I would have to accept my special attitude, my special place in this scheme — otherwise I would have no place in *any* scheme. What was the most difficult was the fact that I was forced to admit something I had always hidden from myself, which the American Negro has had to hide from himself as the price of his public progress; that I hated and feared white people. This did not mean that I loved black people; on the contrary, I despised them, possibly because they failed to produce Rembrandt. In effect,

---

³ *You . . . curse*: From Shakespeare's *The Tempest*; the relationship between Prospero and Caliban is that of master and slave.

I hated and feared the world. And this meant, not only that I thus gave the world an altogether murderous power over me, but also that in such a self-destroying limbo I could never hope to write.

One writes out of one thing only — one's own experience. Everything depends on how relentlessly one forces from this experience the last drop, sweet or bitter, it can possibly give. This is the only real concern of the artist, to recreate out of the disorder of life that order which is art. The difficulty then, for me, of being a Negro writer was the fact that I was, in effect, prohibited from examining my own experience too closely by the tremendous demands and the very real dangers of my social situation.

I don't think the dilemma outlined above is uncommon. I do think, since writers work in the disastrously explicit medium of language, that it goes a little way toward explaining why, out of the enormous resources of Negro speech and life, and despite the example of Negro music, prose written by Negroes has been generally speaking so pallid and so harsh. I have not written about being a Negro at such length because I expect that to be my only subject, but only because it was the gate I had to unlock before I could hope to write about anything else. I don't think that the Negro problem in America can be even discussed coherently without bearing in mind its context; its context being the history, traditions, customs, the moral assumptions and preoccupations of the country; in short, the general social fabric. Appearances to the contrary, no one in America escapes its effects and everyone in America bears some responsibility for it. I believe this the more firmly because it is the overwhelming tendency to speak of this problem as though it were a thing apart. But in the work of Faulkner, in the general attitude and certain specific passages in Robert Penn Warren, and, most significantly, in the advent of Ralph Ellison, [4] one sees the beginnings — at least — of a more genuinely penetrating search. Mr. Ellison, by the way, is the first Negro novelist I have ever read to utilize in language, and brilliantly, some of the ambiguity and irony of Negro life.

About my interests: I don't know if I have any, unless the morbid desire to own a sixteen-millimeter camera and make experimental movies can be so classified. Otherwise, I love to eat and drink — it's my melancholy conviction that I've scarcely ever had enough to eat (this is because it's *impossible* to eat enough if you're worried about the next meal) — and I love to argue with people who do not disagree with me too profoundly, and I love to laugh. I do *not* like bohemia, or bohemians, I do not like people whose principal aim is pleasure, and I do not like people who are *earnest* about anything. I don't like people who like me because I'm a Negro; neither do I like people who find in the same accident grounds for contempt. I love

[4] *Warren . . . Ellison*: Robert Penn Warren (1905–1990), white Southern poet, novelist, and critic who taught literature at Yale University; Ralph Ellison (b. 1914), black novelist who published *Invisible Man* in 1952.

America more than any other country in the world, and, exactly for this reason, I insist on the right to criticize her perpetually. I think all theories are suspect, that the finest principles may have to be modified, or may even be pulverized by the demands of life, and that one must find, therefore, one's own moral center and move through the world hoping that this center will guide one aright. I consider that I have many responsibilities, but none greater than this: to last, as Hemingway says, and get my work done.

I want to be an honest man and a good writer.   10

FROM READING TO REREADING

1. Baldwin began his career writing book reviews — "mostly, as it turned out, about the Negro problem, concerning which the color of my skin made me automatically an expert." What is his tone here? In what ways was "the Negro problem" both an opportunity for Baldwin and an obstacle?

2. Notice how Baldwin suddenly alters his tone in the second-to-last paragraph, when he begins "About my interests." What does that statement suggest about his intended audience and the occasion of the essay?

3. At one point, Baldwin describes himself as "an interloper." Interestingly, a leading European theorist of the essay, Theodore Adorno, once described the essay as the form of interlopers. In what sense did Baldwin's dilemma offer him an advantage as an essayist?

VIRGINIA WOOLF
Professions for Women

Though many of Virginia Woolf's essays were written for very specific occasions
— speeches, book review assignments, club gatherings, and the like — the quality
of her language and intelligence makes her essays far more than "occasional" (the
word critics use to describe essays that are stimulated from without rather than
from within). "Professions for Women" is one such essay; written as a talk for
a particular occasion, it far surpasses its immediate context, and its language
still powerfully speaks to the condition of women in professional life. The essay
reprinted here is a shorter version of the paper that Woolf read to a British
women's organization, the Women's Service League, in 1931. After Woolf's
death, it was collected in The Death of the Moth and Other Essays.

WHEN YOUR SECRETARY invited me to come here, she told me that
your Society is concerned with the employment of women and she
suggested that I might tell you something about my own professional experiences. It is true I am a woman; it is true I am employed; but what
professional experiences have I had? It is difficult to say. My profession is
literature; and in that profession there are fewer experiences for women than
in any other, with the exception of the stage — fewer, I mean, that are
peculiar to women. For the road was cut many years ago — by Fanny Burney,
by Aphra Behn, by Harriet Martineau, by Jane Austen, by George Eliot —
many famous women, and many more unknown and forgotten, have been
before me, making the path smooth, and regulating my steps. Thus, when
I came to write, there were very few material obstacles in my way. Writing
was a reputable and harmless occupation. The family peace was not broken
by the scratching of a pen. No demand was made upon the family purse.
For ten and sixpence one can buy paper enough to write all the plays of
Shakespeare — if one has a mind that way. Pianos and models, Paris, Vienna
and Berlin, masters and mistresses, are not needed by a writer. The cheap-
ness of writing paper is, of course, the reason why women have succeeded
as writers before they have succeeded in the other professions.

But to tell you my story — it is a simple one. You have only got to
figure to yourselves a girl in a bedroom with a pen in her hand. She had only
to move that pen from left to right — from ten o'clock to one. Then it
occurred to her to do what is simple and cheap enough after all — to slip a
few of those pages into an envelope, fix a penny stamp in the corner, and
drop the envelope into the red box at the corner. It was thus that I became

a journalist; and my effort was rewarded on the first day of the following month — a very glorious day it was for me — by a letter from an editor containing a cheque for one pound ten shillings and sixpence. But to show you how little I deserve to be called a professional woman, how little I know of the struggles and difficulties of such lives, I have to admit that instead of spending that sum upon bread and butter, rent, shoes and stockings, or butcher's bills, I went out and bought a cat — a beautiful cat, a Persian cat, which very soon involved me in bitter disputes with my neighbours.

What could be easier than to write articles and to buy Persian cats with the profits? But wait a moment. Articles have to be about something. Mine, I seem to remember, was about a novel by a famous man. And while I was writing this review, I discovered that if I were going to review books I should need to do battle with a certain phantom. And the phantom was a woman, and when I came to know her better I called her after the heroine of a famous poem, The Angel in the House. [1] It was she who used to come between me and my paper when I was writing reviews. It was she who bothered me and wasted my time and so tormented me that at last I killed her. You who come of a younger and happier generation may not have heard of her — you may not know what I mean by the Angel in the House. I will describe her as shortly as I can. She was intensely sympathetic. She was immensely charming. She was utterly unselfish. She excelled in the difficult arts of family life. She sacrificed herself daily. If there was chicken, she took the leg; if there was a draught she sat in it — in short she was so constituted that she never had a mind or a wish of her own, but preferred to sympathize always with the minds and wishes of others. Above all — I need not say it — she was pure. Her purity was supposed to be her chief beauty — her blushes, her great grace. In those days — the last of Queen Victoria — every house had its Angel. And when I came to write I encountered her with the very first words. The shadow of her wings fell on my page; I heard the rustling of her skirts in the room. Directly, that is to say, I took my pen in my hand to review that novel by a famous man, she slipped behind me and whispered: 'My dear, you are a young woman. You are writing about a book that has been written by a man. Be sympathetic; be tender; flatter; deceive; use all the arts and wiles of our sex. Never let anybody guess that you have a mind of your own. Above all, be pure.' And she made as if to guide my pen. I now record the one act for which I take some credit to myself, though the credit rightly belongs to some excellent ancestors of mine who left me a certain sum of money — shall we say five hundred pounds a year? — so that it was not necessary for me to depend solely on charm for my living. I turned upon her and caught her by the throat. I did my best to kill her. My excuse,

---

[1] *The Angel in the House*: Poem by the English poet Coventry Patmore (1823–1896) about the courtship and marriage of a clergyman's daughter. For many, the self-sacrificing heroine represented the epitome of Victorian womanhood.

if I were to be had up in a court of law, would be that I acted in self-defence. Had I not killed her she would have killed me. She would have plucked the heart out of my writing. For, as I found, directly I put pen to paper, you cannot review even a novel without having a mind of your own, without expressing what you think to be the truth about human relations, morality, sex. And all these questions, according to the Angel of the House, cannot be dealt with freely and openly by women; they must charm, they must conciliate, they must — to put it bluntly — tell lies if they are to succeed. Thus, whenever I felt the shadow of her wing or the radiance of her halo upon my page, I took up the inkpot and flung it at her. She died hard. Her fictitious nature was of great assistance to her. It is far harder to kill a phantom than a reality. She was always creeping back when I thought I had despatched her. Though I flatter myself that I killed her in the end, the struggle was severe; it took much time that had better have been spent upon learning Greek grammar; or in roaming the world in search of adventures. But it was a real experience; it was an experience that was found to befall all women writers at that time. Killing the Angel in the House was part of the occupation of a woman writer.

But to continue my story. The Angel was dead; what then remained? You may say that what remained was a simple and common object — a young woman in a bedroom with an inkpot. In other words, now that she had rid herself of falsehood, that young woman had only to be herself. Ah, but what is 'herself'? I mean, what is a woman? I assure you, I do not know. I do not believe that you know. I do not believe that anybody can know until she has expressed herself in all the arts and professions open to human skill. That indeed is one of the reasons why I have come here — out of respect for you, who are in process of showing us by your experiments what a woman is, who are in process of providing us, by your failures and successes, with that extremely important piece of information.

But to continue the story of my professional experiences. I made one pound ten and six by my first review; and I bought a Persian cat with the proceeds. Then I grew ambitious. A Persian cat is all very well, I said; but a Persian cat is not enough. I must have a motor car. And it was thus that I became a novelist — for it is a very strange thing that people will give you a motor car if you will them a story. It is a still stranger thing that there is nothing so delightful in the world as telling stories. It is far pleasanter than writing reviews of famous novels. And yet, if I am to obey your secretary and tell you my professional experiences as a novelist, I must tell you about a very strange experience that befell me as a novelist. And to understand it you must try first to imagine a novelist's state of mind. I hope I am not giving away professional secrets if I say that a novelist's chief desire is to be as unconscious as possible. He has to induce in himself a state of perpetual lethargy. He wants life to proceed with the utmost quiet and regularity. He wants to see the same faces, to read the same books, to do the same things day after day, month after month, while he is writing, so that nothing may break the illusion in which he is living — so that nothing may disturb or disquiet the mysterious nosings about, feelings round, darts, dashes and sudden discoveries of that very shy and illusive spirit, the imagination. I suspect that this state is the same both for men and women. Be that as it may, I want you to imagine me writing a novel in a state of trance. I want you to figure to yourselves a girl sitting with a pen in her hand, which for minutes, and indeed for hours, she never dips into the inkpot. The image that comes to my mind when I think of this girl is the image of a fisherman lying sunk in dreams on the verge of a deep lake with a rod held out over the water. She was letting her imagination sweep unchecked round every rock and cranny of the world that lies submerged in the depths of our unconscious being. Now came the experience, the experience that I believe to be far commoner with women writers than with men. The line raced through the girl's fingers. Her imagination had rushed away. It had sought the pools, the depths, the dark places where the largest fish slumber. And then there was a smash. There was an explosion. There was foam and confusion. The imagination had dashed itself against something hard. The girl was roused from her dream. She was indeed in a state of the most acute and difficult distress. To speak without figure she had thought of something, something about the body, about the passions which it was unfitting for her as a woman to say. Men, her reason told her, would be shocked. The consciousness of what men will say of a woman who speaks the truth about her passions had roused her from her artist's state of unconsciousness. She could write no more. The trance was over. Her imagination could work no longer. This I believe to be a very common experience with women writers — they are impeded by the extreme conventionality of the other sex. For though men sensibly allow themselves great freedom in these respects, I doubt that they realize or can control the extreme severity with which they condemn such freedom in women.

These then were two very genuine experiences of my own. These were two of the adventures of my professional life. The first — killing the Angel in the House — I think I solved. She died. But the second, telling the truth about my own experiences as a body, I do not think I solved. I doubt that any woman has solved it yet. The obstacles against her are still immensely powerful — and yet they are very difficult to define. Outwardly, what is simpler than to write books? Outwardly, what obstacles are there for a woman rather than for a man? Inwardly, I think, the case is very different; she has still many ghosts to fight, many prejudices to overcome. Indeed it will be a long time still, I think, before a woman can sit down to write a book without finding a phantom to be slain, a rock to be dashed against. And if this is so in literature, the freest of all professions for women, how is it in the new professions which you are now for the first time entering?

Those are the questions that I should like, had I time, to ask you. And indeed, if I have laid stress upon these professional experiences of mine, it is because I believe that they are, though in different forms, yours also. Even when the path is nominally open — when there is nothing to prevent a woman from being a doctor, a lawyer, a civil servant — there are many phantoms and obstacles, as I believe, looming in her way. To discuss and define them is I think of great value and importance; for thus only can the labour be shared, the difficulties be solved. But besides this, it is necessary also to discuss the ends and the aims for which we are fighting, for which we are doing battle with these formidable obstacles. Those aims cannot be taken for granted; they must be perpetually questioned and examined. The whole position, as I see it — here in this hall surrounded by women practising for the first time in history I know not how many different professions — is one of extraordinary interest and importance. You have won rooms of your own in the house hitherto exclusively owned by men. You are able, though not without great labour and effort, to pay the rent. You are earning your five hundred pounds a year. But this freedom is only a beginning; the room is your own, but it is still bare. It has to be furnished; it has to be decorated; it has to be shared. How are you going to furnish it, how are you going to decorate it? With whom are you going to share it, and upon what terms? These, I think are questions of the utmost importance and interest. For the first time in history you are able to ask them; for the first time you are able to decide for yourselves what the answers should be. Willingly would I stay and discuss those questions and answers — but not tonight. My time is up; and I must cease.

FROM READING TO REREADING

1. One of the biggest problems Woolf faced in this talk was the differences that she felt existed between an independent writer like herself and people who work in other professions. What are these differences? How does she overcome the problem — how does she bridge the gap?

2. At the heart of Woolf's essay is a poetic image — the "Angel of the House." What does she mean by this image? What does it have to do with her life as a writer and with the quality of her feminism?

3. In rereading, note the violent imagery repeated in the essay. Does it strike you as out-of-keeping for a talk in such a setting? In what ways do you think the violence Woolf alludes to throughout the talk is central to her ideas and position?

From Reading to Writing

1. James Baldwin ends his essay with a statement that George Orwell would agree with: "I want to be an honest man and a good writer." For

Orwell, however, telling the truth may sometimes be in conflict with aesthetic considerations. Does this conflict exist for Baldwin? Write an essay in which you examine Orwell's and Baldwin's essays from the perspective of honesty and style. In what ways are the two writers similar? In what ways do they handle the problems of honesty and art differently?

2. In their essays, both Annie Dillard and Cynthia Ozick are enormously sensitive to their physical surroundings. Consider your own development as a writer. Do you think your physical environment in any way contributes to your writing? In a personal essay, describe either a past or present environment (a room, a library spot, or some other place) and discuss how it has directly or indirectly influenced your own "writing life."

3. The essays by Joan Didion and Virginia Woolf, though they treat different issues, both show writers concerned with keeping in touch with their emotional selves. In what way do you think writing can do this? How closely is your own writing connected to your emotional life? Write an essay in which you discuss a piece of your own writing — a selection from a notebook or journal, or an essay, poem, or story — and describe the person you discover there.

The Essayists

JAMES BALDWIN

I N "NOTES OF A NATIVE SON," James Baldwin writes about a brief exchange between himself, a high-schooler at the time, and his father, a preacher who hoped his son would follow him into the ministry. Really talking to each other for the first time in their lives, the father asks his son a question that seems more like an acknowledgment, "You'd rather write than preach, wouldn't you?" James, who had been a youth minister for three years, answers yes, knowing that his early zeal for preaching has been replaced by a greater love of writing. This episode not only marks the beginning of a career that would span five decades, but, as Jonathan Yardley comments, it also "reminds us that [Baldwin had] always been as much preacher as writer." Baldwin's early exposure to evangelism and religious language exerted a lasting influence on his prose, especially on his essays with their powerful and moving cadences, their remarkable balance of reason and passion, and their tone of moral urgency. Perhaps it was this spiritual quality that led Henry Louis Gates, Jr., to remark that Baldwin's death was "a great loss not only for black people, but to the country as a whole, for which he served as a conscience."

Baldwin was born in 1924 in Harlem, in New York City; he once described his childhood environment as a "bleak fantasy" of poverty and violence. Without the prospect of a college education, Baldwin knew there was very little chance for him to become a writer. He decided that his only hope lay in immersing himself in the artistic and literary life of New York City that at the time flourished in and around Greenwich Village. Shortly after graduating from DeWitt Clinton High School in the Bronx, Baldwin left Harlem and moved to the Village. Almost immediately, he set to work on a novel that later proved "unsalable" but that nevertheless showed enough promise in its unfinished state to earn the twenty-one-year-old writer a Eugene F. Saxton Fellowship in 1945. Throughout the early part of his career Baldwin would continue to receive grants from a number of institutions, including the Guggenheim, Rosenwald, and Ford foundations, the National Institute of Arts and Letters, and *Partisan Review*.

When the Saxton fellowship ended, Baldwin supported himself by "waiting on tables in a Village restaurant and writing book reviews — mostly, as it turned out, about the Negro problem, concerning which the color of my skin made me automatically an expert." In 1948 his essays and reviews were appearing in such periodicals as *The Nation, The New Leader, Commentary,* and *Partisan Review*. Of one of these early pieces Jocelyn Whitehead Jackson writes: "The relative dispassion with which Baldwin details the effects of oppressive . . . life in 'The Harlem Ghetto' becomes in this intensely personal and probing essay a passionate, yet ordered, autobiographical case history." The pattern that Jackson describes could easily be extended to any of these pieces; again and again we find within Baldwin's early work a steady movement back and forth between the carefully reasoned analysis of cultural and social phenomena and the poignant assertion of Baldwin's own identity as a black, as a homosexual, and as an artist in the light of the social conditions he depicts.

In 1948 Baldwin left New York City for Paris, where he would reside for the next nine years. His move to Paris, writes C. W. E. Bigsby, was prompted to a large degree by the desire to "release [himself] from an identity which was no more than a projection of his racial inheritance." Baldwin, however, soon realized that the problems he faced as a writer went far beyond the question of race. In his introduction to *Nobody Knows My Name*, he explains:

> In America, the color of my skin had stood between myself and me; in Europe, that barrier was down. Nothing is more desirable than to be released from an affliction, but nothing is more frightening than to be divested of a crutch. It turned out that the question of who I was was not solved because I had removed myself from the social forces which menaced me — anyway, those forces had become interior, and I had dragged them across the ocean with me. The question of who I was had at last become a personal question, and the answer was to be found in me.

Baldwin recognized that he could not escape the problem of race simply by leaving America. Moreover, he was aware of another, more urgent problem facing him, the problem of forging an original identity for himself through writing. The great danger for the writer of color, as Baldwin saw it, lay in allowing questions of race to obscure questions of selfhood. The search for identity would become a recurrent theme in all of Baldwin's work, but perhaps this theme is more dramatically set forth in his essays, where such questions merge with those of style and where the writer speaks directly to us rather than through fictional characters.

Though Baldwin viewed himself primarily as a novelist, though he tended to use the essay form as "a testing ground for his fiction," we should not regard his essays as secondary or inferior to his fiction. Baldwin's first three novels, *Go Tell It on the Mountain* (1953), *Giovanni's Room* (1956), and *Another Country* (1962) were each subject to a considerable, but mixed reception from the literary establishment. His essays of the same period, however, elicited and continue to elicit high praise. Literary critic Harold Bloom has written: "Whatever the ultimate canonical judgement upon James Baldwin's fiction may prove to be, his non-fictional work clearly has permanent status in American literature."

The contention that Baldwin's talents find their most elegant expression in his essays gains support in Langston Hughes's favorable review of the young writer's first nonfiction work, *Notes of a Native Son*, published in 1955. The prominent African American poet, writer, and central figure in the black literary and artistic movement known as the Harlem Renaissance, wrote of the much younger Baldwin:

> To my way of thinking, he is much better at provoking thought in the essay than he is at arousing emotion in fiction. I much prefer *Notes of a Native Son* to his novel, *Go Tell It on the Mountain*, where the surface

excellence and poetry of his writing did not seem to me to suit the earthiness of his subject-matter. In his essays, words and material suit each other. The thought becomes poetry, and the poetry illuminates the thought.

If Langston Hughes is right about Baldwin's strengths, and many other critics have made similar claims, then the relative success of Baldwin's attempts to forge an identity for himself might be most accurately measured in terms of the skills he rapidly developed as an essayist.

When Baldwin returned to America in 1957, he came back to a very different country from the one he had left almost a decade earlier. The civil rights movement under the leadership of Martin Luther King, Jr., had already begun to make great strides in its goals of legal and economic equality for all minorities. Baldwin played a prominent role in the movement, writing about the difficult issue of race relations and the dehumanizing effects of racism on both victim and oppressor. The latter theme is beautifully condensed into a single sentence in the essay "Fifth Avenue, Uptown": "It is a terrible, and inexorable, law that one cannot deny the humanity of another without diminishing one's own: in the face of one's victim, one sees oneself." But even as Baldwin assumed a greater role in public life, he consistently rejected the attempts of others to label him a "leader" or "spokesperson." In a 1984 interview, Baldwin explained why he could never be "a voice of the people."

> A spokesman assumes that he is speaking for others. I never assumed that I could. What I tried to . . . make clear, was that no society can smash the social contract and be exempt from the consequences, and the consequences are chaos for everybody in society.

In his desire to be "a witness of the truth," Baldwin continued to speak as an individual deeply concerned for the future of his country and its people. When his second collection of essays, *Nobody Knows My Name*. appeared in 1961, Irving Howe praised the essays for their power and clarity of vision; the book clearly belonged to the literature of protest, but it seemed more a cry of anguish than a call for revolt.

The publication in 1963 of *The Fire Next Time*, Baldwin's third work of nonfiction, marked a significant change in the writer's general tone. With all the verbal powers of a biblical prophet, Baldwin predicted a future of racial violence in America unless its people began the long and arduous task of social and political transformation. Pearl K. Bell has said of the book that despite its apocalyptic tone, "the essay was distinguished by its lucid dignity. It was, however, the last time [Baldwin] would keep his distance from the anger and hatred he had warned against" in earlier writings. After 1963 Baldwin's work, according to Donald B. Gibson, grew increasingly "sympathetic to the political perspective." Gibson also notices the beginning of a convergence between the fiction and the essays with regard to ideological content. Baldwin's literary output in this period includes a novel, *Tell Me How Long the Train's Been Gone* (1968), and a long essay, "No Name in the Street" (1972). Both works show the influence of the militant black nationalist movement of the late 1960s with its renunciation of Martin Luther King's credo of nonviolence.

Twenty years earlier, Baldwin had written of his efforts to resist the role of "protest novelist" that he felt was being placed upon him and other black writers by both the white and black communities. To many critics, his later works represent a capitulation to the enormous social pressures of the times in which he lived. These same pressures probably motivated Baldwin to return to Europe. While Baldwin continued to write — he produced two more novels and several works of nonfiction before his life ended in 1987 — he never again achieved the kind of popular or critical success that marked his early career. In 1985 Baldwin's collected nonfiction appeared under the rubric of *The Price of the Ticket*, containing an important introductory essay by the author that looked back over the writer's long and turbulent career.

The divisions and paradoxes that make up James Baldwin's life and achievement form an important part of our understanding of his work. Baldwin embraced his roles as a black and as an American with equal love (and hatred), though he strongly doubted that the two identities could ever be reconciled. Early on, he publicly disavowed the literature of protest, yet later in his career he would consciously sacrifice much of his stylistic elegance in order not to distract the reader from his political message. He was never comfortable with the term "expatriate" and preferred to view himself as a "commuter" between America and Europe. He was not unaware that most of his fame rested on his achievement as an essayist, but this fact never seemed to dampen his enthusiasm for writing fiction; clearly something about writing novels satisfied Baldwin in a way writing essays did not. In one of his last essays, "Here Be Dragons," Baldwin can be observed still struggling with the idea of "a universal duality," of a contradiction at the very heart of our existence. "The human imagination," Baldwin writes, "is perpetually required to examine, control, and redefine reality, of which we must assume ourselves to be the center and the key. Nature and revelation are perpetually challenging each other; this relentless tension is one of the keys to human history and to what is known as the human condition." It was James Baldwin's unique gift as a writer to be able to get as close as possible to the truth of that condition.

Principal Works by James Baldwin

Go Tell It on the Mountain   novel: 1953

The Amen Corner   drama: 1955

Notes of a Native Son   essays: 1955

Giovanni's Room   novel: 1956

Nobody Knows My Name: More Notes of a Native Son   essays: 1961
Another Country   novel: 1962
The Fire Next Time   essays: 1963
Blues for Mister Charlie   drama: 1964
Going to Meet the Man   short stories: 1965
Tell Me How Long the Train's Been Gone   novel: 1968
No Name in the Street   essay: 1972
If Beale Street Could Talk   novel: 1974
The Devil Finds Work   film criticism: 1976
Just Above My Head   novel: 1979
The Evidence of Things Not Seen   nonfiction: 1985
The Price of the Ticket: Collected Nonfiction, 1948–1985   essays: 1985

Selected Criticism of James Baldwin's Essays

BIGSBY, C. W. E. "The Divided Mind of James Baldwin." *Journal of American Studies* 13, no. 3 (December 1979). Also reprinted in Bloom. Less a detailed analysis of Baldwin's work than "an account of a career and a mind instructively divided."

BLOOM, HAROLD, ed. *James Baldwin: Modern Critical Views*. New York: Chelsea House Publishers, 1986. See editor's introduction. An important contribution to our understanding of the prophetic style in Baldwin's essays.

CUNNINGHAM, JAMES. "Public and Private Rhetorical Modes in the Essays of James Baldwin," in *Essays on the Essay: Redefining the Genre*, ed. Alexander J. Butrym. Athens: University of Georgia Press, 1989, pp. 192–204. Cunningham examines the "interlocking relationship" between public and private life in Baldwin's essays.

GIBSON, DONALD M., ed. *Five Black Writers: Essays on Wright, Ellison, Baldwin, Hughes, Leroi Jones*. New York: New York University Press, 1970. The editor's introduction provides a brief but insightful overview of Baldwin's achievement and examines claims that Baldwin is a better essayist than novelist.

JACKSON, JOCELYN WHITEHEAD. "The Problem of Identity in Selected Early Essays of James Baldwin." *Journal of Interdenominational Theological Center* 6 (1978): 1–15. Also reprinted in Standley and Burt. Jackson argues that Baldwin's essays must be understood in the context of an author's quest for identity.

LEVIN, DAVID. "Baldwin's Autobiographical Essays: The Problem of Negro Identity." *The Massachusetts Review* 5 (1964): 239–247. Levin surveys Baldwin's personal essays and analyzes the author's early expressed desire to be "an honest man and a good writer."

MOLLER, KARIN. *The Theme of Identity in the Essays of James Baldwin: An Interpretation*. Gothenberg Studies in English Series, 32. Atlantic Highlands, N.J.: Humanities Press,

1975. A full-length study of the essays focusing on the essayist's attempts to dramatize his discovery of an identity through writing.

STANDLEY, FRED L., and NANCY V. BURT, eds. *Critical Essays on James Baldwin*. Boston: G. K. Hall & Co., 1988. An anthology of reviews and criticism on Baldwin introduced by an overview of the author's literary career.

JOAN DIDION

I N THE 1960s, magazine pieces characterized by exhaustive research, creative organization, and a style more literary than reportorial, began to appear in pages of *Esquire, Harper's, The New Yorker,* and other periodicals. The New Journalism, as this genre came to be known, made no claims to objectivity. The writers who practiced it rarely concealed their attitudes toward their subjects; in fact, in some of the best pieces of this kind, the writer became part of the story. The New Journalism, as developed by writers like Tom Wolfe, Gay Talese, Lillian Ross, and Truman Capote, seemed at times less a type of journalism than a version of the essay. While the non-fiction of Joan Didion is not easily placed into any preestablished category, it shares with the New Journalism a painstaking attention to the selection and placement of detail as well as a deeply personal quality that critics and readers alike find compelling. Besides being "a gifted reporter," Michiko Kakutani writes, Didion "is also a prescient witness, finding in her own experiences parallels of the times. The voice is always precise, the tone unsentimental, the view unabashedly subjective. She takes things personally." For her uncanny ability to record exactly what she sees and feels, Joan Didion is widely regarded as one of the finest essayists now living.

Born in 1934, Didion spent most of her childhood in California's Sacramento Valley. Her ancestors arrived in the region in the 1840s, and, as a child, she took pride in knowing that she lived on the same land that her family had settled five generations earlier. More than one critic has attributed the quality of "hard-boiled individualism" in Didion's essays to her pioneer heritage. Moreover, Sacramento and its environs figure heavily in Didion's work, and it is probable that her deep attachment to a particular region enhances her ability to evoke a strong sense of place in all her writings regardless of the setting.

Although Didion wrote stories from the time she was a little girl, her interest in writing grew more serious when, at the age of fifteen or sixteen, she began to type out stories by Ernest Hemingway "to learn how the sentences worked." As Didion once explained, Hemingway wrote "very direct sentences, smooth rivers, clear water over granite"; she decided to work hard to match that precision and clarity in her own writing. After high school, Didion enrolled at the University of California at Berkeley, where she majored in English literature, periodically submitting original work to the campus literary magazine, *Occident.* Shortly before graduation in 1956, Didion received word that she had won *Vogue* magazine's Prix de Paris contest with a nonfiction piece on San Francisco architecture. Instead of a trip to Paris, she chose a cash prize and a writing job at *Vogue's* New York City offices.

It was at *Vogue,* under the supervision of editor Allene Talmey, that Didion honed her skills as a writer of remarkable precision. Talmey recalls, "At first she wrote captions. I would have her write three hundred to four hundred words and then cut it back to fifty. We wrote long and published short and by doing that Joan learned to write." In one caption for an article on home interiors, Didion wrote:

> Opposite, above: All through the house, color, verve, improvised treasures in happy but anomalous coexistence. Here, a Frank Stella, an Art-Nouveau stained-glass panel, a Roy Lichtenstein. Not shown: A table covered with brilliant oilcloth, a Mexican find at fifteen cents a yard.

The following passage from an essay entitled "In Hollywood" illustrates best what Didion's craft owes to these earlier exercises in the careful use of detail and emphasis:

> At midwinter in the big houses off Benedict Canyon the fireplaces burn all day with scrub oak and eucalyptus, the French windows are opened wide to the subtropical sun, the rooms filled with white phalaenopsis and cymbidium orchids and needlepoint rugs and the requisite scent of Rigaud candles.

Didion would continue to gain valuable experience at *Vogue,* writing features on celebrities and becoming the magazine's film critic; but by 1963 she had grown disillusioned with living in New York. Earlier that year, she had published her first novel, *Run River,* about a failed marriage. The book garnered little public attention and received only a handful of mixed reviews. The following year, Didion married another writer, John Gregory Dunne, and together they decided to move to Los Angeles, where the couple earned a meager living working together on a series of articles for the *Saturday Evening Post.*

Didion's columns for *The Saturday Evening Post* form much of the substance of her first collection of essays, *Slouching Towards Bethlehem,* published in 1968. The volume's title is taken from W. B. Yeats's poem, "The Second Coming," which contains the lines: "Things fall apart, the center can not hold; / Mere anarchy is loosed upon the world." The social upheaval of the late 1960s had begun to affect Didion's ability to write; the collection was a last-ditch attempt to come to terms with the chaos that was threatening her craft. As Didion writes in her preface, she had grown convinced "that writing was an irrelevant act, that the world as I had understood it no longer existed. If I was to work again at all, it would be necessary for me to come to terms with disorder." The essays take the reader to a murder trial in the San Bernardino Valley, to the Haight-Ashbury section of San Francisco to examine the hippie movement, to the tiny wedding chapels that dot the Las Vegas strip. Didion's West is a land of lost hopes and disillusionment. As Alfred Kazin wrote: "The story between the lines of *Slouching Towards Bethlehem* is surely not so much 'California' as it is her ability to make us share her passionate sense of it."

Throughout her career, Didion has been criticized for her sensibility and her method, though these objections seldom stand up on a closer examination of her work. While she has been called a nihilist (one who believes that existence is meaningless) for her bleak studies in the failure of the American Dream, the voice that emerges in these essays is deeply moral.

She traces what she calls the "atomization," or disintegration, of social and cultural values with a melancholy voice that, for Melvin Maddocks, suggests "a last survivor dictating a superbly written wreckage report onto a tape she doubts will ever be played." Another criticism often leveled at Didion is that she fails "to achieve a respectable distance" from her subjects. In her defense, Dan Wakefield has written that her "personality does not self-indulgently intrude itself upon her subjects, it informs and illuminates them."

In 1970 Didion published *Play It as It Lays*, a best-selling novel that earned her a National Book Award nomination. She followed this success with another novel, *A Book of Common Prayer*, in 1977. Both books share themes common to Didion's essays: a deep sense of weariness manifest through passionless relationships and lives without meaning; a desire for order in a world on the brink of total chaos; a knowledge that history has determined for us the course our lives will take. It was not until 1979 that Didion published her second collection of essays, *The White Album*. The title essay finds Didion still trying to come to terms with the events of the 1960s, a decade whose most disturbing aspects are crystallized for her on the famous Beatles album of the same name. In one sense, then, the collection begins where *Slouching Towards Bethlehem* left off. In another sense, however, the book represents an important departure from earlier work.

Didion's early essays possess a strong narrative quality; she is usually telling a story or at least providing enough elements for the reader to assemble one for themselves. In later work, however, she seems to abandon this approach in favor of presenting us with a seemingly random sequence of "disparate images" and "shifting phantasmagoria." These images, she feels, supply the reader with a more accurate representation of our actual experience than a narrative that pretends to explain why and how things happen. Didion's change of approach might owe something to her work as a screenwriter. In the early 1970s, she began to collaborate on screenplays with her husband. A screenwriter, as John Gregory Dunne has pointed out, "must cede to the director certain essential writer's functions — pace, mood, style, point-of-view, rhythm, texture." It is not surprising, then, that Didion finds this work somewhat restricting. And yet the screenwriter's conscious surrendering of control over certain aspects of his or her work may have taught Didion to sacrifice some of the narrative control she previously exerted over the images that make up her essays. Thus, in the title essay of *The White Album*, the reader encounters fifteen brief vignettes linked only loosely by their concern with public events like the murders by the Charles Manson cult, or the student rebellion at San Francisco State, or the trial of the black radical Huey P. Newton, or the funeral of assassinated Robert F. Kennedy. The essay was widely praised as the best short piece yet written on the experience of the 1960s.

While Didion has not published a collection of essays since *The White Album*, she continues to add to the growing list of literary-quality nonfiction that bears her name. One such effort, *Salvador*, chronicles her experiences during a two-week visit to the Central American republic of El Salvador in 1982. The essay offers no solutions to the civil strife that was, at the time of her visit, tearing the small nation apart. Instead, the book, as Juan M. Vasquez explains, "is for those who can appreciate that the way some people live — the way some countries live — is not always believable, but it is all too crushingly real." Many readers complained, however, that the author would not be able to paint an accurate picture of the situation in El Salvador without a longer stay in that country.

In 1984 Didion published a fourth novel, *Democracy*, a work marked by the author's curious mixing of fact and fiction; at several points in the novel, Joan Didion herself appears as a character. Clearly, the writer is experimenting with the limits of fiction, or alternatively, with the limits of fact. As in much of her later work, the boundaries between reality and imagination cannot be easily maintained. In more recent work, Didion takes on America's cities in *Miami*, her 1987 account of the Florida metropolis, and in "New York: Sentimental Journeys," a long essay on the trial of several teenagers accused of raping and beating a jogger in New York City's Central Park.

The poet Robert Frost once said that his poems acted as "momentary stays against confusion," a remark that can quite easily be extended to Joan Didion's essays. She finds that she must write to come to grips with the disorder of the times we inhabit. The essay, then, for Didion is a ritual, a means of facing "the unspeakable peril of the everyday." Moreover, it is a ritual that involves the continual search for the exact word or phrase to describe a particular image or scene. John Leonard has written that "nobody writes better English prose than Joan Didion. Try to rearrange one of her sentences, and you've realized that the sentence was inevitable."

Principal Works by Joan Didion

Run River   novel: 1963

Slouching Towards Bethlehem   essays: 1968

Play It as It Lays   novel: 1970

A Book of Common Prayer   novel: 1977

Telling Stories   short fiction: 1978

The White Album   essays: 1979

Salvador   nonfiction: 1983

Democracy   novel: 1984

Miami   nonfiction: 1987

New York: Sentimental Journey   nonfiction: 1991
[appeared in *The New York Review of Books* on January 17, 1991]

Selected Criticism of Joan Didion's Essays

DAVIDSON, SARA. "A Visit with Joan Didion." *The New York Times Book Review*, April 3, 1977, pp. 1, 35–38. Excellent interview with the essayist. Also in Friedman.

FRIEDMAN, ELLEN G., ed. *Joan Didion: Essays and Conversations*. Princeton, N.J.: Ontario Review Press, 1984. While only one of the essays by various critics collected here treats Didion's nonfiction at length, several comment interestingly on the essays in passing.

HENDERSON, KATHERINE USHER. *Joan Didion*. New York: Ungar, 1981. A brief introductory study of Didion's achievement as a writer with frequent reference to her essays.

JOHNSON, MICHAEL. *The New Journalism*. Lawrence: University of Kansas Press, 1971, pp. 96–100. Considers Didion's essays in the context of journalistic writings by Tom Wolfe, Truman Capote, and Dan Wakefield.

KAKUTANI, MICHIKO. "Joan Didion: Staking Out California." *The New York Times Magazine*, June 10, 1979, pp. 34ff, 44. Interesting profile/interview with Didion shortly before the publication of *The White Album*. Also in Friedman.

WINCHELL, MARK ROYDEN. *Joan Didion*. Rev. ed. Boston: Twayne Publishers, 1989. The first six chapters of this full-length study deal exclusively with Didion's nonfiction.

ANNIE DILLARD

THE REAL WORLD, Annie Dillard contends, has the power to fascinate us more than any imaginative world, and the kind of writer who deals most intimately with the real world is the essayist. "The essayist," Dillard writes, "does what we do with our lives; the essayist thinks about actual things. He can make sense of them analytically or artistically. In either case he renders the real world coherent and meaningful, even if only bits of it, and even if that coherence and meaning reside only inside small texts." While only one of Dillard's seven volumes of nonfiction is strictly speaking a collection of essays, her method of writing most closely resembles that of the essayist. For the essayist, according to Dillard, "no subject matter is forbidden, no structure is proscribed." Dillard's choice of topics ranges from stunt pilots to Santa Claus, from the Galapagos to a total eclipse of the sun, from practical jokes to polar exploration. To the first-time reader of her work her powers of observation are immediately apparent, and like all great essayists Dillard cares passionately about sentences. In a note at the beginning of her collection, *Teaching a Stone to Talk*, she reminds the reader that she does not consider her essays mere "occasional pieces, such as a writer brings out to supplement his real work; instead [they are] my real work, such as it is."

Born in 1945, Dillard grew up in Pittsburgh, Pennsylvania. This fact comes as a surprise to many of Dillard's readers, since so much of her writing is devoted to revealing the mysteries of the natural order. But it was in the Homewood branch of Pittsburgh's Carnegie library system that Dillard as a sixth-grader discovered *The Field Book of Ponds and Streams*, a book that she credits as a major influence on the shape of her career as a writer. One chapter in the small blue-bound volume explained how to make sweep nets, plankton nets, glass-bottomed buckets, and killing jars, how the aspiring naturalist must equip herself for a day of study in "the field," and how a brook might yield its secrets to the careful observer. As Dillard writes, "that anyone lived the fine life described in Chapter Three astonished me." Despite her early interest in natural phenomena, however, readers should not be too quick to label Dillard "a nature writer." As the writer herself maintains "I am no scientist, but a poet and a walker with a background in theology and a penchant for quirky facts." One of Dillard's major themes, then, is the art of "seeing," the cultivation of which allows her to describe in writing a thing's invisible as well as its visible qualities.

In 1963 Dillard left Pittsburgh to attend Hollins College in a rural section of Virginia. There she began a journal whose entries would later be tirelessly revised and condensed into the manuscript of *Pilgrim at Tinker Creek*, her first work of nonfiction. In the book, Dillard records random impressions of life in and around a small Virginia stream, periodically intermixing those impressions with zoological observations and speculations both philosophical and theological. By her own account, *Pilgrim at Tinker Creek* comes closest to "what [Henry David] Thoreau called 'a meteorological journal of the mind.'" We might understand Thoreau's phrase to mean a record of deep solitude and reflection in and about nature. As a *Commentary* critic has remarked: "One of the most pleasing traits of the book is the graceful harmony between scrutiny of real phenomena and the reflections to which it gives rise. Anecdotes of animal behavior become so effortlessly enlarged into symbols by the deepened insight of meditation." Another critic writes that Dillard's prose "reads like poetry because, in fact, it is. . . . She constructs her nonfiction as carefully as a sonnet." When *Pilgrim at Tinker Creek* appeared in 1974, the book received the kind of critical acclaim not often accorded a writer's first published prose (Dillard had published a collection of poems, *Tickets for a Prayer Wheel*, as well in 1974) and won the Pulitzer Prize for general nonfiction.

Dillard's second volume of nonfiction, *Holy the Firm*, appeared three years later. She has said that the spare Christian allegory is her "only interesting work." While only forty-three pages long in manuscript, the narrative took Dillard fifteen months to write. The book is highly structured and underwent endless revision before it reached its final state. Fashioned out of the three days Dillard spent on Lummi Island in Puget Sound, *Holy the Firm* extends many of the more theological reflections found in *Pilgrim at Tinker Creek*. The language of the work often resembles a modern brand of religious mysticism; in one passage Dillard contemplates our place in the cosmos: "How could I have forgotten? Didn't I see the heavens wiped shut just yesterday, on the road walking? Didn't I fall from the dark of the stars to these senselit and noisome days?" Like one of her heroes, the French theologian Teilhard de Chardin, Dillard believes that purity lies not "in separation from but in deeper penetration into the universe. . . . The world is filled, and filled with the Absolute. To see this is to be made free." Dillard's desire to view, if only in its manifestations, the Absolute, or moving force behind all things, imbues her little book with a sense of wonder seldom found in modern literature.

After writing two nonfiction works that sought to penetrate some of the more profound mysteries of our existence, Dillard turned her attention to literary matters. *Living by Fiction*, a book of criticism that explores the condition of modern fiction, appeared in 1982. The work is aimed, as reviewer David Sundelson commented, "at a literate but not scholarly audience — those who 'read and reread the world's good books,'" and it provides "a clear and sympathetic introduction" to some of the more difficult modern novelists. The book could only have been written by one long familiar with the art of careful reading. Since 1966 Dillard has kept a list of all the books she has read with her own impressions of each work. In fact, though committed to the notion that a great teacher can often supply the spark to a young writer's career, she insists that she learned to write "through literature." Thus, for Dillard, the act of reading must be seen as intimately related to the act of writing.

Nineteen eighty-two was also the year that saw the publication of

Teaching a Stone to Talk, Dillard's only collection of essays. Dillard's choice of title hints at the author's view of the paradoxical relation of language to the natural world, a topic that America's first great essayist, Ralph Waldo Emerson, established as one of the central themes of our national literature. Confronted with the silence of nature, Dillard wonders if language can serve as a bridge between humans and their environment. William Howarth has written that Dillard resolves this question by learning to "shed language and accept silence, [by learning] to hear what a wordless, stony existence has to say. Of course, she must use words to convey this very thought, but in her essays the itinerant mood is always contradictory and intuitive." By using the language of silence to speak to what cannot speak to her, Dillard meets nature on its own terms. As an instance of this method, in "Living Like Weasels," Dillard tries to understand a weasel's mind, or "mindlessness," and in the process learns something about herself:

> The weasel lives in necessity and we live in choice, hating necessity and dying at last in its talons. I would like to live as I should, as the weasel lives as he should. And I suspect for me the way is like the weasel's: open to time and death painlessly, noticing everything, remembering nothing, choosing the given with a fierce and pointed will.

In another essay, "In the Jungle," Dillard insists on the centrality of the Napo River and its basin, a particularly remote region of the Ecuadorean wilderness:

> The Napo River: it is not out of the way. It is in the way, catching sunlight the way a cup catches poured water; it is a bowl of sweet air, a basin of greenness, and of grace, and, it would seem, of peace.

Wherever one stands in nature — that is where the center is. What is ambiguous is whether Dillard means to imply that human beings will always consider themselves to be in the middle of things, or that nature itself refuses to acknowledge the man-made distinction between centrality and remoteness. For Dillard, to understand the world, we must first realize that the entire set of relationships (distance, proximity, temporality, opposition, etc.) that help us to order our perceptions of things do not occur in nature but in our minds.

After writing *Encounters with Chinese Writers* (1985), an account of her experience as a member of a U.S. cultural delegation sent to China, Dillard set out to construct a narrative of her early life in Pittsburgh. The result of her labors was *An American Childhood,* published in 1987. There had always been a strong autobiographical element in Dillard's work, but this book was at least on the surface of things a memoir. Dillard has described the process of writing such a book: "You have to take pains in a memoir not to hang on the reader's arm, like a drunk, and say, 'And then I did this and it was so interesting.' I don't write for that reason." The reason she wrote a memoir is contained in the book's epilogue: one's own story holds interest for others to the extent that the teller is able to relate "the moment of opening a life and feeling it touch . . . this speckled mineral sphere, our present world." Put another way, Dillard wants to recount for the reader the process by which she woke up and discovered a place for herself in the world. By embroidering her narrative with the history and topography of Pittsburgh, Dillard avoids the self-indulgence of many other autobiographies. *An American Childhood* takes us from Dillard's birth at the end of World War II to her first years at Hollins College, where her career as a writer began. She admits that the book ends "just about where my experience of the real world ends. I've mostly spent the rest of my time behind a desk."

Dillard's *The Writing Life*, which appeared in 1989, might be said to continue the narrative begun in *An American Childhood*. But in contrast to the vibrancy of childhood experience, the writer's life, as Dillard describes it, "is colorless to the point of sensory deprivation. Many writers do little else but sit in small rooms recalling the real world." Despite this bleak estimate of a writer's existence, *The Writing Life* mostly extols a profession full of risks. In her final chapter, Dillard compares writing to stunt flying. If the risks of writing are those of a very different order from those of flying, then at least Dillard has the stunt pilot's daredevil attitude toward her craft: "One of the few things I know about writing is this: spend it all, shoot it, play it, lose it, all, right away, every time." Perhaps it was this flamboyant energy that moved Eudora Welty to remark in her review of *Pilgrim at Tinker Creek*: "A reader's heart must go out to a young writer with a sense of wonder so fearless and unbridled. It is this intensity of experience that she seems to live in order to declare."

Principal Works by Annie Dillard

Tickets for a Prayer Wheel   poetry: 1974

Pilgrim at Tinker Creek   nonfiction: 1974

Holy the Firm   nonfiction: 1977

Living by Fiction   criticism: 1982

Teaching a Stone to Talk: Expeditions and Encounters   essays: 1982

Encounters with Chinese Writers   nonfiction: 1985

An American Childhood   memoir: 1987

The Writing Life   nonfiction: 1989

Selected Criticism of Annie Dillard's Essays

BISCHOFF, JOAN. "Fellow Rebels: Annie Dillard and Maxine Hong Kingston." *English Journal*, December 1989, pp. 62–67. An extended review essay focusing in part on Dillard's *An American Childhood*.

CALDWELL, GAIL. "Pilgrim's Progress." *The Boston Globe Magazine,* May 8, 1983, p. 11ff. A comprehensive profile of Dillard and her work since *Pilgrim at Tinker Creek.*

CURTIS, C. MICHAEL. [Review of *Holy the Firm*]. *The Atlantic Monthly,* December 1977, pp. 106–107. Review focusing on Dillard's use of the language of the early Christian movement.

HAWKINS, PETER S. "Annie Dillard: Pilgrim at Midstream." *The Christian Century,* June 7, 1989, pp. 592–595. A Yale professor of religion examines Dillard's spiritual development.

TIETJEN, ELAINE. "Perceptions of Nature: Annie Dillard's *Pilgrim at Tinker Creek.*" *North Dakota Quarterly,* Summer 1988, pp. 101–113. A poet and environmentalist looks at the meaning of perception in Dillard's best-known book.

UPDIKE, JOHN. [Review of *The Writing Life*]. *The New Yorker,* December 25, 1989, pp. 106–108. Contains several powerful insights into Dillard's craft.

WEBER, KATHERINE. "Annie Dillard: PW Interviews." *Publishers Weekly,* September 1, 1989, pp. 67–68. The author speaks at length about the writing process.

WELTY, EUDORA. [Review of *Pilgrim at Tinker Creek*]. *The New York Times Book Review,* March 24, 1974, pp. 4–5. The well-known writer of short fiction praises the work for its ambition and poetic richness but wonders whether the book does not suffer from the absence of voices other than Dillard's own.

WYMARD, ELEANOR. "A New Existential Voice: For Annie Dillard the World Is an Epiphany." *Commonweal,* October 24, 1975, pp. 495–496. Argues that Dillard successfully reconciles the creative imagination with Christian faith in the Incarnation in *Pilgrim at Tinker Creek.*

STEPHEN JAY GOULD

SINCE 1974, when his column "This View of Life" became a regular feature in *Natural History* magazine, Stephen Jay Gould has continued to set new standards for the popular scientific essay. Nearly two hundred of these essays have already been collected in five critically praised volumes that, in addition to three book-length studies — of I.Q. testing, geological time, and history — constitute most of Gould's nonacademic writing. A Harvard paleontologist and evolutionary theorist, he has made important contributions to our understanding of the ways new forms of life develop, and many of his writings display this interest in evolutionary principles. But to his readers, Gould is known primarily as a writer whose special talent lies in his uncanny ability to translate the most difficult scientific theories into terms most nonscientists can readily understand. For years he has argued against those who consider popular scientific writing an activity that results in a distortion of actual theories and findings. In the prologue to his most recent collection of essays, *Bully for Brontosaurus*, Gould declares: "We must all pledge ourselves to recovering accessible science as an honorable intellectual tradition. The rules are simple: no compromises with conceptual richness; no bypassing of ambiguity or ignorance; removal of jargon, of course, but no dumbing down of ideas." By following his own rules, Gould's writings have attracted an audience of "perceptive and intelligent" laypersons, evidenced by the thousands of letters he receives each year from nonprofessionals and by the appearance of his books' titles on best-seller lists in newspapers throughout the nation.

Born in New York City in 1941, Gould likes to trace his career back to a visit to the American Museum of Natural History at the age of five. Seeing the museum's *Tyrannosaurus rex* for the first time so impressed the young Gould that he decided to become a paleontologist, though he did not then know the term for scientists who studied prehistoric life through fossil records. After receiving degrees from Antioch College and Columbia University, at the age of twenty-five he went to teach geology and zoology at Harvard. Much of Gould's research revolves around the evolutionary growth patterns of West Indian land snails, far less glamorous creatures than the dinosaurs that fascinated him as a child. But it was his study of snails that contributed to the development, with colleague Niles Eldredge, of the controversial theory of "punctuated equilibrium." The theory, first advanced in 1972, proposes that evolution does not occur gradually as Charles Darwin thought, but in relatively rapid changes affecting isolated groups of a given population. Often such leaps in the evolutionary process are fostered by out-of-the-ordinary events like changes in climate or meteor showers or the appearance of a rival species. While the theory met with heavy opposition at first, very few scientists would now deny its validity.

The unexpected within nature has served as the focus not only of Gould's research but of his writing as well: his use of nature's curiosities to illuminate scientific principles is a strategy common to many of his essays.

Of Gould's literary method, David Quammen remarks: "Every oddity he describes stands on its own as a discrete fact of nature, an individual mystery, as well as yielding an example of some broader principle." The flamingo's "smile," featured in Gould's 1985 collection of the same name, illustrates how the workings of nature are largely made known through nature's imperfections. The title essay begins with the problem: Why has the flamingo's upper jaw come to resemble and to work functionally like a typical bird's lower bill? Such an inversion, according to Darwinian principles, can be accounted for by the fact that the flamingo is an upside down feeder and his inverted bill is the only solution to this upside down orientation. But Gould also finds an important lesson about evolution in the strange example of the flamingo:

> Adaption has a wonderful power to alter an anatomical design. . . . Yet, we should not conclude that Darwinian adaption to local environments has unconstrained power to design theoretically optimum shapes for all situations. Natural selection, as a historical process, can only work with material available. . . . The resulting imperfections and odd solutions, cobbled together with parts on hand, records a process that unfolds in time from unsuited antecedents, not the work of a perfect architect creating ab nihilo [from nothing].

The final sentence reflects Gould's continuing efforts in the name of evolution; he recently appeared in a Little Rock, Arkansas, courtroom to support the teaching of Darwin's theories, while opposing advocates of "creation science," the religious explanation of how life developed on earth.

Gould's defense of Darwinism against the "creationist" view finds elegant expression in his 1983 collection, *Hen's Teeth and Horse's Toes.* His earlier attempts at the popular essay are collected in *Ever Since Darwin* (1977), which "presents the basics of evolutionary theory as a comprehensive world view." A second volume of essays, *The Panda's Thumb* (1980), focused on a series of recent debates and developments in evolutionary science that imparted to the field a new vitality and a greater range of inquiry. Each of these volumes, then, deals extensively, though not exclusively, with some aspect of the ascendance of Darwin's theory of natural selection. *The Flamingo's Smile,* however, represents something of a departure for Gould; widening his focus, the scientist writes that the book "is about history and what it means to say that life is the product of a contingent past, not the inevitable and predictable result of simple timeless laws of nature." The collection was widely viewed as a successful attempt to erase the boundaries between scientific and humanistic studies. As Sue M. Halperin wrote in her review of the volume:

> Gould is both a scientist and a humanist, not merely a scientist whose literary abilities enable him to build a narrow bridge between the two cultures in order to export the intellectual commodities of science to the

other side. [His writing] portrays universal strivings, it expresses creativity, and it reveals Gould to be a student of human nature as well as one of human affairs.

In several essays in *The Flamingo's Smile,* Gould demonstrates how the misuse of science can result in the victimization of human beings as in the cases of the "Hottentot Venus," an African woman placed on display in nineteenth-century Europe, and Carrie Buck, an American woman labeled mentally incompetent and legally sterilized in the 1920s. The lesson of these essays is a simple one: scientific findings are morally neutral; their use is not.

A typical essay by Gould moves from the particular to the general: the particulars come from Gould's personal research or from classic books and papers of science containing the data he wants to study. He always tries to impress upon the reader that "science is not a heartless pursuit of objective information, it is a creative human activity." Accordingly, scientific documents can be read in a way very similar to the way we read literary texts. Raymond A. Solokov has written that Gould's "method is at bottom a kind of textual criticism of the language of earlier biologists, a historical analysis of their metaphors, their concepts of the world." By illustrating how scientists develop and defend their ideas about the world, he is able to render a clearer picture of the scientific process to the general public. While some reviewers have criticized his essays for being repetitive with respect to the key principles and themes that inform them, Gould's diversity of interests prevents the pieces from sounding too much alike. In one collection alone, a reader will find essays on Adam's navel, extraterrestrial beings, the origin of corn, the disappearance of .400 hitters in major league baseball, and nuclear winter.

One label that Gould has consistently tried to avoid is that of "nature writer." Like his contemporary Annie Dillard, he grew up in an urban environment and that experience has greatly influenced his attitude toward nature. As Gould has said of himself in the prologue to his fifth collection of essays, *Bully for Brontosaurus:* "My adult joys have been walks in cities, amidst stunning diversity of behavior and architecture, . . . more than excursions in the woods." His love of the natural derives mainly from the intellectual challenges it offers the human mind, though he is not "insensible to natural beauty." Accordingly, Gould likes to divide writings on natural history into two categories. The first he calls the Franciscan, after St. Francis of Assisi, who praised nature as a way of praising his God. The second category takes its name from the Renaissance scientist Galileo, a student of the heavens and of the physical laws that govern the universe. Franciscan writing is a kind of poetry, exalting "organic beauty by corresponding choice of words and phrase." Gould considers Henry David Thoreau's *Walden* one of the finest examples of the Franciscan mode. While the Galilean tradition, in which Gould places himself, does not deny the beauty of nature, it takes greater delight from comprehending the causes of natural occurrences. Like the Franciscans, the Galileans seek a union with nature, but their method is one of reason, not of poetry.

In recent years, Gould has grown increasingly worried that the myths about human life born out of expectations of progress may actually be harmful to large sections of the world's *Homo sapiens* population. In the case of I.Q. testing, Gould points out in his 1981 study, *The Mismeasure of Man*, our desire to quantify intelligence as a means "to identify children who needed special help so that the help could be given," has given rise to a great number of distorted conceptions about the worth of an individual. The book, Gould wrote, "is about the abstraction of intelligence as a single entity, its location in the brain, its quantification as one number for each individual, and the use of these numbers to rank people in a single series of worthiness, invariably to find that oppressed or disadvantaged groups — races, classes, or sexes — are innately inferior and deserve their status."

But on the whole, Gould is more optimistic about the human condition than many of his colleagues. As someone who believes that our very evolution was an improbability given the number of unlikely events that had to occur in order to bring it about, he has never ceased being amazed at our ability as a species to adapt to new situations, and he holds up a good deal of hope for our future. Of life on earth Gould has said: "Marine species tend to last 5 to 10 million years, and the terrestrial species less. But all bets are off with humans." For Gould, the future of the human race lies in the choices we make about ourselves and our world, and how successfully we make those choices rests upon our knowledge of how we got here in the first place. As a scientist and writer of the first order, he offers his readers that knowledge in the clearest and most elegant way imaginable. For his unique abilities, Gould was cited by *Newsweek* magazine as "a thinker and writer as central to our times as any whose name comes to mind."

Principal Works by Stephen Jay Gould

Ever Since Darwin: Reflections in Natural History   essays: 1977

The Panda's Thumb: More Reflections in Natural History   essays: 1980

The Mismeasure of Man   nonfiction: 1981

Hen's Teeth and Horse's Toes: Further Reflections in Natural History   essays: 1983

The Flamingo's Smile: Reflections in Natural History   essays: 1985

Time's Arrow, Time's Cycle: Myth and Metaphor in the Discovery of Geological Time   nonfiction: 1987

An Urchin in the Storm: Essays About Books and Ideas   criticism: 1987

Wonderful Life: The Burgess Shale and the Nature of History   nonfiction: 1990

Bully for Brontosaurus: Reflections in Natural History   essays: 1991

Selected Criticism of Stephen Jay Gould's Essays

BERNSTEIN, JEREMY. "Who Was Christy Mathewson?" *The New Yorker*, April 12, 1982, pp. 144–153. Another noted scientist-writer reviews Gould's *The Mismeasure of Man*, which he calls "a devastating and often extremely angry attack" on intelligence testing.

HARNACK, WILLIAM J. "Stephen Jay Gould: Linking Our Past and Our Future." *The Humanist*, July/August 1984, pp. 11–12. An informative tribute to the recipient of the 1984 American Humanist Association Distinguished Service Award.

LEVY, DANIEL S. "Evolution, Extinction and the Movies." *Time*, May 14, 1990, pp. 19–20. Gould demonstrates how "creation science" is finally a self-contradictory discipline and explains why human beings are not very significant in the order of things.

LEWONTIN, R. C. "Fallen Angels." *The New York Review of Books*, June 14, 1990, pp. 3–7. This review of Gould's *Wonderful Life: The Burgess Shale and the Nature of History* explores the essayist's conviction that ideology and politics exert a much greater influence over science than has traditionally been thought.

MASUR, LOUIS P. "Stephen Jay Gould's Vision of History." *The Massachusetts Review*, Fall 1989, pp. 467–484. A comprehensive and well-written look at Gould's view of natural and human history.

SMITH, WENDY. "Stephen Jay Gould: PW Interviews." *Publishers Weekly*, October 13, 1989, pp. 32–33. "The distinguished paleontologist argues against simplistic theories of progress in nature."

TIERNEY, JOHN. "Steven Jay Gould: The Rolling Stone Interview." *Rolling Stone*, January 15, 1987, pp. 38–61. Gould lucidly holds forth on a number of issues ranging from rock music to nuclear war.

GEORGE ORWELL

GEORGE ORWELL, the pen name of English writer Eric Arthur Blair (1903–1950), is perhaps best known for his futuristic novel of totalitarianism, *1984*. That novel, along with the political satire *Animal Farm*, effectively established Orwell as the leading political writer and journalist of his time. Critic John Wain has characterized Orwell's work as polemical in nature:

> All of it, in whatever form — novels, essays, descriptive sketches, volumes of autobiography — has the same object: to implant in the reader's mind a point of view, often about some definite, limited topic, but in any case about an issue over which [Orwell] felt it wrong not to take sides.

And Orwell's own estimate of his career seems to confirm Wain's judgment. In "Why I Write," he set forth the major theme of his later work: "Every line of serious work that I have written since 1936 has been written, directly or indirectly, against totalitarianism and for democratic socialism." Although this motif finds its most popular expression in his novels, Orwell's career as a writer officially began with the publication of the essay "A Farthing Newspaper" in 1928, and over the next twenty years he would write almost a hundred others. Moreover, while the critical estimation of his novels has declined in recent years, his essays continue to be accorded the highest praise. Typical of such praise is Irving Howe's, which cited Orwell as "the best English essayist since [William] Hazlitt, perhaps since Dr. [Samuel] Johnson. He was the greatest moral force in English letters during the last several decades."

Orwell was born at Motihari, Bengal, where his father was a minor agent in the colonial administration of British-occupied India. The family returned to England while Orwell was still a child and shortly afterward he was enrolled in private schools until he graduated from Eton in 1921. In Orwell's account of his experiences as a schoolboy, the posthumously published "Such, Such Were the Joys," the writer recalls his painful introduction to some of the harsher aspects of private school education and to the injustices of the English class system. Despite these intimations of deeper problems in the structure of English society, Orwell's early career closely follows the path of a young man in training for what Raymond Williams calls "membership in the administrative middle class of imperialist Britain." After declining to attend university, he joined the Indian Imperial Police and served in Burma for the next five years. Returning to England on leave in 1927, he decided to resign from the colonial police. One reason for this decision was Orwell's desire to become a writer. Another reason was his growing awareness of imperialism's political and moral dangers; in "Shooting an Elephant" he writes: "I had already made up my mind that imperialism was an evil thing and the sooner I chucked my job and got out of it the better."

Within six months of his release from service, Orwell began his firsthand exploration into the lives of ordinary working people. First in London, and later in Paris, he worked hard to establish himself as a writer with pieces on unemployment and homelessness in England. By 1932 he was successful in publishing a first book, *Down and Out in Paris and London*. The book can be described as a series of sketches strung loosely together that depict in great detail the experience of being without money in a modern city. The period of self-imposed poverty during which Orwell gathered material for his book provided him with an important insight prompted also by his experiences in Burma. It seemed to him that modern societies exploited their lower classes in the same way they exploited their colonial subjects. The indignation that Orwell felt as a result of this discovery finds its expression in virtually every work of this early period, culminating in *The Road to Wigan Pier* in 1937. Richard Hoggart has called this work of social criticism and autobiography Orwell's "first directly political book." While mainly an account of the writer's experiences among the poor workers in the north of England, the book also contains a bitter attack on the social policies that had failed to alleviate the terrible conditions under which the lower classes were forced to live and work. While doing research for *Wigan Pier*, Orwell kept a careful diary of his observations and experiences; one such entry begins:

> In the early morning the mill girls clumping down the cobbled street, all in clogs, make a curiously formidable sound, like an army hurrying into battle. I suppose this is the typical sound of Lancashire.

Entries like this one would later be polished into the lucid prose that characterizes all of Orwell's writing. While revising this passage for inclusion in the opening of the book, Orwell would see fit to include himself in the scene.

> The first sound in the mornings was the clumpings of the mill-girls' clogs down the cobbled street. Earlier than that, I suppose, there were factory whistles which I was never awake to hear.

The subjective tone in this passage is an important reminder that Orwell saw the issues he wrote about in a very personal light and that because of his idiosyncratic views he often found himself out of step with those who otherwise shared views similar to his own.

Shortly before the publication of *The Road to Wigan Pier*, Orwell left England once again, this time for Spain, to gather information for articles and to fight on the government side in the civil war. While serving with an English contingent, Orwell was seriously wounded. Though his military career had been cut short, his experiences in Spain continued to exert an important influence on his politics. *Homage to Catalonia*, his intensely personal account of the Spanish civil war and the internal struggles that plagued the leftist militias, is perhaps the pivotal work of Orwell's career. Orwell has said that while writing the book he committed himself to elevating political writing to the level of art. Though his experiences in Spain could have led Orwell to abandon his belief in socialism, as many have suggested they did, he emerged from the conflict with renewed hope and a clearer sense of purpose. In one of the moving passages that concludes *Homage to Catalonia*, Orwell gives elegant expression to his continuing faith in humankind:

> When you have had a glimpse of such a disaster as this — and however it ends, the Spanish War will turn out to have been an appalling disaster, quite apart from the slaughter and physical suffering — the result is not necessarily disillusionment and cynicism. Curiously enough the whole experience has left me with not less but more belief in the decency of human beings.

Between the publication of *Coming Up for Air*, Orwell's last conventional novel, in 1939, and the appearance of the two novels that would win for him worldwide recognition, *Animal Farm* (1945) and *1984* (1949), Orwell continued to work in the essay form. *Inside the Whale and Other Essays* consists of three longer pieces concerned primarily with literature and popular culture. It is in the title essay, written on the eve of the Second World War, that Orwell announces what he sees as the future of human society:

> Almost certainly we are moving into an age of totalitarian dictatorship — an age in which freedom of thought will be at first a deadly sin and later on a meaningless abstraction. The autonomous individual is going to be stamped out of existence.

Another lengthy polemical essay, *The Lion and the Unicorn* (1941), examines the English national character and attempts to locate the prospects for political and social reform within English society. In the volume called *The English People* (1947), Orwell returns to these themes but extends his analysis to include a fascinating discussion of the English language. He relates what he considers to be the defining characteristics of English and in the process provides a keen insight into his own written style:

> To write or even to speak English is not a science but an art. There are no reliable rules: there is only the general principle that concrete words are better than abstract ones, and that the shortest way of saying anything is the best. . . . Whoever writes English is involved in a struggle that never lets up even for a sentence.

Orwell's ideas about language attain their most detailed and lively exposition in his 1946 essay, "Politics and the English Language." He begins the essay by exploring the reasons why English has lost so much of its vitality and precision and proceeds to place the blame for the destruction of the language on politicians who design statements to conceal rather than reveal the truth about any particular issue. This situation, however, is not irreversible. If people cease to make use of hackneyed phrases and circumlocutions, these practices will die out in favor of an English that is precise and reliable as a medium for the communication of ideas.

"Politics and the English Language" is one of the essays collected in the volume called *Shooting an Elephant*. This collection, which appeared in print shortly after Orwell's death from tuberculosis, contains much of his finest work as an essayist. Included here are "A Hanging" and "Shooting an Elephant," the author's recollections of his service in the Indian Imperial Police, which for their descriptive brilliance could easily have found a place in his novel *Burmese Days* (1934). Other essays like "Some Thoughts on the Common Toad" and "A Good Word for the Vicar of Bray" display Orwell's delight in the natural scene. Still others like "Books vs. Cigarettes" and "Decline of the English Murder" take up in great detail some preoccupations of English life. All of the essays bear the mark of a deeply perceptive and flexible intelligence capable of reflecting on just about any subject that interests it.

In the four decades since his death, a dominant picture of Orwell as man and writer has emerged. Lionel Trilling, in his classic essay on *Homage to Catalonia*, "George Orwell and the Politics of Truth," portrayed Orwell as "the man who told the truth." Others besides Trilling have seen Orwell as the disillusioned idealist dedicated only to truth-telling. While the body of Orwell's work makes it difficult to argue that he ever became completely disenchanted with the idea of social reform, books like *Animal Farm* and *1984* do seem to point to an increasing cynicism about modern politics. As evidenced by his creation of Newspeak, the dangerous form English takes in the latter novel, Orwell felt that the ways in which we use language will determine in part whether or not we remain free as thinking individuals. In his own prose, Orwell developed a style that became the model for clear, direct description and exposition. By allowing "the meaning to choose the word," Orwell hoped to create texts from which the reader, with very little effort, could extract the writer's message.

In Orwell's later work, as George Woodcock remarks, "the style grows so near to the subject that one no longer thinks of it as style." It is much to ask of any writer that he sacrifice a more "literary" or ornate style in favor of one better suited to the communication of vital facts. Orwell, who always placed the interests of others before his own, not only made this sacrifice but created a new kind of writing. As Connor Cruise O'Brien writes: "that spare, tough prose has not aged; that clear eye sees more than ours do even if there are things which it cannot see through. . . . What political writer now cares as much as he did, both about what he is writing and about how he is writing it?" Orwell knew that the price of freedom was honesty, but he also knew that saying exactly what one meant, even in a democracy, always required a great deal of moral courage. George Orwell never flinched; and it is for this courage more than any aspect of his writing that his essays remain a dominant model of English prose style.

Principal Works by George Orwell

Down and Out in Paris and London   autobiography: 1933

Burmese Days   novel: 1934

A Clergyman's Daughter   novel: 1935

Keep the Aspidistra Flying   novel: 1937

The Road to Wigan Pier   social criticism/autobiography: 1937

Homage to Catalonia   social criticism/autobiography: 1938

Coming Up for Air   novel: 1939

Animal Farm   novel: 1945

1984   novel: 1949

The Collected Essays, Journalism and Letters of George Orwell   (in four volumes): 1968

Selected Criticism of George Orwell's Essays

BLOOM, HAROLD, ed. *George Orwell: Modern Critical Views*. New York: Chelsea House Publishers, 1987. While this representative collection of critical essays focuses mainly on Orwell's fiction, there are several pieces included on his nonfiction. Several of the pieces appear in Williams 1974 as well.

KEARNS, CLEO McNELLY. "On Not Teaching George Orwell." *College English* 38 (6) February 1977. Reprinted in Bloom. An insightful study of the problems that Orwell poses for undergraduate writers who follow his advice on composition too closely.

SLATER, IAN. *George Orwell: The Road to Airstrip One*. New York: W. W. Norton & Co., 1985. An intelligent account of Orwell's political development through a careful reading of his work including his nonfiction prose.

TRILLING, LIONEL. "George Orwell and the Politics of Truth." *Commentary* 13 (3) March 1952. Reprinted in Bloom and in Williams 1974. One of the most influential essays on Orwell's prose since his death.

WILLIAMS, RAYMOND, ed. *George Orwell: A Collection of Critical Essays*. Englewood Cliffs, N.J.: Prentice-Hall, 1974. A diverse selection of readings on Orwell. Several of the essays appear in Bloom as well.

WILLIAMS, RAYMOND. *Orwell*. New York: Columbia University Press, 1981. A short and brilliant study from a socialist literary critic's perspective.

WOLLHEIM, RICHARD. "Orwell Reconsidered." *Partisan Review* 27 (1) Winter 1960. Reprinted in Bloom. Examines *The Road to Wigan Pier* in the context of the 1930s, an age in which journalism could not be distinguished from literature.

WOODCOCK, GEORGE. *The Crystal Spirit*. London: Jonathan Cape, 1967. See especially "Prose like a Window-Pane," pp. 263–279. Reprinted in Williams 1974. One of the best extended discussions of Orwell's prose style.

CYNTHIA OZICK

"I NEVER MEANT TO WRITE ESSAYS," Cynthia Ozick tells us in the foreword to her first collection of nonfiction, *Art and Ardor*. The desire to do so came upon her suddenly, just after she had finished reading George Orwell's memoir, "Such, Such Were the Joys." Since that moment, Ozick has written and published over a hundred essays. If some take the form of articles or public addresses, they are nevertheless all marked by the same impassioned and intricate prose style, by the conviction that knowledge is arrived at not through preconceived patterns of inquiry, but through invention and imagination — through ardor. For Ozick the essay must be an act governed by intuition; the true essayist starts from scratch with little or no idea where the form will take her. Only by turning her back on what she already knows, by resisting the desire to summarize or explain, can the essayist claim for herself the same sense of discovery experienced by a writer of fiction. This conception of the essay frees it from the stranglehold of strict logic and sober factuality. Ozick, through her own writing, continually reminds us that "nearly every essay, like every story, is an experiment, not a credo."

Born in 1928, Ozick was raised in New York City. In one of her most lyrical essays, "A Drugstore in Winter," she recalls the pleasures of her childhood as the daughter of a Bronx pharmacist during the Great Depression and remembers the forces that shaped her as a writer:

> A writer is dreamed and transfigured into being by spells, wishes, goldfish, silhouettes of trees, boxes of fairy tales dropped in the mud, uncles' and cousins' books, tablets and capsules and powders, papa's Moscow ache, his drugstore jacket with his special fountain pen in the pocket, his beautiful Hebrew paragraphs, his Talmudist's rationalism, his Russian-Gymnasium Latin and German, mama's furnace-heart, her masses of memoirs, her paintings of autumn walks down to the sunny water, her braveries, her reveries, her old, old school hurts.

All of Ozick's personal essays demonstrate her novelist's eye for details that resonate with a significance far beyond the mere fact of their existence. For Ozick, the details of our lives are imbued with hidden meanings. The interpretations we place upon these details, however, cannot be seen as final; certain elements will always remain beyond the limits of human understanding. Commenting on a collection of Ozick's stories, Paul Gray wrote: "She demands nothing less of her prose than the ineffable, yet her language does not simply point a finger at prepackaged symbols or detachable interpretations. With remarkable success, it makes a fist around the unknown."

After high school, Ozick enrolled as a first-year student at New York University. In "Washington Square, 1946," she describes how she mistakenly arrived for classes a day early. Wishing to delay the long subway ride home, Ozick takes a walk in the surrounding neighborhood and ponders the sights around Washington Square: a pretzel vendor, a Chock Full O' Nuts coffee shop, a newsstand. These "three omens," as she calls them, take on allegorical significance; each omen symbolizes an aspect of Ozick's future as a writer and intellectual. The essay nicely illustrates Ozick's skillfull use of literary methods most often associated with fiction. In her foreword to *Metaphor and Memory,* she explains her practice by contending that there is no "commanding difference between essays and stories. . . . A story is a hypothesis, a tryout of human nature under the impingement of certain given materials; so is an essay." The implication is clear; why should the essayist not avail herself of the techniques of fiction as well as those of nonfiction? For all practical purposes, Ozick sees her essays as stories with pretensions toward the truth. The results of this approach offer a stiff challenge to the orthodox notion that essays must witness, persuade, advocate, polemicize, or state the facts in the plainest terms. Ozick's essays are meant to "illuminate" their subjects in just the way that good fiction or poetry does: by engaging the imagination rather than the intellect.

While pursuing a graduate degree in English Literature at Ohio State University, Ozick decided to combine the traditional academic career of teaching and critical writing with the craft of fiction. She left graduate school with an M.A. and soon after dedicated herself to writing novels consciously modeled on the later works of her literary hero Henry James. *Trust,* which would become her first published book, was originally conceived as a shorter work, though by the time it was finished it had grown to more than 650 pages. Thomas R. Edwards has aptly remarked that Ozick "is never in danger of saying too little as a writer." The book, in the process of examining the broader aspects of modern life: history, politics, identity, antisemitism, tended toward abstraction and high seriousness. While most critics agreed that *Trust* was the work of "a highly perceptive intelligence," several were troubled by the author's apparent failure to achieve a balance between her ornate style of writing and the dramatic aspects of her work. Plot and dramatic movement were often sacrificed for stylistic fireworks. And yet, the novel provided Ozick with the themes that have dominated her work ever since: the conflict between reason and imagination, between law and freedom, between religious and secular life. This final theme is strongly indicative of Ozick's own ambivalence toward writing fiction.

"Thou shalt not make unto thee any graven image," the second of the Ten Commandments instructs. The biblical term "graven image" has traditionally been identified with the idols of paganism. But for Ozick, literature itself is a form of idolatry. In this view, fiction and poetry are condemned as dangerous arts that compete with the revealed truths of the Old Testament for our devotion. Moreover, the literary artist becomes a kind of magician whose presumption would lead him to imitate the Creation by fashioning fictive worlds. Since the Second Commandment's ban on idolatry is, for Ozick, the fundamental condition of Judaism, she considers the term *Jewish writer* "a pointed contradiction, in which one arm of the phrase clashes so profoundly with the other as to annihilate it." And yet, as if to deny the very premise she upholds, she has published three novels, four collections of short fiction, and numerous poems. Moreover, her two essay collections, *Art and Ardor* (1983) and *Metaphor and Memory* (1988), are mainly literary in focus. This apparent contradiction has led Ozick to ask herself in vain: "Why do we become what we most desire to contend with?"

The appearance of *The Pagan Rabbi and Other Stories* in 1971 cemented Ozick's reputation as one of our best writers of short fiction. The title story dramatizes, though does not resolve, its author's conflicts about the role of imagination within religious life. Sanford Pinsker characterizes the major tension within the story precisely.

> It is as if the old charges against "Jewish writing" — that everything not Torah [the Hebrew scripture] is levity, that the wider cultural world is both pagan and utterly in conflict with the Jewish imagination, that the fiction writer is himself, or herself, a species of pagan — had been filtered through a consciousness at one and the same time thoroughly literary and uncompromisingly Jewish.

What is true of Ozick's fiction, however, is also true of her essays. Her attacks in *Art and Ardor* on such literary "pagans" as critic Harold Bloom, novelist Philip Roth, and poet Allen Ginsburg usually amount to attacks on aspects of her own writing that she considers antithetical to her goal of remaining firmly within the Jewish tradition. Thus, it is Ozick's conflict over her fictional productions that provides the motive for many of her essays; whether critical or personal, they attempt to explain, justify, and defend her often controversial positions.

By the time *Art and Ardor* was published, Ozick had already added another novel, *The Cannibal Galaxy* (1983), and two more collections of short fiction, *Bloodshed and Three Novellas* (1976) and *Levitations: Five Fictions* (1982), to her list of literary achievements. The tough-minded, mostly polemical essays are marked by a vitality of thought and language. As Barbara Koenig Quart wrote in her review for *The Nation*: "even if one wants to argue with Ozick every step of the way . . . one must start by noting how very well she writes." Her masterly prose style is best described in words Ozick herself uses to recall the style of her literary hero Henry James, a style "nuanced, imbricated with a thousand distinctions and observation, and as idiosyncratically and ecstatically redolent of the spirals of past and future as a garlic clove."

While several of the essays in the collection originally appeared under the lowly rubric of book reviews or introductions to new editions of an author's work, Ozick has always viewed such assignments as occasions for what she calls "essays of ideas." In these essays, she invariably uses another writer's work as a springboard for her own reflections, so that a review of Nobelist Isaac Bashevis Singer's *Collected Stories* gives rise to a meditation on the role of the supernatural in everyday life, or a revaluation of an early work by Truman Capote becomes a discussion of the nature of literary fame. Ozick's tendency to make sweeping generalizations has bothered some critics. Poet Katha Pollitt, though mostly praising *Art and Ardor*, nevertheless declares in her review that "Ozick is fond of grand pronouncements, and she delivers them with such confidence one might almost not notice that many of them are flatly invalid." Pollitt then goes on to attribute these minor flaws to the author's exuberance.

Ozick's enthusiasm for literature carries over into her next volume of essays, *Metaphor and Memory*, which appeared shortly after her third novel *The Messiah of Stockholm* (1987). The title of the collection is taken from Ozick's Phi Beta Kappa Oration delivered at Harvard University. The piece may be considered Ozick's most recent attempt to find a middle ground between art and morality. Metaphor, she explains, "relies on what has been experienced before; it transforms the strange into the familiar." Because it gives us the power to envision what is foreign to our experience in terms we already know, metaphor promotes compassion toward those unlike ourselves:

> Those who have no pain can imagine those who suffer. Those at the center can imagine what it is to be outside. The strong can imagine the weak. Illuminated lives can imagine the dark. Poets in their twilight can imagine the borders of stellar fire. We strangers can imagine the familiar hearts of strangers.

Metaphor, then, is always directed toward clarification, toward knowledge. But the kind of knowledge that Ozick celebrates is never accrued only for its own sake; the pursuit of a knowledge that gives birth to nothing else is merely another form of idolatry. Insofar as they succeed in guiding us toward a greater understanding of our common history and experience, moments of illumination, like those described in the passage above, connect us to our world. As enemies of abstraction, Cynthia Ozick and her metaphors work hard to transform knowledge into wisdom, into ethics. Calling Ozick "the best American writer to emerge in recent years," novelist Edmund White concludes that "her artistic strength derives from her moral energy." The second sentence of *Genesis* reads "And the earth was astonishingly empty." The principle to be drawn from Ozick's essays is that while the imagination may be amoral, the act of writing can never be anything other than a profoundly moral exercise aimed at rescuing life from emptiness.

Principal Works by Cynthia Ozick

Trust   novel: 1966

The Pagan Rabbi and Other Stories   short fiction: 1971

Bloodshed and Three Novellas   short fiction: 1976

Levitation: Five Fictions   short fiction: 1982

The Cannibal Galaxy   novel: 1983
Art and Ardor   essays: 1983
The Messiah of Stockholm   novel: 1987
Metaphor and Memory   essays: 1988
The Shawl   short fiction: 1990

Selected Criticism of Cynthia Ozick's Essays

BLOOM, HAROLD, ed. *Cynthia Ozick: Modern Critical Views*. New York: Chelsea Publishers, 1986. Contains Bloom's fine introductory essay on Ozick's place in the Jewish literary tradition.

KAUVAR, ELAINE M. "An Interview with Cynthia Ozick." *Contemporary Literature* 26 (4) 1985, pp. 376–401. Ozick discusses her ideas about literature and her own work.

LOWIN, JOSEPH. *Cynthia Ozick*. Boston: Twayne Publishers, 1988. A general study with several observations about Ozick's nonfiction interspersed throughout the book.

PINSKER, SANFORD. "Jewish Tradition and the Individual Talent." *The Georgia Review* 37 (3) Fall 1983. Reprinted in Bloom. Attempts to locate Ozick's essays alongside those of other New York Jewish intellectuals while recognizing that Ozick's religious views are not easily reconciled with those of this mainly secular group.

POLLITT, KATHA. "The Three Selves of Cynthia Ozick." *The New York Times Book Review*, May 22, 1983, pp. 63–67. Reprinted in Bloom. A review of *Art and Ardor*; Pollitt focuses upon Ozick's obsession with idolatry, both religious and secular.

LEWIS THOMAS

I N THE EARLY 1970s, a series of remarkable essays began to appear in the *New England Journal of Medicine.* The journal, read mainly by the medical community, traditionally printed long technical papers filled with data aimed at informing scientists and doctors of recent advances in their fields. The essays in question, however, were of a completely different nature. While most contained reflections on medicine and biology, many focused on topics as varied as music, astronomy, language, technology, and social ritual. The essayist's favorite posture was that of an enlightened amateur who enjoyed writing about any subject capable of sparking his seemingly infinite curiosity. Moreover, they were written in a style both elegant and direct, a far cry from the often incomprehensible prose of most scientific articles. Critic Jeffrey Burke pointed to the author's "casual tone — that of the thoughtful mind apparently wandering, yet always to a certain purpose." Author Joyce Carol Oates wrote that these short pieces were "masterpieces of the 'art of the essay.'"

The writer being singled out for such high praise was the eminent physician and medical researcher Lewis Thomas, president of the famous Memorial Sloan-Kettering Cancer Center in New York City. Thomas achieved widespread recognition when his first book, *The Lives of a Cell: Notes of a Biology-Watcher,* a gathering of his essays from the *New England Journal of Medicine,* won the 1974 National Book Award for nonfiction. Since that time, he has published three other collections of essays and a memoir. As Mark Czarnecki has commented, "Scientists who can illuminate their discipline for the general reader are a rare breed. Since his first collection of essays . . . appeared in 1974, Lewis Thomas has established himself as science's most compassionate and comprehensible advocate."

Born in 1913, Thomas first learned about the practice of medicine from his father, a general practitioner in Flushing, New York. The physician continually reminded his son that doctors could actually do very little for their patients.

> It was necessary for him to be available, and to make all these calls at their homes, but I was not to have the idea that he could do anything much to change the course of their illnesses. It was important to my father that I understand this; it was a central feature of the profession, and a doctor should not only be prepared for it but be prepared to be honest with himself about it.

Years later, while Thomas was a medical student at Harvard, the discovery of antibiotics enabled the quick recovery of patients who would certainly have died without them. The arrival of these "miracle drugs" profoundly influenced a whole generation of doctors, including Thomas, who were convinced that medicine had finally grown into a science. The optimism of that period still informs much of Thomas's outlook. Recently, he was asked whether he thought new medical problems would emerge even as old ones disappeared in the wake of scientific advances. Thomas voiced his belief that disease itself is almost a thing of the past, and that many of the remaining problems would be solved within a few decades. His optimism derives, in part, from the positive method of science itself; insofar as it always looks forward, all scientific truth is optimistic. At the same time, however, Thomas is not unaware of the dangers we face as a species. He has written eloquently of our need to preserve the environment and contemplated the consequences of a nuclear holocaust for life on earth. Thomas is a traditional humanist in that he believes that we as human beings hold the keys to our own perfection or destruction.

Thomas began writing essays at the instigation of Franz Ingelfinger, editor of the *New England Journal of Medicine* and a longtime friend of the physician. Ingelfinger had read a copy of Thomas's keynote address at a 1970 medical conference. He was impressed by the talk and suggested that his friend try writing some short pieces for the *Journal*. The terms of their agreement were quite simple. Thomas would write one essay a month, each no longer than the space of one *Journal* page (about 1000 words) in the same general style Thomas had employed at the conference. The essays could focus on any topic and they would be printed, if accepted for publication, without any changes. While Thomas had written nothing "for fun" since graduating medical school, the assignment was an intriguing one. By this time in his career, he had written about two hundred scientific papers, all "composed in the relentlessly flat style required for absolute unambiguity in every word." The opportunity being offered would allow Thomas to break free from the indifferent prose of research journals. But the prospect of writing essays also worried him a little.

Because he was trained as a scientist, Thomas's thinking tended toward the analytical. The example of Montaigne, the first great essayist, however, had shown Thomas that the essay was not a form given to strict organization: "Montaigne simply turns his mind loose and writes whatever he feels like writing." As a result of this method, Montaigne's essays rarely confine themselves to a single idea and even more rarely do they unfold in an orderly fashion. While his editor's instructions that the pieces be short placed certain limits on what Thomas could write, he would try to proceed as much as possible in the manner of his essayist hero. Thomas decided to write without any method at all, writing as quickly as possible without a plan or outline. This unmethodical method resulted in the publication of six essays. At the end of this first sequence of essays, Thomas wrote a letter to Ingelfinger saying he thought it better not to continue, that the journal could probably find another writer better equipped to write this type of piece. To his surprise, the *Journal* refused to release Thomas from his agreement, claiming that the essays had met with a great response from members of the medical community as well as from people whose doctors had passed the essays along to them. One such person was Joyce Carol Oates, who wrote Thomas a letter encouraging him to collect his essays into a volume for publication.

Following Oates's advice, though doubting their wider appeal somewhat, Thomas decided to publish the essays he had written so far under the
title *The Lives of a Cell,* which was also the name of the first essay he wrote.
The book, which appeared in 1974, received almost unanimous praise from
reviewers, though a few scientists were troubled by the hypothesis that runs
through many of the essays. The Gaia hypothesis, first proposed by J. E.
Lovelock and then supported by L. Margulis, views the earth as "a kind of
organism displaying so many instances of interdependency and connectedness as to resemble an enormous embryo still in the process of developing."
The idea is one that appeals to Thomas because it helps to explain how our
planet regulates itself, "maintaining stability in the relative composition of
the constituents in its atmosphere and waters, achieving something like the
homeostasis familiar to students of conventional complex organisms, man
himself for example." Without this mechanism for keeping constant the
earth's constituent elements, life inevitably would be destroyed.

The hypothesis meets its stiffest challenge from evolutionary biologists
who attribute the development of species mainly to chance. They feel that
the suggestion that the earth

> possesses an array of unfathomably complex mechanisms for its own inter-
> nal regulation, and that these mechanisms operating together maintain the
> stability of the whole, carries the implication that the thing was somehow
> designed to work this way.

Denying such design, the Darwinian theory of natural selection is based on
competition between species. Darwinians disagree with the Gaian view proposing that life on earth developed out of cooperation and collaboration
among its different aspects. Acknowledging the strong element of chance in
natural history, Thomas, always optimistic, still likes to imagine that life
could have evolved out of a kind of extended partnership.

Thomas's second collection, *The Medusa and the Snail,* continues this
theme of cooperation in nature. The title essay explores the complex symbiotic relationship between the Medusa, a jellyfish, and the "snail" of the
title, actually a sea slug. Insofar as the two organisms cannot live without
each other, Thomas suggests, they cannot really be considered selves — that
is, separate beings. Thomas's point seems to be that however natural we feel
it is to think of ourselves as autonomous, nature does not always support this
notion. In "Medical Lessons from History," the final essay of the volume,
Thomas strikes an unusually solemn note. After reviewing medicine's progress in this century, he concludes:

> These ought to be the best of times for the human mind, but it is not
> so. . . . I cannot begin to guess at all the causes of our cultural sadness,
> but I can think of one thing that is wrong with us and eats away at us: we
> do not know enough about ourselves.

Only by increasing our scientific knowledge, Thomas believes, can we attain the wisdom necessary for our survival as a species.

In 1983 Thomas published *The Youngest Science,* less a memoir than an account of the maturation of medical science that happens to coincide with Thomas's own career. As one reviewer remarked:

> For his part, Lewis Thomas has seen the modern medicine of his father transformed into an inventive, skillful, practical science of today. He has watched the process, he has partaken of it and now he has written vividly about it. More he could not have done.

Though at times Thomas, a master of the short essay, seems uncomfortable in this complex narrative form, he nevertheless manages to raise most of the central issues facing medicine. These issues range from specialization within the profession to low-cost health care, from bio-ethics to technology, from genetic engineering to medical education. Many of these topics emerge again in Thomas's third essay collection, *Late Night Thoughts on Listening to Mahler's Ninth Symphony.*

Several reviewers found this volume marked by a somber tone not present in Thomas's earlier work. In the opening and closing essays, he imagines the devastation that would be wrought by nuclear war. Another essay in the book considers the far-reaching effects of the federal government's cuts in support for basic scientific research. John Yardley comments that while the essays devoted to subjects like these "are written with great feeling and from an unexceptionable point of view, I find them considerably less interesting than those devoted to biology and scientific method." Thomas is at his best when he turns his attention to the demystification of the scientific method. He understands better than anyone that the future happiness of the human race lies in cooperation between scientists and the nonscientific community, two groups that often seem to be in opposition. He argues that these groups must prevent each other from becoming self-absorbed or isolated. Accordingly, he speaks to both worlds, appealing to the scientific community to keep in mind the needs and interests of the rest of the world, while at the same time explaining the methods and goals of science to nonscientists. In this deeply confusing period in our history, Thomas's essays provide comfort; their emphasis on the interconnection of all living things brings with it a sense of order and harmony seldom felt in modernity. The *New York Times* book reviewer Christopher Lehmann-Haupt puts it best when he writes that Lewis Thomas "is a scientist . . . who makes us feel a little less bad about being alive and human."

Principal Works by Lewis Thomas

The Lives of a Cell: Notes of a Biology-Watcher   essays: 1974
The Medusa and the Snail: More Notes of a Biology-Watcher   essays: 1979

The Youngest Science: Notes of a Medicine-Watcher   memoir: 1983
Late Night Thoughts on Listening to Mahler's Ninth Symphony   essays: 1983
Et Cetera, Et Cetera: Notes of a Word-Watcher   essays: 1990

Selected Criticism of Lewis Thomas's Essays

BERNSTEIN, JEREMY. "A Doctor's Life." *The New Yorker*, February 14, 1983, pp. 109–114. A long review essay of Thomas's *The Youngest Science* that examines the author's career and literary achievement.

BURKE, JEFFREY. "Biological Imperative." *Harper's*, May 1979, pp. 95–96. Some useful insights into Thomas's tone and style.

CZARNECKI, MARK. "Waging War on Disease." *Maclean's Magazine*, March 17, 1983, pp. 59, 61. A rare mixed review of Thomas's *The Youngest Science* that draws attention to the author's humanist and humanitarian tendencies.

HELLENSTEIN, DAVID. "The Muse of Medicine." *Esquire*, March 1984, pp. 72–77. An in-depth profile of Thomas written in a popular style.

OATES, JOYCE CAROL. "Beyond Common Sense." *The New York Times Book Review*, May 26, 1974, pp. 2–3. An important review of *The Lives of a Cell* that first brought Thomas to the attention of many readers.

WADDINGTON, C. H. "The Mysteries of the Libidinous Molecule." *The New York Review of Books*, Vol. XXI, No. 19, November 28, 1974, pp. 4, 6, 8. Another influential early review focusing on Thomas's observations of social behavior.

ALICE WALKER

E ARLY IN HER CAREER, the African American essayist, novelist, and poet
Alice Walker realized that to be a writer often meant being alone.
Taking for granted the inevitable solitude that accompanies all acts of writing,
Walker considers the special kind of loneliness experienced by certain writers
in her 1973 essay "From an Interview":

> The writer — like the musician or painter — must be free to explore,
> otherwise she or he will never discover what is needed (by everyone) to
> be known. This means, very often, finding oneself considered "unaccept-
> able" by masses of people who think that the writer's obligation is not to
> explore or to challenge, but to second the masses' motions, whatever they
> are. Yet the gift of loneliness is sometimes a radical vision of society or
> one's people that has not previously been taken into account.

Alice Walker has spent most of her adult life putting her "gift of loneliness"
to its fullest use, offering her readers a vision of a world few of them have
ever seen. Specifically, Walker forces us to "take account" of the lives of
African American women, a segment of our population that has traditionally
received little attention in our national literature. She is the major proponent
of a brand of feminism she calls the "womanist" tradition. In fact, Walker's
major nonfiction statement of her ideas, *In Search of Our Mothers' Gardens*,
considered by many to be one of the most influential books to appear in
recent years, is subtitled *Womanist Prose*.

For Walker, the term "womanist" is synonymous with "black feminist"
or "feminist of color." It derives from the black folk expression "You acting
womanish" — that is, like a woman — and it refers to the courageous and
willful behavior Walker has so often observed, and written about, in women
of her race. To be a womanist is to appreciate and even prefer "women's
culture, women's flexibility, and women's strength." It also means being
"committed to [the] survival and wholeness of entire people, male and
female." Walker sees the experiences of black women in America as a series
of developments by which these women achieved a degree of control over
their own lives after having been victimized by the dominant culture as well
as by black men for several centuries. But even more horrifying to Walker
than "the external facts and figures of oppression," as Mary Helen Washington writes, is the "terror within; the mutilation of the spirit." Spiritual
disfigurement and the symbolic acts of healing that must follow if a woman
is to be whole again are two of the most important themes in Walker's fiction
and nonfiction. While she has never neglected other issues facing the women
of her race — poverty, exploitation, discrimination — she is most concerned
with the inner lives of the people about and for whom she writes.

Walker was born in Eatontown, Georgia, in 1944. At an early age, she
began to record in a small notebook stories her parents told her along with a
few of her own poems. When she was eight, she was accidentally blinded in
one eye by a shot from her brother's BB gun, an event recorded in her essay

"Beauty: When the Other Dancer Is the Self." She now credits the injury, which in her youth had made her extremely self-conscious and withdrawn, with her ability to study human relationships dispassionately "and to learn to be patient enough to care how they turned out." Her feelings of isolation may also have motivated Walker to excel in school; she became high school valedictorian and won a scholarship to attend Spelman College, a black women's college in Atlanta. After becoming involved in the civil rights movement, which would provide the inspiration for *Meridian*, her second novel, Walker began to resent Spelman's conservative attitude toward the movement. These feelings led her to accept a scholarship to attend the more progressive Sarah Lawrence College in New York State.

Soon after her graduation, Walker published her first volume of poetry, *Once*, a collection that mapped out much of the thematic territory Walker would explore in later works — Africa, suicide, love, civil rights activism, violence against women. Lisel Mueller praised the spare poems in which "feeling is channeled into a style that is direct and sharp, honest speech pared down to essentials." Some of this candor reappears in Walker's first novel, *The Third Life of Grange Copeland*. Published in 1970, the novel portrays, with what one reviewer called "vivid matter-of-factness," the vicious cycle of poverty and violence that has entrapped one Southern black family. Three years later, a collection of short stories, *In Love & Trouble: Stories of Black Women*, won the prestigious Richard and Hilda Rosenthal Award from the American Institute of Arts and Letters, while *Revolutionary Petunias & Other Poems* was nominated for a National Book Award. The former emphasized Walker's commitment to the lives of black women, especially those trapped in poverty and ignorance. Moreover, she dedicated the collection to the memory of Zora Neale Hurston, a black woman writer of an earlier generation who continues to inspire Walker and other African American women writers.

Hurston, an integral figure in the Harlem Renaissance of the 1920s and '30s, is probably best known for her novel *Their Eyes Were Watching God* and a collection of black folklore *Mules and Men*. Of the novel, Walker once wrote: "There is no book more important to me than this one." One reason for Walker's remark might be found in Hurston's original creation of a black female protagonist who, to quote critics Barbara Johnson and H. L. Gates, Jr., "writes herself into being" using the spoken idiom of the black community she inhabits. That Walker should have Celie, the heroine of her most celebrated novel, *The Color Purple*, imitate Hurston's protagonist by writing herself into being demonstrates the younger writer's debt to her predecessor. Walker even pays tribute to Hurston as one of her metaphorical mothers in her essay "In Search of Our Mothers' Gardens." Althought the theme is most fully explored in the case of Hurston, Walker's search for her "mothers" or literary precursors occupies much of her work.

With English novelist and essayist Virginia Woolf, Walker shares the view that the tradition of women has been one of silence as much as one of voice. In Woolf's view, womens' voices have been suppressed to such an extent that they as a group have been denied artistic identity. Walker's vision of the female tradition, however, seems slightly more optimistic than Woolf's. In Dianne E. Sadoff's paraphrase of Walker's belief: black women, historically "forbidden by law to read or write, kept alive the creative spirit among their people and passed on to their daughters that 'living creativity,' the 'notion of song.'" If women could not leave their daughters a written legacy, they could at least provide them with an oral one. One form taken by this legacy was the blues music of the rural South; for Walker, it is the great blues singer Bessie Smith who becomes a paradigm, along with Zora Neale Hurston, for the black female artist, just as singing becomes Walker's metaphor for writing. In *The Color Purple*, it is the female blues singer Shug Avery that embodies both love and creativity, and it is she who enables other women in the novel to find their voices.

By the early 1980s, Walker had begun to come under attack for her "too partisan" fictions. In a review of Walker's second collection of short fiction, *You Can't Keep a Good Woman Down*, Katha Pollitt observes "The black woman is always the most sympathetic character." But Walker has never attempted to hide her consuming interest in the plight of black women or her "womanist" bias. She is content to allow other writers to sing the praises of other groups. Moreover, she has never backed away from her position for fear of offending another group. When *The Color Purple* appeared in 1982 many critics denounced Walker for her unflattering portrayal of black men as cruel perpetrators of sexual and physical abuse on black women. One enraged columnist wrote, "*The Color Purple* can make you see red. That's especially true if you are a man and happen to be black." Several civil rights organizations even picketed the release, by Steven Spielberg, of a film version of Walker's novel. Despite the controversy surrounding the book, Walker was the recipient of both the American Book Award and the Pulitzer Prize for fiction.

For thirteen years, Walker served as contributing editor to *Ms.*, the feminist magazine founded by Gloria Steinem. It was here that she first published many of the essays that would later be collected in two volumes of nonfiction prose, *In Search of Our Mothers' Gardens: Womanist Prose* (1983) and *Living by the Word: Selected Writings 1973–1987* (1988). The first of these volumes traces Walker's search for an identity through the legacy passed on by Southern black women, both literate and illiterate. Accordingly, most of the writing, though it touches on politics and literature, is autobiographical. Though Walker, in the process of writing these essays, considered leaving out certain aspects of her life that she found embarrassing, she ultimately decided against doing so. The result of her decision is the searing honesty that pervades these pieces. As in the essays of George Orwell, there is a strongly didactic element in Walker's prose, and this didacticism, usually in the interest of her "womanist" project, is best served by a style that is both direct and powerful in its rhetoric. Some of the power of Walker's style may be observed in this passage from the essay "Looking for Zora," in which she recounts the aftermath of a first visit to Hurston's neglected and weed-choked gravesite. Unable to express her grief or horror at the grave itself, she explains:

> It is only later, when the pain is not so direct a threat to one's own existence that what was learned in that moment of comical lunacy is understood. Such moments rob us of both youth and vanity. But perhaps they are also times when greater disciplines are born.

One such "discipline" is manifest in Walker's more recent work; her second collection of essays, *Living by the Word* and, to a lesser extent, her 1989 novel *The Temple of My Familiar*, reveal a writer of maturing vision. The anger of her earlier works is still present, but Walker has adopted a more spiritual approach. In an essay called "Everything Is a Human Being," she explores "the Native American view that all of creation is of one substance and therefore deserving of the same respect." Walker's attempt to locate parallels between how we treat each other and how we treat our world and its creatures can be seen as a first step toward a notion of universal connectedness, and by association, universal equality. In a recent interview, she remarked: "It's really fatal to see yourself as separate. You have to feel, I think, more or less equal and valid in order for the whole organism to feel healthy." Walker, perhaps more than any essayist writing today, best exemplifies the role of writer as seer; her message is one of wholeness, of personal salvation. As novelist David Bradley wrote: "There's a world in Alice Walker's eye."

Principal Works by Alice Walker

Once   poetry: 1968

The Third Life of Grange Copeland   novel: 1970

In Love & Trouble: Stories of Black Women   short stories: 1973

Revolutionary Petunias & Other Poems   poetry: 1973

Meridian   novel: 1976

Good Night, Willie Lee, I'll See You in the Morning   poetry: 1979

You Can't Keep a Good Woman Down: Stories   short stories: 1981

The Color Purple   novel: 1982

In Search of Our Mothers' Gardens: Womanist Prose   essays: 1983

Horses Make a Landscape Look More Beautiful   poetry: 1984

Living by the Word: Selected Writings 1973–1987   essays: 1988

The Temple of My Familiar   novel: 1989

Selected Criticism of Alice Walker's Essays

BLOOM, HAROLD, ed. *Alice Walker: Modern Critical Views*. New York: Chelsea House Publishers, 1989. A representative selection of some of the best criticism of Walker's writing; several essays make mention of Walker's nonfiction, though usually in order to elucidate her fiction.

BRADLEY, DAVID. "Novelist Alice Walker: Telling the Black Woman's Story." *The New York Times Magazine*, January 8, 1984, pp. 25–37. A retrospective profile that appeared shortly after the publication of *In Search of Our Mothers' Gardens*.

MAIRS, NANCY. "In Search of 'In Search of Our Mothers' Gardens.'" *The American Voice*, Fall 1989, pp. 76–83. This piece relates the author's attempts as a white woman to understand and to accurately read the Walker essay.

WATKINS, MEL. "Sexism, Racism, and Black Women Writers." *The New York Times Book Review*, June 15, 1986, pp. 1, 35–37. While this essay does not focus only on Walker, it provides the context for much of her nonfiction.

E. B. WHITE

W HEN E. B. WHITE DIED at the age of eighty-six in autumn 1985, the editor of *The New Yorker*, William Shawn, speaking on behalf of the magazine whose urbane style White himself had helped to create, paid tribute to the writer:

> E. B. White was a great essayist, a supreme stylist. His literary style was as pure as any in our language. It was singular, colloquial, clear, unforced, thoroughly American and utterly beautiful. Because of his quiet influence, several generations of this country's writers write better than they might have done.

E(lwyn) B(rooks) White occupies a rare position among the men and women of American letters. Not since Ralph Waldo Emerson and Henry David Thoreau, one of White's literary heroes, had an American writer established a reputation as a popular and critical success almost solely on the basis of his essays and sketches. While he was also known for his writing for children and a best-selling manual of style, it was in his capacity as an essayist that he achieved national recognition. Throughout his career, White worked hard to resurrect the personal essay as a major literary form in the United States. Even though his efforts in the name of the essay were not completely successful — late in life, White remarked that the essayist "must be content in his self-imposed role of second-class citizen" in the republic of letters — he nevertheless managed to win the old form some new respect. Never one to force his ideas upon others, White in his offhand manner probably taught us more about the personal essay than almost anyone. In the preface to his *Selected Essays*, he offers a tongue-in-cheek account of what it takes to be an essayist: "Only a person who is congenitally self-centered has the effrontery and the stamina to write essays." Fortunately for his readers, the "self-centered" White never lost confidence in his ability to share his idiosyncratic view of the world with others.

Born in 1899 to wealthy parents, White grew up in Mount Vernon, New York, an affluent suburb north of Manhattan. While his biographer, Scott Elledge, has tried to play down the nearly idyllic conditions under which White was brought up, from the latter's writings, it seems that the worst he had to endure as a child was severe bouts of hay fever. After completing Mount Vernon high school, White attended Cornell University, where he served as editor-in-chief of *The Cornell Sun*, the campus newspaper. His interest in journalism led him to New York City, where by 1927 he found a job with *The New Yorker*, a recently formed magazine edited by Harold Ross. Only two years before, just nine weeks after the magazine's inaugural issue appeared, White had contributed the first of thousands of pieces he would write for its pages. As Ross once remarked, "there was practically no purpose to which words could be put that White was unable to master." Writing everything from prose sketches to cartoon captions to light verse, White, along with James Thurber, would do more than any other staff writer to shape the magazine's tone, one marked by, according to Herbert Mitgang, "sophisticated wit, irreverence, and necessary candor." His "Notes and Comment" formed the opening section of each issue's "Talk of the Town" column. Paul Gray wrote: "As the magazine prospered, and gossip about its inner workings leaked out, White became the country's best-known anonymous journalist. His casual, pithy approach to a paragraph defined brevity and wit for a generation of aspiring stylists."

By 1929 White had authored *The Lady Is Cold*, a collection of light verse as well as *Is Sex Necessary?*, a satire written with office-mate Thurber. The same year, he married *The New Yorker*'s fiction editor Katherine Sergeant Angell, a woman considered to be "the intellectual soul" of the magazine. While the Whites were happy in Manhattan, they desired greater privacy and a simpler life. In 1933 they purchased a farmhouse in North Brooklin, Maine, and five years later took up residence there on a permanent basis. During this period, White had grown restless at *The New Yorker*. He had approached Ross several times about his desire to write essays on various topics for the magazine, but the editor had been discouraging. White learned that *Harper's Magazine* was eager to allow him to develop his talents as an essayist, and in 1937 he began a monthly column called "One Man's Meat" for the periodical.

The essays White wrote for *Harper's*, fifty-five in all, revealed a very different side of the writer who had made his reputation on sophisticated but light humor pieces and satirical commentary. By the time *Quo Vadimus?*, a collection of sketches written while he was still at *The New Yorker*, appeared in 1939, White had already graduated to a more serious style. An essay like "Once More to the Lake," ostensibly a reflection on the pleasures of nostalgia, surprises the reader with its intimations of mortality and its haunting depiction of what George Core calls "generational likenesses and differences as seen through the lens of memory." The concluding episode of the young boy, White's own son, buckling his cold wet swimming trunks around his waist and the sympathetic chill the father feels in his own groin takes its place alongside some of the finest moments in modern American literature. Another early essay, "The World of Tomorrow," White's account of the 1939 New York World's Fair offers a deeply sardonic view of human progress and sets forth one of White's recurrent themes, the superiority of the natural to the artificial. By the time these pieces were collected into one volume, aptly titled *One Man's Meat*, in 1942, White had already achieved his reputation as one "of the best writers of the familiar essays in English." Before the end of the Second World War, White returned briefly to Manhattan and to *The New Yorker* as a favor to Harold Ross whose staff of writers had been depleted by the war effort. After the war, he went back to Maine, but would continue to appear in the magazine in the form of letters sent from his salt-water farm and other farflung locations.

It is a commonly held notion that White's essays are the product of what *The New Yorker* obituary referred to as the author's "inexplicably sunny inclinations." Such an appraisal is understandable given the nature of his early pieces for *The New Yorker*. White had once written to his brother: "I discovered a long time ago that writing of the small things of the day, the trivial matters of the heart, the inconsequential but near things of this living was the only kind of creative work which I could accomplish with any sincerity or grace. . . . Not till *The New Yorker* came along did I ever find any means of expressing those impertinences and irrelevancies." His immensely successful children's books could only enhance his status as one of America's most cheerful writers. But recently another essayist, Joseph Epstein, has refuted the conventional wisdom about White's mood, announcing that one would have "to search very sedulously indeed to find a gloomier writer than E. B. White." In fact, citing the following passage, Epstein contends that White has a strong penchant for the apocalyptic:

> I think when the end of the world comes the sky will be its old blue self, with white cumulus clouds drifting along. You will be looking out a window, say, at a tree; and then after a bit the tree won't be there any more, and the looking won't be there any more, only the window will be there, in memory — the thing through which the looking has been done.

This sense of doom even carried over to White's personal life. He suffered from severe bouts of depression; he always felt a deep sense of failure about his work at *Harper's* even though the essays he wrote there were the most important he would ever write.

One reason why this side of White is likely to escape even his most devoted readers is the crisp eloquence of his prose. He wrote in a style that was plain in both syntax and vocabulary. White had learned all he would ever need to know about prose style from his Cornell professor William Strunk, whose pamphlet *The Elements of Style* would be edited and published by his former student in 1959. In addition to the basic grasp of the English sentence, White possessed an ear for prose rhythm. In his preface to *The Elements of Style*, he wrote that he was uncomfortable in the role of expert in composition since "the truth is I write by ear, always with difficulty and seldom with any exact notion of what is taking place under the hood." Moreover, for White, the phrase "plain style" did not indicate bland writing. His powers of description rival anyone's. Here is White describing his city backyard:

> The day was clear, with a gentle wind, and the small leaves descended singly and serenely, except now and then when a breeze entered and caused a momentary rain of leaves — what one weather prophet on the radio calls "inner mitten" showers. A school of fish paraded counter-clockwise in the fountain, and on the wall above us hung seed pods of the polygonum vine.

Passages like this are found everywhere in White; that this particular passage is to be found in "Daylight and Darkness," a short meditation on the threat of nuclear war, demonstrates the modulating effect of his style on the darkness of his subject matter.

After *One Man's Meat,* White would publish two more major collections of essays and other pieces: *The Second Tree from the Corner* (1954) and *The Points of My Compass* (1962). In the former, White gives vent to many of his fears about the fragility of peace between nations and the horrible consequences of atomic conflict. In "The Morning of the Day They Did It," he offers his own version of the end of the world. The latter collection contains White's letters to *The New Yorker* written between 1954 and 1961. While he continues to write on American and world politics — his comments on the McCarthy hearings and the House Un-American Activities Committee are some of the most political White ever voiced — most of the essays take up his ambivalence about progress first set forth in the early essay "The World of Tomorrow." While White is unabashedly nostalgic in essays like "The Railroad" and "The Years of Wonder," he cannot be accused of being a sentimentalist. His yearning for the past is not synonymous with a desire for a simpler life. If anything, White's point is that technological advances make things too easy for us, separate us from our world through unnecessary convenience. To paraphrase Thoreau, an invention designed to solve a problem should never be more complicated than the problem itself.

Perhaps his essay "The Ring of Time" best illustrates White's vision of life. Describing a young circus rider, White reflects: "the enchantment grew not out of anything that happened or was performed but out of something that seemed to go round and around and around with the girl, attending her, a steady gleam in the shape of a circle — a ring of ambition, of happiness, of youth." But, White sadly observes, soon the young girl would grow up, "wear makeup," the illusion of timelessness created by her graceful ride around the ring would be shattered. Many of his essays offer images of circularity and eternity commingled with those of the passage of time and decay. Though conscious that his essays are written in time, White writes so that some beauty might survive time's ravages.

Principal Works by E. B. White

The Lady Is Cold   verse: 1929

Is Sex Necessary? (with James Thurber)   satire: 1929

Every Day Is Saturday   commentary: 1934

The Fox of Peapack and Other Poems   verse: 1938

Quo Vadimus?   sketches and stories: 1939

One Man's Meat   essays: 1942

Stuart Little   children's literature: 1945

The Wild Flag   commentary: 1946

Here Is New York   nonfiction: 1949

Charlotte's Web   children's literature: 1952

The Second Tree from the Corner   essays and other pieces: 1954

The Elements of Style (by William Strunk, Jr.; revised and enlarged by E. B. White)   1959

The Points of My Compass   essays: 1962

The Trumpet of the Swan   children's literature: 1970

Selected Criticism of E. B. White's Essays

DENNIS, NIGEL. "Smilin' Through." *The New York Review of Books,* October 27, 1977, pp. 42–43. A retrospective review of White's *Collected Essays.*

ELLEDGE, SCOTT. *E. B. White: A Biography.* New York: W. W. Norton & Co., 1984. The definitive life with important observations about White's style.

EPSTEIN, JOSEPH. "E. B. White, Lite and Dark," in *Partial Payments.* New York: W. W. Norton & Co., 1989. Epstein convincingly argues that White is one of the gloomiest writers in the language.

PLIMPTON, GEORGE, and FRANK H. CROWTHER. "The Art of the Essay I: E. B. White." *The Paris Review,* XLVIII (Fall 1969), pp. 65–88. White talks extensively about style and the craft of writing essays.

SAMPSON, EDWARD C. *E. B. White.* New York: Twayne Publishers, 1974. A comprehensive survey of all of White's nonfiction. Contains an extensive bibliography.

VAN GELDER, ROBERT. *Writers and Writing.* New York: Charles Scribner's Sons, 1946. Contains an early interview with White.

VIRGINIA WOOLF

A N ESSAYIST'S KNOWLEDGE, Virginia Woolf once wrote, must be "so fused by the magic of writing that not a fact juts out, not a dogma tears the surface of the texture." In her own essays, Woolf wore her learning so lightly that we tend to see them as experiments in pure style. As one critic has written, "she seemed to be so carried away by the supremacy of style as to denigrate the importance of content." Perhaps this is why writers on Woolf are more likely to concentrate on her amazing sequence of novels, including *Mrs. Dalloway* (1925), *To the Lighthouse* (1927), *Orlando* (1928), and *The Waves* (1931), and the early feminist tract, *A Room of One's Own* (1929). Style, after all, is one of the most difficult aspects of a literary work to discuss and Virginia Woolf's essays require just such an aesthetic approach. Precisely because the writer's style is nearly inseparable from her own notion of who she is, reading an essay by Woolf leaves us with the feeling of having been engaged in conversation with an utterly charming, utterly brilliant woman. Woolf herself describes this power the good essay has on its readers: "Even things in a book-case change if they are alive; we find ourselves wanting to meet them again; we find them altered. [We know that] come September or May, we shall sit down with them and talk."

Woolf was born in London in 1882, the second daughter of Leslie Stephen, a famous literary personality, and Julia Jackson, who could claim descent from French nobility. She received no formal education, but instead was set free in her father's library to read whatever she liked. Given the prominent place held by Leslie Stephen in the cultural life of late nineteenth-century England, Woolf could hardly avoid being immersed in the period's major intellectual and literary issues. By a very early age, Virginia knew or at least had met most of the great novelists and poets of the time. Throughout her childhood what Woolf called "the pressures of society" exerted themselves fully in the Stephen household:

> We learned the rules of the Victorian game of manners so thoroughly that we have never forgotten them. We still play the game. It is useful; it has beauty, for it is founded upon restraint, sympathy, unselfishness — all civilised qualities.

Woolf would later admit that while she was not at all sure these qualities were always the ones to be emulated in writing, they nevertheless allowed "one to say a great many things which would be inaudible if one marched straight up and spoke out." Though Woolf's "surface manner" might deprive her essays of the candor that makes Orwell's so vibrant, her subtlety and nuance grant them a greater expressiveness.

The highly civilized surroundings of her youth, however, could not mask the unhappiness of Woolf's early life. When she was thirteen, her mother died. Shortly after, Woolf suffered the first of many mental break-downs culminating in her 1941 suicide after many failed attempts. For part of her youth, she was subject to sexual abuse at the hands of her elder half-brother George Duckworth, though she would only report these incidents many years later. Despite these tragedies, by 1904 she had begun writing review essays for the *Times Literary Supplement*. By the time she published her first novel, *The Voyage Out*, a decade later, she had already established herself as one of the most perceptive of English literary critics. A number of her early essays were revised for inclusion in *The Common Reader* (1925), her first collection of nonfiction.

The Common Reader, along with its 1932 sequel of the same title, represents what Woolf considered the best of her essays on literary topics. Envisioning the collection as more than just a compilation, she experimented with the idea of placing the essays in a fictional framework hoping "to envelop each essay in its own atmosphere. To get them into a current of life, & so to shape the book." Moreover, while she had always extolled the virtues of the essay, she would at times find the form somewhat limiting in what she considered its single-topic nature. Finally, Woolf decided to let the essays stand on their own. In addition to the unity derived from theme and style, the essays cohere because present everywhere in them is the *persona*, or fictional speaker, which Phyllis Rose describes as "that of a woman, neither professional critic or scholar, moderately informed, who is modestly, earnestly, trying to illuminate life through the reading of books." Another recent critic, Georgia Johnston, has elegantly demonstrated how Woolf, "by making each essay one part of a larger vision . . . , has used the limiting form of the essay as one might use one poem in a book of poems and has reached beyond that chosen form."

While most of the pieces in the two collections contain the author's reflection of classical and modern fiction, the essay form nevertheless manages to attract some of Woolf's attention. At the time when Woolf was writing these pieces, essays were generally considered to be *about* literature and therefore could not conceivably *be* literature. But Woolf herself never doubted that the essay was a literary form, that its chief aim "is simply that it should give pleasure." In "The Modern Essay," she describes the essay reader's passage "through the most various experiences of amusement, surprise, interest, indignation. . . ." Woolf's claim that the form gives pleasure challenged the more traditional notion that it best served as a vehicle for commentary and information. We might even speculate that in offering this view of the genre she was trying to make a place for the kinds of essays she one day hoped to write or had already written but was afraid to publish. The ideal essay is able to "draw its curtain around us, but it must be a curtain which shuts us in, not out." Moreover, the essayist must "know . . . how to write"; an essayist's style must be able to induce within the reader a kind of hypnotic state: it must be able "to sting us awake and fix us in a trance which is not sleep but rather an intensification of life — a basking with every faculty alert in the sun of pleasure." Woolf's ability to convey with remarkable intensity acts of sensory experience manifests itself most fully in the personal essays that would be collected by her husband Leonard Woolf in the years following her death.

In his introduction to *The Death of the Moth and Other Essays* (1942), Leonard Woolf writes that he has made his selection from a number of essays that, if they had been published all together, would fill several volumes. In fact, Woolf's *Collected Essays* were published in four volumes in 1967. While each of the essays in *The Death of the Moth* was revised as much as eight or nine times by the author herself, it is unlikely that she had begun to arrange them in an order for publication as she had clearly done for *The Common Reader 1 and 2*. Nevertheless, the essays are held together by the same spirit of experimentation that marks her work as a mature novelist and short story writer. In the remarkable "Evening over Sussex: Reflections in a Motor Car," Woolf characteristically plays with our commonplace notion of the unified self. No fewer than six "selves" appear over the course of a few pages that purport to convey the experience of motoring through an evening countryside. Each of the first five "selves" represents one aspect of the particular complex of thoughts and emotions that defines the person called Virginia Woolf. A sixth "self," the most elusive of the group, arises to coordinate the other five:

> Now we have got to collect ourselves: . . . Now I, who preside over the company, am going to arrange in order the trophies which we have all brought in. Let me see: there was a great deal of beauty brought in today: farmhouses, cliffs standing out to sea; marbled fields; mottled fields; red feathered skies; all that. Also there was the disappearance or death of the individual. . . .

Because of Woolf's history of mental illness — for long periods of her life she may have been clinically insane — we might be tempted to conclude that the author is relating the experience of the fragmentation of identity that is often the first sign of mental disturbance. Actually, she is merely demonstrating how the human mind often functions, sympathizing with both sides of an issue at once or simultaneously viewing the same object in very different ways. Some of the finest essays ever written share the impression of a mind in the act of contemplation. Woolf's essays not only share this quality, but go further to record, from an internal perspective, the writer's "stream of thought," the process by which her mind moves associatively from impression to impression.

In her essay "Craftmanship," originally written for a 1938 series of radio broadcasts treating the uses of language and style, Woolf reveals many of her ideas about writing. Paradoxically, she begins by informing us that "words are not useful . . . they hate being useful, . . . it is their nature not to express one simple statement but a thousand possibilities." Beyond the surface meaning of words and phrases lie "so many sunken meanings," and insofar as Woolf thought writers the people most sensitive to this aspect of language, she also felt that they, better than anyone else, could extract or retrieve those meanings. The process by which such retrieval occurs, however, is utterly subjective and each writer will produce a different set of meanings given the same collection of words or phrases. It is for this reason that writers can never succeed at being wholly impersonal. As long as they associate particular feelings, thoughts, and memories with particular arrangements of language, they cannot ever fully transcend the personal bent within their own writing. Woolf's own solution to this problem inherent in words was to indulge their power to draw on our unconscious, to allow the random acts of association to occur right on the page. While this technique confused many readers of her novels who found her style subjective to the point of obscurity, this criticism was never directed to the nonfiction prose, both critical and personal. Her father had once told her "to write in the fewest possible words, as clearly as possible, exactly what one meant," and she rarely departed from this advice in her own essays even while invoking her ideas about the uses of language.

At its best, and it is almost always at its best in her essays, Virginia Woolf's prose reflects her view of experience as a flood of perceptions and sensations originating in the seemingly inconsequential events of an ordinary day. Even the minute struggles of a moth against the onset of death do not escape her eye. Her amazing sensitivity to detail, and the luminous prose it engendered, have made her one of the two or three most influential English stylists of the twentieth century. And this obsession with style shaped Woolf's view of humanity. As Paul West has written: "She saw each individual human life as a complex sentence, short even at its lengthiest, meaningful only in evolutionary terms, but therefore a sample of a process she found 'everlasting and perpetual.'"

Principal Works by Virginia Woolf

The Voyage Out   novel: 1915

Night and Day   novel: 1919

Monday or Tuesday   short fiction: 1921

Jacob's Room   novel: 1922

Mrs. Dalloway   novel: 1925

The Common Reader   criticism: 1925

To the Lighthouse   novel: 1927

Orlando   fictional biography: 1928

A Room of One's Own   essay: 1929

The Waves   novel: 1931

The Common Reader   criticism: 1932

The Years   novel: 1937

Three Guineas   essay: 1938

Between the Acts   novel: 1941
The Death of the Moth and Other Essays   essays: 1942
A Haunted House and Other Short Stories   short fiction: 1944
The Moment and Other Essays   essays: 1947
The Captain's Death Bed and Other Essays   essays: 1950
A Writer's Diary   journal: 1954
Granite and Rainbow   essays: 1958
Collected Essays (4 vols.)   1967

Selected Criticism of Virginia Woolf's Essays

BELL, BARBARA CURRIER, and CAROL OHMANN. "Virginia Woolf's Criticism: A Polemical Preface." *Critical Inquiry*, I (1974), pp. 361–371. A brief and illuminating survey of Woolf's criticism.

BREWSTER, DOROTHY. *Virginia Woolf*. New York: New York University Press, 1962. A general study containing a detailed discussion of the essays.

GORSKY, SUSAN RUBINOW. *Virginia Woolf, Rev. ed*. Boston: Twayne Publishers, 1989. Chapter 2 is a well-writen overview of Woolf's nonfiction.

JOHNSTON, GEORGIA. "The Whole Achievement in Virginia Woolf's *The Common Reader*," in *Essays on the Essay: Redefining the Genre*, ed. Alexander J. Butrym. Athens: University of Georgia Press, 1989, pp. 148–158. Lucidly and convincingly argues for the existence of a structural principle organizing Woolf's first collection of criticism with an interesting discussion of the voice in the essays.

KLAUS, CARL H. "On Virginia Woolf on the Essay." *Iowa Review*, Spring/Summer 1990, pp. 28–34. A thorough close reading of Woolf's "The Modern Essay."

MARCUS, JANE, ed. *New Feminist Essays on Virginia Woolf*. Lincoln: University of Nebraska Press, 1981. An important collection that attempts to trace Woolf's feminism in a number of her works including her nonfiction and essays.

ROSE, PHYLLIS. *Woman of Letters: A Life of Virginia Woolf*. New York: Oxford University Press, 1978. A good critical biography with some discussion of the essays.

ROSENTHAL, MICHAEL. *Virginia Woolf*. New York: Columbia University Press, 1979. Explores Woolf's preoccupation with form, paying special attention in Chapters 14 and 15 to her feminist essays and literary criticism.

ACKNOWLEDGMENTS *(continued from p. iv)*

in *Playboy*, January 1985) and "A Talk to Teachers" (originally published as "The Negro Child — His Self-Image" in *The Saturday Review*, December 21, 1963). Reprinted in *The Price of the Ticket* (New York: St. Martin's/Marek, 1985). Reprinted by permission of the James Baldwin Estate. "If Black English Isn't a Language, Then Tell Me, What Is?" Copyright © 1979/87 by the New York Times Company. Reprinted by permission.

EMILY DICKINSON, excerpt from "There's a Certain Slant of Light," reprinted in "Washington Square, 1946" by Cynthia Ozick. Reprinted by permission of the publishers and the Trustees of Amherst College from *The Poems of Emily Dickinson*, Thomas H. Johnson, Ed. Cambridge, Mass.: The Belknap Press of Harvard University Press. Copyright 1951, © 1955, 1979, 1983 by the President and Fellows of Harvard College.

JOAN DIDION, "John Wayne: A Love Song," "On Going Home," and "On Keeping a Notebook" from *Slouching Towards Bethlehem* by Joan Didion. Copyright © 1965, 1966, 1967, 1968 by Joan Didion. Reprinted by permission of Farrar, Straus and Giroux, Inc. "Insider Baseball." Copyright © 1988 by Joan Didion. From *The Best American Essays 1989*, Ticknor & Fields. First appeared in *The New York Review of Books*. Reprinted by permission of the Wallace Literary Agency, Inc. Excerpt from *Miami* by Joan Didion. Copyright © 1987 by Joan Didion. Reprinted by permission of Simon & Schuster, Inc.

ANNIE DILLARD, "In the Jungle," "Living Like Weasels," and "Total Eclipse" from *Teaching a Stone to Talk: Expeditions and Encounters* by Annie Dillard. Copyright © 1982 by Annie Dillard. Reprinted by permission of HarperCollins Publishers Inc. "Stalking" from *Pilgrim at Tinker Creek* by Annie Dillard. Copyright © 1974 by Annie Dillard. Reprinted by permission of HarperCollins Publishers Inc. Excerpt from *The Writing Life* by Annie Dillard. Copyright © 1989 by Annie Dillard. Reprinted by permission of HarperCollins Publishers Inc. Excerpt from *The Writing Life* by Annie Dillard as it appeared in *The Best American Essays 1989*. Copyright © 1989 by Annie Dillard. Reprinted by permission of HarperCollins Publishers Inc.

STEPHEN JAY GOULD, "Darwin's Middle Road" and "Women's Brains" reprinted from *The Panda's Thumb: More Reflections in Natural History* by Stephen Jay Gould, by permission of W. W. Norton & Company, Inc. Copyright © 1980 by Stephen Jay Gould. "The Dinosaur Rip-off" and "The Streak of Streaks" reprinted from *Bully for Brontosaurus: Reflections in Natural History* by Stephen Jay Gould, by permission of W. W. Norton & Company, Inc. Copyright © 1991 by Stephen Jay Gould. "The Median Isn't the Message" by Stephen Jay Gould. Appeared in *Discover*, June 1985. Reprinted by permission of the author.

GEORGE ORWELL, "Politics and the English Language" by George Orwell. Copyright 1946 by Sonia Brownell Orwell and renewed 1974 by Sonia Orwell. Reprinted from his volume *Shooting an Elephant and Other Essays* by permission of Harcourt Brace Jovanovich, Inc. and the Estate of the late Sonia Brownell Orwell and Martin Secker & Warburg Ltd. "Shooting an Elephant" from *Shooting an Elephant and Other Essays* by George Orwell. Copyright 1950 by Sonia Brownell Orwell and renewed 1978 by Sonia Pitt-Rivers. Reprinted by permission of Harcourt Brace Jovanovich, Inc. and the Estate of the late Sonia Brownell Orwell and Martin Secker & Warburg Ltd. Excerpts from "Such, Such Were the Joys" by George Orwell. Copyright 1952 and renewed 1980 by Sonia Brownell Orwell and reprinted from his volume *Such, Such Were the Joys* by permission of Harcourt Brace Jovanovich, Inc. and the Estate of the late Sonia Brownell Orwell and Martin Secker & Warburg Ltd. "What Is Science?" from *Collected Essays, Journalism, and Letters of George Orwell: In Front of Your Nose, 1945–1950.* Vol. IV, edited by Sonia Brownell

Orwell and Ian Angus. Copyright © 1968 by Sonia Brownell Orwell. Reprinted by permission of Harcourt Brace Jovanovich, Inc. and the Estate of the late Sonia Brownell Orwell and Martin Secker & Warburg Ltd. "Why I Write" from *Such, Such Were the Joys* by George Orwell. Copyright 1953 by Sonia Brownell Orwell and renewed 1981 by Mrs. George K. Perutz, Mrs. Miriam Gross, and Dr. Michael Dickson, Executors of the Estate of Sonia Brownell Orwell. Reprinted by permission of Harcourt Brace Jovanovich, Inc. and the Estate of the late Sonia Brownell Orwell and Martin Secker & Warburg Ltd.

CYNTHIA OZICK, "A Drugstore in Winter" from *Art & Ardor* by Cynthia Ozick. Copyright © 1983 by Cynthia Ozick. Reprinted by permission of Alfred A. Knopf, Inc. "The Question of Our Speech," "The Seam of the Snail," "The Shock of Teapots," and "Washington Square, 1946" from *Metaphor and Memory* by Cynthia Ozick. Copyright © 1989 by Cynthia Ozick. Reprinted by permission of Alfred A. Knopf, Inc. "Science and Letters: God's Work — and Ours." First published in *The New York Times Book Review*, September 27, 1987. Reprinted as "Crocodiled Moats in the Kingdom of Letters" in *Metaphor and Memory* by Cynthia Ozick. Copyright © 1989 by Cynthia Ozick. Reprinted by permission of Alfred A. Knopf, Inc.

LEWIS THOMAS, excerpt from *Et Cetera, Et Cetera: Notes of a Word-Watcher* by Lewis Thomas. Copyright © 1990 by Lewis Thomas. By permission of Little, Brown and Company. "Humanities and Science" from *Late Night Thoughts on Listening to Mahler's Ninth Symphony* by Lewis Thomas. Copyright © 1983 by Lewis Thomas. Used by permission of Viking Penguin, a division of Penguin Books USA Inc. "Scabies, Scrapie" from *The Youngest Science: Notes of a Medicine Watcher* by Lewis Thomas. Copyright © 1983 by Lewis Thomas. Used by permission of Viking Penguin, a division of Penguin Books USA Inc. "The Tucson Zoo," copyright © 1977 by Lewis Thomas. "How to Fix the Premedical Curriculum," copyright © 1978 by Lewis Thomas. From *The Medusa and the Snail* by Lewis Thomas. Used by permission of Viking Penguin, a division of Penguin Books USA Inc.

ALICE WALKER, "Beauty: When the Other Dancer Is the Self" and "In Search of Our Mothers' Gardens" from *In Search of Our Mothers' Gardens*, copyright © 1983 by Alice Walker. Reprinted by permission of Harcourt Brace Jovanovich, Inc. "Brothers and Sisters" and "Looking for Zora," copyright © 1975 by Alice Walker. Reprinted from her volume *In Search of Our Mothers' Gardens* by permission of Harcourt Brace Jovanovich, Inc. "Journey to Nine Miles" from *Living By the Word*, copyright © 1988 by Alice Walker. Reprinted by permission of Harcourt Brace Jovanovich, Inc. "Women" from *Revolutionary Petunias and Other Poems* by Alice Walker, reprinted in "In Search of Our Mothers' Gardens" by Alice Walker. Coyright © 1970 by Alice Walker. Reprinted by permission of Harcourt Brace Jovanovich, Inc.

E. B. WHITE, "Aunt Poo" and "Walden" from *One Man's Meat* by E. B. White. Copyright 1942 by E. B. White. Reprinted by permission of HarperCollins Publishers Inc. "Death of a Pig," coyright 1947 by E. B. White. "Once More to the Lake," copyright 1941 by E. B. White. From *Essays of E. B. White* by E. B. White. Reprinted by permission of HarperCollins Publishers Inc. "Will Strunk" from *The Points of My Compass* by E. B. White. Copyright © 1957, 1962 by E. B. White. Reprinted by permission of HarperCollins Publishers Inc.

VIRGINIA WOOLF, "The Death of the Moth," "Professions for Women," and "Thoughts on Peace in an Air Raid" from *The Death of the Moth and Other Essays* by Virginia Woolf. Copyright 1942 by Harcourt Brace Jovanovich, Inc. and renewed 1970 by Marjorie T. Parsons, Executrix. Reprinted by permission of the publisher and the Executors of the Estate of Virginia Woolf and The Hogarth Press. "Ellen

Index of Authors and Titles